ENCYCLOPAEDIA OF
SWIMMING

Encyclopaedias published by Robert Hale & Co

ASSOCIATION FOOTBALL
Maurice Golesworthy
ATHLETICS   Melvyn Watman
BOWLS   Ken Hawkes and Gerard Lindley
BOXING   Maurice Golesworthy
CHESS   Anne Sunnucks
CRICKET   Maurice Golesworthy
FLAT RACING   Roger Mortimer
GOLF   Webster Evans
MOTOR-CYCLE SPORT   Peter Carrick
MOTOR RACING
Anthony Pritchard and Keith Davey
MOUNTAINEERING   Walt Unsworth
RUGBY FOOTBALL   J. R. Jones
    (*Third edition edited by Maurice Golesworthy*)
RUGBY LEAGUE FOOTBALL   A. N. Gaulton
SHOW JUMPING   Charles Stratton

Encyclopaedia of
SWIMMING

Compiled by
PAT BESFORD

SECOND EDITION

ROBERT HALE & COMPANY

LONDON

ST. MARTIN'S PRESS

NEW YORK

©*Pat Besford 1971 and 1976*
First published in Great Britain 1971
First published in United States of America 1971
New Edition 1976

Robert Hale & Company
Clerkenwell House
Clerkenwell Green
London EC1R 0HT

ISBN 0 7091 5063 6

St. Martin's Press, Inc.
175 Fifth Avenue
New York, N.Y. 10010

Library of Congress Catalog Card Number 76 - 16687

PRINTED IN GREAT BRITAIN BY
CLARKE, DOBLE & BRENDON LTD.,
PLYMOUTH

INTRODUCTION

There has to be a reason for anyone to want to do anything and "my thing" always has been a fascination for the people and their achievements which together make up the history of the sport of swimming.

The idea behind the first edition of this encyclopaedia was to bring together under one cover the many facets of the sport. At the time it seemed a simple, straightforward enterprise but it did not quite work out like that.

This second edition, however, I believed was obviously going to be far, far easier! That, too, proved to be as far from the truth as the original misconception.

Original errors in names, results and records are among the most difficult to sort out and the most time-consuming. As a typical illustration, one famous European champion has four certificates recording major achievements — and on each his name is spelt in a different way!

I am indebted to Erich Kamper, the renowned Olympic historian, whose *Encyclopaedia of the Summer Olympics* and *Who's Who at the Olympics* have been invaluable in attempting to resolve problems of this kind.

But despite all the checking and cross-checking — and here I would express most grateful thanks to Tommy Long for all the hours he sweated over hot proofs — it would be foolish to believe that there will not be mistakes. My apologies in advance and I would be most grateful to hear about them from readers.

PAT BESFORD

London
1976

ACKNOWLEDGEMENTS

So many people in so many different parts of the world have provided information, facts and figures to make this book possible. The help from all the countless swimming enthusiasts is gratefully recorded here and especially from:

Aronne Anghileri (Italy)
Istvan Barany (Hungary)
A.W. Barrett (New Zealand)
Claus Bastian (West Germany)
Alex Bulley (South Africa)
Boris Chernyshev (USSR)
Jock Coutts (Scotland)
Bobby Dawson (USA)*
Klaus Fiedler (East Germany)
Gerald Forsberg (GB)
S.B. Grange (Australia)
Harry Hainsworth (USA)
Fran Heath (Canada)
International Hall of Fame (USA)

Margaret Jarvis (GB)
Erich Kamper (Austria)
Jos van Kuijeren (Netherlands)
Gerhard Lerch (East Germany)
Norris McWhirter (GB)
Ross McWhirter (GB)*
François Oppenheim (France)
Austin Rawlinson (GB)
R. Max Ritter (USA)
Sebastian Salinas (Peru)
Sydney Skilton (GB)
Nick Thierry (Canada)
Vaughan Thomas (Wales)
Belle White (GB)*

* Deceased

ILLUSTRATIONS

Between pages 80 and 81

Between pages 192 and 193

PICTURE CREDITS

Tony Duffy: 2, 12, 13, 14, 15, 16, 23, 24, 25, 27, 28, 30; Associated Press Ltd: 3; Istvan Barany: 4, 5, 6, 19, 20, 21; United Press International: 7, 8; Sportsworld: 11; Press Association: 22; Daily Mirror: 26; C. A. Otten: 29.

ABBREVIATIONS AND NOTES

F.I.N.A. = Fédération Internationale de Natation Amateur
I.O.C. = International Olympic Committee
L.E.N. = Ligue Européenne de Natation

Arg	Argentine	Guat	Guatemala
Aus	Australia	Hun	Hungary
Aut	Austria	It	Italy
Belg	Belgium	Ire	Ireland
Braz	Brazil	Jap	Japan
Can	Canada	Mex	Mexico
China	China P.R.	Neth	Netherlands
Col	Colombia	NZ	New Zealand
Cub	Cuba	Peru	Peru
Czech	Czechslovakia	Pol	Poland
Den	Denmark	Rhod	Rhodesia
E Ger	East Germany*	Rom	Romania
Ecu	Ecuador	Scot	Scotland
Egypt	Egypt	SAf	South Africa
Eire	Eire	Sp	Spain
Eng	England	Swe	Sweden
Fiji	Fiji	USA	United States
Fin	Finland	Urug	Uruguay
Fr	France	Wales	Wales
Ger	Germany*	W Ger	West Germany*
GB	Great Britain	Yugo	Yugoslavia
Gre	Greece	USSR	Soviet Union

*East Germany (German Democratic Republic) and West Germany (German Federal Republic) were accepted by F.I.N.A. as separate national federations in 1950. The I.O.C., however, did not allow separate German teams in the Olympics until the 1968 Games.

m. = metres
y. = yards. If used beside a time, it indicates that the performance for a metric distance was recorded over the equivalent longer yards distance
e. = equalling record
bu. = butterfly. If used beside a time under a breast-stroke heading, it indicates that the over-water arm recovery was used during some or all of the race prior to the separation of breast-stroke and butterfly
uw = under-water If used beside a time under a breast-stroke heading, it indicates that the performance included swimming distances under-water before this was prohibited on 30th April 1957.

Times are indicated as follows: 1:01.1 = 1 min. 1.1 sec. or 1:01.11 = 1 min. 1.11 sec.

Notwithstanding the use of an asterisk (*) for specific cross-reference purposes, the use of an asterisk (*) in the place of the hundredth figure in results and records since the 1970s (viz 1:01.1*) indicates that the time was taken to only one tenth of a second.

Dotted lines have been introduced into various results and record sections to indicate the various phases of development, such as the discontinuation of short-course records, changes in the breast-stroke and butterfly rules, the start of timing to hundredths of a second etc.

This second edition is dedicated
to the memory of Alan Ross McWhirter
statistician, author, colleague and friend
1925 - 1975

International Federation, as approved by the I.O.C., even if the federation rules are more strict than those of the I.O.C.

"Not have received any financial rewards or material benefit in connection with his or her sports participation, except as permitted in the bye-laws to this rule."

The 1974 tidying up, and, in some cases, liberalising of their amateur rules show that the I.O.C. have moved with modern times and needs and given the lead to the I.S.Fs.

The most significant point in the new bye-laws is the clear ruling that an amateur may accept compensation for "broken time", ie to cover financial loss resulting from absence from work through preparing for or competing in an Olympic Games or other international competition provided that this is authorised by his N.O.C. or N.S.F.

Further, a competitor's amateur status will not now be jeopardised if his person, name, picture or sports performances are used in advertising as a result of his I.S.F., N.O.C. and N.S.F. entering into a contract for commercial sponsorship provided that he, personally, does not receive any payment.

But he may not carry advertising material on his person or clothing, other than trade marks on technical equipment or clothing as agreed by the I.O.C. with the I.S.Fs. in the Olympic Games, World or Continental championships and Games under the patronage of the I.O.C.

Further, the I.O.C. no longer places a limit on the number of days during which a competitor may receive food and lodging, transport, pocket money, authorised paid coaching etc. in order to prepare for an Olympic Games or other international competition. It is left to each I.S.F. to decide if they wish to limit the days.

An amateur may be paid as a physical education or sports teacher giving elementary instruction but may not act as a professional coach or trainer in any sport. Nor may an amateur in one sport be or have been a professional athlete in any other sport.

ADMINISTRATION.
See AMATEUR SWIMMING ASSOCIATION; FEDERATION INTERNATIONALE DE NATATION AMATEUR; LIGUE EUROPEENNE DE NATATION.

AGE-GROUP.
The United States were the pioneers of age-group swimming, a system of competition for youngsters of like age. Regarded as a development process and not an end in itself, the pioneering Americans have achieved tremendous international success through following this policy.

At the Mexico Olympics of 1968, 90 per cent of the American team, who won 58 out of a possible 90 swimming medals, were or had been age-group competitors. Altogether, the United States recognized 686 different events for their national age-group rankings.

The most common groups are 10 years and under, 11–12, 13–14 and 15–17 years, but the many countries who have followed the example of the United States choose even single year age-groups if this suits them best.

AMATEUR ATHLETIC UNION OF THE UNITED STATES CHAMPIONS.
See UNITED STATES DIVING, INDOOR AND OUTDOOR CHAMPIONS

AMATEURISM.
The most important law covering amateurism is that of the International Olympic Committee who, in Vienna in October 1974, decided as follows:

"Rule 26: To be eligible for participation in the Olympic Games, a competitor must:

"Observe and abide by the Rules and Regulations of the I.O.C. and in addition the Rules and Regulations of his or her

AMATEUR SWIMMING ASSOCIATION.
The A.S.A., the governing body for the sport in England, are accepted as having been founded on 7 Jan. 1869, though in fact were not known by this name until 17 years after this date (see

Metropolitan Swimming Association).

During the intervening years, continual rows concerning amateur and professionalism caused breakaways and the formation of a rival association. Finally, on 3 Mar. 1886 the warring factions sank their differences and agreed on a set of 135 rules, based on those of the Amateur Athletic Association and the National Cyclists Union, which have been the basis of A.S.A. administration ever since and have been copied by bodies throughout the world.

After 100 years of amateur administration, the A.S.A. appointed their first professional secretary, Norman Sarsfield, in 1970 as successor to Harold Fern (see separate entry), who had been honorary secretary for 49 years.

AMATEUR SWIMMING ASSOCIATION CHAMPIONSHIPS. Although titled the A.S.A. championships (of England), these events, traditionally, have been open to the world. This has been because of the A.S.A.'s leading role in establishing organized competition and, as a result, titles have been won by competitors from Australia, Belgium, Canada, France, Hungary, New Zealand, Sweden, South Africa, the United States and, of course, Scotland, Wales and Ireland.

Until 1934, the events were held at varying venues and different dates around the country which often resulted in small entries, or even swim-overs, because of the time and expense involved. From then on, the bulk of the events have been held at centralized venues—though often the diving has been held separately.

In 1971 short course (see SHORT COURSE) closed British championships were introduced and are held annually in the spring. But the summer long course (see LONG COURSE) "Nationals", open to the world, still remain the high spot of the year in Britain.

The venues and winners of Amateur Swimming Association championships are listed throughout under the well-known abbreviation of A.S.A. champions, diving champions etc.

AMERICAN CHAMPIONS. See UNITED STATES CHAMPIONS.

ANDERSEN, Greta (Denmark, 1928-). As an Olympic champion and also a conqueror of the English Channel, Miss Andersen claims a double place in swimming history. At 20, in the Games of 1948, she won the 100 m. free-style in 66.3, having equalled the Olympic record of 65.9 in a heat. Later she collapsed and had to be dragged from the water during a heat of the 400 m., but recovered in time to help Denmark to silver medals in the free-style relay. The Dane also won the European 400 m. title in 1950 (5:30.9) and placed third in the 100 m. in 1947 and 1950. In addition, she was a member of Danish relay teams who placed first in the 1947 Europeans and second in 1950.

Miss Andersen, at this time recognized as a sprinter and middle-distance competitor, then turned her talents to long distance events and between 1957 and 1964, as a professional, she made the hazardous Channel crossing six times. The first was during a Butlin-sponsored race in 1957 when only two out of 24 starters got across and Greta finished two hours ahead of her male rival.

She held the record for England to France (the more difficult crossing) with 13 hours 14 minutes from 1964-73, yet despite her Olympic success, she broke only one world record, for 100 y. (58.2) in 1949. She married an American and appears in some Channel records as Andersen-Sonnichsen.

A.S.A. CHAMPIONS. The Derby Bath, Blackpool, has been the venue of 18 of the 34 A.S.A. championship meetings since centralization began in 1935. For a number of years all events over 440 yards were excluded from the main meeting, but since 1962 only the long distance event has been held separately. The venues since centralization have been:

1935 South Shore, Blackpool
1936* Empire Pool, Wembley
1937* Scarborough, Yorkshire
1938 Great Yarmouth, Norfolk
1939* Minehead, Somerset
1940–45 No championship meetings
1946* New Brighton, Cheshire
1947* Hastings and St. Leonards, Sussex
1948† Scarborough, Yorkshire
1949 Queen Street, Derby
1950 Kingsway, Lancaster
1951 Kingsway, Lancaster
1952 King Alfred, Hove, Sussex
1953–63* Derby Bath, Blackpool

1964* Crystal Palace, London
1965–70 Derby Bath, Blackpool
1971* Leeds, Yorkshire
1972* Crystal Palace, London
1973* Coventry, Warwickshire
1974 Derby Bath, Blackpool
1975 Coventry, Warwickshire
1976* Crystal Palace, London

* Diving included
† Diving included but bad weather forced postponement and transfer of events to Hastings.

100 y. Free-style. This was the second championship to be instituted and was promoted originally by the South-East London S.C.

1878	Moore, J. S.	1:16¾
1879	Moore, J. S.	1:13¼
1880	Itter, W. R.	1:16¾
1881	Bettinson, G. R.	1:16.0
1882	Depau, C.	1:12¼
1883	Blew Jones, W.	1:11.0
1884	Mayger, J.L.	1:11.2
1885	Mayger, J.L.	1:12.0
1886	Nuttall, Joseph	1:09½
1887	Nuttall, Joseph	1:07.8
1888	Nuttall, Joseph	1:06¼
1889	Lenton, Charles	1:07.8
1890	Evans, William	1:08¾
1891	Evan, William	1:08.4
1892	Tyers, Jack	1:05.8
1893	Tyers, Jack	1:07.6
1894	Tyers, Jack	1:05.6
1895	Tyers, Jack	1:04.0
1896	Tyers, Jack	1:01.4
1897	Tyers, Jack	1:03.6
1898	Derbyshire, Rob	1:00.8
1899	Derbyshire, Rob	1:00.4
1900	Derbyshire, Rob	1:01.0
1901	Derbyshire, Rob	1:01.4
1902	Lane, Freddy (Aus)	1:00.0
1903	Derbyshire, Rob	1:01.6
1904	Derbyshire, Rob	1:00.8
1905	Halmay, Zoltan (Hun)	59.0
1906	Daniels, Charles (USA)	58.6
1907	Daniels, Charles (USA)	55.4
1908	Meyboom, Hermann (Belg)	1:00.6
1909	Radmilovic, Paul	1:01.0
1910	Beaurepaire, Frank (Aus)	59.8
1911	Hardwick, Harold (Aus)	58.6
1912	McGillivray, Peter	57.6
1913	Annison, Harold	1:00.0
1914-19	No events	
1920	Stedman, Ivan (Aus)	58.0
1921	Van Schelle, Martial (Belg)	57.6
1922	Van Schelle, Martial (Belg)	56.6
1923	Van Schelle, Martial (Belg)	57.0

1924	Henry, Ernest (Aus)	58.0
1925	Barany, Istvan (Hun)	55.8
1926	House, J. A. Jnr. (USA)	57.4
1927	Baillie, Charles	56.8
1928	Sampson, Paul	54.4
1929	Brooks, Norman	55.4
1930	Brooks, Norman	56.2
1931	Sutton, Reg	56.2
1932	Brooks, Norman	54.6
1933	Sutton, Reg	56.0
1934	Larson, George (Can)	54.0
1935	Gabrielsen, Roy	55.4
1936	Dove, Freddie	55.0
1937	Dove, Freddie	55.8
1938	Dove, Freddie	55.0
1939	Taylor, Mickey	54.2
1940-45	No events	
1946	Jany, Alex (Fra)	52.0
1947	Kendall, Pat	55.2
1948	Stedman, Ron	55.0
1949	Stedman, Ron	53.7
1950	Kendall, Pat	54.1
1951	Larsson, Goran (Swe)	52.1
1952	Wardrop, Jack	53.4

110 y. Free-style

1953	Roberts, Ron	59.5
1954	Baxter, Geoff	1:00.9
1955	Roberts, Ron	58.5
1956	McKechnie, Neil	58.9
1957	McKechnie, Neil	59.2
1958	Black, Ian	58.3
1959	Black, Ian	58.0
1960	Clarke, Stan	57.8
1961	Martin-Dye, John	57.2
1962	McGregor, Bobby	55.6
1963	McGregor, Bobby	54.1
1964	McGregor, Bobby	53.9
1965	Lord, Bobby	55.2
1966	McGregor, Bobby	53.5
1967	McGregor, Bobby	54.0
1968	McGregor, Bobby	53.9
1969	Windeatt, Malcolm	56.3
1970	Windeatt, Malcolm	55.2

100m. Free-style

1971	Windeatt, Malcolm	55.1
1972	Windeatt, Malcolm	54.3
1973	Cunningham, Colin	54.26
1974	Brinkley, Brian	54.2*
1975	Brinkley, Brian	52.30

220 y. Free-style. Instituted originally by the Swimming Association of Great Britain

1880	Danels, Edward	3:09¾
1881	Danels, Edward	3:14½
1882	Danels, Edward	3:13¼

1883	Cairns, Tom	2:59¼		1951	Larsson, Goran (Swe)	2:12.2
1884	Cairns, Tom	3:02¼		1952	Wardrop, Jack	2:11.2
1885	Cairns, Tom	3:08¼		1953	Roberts, Ron	2:15.8
1886	Nuttall, Joseph	3:04.8		1954	Wardrop, Jack	2:11.7
1887	Nuttall, Joseph	2:59.8		1955	McKechnie, Neil	2:13.8
1888	Nuttall, Joseph	†3:15.6		1956	McKechnie, Neil	2:11.3
1889	Jones, T.	2:57½		1957	McKechnie, Neil	2:12.0
1890	Evans, William	2:51.2		1958	Black, Ian	2:07.2
1891	Evans, William	2:52.0		1959	Black, Ian	2:06.0
1892	Tyers, Jack	2:46.4		1960	Clarke, Stan	2:07.6
1893	Tyers, Jack	2:54.8		1961	Martin-Dye, John	2:06.9
1894	Tyers, Jack	2:49.0		1962	McLachlan, Murray (SAf)	2:05.5
1895	Tyers, Jack	2:41.0		1963	McGregor, Bobby	2:04.8
1896	Tyers, Jack	2:50.2		1964	Grylls, Geoff (SAf)	2:03.5
1897	Tyers, Jack	2:38.8		1965	Grylls, Geoff (SAf)	2:01.6
1898	Derbyshire, Rob	2:42.4		1966	McGregor, Bobby	2:02.6
1899	Lane, Freddy (Aus)	2:38.2		1967	Jarvis, Tony	2:03.4
1900	Lane, Freddy (Aus)/			1968	Jarvis, Tony	2:00.1
	Derbyshire, Rob	2:34.8		1969	Woodroffe, Martyn	2:01.5
1901	Derbyshire, Rob	2:42.0		1970	Borrie, Mike (NZ)	2:02.4
1902	Lane, Freddy (Aus)	2:28.6			†Race afterward declared void.	
1903	Derbyshire, Rob	2:46.0				
1904	Forsyth, Eric	2:37.8		**200m. Free-style**		
1905	Kieran, Barney (Aus)	2:37.2		1971	Brinkley, Brian	2:02.0
1906	Healy, Cecil (Aus)	2:37.4		1972	Brinkley, Brian	1:57.9
1907	Halmay, Zoltan (Hun)	2:34.0				
1908	Beaurepaire, Frank (Aus)	2:37.0		1973	Brinkley, Brian	1:56.68
1909	Battersby, Sydney	2:32.8		1974	Brinkley, Brian	1:57.5*
1910	Beaurepaire, Frank (Aus)	2:30.0		1975	Brinkley, Brian	1:55.59
1911	Hardwick, Harold (Aus)	2:33.6				
1912	Hatfield, Jack	2:30.2				
1913	Hatfield, Jack	2:30.6				
1914–19	No events					
1920	Beaurepaire, Frank (Aus)	2:29.2		1884	Cairns, Tom	6:33.0
1921	Borg, Arne (Swe)	2:29.2		1885	Schlotel, H.	6:48.2
1922	Hatfield, Jack	2:32.2		1886	Schlotel, H.	6:21¼
1923	Borg, Arne (Swe)	2:29.6		1887	Schlotel, H.	6:21.4
1924	Annison, Harold	2:35.0		1888	Nuttall, Joseph	6:16½
1925	Hatfield, Jack	2:34.4		1889	Henry, William	6:04.0
1926	Whiteside, Joe	2:31.0		1890	Evans, William	6:19.2
1927	Dickin, Albert	2:36.0		1891	Evans, William	7:15.0
1928	Whiteside, Joe	2:27.2		1892	Evans, William	7:03.0
1929	Brooks, Norman	2:28.0		1893	Tyers, Jack	6:33.2
1930	Brooks, Norman	2:26.0		1894	Tyers, Jack	7:06.4
1931	Sutton, Reg	2:22.2		1895	Tyers, Jack	6:08.8
1932	Sutton, Reg	2:31.5		1896	Tyers, Jack	6:18.4
1933	Leivers, Bobby	2:23.6		1897	Cavill, Percy (Aus)	4:50.4
1934	Larson, George (Can)	2:20.2		1898	Jarvis, John	6:30.0
1935	Wainwright, Norman	2:18.6		1899	Lane, Freddy (Aus)	6:30.8
1936	Wainwright, Norman	2:17.8		1900	Jarvis, John	†12:55.0
1937	Wainwright, Norman	2:18.6		1901	Billington, David	8:23.2
1938	Wainwright, Norman	2:16.6		1902	Cavill, Richard (Aus)	5:04.8
1939	Wainwright, Norman	2:14.4		1903	Billington, David	6:34.6
1940–45	No events			1904	Billington, David	6:19.0
1946	Jany, Alex (Fra)	2:14.0		1905	Kieran, Barney (Aus)	5:22.2
1947	Hale, Jack	2:20.1		1906	Taylor, Henry	5:42.6
1948	Hale, Jack	2:16.4		1907	Taylor, Henry	4:43.0
1949	Ostrand, Per-Ola (Swe)	2:13.6		1908	Beaurepaire, Frank (Aus)	4:59.4
1950	Wardrop, Jack	2:16.6		1909	Battersby, Sydney	swam over

440 y. Free-style. First promoted by the Portsmouth S.C. and conducted as a salt-water championship until 1934.

1910	Beaurepaire, Frank (Aus)	5:38.6
1911	Hardwick, Harold (Aus)	5:40.4
1912	Hatfield, Jack	4:54.8
1913	Hatfield, Jack	5:43.0
1914–19	No events	
1920	Annison, Harold	5:41.0
1921	Peter, Percy	5:40.0
1922	Peter, Percy	5:46.8
1923	Peter, Percy	5:52.6
1924	Hatfield, Jack	5:52.6
1925	Radmilovic, Paul	5:41.2
1926	Dickin, Albert	5:44.5
1927	Hatfield, Jack	5:51.0
1928	Sampson, Paul	5:30.8
1929	Brooks, Norman	5:39.2
1930	Brooks, Norman	5:41.8
1931	Sutton, Reg	5:27.4
1932	Leivers, Bobby	5:30.4
1933	Sutton, Reg	5:28.0
1934	Leivers, Bobby	5:37.0
1935	Wainwright, Norman	5:05.8
1936	Wainwright, Norman	4:58.4
1937	Wainwright, Norman	5:03.4
1938	Wainwright, Norman	4:59.0
1939	Wainwright, Norman	4:52.6
1940–45	No events	
1946	Hale, Jack	4:56.2
1947	Hale, Jack	5:00.4
1948	Hale, Jack	5:02.4
1949	Ostrand, Per-Ola (Swe)	4:47.5
1950	Wardrop, Jack	4:54.8
1951	Wardrop, Jack	4:49.5
1952	Wardrop, Jack	4:47.2
1953	Sreenan, Bob	4:54.4
1954	Symonds, Graham	4:53.8
1955	McKechnie, Neil	4:47.0
1956	McKechnie, Neil	4:45.8
1957	Sreenan, Bob	4:53.6
1958	Black, Ian	4:28.4
1959	Black, Ian	4:32.9
1960	Martin-Dye, John	4:31.7
1961	Martin-Dye, John	4:34.2
1962	Campion, Dick	4:32.7
1963	Martin-Dye, John	4:31.3
1964	Grylls, Geoff (SAf)	4:24.9
1965	Grylls, Geoff (SAf)	4:22.2
1966	Kimber, Alan	4:24.3
1967	Kimber, Alan	4:23.5
1968	Jarvis, Tony	4:22.0
1969	Jacks, Ron (Can)	4:17.9
1970	Terrell, Ray	4:21.4

† Against strong current

400m. Free-style

1971	Brinkley, Brian	4:18.5
1972	Brinkley, Brian	4:10.2
1973	Brinkley, Brian	4:10.62
1974	Brinkley, Brian	4:08.4*
1975	Brinkley, Brian	4:04.03

500 y. Free-style

1878	Taylor, James (first winner)	8:07¼

Hatfield, Jack won nine times—
1912–13 and, after the war
break, from 1921 to 1927.

1934	Wainwright, Norman (last winner)	5:24.0
1935	Discontinued	

880 y. Free-style. Originally promoted by the *Sporting Life.*

1881	Ainsworth, Dave	14:31½
1882	Ainsworth, Dave	15.16¾
1883	Ainsworth, Dave	14:23½
1884	Bell, G.	14:35½
1885	Schlotel, H.	†13:04½
1886	Schlotel, H.	14:17½
1887	Nuttall, Joseph	14:44.0
1888	Bowden, H.	14:25.4
1889	Standring, J.F.	14:56.8
1890	Evans, William	14:38.0
1891	Greasley, Sam	13:42.4
1892	Greasley, Sam	14:00.8
1893	Tyers, Jack	13:41.0
1894	Tyers, Jack	13:42.4
1895	Tyers, Jack	13:56.0
1896	Not held	
1897	Derbyshire, Rob	13:38.8
1898	Jarvis, John	12:52.0
1899	Jarvis, John	12:45.6
1900	Jarvis, John	12:35.0
1901	Jarvis, John	12:42.4
1902	Cavill, Richard (Aus)	11:50.4
1903	Billington, David	13:10.6
1904	Forsyth, Eric	12:23.0
1905	Kieran, Barney (Aus)	11:28.0
1906	Taylor, Henry	11:25.4
1907	Taylor, Henry	12:16.2
1908	Beaurepaire, Frank (Aus)	12:44.0
1909	Battersby, Sydney	11:47.2
1910	Beaurepaire, Frank (Aus)	11:39.8
1911	Taylor, Henry	12:05.6
1912	Hatfield, Jack	12:21.2
1913	Hatfield, Jack	11:46.4
1914–19	No events	
1920	Annison, Harold	12:21.4
1921	Hatfield, Jack	11:46.4
1922	Hatfield, Jack	11:59.2
1923	Hatfield, Jack	12:15.2
1924	Hatfield, Jack	12:11.4
1925	Hatfield, Jack	11:51.0
1926	Radmilovic, Paul	11:57.4
1927	Peter, Percy	12:02.2
1928	White, S. W.	13:55.0
1929	Taris, Jean (Fra)	11:19.8
1930	Bramhall, Fred	swam over.
1931	Taylor, Arthur	11:33.2
1932	Leivers, Bobby	11:27.4

1933	Wainwright, Norman	11:31.6
1934	Wainwright, Norman	10:57.4
1935	Wainwright, Norman	10:51.6
1936	Leivers, Bobby	10:30.0
1937	Wainwright, Norman	10:26.4
1938	Deane, Kenneth, R.H.	10:47.0
1939	Wainwright, Norman	10:51.4
1940–5	No events	
1946	Hale, Jack	10:27.4
1947	Hale, Jack	10:49.6
1948	Hale, Jack	10:58.6
1949	Wardrop, Jack	10:30.3
1950	Wardrop, Jack	10:29.1
1951	Bland, Donald	10:33.1
1952	Wardrop, Jack	10:03.6
1953	Sreenan, Bob	10:24.6
1954	Symonds, Graham	10:48.4
1955	Sreenan, Bob	10:27.7
1956	McKechnie, Neil	10:12.9
1957	Sreenan, Bob	10:07.8
1958	Sreenan, Bob	10:07.8
1959	Campion, Dick	10:13.5
1960	Campion, Dick	9:56.7
1961	Kennedy, Jim	9:52.6
1962	Campion, Dick	9:47.2
1963	Kennedy, Jim	9:57.6
1964	Milton, Tony	10:13.2
1965	Grylls, Geoff (SAf)	9:15.5
1966	Kimber, Alan	9:09.3
1967	Kimber, Alan	9:13.3
1968	Kimber, Alan	9:12.7
1969	Jacks, Ron (Can)	8:58.0
1970	Treffers, Mark (NZ)	9:03.2
1971	Discontinued	

† Course shorter than 880 y.

One mile Free-style. This was the first official National Championship and was promoted originally by the Metropolitan Swimming Association. From 1869-1872 it was swum in the River Thames over a course from Putney Aquaduct to Hammersmith Bridge. Thereafter it was swum in still water. The first trophy was won outright by Horace Davenport in 1876. Later Davenport paid half of the cost of a replacement trophy which he won three times again. But this time it was a perpetual trophy.

1869	Morris, Tom	27:18.0
1870	Parker, Harry	26:06.4
1871	Parker, Harry	24:35.0
1872	Parker, Harry	29:03.0
1873	Ainsworth, Dave	30:38½
1874	Davenport, Horace	31:09.0
1875	Davenport, Horace	31:30.0
1876	Davenport, Horace	33:08.0
1877	Davenport, Horace	29:25½
1878	Davenport, Horace	31:15¼
1879	Davenport, Horace	34:09.0
1880	Taylor, James	30:38.0
1881	Taylor, James	35:20.0
1882	Taylor, James	32:38.0
1883	Danels, Edward	31:40.6
1884	Bell, G.	31:42¾
1885	Sargent, S.	32:11½
1886	Schlotel, H.	31:32¾
1887	Nuttall, Joseph	30:38.0
1888	Standring, J.F.	34:01½
1889	Bowden, H.	31:00.8
1890	Greasely, Sam	29:32.4
1891	Greasley, Sam	30:33.6
1892	Greasley, Sam	28:18.4
1893	Tyers, Jack	27:21.4
1894	Tyers, Jack	27:51.4
1895	Tyers, Jack	27:33.8
1896	Tyers, Jack	26:46.0
1897	Jarvis, John	32:28.6
1898	Jarvis, John	26:37.2
1899	Jarvis, John	25:13.4
1900	Jarvis, John	26:26.0
1901	Jarvis, John	25:13.8
1902	Jarvis, John	25:32.4
1903	Billington, David	24:56.4
1904	Billington, David	27:18.0
1905	Billington, David	24:42.6
1906	Taylor, Henry	27:09.0
1907	Taylor, Henry	25:04.6
1908	Beaurepaire, Frank (Aus)	25:15.4
1909	Battersby, Sydney	24:01.4
1910	Beaurepaire, Frank (Aus)	24:39.4
1911	Taylor, Henry	†23:35½
1912	Hatfield, Jack	25:02.8
1913	Hatfield, Jack	24:55.2
1914	Hatfield, Jack	24:42.4
1915–19	No events	
1920	Annison, Harold	25:25.0
1921	Hatfield, Jack	24:48.8
1922	Hatfield, Jack	26:46.8
1923	Hatfield, Jack	24:54.0
1924	Hatfield, Jack	25:22.4
1925	Radmilovic, Paul	24:27.0
1926	Radmilovic, Paul	24:27.0
1927	Radmilovic, Paul	25:39.8
1928	Lindsay, D. (NZ)	25:10.8
1929	Hatfield, Jack	25:40.6
1930	Hatfield, Jack	25:30.6
1931	Milton, Freddie	25:28.4
1932	Milton, Freddie	25:58.6
1933	Wainwright, Norman	23:20.6
1934	Wainwright, Norman	23:47.0
1935	Wainwright, Norman	23:19.0
1936	Leivers, Bobby	21:49.4
1937	Wainwright, Norman	22:31.8
1938	Leivers, Bobby	22:07.2
1939	Wainwright, Norman	21:38.8
1940–45	No events	
1946	Hale, Jack	21:47.2

1947	Hale, Jack	21:33.2
1948	Hale, Jack	21:25.2
1949	Bland, Donald	22:13.2
1950	Bland, Donald	21:54.9
1951	Bland, Donald	21:33.8
1952	Wardrop, Jack	20:53.2
1953	Sreenan, Bob	21:11.4
1954	Sreenan, Bob	22:13.2
1955	Sreenan, Bob	21:16.4
1956	Sreenan, Bob	20:57.4
1957	Sreenan, Bob	21:23.2
1958	Black, Ian	19:17.5
1959	Campion, Dick	20:48.2
1960	Campion, Dick	20:00.2
1961	Campion, Dick	19:50.6
1962	Campion, Dick	19:30.2
1963	Martin-Dye, John	20:07.5
1964	Grylls, Geoff (SAf)	19:10.1

† Course 1,755 y. 7 in.

1,650 y. Free-style

1965	Gilchrist, Sandy (Can)	17:33.9
1966	Kimber, Alan	17:52.8
1967	Kimber, Alan	17:33.9
1968	Kimber, Alan	17:48.3
1969	Jacks, Ron (Can)	17:20.8
1970	Treffers, Mark (NZ)	17:04.4

1,500m. Free-style

1971	Mills, John	17:21.5
1972	Brinkley, Brian	16:38.6
1973	Brinkley, Brian	16:41.05
1974	Carter, Jimmy	16:38.6*
1975	Nash, Paul	16:28.19

Long distance. Known originally as the 'Lords and Commons' Race' (1877 to 1879) the first cup having been presented by members of Parliament. It was won outright by Horace Davenport. Each man had to be accompanied by a boat and the race, a dramatic sight, was held in the River Thames, with the current, over a course of between five and six miles, until 1939. After the Second World War, the pollution of the Thames made it dangerous for swimmers, but a race was held in the Serpentine in 1947. It was then discontinued until 1962 when the British Long Distance A.S.A. became associated in the organization. The venues since then have been in the River Ouse (1962-63), River Wear (1964-65) and Trentham Park Lake, Nottingham (1966-75).

1877	Davenport, Horace	1 hr 13:27.0
1878	Davenport, Horace	1 hr 16:10.0
1879	Davenport, Horace	1 hr 22:27.0

1880	Itter, W. R.	1 hr 17:00.0
1881	Richardson, W. R.	1 hr 21:30.0
1882	Huntingdon, F. W.	1 hr 21:00.0
1883	Itter, W. R.	1 hr 15:20.0
1884	Bell, G.	1 hr 19:01.0
1885	Bell, G.	1 hr 24:42.0
1886	France, A. E.	1 hr 20:50.0
1887	France, A. E.	1 hr 18:10.0
1888	France, A. E.	1 hr 17:07.0
1889	Bowden, H.	1 hr 25:50.0
1890	Henry, William	1 hr 15:15.0
1891	Ibbott, A.	1 hr 12:27.0
1892	Drake, Mathew	1 hr 18:40.0
1893	Tyers, Jack	1 hr 17:01.8
1894	Tyers, Jack	1 hr 47:06.0
1895	Race void	–
1896	Green, W.	2 hr 33:15.0
1897	Cavill, Percy (Aus)	1 hr 06:35.0
1898	Jarvis, John	1 hr 07:58.0
1899	Jarvis, John	1 hr 09:45.0
1900	Jarvis, John	1 hr 04:17.0
1901	Jarvis, John	1 hr 09:04.2
1902	Jarvis, John	1 hr 13:27.0
1903	Jarvis, John	1 hr 03:48.2
1904	Jarvis, John	1 hr 07:32.2
1905	Billington, David	1 hr 08:55.0
1906	Jarvis, John	1 hr 03:40.0
1907	Radmilovic, Paul	1 hr 09:15.2
1908	Springfield, F.W. (Aus)	1 hr 10:57.0
1909	Taylor, Henry	1 hr 05:24,0
1910	Battersby, Sydney	1 hr 03:12.4
1911	Champion, Malcolm (NZ)	1 hr 06:11.4
1912	Taylor, Henry	1 hr 04:07.4
1913	Hatfield, Jack	1 hr 05:27.0
1914	Hatfield, Jack	1 hr 05:04.0
1915-19	No events	
1920	Taylor, Henry	1 hr 04:55.0
1921	Hatfield, Jack	1 hr 08:32.0
1922	Peter, Percy	1 hr 07:23.0
1923	Hatfield, Jack	1 hr 16:13.0
1924	Hatfield, Jack	1 hr 08:25.0
1925	Radmilovic, Paul	1 hr 05:06.4
1926	Radmilovic, Paul	1 hr 07:35.0
1927	Pascoe, Ernie	1 hr 11:38.4
1928	Hatfield, Jack	1 hr 04:44.0
1929	Peter, Percy	1 hr 05:02.6
1930	Pascoe, Ernie	1 hr 06:53.8
1931	Hatfield, Jack	57:22.0
1932	Milton, Freddie	53:37.4
1933	Milton, Freddie	1 hr 08:20.0
1934	Deane, Cecil	1 hr 08:52.6
1935	Deane, Cecil	1 hr 03:47.4
1936	Deane, Cecil	1 hr 04:04.8
1937	Deane, Cecil	1 hr 02:57.6
1938	Deane, Cecil	1 hr 05:24.2
1939	Hale, Jack	1 hr 03:59.4
1940-46	No events	

1947	Hale, Jack	1 hr 13:30.2
1948–61	No events	
1962	Kennedy, Jim	1 hr 36:20.0
1963	Milton, Tony	1 hr 35:20.0
1964	Johnson, R.	1 hr 45:57.0
1965	Milton, Tony	1 hr 40:10.0
1966	Milton, Tony	2 hr 36:10.0
1967	Wilson, Andy	2 hr 13:20.0
1968	Metcalfe, Brian	2 hr 21:09.0
1969	Kimber, Alan	2 hr 07:58.0
1970	Metcalfe, Brian	2 hr 16:05.0
1971	Pratten, David	1 hr 56:10.0
1972	Pratten, David	2 hr 02:39.0
1973	Pratten, David	2 hr 04:02.0
1974	Bell, Graham	2 hr 27:51.0
1975	Ashley, Mark	2 hr 10:45.0

150 y. Back-stroke

1903	Call, William	2:06.6
1904	Call, William	2:01.4
1905	Call, William	2:01.6
1906	Unwin, Fred	2:04.0
1907	Unwin, Fred	1:59.2
1908	Unwin, Fred	2:01.0
1909	Unwin, Fred	2:02.2
1910	Weckesser, Maurice (Belg)	1:57.2
1911	Weckesser, Maurice (Belg)	1:58.4
1912	Webster, George	2:00.0
1913	Webster, George	1:59.4
1914	Webster, George	1:54.6
1915–19	No events	
1920	Blitz, Gerard (Belg)	1:55.8
1921	Blitz, Gerard (Belg)	1:55.8
1922	Rawlinson, Austin	1:56.2
1923	Rawlinson, Austin	1:55.8
1924	Rawlinson, Austin	1:48.2
1925	Rawlinson, Austin	1:52.4
1926	Rawlinson, Austin	1:51.8
1927	Besford, John	1:50.0
1928	Besford, John	1:48.2
1929	Trippett, John	1:52.0
1930	Besford, John	1:46.2
1931	Besford, John	1:45.4
1932	Besford, John	1:45.0
1933	Francis, Willy	1:46.0
1934	Francis, Willy	1:45.0
1935	Besford, John	1:46.8
1936	Besford, John	1:48.4
1937	Taylor, Micky	1:46.4
1938	Taylor, Micky	1:46.0
1939	Tyrrell, Ian (SAf)	1:42.0
1940–45	No events	
1946	Vallery, Georges (Fr)	1:38.6

100 y. Back-stroke

1947	Kinnear, Bert	1:04.0
1948	Brockway, John	1:02.6
1949	Brockway, John	1:00.8
1950	Brockway, John	1:01.2
1951	Brockway, John	59.7
1952	Wardrop, Bert	1:00.4

110 y. Back-stroke

1953	Brockway, John	1:08.8
1954	Brockway, John	1:07.2
1955	Brockway, John	1:08.4
1956	Sykes, Graham	1:08.2
1957	Sykes, Graham	1:06.7
1958	Sykes, Graham	1:07.4
1959	Sykes, Graham	1:05.5
1960	Sykes, Graham	1:04.8
1961–63	No events	
1964	Stewart, Brian (SAf)	1:03.9
1965	Stewart, Brian (SAf)	1:03.1
1966	Jones, Roddy	1:02.2
1967	Jones, Roddy	1:03.1
1968	Jones, Roddy	1:02.4
1969	Rushton, Clive	1:02.7
1970	Richards, Mike	1:01.8

100 m. Back-stroke

1971	Richards, Mike	1:02.6
1972	Cunningham, Colin	1:00.3
1973	Cunningham, Colin	1:00.76
1974	Pickell, Stephen (Can)	1:00.8*
1975	Carter, Jimmy	1:00.37

220 y. Back-stroke

1961	Sykes, Graham	2:23.9
1962	Sykes, Graham	2:21.6
1963	Jones, Roddy	2:25.0
1964	Stewart, Brian (SAf)	2:20.1
1965	Hutton, Ralph (Can)	2:16.0
1966	Jackson, Neil	2:18.5
1967	Reynolds, Peter (Aus)	2:17.9
1968	Butler, David	2:17.2
1969	Rushton, Clive	2:16.8
1970	Richards, Mike	2:15.2

200 m. Back-stroke

1971	Richards, Mike	2:15.7
1972	Cunningham, Colin	2:09.5
1973	Cunningham, Colin	2:09.45
1974	Pickell, Stephen (Can)	2:11.9*
1975	Carter, Jimmy	2:10.81

110 y. Breast-stroke

1964	Nicholson, Neil	1:12.6
1965	Hotz, Basil (SAf)	1:12.3
1966	Roberts, Roger	1:11.1
1967	Roberts, Roger	1:10.3
1968	Roberts, Stuart	1:11.5
1969	Mahony, Bill (Can)	1:10.2
1970	Carty, Mark	1:12.1

100 m. Breast-stroke

1971	O'Connell, Malcolm	1:09.8
1972	O'Connell, Malcolm	1:08.1
1973	Wilkie, David	1:07.86
1974	Wilkie, David	1:06.96
1975	Leigh, David	1:08.05

200 y. Breast-stroke

1903	Robinson, William	2:49.8
1904	Robinson, William	2:52.2
1905	Robinson, William	2:49.0
1906	Naylor, F. H.	2:58.4
1907	Courtman, Percy	2:55.4
1908	Courtman, Percy	2:47.2
1909	Courtman, Percy	2:46.2
1910	Julin, Harald (Swe)	2:53.0
1911	Toldi, Odon (Hun)	2:42.0
1912	Courtman, Percy	2:47.8
1913	Courtman, Percy	2:43.0
1914–19	No events	
1920	Lassam, R. G.	2:43.2
1921	Leon, S. (Fra)	2:49.8
1922	De Combe, Joseph (Belg)	2:58.0
1923	Stoney, William	2:51.0
1924	Flint, Reg	2:51.0
1925	Flint, Reg	2:50.0
1926	Bouvier, Henri (Fra)	2:48.2
1927	Van Parys, Louis (Belg)	2:42.4
1928	Flint, Reg	2:42.4
1929	Flint, Reg	2:44.6
1930	Bell, Stanley	2:43.4
1931	Cartonnet, Jacques (Fra)	2:42.2
1932	Cartonnet, Jacques (Fra)	2:39.0
1933	Schoebel, A. (Fra)	2:38.0
1934	Hamilton, Norman	2:43.2
1935	Hamilton, Norman	2:43.6
1936	Hamilton, Norman	2:43.6
1937	Davies, John	2:41.2
1938	Davies, John	2:39.2
1939	Davies, John	2:37.8
1940–45	No events	
1946	Davies, John	2:39.6
1947	Romain, Roy	Bu 2:30.0
1948	Romain, Roy	Bu 2:30.8
1949	Romain, Roy	Bu 2:30.7
1950	Jervis, Peter	2:34.7
1951	Snelling, Deryk	Bu 2:34.0
1952	Jervis, Peter	2:29.8

220 y. Breast-stroke

1953	Jervis, Peter	2:53.0
1954	Jervis, Peter	2:51.3
1955	Walkden, Chris	2:47.3
1956	Walkden, Chris	2:46.0
1957	Day, Brian	2:50.3
1958	Walkden, Chris	2:43.9
1959	Rowlinson, Gerard	2:48.5
1960	Rowlinson, Gerard	2:46.0

1961	Wilkinson, Chris	2:43.9
1962	Wilkinson, Chris	2:43.8
1963	Nicholson, Neil	2:42.2
1964	Hotz, Basil (SAf)	2:39.2
1965	Hotz, Basil (SAf)	2:40.3
1966	Finnigan, David	2:39.4
1967	Roberts, Roger	2:36.1
1968	Roberts, Stuart	2:38.5
1969	Mahony, Bill (Can)	2:33.5
1970	Johnson, Nigel	2:36.1

200 m. Breast-stroke

1971	O'Connell, Malcolm	2:33.7
1972	Wilkie, David	2:28.0
1973	Wilkie, David	2:27.60
1974	Wilkie, David	2:26.3*
1975	O'Brien, Barry	2:31.02

110 y. Butterfly

1964	Slovin, Vincent (SAf)	1:00.4
1965	Sherry, Dan (Can)	58.1
1966	Thurley, John	1:01.7
1967	Norris, Len	1:00.3
1968	Woodroffe, Martyn	59.8
1969	Woodroffe, Martyn	59.2
1970	Woodroffe, Martyn	1:00.1

100 m. Butterfly

1971	Robertson, Bruce (Can)	58.4
1972	Mills, John	59.2
1973	Edwards, Martin	58.90
1974	Brinkley, Brian	58.5*
1975	Brinkley, Brian	57.03

220 y. Butterfly

1953	Barnes, Brian	2:44.2
1954	Hale, Jack	2:39.5
1955	Symonds, Graham	2:36.3
1956	Dickson, Derek	2:43.8
1957	Campion, Dick	2:44.2
1958	Black, Ian	2:25.2
1959	Black, Ian	2:22.7
1960	Blyth, Ian	2:23.5
1961	Jenkins, Brian	2:19.0
1962	Jenkins, Brian	2:16.7
1963	Jenkins, Brian	2:17.6
1964	Slovin, Vincent (SAf)	2:13.6
1965	Sherry, Dan (Can)	2:13.5
1966	Thurley, John	2:15.1
1967	Woodroffe, Martyn	2:15.3
1968	Woodroffe, Martyn	2:11.0
1969	Woodroffe, Martyn	2:09.9
1970	Woodroffe, Martyn	2:10.7

200 m. Butterfly

| 1971 | Mills, John | 2:10.1 |
| 1972 | Brinkley, Brian | 2:05.6 |

1973	Brinkley, Brian	2:07.55
1974	Brinkley, Brian	2:07.3*
1975	Brinkley, Brian	2:05.68

220 y. Individual medley

1966	Kimber, Alan	2:21.8
1967	Reynolds, Peter (Aus)	2:19.8
1968	Woodroffe, Martyn	2:18.9
1969	Woodroffe, Martyn	2:17.6
1970	Woodroffe, Martyn	2:18.2

200 m. Individual medley

1971	Brinkley, Brian	2:19.5
1972	Terrell, Ray	2:11.9
1973	Brinkley, Brian	2:10.95
1974	Wilkie, David	2:12.3*
1975	Brinkley, Brian	2:10.89

440 y. Individual medley

1963	Jenkins, Brian	5:16.9
1964	Lacey, Tom (SAf)	5:06.7
1965	Gilchrist, Sandy (Can)	4:55.3
1966	Kimber, Alan	5:02.0
1967	Kimber, Alan	4:54.8
1968	Woodroffe, Martyn	4:55.5
1969	Woodroffe, Martyn	4:55.1
1970	Woodroffe, Martyn	4:52.5

400 m. Individual medley

1971	Roxborough, Steve (Can)	4:58.1
1972	Terrell, Ray	4:42.7
1973	Brinkley, Brian	4:36.29
1974	Carter, Jimmy	4:42.0*
1975	Carter, Jimmy	4:38.06

Team (club) relay (distances varied)

1909	Wigan
1910	Wigan
1911	Hyde Seal
1912	Hyde Seal
1913	Hyde Seal
1914	Northumberland/Otter finalists (abandoned because of outbreak of war)
1915–19	No events
1920	Hammersmith
1921	Middlesbrough
1922	Penguin
1923	Northumberland (swim over after dead heat with Penguin)
1924	Penguin
1925	Penguin
1926	Penguin
1927	Penguin
1928	South Manchester
1929	Oldham Police
1930	Oldham Police

1931	Oldham Police
1932	Oldham Police
1933	Otter
1934	Oldham Police
1935	Otter
1936	Otter
1937	Otter
1938	Otter
1939–45	No events

Team (county) relay (distances varied)

| 1946 | Yorkshire | 10:01.0 |
| 1947 | Yorkshire | 7:57.2 |

Team (club) relay (distances varied)

1948	Otter	10:54.4
1949	Otter	11:05.4
1950	Blackpool	10:58.7
1951	Sparkhill	10:33.6
1952	Sparkhill	9:37.0
1953	Sparkhill	9:42.5
1954	Coventry	9:38.4

4 x 110 y. Free-style (club) relay

1955	Otter	4:06.5
1956	Otter	4:09.5
1957	Wallasey	4:06.1
1958	York City	4:01.4
1959	York City	4:02.6
1960	Stoke Newington	3:58.2
1961	York City	3:57.3
1962	York City	3:55.6
1963	York City	3:54.1
1964	York City	3:52.2
1965	York City	3:53.3
1966	York City	3:52.6
1967	Otter	3:49.5
1968	Southampton	3:49.9
1969	Southampton	3:48.5
1970	Southampton	3:49.1

4 x 100 m. Free-style relay

1971	Nottingham Northern	3:49.6
1972	Southampton	3:46.5
1973	Southampton	3:45.35
1974	Modernians	3:50.4*
1975	Modernians	3:46.05

Medley (club) relay (distances varied)

1946	Otter	3:46.4
1947	Otter	7:51.2
1948	Otter	7:53.4
1949	Otter	6:52.2
1950	Otter	7:02.0
1951	Penguin	6:56.7
1952	Penguin	7:41.6
1953	Otter	7:46.3
1954	Otter	7:32.2

4 x 110 y. Medley (club) relay

1955	Otter	4:36.5
1956	Stoke Newington	4:46.8
1957	Otter	4:46.4
1958	Stoke Newington	4:44.9
1959	Stoke Newington	4:38.0
1960	Stoke Newington	4:34.3
1961	Otter	4:34.5
1962	York City	4:29.4
1963	York City	4:28.0
1964	Otter	4:25.3
1965	Barracuda	4:26.4
1966	Stoke Newington	4:19.2
1967	Stoke Newington	4:18.4
1968	Southampton	4:19.3
1969	Southampton	4:20.4
1970	Southampton	4:16.0

4 x 100 m. Medley (club) relay

1971	Nottingham Northern	4:13.5
1972	Southampton	4:11.7
1973	Southampton	4:07.40
1974	Millfield School	4:13.0*
1975	Southampton	4:07.57

WOMEN

100 y. Free-style

1901	Thorp, Hilda	1:30.4
1902	Scott, Maggie	1:25.2
1903	Thorp, Hilda	1:27.6
1904	Mackay, Netta	1:25.2
1905	Scott, Maggie	1:25.2
1906	Fletcher, Jennie	1:24.0
1907	Fletcher, Jennie	1:18.0
1908	Fletcher, Jennie	1:18.0
1909	Fletcher, Jennie	1:14.0
1910	Steer, Irene	1:13.6
1911	Fletcher, Jennie	1:15.6
1912	Fletcher, Jennie	1:15.2
1913	Curwen, Daisy	1:13.6
1914-18	No events	
1919	Jeans, Constance	1:11.6
1920	Jeans, Constance	1:14.0
1921	James, Hilda	1:11.0
1922	Jeans, Constance	1:09.2
1923	Jeans, Constance	1:07.4
1924	Jeans, Constance	1:07.2
1925	Jeans, Constance	1:07.2
1926	Laverty, Marion	1:07.4
1927	Hamblen, Mabel	1:08.2
1928	Tanner, Vera	1:06.2
1929	Cooper, Joyce	1:06.0
1930	King, Ellen	1:09.0
1931	Cooper, Joyce	1:05.6
1932	Cooper, Joyce	1:02.8
1933	Calderhead, Sheila	1:07.2
1934	Hughes, Edna	1:06.8

1935	Wadham, Olive	1:03.6
1936	Wadham, Olive	1:02.8
1937	Wadham, Olive	1:03.4
1938	Harrowby, Joyce	1:02.2
1939	Harrowby, Joyce	1:02.6
1940-45	No events	
1946	Riach, Nancy	1:03.0
1947	Riach, Nancy	1:02.4
1948	Wellington, Margaret	1:02.8
1949	Turner, Elizabeth	1:02.4
1950	Linton, "Pip"	1:02.9
1951	Linton, "Pip"	1:03.5
1952	Barnwell, Angela	1:02.2

110 y. Free-style

1953	Botham, Jean	1:09.7
1954	Botham, Jean	1:09.4
1955	Ewart, Fearne	1:08.3
1956	Grant, Virginia (Can)	1:07.0
1957	Wilkinson, Diana	1:05.7
1958	Grinham, Judy	1:06.8
1959	Steward, Natalie	1:05.2
1960	Steward, Natalie	1:04.9
1961	Wilkinson, Diana	1:04.9
1962	Wilkinson, Diana	1:03.3
1963	Wilkinson, Diana	1:03.3
1964	Wilkinson, Diana	1:04.4
1965	Lay, Marion (Can)	1:01.4
1966	Sillett, Pauline	1:02.9
1967	Jackson, Alex	1:02.6
1968	Jackson, Alex	1:01.7
1969	Jackson, Alex	1:03.7
1970	Jackson, Alex	1:01.2

100 m. Free-style

1971	Hill, Lynda	1:02.0
1972	Allardice, Lesley	1:01.2
1973	Allardice, Lesley	1:00.71
1974	Amundrud, Gail (Can)	1:01.0*
1975	Hill, Debbie	1:01.21

220 y. Free-style

1912	Curwen, Daisy	3:08.8
1913	Curwen, Daisy	3:12.4
1914-18	No events	
1919	Jeans, Constance	3:04.0
1920	Jeans, Constance	3:02.6
1921	James, Hilda	3:05.2
1922	James, Hilda	3:10.0
1923	Jeans, Constance	2:54.0
1924	James, Hilda	2:58.6
1925	Jeans, Constance	2:52.8
1926	Mayne, Edith	2:57.8
1927	Cooper, Joyce	2:49.4
1928	Cooper, Joyce	2:46.4
1929	Cooper, Joyce	2:48.0
1930	Yarwood, May	3:09.0
1931	Cooper, Joyce	2:50.6

1932	Cooper, Joyce	2:42.2
1933	Wolstenholme, Beatrice	2:43.8
1934	Kenyon, Mary	2:44.8
1935	Bartle, Olive	2:45.0
1936	Morcom, Gladys	2:43.0
1937	Bartle, Olive	2:42.6
1938	Jeffery, Margaret	2:40.8
1939	Yate, Helen	2:41.6
1940-45	No events	
1946	Riach, Nancy	2:36.0
1947	Gibson, Cathie	2:29.2
1948	Gibson, Cathie	2:32.6
1949	Wellington, Margaret	2:34.2
1950	Linton, "Pip"	2:33.1
1951	Wilkinson, Daphne	2:31.1
1952	Preece, Lillian	2:32.0
1953	Preece. Lillian	2:33.7
1954	Botham, Jean	2:34.3
1955	Grant, Virginia (Can)	2:34.7
1956	Grant, Virginia (Can)	2:20.6
1957	Grinham, Judy	2:30.0
1958	Ferguson, Elizabeth	2:28.6
1959	Steward, Natalie	2:25.6
1960	Steward, Natalie	2:22.1
1961	Wilkinson, Diana	2:21.6
1962	Wilkinson, Diana	2:21.9
1963	Lonsbrough, Anita	2:19.7
1964	Long, Elizabeth	2:21.9
1965	Long, Elizabeth	2:16.1
1966	Cave, Jeanette	2:20.5
1967	Williams, Susan	2:17.2
1968	Jackson, Alex	2:17.6
1969	Ratcliffe, Shelagh	2:17.1
1970	Jackson, Alex	2:14.3

200 m. Free-style

1971	Allardice, Lesley	2:13.9
1972	Allardice, Lesley	2:12.2
1973	Allardice, Lesley	2:11.19
1974	Amundrud, Gail (Can)	2:10.42
1975	Lee, Wendy (Can)	2:09.58

440 y, Free-style

1924	James, Hilda	6:27.0
1925	Laverty, Marion	6:18.8
1926	Laverty, Marion	6:10.6
1927	Laverty, Marion	6:11.4
1928	Cooper, Joyce	6:08.6
1929	Cooper, Joyce	6:15.4
1930	Cooper, Joyce	6:02.4
1931	Cooper, Joyce	5:58.4
1932	Cooper, Joyce	6:00.6
1933	Wolstenholme, Beatrice	6:03.0
1934	Wolstenholme, Beatrice	5:40.6
1935	Wolstenholme, Beatrice	6:00.0
1936	Morcom, Gladys	5:50.4
1937	Bartle, Olive	5:50.0
1938	Jeffery, Margaret	5:43.2

1939	Hutton, Margaret	5:39.8
1940-45	No events	
1946	Riach, Nancy	5:50.0
1947	Gibson, Cathie	5:23.2
1948	Gibson, Cathie	5:39.8
1949	Wellington, Margaret	5:36.4
1950	Wilkinson, Daphne	5:26.2
1951	Wilkinson, Daphne	5:17.6
1952	Wilkinson, Daphne	5:20.4
1953	Wilkinson, Daphne	5:29.8
1954	Brown, Christine	5:33.2
1955	Clarke, Joyce	5:34.8
1956	Girvan, Margaret	5:29.5
1957	Ferguson, Elizabeth	5:33.0
1958	Ferguson, Elizabeth	5:13.1
1959	Steward, Natalie	5:12.9
1960	Long, Elizabeth	5:05.0
1961	Rae, Nan	5:02.8
1962	Long, Elizabeth	4:53.7
1963	Long, Elizabeth	4:52.4
1964	Long, Elizabeth	4:58.5
1965	Long, Elizabeth	4:48.9
1966	Cave, Jeanette	4:52.6
1967	Williams, Susan	4:48.5
1968	Davison, Sally	4:55.8
1969	Williams, Susan	4:51.5
1970	Wright, Judith (NZ)	4:42.6

400 m. Free-style

1971	Allardice, Lesley	4:44.6
1972	Green, June	4:35.4
1973	Green, June	4:37.28
1974	Cliff, Leslie (Can)	4:28.5*
1975	Skilling, Karrie (Can)	4:29.51

880 y. Free-style

1966	Cave, Jeanette	10:23.5
1967	Williams, Susan	9:59.8
1968	Davison, Sally	10:04.1
1969	Williams, Susan	10:06.1
1970	Wright, Judith (NZ)	9:48.5

800 m. Free-style

1971	Green, June	10:00.1
1972	Green, June	9:31.3
1973	Green, June	9:33.87
1974	Cliff, Leslie (Can)	9:12.9*
1975	Skilling, Karrie (Can)	9:10.86

Long Distance. (See men's long distance result for race conditions).

1920	Jeans, Constance	1 hr 12:59.4
1921	Scott, Phyllis,	1 hr 06:55.0
1922	Jeans, Constance	1 hr 07:36.0
1923	James, Hilda	1 hr 09:46.4
1924	James, Hilda	1 hr 11:24.4
1925	Scott, Phyllis	1 hr 11:47.6

1926	Hamblen, Mabel	1 hr 15:17.2
1927	Hamblen, Mabel	1 hr 11:32.0
1928	Hamblen, Mabel	1 hr 09:58.0
1929	Vine-Jackman, Gladys	1 hr 14:07.0
1930	Cooper, Joyce	1 hr 12:57.0
1931	Cooper, Joyce	1 hr 01:56.0
1932	Cooper, Joyce	59:04.2
1933	Cooper, Joyce	1 hr 06:46.8
1934	Browning, Shelagh	1 hr 11:15.8
1935	Browning, Shelagh	1 hr 11:27.4
1936	Browning, Shelagh	1 hr 10:15.0
1937	Allen, M.Y.	1 hr 15:01.0
1938	Bassett-Lowke Vivienne	1 hr 06:13.8
1939	Langer, Ruth	1 hr 14:04.0
1940-47	No events	
1948	Hill, Elizabeth	1 hr 24:56.8
1949-61	No events	
1962	Lynch, Susan	1 hr 52:30.0
1963	Gray, Elaine	1 hr 48:33.0
1964	Gray, Elaine	1 hr 50:03.0
1965	Gray, Elaine	1 hr 52:15.0
1966	Gray, Elaine	2 hr 47:16.0
1967	Gray, Elaine	2 hr 28:58.0
1968	Gray, Elaine	2 hr 33:30.2
1969	Woodall, Bridget	2 hr 35:40.0
1970	Woodall, Bridget	2 hr 40:06.0
1971	Taylor, Val	1 hr 57:40.0
1972	Taylor, Val	2 hr 14:26.0
1973	Taylor, Val	2 hr 09:14.0
1974	Taylor, Val	2 hr 25:50.0
1975	Brook, Wendy	2 hr 08:00.0

150 y. Back-stroke

1920	Morton, Lucy	2:19.0
1921	Spencer, May	2:18.6
1922	Gilbert, Irene	2:16.0
1923	Spencer, May	2:18.4
1924	Shaw, Winifred	2:18.6
1925	King, Ellen	2:04.0
1926	King, Ellen	2:04.6
1927	Barker, M.A.	2:03.8
1928	King, Ellen	1:57.2
1929	Cooper, Joyce	1:59.2
1930	Clifford, Irene	2:05.0
1931	Cooper, Joyce	1:55.4
1932	Welsh, M.	Swim over
1933	McNulty, Margaret	2:04.8
1934	Wolstenholme, Beatrice	1:58.4
1935	Harding, Phyllis	1:56.6
1936	Harding, Phyllis	1:55.0
1937	Frampton, Lorna	1:56.4
1938	Yate, Helen	1:56.6
1939	Bassett-Lowke, Vivienne	1:54.4
1940-45	No events	
1946	Berlioux, Monique (Fr)	1:52.6

100 y. Back-stroke

1947	Gibson, Cathie	1:10.4
1948	Lane, Ngairi (NZ)	1:11.8
1949	Yate, Helen	1:10.2
1950	McDowall, Margaret	1:11.7
1951	McDowall, Margaret	1:09.2
1952	McDowall, Margaret	1:09.8

110 y. Back-stroke

1953	McDowall, Margaret	1:18.6
1954	Symons, Pat	1:16.9
1955	Grinham, Judy	1:15.3
1956	Grinham, Judy	1:04.5
1957	Hoyle, Julie	1:16.0
1958	Grinham, Judy	1:12.9
1959	Edwards, Margaret	1:12.5
1060	Steward, Natalie	1:11.0
1961	Edwards, Margaret	1:13.8
1962	Ludgrove, Linda	1:10.9
1963	Ludgrove, Linda	1:11.7
1964	Ludgrove, Linda	1:09.9
1965	Fairlie, Ann (SAf)	1:08.9
1966	Ludgrove, Linda	1:09.1
1967	Ludgrove, Linda	1:09.5
1968	Burrell, Wendy	1:11.2
1969	Gurr, Donna-Marie (Can)	1:09.1
1970	Stirling, Glenda (NZ)	1:08.7

100 m. Back-stroke

1971	Brown, Jackie	1:10.7
1972	Brown, Jackie	1:09.7
1973	Kelly, Margaret	1:09.98
1974	Cook, Wendy (Can)	1:06.2*
1975	Ladouceur, Ginette (Can)	1:07.44

220 y. Back-stroke

1964	Ludgrove, Linda	2:31.3
1965	Fairlie, Ann (SAf)	2:30.2
1966	Ludgrove, Linda	2:29.0
1967	Ludgrove, Linda	2:29.8
1968	Burrell, Wendy	2:32.8
1969	Gurr, Donna-Marie (Can)	2:28.8
1970	Burrell, Wendy	2:28.9

200 m. Back-stroke

1971	Ashton, Diane	2:30.7
1972	Ashton, Diane	2:29.7
1973	Fordyce, Gillian	2:29.48
1974	Cook, Wendy (Can)	2:23.1*
1975	Ladouceur, Ginette (Can)	2:26.09

110 y. Breast-stroke

1964	Slattery, Jill	1:20.6
1965	Harris, Diana	1:19.2
1966	Harris, Diana	1:19.2
1967	Radnage, Amanda	1:19.1
1968	Harris, Diana	1:18.8

1969	O'Connor, Anne (Eire)	1:19.9
1970	Radnage, Amanda	1:19.5

100 m. Breast-stroke

1971	Harrison, Dorothy	1:18.8
1972	Jarvis, Christine	1:17.4
1973	Jarvis, Christine	1:17.93
1974	Dickie, Sandra	1:16.4*
1975	Kelly, Margaret	1:16.18

200 y. Breast-stroke

1920	Morton, Lucy	3:10.0
1921	Carson, Gladys	3:12.4
1922	Hart, Doris	3:02.8
1923	Hart, Doris	3:03.8
1924	Harrison, Marion	3:07.6
1925	Gilbert, Irene	3:05.0
1926	Morris, E.M.	3:11.2
1927	King, Ellen	3:06.4
1928	King, Ellen	3:10.0
1929	Hinton, Margery	3:08.0
1930	Wolstenholme, Celia	2:56.8
1931	Hinton, Margery	2:56.6
1932	Hinton, Margery	2:56.6
1933	Hinton, Margery	2:58.6
1934	Hinton, Margery	2:57.4
1935	Kingston, Vera	2:53.6
1936	Storey, Doris	2:53.6
1937	Storey, Doris	2:53.8
1938	Storey, Doris	2:49.2
1939	Storey, Doris	2:43.6
1940-45	No events	
1946	Caplin, Jean	3:01.2
1947	Church, Elizabeth	2:52.8
1948	Church, Elizabeth	2:54.2
1949	Caspers, Jennie (Neth)	2:47.1
1950	Gordon, Elenor	2:46.0
1951	Gordon, Elenor	2:45.5
1952	Gordon, Elenor	2:43.0

220 y. Breast-stroke

1953	Grundy, Margaret	3:07.9
1954	Grundy, Margaret	3:03.8
1955	Gordon, Elenor	3:00.1
1956	Gordon, Elenor	2:59.2
1957	Gosden, Christine	2:56.5
1958	Lonsbrough, Anita	2:55.8
1959	Lonsbrough, Anita	2:54.0
1960	Lonsbrough, Anita	2:56.1
1961	Lonsbrough, Anita	2:53.7
1962	Lonsbrough, Anita	2:52.2
1963	Mitchell, Stella	2:52.6
1964	Mitchell, Stella	2:50.5
1965	Mitchell, Stella	2:49.2
1966	Mitchell, Stella	2:49.3
1967	Slattery, Jill	2:49.2
1968	Slattery, Jill	2:49.3
1969	Harrison, Dorothy	2:50.0

1970	Harrison, Dorothy	2:48.8

200 m. Breast-stroke

1971	Harrison, Dorothy	2:51.2
1972	Beavan, Pat	2:46.4
1973	Tamlyn, Caroline	2:47.18
1974	Stuart, Marian (Can)	2:45.1*
1975	Kelly, Margaret	2:42.13

110 y. Butterfly

1953	Ivinson, Margaret	1:24.2
1954	Webb, Fenella	1:24.0
1955	Macadam, Cathy	1:17.7
1956	Morton, Anne	1:17.4
1957	Gosden, Christine	1:16.9
1958	Watt, Sheila	1:14.5
1959	Watt, Sheila	1:13.9
1960	Watt, Sheila	1:12.4
1961	Green, Lesley	1:12.7
1962	Baines, Pat	1:11.3
1963	Stewart, Mary (Can)	1:08.6
1964	Cotterill, Anne	1:10.2
1965	Tanner, Elaine (Can)	1:08.1
1966	Barner, Ann	1:08.8
1967	Barner, Ann	1:08.0
1968	Auton, Margaret	1:08.1
1969	Auton, Margaret	1:08.1
1970	Whiting, Cathy (NZ)	1:08.0

100 m. Butterfly

1971	Jeavons, Jean	1:10.0
1972	Jeavons, Jean	1:06.6
1973	Atkinson, Joanne	1:06.26
1974	Stenhouse, Patti (Can)	1:06.8*
1975	Boivin, Helene (Can)	1:05.22

220 y. Butterfly

1966	Barner, Ann	2:34.7
1967	Barner, Ann	2:36.4
1968	Auton, Margaret	2:32.7
1969	Smith, Vicki (Eire)	2:33.1
1970	Smith, Vicki (Eire)	2:33.7

200 m. Butterfly

1971	Stockley, Clare	2:37.2
1972	Jeavons, Jean	2:23.6
1973	Jeavons, Jean	2:25.17
1974	Stenhouse, Patti (Can)	2:23.5*
1975	Bonner, Julie (Can)	2:22.96

220 y. Individual Medley

1966	Turnbull, Judith	2:37.6
1967	Ratcliffe, Shelagh	2:34.6
1968	Ratcliffe, Shelagh	2:34.7
1969	Ratcliffe, Shelagh	2:34.2
1970	Ratcliffe, Shelagh	2:30.7

200 m. Individual medley

1971	Banks, Denise	2:34.9
1972	Richardson, Sue	2:31.4
1973	Walker, Diane	2:31.81
1974	Cliff, Leslie (Can)	2:27.2*
1975	Boivin, Helen (Can)	2:25.72

440 y. Individual medley

1963	Lonsbrough, Anita	5:37.0
1964	Lonsbrough, Anita	5:39.4
1965	Hounsell, Barbara (Can)	5:35.0
1966	Williams, Susan	5:37.0
1967	Ratcliffe, Shelagh	5:27.7
1968	Ratcliffe, Shelagh	5:31.3
1969	Ratcliffe, Shelagh	5:28.0
1970	Ratcliffe, Shelagh	5:19.1

400 m. Individual medley

1971	Banks, Denise	5:26.9
1972	Walker, Diane	5:17.3
1973	Walker, Diane	5:16.20
1974	Cliff, Leslie (Can)	5:06.12
1975	Richardson, Susan	5:08.82

Free-style (club) relay (various distances)

1948	Beckenham Ladies	4:38.0
1949	Weston,super-Mare	4:36.6
1950	Croydon Ladies	4:40.7
1951	Croydon Ladies	4:39.5

4 x 110 y. Free-style (club) relay

1952	Mermaid	4:57.0
1953	Mermaid	5:01.8
1954	Mermaid	4:59.4
1955	Leander	5:02.3
1956	Mermaid	4:53.3
1957	Kingston Ladies	4:53.0
1958	Kingston Ladies	4:49.8
1959	Beckenham Ladies	4:45.3
1960	Mermaid	4:40.5
1961	Hampstead Ladies	4:40.0
1962	Hampstead Ladies	4:34.3
1963	Hampstead Ladies	4:30.3
1964	Stoke Newington	4:33.2
1965	Hampstead Ladies	4:31.6
1966	Kingston Ladies	4:29.1
1967	Beckenham Ladies	4:26.2
1968	Beckenham Ladies	4:31.8
1969	Beckenham Ladies	4:28.8
1970	Hornchurch	4:25.3

4 x 100 m. Free-style (club) relay

1971	Havering	4:21.9
1972	Cheam Ladies	4:17.3
1973	Havering	4:19.68
1974	Paisley	4:19.5*
1975	Beckenham Ladies	4:13.48

Medley (club) relay (various distances)

1935	Coventry Three Spires	
1936	Bournemouth	
1937	Bournemouth	
1938	Leicester United Ladies	
1939	Armley Ladies	
1940-45	No events	
1946	Mermaid	5:59.2
1947	Beckenham Ladies	5:38.1
1948	Mermaid	5:27.4
1949	Northampton	4:55.2
1950	Hampstead Ladies	4:56.9
1951	Croydon Ladies	4:56.6
1952	Mermaid	5:26.4

4 x 110 y. Medley (club) relay

1953	Mermaid	5:19.0
1954	Mermaid	5:22.7
1955	Mermaid	5:15.0
1956	Leander	5:24.7
1957	Heston	5:21.7
1958	Heston	5:04.9
1960	Heston	5:09.2
1961	Heston	5:04.9
1962	Hampstead Ladies	5:05.5
1963	Hampstead Ladies	4:58.0
1964	Beckenham Ladies	4:51.7
1965	Beckenham Ladies	4:52.2
1966	Beckenham Ladies	4:50.5
1967	Beckenham Ladies	4:48.9
1968	York City	4:55.5
1969	Hartlepool	4:50.4
1970	Beckenham Ladies	4:53.1

4 x 100 m. Medley (club) relay

1971	Southampton	4:53.5
1972	Southampton	4:44.4
1973	Beckenham Ladies	4:46.13
1974	Beckenham Ladies	4:43.5*
1975	Cardiff	4:35.98

A.S.A. CHAMPIONS (SHORT COURSE.

It was 1971 before the A.S.A. followed the pattern set in many other countries and instituted short course (see SHORT COURSE) championships. The idea of these events is to provide competition at the end of the winter training and help the selection of teams for early international matches.

1971	Worthing, Sussex
1972	Grimsby, Lincolnshire
1973	Cheltenham, Gloucestershire
1974	Harrogate, Yorkshire
1975	Manchester, Lancashire
1976	Worthing, Sussex

MEN

100 m. Free-style

1971	Bailey, Mike	55.5
1972	Windeatt, Malcolm	*54.6
1973	Windeatt, Malcolm	53.9
1974	Brinkley, Brian	*53.8
1975	Brinkley, Brian	*53.6
	* 110 y.	

200 m. Free-style

1971	Brinkley, Brian	2:02.5
1972	Brinkley, Brian	*2:00.1
1973	Brinkley, Brian	1:56.9
1974	Brinkley, Brian	*1:54.7
1975	Brinkley, Brian	*1:56.4
	*220 y.	

400 m. Free-style

1971	Brinkley, Brian	4:20.1
1972	Brinkley, Brian	*4:16.2
1973	Brinkley, Brian	4:09.2
1974	Brinkley, Brian	*4:02.9
1975	Brinkley, Brian	*4:07.6
	440 y.	

1,500 m. Free-style

1971	Devlin, Alex	17:40.9
1972	Terrell, Ray	*17:18.4
1973	Brinkley, Brian	16:37.3
1974	Smith, Dean	*16:50.9
1975	Parker, David	*16:40.5
	* 1,650 y.	

100 m. Back-stroke

1971	Richards, Mike	1:00.7
1972	Richards, Mike	*1:01.1
1973	Cunningham, Colin	1:00.7
1974	Cunningham, Colin	*1:00.2
1975	Bunce, Steve	*1:01.0
	* 110 y.	

200 m. Back-stroke

1971	Richards, Mike	2:14.2
1972	Cunningham, Colin	*2:13.5
1973	Cunningham, Colin	2:11.4
1974	Cunningham, Colin	*2:10.6
1975	Lerpiniere, Peter	*2:12.6
	* 220 y.	

100 m. Breast-stroke

1971	Wilkie, David	1:09.8
1972	O'Connell, Malcolm	*1:09.1
1973	O'Connell, Malcolm	1:08.5
1974	Leigh, David	*1:07.0
1975	Leigh, David	*1:06.7
	*110 y.	

200 m. Breast-stroke

1971	Wilkie, David	2:33.5
1972	Wilkie, David	*2:31.6
1973	O'Brien, Barry	2:32.8
1974	Leigh, David	*2:24.3
1975	Leigh, David	*2:28.6
	* 220y.	

100 m. Butterfly

1971	Bailey, Mike	1:00.4
1972	Mills, John	*1:00.3
1973	Edwards, Martin	58.9
1974	Cunningham, Colin	*58.9
1975	Brinkley, Brian	*58.1
	*110 y.	

200 m. Butterfly

1971	Mills, John	2:12.5
1972	Mills, John	*2:09.2
1973	Brinkley, Brian	2:09.6
1974	Brinkley, Brian	*2:06.2
1975	Brinkley, Brian	*2:08.0
	* 220 y.	

Short Individual medley *

1971	Wilkie, David	1:28.9
1972	Terrell, Ray	1:25.8
1973	Terrell, Ray	1:26.1
1974	Brinkley, Brian	2:14.1
1975	Cleworth, Duncan	1:27.2
	* Distances varied	

400 m. Individual medley

1971	Grossman, Steve	4:58.2
1972	Terrell, Ray	*4:50.7
1973	Brinkley, Brian	4:42.2
1974	Prime, Barry	*4:44.8
1975	McClatchey, Alan	*4:46.4
	*440 y.	

WOMEN

100 m. Free-style

1971	Sutherland, Diana	1:02.5
1972	Allardice, Lesley	*1:02.4
1973	Sirs, Judith	1:01.1
1974	Simpson, Jackie	*1:01.2
1975	Hill, Debbie	*1:01.6
	* 110 y.	

200 m. Free-style

1971	Sutherland, Diana	2:16.3
1972	Brown, Moira	*2:14.7
1973	Allardice, Lesley	2:11.7
1974	Edmondson, Sue	*2:11.2
1975	Walker, Diane	*2:13.5
	* 220 y.	

400 m. Free-style

1971	Sutherland, Diana	4:46.3
1972	Green, June	*4:43.7
1973	Green, June	4:35.2
1974	Edmondson, Sue	*4:34.7
1975	Walker, Diane	*4:35.6
	* 440 y.	

800 m. Free-style

1971	Mackie, Andrea	9:55.8
1972	Green, June	*9:40.6
1973	Green, June	9:22.8
1974	Atkinson, Joanne	*9:20.8
1975	Atkinson, Joanne	*9:23.3
	* 880 y.	

100 m. Back-stroke

1971	Brown, Jackie	1:10.1
1972	Bairstow, Pam	*1:10.7
1973	Kelly, Margaret	1:09.7
1974	Kelly, Margaret	*1:08.0
1975	Roughley, Belinda	*1:09.0
	* 110 y.	

200 m. Back-stroke

1971	Burrell, Wendy	2:31.2
1972	Bairstow, Pam	*2:03.4
1973	Ashton, Diane	2:28.8
1974	Kelly, Margaret	*2:26.2
1975	Roughley, Belinda	*2:29.4
	* 220 y.	

100 m. Breast-stroke

1971	Harrison, Dorothy	1:16.8
1972	Jarvis, Christine	*1:17.9
1973	Jarvis, Christine	1:17.5
1974	Gaskell, Christine	*1:15.6
1975	Burnham, Helen	*1:17.6
	* 100 y.	

200 m. Breast-stroke

1971	Harrison, Dorothy	2:49.0
1972	Beavan, Pat	*2:49.1
1973	Tamlyn, Caroline	2:45.3
1974	Gaskell, Christine	*2:43.3
1975	Burnham, Helen	*2:47.4
	* 220 y.	

100 m. Butterfly

1971	Machin, Janice	1:10.4
1972	Jeavons, Jean	*1:08.9
1973	Jeavons, Jean	1:07.3
1974	Atkinson, Joanne	*1:06.7
1975	Atkinson, Joanne	*1:06.5
	* 110 y.	

200 m. Butterfly

1971	Stockley, Clare	2:36.6
1972	Machin, Janice	*2:29.9

1973	Jeavons, Jean	2:26.4
1974	Atkinson, Joanne	*2:26.3
1975	Atkinson, Joanne	*2:24.1
	* 220 y.	

Short Individual medley*

1971	Banks, Denise	1:39.0
1972	Ratcliffe, Shelagh	1:38.0
1973	Banks, Denise	1:35.9
1974	Banks, Denise	2:28.6
1975	Adams, Anne	1:34.9
	* Distances various	

400 m. Individual medley

1971	Anslow, Sharon	5:27.2
1972	Ratcliffe, Shelagh	*5:21.9
1973	Richardson, Sue	5:14.4
1974	Richardson, Sue	*5:14.3
1975	Adams, Anne	*5:13.1
	* 440 y.	

A.S.A. DIVING CHAMPIONS. The first official championship of England, yet open to the world, was a highboard event for men in 1907. Prior to this a National Graceful Diving event for men had been organized by the Royal Life Saving Society (1895). This latter competition was handed on, in 1920, to the Amateur Diving Association—which did a great deal to foster diving from the turn of the century to the mid-thirties. It came under the auspices of the A.S.A. in 1936 following the disbandment of the A.D.A.

Since 1935, the majority of the diving championships have been held at centralized venues as follows:

1935	New Brighton, Cheshire
1936*	Empire Pool, Wembley
1937*	Scarborough, Yorkshire
1938	Empire Pool, Wembley
1939*	Minehead, Somerset
1940-45	No championship meetings
1946*	New Brighton, Cheshire
1947*	Hastings and St. Leonards, Sussex
1948†	Hastings and St. Leonards, Sussex
1949	Hastings and St. Leonards, Sussex
1950	Morecambe and Hersham, Lancashire
1951	New Brighton, Cheshire
1952	New Brighton, Cheshire
1953-63*	Derby Bath, Blackpool
1964*	Crystal Palace, London
1965-67	Crystal Palace, London
1968	Coventry, Warwickshire
1969	Derby Bath, Blackpool
1970	Crystal Palace, London

1971* Leeds, Yorkshire
1972* Crystal Palace, London
1973* Coventry, Warwickshire
1974 Huddersfield, Yorkshire (springboard)
   Wigan, Lancashire(highboard)
1975 Huddersfield, Yorkshire (springboard)
   Crystal Palace, London (highboard)
1976* Crystal Palace, London
   * With swimming championships
   † Originally scheduled for Scarborough with the swimming championships, bad weather forced postponement and transfer of the meeting to Hastings.

MEN

Highboard diving

1907	Smyrk, Harold	
1908	Smyrk, Harold	
1909	Pott, Herbert	
1910	Pott, Herbert	
1911	Pott, Herbert	
1912	Pott, Herbert	
1913	Gaidzik, George (USA)	
1914–19	No events	
1920	Clarke, Harold	
1921	Knight, Reggie	
1922	Knight, Reggie	
1923	Weil, R.	
1924	Weil, R.	
1925	Dickin, Albert	
1926	Dickin, Albert	
1927	Aldous, Jimmy	
1928	Burne, Tommy	
1929	Dickin, Albert	
1930	Wild, George	
1931	Tomalin, Doug	
1932	Heron, Eddie	
1933	Tomalin, Doug	
1934	Tomalin, Doug	
1935	Tomalin, Doug	
1936	Tomalin, Doug	
1937	Tomalin, Doug	
1938	Marchant, Louis	
1939	Tomalin, Doug	
1940–45	No events	
1946	Marchant, Louis	105.43
1947	Brunnhage Lennart (Swe)	101.86
1948	Ward, Gordon	87.83
1949	Heatly, Peter	140.23
1950	Heatly, Peter	147.64
1951	Heatly, Peter	142.18
1952	Turner, Tony	131.25
1953	Tarsey, David	139.59
1954	Turner, Tony	135.43
1955	Squires, Peter	135.00
1956	Tarsey, David	138.33

1957	Heatly, Peter	139.35
1958	Phelps, Brian	139.58
1959	Phelps, Brian	148.61
1960	Phelps, Brian	157.14
1961	Phelps, Brian	148.38
1962	Phelps, Brian	162.23
1963	Kitcher, Tony	161.08
1964	Phelps, Brian	165.55
1965	Phelps, Brian	161.02
1966	Phelps, Brian	165.51
1967	Priestley, David	157.30
1968	Priestley, David	153.45
1969	Gill, Andy	426.40
1970	Drew, Philip	446.60
1971	Gill, Andy	421.20
1972	Dufficy, Frank	439.59
1973	Dufficy, Frank	447.00
1974	Brown, Martyn	461.85
1975	Brown, Martyn	471.10

Springboard diving

1935	Tomalin, Doug	
1936	Hodges, Freddie	
1937	Hodges, Freddie	
1938	Hodges, Freddie	
1939	Hodges, Freddie	
1940–45	No events	
1946	Mulinghausen, Raymond (Fr)	116.30
1947	Kern, Roy	105.90
1948	Heatly, Peter	113.50
1949	Heatly, Peter	174.91
1950	Heatly, Peter	176.51
1951	Turner, Tony	160.67
1952	Turner, Tony	176.60
1953	Turner, Tony	135.14
1954	Turner, Tony	134.20
1955	Tarsey, David	133.43
1956	Tarsey, David	134.02
1957	Squires. Peter	125.14
1958	Collin, Keith	135.00
1959	Squires, Peter	150.39
1960	Phelps, Brian	152.98
1961	Phelps, Brian	154.80
1962	Phelps, Brian	152.39
1963	Collin, Keith	128.69
1964	Young, Denis	139.62
1965	Carter, Frank	135.96
1966	Carter, Frank	145.93
1967	Carter, Frank	140.20
1968	Carter, Frank	135.31
1969	Roberts, Alun	468.25
1970	Thewlis, Joe	475.60
1971	Walls, Chris	478.30
1972	Wetheridge, Brian	474.95
1973	Simpson, Trevor	515.25
1974	Simpson, Trevor	506.65
1975	Snode, Chris	536.55

1 m. Springboard diving

1937	Tomalin, Doug	
1938	Tomalin, Doug	
1939	Thom, Don (Can)	
1940–45	No event	
1946	Hodges, Freddie	135.85
1947	Webb, John	93.16
1948	Elliott, Peter	93.35
1949	Heatly, Peter	128.60
1950	Heatly, Peter	127.32
1951	Heatly, Peter	110.09
1952	Turner, Tony	121.94
1953	Turner, Tony	113.32
1954	Turner, Tony	102.31
1955	Mercer, Frank	110.68
1956	Raanan, Chico (Isr)	106.88
1957	Collin, Keith	120.39
1958	Squires, Peter	124.57
1959	Collin, Keith	132.53
1960	Candler, John	129.21
1961	Young, Denis	130.40
1962	Collin, Keith	125.68
1963	Young, Denis	126.88
1964	Young, Denis	127.39
1965	Young, Denis	123.58
1966	Roberts, Alun	126.03
1967	Carter, Frank	126.35
1968	Roberts, Alun	130.35
1969	Roberts, Alun	440.05
1970	Gill, Andy	425.35
1971	Simpson, Trevor	444.80
1972	Simpson, Trevor	474.55
1973	Simpson, Trevor	471.65
1974	Simpson, Trevor	431.80
1975	Snode, Chris	433.70
1976	Snode, Chris	477.25

Plain diving

1895	Martin, H.
1896	Martin, H.
1897	Sonnemans, V. (Belg)
1898	Martin, H.
1899	Martin, H.
1900	Goldwell, E.
1901	Serrano, R.
1902	Phillips, G.
1903	Tellander, E.
1904	Melville Clark, Gordon
1905	Melville Clark, Gordon
1906	Melville Clark, Gordon
1907	Cane, G.
1908	Aldous, Jimmy/Johansson, Hjalmar (Swe) tie
1909	Johansson, Hjalmar (Swe)
1910	Johansson, Hjalmar (Swe)
1911	Johansson, Hjalmar (Swe)
1912	Yvon, George
1913	Johansson, Hjalmar (Swe)
1914–19	No events
1920	Clarke, Harold

1921	Clarke, Harold	
1922	Clarke, Harold	
1923	Dickin, Albert	
1924	Eve, Richmond (Aus)	
1925	Clarke, Harold	
1926	Dickin, Albert	
1927	Dickin, Albert	
1928	Burne, Tommy	
1929	Dickin, Albert	
1930	Burne, Tommy	
1931	Tomalin, Doug	
1932	Cook, Reggie/Dawsell, Harold (tie)	
1933	Marchant, Louis	
1934	Marchant, Louis	
1935	Marchant, Louis	
1936	Mather, Tommy	
1937	Tomalin, Doug	
1938	Tomalin, Doug	
1939	Redfern, Graham	
1940–45	No events	
1946	Marchant, Louis	49.30
1947	Marchant, Louis	43.70
1948	Marchant, Louis	49.72
1949	Marchant, Louis	47.92
1950	Marchant, Louis	52.81
1951	Redfern, Graham	38.75
1952	Redfern, Graham	47.60
1953	Elliot, Peter	57.28
1954	Tarsey, David	59.11
1955	Squires, Peter	55.98
1956	Squires, Peter	57.79
1957	Phelps, Brian	54.99
1958	Collin, Keith	55.98
1959	Squires, Peter	67.01
1960	Phelps, Brian	60.34
1961	Phelps, Brian	63.77
1962	Discontinued	

WOMEN

Highboard diving

1924	White, Belle	
1925	White, Belle	
1926	White, Belle	
1927	White, Belle	
1928	White, Belle	
1929	White, Belle	
1930	Leach, Dorothy	
1931	Leach, Dorothy	
1932	Leach, Dorothy	
1933	Macready E. 'Dot'	
1934	Cousens, Cecily	
1935	Cousens, Cecily	
1936	Gilbert, Jean	
1937	Gilbert, Jean	
1938	Moulton, Madge	
1939	Slade, Betty	
1940–45	No events	
1946	Child, Edna	34.83
1947	Child, Edna	52.86

1948	Hilder, Maire	61.34
1949	Child, Edna	67.55
1950	Long, Ann	52.04
1951	Cuthbert, Kay	63.59
1952	Long, Ann	67.95
1953	Long, Ann	74.48
1954	Long, Ann	76.92
1955	Welsh, Charmian	69.80
1956	Welsh, Charmian	76.06
1957	Welsh, Charmian	71.06
1958	Welsh, Charmian	83.70
1959	Long, Ann	81.17
1960	Thomas, Norma	77.18
1961	Thomas, Norma	91.03
1962	Austen, Margaret	89.13
1963	Newman, Joy	103.60
1964	Cramp, Frances	95.96
1965	Cramp, Frances	84.91
1966	Cramp, Frances	83.20
1967	Haswell, Mandi	75.23
1968	Haswell, Mandi	86.17
1969	Boys, Beverley (Can)	337.65
1970	Burrow, Shelagh	302.85
1971	Williams, Beverley	318.30
1972	Williams, Beverley	323.90
1973	Koppell, Helen	331.05
1974	Williams, Beverley	343.45
1975	Williams, Beverley	345.00

Springboard diving

1935	Larsen, Katrina	
1936	Slade, Betty	
1937	Slade, Betty	
1938	Slade, Betty	
1939	Slade, Betty	
1940–45	No events	
1946	Child, Edna	97.57
1947	Winterton, Peggy	89.01
1948	Child, Edna	102.79
1949	Child, Edna	101.15
1950	Newman, Denise	106.38
1951	Long, Ann	107.98
1952	Drew, Dorothy Ann	120.84
1953	Welsh, Charmian	117.00
1954	Welsh, Charmian	118.39
1955	Long, Ann	108.31
1956	Long, Ann	112.61
1957	Long, Ann	112.20
1958	Long, Ann	125.40
1959	Watson, Marian	128.48
1960	Ferris, Elizabeth	137.36
1961	Thomas, Norma	141.71
1962	Ferris, Elizabeth	117.18
1963	Newman, Joy	109.08
1964	Rowlatt, Kathy	122.92
1965	Stewart, Judy (Can)	131.13
1966	Dickens, Janet	118.95
1967	Rowlatt, Kathy	135.10
1968	Rowlatt, Kathy	130.91

1969	Boys, Beverley (Can)	370.30
1970	Drake, Alison	354.30
1971	Drake, Alison	358.60
1972	Drake, Alison	430.65
1973	Koppell, Helen	416.60
1974	Koppell, Helen	397.50
1975	Carwardine, Lesley	375.85

1 m. Springboard diving

1949	Child, Edna	89.12
1950	Cuthbert, Kay	68.59
1951	Long, Ann	68.20
1952	Welsh, Charmian	82.89
1953	Welsh, Charmian	84.25
1954	Welsh, Charmian	80.71
1955	Welsh, Charmian	85.38
1956	Welsh, Charmian	80.45
1957	Ferris, Elizabeth	102.56
1958	Welsh, Charmian	99.58
1959	Thomas, Norma	106.85
1960	Cramp, Frances	87.68
1961	Austen, Margaret	95.97
1962	Cramp, Frances	99.57
1963	Leiper (Thomas), Norma	100.54
1964	Francis, Susan	93.30
1965	Francis, Susan	97.11
1966	Froscher, Margo	103.65
1967	Erard (Cramp), Frances	107.66
1968	Froscher, Margo	94.93
1969	Koppell, Helen	295.05
1970	Drake, Alison	310.85
1971	Drake, Alison	336.35
1972	Koppell, Helen	353.40
1973	Drake, Alison	325.65
1974	Koppell, Helen	365.50
1975	Koppell, Helen	334.80
1976	Drake, Alison	375.15

Plain diving

1953	Welsh, Charmian	51.35
1954	Long, Ann	59.85
1955	Long, Ann	52.00
1956	Welsh, Charmian	54.65
1957	Welsh, Charmian	58.71
1958	Long, Ann	59.92
1959	Ferris, Elizabeth	61.13
1960	Ferris, Elizabeth	53.99
1961	Austen, Margaret	60.95
1962	Discontinued	

A.S.A. PLUNGING CHAMPIONS.
See PLUNGING A.S.A. CHAMPIONS.

A.S.A. SYNCHRONIZED SWIM-MING CHAMPIONS. The first championship for this fourth discipline in the swimming programme took place in Walsall in 1975. The winners are:
Solo

1975	Cox, Jacqueline	109.410

Duet
1975 Cox, Jacqueline/Holland,
      Andrea   103.940
Team
1975 Reading Royals   93.344

A.S.A. WATER POLO CHAMP-IONS. See under WATER POLO, CHA-MPIONS.

ATWOOD, Sue (United States, 5 June, 1953-). One of the world's finest back-stroke and medley swimmers and with an outstanding record in American championships, Sue Atwood never won a major title. She took four silvers and a bronze at the Pan American Games of 1971 – being second in the 100 and 200 m. back-stroke, 200 m. medley and 4 x 100 m. medley and third in the 400 m. IM.

The following year, at the Munich Olympics, a new American back-stroke star Melissa Belote (see BELOTE, MEL-ISSA) robbed Miss Atwood of the 200 m. title and the world mark of 2:21.5 she had set in 1969. And by placing third behind the victorious Miss Belote in the 100 m., Miss Atwood did not get the back-stroke berth for the winning U.S.A. medley relay squad.

Miss Atwood won 18 National titles from 1969 to 1973 – at Outdoor meetings the 100 and 200 m. back-stroke in 1969/70/71 and the 400 m. medley in 1970; at the Indoors, the 100 y. back-stroke in 1969, '70, '71 and '73, 200 y. back-stroke, four years 1969-72, 200 y. medley ('71) and 400 y. medley ('71/'72).

AUSTRALIA, AMATEUR SWIM-MING UNION OF. The A.S.U.A. was formed in Sydney on 22 Feb 1909, at a meeting chaired by the late James Taylor and attended by representatives from the state associations of New South Wales, Victoria and South Australia, who became founder members, and of Queensland and Western Australia, who, with Tasmania, became members in 1913;

Although from 1894 to 1909 there was no central controlling authority. Australasian championships took place under an agreement between New South Wales, Victoria, Queensland, Western Australia and the A.S.A. of New Zealand. Combined Australasian teams were entered for the 1908 and 1912 Olympic Games in London and Stockholm. At the latter, a team of three Australians (Hea-ly, Bordman and Hardwick) and one New Zealander (Champion) won the 4 x 200 m. relay gold medals.

AUSTRALIAN CHAMPIONS. Australian championships organized under the auspices of the A.S.U.A. have been held since 1910 (see also AUSTRALIA, AMATEUR SWIMMING UNION OF). No championships were held between 1915-19, because of the First World War, nor from 1941-45. The winners since the Second World War are:

MEN

100 m. Free-style (instituted for 100 y. 1894)

1946*	O'Neill, Frank	1:02.6
1947*	O'Neill, Frank	1:02.2
1948*	Boyd, Warren	1:00.0
1949	Marshall, John	1:00.3
1950*	O'Neill, Frank	59.6
1951*	O'Neill, Frank	1:00.8
1952	Aubrey, Rex	59.2
1953*	Henricks, Jon	57.2
1954*	Henricks, Jon	56.8
1955*	Henricks, Jon	57.2
1956*	Henricks, Jon	55.5
1957*	Devitt, John	56.6
1958*	Devitt, John	55.9
1959*	Konrads, John	55.9
1960*	Devitt, John	55.4
1961	Dickson, David	56.2
1962*	Staples, Charles	56.3
1963*	Dickson, David	55.5
1964	Dickson, David	55.1
1965*	Dickson, David	55.6
1966	Wenden, Michael	54.6
1967*	Doak, Peter	56.7
1968	Wenden, Michael	53.8
1969	Rogers, Greg	54.9
1970	Wenden, Michael	54.0
1971	Wenden, Michael	53.6
1972	Wenden, Michael	53.9
1973	Wenden, Michael	53.6
1974	Rogers, Neil	54.10
1975	Abbott, Rick (USA)	53.1*
1976	Rogers, Neil	53.05

* = 110 y.

200 m. Free-style (instituted 1894)

1946*	Beard, Arthur	2:22.4
1947*	Marshall, John	2:20.3
1948	Marshall, John	2:16.8
1949*	Marshall, John	2:14.3
1950*	O'Neill, Frank	2:14.6
1951*	O'Neill, Frank	2:17.6
1952*	O'Neill, Frank	2:17.2

1953* Henricks, Jon	2:09.8
1954* Henricks, Jon	2:09.9
1955* Rose, Murray	2:11.6
1956* Chapman, Gary	2:05.8
1957* Garretty, Murray	2:11.6
1958* Konrads, John	2:05.1
1959* Konrads, John	2:03.3
1960 Konrads, John	2:01.6
1961 Konrads, John	2:04.5
1962* Windle, Bobby	2:02.9
1963* Windle, Bobby	2:02.8
1964 Windle, Bobby	2:00.0
1965* Dickson, David	2:04.7
1966 Wenden, Michael	2:00.5
1967* Wenden, Michael	2:02.2
1968 Wenden, Michael	1:57.9
1969 Rogers, Greg	1:59.2
1970 Wenden, Michael	1:59.4
1971 Rogers, Greg	1:58.3
1972 Wenden, Michael	1:57.1
1973 Cooper, Brad	1:57.9

1974 Kulasalu, John	1:56.79
1975 Windeatt, Graham	1:55.7*
1976 Kerry, Mark	1:54.33

* = 220 y.

400 m. Free-style (instituted 1894)

1946* Beard, Arthur	5:04.6
1947* Marshall, John	5:02.0
1948* Marshall, John	4:52.2
1949 Marshall, John	4:50.2
1950* Agnew, David	4:53.3
1951* Kelleway, Brian	4:54.3
1952* Beard, John	5:02.2
1953* Chapman, Gary	4:42.6
1954* Chapman, Gary	4:39.3
1955* Rose, Murray	4:47.3
1956* Rose, Murray	4:33.0
1957* Garretty, Murray	4:40.6
1958* Konrads, John	4:21.8
1959* Konrads, John	4:31.2
1960* Konrads, John	4:15.9
1961 Konrads, John	4:25.1
1962* Windle, Bobby	4:25.0
1963* Windle, Bobby	4:23.0
1964 Windle, Bobby	4:17.6
1965* Pick, John	4:24.7
1966 Bennett, John	4:23.6
1967* Bennett, John	4:18.3
1968 Brough, Greg	4:13.6
1969 Brough, Greg	4:13.3
1970 Brough, Greg	4:10.0
1971 Windeatt, Graham	4:07.8
1972 Cooper, Brad	4:01.7
1973 Cooper, Brad	4:07.6

1974 Cooper, Brad	4:01.30
1975 Holland, Steve	4:02.8*
1976 Holland, Steve	3:57.11

* = 440 y.

1,500 m. Free-style (instituted 1937)

1946* Sever, Ken	21:05.0
1947* Marshall, John	20:23.4
1948 Marshall, John	20:35.5
1949 Marshall, John	19:35.2
1950* Kelleway, Brian	20:32.7
1951* Darke, Barry	21:05.7
1952* McCormick, James	20:41.4
1953* Mortenson, Brian	19:47.1
1954* Donohue, James	19:47.1
1955* Winram, Gary	19:14.8
1956* Garretty, Murray	18:33.5
1957* Garretty, Murray	19:04.4
1958* Konrads, John	17:28.7
1959* Konrads, John	18:24.2
1960* Konrads, John	17:11.0
1961 Windle, Bobby	17:37.7
1962* Windle, Bobby	17:53.3
1963* Windle, Bobby	17:59.6
1964 Windle, Bobby	17:09.4
1965* Pick, John	17:04.4
1966 Jackson, Ron	17:37.3
1967* Bennett, John	17:23.6
1968 Brough, Greg	16:51.9
1969 Brough, Greg	16:43.6
1970 Windeatt, Graham	16:23.1
1971 Windeatt, Graham	16:17.8
1972 Cooper, Brad	15:57.7
1973 Badger, Stephen	16:11.1

1974 Holland, Steve	15:57.88
1975 Holland, Steve	15:49.1*
1976 Holland, Steve	15:10.59

* = 1,650 y.

100 m. Back-stroke (instituted 1921 for 100 y.)

1946* Milgate, Rodney	1:15.0
1947* Bourke, Bruce	1:13.4
1948* Bourke, Bruce	1:11.0
1949 Bourke, Bruce	1:11.5
1950* Bourke, Bruce	1:11.9
1951* O'Keefe, Leslie	1:14.5
1952* Barry, Robert	1:10.6
1953* Barry, Robert	1:09.7
1954* Weld, Cyrus	1:08.3
1955* Theile, David	1:07.4
1956* Theile, David	1:05.5
1957* Monckton, John	1:03.9
1958* Monckton, John	1:01.5
1959* Theile, David	1:04.0
1960* Theile, David	1:03.0
1961 Fingleton, Tony	1:05.4
1962* Carroll, Julian	1:05.8
1963* Fingleton, Alan	1:05.4
1964 Byrom, John	1:04.2
1965* Reynolds, Peter	1:02.6
1966 Reynolds, Peter	1:03.7
1967* Reynolds, Peter	1:05.0
1968 Byrom, Karl	1:02.1

1969	Byrom, Karl	1:03.0
1970	Rogers, Neil	1:03.6
1971	Cooper, Brad	1:02.0
1972	Paterson, Ross	1:02.9
1973	Cooper, Brad	1:00.5

1974	Tonelli, Mark	59.55
1975	Tonelli, Mark	59.7*
1976	Tonelli, Mark	58.35

* = 110 y.

200 m. Back-stroke (instituted 1957)

1957*	Monckton, John	2:23.5
1958*	Monckton, John	2:18.8
1959*	Hayres, John	2:26.9
1960*	Carroll, Julian	2:19.7
1961	Carroll, Julian	2:24.9
1962*	Carroll, Julian	2:22.1
1963*	Fingleton, Tony	2:23.5
1964	Reynolds, Peter	2:19.1
1965*	Reynolds, Peter	2:18.1
1966	Reynolds, Peter	2:14.6
1967*	Byrom, Karl	2:19.9
1968	Byrom, Karl	2:14.8
1969	Byrom, Karl	2:15.4
1970	Rogers, Neil	2:17.1
1971	Cooper, Brad	2:12.2
1972	Cooper, Brad	2:10.6
1973	Cooper, Brad	2:11.7

1974	Cooper, Brad	2:07.40
1975	Tonelli, Mark	2:10.5*
1976	Kerry, Mark	2:03.58

* = 220 y.

100 m. Breast-stroke (instituted 1957)

1957*	Gathercole, Terry	1:14.8
1958*	Hunt, Maxwell	1:15.0
1959*	Gathercole, Terry	1:14.1
1960*	Gathercole, Terry	1:15.4
1961	Burton, William	1:14.3
1962*	Burton, William	1:13.9
1963*	O'Brien, Ian	1:11.3
1964	O'Brien, Ian	1:08.1
1965*	O'Brien, Ian	1:11.1
1966	O'Brien, Ian	1:11.8
1967*	Oxer, David	1:15.6
1968	Tonkin, Peter	1:11.2
1969	Jarvie, Paul	1:11.8
1970	Jalmaani, Amman (Phil)	1:10.7
1971	Jarvie, Paul	1:11.7
1972	Jarvie, Paul	1:09.6
1973	Creswick, Michael	1:09.6

1974	Cluer, Nigel	1:10.00
1975	Bohan, Rick (USA)	1:08.3*
1976	Jarvie, Paul	1:07.49

* = 110 y.

200 m. Breast-stroke (instituted 1908)

1946	Johnson, John	3:00.8
1947*	Davies, John	Bu2:58.2
1948*	Davies, John	Bu2:45.9
1949	Shanahan, James	2:53.0
1950*	Hallet, Kevin	2:58.1
1951*	Hawkins, David	2:49.7
1952*	Hawkins, David	2:42.3
1953*	Stott, Graeme	3:02.0
1954*	Gathercole, Terry	2:56.2
1955*	Gathercole, Terry	2:47.0
1956*	Gathercole, Terry	2:45.4
1957*	Gathercole, Terry	2:40.9
1958*	Gathercole, Terry	2:44.7
1959*	Gathercole, Terry	2:47.1
1960*	Gathercole, Terry	2:43.0
1961	Burton, William	2:42.6
1962*	O'Brien, Ian	2:41.8
1963*	O'Brien, Ian	2:37.4
1964	O'Brien, Ian	2:32.6
1965*	O'Brien, Ian	2:38.9
1966	O'Brien, Ian	2:41.6
1967*	Edwards, Gregory	2:41.5
1968	Oxer, David	2:38.9
1969	Gynther, Neil	2:41.7
1970	Gynther, Neil	2:37.0
1971	Jarvie, Paul	2:33.1
1972	Jarvie, Paul	2:31.9
1973	Creswick, Michael	2:42.9

1974	Cluer, Nigel	2:29.45
1975	Bosh, Greg	2:30.6*
1976	Jarvie, Paul	2:21.25

* = 220 y.

100 m. Butterfly (instituted 1957)

1957*	Wilkinson, Brian	1:03.8
1958*	Wilkinson, Brian	1:04.4
1959*	Wilkinson, Brian	1:04.3
1960*	Hayes, Neville	1:03.0
1961	Hayes, Neville	1:01.6
1962*	Berry, Kevin	1:00.1
1963*	Berry, Kevin	59.9
1964	Berry, Kevin	58.8
1965*	Stark, John	1:01.8
1966	Reynolds, Peter	1:00.1
1967*	Dunn, Graham	1:00.9
1968	Cusack, Bob	59.1
1969	Scott, Ken	1:01.3
1970	Rogers, Neil	59.7
1971	Rogers, Neil	58.5
1972	Rogers, Neil	57.5
1973	Coutts, John	1:00.0

1974	Rogers, Neil	56.25
1975	Smith, Peter	58.4*
1976	Rogers, Neil	55.47

* = 110 y.

200 m. Butterfly (instituted 1953)

1953*	Fitzpatrick, Ken	2:56.8
1954*	Sharpe, Ken	2:50.0
1955*	Middleton, Graeme	2:47.6
1956*	Middleton, Graeme	2:36.5
1957*	Wilkinson, Brian	2:33.2
1958*	Wilkinson, Brian	2:27.0
1959*	Wilkinson, Brian	2:24.9
1960*	Hayes, Neville	2:17.9
1961	Hayes, Neville	2:14.7
1962*	Berry, Kevin	2:12.5
1963*	Berry, Kevin	2:13.4
1964	Berry, Kevin	2:06.9
1965*	Stark, John	2:13.4
1966	Stark, John	2:11.7
1967*	Hill, Brett	2:13.7
1968	Hill, Brett	2:13.5
1969	Wilkinson, Rick	2:13.3
1970	Findlay, James	2:10.2
1971	Wilkinson, Rick	2:10.1
1972	Wilkinson, Rick	2:09.9
1973	Tetlow, Peter	2:09.3
1974	Smith, Peter	2:09.22
1975	Tonelli, Mark	2:10.0*
1976	Graff, Jeffrey van de	2:05.85

* = 220 y.

200 m. Individual medley (instituted 1964)

1964	Buck, Terry	2:22.0
1965*	Reynolds, Peter	2:22.3
1966	Reynolds, Peter	2:19.6
1967*	Reid, Peter	2:22.4
1968	Reid, Peter	2:19.8
1969	Findlay, James	2:20.4
1970	Findlay, James	2:18.0
1971	Featherstone, Bruce	2:17.9
1972	Featherstone, Bruce	2:15.3
1973	Tetlow, Peter	2:17.3
1974	Windeatt, Graham	2:12.13
1975	Windeatt, Graham	2:12.0*
1976	Lewis, T.	2:15.87

* = 220 y.

400 m. Individual medley (instituted 1953)

1953*	O'Neill, Frank	5:43.0
1954*	Barry, Robert	5:48.6
1955*	Henricks, Jon	5:55.0
1956*	Weld, Cyrus	5:40.9
1957*	Garretty, Murray	5:37.5
1958*	Wilkinson, Brian	5:37.4
1959*	Kable, Anthony	5:45.4
1960*	Kable, Anthony	5:33.6
1961	Burton, William	5:29.0
1962*	Alexander, Alex	5:23.3
1963*	Ebsary, Bill	5:18.8
1964	Buck, Terry	5:04.0

1965*	Reynolds, Peter	5:03.7
1966	Reynolds, Peter	4:54.0
1967*	Reynolds, Peter	5:06.2
1968	Byrom, Karl	4:58.7
1969	Findlay, James	4:57.4
1970	Findlay, James	4:49.6
1971	Findlay, John	4:51.8
1972	Windeatt, Graham	4:46.6
1973	Martin, Neil	4:44.5
1974	Windeatt, Graham	4:44.11
1975	Dawson, Peter	4:40.7*
1976	Dawson, Peter	4:33.69

* = 440 y.

WOMEN

100 m. Free-style (instituted 1930 for 100 y.)

1946*	West, Dawn	1:12.6
1947*	Davies, Judy-Joy	1:11.9
1948*	Spencer, Denise	1:10.1
1949	McQuade, Marjorie	1:09.9
1950*	McQuade, Marjorie	1:08.5
1951*	McQuade, Marjorie	1:09.0
1952*	McQuade, Marjorie	1:09.5
1953*	McQuade, Marjorie	1:08.4
1954*	Crapp, Lorraine	1:08.2
1955*	Leech, Faith	1:07.6
1956*	Fraser, Dawn	1:04.5
1957*	Morgan, Sandra	1:07.8
1958*	Fraser, Dawn	1:01.5
1959*	Fraser, Dawn	1:01.7
1960*	Fraser, Dawn	1:00.2
1961	Fraser, Dawn	1:01.0
1962*	Fraser, Dawn	1:00.6
1963*	Turner, Jan	1:04.4
1964	Fraser, Dawn	58.9
1965*	Murphy, Janice	1:03.1
1966	Bell, Lynn	1:03.0
1967*	Steinbeck, Janet	1:03.4
1968	Watson, Lynn	1:01.8
1969	Steinbeck, Janet	1:02.5
1970	Watson, Lynn	1:01.7
1971	Gould, Shane	1:00.3
1972	Gould, Shane	1:00.1
1973	Gould, Shane	59.6
1974	Gray, Sonya	58.95
1975	Gray, Sonya	58.8*
1976	Tate, Jenny	59.85

* = 110 y.

200 m. Free-style (instituted 1930)

1946*	Spencer, Denise	2:39.4
1947*	Spencer, Denise	2:37.6
1948*	Spencer, Denise	2:35.0
1949	McQuade, Marjorie	2:35.0
1950*	Davies, Judy-Joy	2:33.3

1951* Davies, Judy-Joy	2:33.1		1975 Gray, Sonya	4:17.9*
1952* McQuade, Marjorie	2:36.0		1976 Wickham, Tracey	4:18.49
1953* McQuade, Marjorie	2:29.6		* = 440 y.	
1954* Crapp, Lorraine	2:30.9			
1955* Fraser, Dawn	2:29.3		**800 m. Free-style** (instituted 1933)	
1956* Fraser, Dawn	2:21.2		1946* Spencer, Denise	12:11.2
1957* Morgan, Sandra	2:29.3		1947 Not held	
1958* Fraser, Dawn	2:14.7		1948 Davies, Judy-Joy	12:08.5
1959* Fraser, Dawn	2:15.3		1949 Spencer, Denise	11:46.9
1960* Fraser, Dawn	2:11.6		1950* Norton, Denise	11:29.8
1961 Fraser, Dawn	2:15.5		1951* Norton, Denise	11:36.5
1962* Fraser, Dawn	2:21.1		1952* Norton, Denise	11:40.9
1963* Konrads, Ilsa	2:18.6		1953* Davies, Judy-Joy	11:14.2
1964 Fraser, Dawn	2:13.1		1954* Davies, Judy-Joy	11:30.2
1965* Herford, Kim	2:19.3		1955* Munro, Jan	11:28.8
1966 Bell, Lynn	2:17.5		1956* Munro, Jan	11:07.4
1967* McDonald, Julie	2:18.0		1957* Giles, Maureen	11:21.8
1968 McDonald, Julie	2:14.2		1958* Konrads, Ilsa	10:16.2
1969 Rillie, Faye	2:15.4		1959* Konrads, Ilsa	10:11.4
1970 Moras, Karen	2:09.8		1960* Konrads, Ilsa	10:17.9
1971 Gould, Shane	2:07.8		1961 Paine, Yvonne	10:29.8
1972 Gray, Helen	2:08.8		1962* Paine, Yvonne	10:37.0
1973 Gould, Shane	2:09.3		1963* Holley, Dawn	10:33.1
-------------------------------			1964 Wainwright, Kathy	10:11.1
1974 Gray, Sonya	2:05.15		1965* Wainwright, Kathy	9:58.2
1975 Gray, Sonya	2:04.9*		1966 Wainwright, Kathy	10:06.4
1976 Gray, Sonya	2:04.90		1967* Wainwright, Kathy	9:54.1
* = 220 y.			1968 Moras, Karen	9:36.9
			1969 Deakes, Christine	9:42.5
			1970 Moras, Karen	9:09.1
400 m. Free-style (instituted 1930)			1971 Moras, Karen	9:16.4
1946* Spencer, Denise	5:48.2		1972 Gould, Shane	9:01.8
1947* Spencer, Denise	5:47.0		1973 Rickard, Virginia	9:13.7
1948* Spencer, Denise	5:31.5		-------------------------------	
1949 Spencer, Denise	5:39.2		1974 Turrall, Jenny	8:54.28
1950* Davies, Judy-Joy	5:23.5		1975 Turrall, Jenny	8:53.9*
1951* Davies, Judy-Joy	5:26.8		1976 Turrall, Jenny	8:50.96
1952* Norton, Denise	5:29.4		* = 880 y.	
1953* Davies, Judy-Joy	5:29.6			
1954* Crapp, Lorraine	5:19.0			
1955* Crapp, Lorraine	5:30.2		**100 m. Back-stroke** (instituted 1930 for	
1956* Crapp, Lorraine	5:05.9		100 y.)	
1957* Morgan, Sandra	5:21.6		1946* Davies, Judy-Joy	1:24.4
1958* Fraser, Dawn	4:55.7		1947* Davies, Judy-Joy	1:21.5
1959* Konrads, Ilsa	4:50.2		1948* Davies, Judy-Joy	1:18.2
1960* Fraser, Dawn	4:47.4		1949 Davies, Judy-Joy	1:20.2
1961 Fraser, Dawn	4:49.7		1950* Davies, Judy-Joy	1:16.6
1962* Fraser, Dawn	4:58.7		1951* Davies, Judy-Joy	1:17.9
1963* Konrads, Ilsa	4:56.7		1952* Davies, Judy-Joy	1:18.0
1964 Fraser, Dawn	4:50.6		1953* Pascall, Margaret	1:18.1
1965* Duncan, Nan	4:54.9		1954* Knight, Dianne	1:18.2
1966 Wainwright. Kathy	4:49.2		1955* Huntingford, Pat	1:18.8
1967* Thorn, Jenny	4:52.7		1956* Beckett, Gergaynia	1:17.5
1968 Moras, Karen	4:39.9		1957* Jackson, Barbara	1:18.1
1969 Moras, Karen	4:34.5		1958* Beckett, Gergaynia	1:14.0
1970 Moras, Karen	4:26.3		1959* Nelson, Ann	1:15.8
1971 Gould, Shane	4:26.2		1960* Wilson, Marilyn	1:13.7
1972 Gould, Shane	4:22.8		1961 Costing, Sue	1:13.2
1973 Gould, Shane	4:31.3		1962 Nelson, Ann	1:13.5
-------------------------------			1963* Woosley, Belinda	1:12.9
1974 Turrall, Jenny	4:23.22			

1964	Woosley, Belinda	1:12.3
1965*	Mabb, Allyson	1:13.7
1966	Mabb, Allyson	1:11.8
1967*	Watson, Lynn	1:12.1
1968	Watson, Lynn	1:09.1
1969	Watson, Lynn	1:09.4
1970	Watson, Lynn	1:09.2
1971	Cain, Debbie	1:07.7
1972	Lewis, Sue	1:08.5
1973	Young, Linda	1:07.4

1974	Cain, Debbie	1:08.02
1975	Robertson, Glenda	1:08.2*
1976	Robertson, Glenda	1:06.26

* = 110 y.

200 m. Back-stroke (instituted 1957)

1957*	Jackson, Barbara	2:50.5
1958*	Beckett, Gergaynia	2:45.1
1959*	Nelson, Ann	2:45.8
1960*	Wilson, Marilyn	2:39.0
1961	Wilson, Marilyn	2:39.6
1962*	Costin, Sue	2:41.7
1963*	Woosley, Belinda	2:38.7
1964	Woosley, Belinda	2:34.5
1965*	Cooper, Vivian	2:37.2
1966	Mabb, Allyson	2:35.0
1968*	Mabb, Allyson	2:34.8
1968	Watson, Lyn	2:28.9
1969	Watson, Lyn	2:31.4
1970	Watson, Lyn	2:28.9
1971	Cain, Debbie	2:28.0
1972	Palmer, Debbie	2:25.0
1973	Young, Linda	2:23.6

1974	Yost, Sandra	2:25.36
1975	Robertson, Glenda	2:24.1*
1976	Robertson, Glenda	2:20.08

* = 220 y.

100 m. Breast-stroke (instituted 1956)

1956*	Whillier, Lynette	1:26.7
1957*	Evans, Barbara	1:26.0
1958*	Lassig, Rosemary	1:25.9
1959*	Lassig, Rosemary	1:23.3
1960*	Lassig, Rosemary	1:22.2
1961	Hogan, Jan	1:25.2
1962*	Hogan, Jan	1:25.2
1963*	Ruygrok, Marguerite	1:22.0
1964	Ruygrok, Marguerite	1:22.8
1965*	Saville, Heather	1:20.1
1966	Saville, Heather	1:18.3
1967*	Saville, Heather	1:21.1
1968	Playfair, Judy	1:17.9
1969	Barnes, Joanne	1:18.1
1970	Whitfield, Beverley	1:18.5
1971	Whitfield, Beverley	1:18.7
1972	Harrison, Dorothy (GB)	1:17.0
1973	Whitfield, Beverley	1:16.5

1974	Whitfield, Beverley	1:17.15

1975	Smith, Allison	1:17.8*
1976	Smith, Allison	1:17.43

* = 110 y.

200 m. Breast-stroke (instituted 1930)

1946*	Lyons, Nancy	3:14.0
1947*	Lyons, Nancy	3:17.8
1948*	Lyons, Nancy	3:09.9
1949	Lyons, Nancy	3:09.8
1950*	Lyons, Nancy	3:09.5
1951*	Uren, Joan	3:12.3
1952*	Lyons, Nancy	3:03.0
1953*	Fehr, Jenny	3:10.6
1954*	Grier, Jane	3:08.3
1955*	Whillier, Lynette	3:08.3
1956*	Evans, Barbara	3:05.4
1957*	Evans, Barbara	3:04.0
1958*	Evans, Barbara	3:02.4
1959*	Lassig, Rosemary	3:00.8
1960*	Lassig, Rosemary	2:57.7
1961	Hogan, Jan	3:02.1
1962*	Hogan, Jan	3:02.3
1963*	Ruygrok, Marguerite	2:54.2
1964	McGill, Linda	2:57.0
1965*	Saville, Heather	2:52.2
1966	Saville, Heather	2:50.8
1967*	Saville, Heather	2:54.6
1968	McKenzie, Sue	2:48.3
1969	Barnes, Joanne	2:49.4
1970	Whitfield, Beverley	2:48.0
1971	Whitfield, Beverley	2:44.9
1972	Harrison, Dorothy (GB)	2:45.0
1973	Whitfield, Beverley	2:42.9

1974	Whitfield, Beverley	2:43.2
1975	Hudson, Judy	2:42.9*
1976	Hudson, Judy	2:41.83

* = 220 y.

100 m. Butterfly (instituted 1955)

1955*	Munro, Jan	1:25.3
1956*	Bainbridge, Beverley	1:16.8
1957*	Bainbridge, Beverley	1:16.0
1958*	Bainbridge, Beverley	1:15.5
1959*	Andrew, Jan	1:15.2
1960*	Fraser, Dawn	1:10.8
1961	Andrew, Jan	1:10.7
1962*	Fraser, Dawn	1:12.8
1963*	McGill, Linda	1:12.8
1964	McGill, Linda	1:11.2
1965*	Groeger, Jill	1:12.3
1966	Groeger, Jill	1:10.4
1967*	George, Lynette	1:11.8
1968	McClements, Lynn	1:09.4
1969	McClements, Lynn	1:08.7
1970	Mabb, Allyson	1:07.2
1971	Funch, Sue	1:07.7
1972	Funch, Sue	1:05.9
1973	Gould, Shane	1:04.4

1974	Cain, Debbie	1:05.01
1975	Stove, Nira	1:05.4*
1976	Hanel, Linda/Smith, Lyle	
	(Dead heat)	1:04.28
	* = 110 y.	

200 m. Butterfly (instituted 1960)

1960*	Andrew, Jan	2:44.1
1961	Andrew, Jan	2:40.5
1962*	McGill, Linda	2:46.0
1963*	McGill, Linda	2:41.5
1964	McGill, Linda	2:37.3
1965*	George, Lynette	2:43.9
1966	Groeger, Jill	2:40.4
1967*	Turner, Cecily	2:39.8
1968	Byrnes, Anne	2:33.3
1969	McClements, Lynn	2:31.1
1970	Robinson, Maree	2:27.0
1971	Robinson, Maree	2:23.5
1972	Neall, Gail	2:23.2
1973	Yost, Sandra	2:21.9
1974	Yost, Sandra	2:20.90
1975	Hudson, Judy	2:20.9*
1976	Ford, Michelle	2:16.55
	* = 220 y.	

200 m. Individual medley (instituted 1953)

1953*	Davies, Judy-Joy	3:06.4
1954*	Munro, Jan	3:06.0
1955*	Munro, Jan	3:05.6
1956*	Bainbridge, Beverley	2:50.2
1957*	Bainbridge, Beverley	2:54.4
1958*	Lassig, Rosemary	2:52.2
1959*	Fraser, Dawn	2:44.2
1960-63	Not held	

1964	McGill, Linda	2:40.7
1965*	Murphy, Jan	2:40.8
1966	Murphy, Jan	2:39.3
1967*	Murphy, Jan	2:40.4
1968	Watson, Lyn	2:35.6
1969	Rickard, Diana	2:36.2
1970	Rickard, Diana	2:31.3
1971	Gould, Shane	2:29.2
1972	Cain, Debbie	2:29.5
1973	Gould, Shane	2:28.5
1974	Cain, Debbie	2:26.35
1975	Hudson, Judy	2:24.8*
1976	Hudson, Judy	2:22.47
	* = 220 y.	

400 m. Individual medley (instituted 1960)

1960*	Colquhoun, Alva	5:54.5
1961	McGill, Linda	5:59.1
1962*	McGill, Linda	5:50.8
1963*	McGill, Linda	5:41.2
1964	McGill, Linda	5:36.4
1965*	Murphy, Jan	5:51.1
1966	Murphy, Jan	5:41.5
1967*	Murphy, Jan	5:41.2
1968	Rickard, Diana	5:32.2
1969	Eddy, Sue	5:31.3
1970	Langford, Denise	5:17.8
1971	Neall, Gail	5:18.5
1972	Neall, Gail	5:09.8
1973	Gould, Shane	5:08.8
1974	Lockyer, Sally	5:07.98
1975	Hudson, Judy	5:05.0*
1976	Hudson, Judy	4:58.60
	* = 440 y.	

brought her total of United States national titles to 14 in three years.

This tally included winning the 200 m. free-style outdoor championship four years in succession (1972-1975), a remarkable feat in the highly-competitive United States swimming set-up.

In 1975, indeed, this talented athlete, trained by Mark Schubert at the Mission Viejo club in California, made a clean sweep of the outdoor and indoor sprint and middle-distance freestyle events (outdoor 100, 200 and 400 m. and indoor 100, 200 and 500 y.)

BABASHOFF, Shirley (United States, 31 Jan, 1957-). On the fringe of individual victories at the 1972 Olympics and 1973 World championships, Shirley Babashoff, born at Whittier, California, finally rose to the top during the U.S. Outdoor championships at Concord in August 1974 when she set world free-style records for 200 m., 2:02.94 (which she equalled to the 100th of a sec. eight days later) and 400 m., 4:15.77. At the Munich Games and in Belgrade the following year, she was the silver-medal bridesmaid behind four different golden brides. In the Olympics she was beaten in the 100 m. by her team-mate Sandy Neilson (see NEILSON, Sandy) and the 200 m. by Australia's Shane Gould (see GOULD, Shane). At the World championships it was East Germany's Kornelia Ender (see ENDER, Kornelia) and America's Keena Rothhammer (see ROTHHAMMER, Keena).

Shirley did win a gold with the U.S. free-style relay squad in Munich, but it was silver again in the same event and the medley relay, behind East Germany in Belgrade.

Undoubtedly, though, it was Shirley the star at the 1975 world championships in Cali, Colombia, where she tackled a mammoth programme of five individual events and two relays.

She sprang the surprise of the meeting in beating world record-holder Ender in the 200 m. free-style after the East German had been 2½ seconds ahead at half distance. The Californian also won the 400 m., was second in the 100 m., third in the 800 m. and fourth in the 200 m. IM. And she anchored American squads to silvers in both relays.

During that year she again broke the 400 m. world record (4:14.76) and

BACHRACH, William (United States, 15 May, 1879-1959). A heavyweight champion coach of outstanding champions, Bill Bachrach counted Johnny Weissmuller, Norman Ross, Arne Borg (Sweden) and Sybil Bauer - all Olympic title-holders and world record-breakers (see biographies) among his Illinois Athletic Club stars. Known as "Bach" or the "Great Bach", this 300 lb. giant habitually wore a bath-robe, appropriately but unusually, for his pool-side coaching stints. His boyhood ambition was to be a great swimmer, but he never won a race, though he did become a great coach.

Bach had a rare talent for getting the best out of his pupils and his advanced ideas on breathing techniques helped Weissmuller, among others, to rise to the top. Bach also is the only coach whose swimmers and divers made a clean sweep of the men's A.A.U. National titles in the same year (1914). His men, at one time, held 95% of world swimming records and his squad won 120 national titles.

BACK-STROKE. The third of the recognised strokes, back-stroke was put in the Olympic programme in 1908 (for men) and in 1924 (for women). The first A.S.A. championship for this style was won in 1903 by William Call.

The early swimmers used an inverted breast-stroke technique with a double arm swing and a frog-leg kick. With the development of front crawl, it was soon realized that an alternating arm action and a flutter leg kick would be as effective on the back as on the front.

It is the only one of the four modern styles in which competitors start in the water. They must stay on their backs throughout the race, except at the turns The F.I.N.A. Rule 67 lays down that:

(a) The competitors shall line up in the water, facing the starting end, with the hands placed on the starting grips. The feet, including the toes, shall be under the surface of the water. Standing in or on the gutter or bending the toes over the lip of the gutter is prohibited.

(b) At the signal for starting and when turning they shall push off and swim upon their backs throughout the race. The hands must not be released before the starting signal has been given.

(c) Any competitor leaving his normal position on the back before the head, foremost hand, or arm has touched, the end of the course for the purpose of turning or finishing, shall be disqualified.

To clarify their ruling about turning in back-stroke events, the F.I.N.A. say that it is permissible to turn over beyond the vertical after the foremost part of the body has touched, for the purpose of executing the turn, but the swimmer must have returned past the vertical to a position on his back before the feet have left the wall.

The most remarkable back-stroke swimmer of the modern era is Roland Matthes of East Germany (See MATTHES, Roland) who won the 100 and 200 m. gold medals at the 1968 and 1972 Olympics. The only other men to win at successive Games were Warren Kealoha of the United States (1920/24) and David Theile from Australia (1956/60). They were victorious in the 100 m. only for there was no 200 m. event in the programme during their years.

In women's Olympic back-stroke competition, no swimmer has won in successive years, although Melissa Belote of the United States (see BELOTE, Melissa) emulated the Matthes double in Munich in 1972.

Three men have won the A.S.A. back-stroke title seven times each. John Besford of Manchester, 1927-28, 1930-32 and 1935-36, John Brockway of Maindee 1948-51 and 1953-55 and Graham Sykes of Coventry successively from 1956-60 (over 110 y.) and 1961-62 (for 200 y.).

BALL, Catie (United States, 30 Sep. 1951-). Holder of all four world breast-stroke records before the 1968 Olympic Games in Mexico City, Miss Ball, from Jacksonville, Florida, was taken ill with a virus infection and failed to win either of the individual golds.

She staved off collapse on the first days of the swimming to take a gold in the United States medley relay team and to struggle into fifth place in the final of the 100 metres. Normally 5 ft. 7 in. and 128 lb, Miss Ball lost 10 lb in weight and was too ill even to start in the heats of the 200 m.

Pan American 100 and 200 m. champion in 1967 and double winner of the United States outdoor titles in 1967 and 1968, Miss Ball broke ten world breast-stroke records between December 1966 and August 1968. These include five successive 100 m. marks from 1:15.6 to 1:14.2. Her other best times were 1:17.0 (110 y.), 2:38.5 (200 m.) and 2:46.9 (220 y.).

BÁRÁNY, István (Hungary, 20 Dec. 1907-). A great competitor in the era when Johnny Weissmuller bestrode the world swimming scene, Dr. Bárány ('Pista' to his friends) became the first European to break the minute for 100 m. (59.8) in coming second to Weissmuller in the 1928 Olympics. He also won a silver in the 4 x 200 m. relay in 1932.

Bárány, a man of many talents, is a doctor of law and political science, worked as a town clerk, journalist, was secretary of the Hungarian Swimming Federation (1957-59) and organized the 1958 European championships in Budapest. He has written 18 books about swimming.

Winner of seven European championship medals—100 m., gold (1926 and 1931); silver (1927); 400 m. gold (1931); 4 x 200 m. silver (1926); bronze (1927) and gold (1931)—his best times were 100 m. (58.4), 200 m. (2:16.0), both European records, and 5:04.0 for 400 m.

BAUER. Sybil (United States, 18 Sep. 1903-31 Jan 1927). The world's first great back-stroke swimmer, Sybil Bauer from Chicago was in a class of her own, as she demonstrated in 1924 when she won the first Olympic 100 m. title for women in Paris by 4.2 sec. in 1:23.2.

A competitor with perfect technique, she had made substantial inroads into the world back-stroke lists before her Olympic victory. These included improving the 100 m. mark by 14.6 sec. in five months and cutting 12 sec from the 150 y. best.

Beautiful and brainy, animated and articulate, this very feminine daughter of Norwegian parents was a leader in the fight to get a full competitive programme into women's university sport. Fifty years later, her successors had fulfilled part of her dream. And when they do succeed finally, Sybil must take part of the credit.

Sybil Bauer died tragically of cancer at the age of 23 at the top of her undefeated swimming career.

BEAUREPAIRE, Sir Frank (Australia, 13 May 1891-29 May 1956). In a swimming career which stretched from 1903 to 1928, Beaurepaire competed in four Olympics–1908, 1912, 1920 and 1924. He won three silver and three bronze medals, the last of these at the age of 33, for 400, 1,500 and 4 x 200 m. free-style. He set eight world records.

And he did this despite three warnings that swimming was dangerous to him as a result of rheumatic fever in childhood. In fact, Beaurepaire swam himself back to health and became one of Australia's outstanding distance free-stylers.

He was Lord Mayor of Melbourne from 1940 to 1942, and knighted at the end of his term of office. Business success made him a millionaire and he was a noted philanthropist, but his great dream of seeing the Olympics in his city was never fulfilled.

Melbourne was awarded the 1956 Games and Beaurepaire was to be Lord Mayor again to host the event. But he died of a heart attack seven months before the opening.

He made many trips to Europe, during which he won ten A.S.A. titles from 220 y. to one mile. His best performances were 200 m. in 2:30.0, 440 y. in 5:23.0 and 1,000 m. in 14:28.0–a mark he set on the way to another world record for one mile, at the age of 30.

BELOTE, Melissa (United States 16 Oct, 1956-). From Silver Springs, Mary land, Melissa Belote, then 15, was the only woman other than Shane Gould (see GOULD, Shane) to win more than one individual title at the 1972 Munich Olympics.

Her golds came in the 100 and 200 m. back-stroke and she won the latter in a world record 2:19.19. She got a third gold in America's winning 4 x 100 m. medley team.

Melissa confirmed her supremacy over 200 m. at the first World championships in Belgrade a year later, winning by 1½ sec. from Holland's Enith Brigitha. But she had to settle for silvers, behind East German competitors in the 100 m. and medley relay.

BENJAMIN, HENRY, NATIONAL MEMORIAL TROPHY. Awarded to the top men's club in England, this trophy was presented to the A.S.A. by the five district associations in 1909 to perpetuate the memory of the late Henry Benjamin, a noted administrator, who was president of the A.S.A. in 1900. Points are awarded for success in A.S.A. long and short course swimming and club water-polo championships.

Otter S.C. have the most wins (13). They were joint holders, with Plaistow United (1933) and Hull Kingston (1947) and won outright in 1935, 1938, 1948-50, 1953, 1955, 1962 and 1963-64. Until 1951, when a trophy was awarded for the top diving club (see MELVILLE CLARK, G., National Memorial Trophy) success in diving championships also counted. The winners have been:

1910	Wigan	29
1911	Hyde Seal	33
1912	Hyde Seal/Middlesbrough	23
1913	Middlesbrough	30
1914-19	Not awarded	
1920	Hammersmith	27
1921	Middlesbrough	32
1922	Penguin	36
1923	Penguin	34
1924	Penguin	23
1925	Weston-super-Mare	28
1926	Penguin	22
1927	Penguin	19
1928	South Manchester	25
1929	Oldham Police	27
1930	Oldham Police	28
1931	Plaistow United	32
1932	Plaistow United	32
1933	Otter/Plaistow United	20
1934	Oldham Police	22
1935	Otter	25
1936	Penguin	23
1937	Otter	27
1938	Otter	34
1939	Hanley	19
1940-46	Not awarded	
1947	Hull Kingston/Otter	24

1948	Otter	20
1949	Otter	27
1950	Otter	15
1951	Penguin	18
1952	Penguin	22
1953	Otter	17
1954	Coventry	17
1955	Otter	19
1956	Wallasey	22
1957	Wallasey	18
1958	Stoke Newington/Wallasey	21
1959	Stoke Newington	30
1960	Stoke Newington	36
1961	York City	31
1962	Otter	41
1963	York City	48
1964	Otter	49
1965	Otter	27
1966	Southampton	49
1967	Southampton	55
1968	Southampton	53
1969	Southampton	33
1970	Southampton	29
1971	St. James's	108
1972	Southampton	149
1973	Southampton	140
1974	Modernian	88
1975	Modernian	102

BERRY, Kevin (Australia, 10 Apr 1945-). The career of butterflyer Kevin Berry was short and successful. In three years, from 1962 to 1964, he won an Olympic title and a relay bronze, three Commonwealth golds and broke 12 world records.

Berry, from Marrickville, Sydney, was 15 in 1960 when he made his first Olympic appearance as Australia's second string in the 200 m. in Rome and did well to place sixth in 2:18.5. Four years later, Berry was world record holder with 2:06.9 and favourite for the Tokyo title. This he duly won, 0.9 ahead of America's Carl Robie, in a new world mark of 2:06.6—a time which took three years to better.

Commonwealth 110 and 220 y. butterfly champion in Perth (Aus) in 1962, Berry, who won six Australian titles, improved the world 200 m. time by 5.9 seconds in 21 months, yet never broke the 100 m. mark, nor was he a member of a world record-breaking relay squad. His best times, all world marks, were 59.0 (110 y.), 2:06.6 (200 m.) and 2:08.4 (220 y.). This last performance, on 12 Jan. 1963, stayed on the record books until the event was discontinued.

BESFORD, John C.P. (Great Britain, 30 Jan. 1911-). Seven times English back-stroke champion between 1927-36, Besford's memorable feat was to win the 1934 European 100 m. title in Magdeburg. For this he received the Hitler trophy, a magnificent bronze eagle, mounted on a bronze globe, surmounting a marble plinth and weighing a hundredweight, a prize which Germany, the host nation, had confidently expected would go to their Ernst Kuppers.

BILLINGTON, David (Great Britain, 1886-4 Feb. 1955). Bacup-born Billington, who at 12 was called "Boy Champion of England", never had the chance to fulfil his early promise.

Though he won 10 National titles between 1901-1905 and beat such notable Australians as Percy Cavill and Barney Kieran, he was suspended as an amateur in 1905 for taking part in a race in the river Seine against professionals.

As a result of this, a new agreement was made between England and France, but the A.S.A. refused to lift the ban on Billington. He was only 19 and who knows what he might have achieved in the 1906 and 1908 Olympics in Athens and London.

BJEDOV, Djurdjica (Yugoslavia, 5 Apr. 1947-). A shock winner of the 100 m. breast-stroke at the 1968 Games—Yugoslavia's first and only Olympic swimming champion—Djurdjica Bjedov almost did not go to Mexico. She was chosen only to make up a medley relay squad. Ironically the team were disqualified for her faulty take-over and did not even reach the final.

Bjedov had no claims to fame. Third in her 200 m. heat in the 1966 European championships was her only commendation. But in Mexico, fit and apparently unaffected by the altitude, she improved as more famous swimmers wilted. She was the fifth fastest qualifier for the 100 m. final and she came through in lane 2 to snatch the gold by one-tenth in an Olympic record of 1:15.8 from Russia's Galina Prosumenschikova, the only European to have won an Olympic swimming title at the 1964 Games.

The slim, pale, dark-haired student from Split, swam from an even more unfavoured position—as seventh qualifier for the final she was in an outside lane—to win the silver for 200 m. in 2:46.4.

This was three seconds better than she had done before, only 2 sec. behind the winner Sharon Wichman (United States) and she beat the Russian again, this time by six tenths.

BLACK, Ian M. (Great Britain, 27 June 1941-). World renown came to Ian Black of Aberdeen in 1958 when, at 17, he won three European titles—two in the space of 40 minutes—in Budapest. He first took the 400 m. free-style, almost without seeming to exert himself, by eight metres. With barely time to dry off, he was back in the water for the 200 m. butterfly. And three days later, he captured the 1,500 m. for a hat-trick of individual golds only once achieved before in these championships, by Arne Borg of Sweden in 1927.

Black's time at the top was short, from 1958 to 1960. But he packed a lot into these three years. He won the 220 y. butterfly gold, and silvers in the 440 y. free-style and 4 x 200 y. relay in the 1958 Empire Games in Cardiff.

The same year, he set European free-style records for 400 m. (4:28.4), 800 m. (9:25.5) and 1,500 m. (18:05.8).

For these achievements he was voted Britain's Sportsman of the Year of 1958 in three national polls.

The fair-haired Scot's only world mark came in 1959 when he became the first holder of the 440 y. medley (5:08.8). The following year he dead-heated with John Konrads of Australia for the bronze medal in the 400 m. free-style in the Rome Olympics, but was judged into fourth place on a technicality. His 4:21.8 then was a European record and he helped Britian to fourth place and to another European record in the 4 x 200 m. free-style relay.

In the A.S.A. championships Black won four titles at each of the meetings of 1958 and 1959—110, 220 and 440 y. free-style and 220 y. butterfly. He also won the mile, a distance he detested, in 1958 and 18 Scottish titles. At one time he held nine of the 18 British records.

BLEIBTREY, Ethelda (United States, 27 Feb. 1902-). America's first woman Olympic swimming champion, Ethelda Bleibtrey had the unique distinction of being the only competitor to win all the swimming events at a single Games.

The fact that there were only three in the Antwerp programme in 1920— the 100, 200 and 4 x 100 m. free-style — cannot dim the feat. Indeed, Miss Bleibtrey would have post-dated by 44 years the first four-golds-at-one-Games achievement of her compatriot Don Schollander (see SCHOLLANDER, Don) in 1964 had there been a back-stroke event for women in Antwerp, for she also was a world-record holder for this stroke.

Swimming over a 100 m. course in what she described as "mud not water", Ethelda took the 100 m. by 3.4 sec (1:13.6) and the 300 m. by 8.8 sec (4:34.0), both world records. And she helped America to victory in the 4 x 100 m. by 29.2 sec. in a world best of 5:11.6, world relay records not being recognised at that time.

The fair-haired New Yorker, who started swimming because of polio and had her first competitive races only two years before her Olympic victories, turned professional at 20, after winning every national American championship from 50 yards to long distance between 1920-1922 in an undefeated amateur career.

BOITEUX, Jean (France, 20 June, 1933-). A surprise Olympic 400 m. winner in Helsinki in 1952, the tall dark-haired Boiteux was close to being disqualified after his victory, for his father leapt into the water to embrace his son before some of the other swimmers had finished. Papa Boiteau's excitement was understandable, for in beating America's Ford Konno by six-tenths in 4:30.7— more than ten seconds faster than the 1948 winning time—his son Jean had become France's first individual Olympic swimming champion.

Boiteaux, who two years before had won silver medals for 400 and 1,500 m. in the European championships in Vienna, later failed to qualify for the final of the Helsinki 1,500 m. He won a slow heat in 19:12.3, missed the final by two seconds and the very real chance of a second medal for France.

BOLOGNA TROPHY. This huge, handsome cup was awarded to the British women's relay team for winning the 4 x 100 m. at the 1927 European championships, in Bologna, Italy. The team consisted of Joyce Cooper and Marion Laverty of England, Ellen King of Scotland and Valerie Davies of Wales.

It was decided by the three countries that the trophy should be put up for an Inter-Country Speed Swimming team contest. Of the 32 meetings, England won 30 and Scotland two before the event was discontinued in 1972.

Year	Venue	Eng-land	Scot-land	Wales
1929	Paisley	19	17	–
1930	Nelson	34	24	14
1931	Rhyl	36	23	13
1933	Dunfermline	32	27	13
1934	Hastings	28	25	17
1935	Newport	35	22	14
1937	Renfrew	35	22	15
1938	Wembley	34	20	18
1939	Barry	36	20	16
1947	Aberdeen	30	28	14
1949	Birmingham	32	25	15
1950	Aberdare	26	30	16
1951	Kilmarnock	24	32	16
1953	Birmingham	33	24	15
1954	Newport	28	27	17
1955	Aberdeen	34	24	14
1956	Gateshead	40	28	16
1957	Newport	39	30	15
1958	Kilmarnock	37	25	19
1959	Liverpool	38	29	17
1960	Newport	40	29	15
1961	Coatbridge	39	25	20
1962	Blackburn	39	25	20
1963	Cardiff	40	25	19
1964	Dumfries	36	28	20
1965	Liverpool	41	21	22
1966	Aberavon	42	20	22
1967	Wishaw·	41	21	22
1968	Grimsby	38	21	25
1969	Aberavon	40	25	19
1970	Edinburgh	56	36	28
1971	Grimsby	56	36	28

BORG, Arne (Sweden, 18 Aug. 1901-). A giant of his time, Borg's theme song could have been wine, women and water. He always did what he felt like doing, and among other things, he liked to swim as did his twin brother Ake, also an international.

His first Olympic appearance was in the 1924 Games where after heats and semi-finals—unheard of these days—he lost the 1,500 m. final to Boy Charlton (Australia) by 34.8 seconds though he was himself 1:41.8 inside the 1920 Olympic record with 20:41.4. But he finished ahead of Charlton, though be-hind Johnny Weissmuller, in the 400 m.

and, such was his versatility, placed fourth in the 100 m.

At the 1928 Games he beat Charlton in the 1,500 m. but was third, behind Alberto Zorilla, the Argentine's only Olympic gold medal swimmer and the Australian in the 400 m. Borg won the 400 and 1,500 m. at the first European championships in 1926 and was second in the 100 m. The following year, he took all three gold medals at the second European meeting. His astonishing 1,500 m. winning time of 19:07.2 was a world record that stood for 11 years—and Borg did this only hours after playing for Sweden, the silver medal winners, in a water-polo match in which he had two teeth knocked out.

Borg set 32 world records between 1921—29 for every free-style distance, from 300 y. up to one mile. As well as his 1,500 m. marks, he swam 400 m. in 4:50.3 in 1925, a time that was not beaten until 1931.

A great patriot, Borg nevertheless did not allow things he thought a waste of time to interfere with his pleasures. Called up for national service during peace time, just as he was setting off on a holiday tour of Spain, he chose Spain. This time even his tremendous popu-larity did not prevent him being sent to prison. Yet his time in cell 306 in Gota prison seems to have been one long round of visits from friends. Food and drink were sent in to him to such a degree that he was 8 kilograms heavier on his release.

BOYS, Beverley (Canada, 4 July 1951-). Winner of three Commonwealth titles, the career of Beverley Boys spans a decade of top level diving. She com-peted in every major event open to her since 1966 (20) and only twice failed to reach the final.

She was just 15 in 1966 when she came second and third respectively in the highboard and springboard at the Commonwealth Games in Jamaica. Four years later, in Edinburgh, she won both titles by clear margins, despite perforating an ear drum on her first practice dive in Scotland. In Christchurch, New Zealand, in 1974, she retained her highboard crown and was second in the springboard for a grand medals total of three golds, two silvers and a bronze.

At the Pan-American Games, Miss

Boys was runner-up in the highboard in 1967 and 1971, also winning a springboard bronze at her second appearance in this event. She was fourth in the highboard at the 1968 Olympics and fifth in the springboard four years later in Munich. And she became the first foreign diver to win an American national title, the indoor highboard crown, in 1969, beating in the process the then Olympic champion, Milena Duchkova, of Czechoslovakia.

BREAST-STROKE. The first of the competitive strokes and the only one in which a prescribed style is laid down, the breast-stroke probably has caused more legislating and officiating trouble than the rest of swimming's problems put together.

The F.I.N.A. Rule 65 states:
  (a) The body shall be kept perfectly on the breast and both shoulders shall be in line with the water surface from the beginning of the first arm stroke after the start and on the turn.
  (b) All movements of the legs and arms shall be simultaneous and in the same horizontal plane without alternating movement.
  (c) Hands shall be pushed forward together from the breast, and shall be brought back on or under the surface of the water.
  (d) In the leg kick the feet shall be turned outwards in the backward movement. A "dolphin" kick is not permitted.
  (e) At the turn, and upon finishing the race, the touch shall be made with both hands simultaneously at the same level, either at, above or below the water level.
  (f) A part of the head shall always be above the general water level, except that at the start and at each turn, the swimmer may take one arm stroke and one leg kick while wholly submerged.

Arguments have ranged from how perfect the movements of the arms and legs must be; whether a swimmer ducking his head into his own bow-wave is swimming under water; to the time, in the early 1930s, when some bright people realized there was nothing in the current rules to prevent the arms being recovered over instead of under the water (see BUTTERFLY).

The interim time (1934-52) during which swimmers could use the over or under water arm technique played havoc with the world records for the butterfly style proved to be the faster.

From 1952-56, the Japanese in particular exploited another loophole in the rules and began to swim great distances under the water. This was immeasurably faster than on the surface and again the world record picture became distorted. But this was ruled out after the 1956 Olympic Games.

In the present day, the sprinting technique, developed especially by the Soviet Union, is causing problems. In order to speed the stroke, it is necessary to shorten both arm and leg actions. As a result, many competitors come perilously close to vertical instead of the lateral movements of this classic style so much beloved by traditionalists.

Only one swimmer, man or woman, has ever won an Olympic breast-stroke title at successive Games. He was Yoshijuki Tsuruta of Japan who was victorious over 200 m. in 1928 and 1932. (see TSURUTA, Yoshijuki).

BRINKLEY, Brian (Great Britain, 28 December 1953-   ). England's most versatile and talented all-round swimmer of the 1970s, Brinkley's problem always was what races to ignore.

At the 1972 Munich Olympics, he was fifth in the 400 m. free-style. A year later, in the Belgrade world championships, he narrowly missed a medal in the 200 m. butterfly. But he began to get into the top placings at the 1974 Commonwealth Games in Christchurch, New Zealand, where he won the 200 m. butterfly and was second in the 200 and 400 m. I.M. And he followed these successes with a silver in the 200 m. butterfly at the European championships in Vienna and another in anchoring Britain, on free-style, to second place in the 4 x 100 m. medley relay.

At the second world championships, in Cali, Colombia, in 1975, the tall powerful Brinkley from Bedford took bronzes in the 200 m. free-style and butterfly and a silver and bronze in the 4 x 200 m. free-style and 4 x 100 m. medley relays respectively. He also captained the British men's team to second overall place, behind the United States . . . an achievement that earned the squad the B.B.C. "Sports Team of the Year" award for 1975.

The versatile Brinkley was England's "Swimmer of the Year" (see YEADEN MEMORIAL TROPHY) for five successive years since appearing on the scene in 1971 and in that time he won 24 long-course National titles and 19 short-course ones for eight different events.

BRITISH COMMONWEALTH GAMES. See COMMONWEALTH GAMES.

BRITISH EMPIRE GAMES. See COMMONWEALTH GAMES.

BRITISH EMPIRE AND COMMON-WEALTH GAMES. See COMMONWEALTH GAMES.

BURTON, Mike (United States, 3 June 1947-). "Mr. Machine" Burton made tremendous inroads into the world figures for the distance free-style events. In less than three years, from Sept. 1966 to Aug. 1969, he improved the 1,500 m. record four times, from 16:41.6 to 16:08.5 and twice, on the way, set world marks for 800 m.

Three years later, at the age of 25 and swimming only as America's third string, Burton won his second successive Olympic 1,500 m. free-style title. And his time at the 1972 Munich Games was a world record of 15:52.58–46.3 sec. faster than in Mexico City in 1968.

Severely injured in a cycling crash with a lorry at 13 which ended his athletics ambitions, Burton has never allowed anything to divert him in his swimming career. He was suffering badly from a stomach complaint in 1967 when he won the World Student 1,500 m. title in Tokyo in only a fraction outside his world record. "Montezuma's revenge" attacked him again during the 1968 Olympics, yet he survived this handicap and that of altitude to win without difficulty, the 400 m. (4:09.0) and 1,500 m. (16:38.9).

Burton, Pan-American 1,500 champion and third in the 400 m. in 1967, is a powerful 5 ft. 9 in. and 153 lb. He was born in Des Moines, Iowa, but has done most of his swimming in California as a member of the Arden Hills club, coached by Sherman Chavoor. In training, he is a demon to his team-mates for he swims on and on and in competition he is perpetual motion.

BUTTERFLY. Butterfly was separated from breast-stroke and became the fourth swimming style in 1952. This was twenty years after enterprising swimmers in the United States had realized there was nothing in the rules to stop them recovering their arms over instead of under the water (see BREAST-STROKE).

At the beginning, butterflyers used the frog-leg kick of breast-stroke with the flying arms technique. It was a tiring style and few were able to do it throughout a 200 m. race. Experiments at the University of Iowa, with a dolphin fish-like kick in 1935, though illegal for competitions, threatened the total extinction of classic breast-stroke.

But when the strokes were divided, up and down leg movement in the vertical plane were permitted. The only breast-stroke similarities now are the simultaneous movements of arms and legs and the rule that the competitor may not swim under water, except for one stroke after the start and at turns.

F.I.N.A. Rule 66 states:

(a) Both arms must be brought forward together over the water and brought backward simultaneously.

(b) The body must be kept perfectly on the breast and both shoulders in line with the surface of the water from the beginning of the first arm stroke, after the start and on the turn.

(c) All movements of the feet must be executed in a simultaneous manner. Simultaneous up and down movements of the legs and feet in the vertical plane are permitted.

(d) When touching at the turn or on finishing a race, the touch shall be made with both hands simultaneously on the same level, and with the shoulders in the horizontal position. The touch may be made at, above, or below the water level.

(e) At the start and at turns, a swimmer is permitted one or more leg kicks and one arm pull under the water, which must bring him to the surface.

CALLIGARIS, Novella (Italy, 27 Dec. 1954-). Italy's only woman swimming star, Novella Calligaris, born in Padua, overcame lack of first-class opposition in her own country to win eight medals in major competition, including a World title.

Petite but extremely courageous, she surprised everyone, except her coach, by winning the first World 800 m. free-style title in Belgrade in 1973 by the handsome margin of 3½ metres in a world record of 8:52.97. She also took two third places, in the 400 m. free-style and medley.

A year earlier, she endeared herself to the crowd at the Olympics in Munich where she was second in the 400 m. free-style and third in the 800 m. free-style and 400 m. medley. Novella bowed out after the European championships in Vienna in 1974 when, though not at her best, she still managed to win a silver and a bronze from the 800 and 400 m. free-style (see also ITALIAN CHAMPIONS).

CANADIAN SWIMMING. The Canadian Amateur Swimming Association was founded in Montreal in 1909 and consists of ten provincial sections — Alberta, British Columbia, Manitoba, New Brunswick, Newfoundland, Nova Scotia, Ontario, Prince Edward Island, Quebec and Saskatchewan.

Montreal had many active swimming organisations in 1909 though none have survived. The oldest known club still in existence is the Vancouver Amateur Swimming Club (1903).

By 1969 the four disciplines of the sport (swimming, diving, synchronised swimming and water-polo) were operating autonomously under an umbrella organisation the Canadian Federation of Amateur Aquatics, later to be known as the Aquatic Federation of Canada.

The A.F.C. is now based, as a resident association, at the new (1971) Government-supported National Sport and Recreation Centre in Ottawa which exists to assist national associations and organisations concerned with the development of Canadian sport and recreation. The services include administration, technical development and promotion and altogether 33 resident and 36 non-resident bodies are benefiting from the many facilities available.

The highly sophisticated aquatics set-up is run by two young executive directors — one responsible for all-over policy and finance and for swimming activities, and the other for diving, synchronised swimming and water-polo — plus three technical directors with special responsibilities for diving, swimming and water-polo.

CANADIAN SWIMMING CHAMPIONS. There has been some difficulty in obtaining the full list of winners of Canadian swimming championships since World War II. The results as known are listed here in the hope that the spaces may be filled in due time.

The centralized venues and lengths of pools are:

Year	Venue	Course
1947	Victoria, B.C.	50 y.
1948	Verdun, Quebec	25 y.
1949	Vancouver, B.C.	25 y.
1950		
1951		
1952	Toronto, Ontario	25 y.
1953	Winnipeg, Manitoba	25 y.
1954	Vancouver, B.C.	55 y.
1955	Montreal, Quebec	25 y.
1956	Toronto, Ontario	50 y.
1957	Vancouver, B.C.	55 y.
1958	Vancouver, B.C.	55 y.
1959	Brantford, Ontario	55 y.
1960	Winnipeg, Manitoba	25 m.
1961	Dorval, Quebec	25 y.
1962	Vancouver, B.C.	55 y.
1963	Montreal, Quebec	50 m.
1964	Vancouver, B.C.	55 y.
1965	Red Deer, Alberta	50 m.
1966	Hamilton, Ontario	55 y.
1967	Winnipeg, Manitoba	50 m.
1968	Winnipeg, Manitoba	50 m.
1969	Pointe Claire, Quebec	50 m.
1970	Winnipeg, Manitoba	50 m.
1971	Edmonton, Alberta	50 m.
1972	Winnipeg, Manitoba	50 m.

1973	Quebec City, Quebec	50 m.
1974	Ottawa, Ontario	50 m.
1975	Calgary, Alberta	50 m.
1976	Vancoucer, BC	50 m.

The winners are:
MEN

100 m. Free-style

1947*	Rowlinson, P. (USA)	53.6
1948*	Salmon, Peter	54.8
1949*	Salmon, Peter	53.2
1950		
1951*	McNamee, Gerry	55.8
1952*	Salmon, Peter	52.6
1953*	McNamee, Gerry	54.1
1954†		
1955*	Park, George	52.0
1956*	Park, George	52.8
1957†		
1958†	Williams, Ken	59.5
1959†	Grout, Cameron	58.8
1960	Pound, Dick	56.9
1961*	Pound, Dick	50.3
1962†	Pound, Dick	57.0
1963	Sherry, Dan	55.6
1964†	Gilchrist, Sandy	56.5
1965	Sherry, Dan	55.9
1966†	Gilchrist, Sandy	56.0
1967	Kasting, Bob	55.4
1968	Finch, Glen	54.8
1969	Kasting, Bob	55.0
1970	Kasting, Bob	54.8
1971	Phillips, Brian	55.4

1972	Phillips, Brian	53.51
1973	Phillips, Brian	53.08
1974	Phillips, Brian	53.37
1975	Pickell, Steve	53.39

    * = 100 y.   † = 110 y.

200 m. Free-style

1947-48	Event not held	
1949*	Gilchrist, Allen	2:01.8
1950		
1951*	McNamee, Gerry	2:02.1
1952*	McNamee, Gerry	2:00.4
1953	Event not held	
1954		
1955	Event not held	
1956†	McNamee, Gerry	2:14.7
1957		
1958†	Slater, Bill	2:14.6
1959†	Rounds, Fred (USA)	2:13.8
1960	Grout, Cameron	2:06.9
1961*	Pound, Dick	1:53.4
1962†	Verth, Tom	2:08.1
1963	Gilchrist, Sandy	2:03.2
1964†	Rose, Murray (Aus)	2:01.9
1965	Hutton, Ralph	2:03.2

1966†	Gilchrist, Sandy	2:02.0
1967	Jacks, Ron	2:03.3
1968	Hutton, Ralph	1:58.9
1969	Kasting, Bob	2:00.7
1970	Bello, Juan (Peru)	2:00.5
1971	Terrell, Ray (GB)	1:59.9

1972	MacKenzie, Ian	1:57.70
1973	MacKenzie, Ian	1:58.54
1974	Robertson, Bruce	1:57.19
1975	Pickell, Steve	1:56.66

    * = 200 y.   † = 220 y.

400 m. Free-style

1947*	Rowlinson, P. (USA)	4:32.8
1948*	Gilchrist, Allen	4:44.3
1949*	Gilchrist, Allen	4:42.7
1950		
1951*	McNamee, Gerry	4:26.4
1952*	McNamee, Gerry	4:18.9
1953*	McNamee, Gerry	4:24.8
1954†		
1955†	Stagman, Charles (USA)	4:48.8
1956†	Slater, Bill	4:49.8
1957		
1958†	Slater, Bill	4:46.4
1959†	Rounds, Fred (USA)	4:46.1
1960	Verth, Tom	4:31.5
1961*	Gilchrist, Sandy	4:35.5
1962		
1963	Gilchrist, Sandy	4:26.0
1964†	Rose, Murray (Aus)	4:16.6
1965	Gilchrist, Sandy	4:26.6
1966†	Hutton, Ralph	4:19.0
1967	Hutton, Ralph	4:19.6
1968	Hutton, Ralph	4:15.7
1969	Smith, George	4:17.5
1970	Kasting, Bob	4:19.7
1971	Terrell, Ray (GB)	4:19.0

1972	Hutton, Ralph	4:10.4*
1973	Buckboro, Deane	4:12.55
1974	Madruga, Djan (Braz)	4:07.54
1975	Ker, Michael	4:08.86

    * = 400 y.   † = 440 y.

1,500 m. Free-style

1947	Event not held	
1948*	Gibson, D.	18:52.8
1949*	Portelance, Jim	18:30.8
1950		
1951*	McNamee, Gerry	18:31.9
1952*	McNamee, Gerry	18:03.1
1953*	McNamee, Gerry	18:21.6
1954†		
1955†	Stagman, Charles (USA)	19:42.3
1956†	Slater, Bill	19:24.4
1957†		
1958†		
1959†	Brackett, Dick (USA)	19:24.9

1960	Slater, Bill	18:59.6	1963	Hutton, Ralph	2:21.3
1961†	Gilchrist, Sandy	18:24.7	1964†	Jacks, Ron	2:20.4
1962†	Webb, Ken (USA)	18:13.9	1965	Stratten, Gaye	2:22.5
1963	Gilchrist, Sandy	18:00.6	1966†	Hutton, Ralph	2:16.2
1964†	Rose, Murray (Aus)	17:14.1	1967	Shaw, Jim	2:16.4
1965	Gilchrist, Sandy	17:48.1	1968	Shaw, Jim	2:14.9
1966†	Hutton, Ralph	17:25.5	1969	Hawes, John	2:17.4
1967	Hutton, Ralph	17:14.8	1970	Crichton, George	2:18.5
1968	Hutton, Ralph	16:51.5	1971	Richards, Mike (GB)	2:14.0

1960　Slater, Bill ... 18:59.6
1961† Gilchrist, Sandy ... 18:24.7
1962† Webb, Ken (USA) ... 18:13.9
1963　Gilchrist, Sandy ... 18:00.6
1964† Rose, Murray (Aus) ... 17:14.1
1965　Gilchrist, Sandy ... 17:48.1
1966† Hutton, Ralph ... 17:25.5
1967　Hutton, Ralph ... 17:14.8
1968　Hutton, Ralph ... 16:51.5
1969　Jacks, Ron ... 17:34.8
1970　Roxborough, Steve ... 17:36.0
1971　Terrell, Ray (GB) ... 17:09.5
- -
1972　Buckboro, Deane ... 16:59.92
1973　Ker, Michael ... 16:35.99
1974　Madruga, Djan (Braz) ... 16:17.47
1975　Badger, Steve (Aus) ... 16:14.23
　　　* = 1,500 y.　　† = 1,650 y.

100 m. Back-stroke
1947* Buckboro, Kel ... 1:09.2
1948* Mingie, Peter ... 1:05.0
1949† Salmon, Peter ... 1:03.0
1950
1951† Mingie, Peter ... 1:03.6
1952* Salmon, Peter ... 1:01.7
1953† McNamee, Gerry ... 1:04.5
1954†
1955* Dolbey, Jerry (USA) ... 58.8
1956* Miller, Don ... 1:05.0
1957†
1958† Wheaton, Bob ... 1:07.6
1959† Verth, Tom ... 1:10.4
1960　Wheaton, Bob ... 1:04.3
1961† Blanchette, Yvon ... 1:01.8
1962† Richards, Charles (USA) ... 1:08.3
1963　Stratten, Gaye ... 1:06.9
1964† Stratten, Gaye ... 1:04.6
1965　Shaw, Jim ... 1:04.2
1966† Hutton, Ralph ... 1:03.5
1967　Shaw, Jim ... 1:02.0
1968　Shaw, Jim ... 1:01.6
1969　Shaw, Jim ... 1:03.5
1970　Kennedy, Bill ... 1:02.0
1971　Richards, Mike (GB) ... 1:01.2
- -
1972　Evans, Clay ... 1:00.38
1973　Pickell, Steve ... 59.90
1974　Pickell, Steve ... 57.60
1975　Pickell, Steve ... 58.38
　　　* = 110 y.　　† = 100 y.

200 m. Back-stroke
1947-56　Event not held
1957
1958† Wheaton, Bob ... 2:30.7
1959† Fisher, Robert ... 2:35.5
1960　Wheaton, Bob ... 2:26.6
1961* Blanchette, Yvon ... 2:17.4
1962† Richards, Charles (USA) ... 2:29.5

1963　Hutton, Ralph ... 2:21.3
1964† Jacks, Ron ... 2:20.4
1965　Stratten, Gaye ... 2:22.5
1966† Hutton, Ralph ... 2:16.2
1967　Shaw, Jim ... 2:16.4
1968　Shaw, Jim ... 2:14.9
1969　Hawes, John ... 2:17.4
1970　Crichton, George ... 2:18.5
1971　Richards, Mike (GB) ... 2:14.0
- -
1972　MacKenzie, Ian ... 2:12.09
1973　MacKenzie, Ian ... 2:10.78
1974　Pickell, Steve ... 2:09.81
1975　Scarth, Mike ... 2:08.10
　　　* = 200 y.　　† = 220 y.

100 m. Breast-stroke
1957* Jubb, Eric ... 1:11.3
1948　Event not held
1949* Salmon, Peter ... 1:02.1
1950
1951* Ross, Bill (USA) ... 1:08.2
1952* Salmon, Peter ... 1:03.5
1953* Crane, R. ... 1:07.0
1954
1955-56　Event not held
1957
1958† Rumpel, Norbert (W Ger) ... 1:17.0
1959　Rabinovitch, Steve ... 1:15.8
1960　Rabinovitch, Steve ... 1:13.3
1961† Nelson, Richard (USA) ... 1:03.4
1962† Rabinovitch, Steve ... 1:14.0
1963　Rabinovitch, Steve ... 1:11.2
1964† Kelso, Jack ... 1:12.8
1965　Chase, Marvin ... 1:13.5
1966† Chase, Marvin ... 1:13.6
1967　Mahony, Bill ... 1:10.8
1968　Mahony, Bill ... 1:09.3
1969　Mahony, Bill ... 1:08.7
1970　Fiolo, Jose (Braz) ... 1:10.7
1971　Mahony, Bill ... 1:09.9
- -
1972　Mahony, Bill ... 1:08.53
1973　Hrdlitschka, Peter ... 1:08.36
1974　Smith, Graham ... 1:08.04
1975　Smith, Graham ... 1:06.38
　　　* = 100 y.　　† = 110 y.

200 m. Breast-stroke
1947* Salmon, Peter ... 2:47.8
1948* Salmon, Peter ... 2:35.0
1949* Ross, Bill (USA) ... Bu2:27.9
1950
1951* Ross, Bill (USA) ... Bu2:34.6
1952* Portelance, Leo ... Bu2:23.4
1953　Gair, Bob ... Bu2:36.7
1954
1955* Bell, Peter ... 2:35.8
1956　Bell, Peter ... 2:52.4
1957

1958†	Rumpel, Norbert (W Ger)	2:49.0
1959†	Rabinovitch, Steve	2:53.5
1960	Rabinovitch, Steve	2:44.4
1961*	Nelson, Richard (USA)	2:23.0
1962†	Rabinovitch, Steve	2:43.3
1963	Rabinovitch, Steve	2:43.3
1964†	Chase, Marvin	2:42.0
1965	Chase, Marvin	2:41.3
1966†	Mahony, Bill	2:38.8
1967	Mahony, Bill	2:33.9
1968	Mahony, Bill	2:31.0
1969	Mahony, Bill	2:30.3
1970	Fowler, K.	2:40.9
1971	Wilkie, David (GB)	2:32.6
1972	Mahony, Bill	2:28.76
1973	Zajac, Mel	2:30.11
1974	Smith, Graham	2:29.28
1975	Smith, Graham	2:25.39

* = 200 y.   † = 220 y.

100 m. Butterfly
1956 and before   Event not held
1957

1958†	Corrigan, M. (USA)	1:06.4
1959†	Grout, Cameron	1:06.6
1960	Grout, Cameron	1:01.5
1961*	Pound, Dick	56.9
1962†	Richards, Charles (USA)	1:03.3
1963	Sherry, Dan	59.3
1964†	Sherry, Dan	59.5
1965	Sherry, Dan	59.1
1966†	Jacks, Ron	1:00.1
1967	Arusoo, Tom	59.5
1968	Jacks, Ron	58.4
1969	Jacks, Ron	59.4
1970	MacDonald, Byron	57.4
1971	Tysick, Graham	59.3
1972	Robertson, Bruce	56.65
1973	Robertson, Bruce	56.60
1974	Robertson, Bruce	56.91
1975	Robertson, Bruce	56.68

* = 100 y.   † = 110 y.

200 m. Butterfly
1954

1955*	Stagman, Charles	2:21.7
1956†	Rutherford, Peter	2:51.3
1957		
1958†	Jacobs, Lorne	2:43.6
1959†	Kitchell, Dick (USA)	2:33.5
1960	Grout, Cameron	2:20.2
1961*	Gretzinger, Richard (USA)	2:13.1
1962†	Richards, Charles (USA)	2:26.8
1963	Sherry, Dan	2:17.8
1964†	Sherry, Dan	2:16.4
1965	Sherry, Dan	2:14.9
1966†	Hutton, Ralph	2:15.3
1967	Arusoo, Tom	2:14.3

1968	Arusoo, Tom	2:11.3
1969	Jacks, Ron	2:12.2
1970	MacDonald, Byron	2:14.4
1971	Tysick, Graham	2:10.6
1972	MacDonald, Byron	2:08.97
1973	MacKenzie, Ian	2:10.20
1974	Rogers, Bruce	2:08.34
1975	Rogers, Bruce	2:06.78

* = 200 y.   † = 220 y.

200 m. Individual medley
1954–63   Event not held

1964†	Leovich, Ted (USA)	2:24.7
1965	Gilchrist, Sandy	2:21.1
1966†	Gilchrist, Sandy	2:20.5
1967	Smith, George	2:20.8
1968	Smith, George	2:16.4
1969	Smith, George	2:13.4
1970	Bello, Juan (Peru)	2:16.7
1971	Terrell, Ray (GB)	2:15.0
1972	Evans, Clay	2:13.29
1973	Brumwell, Dave	2:12.70
1974	Adams, Jim	2:11.53
1975	Pickell, Steve	2:12.62

† = 220 y.

400 m. Individual medley
1954

1955*	Brunell, Frank (USA)	4:54.4
1956*	Slater, Bill	5:11.6
1957		
1958†	Slater, Bill	5:35.1
1959†	Grout, Cameron	5:43.5
1960	Grout, Cameron	5:25.6
1961*	Gretzinger, Richard (USA)	4:49.9
1962†	Webb, Ken (USA)	5:08.3
1963	Gilchrist, Sandy	5:08.8
1964†	Gilchrist, Sandy	4:59.2
1965	Hutton, Ralph	5:00.4
1966†	Gilchrist, Sandy	4:58.1
1967	Gilchrist, Sandy	5:01.4
1968	Gilchrist, Sandy	4:51.8
1969	Smith, George	4:48.0
1970	Bello, Juan (Peru)	4:56.3
1971	Terrell, Ray (GB)	4:45.7
1972	Brumwell, Dave	4:49.85
1973	Brumwell, Dave	4:45.60
1974	Fowlie, Jim	4:37.65
1975	Fowlie, Jim	4:41.00

* = 400 y.   † = 440 y.

WOMEN

100 m. Free-style

1947*	King, Vivian	1:06.3
1948*	Strong, Irene	1:03.0
1949*	Kerr, Catherine	1:04.1
1950		

1951* McNamee, Kay	1:04.7
1952* McNamee, Kay	1:03.6
1953* Wittall, Beth	1:04.3
1954†	
1955* Mann, Shelley (USA)	58.9
1956* Grant, Virginia	58.6
1957†	
1958† Ordogh, Susan (Hun)	1:07.5
1959† Rhoads, Deirdre (USA)	1:07.6
1960 Stewart, Mary	1:05.5
1961* Stewart, Mary	57.2
1962† Wood, Carolyn (USA)	1:04.4
1963 Stewart, Mary	1:04.3
1964† Lay, Marion	1:02.6
1965 Lay, Marion	1:02.2
1966† Lay, Marion	1:02.5
1967 Lay, Marion	1:01.1
1968 Coughlan, Angela	1:01.8
1969 Coughlan, Angela	1:01.8
1970 Coughlan, Angela	1:01.4
1971 Coughlan, Angela	1:01.9
-	-
1972 Rondeau, Mary-Beth	1:00.71
1973 Cook, Wendy	1:00.62
1974 Wright, Judy	58.99
1975 Quirk, Jill	59.01
* = 100 y. † = 110 y.	

200 m. Free-style

1947–50 Event not held	
1951* McNamee, Kay	2:32.2
1952* McNamee, Kay	2:18.5
1953 Event not held	
1954	
1955 Event not held	
1956 Event not held	
1957	
1958† Ramey, Nancy (USA)	2:31.6
1959† Rhoads, Deirdre (USA)	2:31.5
1960 Iwasaki, Margaret	2:27.6
1961* Campbell, Katy	2:09.1
1962† Wood, Carolyn (USA)	2:21.7
1963 Stewart, Mary	2:23.9
1964† Lay, Marion	2:19.6
1965 Lay, Marion	2:18.5
1966† Kennedy, Louise	2:17.9
1967 Coughlan, Angela	2:16.6
1968 Coughlan, Angela	2:13.2
1969 Coughlan, Angela	2:13.2
1970 Couhglan, Angela	2:13.4
1971 Coughlan, Angela	2:12.3
-	-
1972 Rondeau, Mary-Beth	2:10.12
1973 Cliff, Lesley	2:09.98
1974 Jardin, Anne	2:06.75
1975 Amundrud, Gail	2:05.59
* = 200 y. † = 220 y.	

400 m. Free-style

1947* King, Vivian	5:29.8
1948* King, Vivian	5:19.4
1949* McNamee, Kay	5:03.4
1950	
1951	
1952 McNamee, Kay	5:13.8
1953 Whittall, Beth	5:07.8
1954	
1955* Gray, Dougie (USA)	5:09.5
1956† Wittall, Beth	5:22.2
1957	
1958† Ramey, Nancy (USA)	5:32.2
1959† Rhoads, Deirdre (USA)	5:21.4
1960 Campbell, Katy	5:13.4
1961* Campbell, Katy	4:37.1
1962† Thompson, Patty	5:09.7
1963 Pomfret, Lynne	5:03.5
1964† Hounsell, Barbara	4:56.2
1965 Kennedy, Louise	4:52.5
1966† Tanner, Elaine	4:46.4
1967† Tanner, Elaine	4:45.6
1968 Coughlan, Angela	4:39.8
1969 Coughlan, Angela	4:37.3
1970 Coughlan, Angela	4:45.1
1971 Coughlan, Angela	4:37.3
-	-
1972 Rondeau, Mary-Beth	4:36.63
1973 McCaffrey, Ann	4:31.90
1974 Oliver, Mich	4:24.25
1975 Quirk, Wendy	4:25.95
* = 400 y. † = 440 y.	

1,500 m. Free-style

1965 Hughes, Jane	19:35.8
1966† Hughes, Jane	19:28.8
† = 1,650 y.	

800 m. Free-style

1967 Warren, Jeanne	10:01.9
1968 Coughlan, Angela	9:52.3
1969 Coughlan, Angela	9:30.8
1970 Coughlan, Angela	9:51.2
1971 Coughlan, Angela	9:25.8
-	-
1972 Cliff, Leslie	9:31.7*
1973 Cliff, Leslie	9:20.58
1974 Oliver, Mich.	9:06.59
1975 Smith, Shannon	9:03.77

100 m. Back-stroke

1947* Geldard, D.	1:17.6
1948* Court, Joyce	1:15.3
1949* Strong, Irene	1:13.3
1950	
1951* Morgan, J.	1:15.1
1952* Fisher, Lenore	1:12.0
1953* Fisher, Lenore	1:09.8
1954	
1955* Fisher, Lenore	1:07.2
1956* Fisher, Lenore	1:10.8
1957	

1958† Barber, Sara 1:15.3
1959† Barber, Sara 1:15.3
1960　Barber, Sara 1:11.2
1961* Stewart, Mary 1:05.6
1962† Barber, Sara 1:13.4
1963　Weir, Eileen 1:13.1
1964† Weir, Eileen 1:11.2
1965　Weir, Eileen 1:11.0
1966† Tanner, Elaine 1:09.8
1967　Tanner, Elaine 1:08.6
1968　Tanner, Elaine 1:06.7
1969　Gurr, Donna-Marie ... 1:10.0
1970　Goshi, Yuikiko (Jap) .. 1:07.7
1971　Gurr, Donna-Marie ... 1:07.5
- -
1972　Gurr, Donna-Marie ... 1:06.40
1973　Cook, Wendy 1:05.84
1974　Cook, Wendy 1:05.42
1975　Garapick, Nancy 1:05.10
　　　* = 100 y.　　† = 110 y.

200 m. Back-stroke
1958† Barber, Sara 2:49.5
1959† Barber, Sara 2:46.2
1960　Barber, Sara 2:42.6
1961* Conklin, Donna 2:31.7
1962† Gabie, Noel (USA) 2:46.9
1963　Weir, Eileen 2:40.1
1964† Weir, Eileen 2:37.7
1965　Tanner, Elaine 2:36.7
1966† Tanner, Elaine 2:34.1
1967　Tanner, Elaine 2:33.3
1968　Tanner, Elaine 2:26.7
1969　Gurr, Donna-Marie ... 2:29.2
1970　Gurr, Donna-Marie ... 2:27.1
1971　Gurr, Donna-Marie ... 2:30.5
- -
1972　Gurr, Donna-Marie ... 2:22.5*
1973　Cook, Wendy 2:23.13
1974　Cook, Wendy 2:18.69
1975　Garapick, Nancy 2:18.74
　　　* = 200 y.　　† = 220 y.

100 m. Breast-stroke
1949* Strong, Irene Bu1:13.4
1950
1951* Stewart, N. Bu1:17.6
1952* Strong, Irene Bu1:14.0
1953* Stewart, Helen 1:24.2
1954†
1955　Event not held
1956* Stewart, Helen 1:21.9
1957
1958† Ordogh, Susan (Hun) .. 1:25.2
1959† Benson, Bonnie 1:26.7
1960　McHale, Judy 1:24.0
1961* Benson, Bonnie 1:15.0
1962† Glendenning, Alison ... 1:22.3
1963　Glendenning, Alison ... 1:22.6
1964† Colella, Lynn (USA) ... 1:23.7

1965　Wilmink, Marjon 1:23.6
1966† Ross, Donna 1:23.1
1967　Lay, Marion 1:22.6
1968　Dockerill, Sylvia 1:20.5
1969　Wright, Jane 1:19.1
1970　Wright, Jane 1:20.0
1971　Harrison, Dorothy (GB) 1:18.4
- -
1972　Stuart, Marian 1:18.12
1973　Stuart, Marian 1:16.18
1974　Stuart, Marian 1:16.98
1975　Baker, Joann 1:14.70
　　　* = 100 y.　　† = 110 y.

200 m. Breast-stroke
1947* Strong, Irene 2:55.7
1948* Strong, Irene 2:51.0
1949* Strong, Irene 2:48.1
1950
1951* Stewart, N. 2:58.4
1952* Strong, Irene 2:44.3
1953* Peebles, Margaret 3:09.8
1954
1955* Sears, Mary Jane (USA) 2:39.8
1956† Peebles, Margaret 3:21.5
1957
1958† Ordogh, Susan (Hun) .. 3:01.6
1959† Schmidlin, Suzette 3:06.0
1960　McHale, Judy 3:01.6
1961* Wilson, Pam 2:43.7
1962† Glendenning, Alison ... 2:57.2
1963　Wilmink, Marjon 2:56.6
1964† Wilmink, Marjon 2:59.0
1963　Wilmink, Marjon 2:57.6
1966† Ross, Donna 3:01.1
1967　Pumfrey, Mary Pat 2:59.4
1968　Smith, Susan 2:57.5
1969　Dockerill, Sylvia 2:54.4
1970　Nishigawa, Yoshima (Jap) 2:48.6
1971　Harrison, Dorothy (GB) 2:50.7
- -
1972　Stuart, Marian 2:46.7*
1973　Stuart, Marian 2:46.88
1974　Stuart, Marian 2:43.65
1976　Baker, Joann 2:41.78
　　　* = 200 y.　　† = 220 y.

100 m. Butterfly
1954
1955* Sears, Mary Jane (USA) 1:05.6
1956* Wittall, Beth 1:10.0
1957
1958† Ramey, Nancy (USA) .. 1:13.4
1959† Doerr, Susan (USA) 1:17.8
1960　Stewart, Mary 1:13.0
1961* Stewart, Mary 1:02.0
1962† Wood, Carolyn (USA) . 1:09.9
1963　Stewart, Mary 1:08.1
1964† Stewart, Mary 1:08.8
1965　Tanner, Elaine 1:09.6

1966†	Tanner, Elaine	1:06.2
1967	Tanner, Elaine	1:05.9
1968	Tanner, Elaine	1:06.7
1969	Smith, Susan	1:07.5
1970	Aoki, Mayumi (Jap)	1:07.5
1971	Cliff, Leslie	1:08.1
1972	Cliff, Leslie	1:05.95
1973	Pape, Joanne de	1:07.39
1974	Quirk, Wendy	1:04.69
1975	Quirk, Wendy	1:04.41

* = 100 y.   † = 110 y.

200 m. Butterfly

1965	Humeniuk, Marianne	2:40.2
1966†	Tanner, Elaine	2:33.1
1967	Corson, Marilyn	2:31.9
1968	Warren, Jeanne	2:31.6
1969	Warren, Jeanne	2:30.2
1970	Asano, Noriko (Jap)	2:28.4
1971	Cliff, Leslie	2:28.6
1972	McHugh, Jennifer	2:26.9*
1973	McHugh, Jennifer	2:24.83
1974	Nadalutti, Flavia (Braz)	2:20.10
1975	Gibson, Cheryl	2:17.58

† = 220 y.

200 m. Individual medley

1954		
1955*	Mann, Shelley (USA)	2:26.4
1956*	Stewart, Helen	2:41.2
1957		
1958-63	Event not held	
1964†	Hounsell, Barbara	2:40.9
1965	Hounsell, Barabra	2:38.5
1966†	Dowler, Sandra	2:41.1
1967	Dowler, Sandra	2:36.7
1968	Tanner, Elaine	2:31.8
1969	Smith, Susan	2:31.7
1970	Nishigawa, Yoshima (Jap)	2:25.8
1971	Cliff, Leslie	2:31.9
1972	Cliff, Leslie	2:25.77
1973	Cliff, Leslie	2:25.90
1974	Smith, Becky	2:23.63
1975	Smith, Becky	2:24.30

* = 200 y.   † = 220 y.

400 m. Indivudual medley

1958†	Barber, Sara	6:14.1
1959†	Rhoads, Deirdre (USA)	6:03.5
1960	Barber, Sara	5:53.7
1961*	Campbell, Katy	5:19.1
1962†	Stewart, Mary	5:59.9
1963	Pomfret, Lynne	5:46.9
1964†	Hounsell, Barbara	5:33.0
1965	Hounsell, Barbara	5:37.9
1966†	Tanner, Elaine	5:27.2
1967	Tanner, Elaine	5:29.2

1968	Corson, Marilyn	5:30.8
1969	Warren, Jeanne	5:24.9
1970	Nishigawa, Yoshima (Jap)	5:11.8
1971	Cliff, Leslie	5:25.3
1972	Cliff, Leslie	5:11.53
1973	Cliff, Leslie	5:08.17
1974	Smith, Becky	5:02.39
1975	Gibson, Cheryl	4:58.93

* = 400 y.   † = 440 y.

CAPILLA, Joaquín (Mexico, 1928-). Mexico's only Olympic Diving Champion, Capilla earned his gold the hard way by working up from lesser honours. He was third in the highboard at the London Games of 1948. In Helsinki he was second. Finally, in Melbourne, Capilla achieved his golden ambition, by almost the narrowest possible margin, beating Gary Tobian (USA) by three-hundredths of a point. The American, incidentally, also lost the 1960 highboard title by a fraction—0.31 of a point to his team mate Robert Webster. Joaquin, largely trained in the United States, additionally took third place in the springboard in 1956 while his brother Alberto competed for Mexico in the 1952 and '56 Games but won no medals.

CARON, Christine (France, 10 July 1948-). Parisienne 'Kiki' Caron, the darling of French swimming, was one of a long line of world-class back-strokers from France. She broke the European 100 m. record six successive times between 1963-64, of which her 1:08.6 on 14 June 1964 also was a world mark. From 1963-66 she also set five European marks for 200 m. and it was not until April 1970 that her fastest time of 2:27.9 was beaten. At the 1964 Tokyo Olympics, Kiki won the silver medal for the 100 m. (67.9, her best). She swam too at the 1968 Games but failed to reach either back-stroke final. She was champion of Europe in 1966 (100 m. in 68.1).

CHANNEL SWIMMING. Since 25 August, 1875 when Captain Webb made the historic first swimming crossing of the English Channel, from Dover to Calais, this battle of brawn and brain against tides and temperature, has remained the high point in the life of any long distance swimmer (see WEBB, Matthew).

It took thirty-six years, until 1911 for Webb's feat to be emulated, by Yorkshire's Tom Burgess, who was successful at his eleventh attempt. And the proportion of successes to failures is less than 7 per cent. More than 2,000 men and women from forty-plus countries have attempted the Channel marathon, either from France to England—the easier way—or England to France. Of those, only about 150 have shared around 250 successful attempts. These figures are not completely correct, despite the formation in 1927, of the Channel Swimming Association to control and authenticate claims. Some crossings were not made under the supervision of official C.S.A. observers and certain records were lost during the London blitz of World War II, including details of some of the twenty-five successes up to that time.

The first woman to cross was America's Gertrude Ederle, an Olympic swimming medallist, who went from France to England in 14 hr. 39 min. in 1926. Then came the two-way swims. The first man was Britain's Olympic water-polo player Ted Temme who followed his France to England success in 1927 with an England to France safe landing in 1934. America's Florence Chadwick showed that a woman could do it too by crossing from France in 1950 and from England in 1951.

Not for thirty years was Temme's double achievement recognized by the C.S.A. who, in 1964, after irefutable evidence, ratified his performance of 1934. In Miss Chadwick's case, her first swim was not officially observed and does not appear in the C.S.A. lists.

The next stage was the two-way crossing. Antonio Abertondo of Argentine, who once swam 262 miles down the Mississippi, achieved this in 1961—swimming from England to France in 18 hr.

England to France			Hr., min.	Year
First man	Matthew Webb (GB)		21:45	1875
First woman	Florence Chadwick(USA)		16:19	1951
Fastest man	Richard Hart (USA)		9:44	1972
Fastest woman	Lynne Cox (USA)		9:36	1973
Slowest man	Henry Sullivan (USA)		26:50	1923
Slowest woman	Rosemary George (GB)		21:35	1961
France to England				
First man	Enrico Tiraboschi (Ita)		16:33	1923
First woman	Gertrude Ederle (USA)		14:39	1926
Fastest man	Barry Watson (GB)		9:35	1934
Fastest woman	C. Nicholas (Can)		9:45	1975
Slowest man	Philip Mickman (GB)		23:48	1949
Slowest woman	Denize le Pennee (GB)		20:50	1966
Both ways				
First man	Ted Temme (GB)	Fr-Eng		1927
		Eng-Fr		1934
First woman	Florence Chadwick (USA)	Fr-Eng		1950
		Eng-Fr		1951
Two-way crossings				
First man	Antonio Abertondo (Arg)		43:10	1961
Fastest man	Jon Erikson (USA)		29:58	1975
First Briton	Kevin Murphy		35:10	1970
Youngest conquerors				
Boy	Jon Erickson (USA	14	Fr-Eng 11:23	1969
Girl	Abla Khairi (Egypt)	13	Eng-Fr 12:30	1974
Miscellaneous achievements				
First mother	Millie Corson (USA)		Fr-Eng 15:28	1926
First 14 yr-old	Leonore Modell (USA)		Fr-Eng 15:27	1964
Most crossings	Desmond Renford (AUS) Eight (1970, 72, 74, 75 – twice in each)			

50 min., taking a ten-minute rest on French soil and then returning to England in 24 hr. 10 min. for an aggregate time of 43 hr. 10 min.

The first Briton to make the two-way crossing was Kevin Murphy, a 21 year-old reporter on a Hemel Hempstead newspaper, who on 5/6 August 1970 made the double trip in 35 hr. 10 min. He left from Shakespeare Beach on the Kent coast and reached land west of Calais after 15 hr. 35 min. After a 10-min. rest and a cup of coffee, he swam back, to land near Folkestone after 19 hr. 25 min. His first thought after walking ashore was to telephone a story of his swim to his newspaper.

In 1975, the centenary of Webb's historic crossing, Murphy failed by only six miles to complete the first triple swim. He spent 52 hours in the water and had the satisfaction of becoming the first to make the double crossing twice.

The distance as the crow flies is not what makes a crossing so difficult. The shortest distance—Dover to Cap Gris Nez—is only 20½ land (17¾ nautical) miles and racing swimmers will cover half of this, at speed, in training daily. It is the tides and currents that can double the distance actually swum, and bad weather, battering waves, stinging jelly fish, sea-sickness, wind, fog and the cold are additional hazards.

The crucial factor is timing. There are two complete tidal streams or four ebb and flow tides of six hours in a day. So the aim is to start on an out-going tide and land on the opposite shore on an in-going one. Swimming too slowly—or too fast—can catch a swimmer on the wrong tide and throw him miles off course and lose the right homeward tide.

An example of expert timing is Commander Gerald Forsberg, a former officer in the Royal Navy, and an endurance swimmer of no mean ability though he would never claim to be a speed merchant. Forsberg made a crossing of the Channel, one of the most difficult straits of sea-water in the world, almost as a lesson in navigation rather than a deed of daring in the Matthew Webb style.

Forsberg's theories about the twice daily tides, winds, and other factors were put into practice on August 22, 1957 when he set a record of 13 hr. 33 m. for the England to France crossing, 22 min. faster than any other swimmer up to that time. A key factor in his success, on a day when the conditions were far from ideal, was his choice of course and his escort boat was navigated by an oarsman who had a huge compass rigged between his feet.

Channel challengers since have benefitted from the experience and scientific expertise of Forsberg, as the sub-10 hour times demonstrate.

The cost of an attempt can be high. There is up to £200 for the accompanying boat and pilot plus extras for food, lanolin—and swimmers must be well greased to keep out the cold—the C.S.A. official observer's fee etc. And as much again can be spent on living at the coast, maybe for weeks, waiting for favourable sea and weather conditions. These days many swims are sponsored and many aspirants professional.

Great swimming prowess is not the main attribute for the Channel swimmer. Tenacity and grit are far more important. In 1964 American John Starrett, a spastic, and Canadian Robert Cossette, a polio victim, swam from France in 12 hr. 45 min. and 12 hr. 5 min. respectively.

There have been sponsored races—by the *Daily Mail* and later by Butlin Holiday camps. There are relay races with teams of six who must each stay at least one hour at a time in the water. And there is the continuing personal pride of anyone, fast or slow, who can simply say: 'I have swum the Channel.'

CHARLTON, 'Boy' (Australia, 12 Aug. 1907-10 Dec. 1975). The first great Australian of the 1920s, Andrew 'Boy' Charlton won five Olympic middle- and long-distance medals and set five world records between 1923 and 1928. He came from a poor part of Sydney and his talent was recognized by Tom Adrian, himself a noted swimmer, who adopted 'Boy', clothed and fed him and coached him to world fame.

A child prodigy, Charlton won his first race at five and broke his first world record, for 880 y. at 15. By the time of the Paris Olympics of 1924, he was a sturdy 12½ stone and totally dedicated to his sport. But there was near-disaster on the way by boat to Europe. His step-father had a nervous breakdown and threw himself from the liner into the sea. Fortunately Adrian was rescued though he was never a really fit man again.

Nevertheless, in Paris Charlton won the 1,500 m. (20:06.6), was in the Australian 4 x 200 m. silver medal team and took third place in the 400 m. (5:06.6), behind Johnny Weissmuller (USA) and Arne Borg (Swe). In Amsterdam, four years later he was second in the 400 and 1,500 m.

Charlton's three world 880 y. records included a 10:32.0 on 8 January 1927. He also set a mark for 1,000 m. in 13:19.6 on the way to a 20:06.6 world record in winning his 1924 Olympic gold—an improvement of 1:04.8 on the previous figures of Borg. Except when sprinting, Charlton's style had all the external appearance of a classic trudgeon of a decade earlier while incorporating the fundamentals of the crawl of the future.

CLARK, Steve (United States, 17 June 1943-). One of the fastest movers in the water, Steve Clark's special talent was short course racing. He was the first man to swim 50 y. in 21.0, 100 y. in 46.0, 100 m. in 53.0, 200 y. in 1:50.0 and 200 m. in 2:00.0 in a 25 y. pool. Split-second turns—he was there and then he wasn't—were the recipe for Clark's successes.

United States representative at the 1960 and 1964 Olympics, Clark from Oakland, California, who competed for Yale University and the Santa Clara club, never swam in an Olympic individual event though he won the Pan American 100 m. title in 1963.

But in the 1964 Tokyo Games he won three relay golds in world record-breaking American squads. On the first leg of the 4 x 100 m. free-style he clocked 52.9 to equal the world record. On the anchor leg of the medley relay—a berth he won from Don Schollander, later to become the 100 m. champion—he was given a split of 52.4. He was also lead-off swimmer in the 4 x 200 m. relay. Clark's only official world record was 54.4 for 100 m. in 1961.

CLIFF, Leslie (Canada, 11 March, 1955-). Canada's greatest all-round swimmer, Leslie Cliff's major medal successes came from medley events. She won the 200 and 400 m. IM at the 1971 Pan American Games in Cali, Colombia where she also took a gold in Canada's medley relay squad (swimming the butterfly leg). She

repeated her individual gold medal feat at the 1974 Commonwealth Games in Christchurch, New Zealand. In between, she took second place in the 400 m. behind Australia's Gail Neall, at the 1972 Olympic Games in Munich.

If Leslie had not settled for medley, this slim Vancouver girl with the blonde, boyish-cropped hair, could have done well on any single stroke, particularly free-style and butterfly.

COLELLA (United States) **Lynn,** (13 June, 1950-). and **Rick** (14 Dec 1951-). A world-class brother and sister pair are unusual enough in any sport, but the Colellas, from Seattle, State of Washington, are unique for their dedication and long service to swimming.

Lynn, the elder, started racing at 10. She won two golds at the 1971 Pan American Games (200 m. breast-stroke and butterfly) and a bronze (100 m. breast-stroke). At the 1972 Munich Olympics she was second in the 200 m. butterfly and the following year, at the World championships in Belgrade, she was third in the 200 m. breast-stroke and butterfly.

Rick emulated his sister at the 1971 Pan-Americans by winning the 200 m. breast-stroke and also won a bronze in the 400 m. medley. He missed a breast-stroke medal by placing fourth over 200 m. in Munich but picked up a bronze in the 400 m. medley in Belgrade.

His best year was 1975. He placed second behind Britain's David Wilkie, (see WILKIE, David), in the 200 m. breast-stroke at the Cali world championships and took a gold in the medley relay. Then it was on to the Mexico City Pan Americans where Rick retained his 200 m. title, won the 100 m. breast-stroke, took second place in the 400 m. medley and earned two more golds with the 4 x 100 m. free-style and medley squads.

Their all-round abilities in the pool, which made them high-point scorers at U.S. championships, earned both Colellas valuable university scholarships, presented by the Philips Petroleum Company. Rick's two, each worth $1,000, enabled him to graduate in aeronautics and go on to the Washington School of Business Administration. Lynn, who had one $1,000 award, won a degree in electrical engineering and then continued post-graduate studies at the University of Washington.

COLEMAN, Georgia (United States, 23 Jan. 1912-40). The first woman to do a 2½ forward somersault in competition, Georgia Coleman, according to her coach Fred Cady, was: 'a girl who could dive like a man'. After only six months in competitive diving, she won the silver for highboard and the bronze for spring-board at the 1928 Olympics. Four years later, at the Los Angeles Games, she won the springboard and was second again in the highboard. Between 1929-32, Georgia from St. Maries, Idaho, was beaten only once—and that from the 1 m. board—in United States championships. Always smiling, she was only 28 when she died.

COMMONWEALTH GAMES. The idea of holding a four-yearly English Speaking Festival, including sport, was first mooted by the Rev. Ashley Cooper in *The Times* (London) in October 1891. But the concept did not come into being until 1911 when 'Inter-Empire Champ-ionships', mainly at the Crystal Palace, London, were organized as part of the Festival of Empire to mark the Corona-tion of King George V. Teams from Australasia, Canada, South Africa and the United Kingdom took part.

The first practical steps to organize a British Empire Games were taken during the Olympics of 1928 when Mr. M. M. (Bobby) Robinson of Canada called a meeting of Empire representatives in Amsterdam. He was able, through the efforts of Mr. J. H. Crocker, to promise full support, financial and otherwise, from the Hamilton Civic Authorities to hold a Games in Canada in 1930.

The Hamilton Games—based on the ideal that 'they shall be merrier and less stern, and will substitute the stimulus of novel adventure for the pressure of international rivalry'—are regarded as the true starting point of the present series of Games.

As a result of the changing nature of the British Empire and the development of the Commonwealth, the title of this multi-sports occasion has changed a num-ber of times. But the ideals of the first Games in Hamilton remain.

COMMONWEALTH GAMES

No.	Title	Venue	Dates
I	British Empire Games	Hamilton, Canada	16–23 Aug., 1930
II	British Empire Games	London, England	4–11 Aug., 1934
III	British Empire Games	Sydney, Australia	5–12 Feb., 1938
IV	British Empire Games	Auckland, New Zealand	4–11 Feb., 1950
V	British Empire and Commonwealth Games	Vancouver, Canada	30 July-7 Aug., 1954
VI	British Empire and Commonwealth Games	Cardiff, Wales	18–26 July, 1958
VII	British Empire and Commonwealth Games	Perth, Australia	22 Nov.-1 Dec., 1962
VIII	British Empire and Commonwealth Games	Kingston, Jamaica	4–13 Aug., 1966
IX	British Commonwealth Games	Edinburgh, Scotland	16–25 July, 1970
X	British Commonwealth Games	Christchurch, New Zealand	24 Jan.-2 Feb. 1974
XI	Commonwealth Games	Edmonton, Canada	3–12 Aug., 1978

COMMONWEALTH GAMES CHAMPIONS. Because of the different titles under which the Games of the Empire and Commonwealth have been staged (see COMMONWEALTH GAMES), throughout this book the words 'Com-monwealth Games' or 'Commonwealth champion' etc., will refer to the British Empire Games, British Empire and Com-monwealth Games, British Common-wealth Games and Commonwealth Games and the champions and medal winners of these Games.

MEN

100 m. Free-style

1930*	Bourne, Munro (Can)	56.0
1934*	Burleigh, George (Can)	55.0
1938+	Pirie, Robert (Can)	59.6

1950+	Salmon, Peter (Can)	1:00.4
	O'Neill, Frank (Aus)	1:00.6
	Kendall, Pat (Eng)	1:01.8

1954+	Henricks, Jon (Aus)	56.6
	Weld, Cyrus (Aus)	58.5
	Aubrey, Rex (Aus)	58.7

1958+	Devitt, John (Aus)	56.6
	Chapman, Gary (Aus)	56.6
	Shipton, Geoff (Aus)	57.0

1962+	Pound, Dick (Can)	55.8
	McGregor, Bobby (Scot)	56.1
	Dickson, David (Aus)	56.1

1966+	Wenden, Mike (Aus)	54.0
	McGregor, Bobby (Scot)	54.2
	Dickson, David (Aus)	54.6

1970	Wenden, Mike (Aus)	53.06
	Rogers, Greg (Aus)	54.26
	Devenish, Bill (Aus)	54.28

1974	Wenden, Mike (Aus)	52.73
	Robertson, Bruce (Can)	53.78
	Phillips, Brian (Can)	54.11
	* = 100 y. + = 110 y.	

200 m. Free-style

1970	Wenden, Mike (Aus)	1:56.69
	Hutton, Ralph (Can)	1:58.45
	Rogers, Greg (Aus)	1:58.63

1974	Badger, Steve (Aus)	1:56.72
	Robertson, Bruce (Can)	1:57.21
	Wenden, Mike (Aus)	1:57.83

400 m. Free-style

1930*	Ryan, Noel (Aus)	4:39.8
1934+	Ryan, Noel (Aus)	5:03.0
1938+	Pirie, Robert (Can)	4:54.6

1950+	Agnew, David (Aus)	4:49.4
	Johnston, Graham (SAf)	4:51.3
	Lucas, Fred (NZ)	5:02.5

1954+	Chapman, Gary (Aus)	4:39.8
	Wardrop, Jack (Scot)	4:41.5
	Johnston, Graham (SAf)	4:43.3

1958+	Konrads, John (Aus)	4:25.9
	Black, Ian (Scot)	4:28.5
	Winram, Gary (Aus)	4:32.4

1962+	Rose, Murray (Aus)	4:20.0
	Wood, Alan (Aus)	4:22.5
	Windle, Robert (Aus)	4:23.1

| 1966+ | Windle, Robert (Aus) | 4:15.0 |

| | Bennett, John (Aus) | 4:15.8 |
| | Hutton, Ralph (Can) | 4:16.1 |

1970	White, Graham (Aus)	4:08.48
	Hutton, Ralph (Can)	4:08.77
	Brough, Greg (Aus)	4:12.16

1974	Kulasalu, John (Aus)	4:01.44
	Cooper, Brad (Aus)	4:02.12
	Badger, Steve (Aus)	4:04.07
	* = 400 y. + = 440 y.	

1,500 m. Free-style

1930*	Ryan, Noel (Aus)	18:55.4
1934*	Ryan, Noel (Aus)	18:25.4
1938+	Leivers, Bobby (Eng)	19:46.4

1950+	Johnston, Graham (SAf)	19:55.7
	Portelance, James (Can)	20:08.3
	Lucas, Fred (NZ)	20:10.1

1954+	Johnston, Graham (SAf)	19:01.4
	Duncan, Peter (SAf)	19:22.1
	Chapman, Gary (Aus)	19:28.4

1958+	Konrads, John (Aus)	17:45.4
	Winram, Gary (Aus)	18:17.2
	McLachlan, Murray (SAf)	18:19.2

1962+	Rose, Murray (Aus)	17:18.1
	Windle, Robert (Aus)	17:44.5
	Wood, Alan (Aus)	17:55.6

1966+	Jackson, Ron (Aus)	17:25.9
	Gilchrist, Sandy (Can)	17:33.9
	Hutton, Ralph (Can)	17:38.9

1970	Windeatt, Graham (Aus)	16:23.82
	Tavasci, Max (Aus)	16:34.46
	Treffers, Mark (NZ)	16:44.69

1974	Holland, Steve (Aus)	15:34.73
	Treffers, Mark (NZ)	15:59.82
	Badger, Steve (Aus)	16:22.23
	* = 1,500 y. + = 1,650 y.	

100 m. Back-stroke

1930*	Trippett, John (Eng)	1:05.4
1934*	Francis, Willie (Scot)	1:05.2
1938+	Oliver, Percy (Aus)	1:07.9

1950+	Wiid, Jackie (SAf)	1:07.7
	Brockway, John (Wales)	1:08.0
	Kinnear, Bert (Scot)	1:10.8

1954+	Brockway, John (Wales)	1:06.5
	Hurring, Lincoln (NZ)	1:06.9
	Weld, Cyrus (Aus)	1:08.6

1958+	Monckton, John (Aus)	1:01.7
	Hayres, John (Aus)	1:03.5
	Wheaton, Bob (Can)	1:06.5

1962+	Sykes, Graham (Eng)	1:04.5
	Carroll, Julian (Aus)	1:05.4
	Vincent, Wayne (Aus)	1:06.2

1966+ Reynolds, Peter (Aus)	1:02.4	
Hutton, Ralph (Can)	1:02.7	
Jackson, Neil (Eng)	1:03.3	

1970	Kennedy, Bill (Can)	1:01.65
	Richards, Mike (Wales)	1:01.69
	Fish, Erik (Can)	1:02.02

1974	Tonelli, Mark (Aus)	59.65
	Pickell, Steve (Can)	59.88
	Cooper, Brad (Aus)	1:00.17

* = 100 y.   + = 110 y.

200 m. Back-stroke

1962* Carroll, Julian (Aus)	2:20.9	
Fingleton, Tony (Aus)	2:21.0	
Robertson, Alan (NZ)	2:23.0	

1966* Reynolds, Peter (Aus)	2:12.0	
Hutton, Ralph (Can)	2:13.5	
Byrom, Karl (Aus)	2:18.8	

1970	Richards, Mike (Wales)	2:14.53
	Terrell, Ray (Eng)	2:15.48
	Rogers, Neil (Aus)	2:15.63

1974	Cooper, Brad (Aus)	2:06.31
	Tonelli, Mark (Aus)	2:09.47
	Williams, Robert (Aus)	2:09.83

* = 220 y.

100 m. Breast-stroke

1962* O'Brien, Ian (Aus)	1:11.4	
Burton, William (Aus)	1:13.9	
Rabinovitch, Steve (Can)	1:14.1	

1966* O'Brien, Ian (Aus)	1:08.2	
Graham, Tony (NZ)	1:12.9	
Tucker, Mike (Eng)	1:13.9	

1970	Mahony, Bill (Can)	1:09.0*
	Cross, Peter (Can)	1:09.4*
	Jarvie, Paul (Aus)	1:10.0*

1974	Leigh, David (Eng)	1:06.52
	Wilkie, David (Scot)	1:07.37
	Naisby, Paul (Eng)	1:08.52

* = 110 y.

200 m. Breast-stroke

1930* Aubin, Jack (Can)	2:38.4	
1934* Hamilton, Norman (Scot)	2:41.4	
1938+ Davies, John (Eng)	Bu2:51.9	

1950+ Hawkins, David (Aus)	Bu2:54.1	
Romain, Roy (Eng)	Bu2:54.2	
Sharpe, Ron (Aus)	2:56.0	

1954+ Doms, John (NZ)	2:52.6	
Jervis, Peter (Eng)	2:52.6	
Hime, Alan (Eng)	Uw2:52.8	

1958+ Gathercole, Terry (Aus)	2:41.6	
Rocchi, Peter (SAf)	2:44.9	
Walkden, Chris (Eng)	2:47.3	

1962+ O'Brien, Ian (Aus)	2:38.2	
Burton, William (Aus)	2:42.1	
Nicholson, Neil (Eng)	2:42.6	

1966+ O'Brien, Ian (Aus)	2:29.3	
Graham, Tony (NZ)	2:36.9	
Mahony, Bill (Can)	2:38.9	

1970	Mahony, Bill (Can)	2:30.29
	Jarvie, Paul (Aus)	2:30.70
	Wilkie, David (Scot)	2:32.87

1974	Wilkie, David (Scot)	2:24.42
	Leigh, David (Eng)	2:24.75
	Naisby, Paul (Eng)	2:27.36

* = 200 y.   + = 220 y.

100 m. Butterfly

1962* Berry, Kevin (Aus)	59.5	
Hayes, Neville (Aus)	1:02.3	
Meinhardt, Aldwin (Can)	1:02.6	

1966* Jacks, Ron (Can)	1:00.3	
Dunn, Graham (Aus)	1:00.9	
Bewley, Keith (Eng)	1:01.5	

1970	MacDonald, Byron (Can)	58.44
	Arusoo, Tom (Can)	58.98
	Jacks, Ron (Can)	59.01

1974	Rogers, Neil (Aus)	56.58
	MacDonald, Byron (Can)	56.83
	Robertson, Bruce (Can)	56.84

* = 110 y.

200 m. Butterfly

1958* Black, Ian (Scot)	2:22.6	
Symonds, Graham (Eng)	2:25.5	
Wilkinson, Brian (Aus)	2:31.0	

1962* Berry, Kevin (Aus)	2:10.8	
Hayes, Neville (Aus)	2:16.3	
Hill, Brett (Aus)	2:18.7	

1966* Gerrard, David (NZ)	2:12.7	
Hill, Brett (Aus)	2:12.8	
Arusoo, Tom (Can)	2:14.2	

1970	Arusoo, Tom (Can)	2:08.97
	Woodroffe, Martyn (Wales)	2:09.14
	Findlay, James (Aus)	2:09.41

1974	Brinkley, Brian (Eng)	2:04.51
	Seymour, Ross (Aus)	2:06.64
	Coutts, John (NZ)	2:07.03

* = 220 y.

200 m. Individual medley

1970	Smith, George (Can)	2:13.72
	Campbell, Ken (Can)	2:16.57
	Woodroffe, Martyn (Wales)	2:16.64

1974	Wilkie, David (Scot)	2:10.11
	Brinkley, Brian (Eng)	2:12.73
	Terrell, Ray (Eng)	2:13.69

400 m. Individual medley

1962*	Alexander, Alex (Aus)	5:15.3
	Oravainen, John (Aus)	5:16.3
	Kelso, Jack (Can)	5:16.5
1966*	Reynolds, Peter (Aus)	4:50.8
	Hutton, Ralph (Can)	4:51.8
	Gilchrist, Sandy (Can)	4:58.7
1970	Smith, George (Can)	4:48.87
	Terrell, Ray (Eng)	4:49.85
	Findlay, James (Aus)	4:51.92
1974	Treffers, Mark (NZ)	4:35.90
	Brinkley, Brian (Eng)	4:41.29
	Terrell, Ray (Eng)	4:42.94

* = 440 y.

4 x 100 m. Free-style

1962* Australia 3:43.9
(Phelps, Peter; Rose, Murray; Doak, Peter; Dickson, David)
Canada 3:48.3
(Meinhardt, Aldwin; Kelso, Jack, Gilchrist, Sandy; Pound, Dick)
England 3:51.3
(Clarke, Stan; Martin-Dye, John; Clayden, Rodney; Kendrew, Peter)

1966* Australia 3:35.6
(Wenden, Mike; Ryan, John; Dickson, David; Windle, Robert)
Canada 3:42.3
(Kasting, Bob; Hutton, Ralph; Jacks, Ron. Gilchrist, Sandy)
England 3:43.7
(Lord, Bobby; Martin-Dye, John; Jarvis, Tony; Turner, Mike)

1970 Australia 3:36.02
(Rogers, Greg; Devenish, Bill; White, Graham; Wenden, Mike)
Canada 3:37.65
(Hutton, Ralph; Smith, George; Jacks, Ron, Kasting, Bob)
England 3:41.24
(Myall, Ivan; Windeatt, Malcolm, Jarvis, Tony; Terrell, Ray)

1974 Canada 3:33.79
(Robertson, Bruce; MacKenzie, Ian; MacDonald, Gary; Phillips, Brian)
Australia 3:34.26
(Patterson, Ross; Coughlan, Peter; Rogers, Neil; Wenden, Mike)
England 3:38.22
(Cunningham, Colin; Walton, Keith; Terrell, Ray; Brinkley, Brian)

* = 4 x 110 y.

4 x 200 m. Free-style

1930* Canada 8:42.4

1934* Canada 8:40.6
(Larson, George; Hooper, Robert; Pirie, Robert; Burleigh, George)
1938+ England 9:19.0
(Dove, Freddie; Ffrench-Williams, Micky; Leivers, Bobby; Wainwright, Norman)

1950+ New Zealand 9:27.7
(Amos, Michael; Barry, Lyall; Chambers, Noel; Lucas, Fred)
Australia 9:34.5
(O'Neill, Frank; Agnew, David; Beard, John; Kelleway, Brian)
England 9:36.8
(Legg, Ray; Bland, Donald; Kendall, Pat; Hale, Jack)

1954+ Australia 8:47.6
(Chapman, Gary; Aubrey, Rex; Hawkins, David; Henricks, Jon)
Canada 8:56.0
(McNamee, Gerald; Simpson, Edward; Gilchrist, Allen; Park, George)
South Africa 8:56.3
(Ford, Dennis; Stueart, William; Duncan, Peter; Johnston, Graham)

1958+ Australia 8:33.4
(Konrads, John; Wilkinson, Brian; Devitt, John; Chapman, Gary)
Scotland 8:54.2
(Leiper, Jimmy; Still, Athol; Sreenan, Robert; Black, Ian)
Canada 9:01.8
(Grout, Cameron; Bell, Peter; Slater, William; Williams, Ken)

1962+ Australia 8:13.5
(Rose, Murray; Wood, Alan; Strahan, Tony; Windle, Robert)
Canada 8:42.4
(Kelso, Jack; Meinhardt, Aldwin; Pound, Dick; Gilchrist, Sandy)
England 8:46.3
(Kendrew, Peter; Campion, Richard; Clarke, Stan; Martin-Dye, John)

1966+ Australia 7:59.5
(Wenden, Mike; Reynolds, Peter; Dickson, David; Windle, Robert)
Canada 8:15.0
(Kasting, Bob; Jacks, Ron; Hutton, Ralph; Gilchrist, Sandy)
England 8:24.0
(Turner, Mike; Bewley, Keith; Thurley, John; Jarvis, Tony)

1970 Australia 7:50.77
(Rogers, Greg; Devenish, Bill; White, Graham; Wenden, Mike)
Canada 8:00.69

(Jacks, Ron; Kasting, Bob; Smith,
George; Hutton, Ralph)
   England   8:10.60
(Terrell, Ray; Mills, John; Myall, Ivan,
Jarvis, Tony)
1974 Australia   7:50.13
(Kulasalu, John; Nay, Robert;
Badger, Steve; Wenden, Mike)
   England   7:52.90
(Cunningham, Colin; Dexter, Neil;
Terrell, Ray; Brinkley, Brian)
   Canada   7:53.38
(MacKenzie, Ian; MacDonald, Gary;
Fowlie, Jim; Robertson, Bruce)
* = 4 x 200 y.   + = 4 x 220 y.

4 x 100 m. Medley
1934* Canada   3:11.4
(Gazell, Ben; Puddy, William, Bur-
leigh, George)
1938+ England   3:28.2
(Taylor, Micky; Davies, John; Dove,
Freddie)
- -
1950+ England   3:26.6
(Hale, Jack; Romain, Roy; Kendall,
Pat)
   Canada   3:29.4
(Beaumont, Lucien; Salmon, Peter;
Gilchrist, Allen)
   New Zealand   3:30.1
(Mathieson, Peter; Shanahan, John,
Barry, Lyall)
1954+ Australia   3:22.0
(Weld, Cyrus; Hawkins, David; Hen-
ricks, Jon)
   New Zealand   3:26.6
(Hurring, Lincoln; Doms, John; Lucas,
Fred)
   Scotland   3:27.3
(Wardrop, Robert; Service, John;
Wardrop, Jack)
- -
1958++ Australia   4:14.2
(Monckton, John; Gathercole, Terry;
Wilkinson, Brian; Devitt, John)
   Canada   4:26.3
(Wheaton, Robert; Bell, Peter; Park,
George; Grout, Cameron)
   England   4:26.4
(Sykes, Graham; Walkden, Chris;
Symonds, Graham; McKechnie, Neil)
1962++ Australia   4:12.4
(Carroll, Julian; O'Brien, Ian; Berry,
Kevin; Dickson, David)
   England   4:19.9
(Sykes, Graham; Nicholson, Neil;
Glenville, Terry; Kendrew, Peter)
   Canada   4:19.9

(Kelso, Jack; Rabinovitch, Steve;
Meinhardt, Aldwin; Pound, Dick)
1966++ Canada   4:10.5
(Hutton, Ralph; Chase, Leonard;
Jacks, Ron; Gilchrist, Sandy)
   England   4:11.3
(Jackson, Neil; Tucker, Malcolm;
Bewley, Keith; Turner, Mike)
   New Zealand   4:17.5
(Brown, Hilton; Graham, Tony;
Gerrard, Dave; O'Carroll, Paddy)
- -
1970 Canada   4:01.10
(Kennedy, Bill; Mahony, Bill; Mac-
Donald, Byron; Kasting, Bob)
   Australia   4:04.55
(Rogers, Neil; Jarvie, Paul; Findlay,
James; Wenden, Mike)
   Wales   4:08.05
(Richards, Mike; Johnson, Nigel,
Woodroffe, Martyn; Moran, Kevin)
1974 Canada   3:52.93
(Pickell, Steve; Mahony, Bill; Robert-
son, Bruce; Phillips, Brian)
   Australia   3:55.76
(Tonelli, Mark; Cluer, Nigel; Rogers,
Neil; Wenden, Mike)
   England   4:00.48
(Cunningham, Colin; Leigh, David;
Nash, Stephen; Brinkley, Brian)
* = 3 x 100 y.   + = 3 x 110 y.
++ = 4 x 110 y.

Springboard diving
1930 Phillips, Al (Can)
1934 Ray, J. Briscoe (Eng)   117.12
1938 Masters, Ray (Aus)   126.36
- -
1950 Athans, George (Can)   169.21
      Heatly, Peter (Scot)   168.80
      Stewart, Jack (NZ)   168.17
1954 Heatly, Peter (Scot)   146.76
      Turner, Tony (Eng)   145.27
      Stewart, Jack (NZ)   144.98
1958 Collin, Keith (Eng)   126.78
      Patrick, William (Can) 124.61
      Tarsey, David (Eng)   118;81
1962 Phelps, Brian (Eng)   154.14
      Dinsley, Tom (Can)   147.22
      Meissner, Ernest (Can) 145.03
1966 Phelps, Brian (Eng)   154.55
      Wagstaff, Don (Aus)   150.17
      Robb, Chris (Aus)   136.52
1970 Wagstaff, Don (Aus)   557.73
      Sully, Ken (Can)   497.37
      Friesen, Ron (Can)   495.90
1974 Wagstaff, Don (Aus)   531.54

Cranham, Scott (Can)	509.61
Simpson, Trevor (Eng)	489.69

Highboard diving

1930	Phillips, Al (Can)	
1934	Mather, Tommy (Eng)	83.83
1938	Tomalin, Doug (Eng)	108.74
1950	Heatly, Peter (Scot)	156.07
	Athans, George (Can)	145.36
	Murphy, Frank (Aus)	129.40
1954	Patrick, William (Can)	142.70
	Newell, Kevin (Aus)	142.06
	Heatly, Peter (Scot)	141.32
1958	Heatly, Peter (Scot)	147.79
	Phelps, Brian (Eng)	144.49
	Cann, Ray (Eng)	138.50
1962	Phelps, Brian (Eng)	168.35
	Deuble, Graham (Aus)	151.00
	Kitcher, Tony (Eng)	150.81
1966	Phelps, Brian (Eng)	164.57
	Wagstaff, Don (Aus)	148.44
	Robb, Chris (Aus)	141.68
1970	Wagstaff, Don (Aus)	485.73
	Drew, Philip (Eng)	429.24
	Gill, Andy (Eng)	421.47
1974	Wagstaff, Don (Aus)	490.74
	Jackomos, Andrew (Aus)	472.47
	Cranham, Scott (Can)	460.98

WOMEN

100 m. Free-style

1930*	Cooper, Joyce (Eng)	1:07.0
1934*	Dewar, Phyl (Can)	1:03.0
1938+	De Lacey, Evelyn (Aus)	1:10.1
1950+	McQuade, Marjory (Aus)	1:09.1
	Wellington, Margaret (Eng)	1:09.6
	Harrison, Joan (SAf)	1:10.7
1954+	Crapp, Lorraine (Aus)	1:05.8
	Grant, Virginia (Can)	1:06.3
	Harrison, Joan (SAf)	1:08.2
1958+	Fraser, Dawn (Aus)	1:01.4
	Crapp, Lorraine (Aus)	1:03.8
	Colquhoun, Alva (Aus)	1:04.0
1962+	Fraser, Dawn (Aus)	59.5
	Thorn, Robyn (Aus)	1:03.8
	Stewart, Mary (Can)	1:04.4
1966+	Lay, Marion (Can)	1:02.3
	Bell, Lynette (Aus)	1:03.2
	Murphy, Jan (Aus)	1:03.4
1970	Coughlan, Angela (Can)	1:01.22
	Watson, Lynn (Aus)	1:01.45
	Watts, Jenny (Aus)	1:01.80
1974	Gray, Sonya (Aus)	59.13

	Amundrud, Gail (Can)	59.36
	Wright, Judy (Can)	59.46

* = 100 y.   + = 110 y.

200 m. Free-style

1970	Moras, Karen (Aus)	2:09.78
	Coughlan, Angela (Can)	2:10.83
	Jackson, Alex (IOM)	2:13.52
1974	Gray, Sonya (Aus)	2:04.27
	Turrall, Jenny (Aus)	2:06.90
	Amundrud, Gail (Can)	2:07.03

400 m. Free-style

1930*	Cooper, Joyce (Eng)	5:25.4
1934+	Dewar, Phyllis (Can)	5:45.6
1938+	Green, Dorothy (Aus)	5:39.7
1950+	Harrison, Joan (SAf)	5:26.4
	Wellington, Margaret (Eng)	5:33.7
	Norton, Denise (Aus)	5:33.8
1954+	Crapp, Lorraine (Aus)	5:11.4
	Priestley, Gladys (Can)	5:19.6
	Girvan, Margaret (Scot)	5:21.4
1958+	Konrads, Ilsa (Aus)	4:49.4
	Fraser, Dawn (Aus)	5:00.8
	Crapp, Lorraine (Aus)	5:06.7
1962	Fraser, Dawn (Aus)	4:51.4
	Konrads, Ilsa (Aus)	4:55.0
	Long, Elizabeth (Eng)	5:00.4
1966	Wainwright, Kathy (Aus)	4:38.8
	Thorn, Robyn (Aus)	4:44.5
	Herford, Kim (Aus)	4:47.2
1970	Moras, Karen (Aus)	4:27.38
	Langford, Denise (Aus)	4:31.42
	Risson, Robyn (Aus)	4:39.75
1974	Turrall, Jenny (Aus)	4:22.09
	Quirk, Wendy (Can)	4:22.96
	Parkhouse, Jaynie (NZ)	4:23.09

* = 400 y.   + = 440 y.

800 m. Free-style

1970	Moras, Karen (Aus)	9:02.45
	Gray, Helen (Aus)	9:27.48
	Risson, Robyn (Aus)	9:37.89
1974	Parkhouse, Jaynie (NZ)	8:58.49
	Turrall, Jenny (Aus)	8:58.53
	Milgate, Rosemary (Aus)	8:58.59

100 m. Back-stroke

1930*	Cooper, Joyce (Eng)	1:15.0
1934*	Harding, Phyllis, Eng)	1:13.8
1938+	Norton, Pat (Aus)	1:19.5
1950+	Davies, Judy-Joy (Aus)	1:18.6
	Stewart, Jean (NZ)	1:19.1
	Yate, Helen (Eng)	1:20.5

1954+	Harrison, Joan (SAf)	1:15.2
	Symons, Pat (Eng)	1:17.4
	Stewart, Jean (NZ)	1:17.5
1958+	Grinham, Judy (Eng)	1:11.9
	Edwards, Margaret (Eng)	1:12.6
	Gould, Philippa (NZ)	1:13.7
1962+	Ludgrove, Linda (Eng)	1:11.1
	Sargeant, Pam (Aus)	1:11.5
	Lewis, Sylvia (Eng)	1:12.2
1966+	Ludgrove, Linda (Eng)	1:09.2
	Tanner, Elaine (Can)	1:09.9
	Franklin, Janet (Eng)	1:11.8
1970	Watson, Lynn (Aus)	1:07.10
	Cain, Debbie (Aus)	1:07.73
	Gurr, Donna-Marie (Can)	1:08.87
1974	Cook, Wendy (Can)	1:06.37
	Gurr, Donna-Marie (Can)	1:06.55
	Young, Linda (Aus)	1:07.52

* = 100 y.   + = 110 y.

200 m. Back-stroke

1962*	Ludgrove, Linda (Eng)	2:35.2
	Lewis, Sylvia (Eng)	2:36.7
	Sargeant, Pam (Aus)	2:37.5
1966*	Ludgrove, Linda (Eng)	2:28.5
	Tanner, Elaine (Can)	2:29.7
	Macrae, Margaret (NZ)	2:34.7
1970	Watson, Lynn (Aus)	2:22.86
	Gurr, Donna-Marie (Can)	2:24.33
	Cain, Debbie (Aus)	2:26.02
1974	Cook, Wendy (Can)	2:20.37
	Yost, Sandra (Aus)	2:22.07
	Gurr, Donna-Marie (Can)	2:23.74

* = 220 y.

100 m. Breast-stroke

1962*	Lonsbrough, Anita (Eng)	1:21.3
	Haddon, Vivien (NZ)	1:21.3
	Fraser, Dorinda (Eng)	1:21.7
1966*	Harris, Diana (Eng)	1:19.7
	Slattery, Jill (Eng)	1:19.8
	Saville, Heather (Aus)	1:21.6
1970	Whitfield, Beverley (Aus)	1:17.40
	Harrison, Dorothy (Eng)	1:17.60
	Jarvis, Christine (Eng)	1:19.83
1974	Gaskell, Christine (Eng)	1:16.42
	Stuart, Marian (Can)	1:16.61
	Dickie, Sandra (Scot)	1:17.17

* = 110 y.

200 m. Breast-stroke

1930*	Wolstenholme, Celia (Eng)	2:54.8
1934*	Dennis, Clare (Aus)	2:50.2
1938+	Storey, Doris (Eng)	3:06.6

1950+	Gordon, Elenor (Scot)	3:01.7
	Lyons, Nancy (Aus)	3:03.6
	Church, Elizabeth (Eng)	3:10.3
1954+	Gordon, Elenor (Scot)	2:59.2
	Morgan, Mary (SAf)	3:03.3
	Grundy, Margaret (Eng)	3:04.5
1958+	Lonsbrough, Anita (Eng)	2:53.5
	Dyson, Jackie (Eng)	2:58.2
	Gosden, Christine (Eng)	2:58.4
1962+	Lonsbrough, Anita (Eng)	2:51.7
	Enfield, Jackie (Eng)	2:54.7
	Haddon, Vivien (NZ)	2:56.3
1966+	Slattery, Jill (Eng)	2:50.3
	Mitchell, Stella (Eng)	2:50.3
	Haddon, Vivien (NZ)	2:53.9
1970	Whitfield, Beverley (Aus)	2:44.12
	Harrison, Dorothy (Eng)	2:46.18
	Radnage, Mandy (Eng)	2:50.11
1974	Beavan, Pat (Wales)	2:43.11
	Whitfield, Beverley (Aus)	2:43.58
	Smith, Allison (Aus)	2:45.08

* = 200 y.   + = 220 y.

100 m. Butterfly

1958*	Bainbridge, Beverley (Aus)	1:13.5
	Staveley, Tessa (NZ)	1:14.4
	Iwasaki, Margaret (Can)	1:15.9
1962*	Stewart, Mary (Can)	1:10.1
	Cotterill, Anne (Eng)	1:11.2
	McGill, Linda (Aus)	1:11.6
1966*	Tanner, Elaine (Can)	1:06.8
	Gegan, Judy (Eng)	1:09.6
	Barner, Ann (Eng)	1:09.7
1970	Lansley, Diane (Eng)	1:07.90
	Smith, Susan (Can)	1:08.18
	Mabb, Allyson (Aus)	1:08.67
1974	Stenhouse, Patti (Can)	1:05.38
	Wickham, Kim (Scot)	1:05.96
	Yost, Sandra (Aus)	1:06.04

* = 110 y.

200 m. Butterfly

1966*	Tanner, Elaine (Can)	2:29.9
	Corson, Marilyn (Can)	2:34.8
	Barner, Ann (Eng)	2:35.0
1970	Robinson, Maree (Aus)	2:24.67
	Comerford, Jane (Aus)	2:24.95
	Mabb, Allyson (Aus)	2:31.09
1974	Yost, Sandra (Aus)	2:20.57
	Stenhouse, Patti (Can)	2:20.66
	Neall, Gail (Aus)	2:21.66

* = 220 y.

200 m. Individual medley
1970 Langford, Denise (Aus)   2:28.89
      Ratcliffe, Shelagh (Eng) 2:29.65
      Rickard, Diana (Aus)   2:30.80

1974 Cliff, Leslie (Can)   2:24.13
      Smith, Becky (Can)   2:25.17
      Hunter, Susan (NZ)   2:26.18

400 m. Individual medley
1962* Lonsbrough, Anita (Eng)   5:38.8
      McGill, Linda (Aus)   5:46.1
      Cornish, Jennifer (Aus)   5:53.4

1966* Tanner, Elaine (Can)   5:26.3
      Murphy, Jan (Aus)   5:28.1
      Hughes, Jane (Can)   5:34.1
- -
1970 Langford, Denise (Aus)   5:10.74
      Neall, Gail (Aus)   5:15.82
      Ratcliffe, Shelagh (Eng) 5:17.89

1974 Cliff, Leslie (Can)   5:01.35
      Smith, Becky (Can)   5:03.68
      Hunter, Sue (NZ)   5:07.20
      * = 440 y.

4 x 100 m. Free-style
1930* England   4:32.8
      (Joynes, Olive; Cooper, Doreen;
      Harding, Phyllis; Cooper, Joyce)
1934* Canada   4:21.8
      (Dewar, Phyl; Humble, F; Hutton,
      Margaret; Pirie, Irene)
1938+ Canada   4:48.3
      (Dewar, Phyl; Lyon, Dorothy; Bag-
      gley, M.; Dobson, D.)
- -
1950+ Australia   4:44.9
      (Spencer, Denise; Norton, Denise,
      Davies, Judy-Joy; McQuade, Marjory)
      New Zealand   4:48.7
      (Jacobi, Kristin; Bridson, Norma;
      Griffin, Winifred; Hastings, J.)
      England   4:56.0
      (Wood, Grace; Yate, Helen; Preece,
      Lilian; Wellington, Margaret)
1954+ South Africa   4:33.9
      (Loveday, Felicity; Petzer, Machduldt;
      Myburgh, Natalie; Harrison, Joan)
      Canada   4:37.0
      (Grant, Virginia; Priestley, Gladys;
      Stewart, Helen; Whittall, Beth)
      England   4:41.8
      (Ewart, Fearne; Nares-Pillow, Valerie;
      Wilkinson, Daphne; Botham, Jean)
1958+ Australia   4:17.4
      (Fraser, Dawn; Morgan, Sandra;
      Crapp, Lorraine; Colquhoun, Alva)
      Canada   4:30.0
      (Barber, Sarah; Iwasaki, Margaret;

Priestly, Gladys; Sangster, Susan)
      England   4:31.5
      (Grinham, Judy; Marshall, Anne;
      Noakes, Beryl; Wilkinson, Diana)
1962+ Australia   4:11.1
      (Bell, Lyn; Thorn, Robyn; Everuss,
      Ruth; Fraser, Dawn)
      Canada   4:21.1
      (Thompson, Pat; Barber, Sarah;
      Sevigny, Madeleine; Stewart, Mary)
      England   4:21.3
      (Keen, Sandra; Long, Elizabeth;
      Amos, Linda; Wilkinson, Diana)
1966+ Canada   4:10.8
      (Tanner, Elaine; Hughes, Jane; Ken-
      nedy, Louise; Lay, Marion)
      Australia   4:11.1
      (Murphy, Jan; Steinbeck, Janet;
      Smith, M.: Bell, Lynn)
      England   4:17.3
      (Wilkinson, Diana; Cope, Sue; Cave,
      Jeanette; Sillett, Pauline)
- -
1970 Australia   4:06.41
      (Cain, Debbie; Watson, Lynn; Watts,
      Jenny; Langford, Denise)
      Canada   4:12.16
      (Smith, Sue; Hall, Linda; James,
      Karen; Coughlan, Angela)
      England   4:14.9
      (Smith, Kate; Allardice, Lesley;
      Pickering, Sally; Sutherland, Diana)
1974 Canada   3:57.14
      (Amundrud, Gail; Jardin, Ann; Smith,
      Becky; Wright, Judy)
      Australia   4:02.37
      (Turrall, Jenny; Cain, Debbie; And-
      erson, Suzy; Gray, Sonya)
      England   4:05.59
      (Jones, Alyson; Willington, Avis;
      Edmondson, Sue; Allardice, Lesley)
      * = 4 x 100 y.   + = 4 x 110 y.

4 x 100 m. Medley relay
1934* Canada   3:42.0
      (Hutton, Margaret; Haslam, Phyllis;
      Dewar, Phyl)
1938+ England   3:57.7
      (Frampton, Lorna; Storey, Doris;
      Hinton, Margery)
- -
1950+ Australia   3:53.8
      (Davies, Judy-Joy; Lyons, Nancy;
      McQuade, Marjory)
      England   3:56.6
      (Yate, Helen; Church, Elizabeth;
      Wellington, Margaret)
      Scotland   3:58.9

(Girvan, Margaret; Gordon, Elenor; Turner, Elizabeth)

1954+ Scotland 3:51.0
(McDowall, Margaret; Gordon, Elenor; Girvan, Margaret)
South Africa 3:52.7
(Harrison, Joan; Morgan, Mary; Petzer, Machduldt)
Australia 3:55.6
(Knight, Judith; Grier, Jan; Crapp, Lorraine)

1958++ England 4:54.0
(Grinham, Judy; Lonsbrough, Anita; Gosden, Christine; Wilkinson, Diana)
Australia 4:55.1
(Nelson, Anne; Evans, Barbara; Bainbridge, Beverley; Fraser, Dawn)
Canada 5:01.6
(Barber, Sarah; Service, Irene; Iwasaki, Margaret; Priestley, Gladys)

1962++ Australia 4:45.9
(Sargeant, Pam; Ruygrok, Marguerite; McGill, Linda, Fraser, Dawn)
England 4:47.9
(Ludgrove, Linda; Lonsbrough, Anita; Cotterill, Anne; Wilkinson, Diana)
Canada 4:48.1
(Barber, Sarah; Glendenning, Alison; Stewart, Mary; Thompson, Patricia)

1966++ England 4:40.6
(Ludgrove, Linda; Harris, Diana; Gegan, Judy; Sillett, Pauline)
Canada 4:44.5
(Kennedy, Louise; Ross, Dona, Tanner, Elaine; Lay, Marion)
Australia 4:45.7
(Mabb, Allyson; Saville, Heather; Groeger, Jill; Bell, Lyn)

- -

1970 Australia 4:30.66
(Watson, Lynn; Whitfield, Beverley; Mabb, Allyson; Langford, Denise)
England 4:38.94
(Platt, Sylvia; Harrison, Dorothy; Lansley, Diane; Smith, Katie)
Canada 4:39.6
(Gurr, Donna-Marie; Dockerill, Sylvia; Smith, Sue; Coughlan, Angela)

1974 Canada 4:24.77
(Cook, Wendy; Stuart, Marian; Stenhouse, Patti; Amundrud, Gail)
Australia 4:30.55
(Young, Linda; Whitfield, Beverley; Cain, Debbie; Gray, Sonya)
Scotland 4:31.68
(Fordyce, Gillian; Dickie, Sandra; Wickham, Kim; McGlashan, Morag)
* = 3 x 100 y.   + = 3 x 110 y.
++ = 110 y.

Springboard diving

1930	Whitsitt, Oonagh (SAf)	90.10
1934	Moss, Judith (Can)	62.27
1938	Donnett, Irene (Aus)	91.18

- -

1950	Child, Edna (Eng)	126.58
	MacLean, Noeline (Aus)	124.59
	Hunt, Lynda (Eng)	115.38
1954	Long, Ann (Eng)	128.26
	McAulay, Barbara (Aus)	127.74
	McDonald, Irene (Can)	126.19
1958	Welsh, Charmain (Eng)	118.81
	McDonald, Irene (Can)	117.01
	Ferris, Elizabeth (Eng)	113.30
1962	Knight, Susan (Aus)	134.72
	Ferris, Elizabeth (Eng)	132.74
	McArthur, Lorraine (Aus)	135.13
1966	Rowlatt, Kathy (Eng)	147.10
	Boys, Beverley (Can)	134.92
	Knight, Sue (Aus)	134.90
1970	Boys, Beverley (Can)	432.87
	Carruthers, Liz (Can)	391.20
	Morley, Gaye (Aus)	389.04
1974	Shatto, Cindy (Can)	430.88
	Boys, Beverley (Can)	426.93
	York, Teri (Can)	413.83

Highboard diving

1930	Stoneham, Pearl (Can)	39.30
1934	Macready, "Dot" (Eng)	30.74
1938	Hook, Lurline (Aus)	36.47

- -

1950	Child, Edna (Eng)	70.89
	Fawcett, Gwen (Aus)	65.64
	MacLean, Noeline (Aus)	59.93
1954	McAulay, Barbara (Aus)	86.55
	Millar, Eunice (Eng)	79.86
	Long, Ann (Eng)	79.53
1958	Welsh, Charmian (Eng)	77.23
	Long, Ann (Eng)	73.69
	Weiland, Molly (Eng)	65.82
1962	Knight, Sue (Aus)	101.15
	Austen, Margaret (Eng)	98.93
	Plowman, Patricia (Aus)	91.79
1966	Newman, Joy (Eng)	98.87
	Bradshaw, Robyn (Aus)	98.85
	Boys, Beverley (Can)	97.21
1970	Boys, Beverley (Can)	361.95
	Robertson, Nancy (Can)	350.49
	Burrow, Shelagh (Eng)	330.63
1974	Boys, Beverley (Can)	361.95
	Williams, Beverley (Eng)	352.14
	Barnett, Madelaine (Aus)	339.30

COMMONWEALTH GAMES FEDERATION.

A meeting of Empire representatives in Los Angeles on Sunday, 7 Aug. 1932, during the Olympic Games of that year, decided to form a British Empire Games Federation. This was two years after the first British Empire Games had been held in Hamilton, Canada, and the decision was confirmed later in London after British Empire Games Associations had been set up in Australia, Bermuda, Canada, England, India, Newfoundland, New Zealand, Rhodesia, Scotland, South Africa and Wales.

As the character of the Empire changed so did the name of the Federation to the 'British Empire and Commonwealth Games Federation' on 20 July 1952 . . . 'British Commonwealth Games Federation' on 7 Aug. 1966 . . . and 'Commonwealth Games Federation' on 22 Jan. 1974. By the Christchurch Games in January 1974 there was a membership of 45 national associations.

COOK, Wendy (Canada, 15 Sept. 1956-). The only woman world record-breaker at the 1974 Commonwealth Games in Christchurch, Wendy Cook did this (1:04.78) on the opening back-stroke leg of the 4 x 100 m. medley relay. Canada's victory brought her third gold, Wendy having taken already first place in the 100 and 200 m. back-stroke.

A member of the Canadian Dolphin swim club of Vancouver, from which so many Canadian champions have emerged, Miss Cook swam at the 1972 Olympics (5th 100 m.) and took the 100 m. bronze at the 1973 World championships.

In 1974 she won back-stroke titles in three countries. She became the first foreigner to take United States indoor and outdoor titles in the same year (200 m.) and she won the 100 and 200 m. crowns of Britian and Canada, the Canadian 200 m. in a Commonwealth record of 2:28.69.

COOPER, Bradford (Australia, 19 July, 1954-). This fair-haired young man from Queensland will be best remembered for being awarded an Olympic title after being beaten, by one hundredth of a second, in the 1972 Munich 400 m. final (see DeMONT, Rick). And this unfortunate fact, which came about in circumstances not of his making, will always overshadow the other achievements of this fine swimmer.

Be that as it may, Cooper will go down in history as an Olympic champion—even if the German organisers did not amend the official Munich results after DeMont's disqualification.

Cooper was second to DeMont in the World 400 m. championships in 1973 and third, behind Steve Holland (see HOLLAND, Steve) and DeMont, in the 1,500 m. He took the 200 m. back-stroke gold, a silver in the 400 m. free-style and a bronze in the 100 m. back-stroke at the 1974 Commonwealth Games, then announced his retirement from swimming.

COOPER, Joyce (Great Britain, 18 Apr. 1909-). A member of the Mermaid club of London, Joyce Cooper's swimming talent embraced almost the whole range of women's events from 1927 to 1933. In fact, the only style at which she did not excel was breaststroke in which she said: 'I go backwards.'

She was third in the Olympic 100 m. free-style and back-stroke in 1928 and won a silver in the 4 x 100 m. relay. Four years later, in Los Angeles, she was a member of the British relay squad who came third and she also reached the finals of the 400 m. free-style and 100 m. back-stroke.

In European events Joyce won a silver for 100 m. free-style in 1927 and shared the Bologna Trophy (see BOLOGNA TROPHY) with her team-mates who took the relay gold that year. In the 1931 Europeans she was second in the 400 m. free-style, 100 m. back-stroke and the relay and third in the 100 m. free-style.

Miss Cooper, who was born in Ceylon, represented England at the first Empire Games in 1930 when she took three of the four individual titles—100 and 400 y. free-style and 100 y. back-stroke—and a fourth gold in the relay with her sister Doreen also a member of this squad.

She won nineteen A.S.A. titles—100 y. (1929, '31, '32), 220 y. (1927-29 and 1931-32), 440 y. (1928-32), long distance (1930-33) and the 150 y. back-stroke (1929 and '31). Miss Cooper married Olympic rowing medallist John Badcock and has two sons, the elder of whom rowed in the English eight at the 1958 Empire Games.

CRABBE, Buster (United States, 7 Feb. 1910-). Successor to Johnny Weissmuller as the screen Tarzan, Clarence 'Buster' Crabbe was Olympic 400 m. champion in 1932 (4:48.4) having taken third place in the 1,500 m. four years earlier in Amsterdam in 20:28.8, a time he improved to 20:02.7 in placing fifth in 1932. Crabbe's only world record was 10:20.4 for 880 y. (1930) but he won eleven American outdoor titles including the one mile five years in succession (1927-31).

Crabbe's film and television roles— and he appeared in nearly 170 pictures— were all in heroic mould. He was space idol Buck Rogers, legionnaire Captain Gallant conquering the Sahara Desert, Flash Gordon and seventh in a long line of Tarzans.

Born in Oakland, California, his family moved when he was eighteen months to the Hawaiian Islands, where his father became overseer of a pineapple plantation. Crabbe learned to swim at five and later, at Puna Hou High School in Honolulu, he was also an outstanding footballer, basketball player and track athlete.

He returned to the mainland to the University of Southern California and as a first-year law student there won a place in the 1928 Olympic team. He starred in the World's Fair Aquacade in New York before World War II.

CRAPP. Lorraine (Australia, 17 Oct. 1938-). The first girl to break five min. for 400 m. free-style is Lorraine Crapp's special claim to fame. Sixteen years after Ragnhild Hveger had set the world mark of 5:00.1, the blonde Miss Crapp from Sydney in one swim on 15 Aug. 1956, set four world marks for 200 m., 220 y., 400 m., and 440 y. with times of 2:19.3, 2:20.5, 4:50.8 and 4:52.4. She repeated this four-records-in-one-swim effort two months later with 2:18.5, 2:19.1, 4:47.2 and 4:48.6 which are her best times. And as a sideline to her achievements, Miss Hveger's 1940 record was in a 25 m. pool, with

a time advantage through the extra turns of about 5.6 sec. compared with Miss Crapp's 55 y. bath achievement.

Miss Crapp won the 1956 Olympic 400 m. title, beating her team-mate Dawn Fraser by more than 10 y., took the silver, behind Miss Fraser, in the 100 m. and a second gold in the 4 x 100 m. relay.

A style perfectionist and coached by Frank Guthrie, Miss Crapp had to train with men because she was too speedy for the girls, yet she had been written off as a swimmer in 1955, within a few months of winning the 110 and 440 y. titles at the 1954 Commonwealth Games. A severe ear infection brought fears she would never recover her medal-winning form. But recover she did to set 16 individual world records (including 10:30.9 for 800 m. and 10:34.6 for 880 y.) and help the Australian national team to seven more. Her career ended at the 1960 Olympics with a silver in the free-style relay.

CSIK, Ferenc (Hungary, 12 Dec. 1913-29 Mar. 1945). A doctor of medicine, Csik was the shock winner of the Olympic 100 m. free-style in Berlin in 1936 when he succeeded despite the handicap of an outside lane. European champion and record holder for 100 m. in 1934 and winner of thirteen Hungarian individual titles, Cisk was killed during an air raid in 1945 while working as an army surgeon.

CURTIS, Ann (United States, 6 Mar. 1926-). The graceful lady of American swimming after World War II, Ann Curtis —now Mrs. Cuneo—crowned her career by winning the Olympic 400 m. title in London in 5:17.8 and placing second in the 100 m. (66.5) behind Denmark's Greta Andersen. Despite these competitive successes and winning eighteen United States outdoor titles between 1943-48, the only world marks by this tall girl from the San Fransisco Crystal Plunge Club were for yards distances—440 y. in 5:07.9 (25 y. bath) in 1947 and 880 y. in 11:08.6 in 1944.

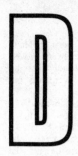

DANIELS, Charles (United States, 12 July 1884-9 Aug 1973). America's first great swimmer, Daniels, who won five medals at the 1904 Olympics in St. Louis and two more at the London Games of 1908, was considered to be a wonder of his age.

The swimming arrangements in St. Louis, where the competitions took place in a lake in the grounds of the World Fair, were somewhat chaotic. Starts were from a raft which often submerged under the weight of the competitors, the turn markers tended to drift and the swimmers found it difficult to keep straight because the lake had no parallel banks for them to follow.

Yet Daniels, then 20, managed to win the 220 and 440 y. and a third gold in the relay, and placed second in the 100 y. and third in the 50 y. dash—the only time this last event was in the Olympic programme. Four years later, he took the 100 m., a race which he had also won at the 1906 Interim Games, and a relay bronze.

He set seven world records between 1907-11 and his best times were 55.8 (100 y.), 68.2 (100 m.), 2:25.4 (200 m.), 2:25.4 (220 y.), 3:57.6 (300 m.) and 7:03.4 (500 m.).

Daniels, an early exponent of the American crawl, had a great influence on the development of the stroke in Britain. He twice won the A.S.A. 100 y. title (1906, '07) and his first world record for this distance (55.4) was set during the 1907 championship race in Manchester.

DAVENPORT, Horace (Great Britain). This great gentleman of early English swimming was not only a champion in the pool but also out of it. He won the A.S.A. mile championship six times from 1874-79 and the Long Distance, or as it was known then 'The Lords and Commons Race' (see AMATEUR SWIMMING ASSOCIATION MILE AND LONG DISTANCE CHAMPIONSHIPS), three times (1877-79). The record he set in winning the mile title in still water in the Welsh Harp in 1877 (29:25½) stood until 1892.

Davenport, a member of the now defunct Ilex and Surbiton Club, also played a vital part in smoothing the troubled waters of the early days of formal swimming administration in England. He was president of the Swimming Association of Great Britain from 1880-83 and of the re-named Amateur Swimming Association from 1890 to 1894.

DeMONT, Richard (United States, 21 April, 1956-). Rick DeMont from San Rafael, California, unfortunately will always be remembered as the man who held an Olympic title for three days, then had it taken away for technical reasons.

The event was the 400 m. free-style at the 1972 Games in Munich, where this slim, 6' 1", beautiful stylist, snatched the touch from Australia's Brad Cooper, by one hundredth of a second, after a storming finish.

The medals were presented, then the medallists and other finalists selected at random, had to undergo dope tests. These tests took at least 48 hours to complete and nothing definite had been decided two days later when DeMont competed in the heats of the 1,500 m. and qualified easily for the final.

This final was the next day, and San Fransisco-born DeMont was seen warming up in preparation for his bid for a second gold medal. Then, without explanation, the line-up for the final was announced, without DeMont, but with the surprise inclusion of Mexico's Guillermo Garcia, the ninth fastest heat man.

DeMont, an asthma sufferer, had been struck out of the final because the tests after the 400 m. had shown that he had minute quantities of ephedrine—a substance banned by the IOC's medical commission—in his body. This had come from a medication he took to control his asthmatic condition.

There was a storm of recrimination, appeals and general drama. The American team doctors, who knew the IOC rules about banned drugs and had been informed about the medications used by DeMont, were blamed for not prescribing an acceptable alternative, as other countries did, for their star distance man.

In the end F.I.N.A. were forced to award the title to runner-up Cooper and take DeMont out of the 1,500 m. final.

One year later, the two men met again in the World 400 m. championship final. And this time DeMont beat Cooper by 0.52 of a second in a world record 3:58.18, to become the first man to break 4 min. for the distance.

DENNIS. Claire (Australia). Olympic 200 m. breast-stroke champion in 1932 in a Games record of 3:06.3, Claire Dennis, from New South Wales, also won the Commonwealth 200 y. title in 1934. She set two world marks, both short course—100 m. in 1:24.6 in 1933 and 200 m. in 3:08.4 in 1932. This latter mark was broken twice, by Lisa Rocke (Germany) and Else Jacobsen (Denmark), before the Berlin Olympics but in the Games, the Dane was only third and the German did not reach the final. Miss Dennis was Australian 200 y. breast-stroke champion in 1931 and from 1933-35, the 1932 event having been cancelled.

DERBYSHIRE, Rob (Great Britain, 29 Nov. 1878-1938). John Henry Derbyshire, from Manchester, was always known as 'Rob'—an abbreviation of his childhood pet name. In the years at the turn of the twentieth century, when British swimmers were supreme, Derbyshire won a gold medal in the 1900 Olympic water-polo tournament, a silver in the 4 x 250 m. relay in the Interim Games in 1906 and another gold in 1908 for the 4 x 200 m. relay at the London Games.

Like most swimmers of his generation, he raced a wide range of distances and won ten A.S.A. titles, including the 100 y. six times from 1898-1901 and 1903-04. He became a baths manager in the north of England and later at Lime Grove Baths, London, where a lane was always set aside, even in busy public time, for serious swimmers. He was the first Briton to break the minute for 100 yards (1907).

DESJARDINS, Pete (United States, 10 Apr. 1907-   ). The 'Little Bronze statue from Florida', Pete was born in Manitoba, Canada, but at an early age moved with his family to Miami Beach where he has lived ever since and eventually became an American citizen.

Double diving medallist in the 1928 Games, he made history then by being the only Olympic competitor to get 10 out of 10 for a dive. This was in the springboard and, in fact, he got the maximum for two dives and his aggregate of judges' marks over the whole test was an amazing 9.2. Not surprisingly, he won this event (by 11 marks) in which he had been second four years earlier, and also took the highboard title.

A compact athlete, standing 5 ft. 3 in., Desjardins, an economics graduate from Stanford University, turned professional and among many notable exhibition tours made four trips to Britain between 1935 and 1938. He travelled always with a typewriter, and his first chore on the train on the way to his next stop was to write a letter of thanks to his last hosts.

He dived in every part of the United Kingdom and in August 1936 alone covered 4,570 miles—an average of 150 miles a day—between engagements, which often involved a thirty-minute solo show of straight and comic dives from plank-like springboards into shallow water.

DEVITT, John (Australia, 4 Feb. 1937-   ). Winner of the Olympic 100 m. in 1960, Devitt is best remembered for the row his victory in Rome caused. And, inevitably, his name always will be linked with American Lance Larson, the man who many thought had won.

The Rome Games were staged in the days before automatic timing and judging. And in the closing stages of this race, Larson, in an adjacent lane to Devitt, had surged forward with amazing speed. Two of the three first place judges gave Devitt their vote. Two of the second place judges put Devitt second. Thus, of the six officials there, three, by implication thought the Australian had won and three favoured the American.

The timekeepers had no doubt. They gave Larson 55.0, 55.1 and 55.1 (for an Olympic record of 55.1) against the 55.2, 55.2 and 55.2 for Devitt. And the unofficial manually-operated judging machine, which recorded the touch on three paper tapes, made Larson the clear winner.

Despite all this evidence, Devitt was awarded the gold in an Olympic record of 55.2, thanks to a judging casting vote by the referee, who technically did not have a vote! Larson got the silver and his time changed to 55.2. Poor Larson was the subject of protests on his behalf for four years. And poor Devitt had to grin and bear it.

The career of Devitt from Sydney started in earnest at the 1956 Melbourne Olympics where he was second to his team-mate Jon Henricks in the 100 m. and won a gold in Australia's winning 4 x 200 m. relay team. As well as his disputed Roman gold, he gained a bronze in the 4 x 200 m. relay in 1960.

Essentially a sprinter, he was Commonwealth 100 m. and relay champion in Cardiff in 1958, broke four world records, for 100 m. (55.2 and 54.6) and 110 y. (55.2 and 55.1) and helped Australian relay teams to ten world marks.

DIBIASI, Klaus (Italy, 6 Oct. 1947-   ), The most dominant diver of all time, Dibiasi competed in three Olympic Games, three European championships and two World championships between 1964 and 1975 and won seven gold and six silver medals from 16 competitions.

His stronger event is the highboard. He won golds at the 1968 and '72 Olympics, 1973 and '75 World championships and 1966 and '74 Europeans and silvers at the 1964 Olympics and 1970 Europeans. From the springboard he was European champion in 1974 and runner-up at the 1968 Olympics, 1970 European and 1973 and '75 World championships.

Dibiasi's achievement in being second and twice first in the highboard at successive Games was something never achieved before by a man or woman in a single Olympic event. He is the first Italian to have won an individual Olympic swimming or diving title and among his many achievements for his country have been seven victories in European Cup competitions.

This tall 5 ft. 11 in. fair-haired man was born in Austria, but in his childhood his Italian parents went to live in Bolzano, in northern Italy. His father Carlo was springboard champion of Italy from 1933 to 1936 and later coached his son to the top of world diving.

Early on Dibiasi had to train outdoors, which in the Italian Dolomites was a chilly business in winter. After his silver success in 1964, an indoor diving tank with a 10 m. board was built for him by the town of Bolzano.

DIVER OF THE YEAR. (See MELVILLE, CLARKE NATIONAL MEMORIAL TROPHY).

DIVING. This complicated sport demands acrobatic ability, the grace of a ballet dancer, iron nerve and a liking for heights.

Competitions are divided into springboard and highboard events (see SPRINGBOARD DIVING, HIGHBOARD DIVING) with prescribed tests. There are five directional groups of dives on the international springboard table and six groups for highboard as follows:

Group 1. Forward. Starting forward and entering forward.

Group 2. Back. Starting backward and entering backward.

Group 3. Reverse. Starting forward with a backward rotation.

Group 4. Inward. Starting backward with a forward rotation.

Group 5. Twist. Starting forward or backward, making from ½ to 2½ twists during straight or somersaulting dives from the groups 1-4 above.

Group 6. Armstand. (Highboard only). Starting with an arm balance (hand-stand) which must be held steadily before the start of the dive or somersault.

There are also four positions in which movements may be performed:

Position (a) Straight. Not bent at knees or hips.

Position (b) Piked. Bent at hips but with knees straight.

Position (c) Tucked. Bunched with hands on knees.

Position (d) Free. Any body position but only applicable to certain more difficult dives with twists.

All dives on the international table have tariff values according to their degree of difficulty. The judge marks the dive without reference to its difficulty and this mark is multiplied by the degree of difficulty to produce the score for the dive (see DIVING JUDGING). Degrees of difficulty range from 1.1 (inward dive

(c) from 5 m.) to 3.0 (forward 3½ somersault (b) from 3 m.).

DIVING JUDGING. Marks in diving are awarded from 0 to 10 on the following basis: completely failed = 0; unsatisfactory = ½-2; deficient = 2½-4½; satisfactory = 5-6; good = 6½-8 and very good = 8½-10.

There are normally five judges, but in events like the Olympic Games there are seven and the dive is marked solely on merit without considering the difficulty of the dive. One highest and one lowest mark are eliminated and the remainder are added together and multiplied by the degree of difficulty (see DIVING). If there are five scoring judges the points are reduced to three judges by dividing by five and multiplying by three. And the final product is the mark for the dive.

The recorders do not have to do lightning calculations in their heads. There are tables to deal with this elaborare procedure from which the score can be extracted within seconds to two decimal points. In major competitions computers are used.

DRUG TAKING IN SWIMMING. There has been legislation against the use of artificial stimulants to improve performances since the earliest days of the Modern Olympics. However, lack of medical knowledge and the ability to detect the use of such substances made the rules little more than pious hopes.

In the mid-1960s a resolution by a sub-committee of the United Nations, plus greater medical interest in the problems of drug-taking turned the spotlight on to this undesirable practice in sport.

Random tests were carried out at some major competitions, including the 1964 and '68 Olympics in Tokyo and Mexico City and the I.O.C., subsequently, drew up a list of banned drugs, the use of which by any competitor would result in disqualification.

It was ruled for the 1972 Games in Munich that medal winners and other competitors, chosen at random during all rounds of competition, would undergo drug tests. This testing, from urine samples, is time-consuming, expensive and, in the case of suspected drug-taking, can take two or more days to resolve.

The taking of drugs had never been considered a serious problem in swimming, as it had been in cycling and it was unfortunate, to say the least, that the I.O.C. decision led to a winner of an Olympic swimming event being deprived of his title (see DeMONT, Rick), the first time in the history of the sport.

DRAVES, Vickie (United States, 31 Dec, 1924-). The first woman to win the Olympic springboard and highboard titles at the same Games–she did it in London in 1948–Victoria Manalo Draves, a twin, had a Filipino father and an English mother.

Born in San Fransisco, her parentage caused her many difficulties before World War II and at one time her club on Nob Hill demanded that she drop her father's surname of Manalo in favour of her mother's maiden name of Taylor. A talented diver before the war, at 16, Vickie's first United States outdoor title success was in 1946 when she won the highboard crown and retained it in 1947 and '48. She never won an outdoor springboard title, but did take the indoor 3 m. championship in 1948.

In the early part of her career, Vickie was coached by Phil Patterson and Jimmy McHugh. But her greatest success came after she had joined the Lyle Draves squad at the Athens club in Oakland. She married Draves in 1946 and he was with her, though not as the team coach, in 1948 when, diving as America's second string, she achieved her historic double at the London Olympics.

DUCHKOVA, Milena (Czechoslovakia, 25 Apr. 1952-). The first Czechoslovakian to win any kind of medal in Olympic pool competitions, Milena had to survive the tensions of occupation of her country by the Soviet Union as well as beat the history of failure. And she did both to win the highboard title in Mexico City.

Only 16 in August 1968, when the Soviet troops occupied Prague, she had to cross the River Vitava over bridges guarded by soldiers with machine guns to do her training and did not know for sure if she could go to the Olympics a week before the team left for Mexico.

But at the Games, the pool crowds were solidly behind her, clapping her every appearance on the board as well as each dive. She won by 4½ marks from Natalia Lobanova (U.S.S.R.) and Duchkova's greatest thrill was to see the Czech flag hoisted above the Russian hammer and sickle at her victory ceremony. Two years after, Milena confirmed her supremacy from the 10 m. platform by winning the European title.

A tiny child—and in Mexico she was only 5 ft. 2½in. and 8 st.—she had been coached since she was seven by Maria Cermakova, who at first was reluctant to give Milena a test because she did not want to take such a little girl as a pupil.

This charming girl went on to win the 1970 European highboard title and come second in the 1972 Olympic and '73 World championships.

DURACK, Fanny (Australia, 27 Oct. 1894-21 March 1956). The first woman Olympic swimming champion, Fanny Durack achieved that honour in 1912 when she won the 100 m. free-style, the only individual event for women, in the Stockholm Games. Racing in an open-air, 100 m. long, specially-built pool in Stockholm harbour, she clipped eight-tenths of a second off the world record, held by Daisy Curwen of England, in winning her heat in 1:19.8 and she beat her team-mate Mina Wylie by 3.2 in 1:22.2 in the final.

In the swimming sense, Fanny was before her time and World War I, which caused the cancellation of the 1916 Games, robbed her of further Olympic honours. She broke nine world records between 1912-18, from 100 yards (by 6.6 seconds) to one mile and was the first to put her name in the record book for 220 and 500 y. and one mile.

She started her career as a breaststroke swimmer—the only style for which there was an Australian championship for women at that time. In fact, Fanny never held a national title though she won the first New South Wales 100 m. breaststroke championship in 1906. Later she swam the trudgen and crawl and her demonstrations around the world did a great deal to promote women's swimming.

Her best times were 66.0 (100 y.), 1:16.2 (100 m.), 2:56.0 (220 y.), 4:43.6 (300 m.), 8:08.2 (500 y.) and 26:08.0 (one mile). It was many years before her standards were equalled.

DUTCH SWIMMING CHAMPIONS. Holland's women have always played an important part in the development of world swimming and particularly in major competitions. In fact, the medal record of the Netherlands at European championships—29 gold, 27 silver and 16 bronze—is second only to East Germany.

They have produced as many world record-breaking women backstrokers as the United States with this crop: Willy van den Turk (1927), Marie Braun (1929/30). Rie Mastenbroek (1934/36), Dina Senff (1936), Cornelia Kint (1938/39), Iet van Feggelen (1938), Geertje Wielema (1950)', Lenie de Nijs (1957) and Ria van Velsen (1958/59).

But Holland's most famous swimmer is Ada Kok (see KOK, Ada), the butterflyer extraordinary, whose world record of 1:4.5 for 100 m. in 1965 stood for five years.

The winners of Dutch championships since 1960 are:

MEN

100 m. Free-style

Year	Name	Time
1960	Kroon, Ronnie	56.7
1961	Kroon, Ronnie	57.8
1962	Kroon, Ronnie	57.0
1963	Baalen, Vinus van	56.8
1964	Kroon, Ronnie	55.6
1965	Sitters, Bert	56.6
1966	Jiskoot, Jan	56.4
1967	Langerhorst, Dick	55.6
1968	Langerhorst, Dick	55.2
1969	Langerhorst, Dick	56.1
1970	Schoutsen, Bob	55.1
1971	Prijdekker, Peter	55.4
1972	Schoutsen, Bob	54.3
1973	Beele, Ruud	56.22
1974	Beele, Ruud	56.19
1975	Ressang, Karim	54.92

200 m. Free-style (instituted 1961)

Year	Name	Time
1961	Bontekoe, Johan	2:08.9
1962	Bontekoe, Johan	2:09.1
1963	Bontekoe, Johan	2:06.1
1964	Bontekoe, Johan	2:04.7
1965	Oudt, Aad	2:04.7
1966	Langerhorst, Dick	2:05.0
1967	Langerhorst, Dick	2:02.0
1968	Langerhorst, Dick	2:00.4
1969	Langerhorst, Dick	2:04.0
1970	Prijdekker, Peter	2:01.1
1971	Prijdekker, Peter	1:59.4
1972	Hamburg, Roger van	1:58.8

1973	Mulder, Henk	2:00.94
1974	Elzerman, Henk	2:02.27
1975	Elzerman, Henk	1:59.53

400 m. Free-style

1960	Bontekoe, Johan	4:41.9
1961	Bontekoe, Johan	4:45.4
1962	Bontekoe, Johan	4:37.5
1963	Bontekoe, Johan	4:31.5
1964	Bontekoe, Johan	4:27.8
1965	Langerhorst, Dick	4:26.6
1966	Langerhorst, Dick	4:23.2
1967	Langerhorst, Dick	4:19.6
1068	Langerhorst, Dick	4:20.0
1969	Hamburg, Roger van	4:20.9
1970	Prijdekker, Peter	4:21.3
1971	Klooster, Ton van	4:15.3
1972	Klooster, Ton van	4:09.7
1973	Klooster, Ton van	4:14.02
1974	Elzerman, Henk	4:13.74
1975	Elzerman, Henk	4:11.53

1,500 m. Free-style

1960	Bontekoe, Johan	19:15.5
1961	Bontekoe, Johan	19:13.5
1962	Bontekoe, Johan	
1963	Bontekoe, Johan	18:22.0
1964	Bontekoe, Johan	18:36.4
1965	Langerhorst, Dick	18:07.6
1966	Langerhorst, Dick	17:41.9
1967	Langerhorst, Dick	17:30.0
1968	Langerhorst, Dick	17:40.1
1969	Hanburg, Roger van	17:18.8
1970	Klooster, Ton van	17:46.3
1971	Klooster, Ton van	16:50.9
1972	Klooster, Ton van	16:28.5
1973	Klooster, Ton van	17:01.00
1974	Elzerman, Henk	16:31.10
1975	Elzerman, Henk	16:11.2*

100 m. Back-stroke

1960	Jiskoot, Jan	1:07.0
1961	Jiskoot, Jan	1:05.6
1962	Weetling, Jan	1:06.4
1963	Osch, Henri van	1:06.2
1964	Osch, Henri van	1:03.6
1965	Schillemans, Peter	1:04.7
1966	Beek, Rinus van	1:05.5
1967	Jonker, Peter	1:04.2
1968	Schoutsen, Bob	1:01.6
1969	Schoutsen, Bob	1:03.6
1970	Schoutsen, Bob	1:01.1
1971	Schoutsen, Bob	1:01.4
1972	Schoutsen, Bob	1:01.0
1973	Ressang, Karim	1:00.88
1974	Ressang, Karim	1:00.86
1975	Ressang, Karim	1:00.97

200 m. Back-stroke (instituted in 1962)

1962	Weeteling, Jan	2:23.2
1963	Osch, Henri van	2:22.5
1964	Osch, Henri van	2:18.4
1965	Osch, Henri van	2:20.9
1966	Osch, Henri van	2:22.7
1967	Beek, Rinus van	2:18.2
1968	Schoutsen, Bob	2:15.4
1969	Schoutsen, Bob	2:13.6
1970	Schoutsen, Bob	2:15.0
1971	Schoutsen, Bob	2:14.8
1972	Schoutsen, Bob	2:12.1
1973	Ressang, Karim	2:12.75
1974	Ressang, Karim	2:11.94
1975	Ressang, Karim	2:13.37

100 m. Breast-stroke (instituted in 1962)

1962	Mensonides, Wieger	1:13.4
1963	Mensonides, Wieger	1:13.0
1964	Vriens, Hemmie	1:12.5
1965	Vriens, Hemmie	1:14.0
1966	Oest, Arthur van	1:12.2
1967	Mensonides, Wieger	1:12.5
1968	Uittenhout, Kees	1:12.1
1969	Uittenhout, Kees	1:13.9
1970	Uittenhout, Kees	1:13.9
1971	Uittenhout, Kees	1:11.7
1972	Hond, Ronald	1:10.9
1973	Elzerman, Hans	1:09.94
1974	Hond, Ronald	1:10.60
1975	Hond, Ronald	1:11.52

200 m. Breast-stroke

1960	Mensonides, Wieger	2:41.9
1961	Mensonides, Wieger	2:43.0
1962	Mensonides, Wieger	2:37.5
1963	Mensonides, Wieger	2:40.1
1964	Mensonides, Wieger	2:40.0
1965	Spijkerman, Hans	2:42.1
1966	Oest, Arthur van	2:41.5
1967	Oest, Arthur van	2:36.0
1968	Spoor, Harm	2:36.9
1969	Nijhuis, Addie	2:38.3
1970	Elzerman, Hans	2:39.6
1971	Elzerman, Hans	2:36.1
1972	Woutering, Robin	2:34.9
1973	Elzerman, Hans	2:30.95
1974	Woutering, Robin	2:32.46
1975	Woutering, Robin	2:36.30

100 m. Butterfly

1960	Korteweg, Gerrit	1:04.1
1961	Not held	
1962	Jiskoot, Jan	1:02.3
1963	Jiskoot, Jan	1:02.4
1964	Jiskoot, Jan	1:00.6
1965	Jiskoot, Jan	1:02.1

1966	Jiskoot, Jan	1:00.9
1967	Langerhorst, Dick	1:01.3
1968	Langerhorst, Dick	1:01.5
1969	Drenth, Elt	1:00.7
1970	Rood, Arnold	59.4
1971	Rood, Arnold	59.9
1972	Rood, Arnold	59.3
1973	Rood, Arnold	1:00.07
1974	Rood, Arnold	59.55
1975	Woutering, Ronald	1:00.66

200 m. Butterfly (instituted 1961)

1961	Sitters, Bert	2:39.1
1962	Sitters, Bert	2:30.0
1963	Jiskoot, Jan	2:21.3
1964	Langerhorst, Dick	2:18.2
1965	Langerhorst, Dick	2:21.8
1966	Langerhorst, Dick	2:20.1
1967	Langerhorst, Dick	2:14.0
1968	Langerhorst, Dick	2:13.5
1969	Drenth, Elt	2:14.2
1970	Rood, Arnold	2:16.9
1971	Rood, Arnold	2:15.6
1972	Hamburg, Roger van	2:12.0
1973	Pijper, Ruud	2:14.22
1974	Rood, Arnold	2:12.22
1975	Woutering, Ronald	2:12.18

200 m. Individual medley (instituted 1967)

1967	Boer, Wim de	2:24.2
1968	Schillemans, Pieter	2:22.9
1969	Kruysdijk, Francois van	2:20.6
1970	Kruysdijk, Francois van	2:21.6
1971	Kruysdijk, Francois van	2:17.8
1972	Hamburg, Roger van	2:13.9
1973	Elzerman, Hans	2:16.48
1974	Elzerman, Hans	2:16.44
1975	Ressang, Karim	2:17.61

400 m. Individual medley (instituted 1962)

1962	Jiskoot, Jan	5:20.7
1963	Jiskoot, Jan	5:16.3
1964	Jiskoot, Jan	5:04.0
1965	Jiskoot, Jan	5:18.6
1966	Jiskoot, Jan	5:09.7
1967	Mulder, Wim	5:08.5
1968	Mulder, Wim	5:04.1
1969	Hamburg, Roger van	5:01.8
1970	Klooster, Ton van	5:11.7
1971	Klooster, Ton van	4:54.1
1972	Woutering, Robin	4:57.9
1973	Elzerman, Hans	4:48.67
1974	Elzerman, Hans	4:53.30
1975	Woutering, Ronald	4:52.32

WOMEN

100 m. Free-style

1960	Terpstra, Erica	1:05.0
1961	Lasterie, Adrie	1:03.7
1962	Tigelaar, Ineke	1:04.3
1963	Terpstra, Erica	1:03.6
1964	Terpstra, Erica	1:02.8
1965	Beumer, Toos	1:02.4
1966	Mulder, Corrie	1:04.6
1967	Bos, Nel	1:01.9
1968	Hemert, Mirjam van	1:03.7
1969	Kuilenburg, Yvonne van	1:03.1
1970	Kuilenburg, Yvonne van	1:02.4
1971	Rijnders, Anke	1:01.2
1972	Bunschoten, Hansje	1:00.4
1973	Brigitha, Enith	58.76
1974	Brigitha, Enith	57.90
1975	Brigitha, Enith	57.53

200 m. Free-style (instituted 1966)

1966	Bos, Nel	2:18.0
1967	Bos, Nel	2:18.0
1968	Maaneman, Dolly	2:20.5
1969	Kuilenburg, Yvonne van	2:16.7
1970	Kuilenburg, Yvonne van	2:15.0
1971	Rijnders, Anke	2:10.6
1972	Bunschoten, Hansje	2:08.5
1973	Bunschoten, Hansje	2:09.25
1974	Brigitha, Enith	2:06.08
1975	Brigitha, Enith	2:05.48

400 m. Free-style

1960	Lagerberg, Tineke	4:57.4
1961	Lasterie, Adrie	4:57.4
1962	Lasterie, Adrie	4:56.7
1963	Tigelaar, Ineke	5:03.7
1964	Tigelaar, Ineke	4:58.2
1965	Kok, Ada	4:59.6
1966	Kok, Ada	4:54.1
1967	Kok, Ada	4:57.3
1968	Kok, Ada	4:54.7
1969	Kuilenburg, Yvonne van	4:53.6
1970	Boer, Linda de	4:41.9
1971	Bunschoten, Hansje	4:33.3
1972	Bunschoten, Hansje	4:27.8
1973	Bunschoten, Hansje	4:32.54
1974	Maas, Annelies	4:28.21
1975	Brigitha, Enith	4:23.60

800 m. Free-style (instituted 1967)

1967	Kok, Ada	10:22.6
1968	Maaneman, Dolly	10:21.6
1969	Boer, Linda de	9:59.5
1970	Telkamp, Sia	10:23.7
1971	Boer, Linda de	9:25.0
1972	Bunschoten, Hansje	9:17.7

1973	Bunschoten, Hansje	9:19.0*
1974	Damen, Jose	9:10.66
1975	Damen, Jose	9:02.8*

100 m. Back-stroke

1960	Dobber, Rini	1:12.8
1961	Winkel, Corrie	1:12.3
1962	Velsen, Ria van	1:10.2
1963	Velsen, Ria van	1:11.3
1964	Velsen, Ria van	1:10.4
1965	Buter, Cobie	1:11.9
1966	Sikkens, Cobie	1:11.3
1967	Buter, Cobie	1:10.2
1968	Sikkens, Cobie	1:09.5
1969	Buter, Cobie	1:11.8
1970	Buter, Cobie	1:09.4
1971	Vermaat, Marianne	1:08.9
1972	Vermaat, Marianne	1:08.4
1973	Brigitha, Enith	1:06.42
1974	Eijk, Paula van	1:07.35
1975	Eijk, Paula van	1:07.97

200 m. Back-stroke (instituted 1967)

1967	Sikkens, Cobie	2:31.5
1968	Sikkens, Cobie	2:29.7
1969	Plantinga, Mia	2:36.2
1970	Groen, Annemarie	2:31.5
1971	Groen, Annemarie	2:29.4
1972	Groen, Annemarie	2:26.6
1973	Elzerman, Jozien	2:25.57
1974	Brigitha, Enith	2:21.84
1975	Peeters, Wilke	2:25.63

100 m. Breast-stroke (instituted 1962)

1962	Bimolt, Klenie	1:21.9
1963	Bimolt, Klenie	1:19.9
1964	Bimolt, Klenie	1:18.0
1965	Bimolt, Klenie	1:20.3
1966	Kok, Gretta	1:19.2
1967	Bimolt, Klenie	1:20.1
1968	Janus, Marjan	1:19.2
1969	Janus, Marjan	1:21.7
1970	Riet, Alie te	1:20.5
1971	Riet, Alie te	1:19.8
1972	Riet, Alie te	1:19.0
1973	Gramme, Corrie	1:17.87
1974	Mazereeuw, Wijda	1:18.38
1975	Mazereeuw, Wijda	1:16.40

200 m. Breast-stroke

1960	Haan, Ada den	2:53.2
1961	Heukles, Bettie	2:53.0
1962	Bimolt, Klenie	2:53.3
1963	Bimolt, Klenie	2:49.3
1964	Bimolt, Klenie	2:49.9
1965	Bimolt, Klenie	2:51.4
1966	Kok, Gretta	2:49.7

1967	Bimolt, Klenie	2:50.5
1968	Bimolt, Klenie	2:53.6
1969	Pentermann, Hennie	2:51.3
1970	Riet, Alie te	2:53.9
1971	Riet, Alie te	2:47.1
1972	Riet, Alie te	2:47.6
1973	Riet, Alie te	2:46.34
1974	Mazereeuw, Wijda	2:45.07
1975	Mazereeuw, Wijda	2:42.15

100 m. Butterfly

1960	Voorbij, Atie	1:11.7
1961	Heemskerk, Marianne	1:12.4
1962	Kok, Ada	1:10.5
1963	Kok, Ada	1:09.9
1964	Kok, Ada	1:06.2
1965	Kok, Ada	1:06.2
1966	Kok, Ada	1:06.3
1967	Kok, Ada	1:05.8
1968	Kok, Ada	1:05.6
1969	Janzen, Marie-José	1:09.2
1970	Buys, Frieke	1:10.3
1971	Rijnders, Anke	1:07.3
1972	Buys, Frieke	1:06.7
1973	Segaar, Annette,	1:07.44
1974	Damen, José	1:05.40
1975	Verkerk, Judith	1:07.96

200 m. Butterfly (instituted 1967)

1967	Kok, Ada	2:22.5
1968	Kok, Ada	2:21.1
1969	Janzen, Marie-José	2:40.5
1970	Veeken, Anke van de	2:40.2
1971	Zandvoort, Truus	2:30.5
1972	Buys, Frieke	2:27.4
1973	Damen, José	2:22.79
1974	Aggenbach, Yolanda	2:20.90
1975	Wolthius, Tineke	2:28.38

200 m. Individual medley (instituted 1967)

1967	Heukels, Bettie	2:37.7
1968	Pentermann, Hennie	2:33.6
1969	Pentermann, Hennie	2:33.0
1970	Pentermann, Hennie	2:33.2
1971	Pentermann, Hennie	2:31.1
1972	Mazereeuw, Wijda	2:29.4
1973	Mazereeuw, Wijda	2:30.80
1974	Brigitha, Enith	2:27.24
1975	Brigitha, Enith	2:26.27

400 m. Individual medley (instituted 1962)

1962	Lasterie, Adrie	5:37.5
1963	Lasterie, Adrie	5:41.2
1964	Heukels, Bettie	5:29.8

1965	Heukels, Bettie	5:33.9
1966	Heukels, Bettie	5:30.2
1967	Heukels, Bettie	5:32.2
1968	Pentermann, Hennie	5:26.6
1969	Pentermann, Hennie	5:24.1
1970	Pentermann, Hennie	5:23.4

1971	Pentermann, Hennie	5:23.8
1972	Lassooij, Gerda	5:15.4
1973	Damen, José	5:14.24
1974	Damen, José	5:07.08
1975	Maas, Annelies	5:14.35

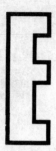

1960	Rostock
1961	Karl-Marx-Stadt
1962	Magdeburg
1963	Magdeburg
1964	Piesteritz
1965	Piesteritz and East Berlin
1966	Rostock
1967	East Berlin
1968	Leipzig
1969	East Berlin
1970	Brandenburg/Havel
1971	Rostock
1972	Leipzig
1973	East Berlin
1974	Rostock
1975	Piesteritz

EAST GERMAN CHAMPIONS.

The German Democratic Republic (East Germany) became affiliated to F.I.N.A. as a separate national federation from the German Federal Republic (West Germany) in 1950. Although from this time the two Germanys were able to participate independently under F.I.N.A. rules, it was not until 1968, at the Games in Mexico City, that the I.O.C. allowed East and West Germany to have spearate teams in the Olympics.

East Germany's first winners of major pool titles were Klaus Bodinger and Jutta Langenau who became gold medallists for 200 m. breast-stroke and 100 m. butterfly respectively at the 1954 European championships in Turin.

Frank Wiegand was voted the outstanding competitor at the 1966 European meeting in Utrecht for his victories in the 400 m. free-style and medley, the former in world record time. But the man who really put G.D.R. swimming on the map was Roland Matthes (see MATTHES, Roland) in winning the 100 and 200 m. back-stroke at the 1968 Mexico Olympics.

The East German girls were slower to emerge but by the world championships in Belgrade in 1973 they were capable of winning 10 of the 14 titles at stake. The following year, in Vienna, they took all but one of the swimming gold medals and 10 out of 12 silver medals.

In July '75 they were again the top nation, at the world championships in Cali, Colombia, where they won 10 out of 14 titles and scored 191 points to the 150 of the United States.

The venues and winners of the East German championships since 1960 are:

MEN

100 m. Free-style

1960	Wiegand, Frank	56.9
1961	Wiegand, Frank	57.0
1962	Gregor, Horst-Gunther	57.2
1963	Wiegand, Frank	55.4
1964	Wiegand, Frank	56.0
1965	Wiegand, Frank	54.2
1966	Gregor, Horst-Gunther	54.8
1967	Poser, Udo	54.8
1968	Gregor, Horst -Gunther	55.3
1969	Poser, Udo	54.5
1970	Matthes, Roland	54.5
1971	Matthes, Roland	53.2
1972	Matthes, Roland	53.6
1973	Pyttel, Roger	52.78
1974	Pyttel, Roger	53.55
1975	Pyttel, Roger	53.04

200 m. Free-style (instituted 1961)

1961	Wiegand, Frank	2:10.1
1962	Herbst, Joachim	2:08.9
1963	Wiegand, Frank	2:08.9
1964	Wiegand, Frank	2:04.8
1965	Wiegand, Frank	1:59.3
1966	Wiegand, Frank	1:59.6
1967	Poser, Udo	1:58.9
1968	Matthes, Roland	2:00.1
1969	Herbst, Joachim	2:00.2
1970	Unger, Lutz	1:59.6
1971	Poser, Udo	1:58.0
1972	Poser, Udo	1:58.3
1973	Pyttel, Roger	1:55.06
1974	Pyttel, Roger	1:55.56
1975	Pyttel, Roger	1:56.43

400 m. Free-style

1960	Englehardt, Heina	4:04.4
1961	Wiegand, Frank	4:42.1
1962	Herbst, Joachim	4:35.6

1963	Wiegand, Frank	4:28.5
1964	Wiegand, Frank	4:28.5
1965	Wiegand, Frank	4:20.9
1966	Muller, Alfred	4:25.0
1967	Poser, Udo	4:16.0
1968	Mitbauer, Heinz	4:22.6
1969	Sperling, Wolfram	4:16.0
1970	Unger, Lutz	4:15.9
1971	Sperling, Wolfram	4:12.4
1972	Sperling, Wolfram	4:09.4
1973	Pyttel, Roger	4:06.58
1974	Pyttel, Roger	4:07.30
1975	Strohbach, Rainer	4:04.69

1,500 m. Free-style

1960	Kutschke, Karl - H	18:51.9
1961	Hunga, Heinz	19:09.4
1962	Herbst, Joachim	18:59.8
1963	Klink, Martin	18:35.2
1964	Wiegand, Frank	17:52.8
1965	Wiegand, Frank	17:52.2
1966	Wiegand, Frank	17:29.1
1967	Muller, Alfred	17:25.4
1968	Mann, Karl - R	17:03.8
1969	Sperling, Wolfram	17:05.7
1970	Sperling, Wolfram	16:59.6
1971	Sperling, Wolfram	16:56.4
1972	Freudenberg, Axel	16:37.1
1973	Meier, Andras	16:32.05
1974	Pfuetze, Frank	16:26.12
1975	Strohbach, Rainer	16:14.03

100 m. Back-stroke

1960	Wagner, Wolfram	1:03.0
1961	Wagner, Wolfram	1:03.6
1962	Dietze, Jurgen	1:03.7
1963	Wagner, Wolfram	1:04.0
1964	Dietze, Jurgen	1:01.9
1965	Dietze, Jurgen	1:02.4
1966	Dietze, Jurgen	1:02.0
1967	Rother, Joachim	1:02.7
1968	Matthes, Roland	59.3
1970	Matthes, Roland	58.3
1971	Matthes, Roland	58.3
1972	Matthes, Roland	56.8
1973	Wanja, Lutz	1:00.33
1974	Matthes, Roland	57.39
1975	Matthes, Roland	57.80

200 m. Back-stroke (instituted 1961)

1961	Wagner, Wolfram	2:20.6
1962	Wagner, Wolfram	2:21.7
1963	Wagner, Wolfram	2:20.0
1964	Wagner, Wolfram	2:18.3
1965	Rother, Joachim	2:16.7
1966	Kunze, Roland	2:17.0
1967	Rother, Joachim	2:13.2

1968	Matthes, Roland	2:07.5
1969	Matthes, Roland	2:06.4
1970	Matthes, Roland	2:07.4
1971	Matthes, Roland	2:06.9
1972	Matthes, Roland	2:02.8
1973	Wanja, Lutz	2:10.46
1974	Matthes, Roland	2:04.84
1975	Matthes, Roland	2:05.85

100 m. Breast-stroke (instituted 1961)

1961	Tittes, Gunter	1:11.8
1962	Henninger, Egon	1:12.3
1963	Henninger, Egon	1:09.8
1964	Henninger, Egon	1:10.2
1965	Henninger, Egon	1:08.5
1966	Henninger, Egon	1:08.8
1967	Katzur, Klaus	1:11.5
1968	Henninger, Egon	1:07.3
1969	Henninger, Egon	1:08.3
1970	Henninger, Egon	1:08.1
1971	Katzur, Klaus	1:07.9
1972	Katzur, Klaus	1:07.7
1973	Glas, Jurgen	1:08.34
1974	Sperling, Wolfram	1:08.96
1975	Arnicke, Gregor	1:09.20

200 m. Breast-stroke

1960	Henninger, Egon	2:39.0
1961	Henninger, Egon	2:40.2
1962	Henninger, Egon	2:40.1
1963	Henninger, Egon	2:36.5
1964	Messner, Wilhelm	2:37.2
1965	Katzur, Klaus	2:31.4
1966	Henninger, Egon	2:32.0
1967	Katzur, Klaus	2:34.4
1968	Henninger, Egon	2:28.2
1969	Katzur, Klaus	2:27.2
1970	Henninger, Egon	2:29.3
1971	Appelt, Dieter	2:31.2
1972	Katzur, Klaus	2:26.2
1973	Glas, Jurgen	2:26.02
1974	Walter, Michael	2:29.34
1975	Glas, Jurgen	2:28.78

100 m. Butterfly (instituted 1961)

1961	Bachmann, Jurgen	1:04.9
1962	Gregor, Horst-Gunther	1:02.3
1963	Gregor, Horst-Gunther	1:01.1
1964	Somer, Peter	1:01.1
1965	Somer, Peter	59.3
1966	Gregor, Horst-Gunther	59.3
1967	Schock, Guntram	1:00.3
1968	Schock, Guntram	1:00.2
1969	Poser, Udo	58.1
1970	Poser, Udo	1:00.4
1971	Matthes, Roland	56.1
1972	Matthes, Roland	56.5

1973	Pyttel, Roger	57.08
1974	Pyttel, Roger	56.62
1975	Pyttel, Roger	56.17

200 m. Butterfly

1960	Millow, Ulrich	2:22.7
1961	Sieber, Wolfgang	2:23.2
1962	Frischke, Volker	2:21.6
1963	Frischke, Volker	2:20.2
1964	Gregor, Horst-Gunther	2:16.4
1965	Gregor, Horst-Gunther	2:14.9
1966	Gregor, Horst-Gunther	2:11.5
1967	Poser, Udo	2:14.7
1968	Gregor, Horst-Gunther	2:14.0
1969	Poser, Udo	2:08.1
1970	Poser, Udo	2:12.7
1971	Flockner, Hartmut	2:09.8
1972	Pyttel, Roger	2:06.9
1973	Flockner, Hartmut	2:06.02
1974	Pyttel, Roger	2:05.40
1975	Pyttel, Roger	2:02.39

200 m. Individual medley (instituted 1967)

1967	Baldermann, Gunter	2:19.7
1968	Matthes, Roland	2:13.9
1969	Matthes, Roland	2:14.8
1970	Matthes, Roland	2:12.8
1971	Tuerpe, Bertram	2:16.0
1972	Sperling, Wolfram	2:11.1
1973	Pyttel, Roger	2:10.06
1974	Lietzmann, Christian	2:08.35
1975	Wanja, Lutz	2:12.15

400 m. Individual medley (instituted 1962)

1962	Bachmann, Jurgen	5:16.6
1963	Pfeifer, Wolfgang	5:11.7
1964	Wiegand, Frank	5:03.2
1965	Katzur, Klaus	4:59.9
1966	Wiegand, Frank	4:55.4
1967	Baldermann, Gunter	5:00.7
1968	Pechmann, Matthias	4:56.4
1969	Pechmann, Matthias	4:48.8
1970	Pechmann, Matthias	4:47.6
1971	Tuerpe, Bertram	4:48.3
1972	Sperling, Wolfram	4:38.9
1973	Sperling, Wolfram	4:37.71
1974	Lietzmann, Christian	4:34.74
1975	Bohmert, Steffen	4:41.63

WOMEN

100 m. Free-style

1960	Steffin, Christel	1:04.3
1961	Pechstein, Heidi	1:05.5
1962	Schumacher, Rita	1:05.4
1963	Schumacher, Rita	1:04.5
1964	Pechstein, Heidi	1:03.9
1965	Grunert, Martina	1:02.6
1966	Schumacher, Rita	1:02.5
1967	Perthes, Gabriele	1:03.9
1968	Grunert, Martina	1:01.4
1969	Wetzko, Gabriele	1:00.6
1970	Wtezko, Gabriele	1:01.1
1971	Wetzko, Gabriele	1:00.8
1972	Wetzko, Gabriele	1:00.2
1973	Ender, Kornelia	58.25
1974	Ender, Kornelia	57.51
1975	Ender, Kornelia	56.65

200 m. Free-style (instituted 1961)

1961	Pechstein, Heidi	2:25.0
1962	Zimmermann, Helga	2:25.5
1963	Zimmermann, Helga	2:22.2
1964	Grunert, Martina	2:22.1
1965	Grunert, Martina	2:18.5
1966	Not held	
1967	Pechstein, Heidi	2:16.3
1968	Wetzko, Gabriele	2:15.2
1969	Wetzko, Gabriele	2:12.7
1970	Tuelling, Karin	2:13.8
1971	Wetzko, Gabriele	2:10.7
1972	Eife, Andrea	2:08.1
1973	Eife, Andrea	2:05.70
1974	Franke, Angela	2:05.25
1975	Ender, Kornelia	2:02.36

400 m. Free-style

1960	Zimmermann, Helga	5:04.3
1961	Weiss, Gisela	5:14.0
1962	Zimmermann, Helga	5:08.0
1963	Zimmermann, Helga	4:57.0
1964	Grunert, Martina	4:59.0
1965	Grunert, Martina	4:56.6
1966	Wanke, Jutta	4:57.0
1967	Pechstein, Heidi	4:48.9
1968	Wetzko, Gabriele	4:44.9
1969	Wetzko, Gabriele	4:38.7
1970	Tuelling, Karin	4:40.8
1971	Wegner, Gudrun	4:36.2
1972	Eife, Andrea	4:29.3
1973	Eife, Andrea	4:27.96
1974	Franke, Angela	4:22.19
1975	Bruckner, Ute	4:20.86

800 m. Free-style (instituted 1967)

1967	Pechstein, Heidi	10:02.5
1968	Goral, Sigrid	9:43.5
1969	Neugebauer, Karin	9:47.4
1970	Neugebauer, Karin	9:33.8
1971	Tuelling, Karin	9:26.4
1972	Wegner, Gudrun	9:10.5
1973	Wegner, Gudrun	9:11.93

| 1974 | Dörr, Cornelia | 9:02.86 |
| 1975 | Dörr, Cornelia | 8:56.59 |

100 m. Back-stroke

1960	Schmidt, Ingrid	1:12.2
1961	Schmidt, Ingrid	1:12.2
1962	Holletz, Veronika	1:11.9
1963	Schmidt, Ingrid	1:10.9
1964	Nerger, Petra	1:11.9
1965	Holletz, Veronika	1:12.2
1966	Kohler, Brigitte	1:11.7
1967	Boes, Susanne	1:12.7
1968	Hofmeister, Barbara	1:11.0
1969	Hofmeister, Barbara	1:09.3
1970	Hofmeister, Barbara	1:09.2
1971	Hofmeister, Barbara	1:10.4
1972	Hilger, Susanne	1:08.4

1973	Richter, Ulrike	1:07.00
1974	Richter, Ulrike	1:04.43
1975	Richter, Ulrike	1:03.52

200 m. Back-stroke (instituted 1963)

1963	Schmidt, Ingrid	2:32.2
1964	Nerger, Petra	2:34.1
1965	Kohler, Brigitte	2:35.8
1966	Kohler, Brigitte	2:34.0
1967	Kohardt, Doris	2:34.0
1968	Kohardt, Doris	2:33.5
1969	Hofmeister, Barbara	2:29.9
1970	Hofmeister, Barbara	2:28.6
1971	Hofmeister, Barbara	2:28.5
1972	Herbst, Christine	2:25.7

1973	Eife, Andrea	2:22.34
1974	Richter, Ulrike	2:18.41
1975	Treiber, Birgit	2:16.10

100 m. Breast-stroke (instituted 1961)

1961	Beyer, Karin	1:19.8
1962	Beyer, Karin	1:19.6
1963	Grimmer, Barbel	1:20.0
1964	Grimmer, Barbel	1:20.2
1965	Grimmer, Barbel	1:19.7
1966	Hansel, Marion	1:20.1
1967	Dehmlow, Martina	1:20.3
1968	Wittke, Eva	1:19.6
1969	Solsky, Christina	1:19.4
1970	Schuchardt, Brigitte	1:18.1
1971	Vogel, Renate	1:17.9
1972	Schuchardt, Brigitte	1:16.4

1973	Vogel, Renate	1:15.30
1974	Vogel, Renate	1:14.58
1975	Anke, Hannelore	1:12.93

200 m. Breast-stroke

1960	Goebel, Barbara	2:53.0
1961	Beyer, Karin	2:54.1
1962	Beyer, Karin	2:51.0

1963	Grimmer, Barbel	2:49.4
1964	Grimmer, Barbel	2:52.7
1965	Grimmer, Barbel	2:47.9
1966	Grimmer, Barbel	2:52.5
1967	Wittke, Eva	2:52.8
1968	Wittke, Eva	2:50.0
1969	Schuchardt, Brigitte	2:50.0
1970	Schuchardt, Brigitte	2:45.1
1971	Vogel, Renate	2:43.5
1972	Schuchardt, Brigitte	2:45.4

1973	Anke, Hannelore	2:44.19
1974	Schott, Anne-Kathrin	2:37.89
1975	Anke, Hannelore	2:38.02

100 m. Butterfly

1960	Fuhrmann, Barbel	1:13.9
1961	Fuhrmann, Barbel	1:12.5
1962	Fuhrmann-von Fircks, Barbel	1:10.7
1963	Noack, Ute	1:08.8
1964	Noack, Ute	1:09.6
1965	Lindner, Helga	1:10.2
1966	Lindner, Helga	1:09.6
1967	Strubing, Christina	1:10.1
1968	Lindner, Helga	1:08.5
1969	Lindner, Helga	1:06.8
1970	Lindner, Helga	1:07.6
1971	Lindner, Helga	1:07.0
1972	Kother, Rosemarie	1:04.9

1973	Ender, Kornelia	1:02.31
1974	Ender, Kornelia	1:02.86
1975	Ender, Kornelia	1:01.33

200 m. Butterfly (instituted 1963)

1963	Fuhrmann-von Fircks, Barbel	2:37.3
1964	Noack, Ute	2:39.4
1965	Lindner, Helga	2:34.7
1966	Lindner, Helga	2:32.7
1967	Strubing, Christina	2:35.0
1968	Lindner, Helga	2:27.2
1969	Lindner, Helga	2:22.3
1970	Lindner, Helga	2:23.0
1971	Lindner, Helga	2:22.1
1972	Kother, Rosemarie	2:19.5

1973	Kother, Rosemarie	2:16.03
1974	Kother, Rosemarie	2:15.96
1975	Kother, Rosemarie	2:14.83

200 m. Individual medley (instituted 1967)

1967	Seydel, Marianne	2:34.7
1968	Seydel, Marianne	2:32.3
1969	Grunert, Martina	2:30.7
1970	Grunert, Martina	2:29.1
1971	Ender, Kornelia	2:30.8
1972	Ender, Kornelia	2:28.1

1973	Ender, Kornelia	2:23.40
1974	Franke, Angela	2:21.46
1975	Tauber, Ulrike	2:18.83

400 m. Individual medley (instituted 1962)

1962	Blank, Harriet	5:42.7
1963	Zimmermann, Helga	5:42.3
1964	Holletz, Veronika	5:39.8
1965	Holletz, Veronika	5:31.4
1966	Pechstein, Heidi	5:28.6
1967	Wittke, Eva	
1968	Steinbach, Sabine	5:21.1
1969	Baumann, Sabine	5:23.0
1970	Stolze, Evelyn	5:17.7
1971	Schuchardt, Brigitte	5:17.5
1972	Stolze, Evelyn	5:11.9
1973	Wegner, Gudrun	5:05.37
1974	Tauber, Ulrike	4:57.76
1975	Tauber, Ulrike	4:52.2*

EDERLE, Gertrude (United States, 23 Oct. 1906-). Ederle has two claims to fame, as an Olympic medallist and a conqueror of the English Channel. Her Olympic successes were in 1924 when she won bronze medals in the 100 and 400 m. free-style and a gold in America's winning free-style relay team. In her amateur swimming days she also broke nine world records—from 100 to 500 m., her times being: 72.8 (100 m.), 2:45.2 (200 m. s/c), 2:46.8 (220 y. s/c), 3:58.4 (100 y.), 5:53.2 (400 m.), 5:54.6 (400 y.), 6:45.2 (500 y.), 7:22.2 (500 m.) and 13:19.0 (880 y.).

Gertrude turned professional in 1925 —after winning six United States outdoor titles—and a year later became the first woman to swim the English Channel. Her 14 hr. 39 min. from France to England, fifty-one years after Matthew Webb had made the first crossing, was faster than any man before her.

EDWARDS, Margaret (Great Britain, 28 Mar. 1939-). Unlucky is the word to describe Margaret Edwards from Heston, whose years among the top backstrokers in the world coincided with the era of an even greater British back-stroke swimmer Judy Grinham (see GRINHAM, Judy).

Petite, dark-haired Margaret was overshadowed physically by her Middlesex county team-mate Judy, yet she broke four world records and won Olympic, European and Commonwealth medals.

She was third behind Judy in the 1956 Olympic 100 m. only months after being in a plaster cast because of a slipped disc. And she was second to her great rival in the 1958 Commonwealth Games in Cardiff and European championships in Budapest.

Blue-eyed Margaret set her first world mark for 110 y. (1:13.5) in Blackpool in 1957 and, swimming again ten minutes later in a relay, lost her record to Gretje Kraan of Holland. Margaret set new figures in a heat at the Cardiff Games (1:12.3), then watching from the bathside, saw Judy clip this to 1:11.9 in the final.

The best tribute to Margaret comes from her old rival Judy, who says: 'I could never have achieved the things I did if Margaret had not been there to challenge all the time.'

ELECTRICAL TIMING. See TIMING.

EMPIRE GAMES. See COMMONWEALTH GAMES.

EMPIRE GAMES CHAMPIONS. See COMMONWEALTH GAMES CHAMPIONS.

ENDER, Kornelia (East Germany, 25 Oct. 1958-). This tall (5' 10''/178 cm.) and powerful girl was only 14 when she became the first European in 17 years to be the fastest sprinter in the world and follow in the famous steps of Australia's great Lorraine Crapp, Dawn Fraser and Shane Gould (see biographies).

It was on 13 July, 1973 that Ender took 0.25 of a sec. off Gould's world record with 58.25. And in the following two years with seven more unchallenged marks, she took her time down to 56.22.

Super-fit Kornelia compiled a formidable medal list in the three years to 1975 . . . four golds (100 m. free-style and butterfly, free-style and medley relays) and a silver (200 m. medley) at the first World championships in Belgrade 1973 . . . four golds (100/200 m. free-style and both relays) at the European championships in Vienna, '74 . . . four golds (100 m. free-style and butterfly and both relays) and a silver (200 m. free-style) at the World championships in Cali in 1975, to add to the three silvers (200 m. medley and both relays) at the 1972 Munich Olympic Games.

Mark Spitz of the United States proudly wearing the seven gold medals he won at the 1972 Olympic Games in Munich. This was the highest number gained by any competitor in any sport at a single Games. He won the 100 and 200 m. freestyle and butterfly and was in America's three winning relay teams. Spitz also won two more golds, in relays, in 1968

The victorious East German medley relay squad: (*from the left*) Kornelia Ender (free-style), Rosemary Kother (butterfly), Renate Vogel (breast-stroke) and Ulrike Richter (back-stroke), who cut four seconds off the world record in winning this event at the first World championships in Belgrade in 1973

Australian free-style world-record breakers: (*left to right*) Ilsa Konrads, Sandra Morgan, Lorraine Crapp and Dawn Fraser. Miss Konrads set 12 distance world records; Miss Morgan was a member of two Australian record-breaking relay teams; Miss Crapp was the first woman to break five minutes for 400 m.; and Miss Fraser, winner of the 100 m. at three Olympics, was the first woman to go under the minute for this distance

The Olympic trail-blazers. Alfréd Hajós (*top left*), of Hungary, the first Olympic swimming champion who won two titles in Athens in 1896, almost bowed down under the weight of his medal haul; his countryman, Zoltán Halmay (*right*) winner of seven medals at three Games between 1900 and 1908 and (*below*) Britain's John Jarvis, Olympic 1,000 and 4,000 m. gold medallist in 1900 and the self-styled amateur swimming champion of the world with his collection of trophies

Johnny Weissmuller of the United States (*right*), winner of five Olympic golds, with Australia's Boy Charlton, the 1,500 m. champion, at the 1924 Games in Paris and (*below*), a life-time later, Weissmuller with his young countryman Don Schollander, who won the 100 and 400 m. free-style titles and a third gold in the 4 x 200 m. relay at the 1964 Tokyo Olympics—a hat-trick that Johnny had achieved 40 years earlier. Schollander also won a fourth gold in the 4 x 100 m. free-style relay in Japan —an event not in the Olympic programme in Weissmuller's day

British Olympic champions, separated by 48 years! *Above*, the first Olympic women's relay champion team, the British squad, at the 1912 Games in Stockholm. The swimmers were (*left to right*) Bella Moore, Jennie Fletcher—who also won the individual 100 m. bronze—Annie Speirs and Irene Steer. In the centre is the chaperone Clara Jarvis, a sister of Olympic champion John Jarvis. *Left*, the moment of sheer delight for Anita Lonsbrough after her victory in the 200 m. breaststroke at the 1960 Games

Right
Smiling Shane Gould, from Australia, on the medal rostrum with her Koala bear mascot, the way she will be remembered always by the thousands who saw her triple gold medal triumphs at the Munich Olympic Games of 1972

America's world record-breaking trio: Tim Shaw (*top*), winner of three titles at the second World championships in Cali, Colombia, in 1975 and the Furniss brothers—Steve (*centre*), the elder, the 200 and 400 m. medley Pan-American champion in 1971 and 1975, and Bruce (*below*), who took away world records from both Tim and Steve in 1975

Her Belgrade performance earned her a special trophy as the outstanding individual competitor of the meeting. She was the most successful woman in Austria and might well have won a fifth title, the 100 m. butterfly, for which she was then the world record-holder, had the programme not made it difficult for her to tackle this event.

And in Cali she, again, was the top performer, man or woman and received another special award.

Between April 1973 and August 1975, Ender broke 15 world marks—eight for 100 m. free-style, two for 200 m. free-style, four for 100 m. butterfly and one for 200 m. medley.

Her fastest times are 100 m. free-style 56.22, 200 m. free-style 2:02.27, 100 m. butterfly 1:01.24 and 200 m. medley 2:23.01.

ENGLISH DIVER OF THE YEAR. See HEARN, GEORGE, CUP.

ENGLISH DIVING CHAMPIONS. See A.S.A. DIVING CHAMPIONS.

ENGLISH DIVING CLUB OF THE YEAR. See MELVILLE CLARKE, NATIONAL MEMORIAL TROPHY, and WHITE, BELLE, NATIONAL MEMORIAL TROPHY.

ENGLISH PLUNGING CHAMPIONS. See A.S.A. PLUNGING CHAMPIONS.

ENGLISH SWIMMER OF THE YEAR. See YEADEN MEMORIAL TROPHY.

ENGLISH SWIMMING CHAMPIONS. See A.S.A. SWIMMING CHAMPIONS.

ENGLISH SWIMMING CLUB OF THE YEAR—MEN. See BENJAMIN, HENRY, NATIONAL MEMORIAL TROPHY.

ENGLISH SWIMMING CLUB OF THE YEAR—WOMEN. See FERN, HAROLD, NATIONAL TROPHY.

ENGLISH WATER-POLO CHAMPIONS. See A.S.A. WATER-POLO, CHAMPIONS.

ENGLISH SYNCHRONIZED SWIMMING CHAMPIONS. See A.S.A. SYNCHRONIZED SWIMMING CHAMPIONS.

EUROPEAN CHAMPIONSHIPS. The first European Championships were held in Budapest in 1926 through the initiative of Hungary, who had pressed for the inauguration of such a Continental event before the First World War. At that time no official European body existed to give title to the competitions. But as a result of this first meeting a European Swimming League was founded (see LIGUE EUROPENNE DE NATATION). The venues and dates of the European championships are:

No.	Venue	Dates
I	Budapest, Hungary	18 Aug.—22 Aug., 1926
II	Bologna, Italy	31 Aug.—4 Sept., 1927
III	Paris, France	23 Aug.—30 Aug., 1931
IV	Magdeburg, Germany	12 Aug.—19 Aug., 1934
V	London, England	6 Aug.—13 Aug., 1938
VI	Monte Carlo, Monaco	10 Sept.—14 Sept., 1947
VII	Vienna, Austria	20 Aug.—27 Aug., 1950
VIII	Turin, Italy	31 Aug.—5 Sept., 1954
IX	Budapest, Hungary	31 Aug.—6 Sept., 1958
X	Leipzig, East Germany	18 Aug.—25 Aug., 1962
XI	Utrecht, Netherlands	20 Aug.—27 Aug., 1966
XII	Barcelona, Spain	5 Sept.—12 Sept., 1970
XIII	Vienna, Austria	18 Aug.—25 Aug., 1974
XIV	Jönköping, Sweden	13 Aug.—21 Aug., 1977

EUROPEAN CHAMPIONSHIPS MEDALLISTS

MEN

100 m. Free-style

1926	Barany, Istvan (Hun)	1:01.0
1927	Borg, Arne (Swe)	1:00.0
1931	Barany, Istvan (Hun)	59.8
1934	Csik, Ferenc (Hun)	59.7
1938	Hoving, Karl (Neth)	59.8
1947	Jany, Alex (Fr)	56.9
	Olsson, Per-Ola (Swe)	58.8
	Szathmári, Elemér (Hun)	59.6
1950	Jany, Alex (Fr)	57.7
	Larsson, Göran (Swe)	59.4
	Tjebbes, Joris (Neth)	1:00.0
1954	Nyéki, Imre (Hun)	57.8
	Balandin, Lev (USSR)	58.2
	Kádas, Géza (Hun)	58.3
1958	Pucci, Paolo (Ita)	56.3
	Polevoj, Victor (USSR)	56.9
	Dobai, Gyula (Hun)	57.5
1962	Gottvalles, Alain (Fr)	55.0
	Lindberg, Per-Ola (Swe)	55.5
	Kroon, Ronnie (Neth)	55.5
1966	McGregor, Bobby (GB)	53.7
	Ilichev, Leonid (USSR)	54.3
	Poser, Udo (E Ger)	54.8
1970	Rousseau, Michel (Fr)	52.9
	Matthes, Roland (E Ger)	53.5
	Kulikov, Georgy (USSR)	53.7
1974	Nocke, Peter (W Ger)	52.18
	Bure, Vladimir (USSR)	52.19
	Steinbach, Klaus (W Ger)	53.31

200 m. Free-style

1970	Fassnacht, Hans (W Ger)	1:55.2
	Larsson, Gunnar (Swe)	1:55.7
	Kulikov, Georgy (USSR)	1:56.6
1974	Nocke, Peter (W Ger)	1:53.10
	Steinbach, Klaus (W Ger)	1:53.72
	Samsonov, Aleksandr (USSR)	1:53.74

400 m. Free-style

1926	Borg, Arne (Swe)	5:14.2
1927	Borg, Arne (Swe)	5:08.6
1931	Barany, Istvan (Hun)	5:04.0
1934	Taris, Jean (Fr)	4:55.5
1938	Borg, Bjorn (Swe)	4:51.6
1947	Jany, Alex (Fr)	4:35.2
	Mitró, György (Hun)	4:50.4
	Bartusek, Miloslav (Czech)	4:51.4
1950	Jany, Alex (Fr)	4:48.0
	Boiteux, Jean (Fr)	4:50.1
	Lehmann, Heinz (Ger)	4:51.2
1954	Csordas, György (Hun)	4:38.8
	Romani, Angelo (Ita)	4:40.4
	Ostrand, Per-Ola (Swe)	4:40.9
1958	Black, Ian (GB)	4:31.3
	Nikitin, Boris (USSR)	4:36.2
	Galetti, Paolo (Ita)	4:38.1
1962	Bontekoe, Johan (Neth)	4:25.6
	Rosendahl, Hans (Swe)	4:25.8
	Wiegand, Frank (E Ger)	4:26.8
1966	Wiegand, Frank (E Ger)	4:11.1
	Belits-Geiman, Semeòn (USSR)	4:13.2
	Mosconi, Alain (Fr)	4:13.6
1970	Larsson, Gunnar (Swe)	4:02.6
	Fassnacht, Hans (W Ger)	4:03.0
	Esteva, Santiago (Sp)	4:08.3
1974	Samsonov, Aleksandr (USSR)	4:02.11
	Gingsjö, Bengt (Swe)	4:03.79
	Krylov, Andrey (USSR)	4:04.32

1,500 m. Free-style

1926	Borg, Arne (Swe)	21:29.2
1927	Borg, Arne (Swe)	19:07.2
1931	Halasy, Oliver (Hun)	20:49.0
1934	Taris, Jean (Fr)	20:01.5
1938	Borg, Bjorn (Swe)	19:55.6
1947	Mitró, György (Hun)	19:28.0
	Voros, Ferenc (Hun)	20:07.0
	Stipetic, Marjan (Yug)	20:08.5
1950	Lehman, Heinz (Ger)	18:34.6
	Boiteux, Jean (Fr)	18:39.0
	Bernardo, Joseph (Fr)	20:06.7
1954	Csordas, György (Hun)	18:57.8
	Schuszter, György (Hun)	19:05.6
	Lavrinenko, Vladimir (USSR)	19:10.6
1958	Black, Ian (GB)	18:05.8
	Katona, József (Hun)	18:13.0
	Androsov, Gennady (USSR)	18:30.2
1962	Katona, Jozsef (Hun)	17:49.5
	Torres, Miguel (Sp)	17:55.6
	Campion, Richard (GB)	17:59.8
1966	Belits-Geiman, Semeòn (USSR)	16:58.5
	Kimber, Alan (GB)	17:13.2
	Pletnev, Aleksandr (USSR)	17:17.9

1970	Fassnacht, Hans (W Ger)	16:19.9
	Lampe, Werner (W Ger)	16:25.6
	Esteva, Santiago (Sp)	16:35.7

1974	Pfuetz, Frank (E Ger)	15:54.57
	Carter, Jimmy (GB)	15:54.78
	Evgrafov, Igor (USSR)	16:04.42

100 m. Back-stroke
1926	Frolich, Gustav (Ger)	1:16.0
1927	Lundahl, Eksil (Swe)	1:17.4
1931	Deutsch, Gerhard (Ger)	1:14.8
1934	Besford, John (GB)	1:11.7
1938	Schlauch, Hans (Ger)	1:09.0

1947	Vallerey, Georges (Fr)	1:07.6
	Valent, Gyula (Hun)	1:10.5
	Kovar, Jiri (Czech)	1:10.5

1950	Larsson, Göran (Swe)	1:09.4
	Kievit, Kees (Neth)	1:09.7
	Skanata, Boris (Yug)	1:10.8

1954	Bozon, Gilbert (Fr)	1:05.1
	Magyar, László (Hun)	1:05.3
	Brockway, John (GB)	1:05.9

1958	Christophe, Robert (Fr)	1:03.1
	Barbier, Leonid (USSR)	1:03.9
	Wagner, Wolfram (E Ger)	1:05.5

| 1962 | No event |
| 1966 | No event |

1970	Matthes, Roland (E Ger)	58.9
	Esteva, Santiago (Sp)	59.9
	Schoutsen, Bob (Neth)	1:00.4

1974	Matthes, Roland (E Ger)	58.21
	Wanja, Lutz (E Ger)	58.66
	Verrasztó, Zoltán (Hun)	58.78

200 m. Back-stroke
1962	Barbier, Leonid (USSR)	2:16.6
	Wagner, Wolfgang (E Ger)	2:17.9
	Csikány, József (Hun)	2:18.5

1966	Gromak, Yury (USSR)	2:12.9
	Monzo, Jamie (Sp)	2:15.7
	Rother, Joachim (E Ger)	2:16.7

1970	Matthes, Roland (E Ger)	2:08.8
	Esteva, Santiago (Sp)	2:09.7
	Werner, Volker (E Ger)	2:11.5

1974	Matthes, Roland (E Ger)	2:04.64
	Verrasztó, Zoltán (Hun)	2:04.96
	Rudolf, Robert (Hun)	2:07.52

100 m. Breast-stroke
1970	Pankin, Nikolay (USSR)	1:06.8
	Menu, Roger-Philippe (Fr)	1:07.8
	Klees, Rolf (W Ger)	1:08.1

1974	Pankin, Nikolay (USSR)	1:05.63
	Kusch, Walter (W Ger)	1:06.04
	Leigh, David (GB)	1:06.17

200 m. Breast-stroke
1926	Rademacher, Erich (Ger)	2:52.6
1927	Rademacher, Erich (Ger)	2:55.2
1931	Reingoldt, Toivi (Fin)	2:52.2
1934	Sietas, Erwin (Ger)	2:49.0
1938	Balke, Joachim (Ger)	2:45.8

1947	Romain, Roy	Bu2:40.1
	Nemeth, Sándor (Hun)	Bu2:41.6
	Cerer, Anton (Yug)	Bu2:46.2

1950	Klein, Herbert (Ger)	Bu2:38.6
	Lusien, Maurice (Fr)	Bu2:40.9
	Rask, Bengt (Swe)	Bu2:43.8

1954	Bodinger, Klaus (E Ger)	2:40.9
	Petrusewicz, Marek (Pol)	2:42.5
	Utassy, Sándor (Hun)	2:43.4

1958	Kolesnikov, Leonid (USSR)	2:41.1
	Lazzari, Roberto (Ita)	2:41.3
	Bodinger, Klaus (E Ger)	2:41.4

1962	Prokopenko, Georgy (USSR)	2:32.8
	Karetnikov, Ivan (USSR)	2:33.2
	Empel, Rob van (Neth)	2:38.1

1966	Prokopenko, Georgy (USSR)	2:30.0
	Tutakaef, Aleksandr (USSR)	2:30.3
	Henninger, Egon (E Ger)	2:30.5

1970	Katzur, Klaus (E Ger)	2:26.0
	Pankin, Nikolay (USSR)	2:26.1
	Kusch, Walter (W Ger)	2:28.2

1974	Wilkie, David (GB)	2:20.42
	Pankin, Nikolai (USSR)	2:22.84
	Leigh, David (GB)	2:23.79

Bu = won on butterfly before the separation of breast-stroke and butterfly in 1954.

100 m. Butterfly
1970	Lampe, Hans (W Ger)	57.6
	Poser, Udo, (E Ger)	57.9
	Nemshilov, Vladimir (USSR)	58.0

1974	Pyttel, Roger (E Ger)	55.90
	Matthes, Roland (E Ger)	56.68
	Meeuw, Folkert (W Ger)	57.60

200 m. Butterfly
1954	Tumpek, György (Hun)	2:32.2
	Fejer, Zsolt (Hun)	2:35.1
	Martinchik, Vagyin (USSR)	2:36.3

1958	Black, Ian (GB)	2:21.9
	Pazdirek, Pavel (Czech)	2:22.6
	Symonds, Graham (GB)	2:25.8
1962	Kuzmin, Valentin (USSR)	2:14.2
	Jenkins, Brian (GB)	2:15.6
	Sieber, Wolfgang (E Ger)	2:18.0
1966	Kuzmin, Valentin (USSR)	2:10.2
	Gregor, Horst (E Ger)	2:10.6
	Skavronsky, Anatoly (USSR)	
		2:11.2
1970	Poser, Udo (E Ger)	2:08.0
	Meeuw, Folkert (W Ger)	2:08.2
	Flockner, Hartmut (E Ger)	2:09.6

- -

1974	Hargitay, András (Hun)	2:03.08
	Brinkley, Brian (GB)	2:04.13
	Flöckner, Hartmut (E Ger)	
		2:04.55

200 m. Individual medley
1970	Larsson, Gunnar (Swe)	2:09.3
	Pechmann, Matthias (E Ger)	
		2:13.5
	Ljungberg, Hans (Swe)	2:14.3

- -

1974	Wilkie, David (GB)	2:06.32
	Lietzmann, Christian (E Ger)	
		2:07.61
	Hargitay, András (Hun)	2:09.08

400 m. Individual medley
1962	Androsov, Gennady (USSR)	
		5:01.3
	Jiskoot, Jan (Neth)	5:05.5
	Bachman, Jurgen (E Ger)	5:05.9
1966	Wiegand, Frank (E Ger)	4:47.9
	Dunaev, Andrey (USSR)	4:48.7
	Katzur, Klaus (E Ger)	4:55.7
1970	Larsson, Gunnar (Swe)	4:36.2
	Fassnacht, Hans (W Ger)	4:36.9
	Pechmann, Matthias (E Ger)	
		4:40.6

- -

1974	Hargitay, András (Hun)	4:28.89
	Lietzmann, Christian (E Ger)	
		4:30.32
	Smirnov, Andrey (USSR)	4:32.48

4 x 100 m. Free-style relay
1962 France   3:43.7
(Gropaiz, Gerard; Christophe, Robert; Curtillet, Jean-Pasqual; Gottvalles, Alain)
     Great Britain   3:44.7
(Clarke, Stan; Kendrew, Peter; Martin-Dye, John; McGregor, Bobby)
     Sweden   3:45.0
(Svensson, Mats; Lundin, Jan; Nord-Wall, Bengt; Lindberg, Per-Ola)

| 1966 | East Germany | 3:36.8 |

(Wiegand, Frank; Poser, Udo; Gregor, Horst-G; Sommer, Peter)
     USSR   3:37.5
(Ilichev, Leonid; Mazanov, Victor; Kulikov, Georgy; Shuvalov, Vladimir)
     Sweden   3:39.0
(Eriksson, Lester; Jansson, Göran; Eriksson, Ingvar; Lundin, Jan)

1970 USSR   3:32.3
(Bure, Vladimir; Mazanov, Victor Kulikov, Georgy; Ilichev, Leonid)
     West Germany   3:34.1
(Schiller, Jurgen; Jacob, Rainer; Meeuw, Folkert; Fassnacht, Hans)
     East Germany   3:34.6
(Matthes, Roland; Unger, Lutz; Seebald, Frank; Poser, Udo)

- -

1974 West Germany   3:30.61
(Steinbach, Klaus; Schiller, Gerhard; Meier, Kersten; Nocke, Peter)
     USSR   3:32.01
(Bure, Vladimir; Samsonov, Aleksandr; Ribakov, Anatoli; Kulikov, Georgy)
     East Germany   3:32.54
(Pyttel, Roger, Matthes, Roland; Hartung, Wilfried; Wanja, Lutz)

4 x 200 m. Free-style relay
1926 Germany   9:57.2
(Heitmann, August; Berges, Friedel; Rademacher, Joachim; Heinrich, Herbert)
1927 Germany   9:49.6
(Heitmann, August; Berges, Friedel; Rademacher, Joachim; Heinrich, Herbert)
1931 Hungary   9:34.0
(Szabados, Laszlo; Szekely, Andras; Wanie, Andras; Barany, Istvan)
1934 Hungary   9:30.2
(Grof, Odon; Csik, Ferenc; Marothy, Andras; Lengyel, Arpad)
1938 Germany   9:17.6
(Birr, Werner; Plath, Werner; Heimlich, Arthur; Freese, Hans)

- -

1947 Sweden   9:00.5
(Olsson, Per-Ola; Ostrand, Per-Ola; Lunden, Martin; Johansson, Olle)
     France   9:00.7
(Vallerey, Georges; Babey, Charles; Vallerey, Jehan; Jany, Alex)
     Hungary   9:01.0
(Nyéki, Imre; Mitró, György; Kádas, Géza; Szathmári, Elemér)
1950 Sweden   9:06.5
(Synnerholm, Tore; Larsson, Göran; Ostrand, Per-Ola; Johansson, Olle)

France   9:10.0
(Blioch, Willy; Boiteux, Jean; Bernardo, Joseph; Jany, Alex)
Yugoslavia   9:12.7
(Vidovic, Branko; Stipetic, Mis; Quinc, Andrej; Stipetic, Marjan)
1954 Hungary   8:47.8
(Till, Laszló; Kádas, Géza; Dömötör, Zoltan; Nyeki, Imre)
France   8:54.1
(Boiteux, Jean; Montserret, Guy; Bozon, Gilbert; Eminente, Aldo)
USSR   8:55.9
(Struzanov, Nikolay; Abovjan, Yury; Balandin, Lev; Kurrennov, Vjatcheslav)
1958 USSR   8:33.7
(Nikolayev, Gennadi; Luzkovski, Igor; Struzanov, Vladimir; Nikitin. Boris)
Italy   8:41.2
(Dennerlein, Fritz; Galetti, Paolo; Romani, Angelo; Pucci, Paolo)
Hungary   8:45.3
(Katona, József; Nyéki, Imre; Muller, Dobai, Gyula)
1962 Sweden   8:18.4
(Rosendhal, Hans; Svensson, Mats; Bengtsson, Lars-Eric; Lindberg, Per-Ola)
France   8:20.4
(Gropaiz, Gerard; Gottvalles, Alain; Curtillet, Jean-Pasqual; Christophe, Robert)
East Germany   8:24.6
(Herbst, Jochen; Klink, Martin; Wiegand, Frank; Frischke, Volker)
1966 USSR   8:00.2
(Ilichev, Leonid; Belits-Geiman, Semeòn; Pletnev, Aleksandr; Novikov) Eugeny)
East Germany   8:01.6
(Gregor, Horst-G; Muller, Alfred; Poser, Udo; Wiegand, Frank)
Sweden   8:04.3
(Eriksson, Lester; Ferm, Olle; Eriksson, Ingvar; Lundin, Jan)
1970 West Germany   7:49.5
(Lampe, Werner; von Schilling, Olaf; Meeuw, Folkert; Fassnacht, Hans)
USSR   7:52.8
(Kulikov, Georgy; Anarbaev, Achmet; Samsonov, Aleksandr; Bure, Vladimir)
East Germany   7:54.5
(Unger, Lutz; Hartung, Wilfried; Matthes, Roland; Poser, Udo)

1974 West Germany   7:39.70
(Steinbach, Klaus; Lampe, Werner; Meeuw, Folkert; Nocke, Peter)
USSR   7:42.06
(Samsonov, Aleksandr; Krylov, Andrey; Aboimov, Victor; Kulikov, Georgy)
Sweden   7:43.10
(Zarnowiecki, Bernt; Bellbring, Anders; Petterson, Peter; Gingsjö, Bengt)

4 x 100 Medley relay
1958 USSR   4:16.5
(Barbier, Leonid; Minaschkin, Vladimir; Semjenkov, Vitlay; Polevoi, Victor)
Hungary   4:20.4
(Magyar, László; Kunsagi, György; Tumpek, György; Dobai, Gyula)
Italy   4:21.9
(Elsa, Gilberta; Lazzari, Roberto; Dennerlein, Fritz; Pucci, Paolo)
1962 East Germany   4:09.0
(Dietze, Jurgen; Henninger, Egon; Gregor, Horst-G; Wiegand, Frank)
USSR   4:10.3
(Siymar, Veiko; Kuzmin, Valentin; Kolesnikov, Leonid; Konoplev, Victor)
Netherlands   4:10.9
(Weeteling, Jan; Mensonides, Wieger; Jiskoot, Jan; Kroon, Ronnie)
1966 USSR   4:02.4
(Mazanov, Victor; Prokopenko, Georgy; Kuzmin, Valentin; Illichev, Leonid)
East Germany   4:02.9
(Dietze, Jurgen; Henninger, Egon; Gregor, Horst-G; Wiegand, Frank)
Hungary   4:05.9
(Csikány, József; Lenki, Ferenc, Gyulás, Ákos; Szentirmai, István)
1970 East Germany   3:54.4
(Matthes, Roland; Katzur, Klaus; Poser, Udo; Unger, Lutz)
France   3:57.6
(Berjeau, Jean-Paul; Menu, Roger-Philippe; Mosconi, Alain; Rousseau, Michel)
USSR   3:58.0
(Krasko, Victor; Pankin, Nicolay; Nemshilov, Vladimir; Ilichev, Leonid)
1974 West Germany   3:51.57
(Steinbach, Klaus; Kusch, Walter; Meeuw, Folkert; Nocke, Peter)
Great Britain   3:54.13
(Cunningham, Colin; Wilkie, David; Nash, Steve; Brinkley, Brian)

USSR 3:54.37
(Potiakin, Igor; Pankin, Nicolay; Sharigin, Victor; Bure, Vladimir)

Springboard diving

1926	Mundt, Arthur (Ger)	186.42
1927	Riebschlager, Ewald (Ger)	172.86
1932	Riebschlager, Ewald (Ger)	136.22
1934	Esser, Leon (Ger)	137.74
1938	Weiss, Erhard (Ger)	148.02
1947	Heinkele, Roger (Fr)	126.71
	Johanson, Svante (Swe)	118.58
	Hidvégi, László (Hun)	114.40
1950	Aderhold, Hans (W Ger)	183.60
	Hernandez, Guy (Fr)	174.66
	Sobeck, Werner (W Ger)	167.98
1954	Brener, Roman (USSR)	153.20
	Udalov, Gennady (USSR)	141.61
	Pire, Christian (Fr)	136.97
1958	Ujvári, László (Hun)	141.17
	Rosenfeldt, Horst (W Ger)	139.77
	Brener, Roman (USSR)	139.99
1962	Mrkwicka, Kurt (Aut)	147.21
	Pophal, Dieter (E Ger)	145.70
	Polulyakh, Boris (USSR)	145.20
1966	Safonov, Mihail (USSR)	155.27
	Andersson, Tord (Swe)	146.30
	Cagnotto, Giorgio (Ita)	146.21
1970	Cagnotto, Giorgio (Ita)	555.21
	Dibiasi, Klaus (Ita)	534.72
	Vasin, Vladimir (USSR)	529.80
1974	Dibiasi, Klaus (Ita)	603.51
	Cagnotto, Giorgio (Ita)	593.94
	Strahov, Viacheslav (USSR)	583.71

Highboard diving

1926	Luber, Hans (Ger)	110.80
1927	Luber, Hans (Ger)	114.86
1931	Staudinger, Josef (Aut)	111.82
1934	Stork, Hermann (Ger)	98.99
1938	Weiss, Erhard (Ger)	124.67
1947	Christiansen, Thomas (Den)	105.55
	Brunnhage, Lennart (Swe)	95.85
	Marchant, Louis (GB)	95.32
1950	Haase, Günther (W Ger)	158.13
	Sobeck, Werner (W Ger)	141.54
	Christiansen, Thomas (Den)	140.94
1954	Brener, Roman (USSR)	144.01
	Tchatchba, Mihail (USSR)	142.06
	Heatly, Peter (GB)	133.59

1958	Phelps, Brian (GB)	143.74
	Tchatchba, Mihail (USSR)	136.57
	Marton, Jenö (Hun)	134.68
1962	Phelps, Brian (GB)	150.81
	Sperling, Rolf (E Ger)	148.24
	Galkin, Gennady (USSR)	143.18
1966	Dibiasi, Klaus (Ita)	162.92
	Phelps, Brian (GB)	152.01
	Kowalewski, Jerzy (Pol)	143.13
1970	Matthes, Lothar (E Ger)	454.74
	Dibiasi, Klaus (Ita)	444.18
	Cagnotto, Giorgio (Ita)	435.36
1974	Dibiasi, Klaus (Ita)	562.33
	Hoffmann, Falk (E Ger)	557.28
	Gendrikson, Aleksandr (USSR)	522.61

Water-polo

1926 Hungary
(Barta, Istvan; Fazekas, Tibor; Hommonai, Marton; Kesseru, Alajos; Kesseru, Ferenc; Vertesy, Josef; Wenk, Janos)

1927 Hungary
(Barta, Istvan; Fazekas, Tibor; Hommonai, Marton; Kesseru, Alajos; Kesseru, Ferenc; Vertesy, Josef; Wenk, Janos; Czelle, Laszlo)

1931 Hungary
(Brody, Gyorgy; Ivady, Sandor; Hommonai, Marton; Halasy, Oliver; Vertsey, Josef; Nemeth, Janos; Kesseru, Alajos; Barta, Istvan; Sarkany, Miklos; Kesseru, Ferenc; Bozsi, Mihaly)

1934 Hungary
(Brody, Gorgy; Sarkany, Miklos; Hommonai, Marton; Halasy, Oliver; Brandi, Jeno; Ivadi, Sandor; Kesseru, Alajos; Nemeth, Janos; Vertesy, Josef; Kusinzky, Gyorgy; Boszi, Mihaly)

1938 Hungary
(Mezei, Ferenc; Mezei, Istvan; Sarkany, Miklos; Molnar, Istvan; Tolnai, Josef; Halassy, Oliver; Kanasy, Gyula; Kidleghy, Kalman; Brandi, Jeno; Bozsi, Mihaly; Nemeth, Janos)

1947 Italy
(Buonocore, Pasquale; Bulgarelli, Emilio; Maioni, Mario; Ognio, Geminio; Arena, Gildo; Ghira, Aldo; Signori, Giacomo; Soracco, Hugo; Pandolfini, Tullo; Pandolfini, Gianfranco; Gaorsi, Giovanni)
Sweden
Belgium

1950 Netherlands
(Van Gelder, Max; Brassem, Cor; Keetelaar, Henni; Bijslma, Gerrit; Koorevaar, Nijs; Van Feggelen, Rudi; Smol, Fritz)
Sweden
Yugoslavia

1954 Hungary
(Jeney, Laszlo; Gyarmati, Dezso; Hevesi, Istvan; Markovits, Kalman; Bolvari, Antal; Martin, Miklos; Karpati, Gyorgy; Boros, Otto; Szabo, Aladar; Szivos, Istvan; Vizvari, Gyorgy)
Yugoslavia
Italy

1958 Hungary
(Boros, Otto; Molnar, Endre; Hevesi, Istvan; Markovits, Kalman; Kanizsa, Tivadar; Domotor, Zoltan; Karpaty, Gyorgy; Jeney, Laszlo; Mayer, Mihaly; Csillay, Gyorgy; Katona, A.)
USSR
Yugoslavia

1962 Hungary
(Boros, Otto; Mayer, Mihaly; Gyarmati, Dezso; Markovits, Kalman; Karpati, Gyorgy; Domotor, Zoltan; Felkai, Laszlo; Tanizsa, Tivadar; Konrad II, Janos; Pocsik, Denes; Ambrus, Miklos)
Yugoslavia/
USSR (tied)

1966 USSR
(Guliaev, Vadim; Grabovski, Igor; Grishin, Boris; Dolgushin, Aleksandr; Kusnezov, Vladimir; Pushkarev, Valeri; Popov, Boris; Zhmudski, Vadim; Semzov, Josif; Osipov, Leonid; Semenov, Vladimir)
East Germany
Yugoslavia

1970 USSR
(Bovin, Oleg; Guilaev, Vadim; Akimov, Anatoli; Dreval, Aleksandr; Dolgushin, Aleksandr; Semenov, Vladimir; Shildovski, Aleksandr; Barkalov, Aleksei; Osipov, Leonid; Skok, Viacheslav)
Hungary
Yugoslavia

1974 Hungary
(Cservenyak, Tibor; Farago, Tamas; Gorgenyi, István; Bodnär, András; Sárosi, László; Csapo, Gabor; Szivos, István; Kasas, Zoltán; Horkai, György; Konrád III, Ferenc; Molnár, Endre)

USSR
Yugoslavia

WOMEN

100 m. Free-style
1927	Vierdag, Marie (Neth)	1:15.0
1931	Godard, Yvonne (Fr)	1:10.0
1934	Ouden, Willy den (Neth)	1:07.1
1938	Hveger, Ragnhild (Den)	1:06.2
1947	Nathansen, Fritze (Den)	1:07.8
	Termeulen, Hannie (Neth)	1:08.1
	Andersen, Greta (Den)	1:08.3
1950	Schumacher, Irma (Neth)	1:06.4
	Vaessen, Marie-Louise (Neth)	
		1:07.1
	Andersen, Greta (Den)	1:07.9
1954	Szöke, Katalin (Hun)	1:05.8
	Temes, Judit (Hun)	1:06.7
	Wielema, Gertje (Neth)	1:07.3
1958	Jobson, Kate (Swe)	1:04.7
	Gastelaars, Cockie (Neth)	1:05.0
	Grinham, Judy (GB)	1:05.4
1962	Pechstein, Heidi (E Ger)	1:03.3
	Wilkinson, Diana (GB)	1:03.3
	Tigelaar, Ineke (Neth)	1:03.3
1966	Grunert, Martina (E Ger)	1:01.2
	Túróczy, Judit (Hun)	1:02.1
	Sillett, Pauline (GB)	1:02.5
1970	Wetzko, Gabriele (E Ger)	59.6
	Segrt, Mirjana (Yugo)	1:00.8
	Jackson, Alex (GB)	1:00.8
1974	Ender, Kornelia (E Ger)	56.96
	Franke, Angela (E Ger)	57.82
	Brigitha, Enith (Neth)	58.10

200 m. Free-style
1970	Wetzko, Gabriele (E Ger)	2:08.2
	Segrt, Mirjana (Yugo)	2:11.0
	Nieber, Yvonne (E Ger)	2:12.8
1974	Ender, Kornelia (E Ger)	2:03.22
	Brigitha, Enith (Neth)	2:03.73
	Eife, Andrea (E Ger)	2:05.04

400 m. Free-style
1927	Braun, Marie (Neth)	6:11.8
1931	Braun, Marie (Neth)	5:42.0
1934	Mastenbroek, Rie (Neth)	5:27.4
1938	Hveger, Ragnhild (Den)	5:09.0
1947	Harup, Karen M. (Den)	5:18.2
	Gibson, Cathy (GB)	5:19.0
	Caroen, Fernande (Bel)	5:20.9
1950	Andersen, Greta (Den)	5:30.9
	Schumacher, Irma (Neth)	5:31.9
	Thomas, Colette (Fr)	5:37.4

1954	Sebo, Agote (Hun)	5:14.4
	Gyenge, Valéria (Hun)	5:16.3
	Ligorio, Esa (Yugo)	5:18.7
1958	Koster, Jans (Neth)	5:02.6
	Schimmel, Corrie (Neth)	5:02.6
	Rae, Nan (GB)	5:07.7
1962	Lasterie, Adrie (Neth)	4:52.4
	Tigelaar, Ineke (Neth)	4:57.3
	Ljunggren, Elizabeth (Swe)	4:58.1
1966	Mandonnaud, Claude (Fr)	4:48.2
	Kok, Ada (Neth)	4:48.7
	Sosnova, Tamara (USSR)	4:50.1
1970	Sehmisch, Elke (E Ger)	4:32.9
	Jonsson, Gunilla (Swe)	4:36.8
	Tuelling, Karen (E Ger)	4:38.0
1974	Franke, Angela (E Ger)	4:17.83
	Dörr, Cornelia (E Ger)	4:19.72
	Calligaris, Novella (Ita)	4:22.92

800 m. Free-style

1970	Neugebauer, Karin (E Ger)	9:29.1
	Boer, Linda de (Neth)	9:35.7
	Calligaris, Novella (Ita)	9:38.8
1974	Dörr, Cornelia (E Ger)	8:52.45
	Calligaris, Novella (Ita)	8:57.93
	Wegner, Gudrun (E Ger)	8:59.79

100 m. Back-stroke

1927	Turk, Willy van den (Neth)	1:24.6
1931	Braun, Marie (Neth)	1:22.8
1934	Mastenbroek, Rie (Neth)	1:20.3
1938	Kint, Cor (Neth)	1:15.0
1947	Harup, Karen (Den)	1:15.9
	Gibson, Cathy (GB)	1:16.5
	Koster (nee van Feggelen), Iet, (Neth)	1:18.0
1950	Horst, Ria van der (Neth)	1:17.1
	Herrbruck, Gertrud (W Ger)	1:17.8
	Galliard, Greet (Neth)	1:17.9
1954	Wielema, Gertje (Neth)	1:13.2
	Korte, Joke de (Neth)	1:13.6
	Symons, Pat (GB)	1:17.3
1958	Grinham, Judy (GB)	1:12.6
	Edwards, Margaret (GB)	1:12.9
	Victorova, Larisa (USSR)	1:13.9
1962	Velsen, Ria van (Neth)	1:10.5
	Winkel, Corrie (Neth)	1:10.7
	Holletz, Veronika (E Ger)	1:11.3
1966	Caron, Christine (Fr)	1:08.1
	Ludgrove, Linda (GB)	1:08.9
	Balaban, Christine (Rom)	1:09.7

1970	Lekveishvili, Tinatin (USSR)	1:07.8
	Gyarmati, Andrea (Hun)	1:07.9
	Buter, Cobie (Neth)	1:08.5
1974	Richter, Ulrike (E Ger)	1:03.03
	Tauber, Ulrike (E Ger)	1:05.07
	Brigitha, Enith (Neth)	1:05.94

200 m. Back-stroke

1970	Gyarmati, Andrea (Hun)	2:25.5
	Hofmeister, Barbara (E Ger)	2:26.6
	Lekveishvili, Tinatin (USSR)	2:27.1
1974	Richter, Ulrike (E Ger)	2:17.35
	Tauber, Ulrike (E Ger)	2:18.72
	Brigitha, Enith (Neth)	2:21.33

100 m. Breast-stroke

1970	Stepanova, Galina* (USSR)	1:15.6
	Frommater, Uta (W Ger)	1:16.9
	Grebennikova, Alla (USSR)	1:16.9
1974	Justen, Christel (W Ger)	1:12.55
	Vogel, Renate (E Ger)	1:13.69
	Kaczander, Agnes (Hun)	1:14.95

* nee Prozumenshikova

200 m. Breast-stroke

1927	Schrader, Hilde (Ger)	3:20.4
1931	Wolstenholme, Celia (GB)	3:16.2
1934	Genenger, Martha (Ger)	3:09.1
1938	Sorensen, Inge (Den)	3:05.4
1947	Vliet, Nel van (Neth)	2:56.6
	Székely, Eva (Hun)	2:57.9
	Groot, Jannie de (Neth)	3:00.5
1950	Vergauwen, Raymonde (Bel)	3:00.1
	Bonnier, Lies (Neth)	3:01.8
	Groot, Jannie de (Neth)	3:02.2
1954	Happe, Ursula (W Ger)	2:54.9
	Hansen, Jytte (Den)	2:55.0
	Killermann, Klára (Hun)	2:55.8
1958	Haan, Ada den (Neth)	2:52.0
	Lonsbrough, Anita (GB)	2:53.5
	Urselmann, Wiltrud (W Ger)	2:53.8
1962	Lonsbrough, Anita (GB)	2:50.2
	Bimolt, Klenie (Neth)	2:51.2
	Kuper, Ursula (E Ger)	2:52.2
1966	Prozumenshikova, Galina (USSR)	2:40.8
	Poznyakova, Irina (USSR)	2:41.9
	Slattery, Jill (GB)	2:47.9

1970 Stepanova, Galina* (USSR)
                                 2:40.7
      Grebennikova, Alla (USSR)
                                 2:43.5
      Harrison, Dorothy (GB)   2:45.6
- -
1974 Linke, Karla (E Ger)   2:34.99
      Schott, Anne-Katrin (E Ger)
                                 2:38.88
      Yourchenia, Marina (USSR)
                                 2:42.04
      * nee Prozumenshikova

100 m. Butterfly
1954 Langenau, Jutta (E Ger)   1:16.6
      Littomeritzky, Mária (Hun) 1:18.6
      Happe, Ursula (W Ger)   1:18.9
1958 Lagerberg, Tineke (Neth)   1:11.9
      Voorbij, Atie (Neth)   1:12.1
      Skupilova, Maria (Czech)   1:14.3
1962 Kok, Ada (Neth)   1:09.0
      Noack, Ute (E Ger)   1:10.0
      Heemskerk, Marianne (Neth)
                                 1:10.3
1966 Kok, Ada (Neth)   1:05.6
      Hustede, Heike (W Ger)   1:06.3
      Pyrhonen, Ella (Fin)   1:07.8
1970 Gyarmati, Andrea (Hun)   1:05.0
      Lindner, Helga (E Ger)   1:05.4
      Koch, Edeltraud (W Ger)   1:05.8
- -
1974 Kother, Rosemarie (E Ger) 1:01.99
      Leucht, Anne-Katrin (E Ger)
                                 1:03.63
      Andersson, Gunilla (Swe)   1:04.67

200 m. Butterfly
1970 Lindner, Helga (E Ger)   2:20.2
      Segrt, Mirjana (Yugo)   2:24.5
      Stolze, Evelyn (E Ger)   2:25.6
- -
1974 Kother, Rosemarie (E Ger) 2:14.45
      Leucht, Anne-Katrin (E Ger)
                                 2:18.45
      Schwarzfeldt, Barbara (W Ger)
                                 2:19.71

200 m. Individual medley
1970 Grunert, Martina (E Ger)   2:27.6
      Stolze, Evelyn (E Ger)   2:29.3
      Ratcliffe, Shelagh (GB)   2:29.6
- -
1974 Tauber, Ulrike (E Ger)   2:18.97
      Hübner, Andrea (E Ger)   2:23.97
      Fetisova, Trina (USSR)   2:25.40

400 m. Individual medley
1962 Lasterie, Adrie (Neth)   5:27.8
      Lonsbrough, Anita (GB)   5:32.3
      Egerváry, Márta (Hun)   5:33.3
1966 Heukels, Betty (Neth)   5:25.0
      Pechstein, Heidi (E Ger)   5:26.0
      Hazieva, Ludmila (USSR)   5:28.4
1970 Stolze, Evelyn (E Ger)   5:07.9
      Schuchardt, Brigitte (E Ger)
                                 5:18.3
      Ratcliffe, Shelagh (GB)   5:19.6
- -
1974 Tauber, Ulrike (E Ger)   4:52.42
      Wegner, Gudrun (E Ger)   4:58.78
      Richardson, Susan (GB)   5:06.71

4 x 100 m. Free-style relay
1927 Great Britain   5:11.6
      (Laverty, Marion; King, Ellen; Davies,
      Valerie; Cooper, Joyce)
1931 Netherlands   4:55.0
      (Baumeister, Truus; Ouden, Willy den;
      Vierdag, Marie; Braun, Marie)
1934 Netherlands   4:41.5
      (Selbach, Jopie; Ouden, Willy den;
      Timmermann, Ans; Mastenbroek, Rie)
1938 Denmark   4:31.4
      (Arndt, Eva; Ove-Petersen, Birte;
      Kraft, Gunvor; Hveger, Ragnhild)
- -
1947 Denmark   4:32.3
      (Andersen, Greta; Svendsen, Eva;
      Harup, Karen; Nathansen, Fritze)
      Netherlands   4:36.0
      (Termeulen, Hannie; Schumacher,
      Irma; Vaessen, Marie-Louise; Mars-
      man, Margot)
      Great Britain   4:37.1
      (Gibson, Cathy; Preece, Lillian; Riach,
      Nancy; Wellington, Margaret)
1950 Netherlands   4:33.9
      (Mauser, Ann; Termeulen, Hannie;
      Vaessen, Marie-Louise; Schumacher,
      Irma)
      Denmark   4:43.1
      (Olsen, Greta; Madsen, Ulla; Petersen,
      Mette; Andersen, Greta)
      Sweden   4:44.7
      (Lundqvist, Marianne; Tidholm, Gis-
      ela; Fredin, Ingegard; Ahlgren, Elisa-
      beth)
1954 Hungary   4:30.6
      (Gyenge, Valéria; Sebo, Agota; Temes,
      Judit; Szöke, Katalin)
      Netherlands   4:33.2
      (Zandvliet, Loes; Korte, Joke de;
      Balkenende, Hettie; Wielema, Gertje)

West Germany   4:37.2
(Jansen, Kate; Netz, Gisela von;
Klomp, Birgit; Rechlin, Elisabeth)

1958 Netherlands   4:22.9
(Schimmel, Corrie; Lagerberg, Tineke;
Kraan, Greetje; Gastelaars, Cockie)
Great Britain   4:24.2
(Grinham, Judy; Ferguson, Elspeth;
Samuel, Judy; Wilkinson, Diana–
Sweden   4:28.5
(Eriksson, Barbro; Anderson, B; Lars-
sson, Karin; Jobson, Kate)

1962 Netherlands   4:15.1
(Gastelaars, Cockie; Lasterie, Adrie;
Terpstra, Erica; Tigelaar, Ineke)
Great Britain   4:16.3
(Amos, Linda; Brenner, Adrienne;
Thompson, Jenny; Wilkinson, Diana)
Hungary   4:17.5
(Frank, Mária; Kovács, Edit; Mad-
arász, Csilla; Takács, Katalin)

1966 USSR   4:11.3
(Sipchenko, Natalia; Rudenka, Anto-
nia; Ustinova, Natalia; Sosnova, Tam-
ara)
Sweden   4:12.2
(Gustavsson, Ingrid; Jafvert,   ;
Lilja, Ann-Charlotte; Hagberg, Ann-
Christine)
Netherlands   4:12.8
(Beumer, Toos; Hemert, Mirjam van;
Weeteling, Bep; Schaap,   )

1970 East Germany   4:00.8
(Wetzko, Gabriele; Komor, Iris; Seh-
misch, Elke; Schulze, Carola)
Hungary   4:02.7
(Gyarmati, Andrea; Túróczy, Judit;
Kovács, Edit; Patoh, Magdolna)
Sweden   4:07.4
(Berglund, Elisabeth; Andersson, Lot-
ten; Zarnowiecki, Anita; Jonsson,
Gunilla)
- -
1974 East Germany   3:52.48
(Ender, Kornelia; Franke, Angela;
Eife, Andrea; Hübner, Andrea)
Netherlands   3:57.08
(Rijnders, Anke; Pors, Ada; Stel,
Veronika; Brigitha, Enith)
France   3:57.61
(Mandonnaud, Claude; Noach, Sylvie
le; Schertz, Chantal; Berger, Guylaine)

4 x 100 m. Medley relay
1958 Netherlands   4:52.9
(Nijs, Lenie de; Haan, Ada den;
Voorbij, Atie; Gastelaars, Cockie)

USSR   4:53.2
(Victorova, Larisa; Uusmees, Esme;
Kamaeva, G   ; Voog, Ulvi)
Great Britain   4:54.2
(Grinham, Judy; Lonsbrough, Anita;
Gosden, Christine; Wilkinson, Diana)

1962 East Germany   4:40.1
(Schmidt, Ingrid; Göbel, Barbara;
Noack, Ute; Pechstein, Heidi)
Netherlands   4:42.9
(Velsen, Ria van; Bimolt, Klenie; Kok,
Ada; Tigelaar, Ineke)
Great Britain   4:46.2
(Ludgrove, Linda; Lonsbrough,
Anita; Cotterill, Anne; Wilkinson,
Diana)

1966 Netherlands   4:36.4
(Sikkens, Coby; Kok, Gretta; Kok,
Ada; Beumer, Toos)
USSR   4:38.2
(Mihailova, Natalia; Prozumenshikova,
Galina; Devjatova, Tatjana; Rudenko,
Antonia)
Great Britain   4:38.4
(Ludgrove, Linda; Harris, Diane;
Gegan, Judy; Sillett, Pauline)

1970 East Germany   4:30.1
(Hofmeister, Barbara; Schuchardt,
Brigitte; Lindner, Helga; Wetzko,
Gabriele)
USSR   4:31.3
(Lekveishvili, Tinatin; Stepanova, Gal-
ina; Tutaeva, Valentina; Zolotnotz-
kaja, Tatjana)
West Germany   4:33.4
(Kraus, Angelika; Frommater, Uta;
Nagel, Heike; Reineck, Heidi)
- -
1974 East Germany   4:13.78
(Richter, Ulrike; Vogel, Renate;
Kother, Rosemarie; Ender, Kornelia)
West Germany   4:23.50
(Grieser, Angelika; Justen, Christel;
Jasch, Beate; Weber, Jutta)
Sweden   4:23.90
(Lundberg, Gunilla; Pettersson, Jean-
ette; Andersson, Gunilla; Olsson,
Diana)

Springboard diving
1927 Bornett, Clara (Aut)   103.32
1931 Jordan, Olga (Ger)   77.00
1934 Jensch-Jordan, Olga (Ger)   74.78
1938 Slade, Berry (GB)   103.60
- -
1947 Moreau, Mady (Fr)   100.43
     Staudinger, Alma (Aut)   90.67
     Aubert-Pinci, Jeanne (Fr)   88.78

1950	Moreau, Mady (Fr)	155.58
	Pelissard, Nicole (Fr)	140.64
	Christophersen, Birte* (Den)	
		129.63
1954	Tchumitcheva, Valentina	
	(USSR)	129.45
	Hansson, Birte* (Swe)	126.24
	Zsigalova, Lubov (USSR)	125.30
1958	Krutova, Ninel (USSR)	124.22
	Welsh, Charmian (GB)	123.42
	Dedova, Valentina (USSR)	122.75
1962	Krämer, Ingrid (E Ger)	153.57
	Lanzke, Christiane (E Ger)	137.78
	Kuznetsova, Natily (USSR)	133.78
1966	Baklanova, Vera (USSR)	135.59
	Reinhard, Delia (E Ger)	136.05
	Fedosova, Tamara (USSR)	133.23
1970	Becker, Heidi (E Ger)	420.63
	Janicke, Marina (E Ger)	407.22
	Safonova, Tamara (USSR)	405.60
1974	Knape, Ulrika (Swe)	465.57
	Kalinina, Irina (USSR)	460.17
	Safonova, Tamara (USSR)	455.34

* later represented Sweden under her married name Hansson.

Highboard diving

1927	White, Belle (GB)	36.04
1931	Epply, Madie (Aut)	34.28
1934	Schieche, Hertha (Ger)	35.43
1938	Becken, Inge (Den)	37.09
1947	Pelissard, Nicole (Fr)	60.03
	Zsagot, Iren (Hun)	59.86
	Staudinger, Alma (Aut)	59.02
1950	Pelissard, Nicole (Fr)	85.67
	Staudinger, Alma (Aut)	82.38
	Christophersen, Birte* (Den)	
		82.31
1954	Karakasjanc, Tatiana (USSR)	
		79.86
	Hansson, Birte* (Swe)	72.17
	Pfarrhofer, Eva (Aut)	65.68
1958	Karezkaite, Aldona (USSR)	81.14
	Gorochovskaja, Raisa (USSR)	
		80.93
	Hansson, Birte* (Swe)	80.34
1962	Krämer, Ingrid (E Ger)	107.96
	Krutova, Ninel (USSR)	95.92
	Schope, Gabriele (E Ger)	90.88
1966	Kusnetsova, Natalia (USSR)	
		100.93
	Pertmayr, Inge (Aut)	94.52
	Krauss, Gabriele (E Ger)	91.22

1970	Duchkova, Milena (Czech)	336.33
	Janicke, Marina (E Ger)	329.85
	Fiedler, Sylvia (E Ger)	322.26
1974	Knape, Ulrika (Swe)	408.87
	Kalinina, Irina (USSR)	399.54
	Vaytsehovskaia, Elena (USSR)	
		366.12

* later represented Sweden under married name Hansson.

NATIONAL PLACINGS

Europa Cup (Best nation in men's events)

1926	Germany	132 points
1927	Germany	111 points
1931	Hungary	114 points
1934	Germany	118 points
1938	Germany	145 points
1947	Hungary	79 points
1950	France	87 points
1954	Hungary	140 points
1958	U.S.S.R.	135 points
1962	U.S.S.R.	116 points
1966	U.S.S.R.	212 points
1970	East Germany	168 points
1974	U.S.S.R.	155 points

Bredius Cup (Best nation in women's events)

1934	Netherlands	88½ points
1938	Denmark	100 points
1947	Denmark	72 points
1950	Netherlands	92 points
1954	Hungary	87 points
1958	Netherlands	123 points
1962	Netherlands	137 points
1966	U.S.S.R.	112 points
1970	East Germany	230 points
1974	East Germany	295 points

Fern Cup (Best diving nation)

1966	U.S.S.R.	47 points
1970	East Germany	48 points
1974	U.S.S.R.	41 points

EUROPEAN CUPS. A number of single discipline international competitions have been developed under the aegis of L.E.N. These provide valuable competition and experience outside the major championships and Games. (see EUROPEAN DIVING CUPS, EUROPEAN SWIMMING CUPS etc.)

EUROPEAN DIVING CUPS
Instituted in 1963 and held every two years, the venues and winners have been:
1963 Leipzig, East Germany
1965 Salzburg, Austria

1967 Helsinki, Finland
1969 Bolzano, Italy
1971 London England
1973 Leningrad, U.S.S.R.
1975 Skövde, Sweden
1976 Edinburgh, Scotland

MEN

Springboard diving

1963	Polulyakh, Boris (USSR)	152.85
1965	Safonov, Mihail (USSR)	477.77
1967	Cagnotto, Giorgio (Ita)	441.03
1969	Dibiasi, Klaus (Ita)	563.07
1971	Dibiasi, Klaus (Ita)	549.51
1973	Dibiasi, Klaus (Ita)	609.03
1975	Cagnotto, Giorgio (It)	569.25

Highboard diving

1963	Volker, Gerd (E Ger)	160.81
1965	Dibiasi, Klaus (Ita)	481.87
1967	Dibiasi, Klaus (Ita)	504.21
1969	Cagnotto, Giorgio (Ita)	467.19
1971	Dibiasi, Klaus (Ita)	482.34
1973	Mihaylin, Nikolay (USSR)	542.22
1975	Dibiasi, Klaus (It)	538.89

WOMEN

Springboard diving

1963	Krämer, Ingrid (E Ger)	151.15
1965	Fedosova, Tamara (USSR)	427.94
1967	Gulbin (nee Krämer), Ingrid (E Ger)	429.33
1969	Knape, Ulrika (Swe)	381.45
1971	Janicke, Marina (E Ger)	406.62
1973	Safonova, Tamara (USSR)	454.84
1975	Knape, Ulrika (Swe)	467.49

Highboard diving

1963	Krämer, Ingrid (E Ger)	111.93
1965	Kusnetsova, Natalia (USSR)	299.78
1967	Duchkova, Milena (Czech)	282.48
1969	Pertmayr, Inge (Aut)	304.53
1971	Duchkova, Milena (Czech)	343.08
1973	Janicke, Marina (E Ger)	372.84
1975	Knape, Ulrika (Swe)	393.27

EUROPEAN SWIMMING CUPS.
Instituted in 1969, with separate team
contests for men and women, the European Swimming Cups are held every two
years. The events, over metric distances,
are; free-style—100, 200, 400, 800
(women)/1,500 (men), 4 x 100 and 4 x
200 (men); back-stroke/breast-stroke
and butterfly—100 and 200; medley—
200, 400 and 4 x 100. Each country
may enter one competitor or team for

each event. The interest in these exciting international clashes has resulted
in "A", "B" and "C" group meetings
having to be organised with promotion
and relegation between the groups. The
venues and winners of Group "A" are:

GROUP "A" (MEN)
1969 Wurzburg, West Germany. East
      Germany 136; U.S.S.R. 124;
      West Germany 117.
1971 Uppsala, Sweden. U.S.S.R. 121;
      East Germany 117; West Ger-
      many 111.
1973 East Berlin, East Germany. East
      Germany 140; U.S.S.R. 122;
      West Germany 96.
1975 Moscow, U.S.S.R. U.S.S.R. 125;
      Great Britain 116. East Ger-
      many 99
1976 Pescara, Italy

GROUP "A" (WOMEN)
1969 Budapest, Hungary. East Germany
      128; U.S.S.R. 90; Hungary 82.
1971 Bratislava, Czechoslovakia. East
      Germany 118; Netherlands
      101; U.S.S.R. 95.
1973 Utrecht, Netherlands. East Ger-
      many 128; Netherlands 99;
      West Germany 82.
1975 Leeds, England. East Germany
      135; Holland 85; U.S.S.R. 78.
1976 Crystal Palace, England

EUROPEAN SWIMMING LEAGUE.
See LIGUE EUROPEENNE DE NAT-
ATION.

**EUROPEAN SYNCHRONIZED
SWIMMING CHAMPIONS.** The first
European championships took place in
Amsterdam in October 1974 when the
medal winners were:
Solo
1974 Holland, Jane (GB)   93.82
      Honsbeek, Angelike (Neth)   82.04
      Serwonski, B (W Ger)   79.32
Duet
1974 Holland, Jane/
      Lane, Jennifer (GB)   85.50
      Serwonski, B
      Mackle, B   (W Ger)   82.41
      Honsbeek, Angelike/
      Gulvers, Helma (Neth)   78.01

Team
1974   Great Britain   88.490
     (Holland, Jane; Cox, Jacqueline;
     Mitchell, Josephine; Davis, Nicky;
     Lane, Jennifer; Horne, Linda; Russell,
     Anne; Shaikh, Doreen)
        West Germany   85.293
        Netherlands   78.859

Top Nation
1974   Great Britain   39 pts

EUROPEAN WATER-POLO CUP-WINNERS CUP. A tournament between the winners of National club cup-winners began in 1974.

The competition is organised on a league basis with preliminary, semi-final (if required) and final pools and the various rounds are usually decided respectively, in October, November and December of each year. The winners are:
1974   FTC of Budapest, Hungary
1975   Mladost of Zagreb, Yugoslavia

EUROPEAN WATER-POLO CUP FOR NATIONAL CHAMPIONS. A tournament between the winners of

National club leagues began in 1963.

The competition is organised on a league basis with preliminary, semi-final, and final pools and the various rounds are usually decided, respectively, in October, November and December of each year. The winners are:
1963   Partizan of Belgrade, Yugoslavia
1964   Pro-Recco of Genoa, Italy
1965   Partizan of Belgrade, Yugoslavia
1966   Partizan of Belgrade, Yugoslavia
1967   Mladost of Zagreb, Yugoslavia
1968   Mladost of Zagreb, Yugoslavia
1969   Mladost of Zagreb, Yugoslavia
1970   Partizan of Belgrade, Yugoslavia
1971   Mladost of Zagreb, Yugoslavia
1972   O.S.C. of Budapest, Hungary
1973   Marina of Moscow, U.S.S.R.
1974   Partizan of Belgrade, Yugoslavia
1975   Partizan of Belgrade, Yugoslavia

EUROPEAN WATER-POLO (NATIONAL TEAM) CUPS. A variety of international tournaments have been held since 1929 in which the cream of Europe's water-polo nations have competed. The venues and winners are:

Copa Klebelsberg

1929	Budapest, Hungary	Hungary
1930	Nürenberg, West Germany ⸗	Hungary
1935	Brussels, Belgium	Hungary

Copa Horthy

1937	Budapest, Hungary	Hungary
1939	Doetinchem, Netherlands	Germany

Trofeo Italia

1949	Milan/Genoa, Italy	Netherlands
1953	Nijmegen, Netherlands	Netherlands
1957	Zagreb, Yugoslavia	U.S.S.R.
1961	Moscow, U.S.S.R.	Hungary
1965	Budapest, Hungary	Hungary

Copa Hungaria

1969	Budapest, Hungary	Italy
1973	Pescara, Italy	Hungary

EUROPEAN YOUTH CHAMPION-SHIPS. European swimming championships for boys and girls of 15 years and under were instituted in 1967. Springboard diving for the same age group was also held that year but the age was raised to under 16 in 1969 and highboard diving was added in 1971.

András Hargitay of Hungary (see HARGITAY, András) gained a remark-

able six gold medals—out of a possible 10—at the 1971 meeting in Rotterdam. The venues and winners are:
1967   Linköping, Sweden
1969   Vienna, Austria
1971   Rotterdam, Holland
1973   Leeds, England
1975   Geneva, Switzerland
1976   Oslo, Norway

BOYS

100 m. Free-style
1967	Grivennikov, Igor (USSR)	56.3
1969	Comas, Jorge (Sp)	55.6
1971	Hargitay, András (Hun)	55.8
1973	Dragunov, Leonid (USSR)	55.7
1975	Arvidsson, Par (Swe)	54.45

400 m. Free-style
1967	Borloi, Matyas (Hun)	4:28.1
1969	Hamburg, Roger van (Neth)	4:24.7
1971	Hargitay, András (Hun)	4:28.1
1973	Parinov, Valentin (USSR)	4:08.7
1975	Nagy, Sandor (Hun)	4:08.49

1,500 m. Free-style
1967	Esteva, Santiago (Sp)	17:49.8
1969	Hamburg, Roger van (Neth)	17:31.1
1971	Kuil, Rene van de (Neth)	17:16.3
1973	Parinov, Valentin (USSR)	16:12.3
1975	Nagy, Sandor (Hun)	16:16.90

100 m. Back-stroke
1967	Davidov, Grigory (USSR)	1:03.3
1969	Milos, Predrag (Yugo)	1:04.9
1971	Wanja, Lutz (E Ger)	1:02.9
1973	Tauber, Michael (E Ger)	1:03.4
1975	Tolko, Miloslav (Czech)	1:02.43

200 m. Back-stroke
1967	Davidov, Grigory (USSR)	2:16.2
1969	Nistri, Massimo (It)	2:19.0
1971	Wanja, Lutz (E Ger)	2:16.2
1973	Tauber, Michael (E Ger)	2:14.1
1975	Karataev, Sergei (USSR)	2:10.60

100 m. Breast-stroke
1967	Ivanov, Sergei (USSR)	1:13.5
1969	Poljakov, Alexander (USSR)	1:12.0
1971	Anajev, Aleksandr (USSR)	1:10.7
1973	Bystrickiy, Sergey (USSR)	1:09.5
1975	Arnicke, Gregor (E Ger)	1:08.55

200 m. Breast-stroke
1967	Turpe, Bertram (E Ger)	2:37.6
1969	Hargitay, András (Hun)	2:38.2
1971	Hargitay, András (Hun)	2:33.3
1973	Tarasov, Vladimir (USSR)	2:28.4
1975	Dementiev, Andrei (USSR)	2:30.52

100 m. Butterfly
1967	Cseh, Laszlo (Hun)	1:01.9
1969	Lenarczyk, Udo (W Ger)	1:01.0
1971	Hargitay, András (Hun)	58.7
1973	Broscienski, Peter (E Ger)	1:00.7
1975	Griffith, Alessandro (It)	59.51

200 m. Butterfly
1967	Freygang, Roland (E Ger)	2:22.1
1969	Shestopalov, Vladimir (USSR)	2:18.9
1971	Hargitay, András (Hun)	2:08.1
1973	Gorelik, Mihail (USSR)	2:12.8
1975	Griffith, Alessandro (It)	2:09.02

200 m. Individual medley
1967	Davidov, Grigory (USSR)	2:19.2
1969	Hargitay, András (Hun)	2:21.5
1971	Hargitay, András (Hun)	2:14.1
1973	Bohmert, Steffan (E Ger)	2:19.1
1975	Glukhov, Vladimir (USSR)	2:14.94

Springboard diving
1967	Hoffmann, Falk (E Ger)	288.90
1969	Lieberum, Hans (E Ger)	334.20
1971	Taubert, Frank (E Ger)	309.81
1973	Wascow, Dieter (E Ger)	323.20
1975	Nemtsanov, Sergey (USSR)	448.11

Highboard diving
1971	Stajkovic, Niki (Aut)	254.58
1973	Stajkovic, Niki (Aut)	264.60
1975	Nemtsanov, Sergey (USSR)	442.17

GIRLS

100 m. Free-style
1967	Grebets, Lidia (USSR)	1:02.6
1969	Wetzko, Gabriele (E Ger)	1:00.1
1971	Rijnders, Anke (Neth)	1:00.4
1973	Bunschoten, Hansje (Neth)	1:01.3
1975	Ran, Ineke (Neth)	58.90

400 m. Free-style
1967	Kock, Vera (Swe)	4:55.2
1969	Wetzko, Gabriele (E Ger)	4:36.1
1971	Bunschoten, Hansje (Neth)	4:31.7
1973	Bunschoten, Hansje (Neth)	4:29.1
1975	Jaeger, Regina (E Ger)	4:25.18

800 m. Free-style
1967	Kock, Vera (Swe)	10:13.4
1969	Neugebauer, Karin (E Ger)	9:30.8

1971	Bunschoten, Hansje (Neth)	9:26.0
1973	Bunschoten, Hansje (Neth)	9:21.1
1975	Thumer, Petra (E Ger)	8:59.31

100 m. Back-stroke
1967	Steinbach, Sabine (E Ger)	1:11.1
1969	Gyarmati, Andrea (Hun)	1:09.1
1971	Elzerman, Jozien (Neth)	1:09.4
1973	Grieser, Angelika (W Ger)	1:08.6
1975	Treiber, Birgit (E Ger)	1:04.84

200 m. Back-stroke
1967	Hammarsten, Britt- Marie (Swe)	2:34.4
1969	Hofmeister, Barbara (E Ger)	2:28.1
1971	Hilger, Susanne (E Ger)	2:27.6
1973	Grieser, Angelika (W Ger)	2:25.4
1975	Treiber, Birgit (E Ger)	2:19.68

100 m. Breast-stroke
1968	Pozdnyakova, Irina (USSR)	1:19.4
1969	Rusanova, Lubov (USSR)	1:19.1
1971	Siewert, Patricia (W Ger)	1:19.1
1973	Luskatova, Olga (USSR)	1:17.1
1975	Linke, Karla (E Ger)	1:15.78

200 m. Breast-stroke
1967	Pozdnyakova, Irina (USSR)	2:47.0
1969	Rusanova, Lubov (USSR)	2:50.5
1971	Anke, Hannelore (E Ger)	2:47.9
1973	Luskatova, Olga (USSR)	2:47.6
1975	Linke, Karla (E Ger)	2:40.56

100 m. Butterfly
1967	Gyarmati, Andrea (Hun)	1:10.1
1969	Gyarmati, Andrea (Hun)	1:06.1
1971	Rijnders, Anke (Neth)	1:05.8
1973	Loos, Birgit (E Ger)	1:06.1
1975	Jank, Marina (E Ger)	1:02.41

200 m. Butterfly
1967	Steinbach, Sabine (E Ger)	2:31.0
1969	Stolze, Evelyn (E Ger)	2:33.7
1971	Kother, Rosemarie (E Ger)	2:25.6
1973	Popova, Natalia (USSR)	2:21.3
1975	Fiebig, Anett (E Ger)	2:20.02

200 m. Individual medley
1967	Steinbach, Sabine (E Ger)	2:32.0
1969	Schuchardt, Brigitte (E Ger)	2:32.3
1971	Ender, Kornelia (E Ger)	2:31.6
1973	Tauber, Ulrike (E Ger)	2:26.1
1975	Treiber, Birgit (E Ger)	2:23.00

Springboard diving
1967	Duchkova, Milena (Czech)	305.40
1969	Semina, Alla (USSR)	313.47
1971	Knape, Ulrika (Swe)	303.45
1973	Kalinina, Irina (USSR)	315.30
1975	Piotraschke, Renate (W Ger)	397.14

Highboard diving
1971	Knape, Ulrika (Swe)	243.24
1973	Williams, Beverley (GB)	251.15
1975	Piotraschke, Renate (W Ger)	319.02

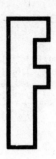

FARRELL, Jeff (United States, 28 Feb. 1937–). An appendicectomy six days before the American Olympic trials of 1960 should have ended Jeff Farrell's medal ambitions. But this naval officer did not give up. He was out of bed within twenty-four hours, training within three days, competed in the trials, and though he 'failed' to win an individual event place he was picked for the relays.

In Rome he swam as anchor man in the 4 x 200 m. free-style and 4 x 100 m. medley and brought his squad home first in world record times of 8:10.2 and 4:05.4. The 1959 Pan American 100 m. champion (56.3), the Olympic sprint gold could well have been Farrell's had not fate intervened. His medley relay split was an unpressed 54.9 as the Americans beat Australia by 6.6 seconds, as against John Devitt's 100 m. winning time of 55.2.

FASSNACHT, Hans (West Germany, 28 Nov. 1950–). One of the new breed of American-trained Europeans, Hans Fassnacht stepped from relative obscurity to a world record-breaker in a matter of eight months . . . from a seventh place in the 1968 Olympic 400 m. (4:18.1) to a world record 4:04.0 in Louisville on 14 Aug. 1969. This stood until the following August, when John Kinsella (USA) clocked 4:02.8.

As a member of the Don Gambril squad at California State College, Fassnacht trained on what he called 'hard sprints', but which, in fact were 15 x 400 m. repetitions with 10 seconds' rest, or 5 x 1,500 m., finishing with his fastest time on his fifth swim. He did 12–15 kilometres a day, seven days a week. In 1969 this work brought him, as well as his world record, European free-style

records for 200 m. (1:56.5), 1,500 m. (16:32.1) and for 400 m. medley (4:42.5). Despite collapsing during an air flight in 1970, when he had difficulty in breathing, Fassnacht was soon back in the water . . . covering 18 kilometres a day!

In the 1966 European championships in Utrecht, the West German was fifth in the 1,500 m. (17:28.6). At the 1970 Barcelona Europeans Fassnacht was considerably more successful.

His medal tally was three golds and three silvers. He won the 200 m. free-style in 1:55.2 and the 1,500 m. in 16:19.9–both European records–and, en route for the longer distance, he also broke the European record for 800 m. with 8:41.4. And he helped West Germany to a European record-breaking victory in the 4 x 200 m. free-style relay with a remarkable anchor leg 'split' of 1:54.4.

Fassnacht's silvers came in the 400 m. free-style (in which he lost his European record to Gunnar Larsson of Sweden but, in clocking 4:03.0, put up the third best time of all time), the 400 m. medley and the 4 x 100 m. free-style.

A year later, Fassnacht demonstrated his versatility in taking six tenths off the four-day-old world 200 m. butterfly record of Mark Spitz with 2:3.3. But he never swam as well again and at West Germany's Olympics in Munich in 1972 his best effort was joint fifth in the 200 m. butterfly, four secs. behind Spitz, and he did not even qualify for the finals of the 400 and 1,500 m. freestyle.

FEDERATION INTERNATIONALE DE NATATION AMATEUR. The world governing body for swimming, was founded in London, during the 1908 Olympic Games, by accident rather than design. The initiative came from an Englishman, George W. Hearn (see HEARN, GEORGE W.), then President of the A.S.A. who thought this was a good opportunity to talk over the problems of the sport, particularly about amateurism. What resulted was an official world federation.

Eight nations were represented at the historic founding-day meeting at the Manchester Hotel, on 19 July–Belgium, Denmark, Finland, France, Germany, Great Britain and Ireland, Hungary and Sweden. Of those present, R. Max Ritter, later an American citizen but at that time representing Germany, was still actively concerned with swimming administration in 1970. The first aims of F.I.N.A. were to draw up rules for the conduct of swimming, diving and water-polo events, to set up world record lists and to take on the responsibility for the organization of the swimming events at Olympic Games.

Now the influence and power that F.I.N.A. exert over swimming are unchallenged and no international contests can be organized except under the laws of the Federation. From eight, the F.I.N.A. membership has grown to more than 100 affiliated nations. The official languages of the Federation are English and French but in the case of interpretation of rules the English text is accepted. Yet the Federation is known by its French title and not the English version of the International Amateur Swimming Federation.

FERGUSON, Cathy Jean (United States, 17 July 1948–).

There were six world record-breakers in the line-up for the final of the 1964 Olympic 100 m. back-stroke in Tokyo, but after a world record-breaking 67.7 seconds, the freckle-faced Californian Cathy Ferguson emerged as Olympic champion, The beaten record-breakers were Christine Caron (France), Ginny Duenkel (USA), Sato Tanaka (Japan) and Linda Ludgrove and Jill Norfolk (GB). The sixth was Miss Ferguson.

That individual performance gave the tall (5 ft 8 in.) and slim high school girl from Burbank the back-stroke berth in the United States medley relay squad–and another gold.

A product of the United States age-group competitive system, Miss Ferguson's career took in age-group records from 11 years upwards. In four seasons she improved her 100 m. back-stroke by 8.4 seconds to her Tokyo world record and her 200 m. time came down by 7.6 to a world record 2:27.4 in a single year.

FERN, Harold E. (Great Britain, 20 Apr. 1881–21 Aug. 1974).

An era unparalleled in sports administration ended in March, 1970 when Harold Fern retired after 49 years as honorary secretary of the A.S.A. No sports governing body in the world has received service to approach the length and quality given to swimming by Alderman Fern.

Honorary secretary of the Southern District in 1905, at 24, he held this office until his election as England's top administrator in 1921. Fern was elected President of F.I.N.A. in 1936 and held this office through World War II until 1948. Between 1940 and 1946 he was also honorary secretary and treasurer and he was treasurer again from 1948–60.

He became a Life President of F.I.N.A. and also of L.E.N. and was honoured by the Fort Lauderdale International Hall of Fame (see HALL OF FAME) as an outstanding contributor in 1974, a few months before his death in his 94th year.

The number of affiliated clubs increased almost 100 per cent–from 875 to 1,629–during his years in office, and the financial assets from £339 18s. 2d. in 1921 to more than £140,000, making the A.S.A. one of the wealthiest amateur governing bodies in Britain.

For his services to swimming and to the Hertfordshire County Council, of which he was a member for fifty years, Fern was honoured with both an O.B.E. and a C.B.E., but his real accolade is the healthy state of his association as he left it.

FERN, Harold, National Trophy.

This trophy was presented to the A.S.A. in 1961 by Alderman Harold Fern (see FERN, HAROLD) to enable a national award for women's clubs to be instituted on similar lines to the top men's club award (see BENJAMIN, HENRY, MEMORIAL TROPHY) which had been in existence since 1910.

Points are awarded for success in A.S.A. long and short-course swimming championships and the award is open to English women's clubs or women's sections of mixed clubs. Winners:

1962	Hampstead Ladies	21 points
1963	Hampstead Ladies	27 points
1964	Beckenham Ladies/	
	Stoke Newington (tie)	24 points
1965	Beckenham Ladies	26 points
1966	Beckenham Ladies	33 points
1967	York City Bath	31 points
1968	Beckenham Ladies	24 points
1969	Beckenham Ladies	21 points
1970	Beckenham Ladies	21 points
1971	Havering	71 points
1972	Hull Olympic	60 points
1973	Beckenham Ladies	65 points

1974 Beckenham Ladies   69 points
1975 Beckenham Ladies   108 points

FLETCHER, Jennie (Great Britain, 19 March, 1890—1967). Jennie from Leicester was Britain's first woman Olympic medallist. She won the bronze behind two Australians in the 100 m. in Stockholm in 1912 (1:27.0)—the first time events for women had been included—and was a member of the British squad who won the relay by 12 sec. from Germany. She was six times A.S.A. 100 y. champion, from 1906—09 and 1911—12, her fastest time being in 1909 (1:14.0).

FRASER, Dawn (Australia, 4 Sept. 1937—). It would take a book—and she has written one—to do justice to Dawn Fraser, the queen of swimming and the only pool competitor to win the same Olympic title—100 m. free-style—at three successive Games. An independent stormy petrel, who had more than one clash with officialdom, her final punishment of ten years' suspension for misbehaviour during the 1964 Olympics was hardly the reward Australian swimming circles owed their greatest champion. The high-handed undemocratic way in which the Australian A.S.U. treated Miss Fraser in 1964 shocked the sporting world. It came shortly after the 27-year-old star had been named 'Australian of the Year' and been honoured with a ceremonial drive around Melbourne race-course on one of the big race days. Two of the incidents in which she was involved were appearing in the parade at the opening ceremony against orders, because of her early races, and being involved in a Japanese flag-purloining prank, but she, along with the other three disciplined swimmers, was not allowed to appear in her own defence.

Miss Fraser, sprinter extraordinary, won her first Olympic 100 m. gold in 1956 when she beat her team-mate Lorraine Crapp by 0.3 in a world record 62.0. Superb form in Rome, four years later, enabled her to keep her crown, clocking 61.2, finishing 3 metres ahead of America's Chris von Saltza. And she wrote her final piece of history in Tokyo on 13 Oct. 1964, when she came home 0.4 ahead of Sharon Stouder (USA) in 59.5.

She reached the 400 m. final in each of these Games, coming second to Miss Crapp in 1956 (5:02.5), fifth in 1960 (4:58.3) and fourth in 1964 in her fastest 4:47.6. And she collected four relay medals—free-style gold in Melbourne, free-style and medley silvers in Rome and a free-style silver in Tokyo.

Dawn, originally from Adelaide, was the first woman to break the minute for 100 m. and 110 y. and her twenty-seven individual world records included nine successive marks for 100 m. In her remarkable ten-year career, Miss Fraser won eight Commonwealth medals, six of them gold—110 y. (1958/62), 440 y. (1962), 4 x 110 y. free-style (1958/62) and medley relay (1962)—plus two silvers in the 440 y. and medley relay in 1958.

She won twenty-three Australian titles—the 100 m. (7 times) and 200 m. (8), 400 m. (5), 100 m. butterfly (2) and 200 m. medley (1). The best of her many world record times were: 100 y. (56.9), 100 m. (58.9), 110 y. (59.5), 200 m. and 220 y. (2:11.6).

FREE-STYLE. There are no special rules for free-style swimming, in fact, the words mean exactly what they say—that the style is the free choice of the competitor. But in modern usage, the free choice in free-style is almost always front crawl, the fastest stroke in the water. Only in the context of medley races, individual and relay, is there a special regulation concerning free-style. And it is a negative ruling. It says that free-style is any style other than butterfly, breast-stroke or back-stroke; which, again, means that free-style is front crawl.

FRENCH CHAMPIONS. The first championships were held in 1899, but the Fédération Française de Natation was not founded until 22 years later, the events up to 1921 being organised by the swimming section of the National amateur all-sports body. From 1908, the championships were organised under the laws of F.I.N.A., the French National amateur all-sports body having been one of the founders of the International Federation.

Two French swimmers have won Olympic titles, Devendeville in the underwater event in 1900 and Jean Boiteux (see BOITEUX, Jean) for 400 m. free-style in 1952. But ten French swimmers won a total of 14 European titles of whom Alex Jany (see JANY, Alex) gained four golds in the 100 and 400 m. free-style in 1947 and 1950.

France's five European gold medals for diving include doubles in 1947 and 1950 by Mady Moreau (springboard) and Nicole Pelissard (highboard). France were also winners of the Olympic water-polo in 1924.

Jean Taris (free-style) and Jacques Cartonnet (breast-stroke) each broke eight world records in the French total of 43 by nine men and seven women. And Jany and Christine Caron (see CARON, Christine) claimed 11 European records apiece for freestyle and back-stroke respectively in France's total of 125 marks.

The venues and winners of (all long-course) championships since 1960 are:

1960 Paris
1961 Paris
1962 Paris
1963 Paris
1964 Paris and Clermont-Ferrand
1965 Paris and Beziers
1966 Paris
1967 Paris and Montelimar
1968 Paris and Aix-en-Provence
1969 Paris and Le Mans
1970 Paris and Tours
1971 Paris and Morzine
1972 Vittel
1973 Vittel
1974 Vittel and Paris
1975 Paris

MEN

100 m. Free-style

1960	Christophe, Robert	57.6
1961	Gropaiz, Gerard	57.2
1962	Gottvalles, Alain	55.6
1963	Gottvalles, Alain	56.1
1964	Gottvalles, Alain	54.3
1965	Luyce, Francis	56.6
1966	Gruener, Bernard	55.8
1967	Rousseau, Michel	54.3
1968	Rousseau, Michel	54.4
1969	Vigne, Gilles	54.6
1970	Rousseau, Michel	53.4
1971	Rousseau, Michel	52.7
1972	Rousseau, Michel	52.6
1973	Rousseau, Michel	52.80
1974	Rousseau, Michel	52.61
1975	Rousseau, Michel	53.20

200 m. Free-style

1960	Curtillet, Jean-Pascal	2:09.0
1961	Gropaiz, Gerard	2:10.6
1962	Gottvalles, Alain	2:05.2
1963	Gropaiz, Gerard	2:05.2
1964	Curtillet, Jean-Pascal	2:03.2
1965	Luyce, Francis	2:01.7
1966	Mosconi, Alain	2:01.1
1967	Mosconi, Alain	1:59.2
1968	Mosconi, Alain	1:59.8
1969	Mosconi, Alain	2:00.8
1970	Rousseau, Michel	1:59.3
1971	Rousseau, Michel	1:58.5
1972	Rousseau, Michel	1:57.5
1973	Rousseau, Michel	1:57.29
1974	Rousseau, Michel	1:54.61
1975	Lazzaro, Marc	1:58.73

400 m. Free-style

1960	Curtillet, Jean-Pascal	4:40.2
1961	Montserret, Guy	4:38.9
1962	Curtillet, Jean-Pascal	4:38.4
1963	Pommat, Jean	4:32.1
1964	Luyce, Francis	4:25.5
1965	Luyce, Francis	4:23.7
1966	Mosconi, Alain	4:24.0
1967	Mosconi, Alain	4:16.4
1968	Ravelinghein, Jean-François	4:20.2
1969	Vigorito, François	4:17.6
1970	Mosconi, Alain	4:19.4
1971	Mosconi, Alain	4:16.9
1972	Mosconi, Alain	4:16.6
1973	Lazzaro, Marc	4:12.91
1974	Lazzaro, Marc	4:08.82
1975	Lazzaro, Marc	4:10.84

1,500 m. Free-style

1960	Curtillet, Jean-Pascal	19:44.6
1961	Montserret, Guy	18:58.4
1962	Bayon, Georges	18:56.1
1963	Bayon, Georges	18:31.6
1964	Luyce, Francis	18:13.0
1965	Luyce, Francis	17:48.1
1966	Mosconi, Alain	17:45.7
1967	Mosconi, Alain	17:22.9
1968	Luyce, Francis	17:23.0
1969	Ravelinghien, Jean-François	17:27.7
1970	Ravelinghien, Jean-François	17:25.3
1971	Ravelinghien, Patrice	17:32.8
1972	Ravelinghien, Patrice	17:28.1
1973	Lalot, Thierry	16:43.15
1974	Lazzaro, Marc	16:36.25
1975	Andraca, Pierre	16:34.63

100 m. Back-stroke

1960	Christophe, Robert	1:03.3
1961	Christophe, Robert	1:06.0
1962	Raffy, Claude	1:03.1
1963	Christophe, Robert	1:02.5
1964	Christophe, Robert	1:03.9
1965	Moreau, Gilles	1:05.1
1966	Vicente, Bernard	1:02.5
1967	Vicente, Bernard	1:03.0
1968	Durand-Bailloud, Jean	1:04.3
1969	Vicente, Bernard	1:02.2
1970	Berjeau, Jean-Paul	1:02.3
1971	Berjeau, Jean-Paul	1:02.4
1972	Berjeau, Jean-Paul	1:00.9
1973	Berjeau, Jean-Paul	1:01.94
1974	Meslier, Franck	1:02.23
1975	Beylot-Bourcelot, Lionel	1:02.18

200 m. Back-stroke (Instituted 1961)

1961	Christophe, Robert	2:21.4
1962	Christophe, Robert	2:21.6
1963	Raffy, Claude	2:20.2
1964	Bertin, Michel	2:19.4
1965	Pouzin, Philippe	2:20.1
1966	Pouzin, Phillipe	2:17.5
1967	Randaxhe, Pierre	2:18.8
1968	Moreau, Gilles	2:19.9
1969	Berjeau, Jean-Paul	2:16.7
1970	Berjeau, Jean-Paul	2:13.7
1971	Berjeau, Jean-Paul	2:12.3
1972	Berjeau, Jean-Paul	2:10.4
1973	Berjeau, Jean-Paul	2:13.57
1974	Meslier, Franck	2:13.18
1975	Beylot-Bourcelot, Lionel	2:11.67

100 m. Breast-stroke

1960	Boullanger, Roland	1:17.7
1961	Kiehl, Georges	1:16.1
1962	Kiehl, Georges	1:16.5
1963	Kiehl, Georges	1:13.3
1964	Kiehl, Georges	1:13.6
1965	Kiehl, Georges	1:12.2
1966	Kiehl, Georges	1:10.6
1967	Kiehl, Georges	1:11.9
1968	Kiehl, Georges	1:12.3
1969	Menu, Roger-Philippe	1:08.5
1970	Menu, Roger-Philippe	1:07.4
1971	Menu, Roger-Philippe	1:08.1
1972	Menu, Roger-Philippe	1:07.6
1973	Combet, Bernard	1:07.51
1974	Combet, Bernard	1:07.41
1975	Combet, Bernard	1:05.66

200 m. Breast-stroke

1960	Audoly, Richard	2:47.4
1961	Kiehl, Georges	2:46.0
1962	Kiehl, Georges	2:46.7
1963	Kiehl, Georges	2:41.2
1964	Ramoïno, Patrick	2:38.8
1965	Kiehl, Georges	2:37.0
1966	Kiehl, Georges	2:37.0
1967	Kiehl, Georges	2:35.0
1968	Kiehl, Georges	2:39.1
1969	Menu, Roger-Philippe	2:34.0
1970	Menu, Roger-Philippe	2:30.6
1971	Menu, Roger-Philippe	2:31.0
1972	Menu, Roger-Philippe	2:31.7
1973	Combet, Bernard	2:33.02
1974	Combet, Bernard	2:28.69
1975	Combet, Bernard	2:27.20

100 m. Butterfly

1960	Pommat, Jean	1:05.4
1961	Pommat, Jean	1:05.0
1962	Mack, Yves	1:02.4
1963	Pommat, Jean	1:01.9
1964	Pommat, Jean	1:02.0
1965	Pommat, Jean	59.8
1966	Mosconi, Alain	1:00.3
1967	Mosconi, Alain	59.7
1968	Mosconi, Alain	1:01.9
1969	Mosconi, Alain	1:00.6
1970	Mosconi, Alain	1:00.1
1971	Mosconi, Alain	58.5
1972	Mosconi, Alain	59.0
1973	Calabuig, Christian	1:00.41
1974	Buttet, Serge	1:00.00
1975	Buttet, Serge	58.25

200 m. Butterfly

1960	Pirolley, René	2:30.8
1961	Vidil, Henri	2:30.5
1962	Pommat, Jean	2:24.5
1963	Pommat, Jean	2:23.2
1964	Pommat, Jean	2:24.9
1965	Pommat, Jean	2:17.8
1966	Mosconi, Alain	2:19.2
1967	Mosconi, Alain	2:17.6
1968	Mosconi, Alain	2:18.4
1969	Ravelinghien, Jean-François	2:17.3
1970	Mosconi, Alain	2:12.2
1971	Ravelinghien, Patrice	2:14.4
1972	Ravelinghien, Patrice	2:13.4
1973	Ravelinghien, Patrice	2:11.84
1974	Ravelinghien, Patrice	2:12.88
1975	Ravelinghien, Patrice	2:11.11

200 m. Individual medley (instituted 1967)

1967	Mosconi, Alain	2:21.1
1968	Rousseau, Michel	2:19.7
1969	Mosconi, Alain	2:21.3
1970	Mosconi, Alain	2:20.6

| 1971 | Mosconi, Alain | 2:18.7 |
| 1972 | Baehr, Pierre | 2:16.8 |

1973	Rousseau, Michel	2:15.79
1974	Moreau, Patrick	2:15.00
1975	Plançon, Gilles	2:15.83

400 m. Individual medley (Instituted 1962)

1962	Bertsch, Marc	5:27.1
1963	Louvet, Marcel	5:22.1
1964	Louvet, Marcel	5:18.9
1965	Mosconi, Alain	5:07.9
1966	Mosconi, Alain	5:04.2
1967	Mosconi, Alain	5:04.9
1968	Ravelinghien, Jean-François	5:05.5
1969	Ravelinghien, Jean-François	5:02.4
1970	Haymann, Patrick	5:05.5
1971	Haymann, Patrick	5:02.7
1972	Berjeau, Jean-Paul	4:55.2

1973	Moreau, Patrick	4:55.10
1974	Moreau, Patrick	4:50.87
1975	Delamare, Philippe	4:49.00

WOMEN

100 m. Free-style

1960	Frost, Heda	1:05.9
1961	Gaillot, Marie-Laure	1:05.8
1962	Ducoulombier (nee Frost), Heda	1:07.4
1963	Dorleans, Danièle	1:06.8
1964	Pietri, Monique	1:04.1
1965	Pommat, Brigitte	1:04.8
1966	Mandonnaud, Claude	1:03.1
1967	Dorleans, Daniele	1:02.8
1968	Mandonnaud, Claude	1:01.7
1969	Mandonnaud, Claude	1:03.8
1970	Mandonnaud, Claude	1:00.9
1971	Mandonnaud, Claude	1:02.2
1972	Berger, Guylaine	1:01.5

1973	Berger, Guylaine	1:00.71
1974	Berger, Guylaine	59.22
1975	Berger, Guylaine	58.46

200 m. Free-style (Instituted 1962)

1962	Ducoulombier (nee Frost), Heda	2:26.1
1963	Vanacker, Annie	2:24.6
1964	Not held	
1965	Vanacker, Annie	2:21.7
1966	Mandonnaud, Claude	2:17.4
1967	Dorleans, Danièle	2:16.0
1968	Mandonnaud, Claude	2:12.4
1969	Mandonnaud, Claude	2:14.3
1970	Mandonnaud, Claude	2:12.6

| 1971 | Mandonnaud, Claude | 2:13.8 |
| 1972 | Mandonnaud, Claude | 2:14.8 |

1973	Mandonnaud, Claude	2:10.87
1974	Mandonnaud, Claude	2:08.47
1975	Berger, Guylaine	2:08.15

400 m. Free-style

1960	Frost, Heda	5:04.6
1961	Frost, Heda	5:08.8
1962	Vanacker, Annie	5:04.6
1963	Vanacker, Annie	5:08.0
1964	Vanacker, Annie	5:02.9
1965	Vanacker, Annie	5:03.4
1966	Mandonnaud, Claude	4:56.2
1967	Mollier, Dominique	4:52.9
1968	Mandonnaud, Claude	4:41.1
1969	Mandonnaud, Claude	4:45.7
1970	Mandonnaud, Claude	4:48.1
1971	Mandonnaud, Claude	4:44.5
1972	Mandonnaud, Claude	4:52.0

1973	Reynaud, Martine	4:50.65
1974	Mandonnaud, Claude	4:33.41
1975	Leroy, Isabelle	4:37.61

800 m. Free-style (Instituted 1967)

1967	Dorleans, Daniele	10:07.0
1968	Kersaudy, Marie-José	9:45.5
1969	Mandonnaud, Claude	10:04.6
1970	Anewy, Maria-Dolores	9:56.2
1971	Mandonnaud, Claude	10:05.0
1972	Reynaud, Martine	9:56.9

1973	Le Noach, Sylvie	9:52.34
1974	Mandonnaud, Claude	9:37.36
1975	Leroy, Isabelle	9:22.97

100 m. Back-stroke

1960	Piacentini, Rose-Marie	1:11.4
1961	Piacentini, Rose-Marie	1:11.5
1962	Piacentini, Rose-Marie	1:12.6
1963	Caron, Christine	1:10.4
1964	Caron, Christine	1:08.7
1965	Caron, Christine	1:08.7
1966	Caron, Christine	1:07.9
1967	Caron, Christine	1:09.2
1968	Caron, Christine	1:08.5
1969	Canet, Sylvie	1:10.3
1970	Desobry, Françoise	1:11.5
1971	Caron, Christine	1:09.2
1972	Le Noach, Sylvie	1:07.5

1973	Le Noach, Sylvie	1:08.10
1974	Le Noach, Sylvie	1:07.19
1975	Le Noach, Sylvie	1:07.67

200 m. Back-stroke (Instituted 1961)

| 1961 | Piacentini, Rose-Marie | 2:38.2 |
| 1962 | Caron, Christine | 2:36.6 |

1963	Caron, Christine	2:34.8
1964	Not held	
1965	Caron, Christine	2:33.4
1966	Caron, Christine	2:29.2
1967	Caron, Christine	2:35.3
1968	Duprez, Benedicte	2:28.4
1969	Canet, Sylvie	2:33.7
1970	Beraud, Christine	2:35.0
1971	Beraud, Christine	2:30.6
1972	Le Noach, Sylvie	2:24.5
1973	Le Noach, Sylvie	2:26.48
1974	Le Noach, Sylvie	2:22.63
1975	Le Noach, Sylvie	2:23.83

100 m. Breast-stroke

1960	Mirkowitch, Amélie	1:23.0
1961	Mirkowitch, Amélie	1:23.4
1962	Pialat, Michele	1:22.5
1963	Mirkowitch, Amélie	1:21.8
1964	Varvenne, Nicole	1:23.7
1965	Dorleans, Danièle	1:22.1
1966	Macaire, Nathalie	1:21.8
1967	Macaire, Nathalie	1:23.8
1968	Gastaldello (nee Mirkowitch), Amélie	1:21.2
1969	Arène, Veronique	1:20.8
1970	Huin, Dominique	1:21.8
1971	Huin, Dominique	1:19.6
1972	Claret, Martine	1:19.7
1973	Leclerc, Viviane	1:19.97
1974	Schmitt, Muriel	1:18.37
1975	De Susini, Annick	1:18.11

200 m. Breast-stroke

1960	Mirkowitch, Amélie	2:56.5
1961	Mirkowitch, Amélie	2:58.9
1962	Pialat, Michèle	2:57.3
1963	Varvenne, Nicole	2:56.2
1964	Varvenne, Nicole	2:58.7
1965	Guerder, Josiane	2:57.3
1966	Macaire, Nathalie	2:56.3
1967	Macaire, Nathalie	2:59.0
1968	Gastaldello (nee Mirkowitch), Amelie	2:55.8
1969	Macaire, Nathalie	2:56.1
1970	Huin, Dominique	2:54.4
1971	Huin, Dominique	2:53.4
1972	Trinquart, Geneviève	2:54.6
1973	Leclerc, Viviane	2:50.49
1974	Schmitt, Muriel	2:49.31
1975	Schmitt, Muriel	2:47.30

100 m. Butterfly

1960	Caron, Annie	1:17.1
1961	Caron, Annie	1:17.8
1962	Libourel, Colette	1:16.8
1963	Hannequin, Danièle	1:18.2
1964	Dorleans, Danièle	1:17.8
1965	Caron, Christine	1:15.8
1966	Prudholme, Michèle	1:14.4
1967	Grojean, Catherine	1:11.6
1968	Grojean, Catherine	1:11.1
1969	Le Cornec, Frederique	1:11.2
1970	Noel, Jacqueline	1:10.6
1971	Salembier, Marie-Domenique	1:10.7
1972	Castiau, Josiane	1:08.7
1973	Langumier, Florence	1:10.07
1974	Pistre, Annette	1:08.78
1975	Clug, Patricia	1:08.13

200 m. Butterfly (Instituted 1967)

1967	Caron, Christine and Prudholme, Michèle (deat heat)	2:45.0
1968	Le Cornec, Frédérique	2:41.5
1969	Le Cornec, Frédérique	2:40.9
1970	Bourlet, Sonia	2:36.8
1971	Salembier, Marie-Domenique	2:34.5
1972	Salembier, Marie-Dominique	2:35.3
1973	Vanpouille, Veronique	2:31.57
1974	Marichal, Sylvie	2:30.71
1975	Clug, Patricia	2:25.57

200 m. Individual medley (instituted 1967)

1967	Dorleans, Danièle	2:36.0
1968	Dorleans, Danièle	2:35.3
1969	Canet, Sylvie	2:38.4
1970	Mandonnaud, Claude	2:34.4
1971	Mandonnaud, Claude	2:34.1
1972	Cartier, Martine	2:36.2
1973	Amiand, Dominique	2:33.00
1974	Carpentier, Caroline	2:31.67
1975	Amiand, Dominique	2:28.86

400 m. Individual medley (Instituted 1962)

1962	Gaillot, Marie-Laure	6:03.5
1963	Vanacker, Annie	5:55.3
1964	Dorleans, Danièle	5:44.1
1965	Dorleans, Danièle	5:41.6
1966	Dorleans, Danièle	5:40.5
1967	Dorleans, Danièle	5:35.9
1968	Kersaudy, Marie-José	5:34.6
1969	Noel, Jacqueline	5:45.7
1970	Lichtenstein, Martine	5:35.8
1971	Lichtenstein, Martine	5:39.2
1972	Amiand, Dominique	5:31.3
1973	Amiand, Dominique	5:27.20
1974	Carpentier, Caroline	5:23.50
1975	Amiand, Dominique	5:20.86

FRONT CRAWL. The fastest means of swimming propulsion, the front crawl, is not mentioned in the rule book of F.I.N.A. This is a strange anomaly for there are more races and records for front crawl swimmers than for any other style, but they all come under the heading of free-style (see FREE–STYLE).

There have been many stages in the development of the front crawl, with its alternating arm stroke and six-beat leg kick. There was side stroke and then the English overarm or side overarm which were developments from the breaststroke. By changing position from prone to side the swimmer could lift one arm out over the water on recovery thus speeding his action. The leg movement changed too, the principles of prone frog kick becoming a side-on scissor blades action.

The trudgen, demonstrated by John Trudgen in London in 1873, was the first style in which both arms were recovered over the water. There were many faults in Trudgen's technique, but the Australians refined this style and their Richard Cavill, using a vertical leg action, bending from the knee, pioneered the Australian crawl. The United States improved the leg kick–after experimenting with eight- and even twelve-beat actions, they settled for the six-beat–and breathing techniques and the embryo of the 'modern' American crawl, now used the world over, was born.

As scientific knowledge of stroke technique grew, it was realised that the leg kick did not contribute as much to propulsion as had been assumed, particularly in relation to the effort expended. Many modern swimmers use their legs now only to a limited degree and some, especially the longer distance experts, use them only as a counter-balance.

FURNISS BROTHERS. (United States). Steve (12 Dec. 1952-   ) and Bruce (27 May 1957-   ), from Santa Ana, California, are a rare breed of world record-breaking brothers.

Steve, the older and bigger (6′ 3″/ 1.91 m), first made his mark at the Pan-American Games of 1971 when he won the 200 and 400 m. medley titles, which he retained at the Pan-Ams of 1975.

He took the 200 m. medley bronze at the 1972 Munich Olympics and failed by only three hundredths of a second to win the world crown for this event in Cali, Colombia, in 1975.

Bruce, the younger and smaller (5′ 11″ /1.80m) came into big-time swimming in 1975. He was runner-up behind his team-mate Tim Shaw (see SHAW, Tim), in the world 200 and 400 m. free-style in Cali and won a gold in the 4 x 100 m. free-style relay. Unfortunately, he had the sad distinction of taking the 'flyer' on the last leg of the 4 x 200 m. free-style relay which resulted in America losing this world title and a world record by disqualification.

Steve was the first Furniss world record-breaker in 1974, when he equalled the 200 m. medley figures of Britain's David Wilkie (see WILKIE, David) with 2:06.32.

Bruce put his name in the record book on 18 June, 1975 when he cut the 200 m. free-style time twice in one day (1:51.41 and 1:50.89). He improved this to 1:50.32 on August 21 and, two days later, took the American title and his elder brother's shared world 200 m. medley record with 2:06.08.

FURUHASHI, Hironashin (Japan, 16 Sept. 1928–). Japan's Hironashin Furu - hashi was known as the 'Flying Fish' not, as most people thought, because of his undoubted speed in the water but because he belonged to the Tobiuo swimming club in Tokyo and 'Tobiuo' means 'Flying Fish' in Japanese. The world's greatest middle and long distance free-styler in 1948/49, Furuhashi never won an Olympic medal. The reason was that Japan, not yet admitted to re-membership of F.I.N.A. after World War II, were excluded from the 1948 Games.

The Japanese had their own way of dealing with this situation. Within minutes of America's Jimmy McLane winning the Olympic 1,500 m. gold medal in London in 19:18.5, news came that Furuhashi had taken 21.8 seconds off the ten-year-old world record of his compatriot Tomikatsu Amano with a time of 18:37.0. Another 'flash' brought the news that Furuhashi had clipped 2.2 from the world 400 m. mark with 4:33.0 which was eight seconds better than the winning time of Bill Smith (USA) in London.

A most unorthodox swimmer, with a deep, rolling style and trailing one leg, Furuhashi's 1948 world best times were not ratified because Japan were not in good standing with F.I.N.A. But he went on to break six official world records— two for 400 m. (best 4:33.3), three for 800 m. (finally 9:35.5) and 1,500 m. (18:19.0). This last mark stood for seven years.

Although Japan were allowed to take part in the 1952 Olympics, Furuhashi, then 24, was past his peak and eighth and last in the 400 m. final was his lone claim to Olympic fame. A graduate of Nihon University in Tokyo, Furuhashi is a professor of athletics at the university and a member of the Japanese Olympic Committee and the F.I.N.A.

FURUKAWA, Masaru (Japan, 6 Jan. 1936–). Furukawa's career at the top of the world breast-stroke rankins (1954– 56) coincided with the brief era when swimming long distances underwater— pioneered by the Japanese—was permitted. And a change of the F.I.N.A. rules prohibiting under-water swimming swept this Nihon University student out of the world rankings almost as quickly as he had gone into them.

Breast-stroke and butterfly were made separate strokes in 1952. Then, in search for speed, some breast-stroke swimmers discovered the advantages of racing great distances under water. Furukawa, with his big lung capacity, exploited this loop-hole in the laws brilliantly.

Twice on the same day he broke the world 200 m. record (10 April 1954). But his remarkable day was 1 October 1955 when he broke all four world records in two swims in one afternoon. In Tokyo, Furukawa set new figures for 200 m. and 220 y. (2:31.0 and 2:31.9) by taking his first breath at the 25 m. turn, breathing again just before the second turn and taking only three breaths on each of his other six laps. Later he swam 100 y. and 100 m. in 61.4 and 68.2 taking only five breaths during the whole of his race.

His only long course world record was in August 1955 when he swam 200 m. in 2:33.7. It took six years for a competitor (Chet Jastremski, USA) swimming on the surface to better this time by a tenth.

Furukawa won the Olympic 200 m. title in 1956 but at the end of the Melbourne Games F.I.N.A. put an end to the under-water era and an end, too, to Furukawa's time at the top.

GATHERCOLE, Terry (Australia, 25 Nov. 1935–).

Gathercole, from Sydney, was the world's best for breast-stroke in the years immediately following the separation of butterfly from breast-stroke and the ruling out of underwater swimming (see BREAST-STROKE). His effective time at the top covered two months, June and July of 1958 when, at 23, he set six world records, won the Commonwealth 220 y. title and a second gold in the medley relay in the Cardiff Games.

His best times set on 28 June 1958– 1:12.4 (110 y.) and 2:36.5 (200 m. and 220 y.)–stood in the world record book until 1961.

Gathercole swam in two Olympics. In 1956 he was fourth in the 200 m. breast-stroke in 2:38.7, four seconds behind the winner, underwater expert Masaru Furu-kawa. In Rome in 1960 he was sixth (2:40.2), but won a silver medal in the medley relay which was in the Olympic programme for the first time.

A former plumber, Gathercole turned to training swimmers and be coach to Australian teams at Olympic and Commonwealth Games and World championships.

GESTRING , Marjorie (United States, 18 Nov. 1922–).

The youngest competitor to win an Olympic title in the pool, Marjorie Gestring was only 13 years and 9 months in early August 1936 when she came first in the springboard diving in Berlin. A tall, slim and graceful girl, Marjorie, from Los Angeles, beat her team mate Katherine Rawls, four years her senior, by less than one point.

GORDON, Elenor (Great Britain, 10 May 1933–).

Helen Orr Gordon, known as Elenor, from Hamilton was one of Scotland's outstanding women swimmers in the 1950s' Her bronze medal in the 200 m. breast-stroke (2:57.6) at the 1952 Olympics was the highlight of her career but she also won the Commonwealth 220 y. titles in 1950 and '54, a medley relay bronze in 1950 and an unexpected medley relay gold in 1954– the first and only time a Scottish squad had won a relay title.

She first swam for Britain, age 14, at the 1947 European championship, and appeared in three Olympics (1948, '52 and '56, the latter, after her marriage, as Mrs. McKay).

This pretty and petite, dark-haired girl won five A.S.A. breast-stroke titles between 1950–56 and was undefeated in the Scottish championships from 1947–57 (eleven years).

GOULD, Shane Elizabeth (Australia, 23 Nov. 1956–).

Undoubtedly the golden girl of the 1972 Olympics, Shane Gould won three golds, all in world record times, a silver and a bronze in Munich. And if there had been a prize for popularity at the Games, this smiling, good-mannered, golden-haired lovely from Sydney would have walked away with it.

Shane was tipped to win as many as five titles. But for a 15-year-old, even one as talented as Gould, this mammoth target involving 11 races in eight days really was a bit too much.

She opened with victory in the 200 m. medley (2:23.07), her outside chance event. Then, the following day, Shane had to settle for the bronze in the 100 m. free-style for which she had seemed to be a certain winner. Probably her medley success brought about this anti-climax, yet the winner Sandy Neilson (USA) did not break Gould's world record (58.5 sec).

Shane was an easy winner of the 400 m. free-style (4:19.04), her third final in successive days. Then, after one day's rest, she tackled the 200 m. and led all the way to win her third gold (2:03.56).

It was a very tired girl who came out for the final of the 800 m. Nevertheless her 8:56.39 was her best time and the American winner, Keena Rothhammer (see ROTHHAMMER, Keena), had to set a world record to beat the Australian girl.

Shane set 11 world records between April 30, 1971 and 11 Feb. 1973 and for eight months (Dec. 1971–Aug. 1972) held the world marks for all five free-style distances – 100, 200, 400, 800 and 1,500 m. Her final world mark, in fact, gave her another special place in swimming's history for her 16:56.9 for 1,500 m. in Adelaide made her the first woman to break 17 min.

Shane, so called after her Welsh-born grandmother who was aptly named Shane Fish, later became disenchanted with the constant training, early rising and strict dieting, and there were fundamental differences of opinion between her parents on the one hand and the demands and discipline of her sport on the other.

In an attempt to revive her spirits and rekindle her interest in swimming, Shane spent several months in California. But, in the end, 2½ years after she burst on the scene like a beautiful rocket, Shane Gould retired from competitive swimming at 16 years and 9 months.

GRINHAM, Judy (Great Britain, 5 Mar. 1939–). The first Briton to win an Olympic swimming gold medal for thirty-two years, Judith Brenda Grinham–but always known as Judy–stepped into a new world on 5 Dec. 1956 when, at 17, she won the 100 m. back-stroke in Melbourne, Lucy Morton had been the last British Olympic champion, way back in 1924, and Judy's Melbourne victory ended starvation time and opened up a new era for her country.

This win, in fact, was just the beginning of an amazing career for this unsophisticated but determined girl from Neasden, who went on to take the back-stroke golds at the 1958 Commonwealth Games and European championships–the first time this kind of hat-trick had been achieved. That year Judy also won a gold in England's world record-breaking medley relay team and a bronze in the free-style relay in Cardiff. And in the Budapest European championships, she added to her medal store with a 100 m. free-style bronze–one of her proudest achievements–and a silver and bronze in the free-style and medley relays respectively.

Her Olympic winning time of 1:12.9 became the first long course world record for 100 m. back-stroke. Later she cut this to 1:11.9, a time which was also a world mark for the two feet longer 110 y.

Judy won three A.S.A. back-stroke titles (1955, '56, '58) while her brief excursion into the free-style field, because she was sick of back-stroke, brought her the National 220 y. title in 1957 and the 110 y. crown in 1958.

For her Melbourne achievements, Judy was voted Britain's sportswoman of 1956. Many thought her swimming achievements were worthy also of a place in a Royal honours list. Unfortunately her era was just before awards to sports stars became commonplace.

Judy Grinham retired from competition on her twentieth birthday, already a legend and one that will remain for ever in British, if not world, swimming history.

GUNDLING, Beulah (United States). The high priestess of synchronized swimming and Pan American solo champion in 1955, Mrs. Gundling and her husband Henry, founders of the International Academy of Aquatic Art, played a most important part in popularising this artistic branch of water sport. They travelled the world giving lectures and demonstrations and their efforts were rewarded in 1952 when F.I.N.A. accepted synchronized swimming as one of their official activities.

GURR, Donna-Marie (Canada, 18 Feb. 1955–). One of international swimming's characters, this slim, courageous girl from Vancouver won medals for back-stroke at four major meetings. Her first successes, second place in the 200 m. and third in the 100 m., came at the 1970 Commonwealth Games, yet it was a near-miracle that she was in Edinburgh at all.

Eight months before these Games, loose chippings of bone and cartilage were discovered at the base of Donna-Marie's left thigh. This should have been the end of her swimming for a year. Instead this pale-faced little blonde insisted on having a plaster she could wear in the water and she just kept training.

Her peak came at the Pan-American Games of 1971 when she won three golds, in the 100 and 200 m. and medley relay. The 200 m. provided a rare drama.

Half-way through the final all the lights in the pool went out so the race had to be reswum and it was the Canadian whose nerve held out best.

She fought her way to a 200 m. bronze at the 1972 Olympics and closed her fine swimming career with a 100 m. silver and 200 m. bronze at the 1974 Commonwealth Games.

GYARMATI FAMILY (Hungary).
Dezso (24 Oct. 1927), Éva (3 Apr.1927) and their daughter Andrea (15 May 1954) are perhaps the most remarkable swimming family in the world.

Father Dezso ranks among the greatest of water-polo players. He won medals at five Olympics—golds in 1952, 1956 and 1964, a silver in 1948 and a bronze in 1960. He was a member of Hungary's European champion teams of 1954 and 1962. He could play as well with his right hand as his left, and at back as well as forward.

Mother Éva Székely (always known in the swimming world by her maiden name) was in the 1948, '52 and '56 Games. She was Olympic breast-stroke champion (using the over water arm recovery before the division of butterfly) and sixth in the 400 m. free-style in 1952. Four years later, using the orthodox underwater arm recovery, she came second in the 200 m. breast-stroke. Runner-up in the European 200 m. breast-stroke in 1947, world record-holder for 100 m. breast-stroke (1:16.9)— using butterfly) and 400 m. medley (5:40.8), versatile Éva won twenty-nine Hungarian titles.

Daughter Andrea has taken the best from each of her parents. She has her father's passionate love for the water. Her mother, who is her coach, has handed down determination and application.

Andrea's first success came at 13, when she won the European Youth 100 m. butterfly title. A year later, at the 1968 Olympic Games she was fifth in the 100 m. back-stroke and butterfly. And a year after this, she retained her Youth butterfly title and was also first in the 100 m. back-stroke.

The year of 1970 brought the third Gyarmati major gold medals in her own right. In the European championships in Barcelona, this delightful daughter of charming and successful parents won the 200 m. back-stroke in a European record of 2:25.5 and the 100 m. butterfly in 65.0. She was also second in the 100 m. back-stroke and swam the first leg (60.3) in Hungary's 4 x 100 m. silver medal free-style relay team.

At Munich in 1972 there were great hopes that Andrea would become the third member of her family to win an Olympic gold medal, particularly after she had broken the world record with 1:3.80 in a semi-final of the 100 m. butterfly. Although she improved this to 1:3.73 in the final, two other girls swam faster — Mayumi Aoki (Jap) with a world record 1:3.34 and Roswitha Beier (EGer) 1:3.61.

The young Gyarmati also took a silver in the 100 m. back-stroke in Munich and a bronze for 200 m. back-stroke at the world championships in Belgrade the following year.

Yet even though she did not win an Olympic gold, Andrea did bring one to add to the family collection in 1973 when she married Hungary's Milhaly Hesz, the 1968 Olympic Kayak canoe singles champion.

HAJÓS, Alfréd (Hungary, 1 Feb. 1878-12 Nov. 1955). The first Olympic swimming champion. Alfréd Hajós won two out of the three golds (100 and 1,200 m.) at the Athens Games of 1896. Born Arnold Guttmann, in Budapest, his swimming pseudonym eventually became his legal name. A noted architect, Hajos designed the indoor pool on Margaret Island in the Danube, dividing Buda and Pest, and many other stadia and hydrophatic installations. Twice a member of the Hungarian national soccer team, Hajós won the silver medal for sports architecture at the 1924 Olympics (the first prize was not awarded) and was elected to the Fort Lauderdale Hall of Fame in 1966.

No world records were ratified in his day and Hajós's Olympic winning time of 1:22.2 for 100 m. did not compare with the 61.4 of England's Jack Tyers (who did not swim in Athens) in taking the A.S.A. 100 y. title that year. But the Hungarian's 18:22.2 for 1,200 m., in beating Antoine Papanos of Greece by 1:41.2, was infinitely superior to the performances by English distance swimmers.

HALASY, Olivér (Hungary, 31 July 1909-10 Sept. 1946). Born Haltmayer, in Ujpest, just north of Budapest, Halasy lost his left foot in a childhood tramway accident, yet became the world's best water-polo half-back of the 1930s. An auditor by profession, Halasy was a member of the Hungarian gold medal teams at the 1932 and '36 Olympics, having won a water-polo silver in 1928, and won more golds at the European championships of 1931, '34 and '38. He also took the European 1,500 m. freestyle in 1931 (20:49.0) and twenty-five Hungarian individual swimming titles.

Halasy was shot dead while returning to his home by taxi late at night when only 37.

HALL, Gary (United States, 7 Aug. 1951-). World record breaking is always a surprise but in relation to Gary Hall's decimation of the 400 m. medley figures in 1969, astonishment was a mild word. The Californian took three-tenths off the year-old mark of his fellow American, Olympic champion Charles Hickcox and in clocking 4:38.7 was ten seconds faster than his own silver medal time in Mexico. Five weeks later he improved 4.8 secs to 4:33.9. The same summer Hall broke the world records for 200 m. back-stroke and medley with 2:06.6 and 2:09.6 respectively.

Hall's versatile talent takes in a 4:08.5 for 400 m. free-style and 1,500 m. in 16:32.8.

In August, 1970, Hall demonstrated his all-round swimming ability further, by breaking the world record for 200 m. butterfly, in the American championships, with 2:05.0. At the same meeting he reduced his 200 m. medley time to 2:09.5 (but this world mark was beaten two weeks later by Sweden's Gunnar Larsson in the European championships) and the 400 m. medley world record to 4:31.0

He attained his finest medley form in early August 1972 when he equalled Larsson's 200 m. world record (2:9.30) and set new figures for 400 m. (4:30.81), which stood for two years, during the American championships in Chicago. But at the Munich Olympics four weeks later, Hall had "gone over the top" and although he held winning and potential world record-breaking leads at half distance in both medley finals, he "blew up" in heart-breaking fashion and finished in fourth and fifth place respectively in the 200 and 400 m.

HALL OF FAME. Founded in 1965 to further the interests of all aquatic activities and to honour outstanding personalities in swimming, the Hall of Fame is a non-profit making educational corporation. The citizens of Fort Lauderdale, Florida, collected $1,190,000 to pay for the building of the vast hall and the 50 m. swimming pool.

In 1968, F.I.N.A. decided that this unique foundation should be known as the International Hall of Fame. Those who have been honoured and the year of their recognition are:

Contrib. = Outstanding Contributor

A – Andersen, Greta (Den) Swim/Channel Swim (1969); Anderson, Miller (USA) Dive (1967); Armbruster, Dave, (USA) Coach (1969).

B – Bachrach, Bill (USA) Coach (1966); Ball, Catie (USA), Swim (1975); Bathe, Walther (Ger) Swim (1970); Bauer, Carl (USA) Contrib. (1967); Bauer, Sybil (USA) Swim (1967); Beaurepaire, Sir Frank (Aus) Swim (1967); Bleibtrey, Ethelda (USA) Swim (1967); Borg, Arne (Swe) Swim (1966); Brandsten, Greta (Swe) Dive (1973); Brandsten, Ernst (Swe/USA) Coach (1966); Braun, Ma (Neth) Coach (1967); Brauninger, Stan (USA) Coach (1971); Breen, George (USA) Swim (1974); Browning, Skippy (USA) Dive (1974).

C – Cady, Fred (USA) Coach (1969); Cann, Tedford (USA) Swim (1967); Capilla, Joaquin (Mex) Dive (1975); Carlile, Forbes (Aus) Coach (1975); Cavill Family (Aus) Swim (1970); Chadwick, Florence (USA) Channel Swim (1970); Charlton, Boy (Aus) Swim (1971); Clark, Steve (USA) Swim (1966); Coleman, Georgia (USA) Dive (1971); Corsan, George Sen. (USA) Contrib. (1971); Counsilman, James (USA) Coach (1975); Cousteau, Jacques-Yves (Fr) Contrib. (1967); Crabbe, Buster (USA) Swim (1965); Crapp, Lorraine (Aus) Swim (1971); Cummins, Bert (GB) Contrib. (1974); Curtis, Ann (USA) Swim (1966).

D – Daniels, Charles (USA) Swim (1965); Daughters, Ray (USA) Coach (1971); Degener, Dick (USA) Dive (1971); Desjardins, Pete (USA) Dive (1966); Dorfner, Olga (USA) Swim (1970); Draves, Vickie (USA) Dive (1969); Durack, Fanny (Aus) Swim (1967).

E – Ederle, Gertrude (USA) Swim/Channel Swim (1965); Epstein, Charlotte (USA) Contrib. (1974).

F – Farrell, Jeff (USA) Swim (1968) Fern, Harold (GB) Contrib. (1974); Finney, Claire (USA) Swim (1970); Fletcher, Jenny (GB) Swim (1971);

Ford, Alan (USA) Swim (1966); Franklin, Benjamin (USA) Contrib. (1968); Fraser, Dawn (Aus) Swim (1965); Fullard-Leo, Ellen (Hawaii) Contrib. (1947); Furuhashi, Hironashin (Jap) Swim (1967).

G – Gestring, Marjorie (USA) Dive (1975); Goodwin, Budd (USA) Swim (1971); Gundling, Beulah (USA) Syncho Swim (1965); Gyarmati, Dezso (Hun) W-Polo/Coach (1975).

H – Hajos, Alfred (Hun) Swim (1966); Halmay, Zoltan (Hun) Swim (1968); Handley, Lou de B (USA) Coach (1967); Handy, Jamison, (USA) Contrib. (1965); Harlan, Bruce (USA) Dive (1973); Harup, Karen (Den) Swim (1974); Hebner, Harry (USA) Swim (1968); Henricks, Jon (Aus) Swim (1973); Henry, William (GB) Contrib. (1974); Hickcox, Charles (USA) Swim (1975); Higgins, John (USA) Swim (1971); Hill (nee Poyton), Dorothy (USA) Dive (1968); Hodgson, George (Can) Swim (1968); Holm, Eleanor (USA) Swim (1966); Hommonai, Marton (Hun) W-Polo (1971); Hough, Richard (USA) Swim (1970); Hunyadfi, Stefin (Hun) W-Polo/Coach (1969); Hveger, Ragnhild (Den) Swim (1966).

J – Jarvis, John (GB) Swim (1968).

K – Kahanamoku, Duke (USA) Swim (1965); Kaufman, Beth (USA) Contrib. (1967); Kealoha, Warren (USA) Swim (1968); Kellerman, Annette (USA) Contrib. (1974); Kennedy, Edward (USA) Contrib. (1966); Kiefer, Adolph (USA) Swim (1965); Kieran, Barney (Aus) Swim (1969); Kint, Cor (Neth) Swim (1971); Kiputh, Bob (USA) Coach (1965); Kitamura, Kusuo (Jap) Swim (1965); Kojac, George (USA) Swim (1968); Kok, Ada (Neth) Swim (1975); Kolb, Claudia (USA) Swim (1974)j Konno, Ford (USA) Swim (1971); Konrads, John and Ilsa (Aus) Swim (1971); Kramer, Ingrid, (E Ger) Dive (1974).

L – Lackie, Ethel (USA) Swim (1969); Lane, Freddy (Aus) Swim (1969); Laufer, Walter (USA) Swim

(1973); Lee, Sammy (USA) Dive
(1968); Longfellow, William (USA)
Contrib. (1965); Louhring, Fred
(USA) Contrib. (1974).

M – McCaffree, Charles (USA) Contrib.
(1975); McCormick, Pat (USA)
Dive (1965); McDermott, Michael
"Turk" (USA) Swim (1969);
McKinney, Frank (USA) Swim
(1974); McLane, James (USA)
Swim (1970); Madison, Helene
(USA) Swim (1966); Maioni, Mario
(It) W-Polo (1971); Mann, Matt II
(USA) Coach (1965)j Mann, Shelly
(USA) Swim (1966); Marshall,
John (Aus) Swim (1973); Masten-
broek, Rie (Neth) Swim (1968);
Meany, Helen (USA) Dive (1971);
Medica, Jack (USA) Swim (1966);
Morris, Pam Synchro Swim (1965).

N – Nakama, Ken (USA) Swim (1974);
Nemeth, Janos (Hun) W-Polo
(1969); Neuschaefer, Al (USA)
Coach (1967); Norelius, Martha
(USA) Swim (1967); Novak, Eva
and Ilona (Hun) Swim (1973).

O – O'Connor, Wally (USA) W-Polo
(1966); Ouden, Willy den (Neth)
Swim (1970); Oyakawa, Yoshi
(USA) Swim (1973).

P – Padou, Henri (Fr) W-Polo (1970);
Patnik, Al (USA) Dive (1969);
Peppe, Mike (USA) Coach (1966);
Pinkston, Betty Becker (USA)
Dive (1967); Pinkston, Clarence
(USA) Dive/Coach (1966).

R – Rademacher, Erich (Ger) Swim/
W-Polo (1971); Radmilovic, Paul
(GB) W-Polo/Swim (1967); Rau-
sch, Emil (Ger) Swim (1968);
Rawls, Katherine (USA) Swim/
Dive (1965); Riggin, Aileen (USA)
Dive/Swim (1967); Ris, Wally
(USA) Swim (1966); Ritter, R.
Max (Ger/USA) Contrib. (1965);
Robie, Carl (USA) Swim (1975);
Robinson, Tom (USA) Coach
(1974); Rose, Murray (Aus) Swim
(1965); Ross, Norman (USA)
Swim (1967); Ruuska, Sylvia
(USA) Swim (1975).

S – Sakamoto, Soichi (USA) Coach
(1966); Saltza, Chris von (USA)
Swim (1966); Sava, Charlie (USA)
Coach (1970); Schaeffer, E. Car-
roll (USA) Swim (1968); Schol-
lander, Don (USA) Swim (1965);
Silvia, Charles (USA) Contrib.
Smith, Bill (USA) Swim (1966);

Spence Brothers, Walter, Wallace
and Leonard (USA) Swim (1967);
Stender, Jan (Neth) Coach (1973);
Stouder, Sharon (USA) Swim
(1972); Szekely, Eva (Hun) Swim
(1975).

T – Taylor, Henry (GB) Swim (1969);
Theile, David (Aus) Swim (1968);
Troy, Mike (USA) Swim (1971);
Tsuruta, Yoshijuki (Jap) Swim
(1968); Trudgen, John (GB) Con-
trib. (1974).

V – Varona, Donna de (USA) Swim
(1969); Verdeur, Joe (USA) Swim
(1966); Vliet, Nel van (Neth) Swim
(1973).

W – Wainwright, Helen (USA) Swim/
Dive (1972); Webb, Matthew (GB)
Channel Swim (1965); Webster,
Robert (USA) Dive (1970); Weis-
muller, Johnny (USA) Swim
(1965); White, Albert (USA) Dive
(1965); Wickham Brothers (Fiji)
Contrib. (1974); Williams, Esther
(USA) Contrib. (1966); Wylie,
Mina (Aus) Swim (1974).

Y – Yorzyk, Bill (USA) Swim (1971)

Z – Zorilla, Albert (Arg) Swim (1975).

HALMAY, Zoltán (Hungary, 18 June
1881-20 May 1956). Wrongly listed in
many history books as de Halmay or
von Halmay, Zoltán Halmay's swimming
talents covered the whole range of events
from 50 y. to 4,000 m. Between 1900
and 1908 he won seven Olympic medals
at three Games–two silvers (200 and
4,000 m.) and a bronze (1,000 m.) in
1900, two golds (50 and 100 y.) in 1904
and two silvers (100 and 4 x 200 m.) in
1908. He also won the silver for 100 m.
at the 1906 Interim Games and was the
first world record-holder for this distance.
His 65.8 set on 3 Dec. 1905 stood for
4½ years.

Halmay, a factory manager from
Budapest, was involved in a row and an
historic swim-off before being acclaimed
winner of the Olympic 50 y. in St. Louis.
In the final, he appeared to have beaten
his American rival Scott Leary by a foot,
but the judges were split on who was
first. A bath-side brawl involving everyone in sight was resolved by the chairman of the jury who ruled the two men
would race again. This time Halmay
made no mistake and won by 0.6 in 28.0
sec.

His Olympic medal-winning times–

100 y. 68.2, 200 m. 2:31.0, 1,000 m. 15:16.4 and 4,000 68:55.4—were miraculous in their era. And he did all this swimming with arms only and without any leg movements.

HARDING, Phyllis (Great Britain, 15 Dec. 1907-   ). An outstanding backstroker, Phyl Harding is the only woman swimmer to have competed at four Olympic Games. She was second in the 100 m. (1:27.4) in 1924 at 17. She was unplaced in 1928, but four years later came fourth behind Britain's bronze medal winner Valerie Davies. And in 1936, in Berlin, she was seventh in the final in her fastest 1:21.5

Her three European championship appearances included bronzes in 1927— the first year women's events were in the programme—and 1931 and fourth in 1934. The Commonwealth Games did not begin until Miss Harding's seventh international season. At the 1930 first meeting she was third in the 100 y. and in 1934, at 26, she won a gold in 1:13.8 and also a silver in the medley relay.

Miss Harding's astonishing career brought her only two A.S.A titles, (1935/36) but, of course, her twelve years at the top were also those of three other great British swimmers—Joyce Cooper, Valerie Davies and Ellen King— who themselves were Olympic backstroke medallists.

HARGITAY, András (Hungary, 17 March, 1956-   ). This tall, serious young man from Budapest, who took third place at the 1972 Munich Olympics, proved himself the finest 400 m. medley swimmer a year later in Belgrade where he won the World title. And he confirmed his supremacy 12 months later, in Vienna, by taking the European championship in a world record (4:28.89). He underlined his position in 1975, in Cali, by retaining his title and also winning the 200 m. medley.

Hargitay has two great assets. One is his tremendous stamina, which he demonstrated in shattering fashion at the 1973 European Cup by winning the 200 m. butterfly and, just seven mins. later, the 400 m. medley.

The second is Hargitay's complete range of swimming talent. Unlike some of his contemporaries, he has no weak stroke in his repertoire.

The Magyar's medal tally takes in six (out of a possible 10) golds at the European Youth championships in Rotterdam in 1971, bronzes for the 200 m. medley at the '73 World and '74 European championships and a gold for 200 m. butterfly to go with his medley victories in Vienna and Cali.

HARRISON, Joan (South Africa, 29 Nov. 1935-   ). South Africa's only Olympic pool champion. Joan Harrison's win in the 100 m. back-stroke (1:14.3—a Games record) in 1952 so excited her team manager Alex Bulley that he collapsed as she touched first. And in that Helsinki Olympics she came close to a second gold medal for free-style. This 100 m. final was a dramatic affair with the South African one of three different leaders in the last 10 m. In the end, Joan was placed fourth in 67.1, a time also given to the third and fifth swimmers, only three-tenths behind Hungarian winner Katalin Szoke.

Joan was only 14, in 1950, when she took the Commonwealth 440 y. title in 5:26.4, more than seven seconds ahead of England's Margaret Wellington and came third in the 110 y. (70.7) in Auckland. Her final successes came in the 1954 Commonwealth Games in Vancouver where she won two golds (110 y. back-stroke and free-style relay) a silver (medley relay) and a bronze (110 y. free-style). But like many great racers, Joan Harrison never broke a world record.

HATFIELD, Jack (Great Britain, 15 Aug. 1893-1965). John Gatenby Hatfield, but known as Jack in the swimming world, won forty A.S.A. titles during his amazing 20-year career from 1912 to 1931. He was silver medallist behind Canada's George Hodgson in the 1912 Olympic 400 and 1,500 m. freestyle and was fifth and fourth respectively in these events in the Olympics of 1924 when he was 31 years old. Hatfield was also a member of Britain's bronze medal 4 x 200 m. relay squad in 1912 in Stockholm.

His English championship successes and best times in each were: 220 y. (1912–2:30.2, 1913, '22, '25); 440 y. (1912–4:54.8, 1913, '24, '27); 500 y. (1912, '13, '21, '22–6:11.4, 1923–27); 880 y. (1912, '13–11:46.4, 1921–25); one mile (1912, '13, '14–24:42.4, 1921-

24. 1929–30) long distance (1913–14, 1921, '23, '24, '28, '31–57:22.0 sec.)

Hatfield broke four world records: 300 y. in 3:26.4 (1913), 400 m. in 5:21.6 (1912), 500 y. 6:02.8 (1913), 500 m. 6:56.8 (1912).

HEARN, George (Great Britain, d. 10 Dec. 1949). The father of organized world swimming, George Hearn from England's West Country was President of the A.S.A. in 1908 when he called a meeting of nationas taking part in the London Olympics to discuss their mutual problems. At this meeting it was decided to found the International Amateur Swimming Federation (see F.I.N.A.). Hearn, who had been hon. secretary of the A.S.A. from 1903/07, became the first secretary/treasurer of the new world organization and held those offices until 1928. He was then made a life honorary president.

HEARN, George, Cup. This trophy was purchased from the widow of George Hearn (see previous entry) by Mr. T.E. H. Tanton and presented, through the *Swimming Times* to the A.S.A. in 1954. It is awarded to the English diver whose performance is judged the best of the year. Winners:

1954 Long, Ann (Ilford)
1955 Welsh, Charmian (Durham City)
1956 Tarsey, David (Ealing)
1957 Welsh, Charmian (Durham City)
1958 Phelps, Brian (Highgate)
1959 Phelps, Brian (Highgate)
1960 Phelps, Brian (Highgate)
1961 Ferris, Elizabeth (Mermaid)
1962 Phelps, Brian (Highgate)
1963 Austen, Margaret (Isleworth)/
      Newman, Joy (Isander) (tie)
1964 Phelps, Brian (Highgate)
1965 Rowlatt, Kathy (Leyton)
1966 Phelps, Brian (Highgate)
1967 Rowlatt, Kathy (Leyton)
1968 Rowlatt, Kathy (Leyton)
1969 Wetheridge, Brian (Metropolitan)
1970 Thewlis, Joe (Luton)
1971 Koppell, Helen (Coventry)
1972 Drake, Alison (Basildon)
1973 Drake, Alison (Basildon)
1974 Williams, Beverley (Hillingdon)
1975 Snode, Christopher (Highgate)

HEATLY, Peter (Great Britain, 9 June 1924-). Scotland's only home-produced diver of real class, Heatly coached himself to medal successes at three Commonwealth Games and a European championship and to participation in two Olympics.

Swimming was his first love. He won Scottish 440 and 880 y. titles in 1946 and might have earned a place in the British swimming team for the 1948 Olympics. But Heatly decided he had better long term prospects in diving and a fifth place from the highboard at the London Games was his first reward.

In the Commonwealth Games, he won the highboard in 1950 and was second in the springboard; won the springboard and was third in the highboard in 1954 and regained his highboard crown in 1958. But his finest fighting effort was in the European championships of 1954 when he just got into the final as twelfth and last qualifier and then pulled back to take the bronze medal on his final dive. Unaccountably, he was left out of the British team for the 1956 Olympics which caused a small storm at the time.

Two engineering degrees, his own engineering and contracting firm, membership of the Edinburgh Town Council and the Vice-Chairmanship of the Organizing Committee for the 1970 Commonwealth Games in Edinburgh are among Heatly's other achievements. He won twenty-eight diving Scottish titles, ten A.S.A. titles and is Britain's representative on the F.I.N.A. international diving committee.

In 1971 he was awarded the C.B.E. for his services to sport and four years later became chairman of the Scottish Sports Council.

HENCKEN, John (United States, 29 May, 1954-). One of the rare breed of superb competitors, Hencken, born in Culver City, California, is a record-breaker who also wins the big events. At the Olympic Games in Munich (1972) he took the 200 m. breast-stroke in a world best 2:21.55 and he followed this with a world record-breaking victory (1:04.02) in the 100 m. at the World championships in Belgrade the next year.

In Munich he was also the 100 m. bronze medallist while in Belgrade, where he also won a gold in the Medley relay, he came second behind the man he had beaten into the silver medal spot in Munich, Britain's David Wilkie (see WILKIE, David) in the 200 m.

Hencken, winner of eight United States breast-stroke titles between 1972-1975, set four world marks for 100 m. (from 1:05.68 in 1972 to 1:03.88 in '74) and five for 200 m. (2:22.79, '72 to 2:18.21, '74) in those years.

The American, although winning two U.S. short-course titles in the spring of 1975, opted out of competing in the World championships and Pan-American Games that year.

HENRICKS, Jon (Australia, 6 June 1934-). One of the world's great sprinters, Jon Henricks from Sydney proved this in winning the 1956 Olympic 100 m. in 55.4 and taking a second gold in the Australian 4 x 200 m. team. Yet, strangely, the 6 ft. and 12 st. fair-haired Henricks was trained as a distance swimmer in the early days, though against his own inclinations.

He missed the 1952 Olympic because of ear trouble and, on the way to Rome in 1960, an illness which hit many of the Australian team robbed him of a possible second 100 m. gold. He was, in fact, one of the favourites, but did not get through the semi-finals and was not well enough to swim at all in the relay.

Henricks was a triple gold medallist (110 y., 4 x 220 y. free-style and 3 x 110 y. medley) in the 1954 Commonwealth Games in Vancouver and won six Australian titles—110 y. from 1953—56 and 220 y. in 1952—54.

HENRY, William (Great Britain, b. 29 June 1859). First co-honorary secretary, with Archibald Sinclair, of the Royal Life Saving Society, William Henry of London worked hard and long to encourage the teaching of life saving and resuscitation. He was also co-author, with Sinclair, of the Badminton Library *Book of Swimming,* published first in June 1893 and revised in December 1894 which gives, to those lucky enough to have a copy now, an encyclopaedic and fascinating picture of the sport in the last century.

He was also a member of the small team—the others were George Hearn, Hjalmar Johansson and Max Ritter (see separate entries)—who drew up the first code of conduct for Olympic swimming events in preparation for the 1908 Games in London.

This remarkable, dapper gentleman,

with his neat military moustache, was a practising as well as a theoretical swimming enthusiast. He won the A.S.A. quarter-mile salt water amateur championship in 1889, the long distance in 1890 and was 100 m. champion of Europe in 1896. A water-polo international, he played for England against Scotland in 1890 and 1892, captaining the team on the latter occasion. He was also one of Britain's finest scientific swimmers.

In 1900, Henry, a member of the Amateur and Zephyr clubs, was in the British team for the 1900 Olympic Games in Paris where he came sixth in the 200 m. obstacle race.

Six years later, at the Interim Games in Athens, at the age of 47, he won a bronze in the 4 x 250 m. relay. He is the oldest competitor to win an Olympic swimming medal.

HICKCOX, Charles (United States, 6 Feb. 1947-). A talented medley man with a leaning towards back-stroke, Hickcox from Phoenix, Arizona, won three golds and a silver at the 1968 Olympics. His medley racing stint in Mexico, with all the problems of altitude, was tremendously hard. Yet Hickcox took the 200 and 400 m. titles in 2:12.0, one second ahead of Greg Buckingham (USA) and 4:48.4, three-tenths in front of his other medley team-mate Gary Hall. The presentation ceremony for the 200 m. medley was most dramatic, for Hickcox had to support his bronze medal-winning team-mate John Ferris, suffering from the effects of altitude, who finally collapsed at the foot of the rostrum and had to be given oxygen.

Hickcox was also second to East Germany's Roland Matthes in the 100 m. back-stroke (60.2 to the 58.7 of Matthes) and he led off the United States medley relay team to victory and a world record of 3:54.9.

His five individual world marks (set between 28 Aug. 1967 and 30 Aug. 1968) included three for back-stroke—100 m. 59.3 and 59.1 and 200 m. 2:09.4, all set during his three gold medal winning appearances in the 1967 World Student Games in Tokyo. His third gold came in the medley relay.

Two months before Mexico, Hickcox set world medley marks for 200 m. (2:10.6) and 400 m. (4:39.0). He was

Pan-American 100 m. back-stroke champion in 1967, runner-up in the 200 m. and a member of the United States 4 x 200 m. free-style gold medal team. He won four United States outdoor titles— 100 and 200 m. back-stroke in both 1966 and '67.

Another member of the Hickcox family emerged on the swimming scene in 1974. This was young Tom, who had not been among America's top 25 sprinters the year before, yet came through to win the U.S. Outdoor 100 m. title in 52.16. A week later, he clocked 51.59 only 0.37 sec. outside the world record, in a match against East Germany.

HIGHBOARD DIVING. The highboards, which are rigid platforms, are 5, 7½ and 10 m. above the water level. However, in major competitions it is unusual for competitors to use anything but the highest one.

The international test for men consists of four voluntary dives with a total degree of difficulty not exceeding 7.5 and six voluntary dives without limit. The women's test is four voluntary dives with a total tarrif value of 7.5 and four voluntary dives without limit.

In each section, each dive must be selected from a different group (see DIVING).

HILL, (nee POYNTON), Dorothy (United States, 17 July 1915-   ). Silver medallist for springboard diving in the 1928 Olympics—two weeks after her thirteenth birthday—Dorothy Poynton from Salt Lake City won the highboard gold in 1932 and retained her title (as Mrs. Hill) in Berlin in 1936 when she also took the bronze medal from the springboard.

HISTORY OF SWIMMING. Swimming was not in the programme of the Ancient Olympic Games, though the sport of swimming was not unknown to the Greeks and races took place in Japan in 36 B.C., during the reign of Emperor Suigiu.

Japan was the first country to organize swimming nationally and an Imperial edict in 1603 made it compulsory in schools; there were even inter-college competitions and a three-day swimming meeting was organized in 1810. But Japan was a closed country and it was

left to the Anglo-Saxon countries to lead the world in modern swimming development.

The first swimming organization in England was the National Swimming Society, founded in London by John Strachan in 1837 when the metropolis had six indoor baths, all of which, surprisingly, had diving boards. The first indoor bath in England was built in Liverpool in 1828 at St. George's Pierhead.

It was in Australia that the first modern swimming championship was organized—in 1846, at the Robinson baths in Sydney where the 440 y. event was won by W. Redman in 8:43.0. In Australia, too, a so-called 'world championship' 100 y. race was held at St. Kilda, a suburb of Melbourne, on 9 Feb. 1858. This was won by Australia's Jo Bennett from Sydney, who beat Charles Stedman of England.

There was no amateur or professional distinction about swimming competitions prior to 1869. But there were a great number of aquatic activities in Britain . . . races for money prizes or side bets and ornamental and trick swimming demonstrations. Harold Kenworthy beat Indians of the Ojibwa tribe at the Holborn baths in 1884 and Fred Beckwith, English professional champion, defeated Deerfoot, a Seneca Indian, in 1861.

The Amateur Swimming Association, founded on 7 Jan. 1869 under the then title of the Metropolitan Swimming Club Association (see separate entries) is considered to be the first national swimming association. And on 11 Feb. 1869, the M.S.C.A. defined as 'amateur' and established rules for competition. The first National amateur champion was Tom Morris, who won a mile race, downstream, between Putney Aqueduct and Hammersmith Bridge in 1869. The first official record approved by the M.S.C.A. was Winston Cole's 100 y. in 1:15.0 in 1871.

On the Continent, the German Federation was founded in 1882, and the French in 1899. The New Zealand A.S.A. (1890) preceded by one year, the formation of the A.S.A. of New South Wales. These two associations co-operated in the organization of Australasian championships until the Australian Amateur Swimming Union was founded in

1909. Combined Australasian teams, in fact, took part in the Olympics up to 1912.

The United States held their first championships in 1877, the distance was one mile and it was won by R. Weissenboth. Until 1888, American championships were organized by the New York Athletic Club. Events for women were not introduced in the United States until 1916. Scotland anticipated American, and indeed English action, by holding their first national championship for women in 1892–a 200 y. event won by E. Dobbie of Glasgow in 4:25.0.

In 1889, the Erste Wiener Amateur Swim Club of Vienna held two races (60 and 500 m.) under the title of European championships, and these continued annually until 1903. In 1896, at the first Olympic Games in Athens, three swimming races were held in the bay of Zea, neat Piraeus. Around 1900, events described as world championships were also organized.

The Federation Internationale de Natation Amateur was founded in London on 19 July 1908 and established that year the first list of official world swimming records. In 1912 women's events were added to the Olympic programme and Fanny Durack of Australia and Greta Johansson of Sweden became the first swimming and diving champions.

European championships were first held in 1926 (for men) and the following year women's races were added and the European Swimming League (see LIGUE EUROPEENNE NATATION) was founded. The first Commonwealth Games (known then as the British Empire Games) took place in 1930.

HODGSON, George (Canada, b. 12 Oct. 1893-). Canada's only Olympic swimming champion, George Ritchie Hodgson was undefeated in his three years of racing culminating in his 400 and 1,500 m. world record-breaking victories in the Stockholm Games of 1912.

Hodgson, who learned to swim in the Laurentian mountain lakes, never had a swimming lesson or a coach . . . being in 'good physical shape' was his way to success. In Stockholm he set world records for 1,000 y. and m. on the way to his gold medal. And having beaten

Britain's Jack Hatfield by 39 sec., Hodgson swam on a further 109 m. to break the world record for one mile.

A day later, the Canadian beat Hatfield again, by 1.4 sec. to win the 400 m. championship. His world record of 5:24.4 in the 100 m. salt-water pool in Stockholm harbour fell to the Briton three months later in an indoor, 100 ft. bath swim. But Hodgson's 1,500 m. mark of 22:00.0 remained on the books for eleven years.

Hodgson won the one mile in the Inter-Empire championships of 1911 to celebrate the coronation of King George V. The course at London's old Crystal Palace, as he recalls, was: 'without lanes or guiding lines on the bottom and the turn was on a log boom across one end'. The Canadian retired at 18, after his Stockholm golden double, the undisputed, undefeated champion of the world.

HOLLAND, Steve (Australia, 31 May, 1958-). Holland's claim to fame always will be that he swam a mile (1,609.344 m.) to win the 1,500 m. free-style at the first World championships in Belgrade in 1973! Then, at 15, he was taking part in his first major competition on his first trip outside Australia.

Holland went into the lead at 500 m., ahead of World 400 m. champion Rick DeMont (USA) and Olympic 400 m. champion Brad Cooper (Aus) (see COOPER, Brad and DeMONT, Rick) and former world record-holder John Kinsella (USA), and steadily pulled away from his experienced rivals. He finished to tumultuous cheers five m. ahead of DeMont with Cooper trailing a further 13 m. back.

Suddenly the cheers turned to gasps, for Holland had not stopped swimming. He tore up the bath again, ignored all efforts by officials to stop him at the turn, and raced back. DeMont, Cooper and Kinsella bemused, but not willing to take a chance that their own lap counting was right and Holland's wrong, were forced to follow their young rival and they, too, swam another 100 m.

And still Holland did not stop. He turned again and set off on yet another 100 m., but this time the frantic officials managed to pull him up after he had swum about 10 m.

Holland's reason for not stopping was

that there should have been a bell or whistle to signal the last 100 m. This hadn't been given and he was going to swim on . . . and on . . . until he did get a signal.

The Brisbane-born boy won in a world record of 15:31.85, which cut six sec. off the mark he had set a month earlier, and put up an 800 m. record (8:16.27) on the way. Four months later, he won the Commonwealth 1,500 m. title in Christchurch, New Zealand, watched by Queen Elizabeth II and other members of the royal family. But this time he knew when to stop swimming.

Holland did not defend his 1,500 m. world title in Cali, Colombia in 1975.

HOLM-JARRETT, Eleanor (United States, 6 Dec. 1913-). Eleanor Holm, later Mrs. Jarrett, qualified for American teams at three Olympics and swam at two. In 1928, at 14, she was fifth in the 100 m. back-stroke in Amsterdam. Four years later she won this event (1:19.4) at the Los Angeles Games. Picked for the 1936 Olympics, she was disciplined for her behaviour on the boat to Europe and was sent home without setting even a toe in the Berlin pool.

Eleanor Holm won twenty-nine American championships and broke seven world back-stroke records. Her best times were 1:16.3 (100 m. s/c), 1:52.0 (150 y. l/c) and 2:48.7 (200 m. s/c). Her American 100 and 200 m. back-stroke records stood for more than sixteen years and she was also an outstanding individual medley competitor.

After her Berlin disappointment, she turned professional and starred with Johnny Weissmuller and Buster Crabbe in Aquacades and films having been born not only with an exceptional swimming talent but also the glamour to succeed in show business.

HUNGARIAN CHAMPIONS. Hungary and Hungarian competitors have exerted a tremendous influence on the modern development of swimming. As early as the 1820s, Hungarian students of classical philology had drawn attention to the ancient Olympics and National Games of the classical Greeks. And Ferenc Kemény, who is regarded as the virtual father of the Hungarian Olympic movement, was a faithful supporter of Baron Pierre de Coubertin, founder of the Olympic Games of the Modern era, during the 12 years leading up to the holding of the first Games in Athens in 1896.

Hungary's Alfréd Hajós (see HAJÓS, Alfréd) was the first Olympic swimming champion, winning the 100 and 1,200 m. titles in Greece. And Magyar swimmers have competed in every Olympics since, except the Games in Antwerp in 1920, when their country was excluded for political reasons. In 1952, their women received a special trophy for winning four of the five titles in Helsinki.

Hungary, too, were the initiators of the first European swimming championships in 1926 when István Bárány (see BÁRÁNY, István) took the 100 m. title.

In recent years, Hungary's National championships have been dominated by a succession of outstanding competitors— like Jozsef Csikány, winner of the 100 m. back-stroke title eight years in succession (1960-67) and Judit Túróczy, 200 m. free-style seven times (1964-70). Multi-title winners in a variety of events are András Hargitay (see HARGITAY, András) who took 28 championships in eight different events between 1970 and '75 and Andrea Gyarmati (see GYARMATI FAMILY) 28 titles in seven (1967-73).

MEN

100 m. Free-style

1960	Dobai, Gyula	56.3
1961	Dobai, Gyula	55.7
1962	Dobai, Gyula	56.0
1963	Dobai, Gyula	55.2
1964	Dobai, Gyula	54.8
1965	Szall, Antal	55.7
1966	Csaba, László	56.6
1967	Kucsera, Gabor	56.1
1968	Csatlos, Csaba	55.4
1969	Szentirmai, István	55.7
1970	Szentirmai, István	54.6
1971	Szentirmai, István	54.0
1972	Szentirmai, István	54.2
1973	Szentirmai, István	55.0
1974	Hamori, Jeno	54.94
1975	Verrasztó, Zoltán	55.2*

200 m. Free-style

1960	Katona, József	2:06.5
1961	Dobai, Gyula	2:06.4

1962	Katona, József	2:06.9
1963	Dobai, Gyula	2:04.9
1964	Dobai, Gyula	2:02.5
1965	Dobai, Gyula	2:04.8
1966	Csaba, László	2:04.6
1967	Jaczo, László	2:05.2
1968	Borloi, Matyas	2:02.7
1969	Borloi, Mátyás	2:00.6
1970	Borloi, Mátyás	1:59.1
1971	Hargitay, András	1:59.9
1972	Hargitay, András	1:59.2
1973	Verrasztó, Zoltán	2:00.1
1974	Hargitay, András	1:59.44
1975	Verrasztó, Zoltán	1:59.30

400 m. Free-style

1960	Katona, József	4:32.3
1961	Katona, József	4:29.8
1962	Katona, József	4:33.2
1963	Katona, József	4:28.4
1964	Dobai, Gyula	4:34.2
1965	Katona, József	4:26.3
1966	Jaczó, László	4:32.4
1967	Kosztolánczy, György	4:27.8
1968	Borlói, Mátyás	4:25.2
1969	Borlói, Mátyás	4:21.3
1970	Hargitay, András	4:13.5
1971	Hargitay, András	4:18.9
1972	Verrasztó, Zoltán	4:20.0
1973	Hargitay, András	4:13.4
1974	Hargitay, András	4:12.81
1975	Tóth, Csaba	4:12.95

1,500 m. Free-style

1960	Katona, József	18:17.2
1961	Katona, József	18:49.5
1962	Katona, József	19:15.1
1963	Katona, József	17:49.6
1964	Ali, Csaba	18:30.3
1965	Katona, József	17:59.9
1966	Kosztolánczy, György	18:18.5
1967	Kosztolánczy, György	17:54.6
1968	Hevesi, László	17:45.1
1969	Deli, György	18:14.3
1970	Hargitay, András	17:29.6
1971	Tóth, Csaba	17:25.6
1972	Soós, Csaba	17:22.7
1973	Tóth, Csaba	16:48.6
1974	Tóth, Csaba	16:28.89
1975	Tóth, Csaba	16:15.45

100 m. Back-stroke

1960	Csikány, József	1:04.5
1961	Csikány, József	1:03.9
1962	Csikány, József	1:03.6
1963	Csikány, József	1:04.6
1964	Csikány, József	1:02.9

1965	Csikány, József	1:04.3
1966	Csikány, József	1:02.6
1967	Csikány, József	1:03.3
1968	Cseh, László	1:02.5
1969	Cseh, László	1:01.2
1970	Cseh, László	1:00.9
1971	Cseh, László	59.9
1972	Cseh, László	59.6
1973	Cseh, László	59.7
1974	Verrasztó, Zoltán	59.6
1975	Verrasztó, Zoltán	59.67

200 m. Back-stroke

1961	Csikány, József	2:20.9
1962	Csikány, József	2:20.1
1963	Csikány, József	2:22.6
1964	Csikány, József	2:18.1
1965	Csikány, József	2:20.6
1966	Csikány, József	2:18.8
1967	Borlói, Mátyás	2:18.1
1968	Borlói, Mátyás	2:16.5
1969	Borlói, Mátyás	2:18.1
1970	Borlói, Mátyás	2:13.9
1971	Cseh, László	2:12.1
1972	Verrasztó, Zoltán	2:12.1
1973	Verrasztó, Zoltán	2:07.3
1974	Verasztó, Zoltán	2:06.37
1975	Verrasztó, Zoltán	2:06.35

100 m. Breast-stroke

1960	Kunsági, György	1:14.8
1961	Lenkei, Ferenc	1:14.1
1962	Ulrich, Andras	1:13.7
1963	Lenkei, Ferenc	1:12.9
1964	Lenkei, Ferenc	1:11.0
1965	Lenkei, Ferenc	1:12.1
1966	Lenkei, Ferenc	1:10.7
1967	Lenkei, Ferenc	1:11.3
1968	Szabó, Sándor	1:09.7
1969	Szabó, Sándor	1:09.8
1970	Ali, Csaba	1:11.3
1971	Szabó, Sándor	1:08.3
1972	Szabó, Sándor	1:09.3
1973	Nagy, József	1:09.3
1974	Szabó, Sándor	1:08.3
1975	Vermes, Albán	1:09.66

200 m. Breast-stroke

1960	Kunsági, György	2:43.1
1961	Lenkei, Ferenc	2:45.5
1962	Ulrich, Andras	2:46.3
1963	Lenkei, Ferenc	2:40.9
1965	Lenkei, Ferenc	2:36.8
1965	Lenkei, Ferenc	2:39.4
1966	Lenkei, Ferenc	2:37.0
1967	Somlai, Lajos	2:38.6
1968	Szabó, Sándor	2:37.0
1969	Szabó, Sándor	2:36.0

1970	David, Gyula	2:35.3
1971	Hargitay, András	2:32.7
1972	Tóth, János	2:32.2
1973	Hargitay, András	2:30.0
1974	Hargitay, András	2:31.91
1975	Hargitay, András	2:28.59

100 m. Butterfly

1960	Kiss, László	1:04.6
1961	Gulrich, József	1:03.5
1962	Gulrich, József	1:00.2
1963	Gulrich, József	1:00.9
1964	Gulrich, József	1:00.6
1965	Csaba, Gábor	1:01.9
1966	Gyulás, Ákos	1:00.6
1967	Lázár, Peter	1:01.4
1968	Kosztolánczy, György	1:02.6
1969	Szentirmai, István	59.9
1970	Szentirmai, István	58.8
1971	Szentirmai, István	57.4
1972	Szentirmai, István	58.1
1973	Szentirmai, István	59.2
1974	Hargitay, András	58.37
1975	Szentirmai, István	58.32

200 m. Butterfly

1960	Várzsegi, Lajos	2:31.4
1961	Katona, József	2:27.3
1962	Katona, József	2:22.9
1963	Kiricsi, János	2:20.7
1964	Kiricsi, János	2:21.4
1965	Ali, Csaba	2:17.8
1966	Ali, Csaba	2:18.9
1967	Ali, Csaba	2:16.8
1968	Ali, Csaba	2:17.2
1969	Ali, Csaba	2:17.2
1970	Hargitay, András	2:13.4
1971	Soós, Csaba	2:17.1
1972	Soós, Csaba	2:14.3
1973	Hargitay, András	2:08.9
1974	Hargitay, András	2:08.5
1975	Hargitay, András	2:07.89

200 m. Imdividual medley (instituted 1966)

1966	Lenkei, Ferenc	2:19.2
1967	Lázár, Péter	2:20.6
1968	Lázár, Péter	2:17.1
1969	Szentirmai, István	2:17.5
1970	Csinger, Márton	2:15.0
1971	Hargitay, András	2:12.6
1972	Hargitay, András	2:11.9
1973	Hargitay, András	2:11.6
1974	Hargitay, András	2:11.64
1975	Hargitay, András	2:08.67

400 m. Individual medley

1960	Várszegi, Lajos	5:18.7
1961	Bodóki, Csaba	5:25.3
1962	Lenkei, Ferenc	5:17.2
1963	Ali, Csaba	5:07.1
1964	Kosztolánczy, György	5:05.7
1965	Ali, Csaba	5:01.2
1966	Lázár, Péter	5:05.5
1967	Kosztolánczy, György	5:00.4
1968	Lázár, Péter	4:56.6
1969	Borlói, Mátyás	4:52.0
1970	Hargitay, András	4:48.2
1971	Hargitay, András	4:41.7
1972	Hargitay, András	4:40.0
1973	Hargitay, András	4:38.8
1974	Hargitay, András	4:35.86
1975	Hargitay, András	4:34.32

WOMEN

100 m. Free-style

1960	Madarász, Csilla	1:03.4
1961	Frank, Mária	1:04.8
1962	Takács, Katalin	1:03.4
1963	Madarász, Csilla	1:04.1
1964	Madarász, Csilla	1:03.2
1965	Túróczy, Judit	1:01.5
1966	Túróczy, Judit	1:02.7
1967	Kovács, Edit	1:03.6
1968	Túróczy, Judit	1:00.6
1969	Túróczy, Judit	1:00.0
1970	Gyarmati, Andrea	1:00.6
1971	Gyarmati, Andrea	1:00.6
1972	Gyarmati, Andrea	1:00.9
1973	Gyarmati, Andrea	1:00.3
1974	Pelle, Judit	1:01.66
1975	Bedekovics, Krisztina	1:00.72

200 m. Free-style (instituted 1961)

1961	Frank, Mária	2:23.6
1962	Frank, Mária	2:24.2
1963	Frank, Mária	2:20.6
1964	Túróczy, Judit	2:21.6
1965	Túróczy, Judit	2:19.5
1966	Túróczy, Judit	2:20.0
1967	Túróczy, Judit	2:18.1
1968	Túróczy, Judit	2:15.1
1969	Túróczy, Judit	2:14.2
1970	Túróczy, Judit	2:16.7
1971	Gyarmati, Andrea	2:14.4
1972	Gyarmati, Andrea	2:14.9
1973	Gyarmati, Andrea	2:12.9
1974	Pelle, Judit	2:13.57
1975	Pelle, Judit	2:16.00

400 m. Free-style

Year	Name	Time
1960	Madrász, Csilla	5:13.1
1961	Frank, Mária	5:15.7
1962	Frank, Mária	5:12.2
1963	Frank, Mária	5:08.4
1964	Takács, Katalin	5:07.7
1965	Gágyor, Vera	5:11.7
1966	Soltész, Ágnes	5:13.3
1967	Fodor, Judit	5:07.4
1968	Törzs, Mária	5:11.1
1969	Törzs, Mária	4:59.6
1970	Eckel, Edit	4:57.4
1971	Gyarmati, Andrea	4:47.6
1972	Gyarmati, Andrea	4:50.9
1973	Gyarmati, Andrea	4:44.8
1974	Lázár, Eszter	4:39.53
1975	Lázár, Eszter	4:36.61

800 m. Free-style (instituted 1965)

Year	Name	Time
1965	Takács, Katalin	10:48.2
1966	Fodor, Judit	10:53.9
1967	Fodor, Judit	10:37.5
1968	Fodor, Judit	10:36.1
1969	Eckel, Edit	10:25.5
1970	Eckel, Edit	10:23.7
1971	Kiss, Éva	10:00.1
1972	Törzs, Mária	10:00.7
1973	Lázár, Eszter	9:55.5
1974	Lázár, Eszter	9:31.63
1975	Lázár, Eszter	9:30.77

100 m. Back-stroke

Year	Name	Time
1960	Madarász, Csilla	1:13.3
1961	Korényi, Olga	1:14.3
1962	Korényi, Olga	1:13.3
1963	Balla, Mária	1:11.2
1964	Balla, Mária	1:11.9
1965	Korényi, Olga	1:12.0
1966	Balla, Mária	1:11.7
1967	Balla, Mária	1:11.1
1968	Balla, Mária	1:10.4
1969	Gyarmati, Andrea	1:12.6
1970	Baranyi, Judit	1:11.5
1971	Gyarmati, Andrea	1:08.4
1972	Gyarmati, Andrea	1:08.2
1973	Gyarmati, Andrea	1:06.9
1974	Czövek, Zsuzsa	1:08.5
1975	Verrasztó, Gabriella	1:06.94

200 m. Back-stroke (instituted 1961)

Year	Name	Time
1961	Takács, Katalin	2:45.4
1962	Egerváry, Márta	2:38.1
1963	Balla, Mária	2:35.2
1964	Balla, Mária	2:36.2
1965	Túróczy, Judit	2:36.8
1966	Túróczy, Judit	2:33.0
1967	Balla, Mária	2:34.0
1968	Pók, Edina	2:40.2
1969	Túróczy, Judit	2:34.3
1970	Gyarmati, Andrea	2:26.9
1971	Gyarmati, Andrea	2:29.1
1972	Gyarmati, Andrea	2:26.6
1973	Gyarmati, Andrea	2:23.1
1974	Czövek, Zsuzsa	2:26.10
1975	Verrasztó, Gabriella	2:23.66

100 m. Breast-stroke

Year	Name	Time
1960	Killermann, Klára	1:21.2
1961	Egerváry, Márta	1:24.8
1962	Egerváry, Márta	1:23.2
1963	Egerváry, Márta	1:21.3
1964	Kovács, Zsuzsa	1:22.9
1965	Brandi, Mária	1:22.2
1966	Kovács, Zsuzsa	1:22.9
1967	Kovács, Edit	1:20.1
1968	Kovács, Edit	1:19.7
1969	Kovács, Edit	1:19.0
1970	Kovács, Edit	1:20.1
1971	Mate, Maria	1:18.8
1972	Kaczander, Ágnes	1:18.0
1973	Kiss, Éva	1:17.4
1974	Kaczander, Ágnes	1:16.38
1975	Ludányi, Mária	1:16.32

200 m. Breast-stroke

Year	Name	Time
1960	Killermann, Klára	2:52.7
1961	Egerváry, Márta	3:03.9
1962	Egerváry, Márta	3:00.4
1963	Egerváry, Márta	2:57.8
1964	Egerváry, Márta	2:58.6
1965	Egerváry, Márta	2:58.1
1966	Máté, Mária	2:58.4
1967	Egerváry, Márta	2:56.7
1968	Egerváry, Márta	2:54.5
1969	Prutz, Éva	2:56.7
1970	Kaczander, Ágnes	2:50.8
1971	Kiss, Éva	2:47.9
1972	Kaczander, Ágnes	2:46.3
1973	Kiss, Éva	2:42.4
1974	Kaczander, Ágnes	2:43.69
1975	Kiss, Éva	2:46.33

100 m. Butterfly

Year	Name	Time
1960	Egerváry, Márta	1:15.3
1961	Egerváry, Márta	1:12.8
1962	Egerváry, Márta	1:11.6
1963	Egerváry, Márta	1:10.9
1964	Tölgyesi, Ida	1:13.1
1965	Egerváry, Márta	1:10.6
1966	Kovács, Edit	1:12.0
1967	Gyarmati, Andrea	1:09.2
1968	Gyarmati, Andrea	1:07.6
1969	Gyarmati, Andrea	1:06.1
1970	Gyarmati, Andrea	1:06.0

1971	Gyarmati, Andrea	1:04.8
1972	Gyarmati, Andrea	1:05.6
1973	Gyarmati, Andrea	1:05.0
1974	Kaczander, Ágnes	1:06.22
1975	Ludányi, Mária	1:05.96

200 m. Butterfly (instituted 1962)

1962	Egerváry, Márta	2:42.7
1963	Egerváry, Márta	2:43.7
1964	Egerváry, Márta	2:44.2
1965	Gágyor, Vera	2:41.9
1966	Gágyor, Vera	2:46.1
1967	Egerváry, Márta	2:39.2
1968	Gyarmati, Andrea	2:34.6
1969	Kovács, Edit	2:39.0
1970	Gyarmati, Andrea	2:28.3
1971	Gyarmati, Andrea	2:30.3
1972	Kaczander, Ágnes	2:29.9
1973	Kiss, Éva	2:27.1
1974	Kaczander, Ágnes	2:23.81
1975	Kiss, Eva	2:25.42

200 m. Individual medley (instituted 1966)

1966	Túróczy, Judit	2:37.1
1967	Túróczy, Judit	2:37.3
1968	Túróczy, Judit	2:30.5
1969	Túróczy, Judit	2:33.7
1970	Túróczy, Judit	2:30.9
1971	Túróczy, Judit	2:29.7
1972	Túróczy, Judit	2:31.4
1973	Kaczander, Ágnes	2:30.4
1974	Kaczander, Ágnes	2:27.71
1975	Verraszto, Gabriella	2:26.10

400 m. Individual medley (instituted 1961)

1961	Egerváry, Márta	5:56.2
1962	Egerváry, Márta	5:45.3
1963	Egerváry, Márta	5:47.5
1964	Egerváry, Márta	5:40.3
1965	Egerváry, Márta	5:35.5
1966	Túróczy, Judit	5:41.3
1967	Egerváry, Márta	5:36.7
1968	Egerváry, Márta	5:33.6
1969	Túróczy, Judit	5:34.3
1970	Kaczander, Ágnes	5:27.8
1971	Kiss Éva	5:21.0
1972	Kaczander, Ágnes	5:17.4
1973	Kiss, Éva	5:17.0
1974	Kaczander, Ágnes	5:14.99
1975	Ernszt, Ágnes	5:15.11

HUTTON, Ralph (Canada, 6 Mar. 1948 −). They call Ralph Hutton the 'Iron Man' and his non-stop stint at the 1966 Commonwealth Games in Jamaica supports this nickname. He competed in thirteen races, swam 3½ miles in six days and collected one gold, five silver and two bronze medals from his marathon effort. The versatile Hutton from Ocean Falls, but who had done much of his swimming in the United States, was in the Canadian winning medley team (swimming back-stroke), was second in the 110 and 220 y. back-stroke, 440 y. medley and 4 x 110 and 4 x 220 y. free-style relays. He was third in the 440 y. and 1,650 y. free-style.

But it was for free-style that he made his world mark−with a 400 m. world record of 4:06.5 on 1 Aug. 1968. But at the Mexico Olympics two months later the Canadian had to bow to America's Mike Burton, who took the gold in 4:09.9 to Hutton's 4:11.7.

Hutton, who at 16, had swum in eight of the ten events at the 1964 Olympics also took part in the 1972 Games in Munich, where he reached two finals.

He was in Canada's team at three Pan-American Games (1963, '67, '71), winning a gold for 200 m. back-stroke on his second appearance (his only major individual victory), eight silvers and three bronzes for a total of 12 medals. He also brought his Commonwealth medal tally to 12 in Edinburgh in 1970.

With a grand total of 25 medals, 18 of them silvers, from eight appearances at major events between 1963-1972, Hutton must be swimming's champion runner-up.

HVEGER, Ragnhild (Denmark, 10 Dec. 1920-). 'The greatest swimmer who never won an Olympic title' is not an extravagant tag to tie around the fame of Ragnhild Hveger. Denmark's 'Golden Torpedo' broke forty-two individual world records for fifteen different free-style distances plus three for back-stroke between 1936 and 1942. Ten years later, after seven years in retirement and at the age of 32, Hveger was still good enough to place fifth in the 1952 Olympic 400 m. final only 4.8 seconds behind the winner.

She showed her budding talent at 13 when the Danish championships took place in her home town of Elsinore. Unknown Ragnhild had never been in a race before, yet she won the 400 m. title.

World War II cost her an Olympic crown. In September, 1940, about the time the cancelled XIIth Games should have taken place, Hveger at the peak of her brilliance set her eighth 400 m. world mark with 5:00.1. It took sixteen years for a girl to break five minutes.

The Dane, at 15, won the 400 m. silver medal at the 1936 Berlin Olympics. At the 1938 European championships she took three golds—an unforgettable half a length of the 50 m. pool victory in the 400 m. (clearly her favourite distance), the 100 and 4 x 100 m. freestyle.

Hveger's world record list include 59.7 (100 y.), 2:21.7 (200 m.), 2:22.6 (220 y.), 3:25.6 (300 y.), 3:42.5 (300 m.), 5:00.1 (400 m.), 5:11.4 (440 y.), 5:53.0 (500 y.), 6:27.4 (500 m.), 10:52.5 (800 m.), 11:08.7 (880 y.), 12:36.0 (1,000 y.), 13:54.4 (1,000 m.), 20:57.0 (1,500 m.) and 23:11.5 (one mile) and for back-stroke 2:41.3 and 5:38.2 for 200 and 400 m. respectively.

1971	Milan	18-21 Sept.
1972	Turin	23-26 July
1973	Leghorn	31 July-2 Aug.
1974	Florence	15-18 Sept.
1975	Padua	8-11 Sept.

MEN

100 m. Free-style

1960	Perondini, Giorgio	58.1
1961	Della Savia, Ezio	57.9
1962	Dennerlein, Fritz	57.7
1963	Bianchi, Bruno	56.8
1964	Bianchi, Bruno	56.9
1965	Boscaini, Pietro	55.4
1966	Borracci, Massimo	56.4
1967	Boscaini, Pietro	55.7
1968	Boscaini, Pietro	54.9
1969	Boscaini, Pietro	56.6
1970	Pangaro, Roberto	55.0
1971	Nardini, Fabrizio	55.5
1972	Pangaro, Roberto	54.9
1973	Pangaro, Roberto	54.6
1974	Pangaro, Roberto	53.66
1975	Guarducci, Marcello	53.43

200 m. Free-style

1960	Dennerlein, Fritz	2:08.7
1961	Dennerlein, Fritz	2:06.1
1962	Orlando, Giovanni	2:05.4
1963	Orlando, Giovanni	2:06.1
1964	De Gregorio, Sergio	2:05.9
1965	De Gregorio, Sergio	2:01.1
1966	Borracci, Massimo	2:05.1
1967	Borracci, Massimo	2:03.9
1968	Boscaini, Pierto	2:01.7
1969	La Monica, G. Piero	2:05.4
1970	Pangaro, Roberto	2:02.2
1971	Targetti, Riccardo	2:01.9
1972	Cinquetti, Arnaldo	1:59.0
1973	Pangaro, Roberto	1:59.4
1974	Pangaro, Roberto	1:57.68
1975	Guarducci, Marcello	1:57.42

400 m. Free-style

1960	Dennerlein, Fritz	4:37.5
1961	Dennerlein, Fritz	4:32.0
1962	Orlando, Giovanni	4:31.1
1963	Spangaro, P.Paolo	4:32.2
1964	De Gregorio, Sergio	4:29.8
1965	De Gregorio, Sergio	4:24.4
1966	Siniscalco, Riccardo	4:31.5
1967	Siniscalco, Riccardo	4:26.8
1968	Nardini, Fabrizio	4:30.1
1969	La Monica, G. Piero	4:29.8
1970	Pangaro, Roberto	4:24.0
1971	Grassi, Sandro	4:19.6

INTER-COUNTRY SPEED SWIMMING CONTEST. See BOLOGNA TROPHY.

INTERNATIONAL AMATEUR SWIMMING FEDERATION. See FEDERATION INTERNATIONALE DE NATATION AMATEUR.

INTERNATIONAL HALL OF FAME. See HALL OF FAME.

ITALIAN CHAMPIONS. First held in 1919, the Italian swimming championships in recent years have been dominated by Novella Calligaris (see CALLIGARIS, Novella), the World 800 m. free-style champion of 1973. This slim girl won 36 out of the total of 72 individual Italian titles decided in the six years between 1968 and 1973. Novella's brother Mauro also won National swimming crowns.

Italian swimming suffered a sad loss in 1966 when a plane carrying members of the National team crashed near Bremen. Those who died included Bruno Bianchi, Sergio de Gregorio, Luciana Massenzi, Dino Rora and Carmen Longo, all Italian champions.

The venues and winners of championships since 1960 are:

1960	Rome	28-31 July
1961	Turin	18-20 Aug.
1962	Rome	3-5 Aug.
1963	Milan	22-25 Aug.
1964	Naples	30 July-2 Aug.
1965	Milan	7-10 Aug.
1966	Turin	28-31 July
1967	Florence	9-12 Aug.
1968	Milan	20-23 Aug.
1969	Naples	7-10 Aug.
1970	Catania	19-22 Sept.

1972	Cinquetti, Arnaldo	4:13.6
1973	Cinquetti, Arnaldo	4:18.0
1974	Marugo, Lorenzo	4:13.55
1975	Affronte, Sergio	4:14.43

1,500 m. Free-style

1960	Rosi, Massimo	18:44.3
1961	Orlando, Giovanni	18:43.7
1962	Orlando, Giovanni	18:16.0
1963	Orlando, Giovanni	18:27.8
1964	Orlando, Giovanni	18:53.9
1965	De Gregorio, Sergio	17:57.8
1966	Siniscalco, Riccardo	18:24.2
1967	Frandi, Fabio	17:55.6
1968	Alibertini, Sergio	18:05.8
1969	Alibertini, Sergio	17:52.8
1970	Irredento, Sergio	17:30.1
1971	Barelli, Luigi	17:11.9
1972	Irredento, Sergio	16:46.6
1973	Irredento, Sergio	17:05.7
1974	Marugo, Lorenzo	16:46.43
1975	Bellon, Stefano	16:41.81

100 m. Back-stroke

1960	Avallone, Giuseppe	1:05.6
1961	Schollmeier, Christian	1:05.3
1962	Rora, Dino	1:04.8
1963	Rora, Dino	1:03.0
1964	Rora, Dino	1:03.2
1965	Rora, Dino	1:02.6
1966	Della Savia, Ezio	1:05.5
1967	Del Campo, Franco	1:02.0
1968	Del Campo, Franco	1:02.4
1969	Chino, Franco	1:02.9
1970	Chimisso, Roberto	1:02.3
1971	Forti, Paolo	1:02.9
1972	Bosco, Simone	1:03.3
1973	Cianchi, Lapo	1:02.6
1974	Cianachi, Lapo	1:02.05
1975	Bisso, Enrico	59.84

200 m. Back-stroke (instituted 1961)

1961	Rora, Dino	2:24.9
1962	Rora, Dino	2:23.6
1963	Rora, Dino	2:21.5
1964	Rora, Dino	2:17.8
1965	Rora, Dino	2:18.7
1966	Della Savia, Ezio	2:20.4
1967	Chino, Franco	2:16.4
1968	Del Campo, Franco	2:13.8
1969	Chino, Franco	2:18.1
1970	Calligaris, Mauro	2:15.8
1971	Calligaris, Mauro	2:15.0
1972	Nistri, Massimo	2:12.8
1973	Nistri, Massimo	2:14.5
1974	Nistri, Massimo	2:11.48
1975	Cianchi, Lapo	2:10.96

100 m. Breast-stroke (instituted 1961)

1961	Contrada, Sergio	1:15.2
1962	Lazzari, Roberto	1:13.9
1963	Gross, Gianni	1:11.5
1964	Gross, Gianni	1:12.0
1965	Gross, Gianni	1:11.3
1966	Gross, Gianni	1:11.1
1967	Gross, Gianni	1:11.2
1968	Sacchi, Massimo	1:10.8
1969	Daneri, Andrea	1:13.2
1970	Daneri, Andrea	1:12.6
1971	Daneri, Andrea	1:10.0
1972	Mingione, Edmondo	1:09.7
1973	Lalle, Giorgio	1:10.8
1974	Lalle, Giorgio	1:07.57
1975	Lalle, Giorgio	1:09.24

200 m. Breast-stroke

1960	Lazzari, Roberto	2:43.6
1961	Contrada, Sergio	2:43.9
1962	Contrada, Sergio	2:42.1
1963	Gross, Gianni	2:40.2
1964	Caramelli, Cesare	2:41.5
1965	Gross, Gianni	2:37.4
1966	Gross, Gianni	2:39.9
1967	Giovannini, Maurizio	2:39.2
1968	Sacchi, Massimo	2:38.3
1969	Benanti, Enrico	2:41.5
1970	Di Pietro, Michele	2:37.3
1971	Daneri, Andrea	2:37.2
1972	Di Pietro, Michele	2:33.7
1973	Lalle, Giorgio	2:31.5
1974	Lalle, Giorgio	2:28.12
1975	Lalle, Giorgio	2:29.95

100 m. Butterfly (instituted 1961)

1961	Fossati, Giampiero	1:03.4
1962	Rastrelli, Antonello	1:02.8
1963	Rastrelli, Antonello	1:02.4
1964	Rastrelli, Antonello	1:01.1
1965	Fossati, Giampiero	1:01.0
1966	Fossati, Giampiero	1:01.3
1967	Attanasio, Antonio	1:01.6
1968	Attanasio, Antonio	1:00.3
1969	Attanasio, Antonio	1:00.7
1970	D'Oppido, Michele	1:00.2
1971	Tozzi, Angelo	1:00.4
1972	D'Oppido, Michele	1:00.1
1973	Tozzi, Angelo	1:01.0
1974	Barelli, Paolo	58.45
1975	Barelli, Paolo	58.52

200 m. Butterfly

1960	Dennerlein, Fritz	2:22.2
1961	Dennerlein, Fritz	2:19.9
1962	Dennerlein, Fritz	2:16.2
1963	Dennerlein, Fritz	2:15.2

1964	Rastrelli, Antonello	2:17.4
1965	Fossati, Giampiero	2:16.0
1966	Fossati, Giampiero	2:17.4
1967	Fossati, Giampiero	2:13.9
1968	Tozzi, Angelo	2:14.1
1969	Palumbo, Ladislao	2:15.2
1970	Tozzi, Angelo	2:15.8
1971	Tozzi, Angelo	2:11.7
1972	Tozzi, Angelo	2:10.1
1973	Tozzi, Angelo	2:11.7
1974	Tozzi, Angelo	2:10.81
1975	Griffith, Alessandro	2:09.92

200 m. Individual medley (instituted 1966)

1966	Pagnini, Pietro	2:23.6
1967	D'Oppido, Michele	2:21.9
1968	D'Oppido, Michele	2:17.9
1969	D'Oppido, Michele	2:20.7
1970	D'Oppido, Michele	2:17.7
1971	D'Oppido, Michele	2:17.1
1972	Marugo, Lorenzo	2:15.7
1973	Marugo, Lorenzo	2:16.3
1974	Marugo, Lorenzo	2:14.25
1975	Barelli, Paolo	2:14.34

400 m. Individual medley (instituted 1962)

1962	Dennerlein, Fritz	5:11.2
1963	Dennerlein, Fritz	5:11.3
1964	Orlando, Giovanni	5:15.0
1965	Orlando, Giovanni	5:13.0
1966	D'Oppido, Antonio	5:08.7
1967	Spinola, Francesco	5:06.7
1968	D'Oppido, Michele	5:00.2
1969	Calligaris, Mauro	5:01.3
1970	Calligaris, Mauro	5:02.5
1971	Marugo, Lorenzo	4:56.0
1972	Calligaris, Mauro	4:49.4
1973	Marugo, Lorenzo	4:51.5
1974	Marugo, Lorenzo	4:46.07
1975	Marugo, Lorenzo	4:46.93

WOMEN

100 m. Free-style

1960	Saini, Paola	1:05.9
1961	Saini, Paola	1:05.4
1962	Saini, Paola	1:03.6
1963	Beneck, Daniela	1:04.5
1964	Beneck, Daniela	1:04.1
1965	Beneck, Daniela	1:03.0
1966	Beneck, Daniela	1:03.3
1967	Strumolo, Maria A.	1:02.9
1968	Strumolo, Maria A.	1:02.8
1969	Calligaris, Novella	1:04.2
1970	Calligaris, Novella	1:03.7

1971	Calligaris, Novella	1:02.9
1972	Calligaris, Novella	1:02.5
1973	Podesta, Laura	1:02.3
1974	Bortolotti, Laura	1:01.69
1975	Dessy, Elisabetta	1:02.62

200 m. Free-style (instituted 1966)

1966	Beneck, Daniela	2:22.5
1967	Strumolo, Maria A.	2:20.5
1968	Sacchi, Mara	2:18.8
1969	Calligaris, Novella	2:17.6
1970	Calligaris, Novella	2:16.8
1971	Calligaris, Novella	2:12.1
1972	Calligaris, Novella	2:09.2
1973	Calligaris, Novella	2:12.0
1974	Bortolotti, Laura	2:11.22
1975	Pandini, Giuditta	2:13.28

400 m. Free-style

1960	Saini, Paola	5:17.7
1961	Saini, Paola	5:12.8
1962	Beneck, Daniela	5:04.8
1963	Beneck, Daniela	5:05.3
1964	Beneck, Daniela	5:01.8
1965	Beneck, Daniela	4:58.4
1966	Beneck, Daniela	4:58.5
1967	Scassellati, Giovanna	5:01.4
1968	Calligaris, Novella	4:52.0
1969	Calligaris, Novella	4:42.7
1970	Calligaris, Novella	4:44.8
1971	Calligaris, Novella	4:33.6
1972	Calligaris, Novella	4:26.7
1973	Calligaris, Novella	4:39.7
1974	Bortolotti, Laura	4:36.33
1975	Pandini, Giuditta	4:34.90

800 m. Free-style (instituted 1966)

1966	Beneck, Daniela	10:29.4
1967	Scassellati, Giovanna	10:22.1
1968	Calligaris, Novella	9:56.7
1969	Calligaris, Novella	9:38.0
1970	Calligaris, Novella	10:01.6
1971	Calligaris, Novella	9:29.1
1972	Calligaris, Novella	9:06.0
1973	Calligaris, Novella	9:11.6
1974	Bortolotti, Laura	9:25.26
1975	Pandini, Giuditta	9:17.06

100 m. Back-stroke

1960	Serpilli, Daniela	1:17.0
1961	Segrada, Mirella	1:17.8
1962	Massenzi, Luciana	1:16.3
1963	Cutolo, Raffaella	1:17.0
1964	Cutolo, Raffaella	1:16.9
1965	Massenzi, Luciana	1:12.6

1966	Dapretto, Luciana	1:12.7
1967	Dapretto, Luciana	1:12.6
1968	Spitoni, Cinzia	1:14.7
1969	Spitoni, Cinzia	1:12.8
1970	Bigazzi, Rita	1:12.0
1971	Finesso, Sandra	1:10.3
1972	Finesso, Sandra	1:10.9
1973	Torrisi, Patrizia	1:10.7
1974	Roncelli, Antonella	1:07.21
1975	Roncelli, Antonella	1:06.64

200 m. Back-stroke (instituted 1966)

1966	Dapretto, Luciana	2:39.4
1967	Dapretto, Luciana	2:36.4
1968	Rasi, Raffaella	2:42.2
1969	Spitoni, Cinzia	2:36.8
1970	Tarantino, Cristina	2:32.8
1971	Bassanese, Emanuela	2:33.8
1972	Finesso, Sandra	2:31.9
1973	Calligaris, Novella	2:31.3
1974	Roncelli, Antonella	2:25.94
1975	Roncelli, Antonella	2:23.7*

100 m. Breast-stroke (instituted 1961)

1961	Marcellini, Luciana	1:23.9
1962	Marcellini, Luciana	1:23.5
1963	Marcellini, Luciana	1:22.8
1964	Schiezzari, Laura	1:22.8
1965	Schiezzari, Laura	1:20.5
1966	Bosio, Loredana	1:21.1
1967	Schiezzari, Laura	1:21.0
1968	Tricarico, M. Rosaria	1:21.7
1969	Tricarico, M. Rosaria	1:23.3
1970	Morozzi, Paola	1:22.7
1971	Miserini, Patrizia	1:20.8
1972	Miserini, Patrizia	1:20.5
1973	Morozzi, Paola	1:21.3
1974	Bolla, Paola	1:21.43
1975	Corniani, Iris	1:19.56

200 m. Breast-stroke

1960	Zennaro, Elena	3:01.6
1961	Marcellini, Luciana	2:58.5
1962	Marcellini, Luciana	2:59.2
1963	Marcellini, Luciana	2:55.3
1964	Marcellini, Luciana	2:58.0
1965	Longo, Carmen	2:55.7
1966	Schiezzari, Laura	2:58.7
1967	Tricarico, M. Rosaria	2:56.4
1968	Tricarico, M. Rosaria	2:54.4
1969	Tricarico, M. Rosaria	2:57.4
1970	Tripi, Monica	2:54.3
1971	Miserini, Patrizia	2:50.9
1972	Miserini, Patrizia	2:51.0
1973	Morozzi, Paola	2:54.3
1974	Bolla, Paola	2:50.94
1975	Corniani, Iris	2:50.29

100 m. Butterfly

1960	Beneck, Anna	1:17.1
1961	Saini, Paola	1:15.2
1962	Saini, Paola	1:13.3
1963	Cecchi, Annamaria	1:13.5
1964	Cecchi, Annamaria	1:15.0
1965	Noventa, Elisabetta	1:13.4
1966	Cecchi, Annamaria	1:12.6
1967	Tomassini, Daniela	1:12.8
1968	Colombo, Cinzia	1:11.2
1969	Palmieri, Marta	1:12.0
1970	Palmieri, Marta	1:10.9
1971	Talpo, Donatella	1:09.0
1972	Talpo, Donatella	1:07.2
1973	Talpo, Donatella	1:07.3
1974	Talpo, Donatella	1:06.06
1975	Schiavon, Donatella	1:05.66

200 m. Butterfly (instituted 1966)

1966	Bellani, Annalisa	2:43.3
1967	Bellani, Annalisa	2:41.1
1968	Fill, Cristina	2:39.3
1969	Calligaris, Novella	2:35.8
1970	Sordelli, Susanna	2:37.7
1971	Calligaris, Novella	2:31.0
1972	Calligaris, Novella	2:26.0
1973	Calligaris, Novella	2:25.4
1974	Corsi, Marina	2:23.90
1975	Rampazzo, Cinzia	2:21.25

200 m. Individual medley (instituted 1966)

1966	Sacchi, Mara	2:44.2
1967	Colombo, Cinzia	2:41.2
1968	Colombo, Cinzia	2:39.2
1969	Calligaris, Novella	2:38.8
1970	Calligaris, Novella	2:37.5
1971	Calligaris, Novella	2:37.1
1972	Calligaris, Novella	2:34.6
1973	Calligaris, Novella	2:27.8
1974	Roncelli, Antonella	2:32.23
1975	Roncelli, Antonella	2:29.54

400 m. Individual medley (instituted 1962)

1962	Beneck, Anna	5:59.2
1963	Noventa, Elisabetta	5:55.9
1964	Noventa, Elisabetta	5:53.3
1965	Noventa, Elisabetta	5:51.8
1966	Tomassini, Daniela	5:50.7
1967	Colombo, Cinzia	5:45.9
1968	Tomassini, Daniela	5:44.3
1969	Calligaris, Novella	5:30.4
1970	Calligaris, Novella	5:31.6

1971	Calligaris, Novella	5:22.8
1972	Calligaris, Novella	5:17.0
1973	Calligaris, Novella	5:10.9
1974	Roncelli, Antonella	5:17.81
1975	Roncelli, Antonella	5:15.26

JANY, Alex (France, 5 Jan. 1929–).
Named as the best swimming prospect in
the world in 1947, Alex Jany, son of a
baths superintendent in Toulouse, failed
to live up to his reputation at the 1948
Olympics. This 6 ft. 2 in. and 16 st.
giant, was only fifth in the 100 m.
(58.3, 1 sec. behind American winner
Wally Ris) having been head and shoulders
in front at 60 m. He was only sixth in the
400 m. though he pulled France into
third place in the relay.

But the London Games was one of
Jany's few swimming failures. The year
before, in the European championships
in Monte Carlo, he won the 100 m. by
2.4 in 57.3 and the 400 m. by 15.2 in
4:35.2–a world record. And he swam
his heart out for France in the 4 x 200
m. relay. As anchorman, he took over a
10 m. deficit behind Sweden and though
he closed the gap inexorably he lost the
gold by 0.2 at the touch. When he
realized he had 'failed', he clung to the
bath end and wept. Jany retained his
100 and 400 m. European titles in
Vienna in 1950, but France had to be
satisfied with second place in the relay,
again behind Sweden.

Jany broke five world records: 100 m.
(55.8 s/c 1947), 200 m. (2:05.4 s/c
1946), 300 y. (3:03.0 s/c 1948), 300 m.
(3:21.0 1947), 400 m. (4:25.2 1947). In
1947 he competed in the A.S.A. championships at New Brighton and won the
100 and 220 y. titles.

JARVIS, John (Great Britain, 24 Feb.
1872–9 May 1933). John Arthur Jarvis–
Arthur to his family, but John to
the swimming world–called himself the
'Amateur Swimming Champion of the
World' and he won 108 titles to justify
his claim.

In the 1900 Olympics in Paris he won
the 1,000 and 4,000 m. gold medals and
is credited in some records with having
also won the 100 m., though in every
other Olympic book of reference this
event does not appear to have taken
place, certainly within the official swimming programme. At any rate, swimming
in the River Seine, Jarvis, from Leicester,
took the 1,000 m. in 13:40.2 finishing
an astonishing 1:13.2 ahead of Austria's
Otto Wahle. But his 4,000 m. victory was
even more amazing. Jarvis was timed in
58:24.0–more than 10½ minutes ahead
of Hungary's Zoltan Halmay.

There were no British competitors at
the 1904 Games in St. Louis, but at the
1906 Interim Games Jarvis was second in
the 1,500 m. and third in the 400 m.

Jarvis, a non-smoker and virtual teetotaller, and his professional rival Joey
Nuttall used the right overarm side-
stroke and developed a special kick
which became known as the Jarvis-
Nuttall kick. Using it Jarvis set many
world bests though he was never credited
with an official record. His efficient
technique won for him twenty-four A.S.A.
titles–440 y. (1898, 1900), 500 and
880 y. (1898, '99, 1900, '01), mile
(1897–1902 = 6), long distance (1898–
1904 and 1906 = 8). He was also plunging champion in 1904.

His international and national successes included winning the Queen Victoria Diamond Jubilee one mile championship (1897), the German Kaiser's championship of Europe, the Emperor of
Austria's world championship (in Vienna),
the King of Italy's world distance championship, the Queen of the Netherlands'
world 4,000 m. championship, the King
Edward VII Coronation Cup one mile
(handed to him by the King) and two
gold cups for 15-mile River Thames
swims, open to the world.

Jarvis, later referred to as Professor
Jarvis, did a great deal to promote life-
saving. He saved many lives, once rescuing
twin sisters, and he introduced life-saving
techniques to Italy on one of his many
international tours. He was an English
water-polo international from 1894 to
1904, though he did not play for Britain
in the Olympic Games. Three of his daughters became swimming teachers while
his sister Clara was chaperone to the British women's team who won the relay gold
medals at the 1912 Stockholm Olympics.

Jarvis was honoured by the Hall of Fame in 1968.

JASTREMSKI, Chet (United States, 12 Jan. 1941–). A great breast-stroke swimmer of his time, Chester Jastremski was also one of the unluckiest. A pioneer of the modern fast-stroking sprint style, he made devastating inroads into the world records lists, yet missed selection for the 1960 Olympics owing to a rule misinterpretation and was only third in the 1964 Games 200 m. though at that time he was the world record holder.

In six weeks from 2 July–20 Aug. 1961, the stocky student (5 ft 9 in, 11 st. 11 lb.) who lived in Giant Street, Toledo, broke the world 100 m. mark six times– from 1:11.1 to astonishing 1:07.8 and 1:07.5 on the same day. He also took the 200 m. world record from 2:33.6 to 2:28.2 in three bites.

Jastremski, of Polish extraction, then a medical student at Indiana University and a pupil of Doc Jim Counsilman, became the first man to break the minute for 100 y. breast-stroke (s/c) with 59.6 in April 1961.

JOHANSSON, Hjalmar (Sweden 20 Jan. 1874-30 Sept. 1937). A pioneer of diving, Hjalmar Johansson won the Olympic high plain championship in 1908 at the age of 34. His speciality was the forward dive which he performed with arms held wide in flight instead of stretching them above his head as in the English header. This variation, known as the 'Swedish swallow' is the only version of the plain dive used in modern competition. The Swede won the silver medal in this event in 1912 and was fourth in the high fancy event while his wife, Greta Johansson became the first woman Olympic diving champion (for plain diving). He was also 6th in the 100 m. free-style and highboard diving at the 1906 Interim Games in Athens.

Johansson had been champion of Sweden since 1897 except for the two years he spent in London prior to the 1908 Games. And during those years, he helped to draw up the Olympic code of conduct for diving competitions, the prototype of the modern international diving regulations.

KAHANAMOKU, Duke (United States, 24 Aug. 1890–22 Jan. 1968). Duke was his christian name and ducal was Kahanamoku's swimming talent. He came out of the Hawaiian Islands in 1911, a superbly conditioned athlete who could plane on the surface of the water as no man of his size had ever done before.

An island king in many movies, Kahanamoku had Hawaiian royal blood. He was born in Princess Ruth's palace in Honolulu during a visit of the Duke of Edinburgh, second son of Queen Victoria. And his father Captain Kahanamoku christened him Duke to celebrate the occasion.

He swam in four Olympics and it would have been five had not the 1916 meeting been cancelled. In 1912 he won the 100 m. free-style (63.4) and a silver in America's relay team. He retained his sprint title in 1920 in a world record 60.4, after the final had been re-swum following Australian protests that their man, William Harold, had been boxed in. . . there were no lane ropes in those days. It was Duke's 30th birthday. And he anchored America to world best time golds in the relay. Duke missed an historic hat-trick of sprint golds in 1924, when Johnny Weissmuller, the American heir to his swimming kingdom, beat him into second place, by 2.4, with the first sub-minute Games record (59.0). Despite this confirmation of his form, Duke did not swim in America's winning relay squad. But he was back in the team again in 1928, at 38, though this time he went home medalless. He was also on the American water-polo team strength at the 1932 Olympics, but did not play.

Essentially a sprinter, Duke's first world record came just after he had won his first Olympic gold, when on 20 July 1912 he clocked 61.6 for 100 m. on a straight course. He followed this with four 100 y. marks (54.5, 53.8, 53.2 and 53.0) between 5 July 1913 and 5 Sept. 1917. He clipped his four-year-old 100 m. time to 61.4 in 1918 and finally to 60.4 in retaining his Olympic crown in Antwerp.

KEALOHA, Warren (United States, 3 March 1903-8 Sept. 1972). The first man to win an Olympic back-stroke title at two successive Games–the others being David Theile and Roland Matthes (see THEILE and MATTHES), the smiling Hawaiian, at 17 the baby of the 1920 American team, took the 100 m. crown in Antwerp by one second (1:15.2), Four years later, in Paris, his winning margin was 2.2 sec. and his first place time 1:13.2.

Kealoha was the world's No.1 back-stroker from 1920 to '26, taking his record down from 1:14.8 (his heat time in Antwerp) to 1:11.4. He also set a 150 y. record (1:44.8) which stood for four years.

If getting from Honolulu to the U.S. trials had not been so difficult, Kealoha might have challenged for gold again in 1928. As it was, it was almost necessary to break a world record to persuade Hawaii to meet the cost of sending swimmers to the mainland. And after arriving by boat, and out of shape, men like Kealoha had to beat all comers on the West Coast, in Chicago and New York before being chosen for the Olympics.

Despite all this, Warren's brother Pua (14 Nov. 1902-1973) was also in the U.S. team in Antwerp where he was second in the 100 m. free-style, fourth in the 1,500 m. and a member of the winning 4 x 200 m. squad. Pua was a reserve at the 1924 Games.

KIEFER, Adolph (United States, 27 June 1918–). Olympic 100 m. back-stroke champion in 1936, Kiefer's winning time (65.9) in Berlin stood until 1952 when America's Yoshinobu Oyakawa trimmed it by 0.2 in Helsinki. Chicago-born Kiefer broke seventeen world marks from 100 y. to 400 m. in his long career at the top from 1935–44. These included cutting the 100 m. time from 67.0 to 64.8 in four record swims in three months (20 Oct. 1935–18 Jan. 1936). His other best times were 56.8 (100 y., 1944), 1:30.4 (150 y., 1941), 2:19.3 (200 m. 1944) and 5:10.9 (400 m., 1941).

KIERAN, Barney (Australia, 1887–22 Sept. 1905). One of the first great trudgen (double over-arm) swimmers, Bernard Bede Kieran's death at 19, following an appendicectomy, was a tragedy for swimming. His performances in his short, three-year racing life, were phenomenal. They included world best times for almost all the free-style distances, though only one, for 500 y. in 6:07.2–which stood for eight years– was ratified retrospectively as a world record when, in 1908, F.I.N.A. was founded and created the first official world list.

Despite the suspicions in Europe and in England in particular, there is little doubt of the authenticity of Kieran's times. His Australian records included 2:28.4 (220 y.) in 1905 which beat the ratified world mark of his compatriot Freddy Lane by 0.2 and was 3.2 faster than the first world record for the four feet shorter 200 m. by Otto Scheff in 1908. Technically, the first man to swim 200 m. faster than Kieran was Charles Daniels (USA) in 1911. (See WORLD RECORDS, introduction).

Kieran from New South Wales did 5:19.0 for 440 y. (1905), which was 17.8 better than the first ratified world 400 m. record in 1908 and 7.4 faster than the first official 440 y. mark. Also in 1905, he clocked 11:11.6 for 880 y., an Australian record. Yet the year after Kieran's death, the first world mark was awarded to England's Henry Taylor with 11:25.4. And Kieran's 23:16.8 for one mile the same year was 2:07.6 faster than the first official world mark and it was not until 1924 that Arne Borg put up a better performance.

Kieran won nine Australian titles– 220, 440 y. and one mile twice each and the 880 y. three times. He died during the Australian championships in Brisbane soon after a most successful visit to England. Although out of training, after months on a ship, he won the A.S.A. 220, 440, 500 and 880 y. titles.

Without any Olympic medals to his credit–he was only coming to the fore in 1904 and was dead before the 1906

Interim Games–and only one world record to mark his passing in the F.I.N.A. lists, Kieran's name and fame were recorded for posterity by his election to the Hall of Fame in 1969.

KING, Ellen (Great Britain, 16 Jan. 1909–). A tremendously versatile swimmer, Ellen King of Scotland competed in the era from 1924–31 when Britain's women competitors challenged the world. Her Olympic medal successes were for back-stroke and free-style relay, but she was also more than competent on breast-stroke.

Ellen, from Edinburgh, swam in her first Games in 1924, at 15, when she was sixth in the 100 m. back-stroke final. Four years later, she was second in 1:22.2, only 0.2 behind the winner Marie Braun, of Holland. In Amsterdam Ellen also won a silver in the relay.

She was the Scottish member of the British quartette–the others were Joyce Cooper and Marion Laverty of England and Valerie Davies of Wales–who won the first European 4 x 100 m. free-style title in 1927 in Italy and their prize was the Bologna Trophy (see BOLOGNA TROPHY). And she swam in the first Commonwealth Games in Hamilton and came second in the 100 y. free-style, third in the 200 m. breast-stroke and free-style relay.

KIPHUTH, Bob (United States, 17 Nov. 1890–7 Jan. 1967). The most highly honoured of all America's great coaches, Robert John Herman Kiphuth, born in Tonawanda, New York, gave his entire life to swimming. And his life's work was crowned with the 'Medal of Freedom', America's highest civilian award The citation speaks for itself . . . 'He has inspired generations of athletes with high ideals of achievement and sportsmanship.' Bob Kiphuth received his medal from President Johnson at the White House on 6 Dec. 1963.

His physical education teaching career began in 1914 when, at 23, he went to Yale University as an instructor and he stayed there until his death in 1967. He was head coach from 1918 until mandatory retirement in 1959 when he became Professor Emeritus of Physical Education and Director Emeritus of the university's Payne Whitney gymnasium.

Professor Kiphuth attended every

Olympic Games from 1924–64, at four of which (1928–48) he was coach to the American team. He preached his gospel of swimming around the world–in France, Germany, Holland, Sweden, Britain Japan, Austria, Hungary, Cuba, Hawaii, Mexico, Iceland, Israel, Hong Kong, Thailand, India, Turkey, Greece, Italy, Spain . . . you name it, Bob went to it.

An honorary Masters of Arts and Doctor of Law, Honoured by the Emperor of Japan with the order of the Sacred Treasure, member of the United States National Olympic and Swimming Committees, Bob Kiphuth, non-smoker and teetotaller, a quiet, kindly man with a great sense of humour, believed ferociously in amateurism. Any swimming stars who went to Yale on scholarships got them for academic and not sporting merit.

The successes of his Yale University swimming teams, who were beaten only ten times in inter-collegiate matches in forty-two years, is tremendous testimony to his swimming knowledge. Yale, in this time, won the Eastern Inter-collegiate league thirty-eight times. Between 1949 and 1957. Yale were high point team at seven National indoor championships meetings (1949, 1951–55, 1957) while the New Haven Swim Club (Yale's summer season club title) were top at five outdoor championships (1950–51, '53, '55–56).

His epitaph, in the words of President Kingman Brewster of Yale, could not be more fitting: 'To Bob Kiphuth athletics was an integral part of learning and all learning was an exercise in self-fulfilment and self-discipline. Generations of students and colleagues have outdone themselves because of the values he inspired and the standards he set.

KITAMURA, Kusuo (Japan, 9 Oct. 1917–). The youngest man to win an Olympic swimming title, Kitamura was only 14 in 1932 when he took the 1,500 m. in Los Angeles. He was the first in the trend towards younger and younger champions and his success, like those who have followed, was the result of careful nutrition, training and stroke mechanics.

His 19:12.4, in beating his team-mate Shozo Makino by 1.7 and Jim Christy, the best from the United States, by 17.1, was 5.2 outside the 1927 world record of Sweden's Arne Borg–a world mark which

stood for another six years. But Kitamura's was a remarkable performance and stood as a Games record until 1952.

Kitamura, in fact, only broke one world mark, for 1,000 m. (12:42.6) in 1933. He became Chairman of the Foreign Relations committee of the Japanese Swimming Federation and was one of the first foreign swimmers to be honoured by the Hall of Fame (1965).

KNAPE, Ulrika (Sweden, 26 April, 1955–). Without doubt, the world's No. 1 diver of the 1970s, Ulrika Knape, fair-haired, beautiful and long-limbed like so many Swedes, won seven major diving medals out of a possible eight in four years from 1972 to 1975.

Her first, two gold and a silver, came at the 1972 Olympics in Munich where she beat defending champion Milena Duchkova of Czechoslovakia (see DUCH-KOVA, Milena) by 20 points in the highboard and was second to America's Micki King in the springboard. And Miss Knape took similar placings the following year at the first World championships in Belgrade, again beating Duchkova for the highboard crown by a handsome margin.

It was a double gold for the Swedish girl at the 1974 European championships in Vienna and she maintained her medal-winning highboard form, although only the bronze, at the World championships in Cali, Colombia in 1975.

KOK, Ada (Netherlands, 6 June 1947–). This gentle giant, Ada Kok, overshadowed Dutch and world butterfly swimming in the 1960s. And though she retired in 1968, after winning an Olympic gold for 200 m. in Mexico City, the records she set between 1963–67 remained unchallenged as swimming went into the 1970s.

The 6 ft. 0 in. 13 st. Dutch girl from the Hague won her first golds in the 1962 European championships, in the 100 m. (69.0) and medley relay. She retained her 100 m. title four years later in Utrecht (65.6), swam the vital leg in Holland's medley relay win and for the first–and last–time showed her free-style power by taking the 400 m. silver medal (4:48.7), having been entered in this event only for a warm-up swim.

Between these European successes, there had been disappointment in Ada's silver–which all Holland had hoped would be a gold—in the 100 m. butterfly at the 1964 Tokyo Olympics. She was world record-holder at the time with the 65.1 for 110 y. (equal to 64.4 for 100 m.) set at Blackpool four months before the Games. But in the big race she could do only 65.6 in finishing 0.9 behind Sharon Stouder (USA). Ada out-swam the American on the butterfly leg of the medley relay (65.0 to Stouder's 66.1), but the superior strength of the rest of the United States squad left Holland again with the silvers.

After seven years at the top of butterfly swimming, Mexico seemed the last chance for Holland's popular Ada to win that elusive Olympic title. So the despondency was extreme as she finished fourth in the 100 m. But, three days later, she fought back to take the new 200 m. title in 2:24.7, having been 1.4 behind runner-up Helga Lindner (East Germany) at half distance.

Ada broke nine individual world butterfly records between September 1963 and August 1967: 100 m. 66.1, 65.1, 64.5; 110 y. 65.1; 200 m. 2:25.8, 2:25.3, 2:22.5, 2:21.0 (the last time was also a record for 220 y.) In medley relay swimming she was magnificent and Holland were seldom beaten in this event in all the years that Ada, who could turn impossible deficits into winning leads, was in the team.

KOLB, Claudia (United States, 19 Dec. 1949–). At 14, swimming in the 200 m. breast-stroke, Claudia Kolb won an unexpected silver medal in the 1964 Olympics. It was a courageous effort, for she had qualified for the final only as fifth best and with 25 m. to go she was in fourth place. Then, suddenly Claudia sprinted like mad for 10 m. to swim into second place (2:47.6) splitting the mighty Russian pair Prosumenschikova (2:46.4) and Babanina (2:48.6).

Four years later, at the Mexico Games, Claudia was the best in the world for the medley individual and she won the 200 and 400 m. gold medals with almost contemptuous ease—the former (2:24.7) by 4.1 from her team-mate Sue Pedersen and the latter by a huge 13.7 from another American Lynn Vidali.

She was the first holder of the world record for 200 m. medley with her 2:27.8 on 21 Aug. 1966. Two years and four world records later, she had brought her

time down to 2:23.5. She broke the 400 m. world record four times, taking it from 5:11.7 in July 1967 to 5:04.7 in Aug. 1968.

Claudia, from the George Haines stable at Santa Clara, twice (1964, '65) won the United States outdoor 100 and 200 m. breast-stroke titles (best winning times 1:17.1 and 2:48.6 in dead-heating with Cynthia Goyette in 1965). She won the 200 m. medley four times (1965– 68) and the 400 m. medley twice (1966–67).

KONRADS, John (Australia, 21 May 1942–) and **KONRADS, Ilsa** (Australia, 29 Mar. 1944–). Born in Riga, Latvia, John and Ilsa Konrads fled with their parents to Germany (1944) before emigrating to Australia (in 1949) where their extraordinary swimming talents came to bloom. Their ability and the expert coaching of Don Talbot brought them a total of thirty-seven world records between Jan. 1958 and Feb. 1960, most of them metric-linear marks with times taken for the longer yards distances

John contracted polio while the family were living in a refugee camp near Stuttgart before going to Sydney. Despite the illness he became more successful than his sister, though it was Ilsa, at 13, who first put the name of Konrads into the world record book. On 9 Jan. 1958 she set new figures for 800 m. and 880 y.

Two days later, John broke the men's world records for the same distance and in two more swims in the next seven days added the 200 m., 220 y., 400 m., and 440 y. Altogether he set twenty-five world marks, won three Olympic medals in 1960—a gold for 1,500 m., and bronzes in the 400 and 4 x 200 m.—and was a triple gold medal winner at the Cardiff Commonwealth Games (440, 1,650 and 4 x 220 y.) in 1958.

Ilsa won the 440 y. in Cardiff to make the Konrads the only brother—sister individual champions in the history of the Games and she came second to Dawn Fraser in this event in Perth in 1962. She also gained an Olympic relay silver in 1960.

John was a member of Australia's Olympic teams for the 1956, '60 and '64 Games, though he was only a stand-by at the first and past his peak for the third. Ilsa swam in the 1960 and 1964 Games, but a fourth place in the 400 m. on her first appearance was her best individual Olympic effort.

Their best times were—John: 2:02.2 (200 m.), 2:01.6 (220 y.), 4:15.9 (400 m. and 440 y.), 8:59.6 (the first man under nine minutes for 800 m. and 880 y.), 17:11.0 (1,500 m. and 1,650 y.); Ilsa: 4:45.4 (400 m./440 y.), 10:11.4 (800 m./880 y.), 19:25.7 (1,500 m./1,650 y.).

KOTHER, Rosemarie (East Germany, 27 Feb. 1956–). Winner of two golds and a silver at the 1973 World championships and three golds at the 1974 Europeans, this stocky 5'6"/167cm) powerful girl changed the face of women's butterfly swimming.

In Belgrade she trimmed the world 200 m. figures in a heat (2:15.45) and slashed them to 2:13.76 in winning the final. She took her second gold in East Germany's world record-breaking medley relay team and was second in the 100 m.

A year later, in Vienna, she won the 100 and 200 m. titles, the former with heat and final world records of 1:02.09 and 1:01.99, and she picked up a third gold in the medley relay. Ten days later, in Concord, Calif., she cut her 100 m. time to 1:01.88 during a match against the United States.

Rosemarie improved her 100 m. time by another eight hundredths of a second at the 1975 World championships in Cali, but had to settle for the silver behind her star team-mate Kornelia Ender (see ENDER, Kornelia). She retained her 200 m. crown by a second and though her 2:13.82 was just outside her year-old world record, no other swimmer came within a second of her 1974 best.

On her return from Cali, Rosemarie married Ranier Gabriel, a Berlin-based Government official.

KRÄMER, Ingrid (East Germany, 29 July 1943–). Dresden's diving star Ingrid competed in three Olympics under three different names. In 1960, as Miss Krämer she won the golden double beating America's Paula Jean Pope in both the highboard and springboard by 2.34 and 14.57 points respectively.

In Tokyo in 1964, as Mrs. Engel-Krämer, the German retained her springboard title by nearly seven points from Jeanne Collier (USA), but lost the highboard narrowly to America's Lesley Bush. Divorced and re-married, Ingrid Gulbin-Kramer was only fifth in the springboard in Mexico and did not dive in the highboard.

Ingrid's first big diving occasion was, at 15, in the 1958 European championships. A slim child, with beautiful feet, she came fourth in the springboard and eighth in the highboard. Four hears later she had two sweeping wins, taking the springboard by 14.79 and the highboard by 12.04 point margins.

L

LANE, Freddy (Australia, 2 Feb. 1880-14 May 1969). The only Australian swimmer in the 1900 Olympics, Lane won the 200 m. title (2:25.2), by 5.8 seconds from Hungary's Zoltan Halmay, and also the 200 m. obstacle gold medal (the only time this event was in the programme) in the River Seine in Paris. He swam a double over-arm stroke, similar to the trudgen but with a narrow kick, which was considered to be too strenuous for distance racing until Lane won the New South Wales mile title, using this style throughout, in 1899. The fact that the rugged Lane, all 9½ stone of him, who died at the ripe old age of 89, was exhausted after some of his longer races, caused considerable concern and there were strong warnings 'never to use the trudgen except for short distance races'.

Lane, from Sydney, swam three seasons in English championships. In 1899 he won the 220 and 440 y. titles. In 1900 he dead-heated with his compatriot Frank Beaurepaire in the 220 y. in a world best 2:34.8. In July 1902, in Manchester, he took the 100 y., beating Australia's Dick Cavill and England's Rob Derbyshire, to become the first man to clock one minute flat, and he won the 220 y. in 2:28.6 (later ratified as the first world record). In October of that year, in Leicester, he astounded the swimming world by breaking the minute for 100 y. (59.6).

In fact, Lane won more English titles than Australian ones—the 100 y. (in 1898 and 1902) and the 220 y. (1902), plus two national 100 y. records of 67.6 (1898) and 60.6 (1902) were his only claims to fame at home. He belonged, of course, to the era before the world-wide system of record ratification had been regularised—thus his minute-breaking 100

y. in Leicester does not appear in the Australia record book. Had F.I.N.A., in establishing their first world record list in 1908, been able to carry out an accurate retrospective investigation of performances and had there not been suspicion in Europe of the veracity of Australian times in those days, the names of Lane and his compatriot Barney Kieran (see KIERAN, BARNEY) would have had an even more important place in the history of the sport. As it is, Lane was honoured by the Hall of Fame in 1969.

LANGFORD, Denise (Australia, 31 Dec. 1955–). This fair-haired student from Newtown, New South Wales, was one of the outstanding competitors at the 1970 Commonwealth Games in Edinburgh where she won more medals than any other woman swimmer—four golds and a silver.

She took the 200 and 400 m. medley in Commonwealth records of 2:28.9 and 5:10.7 and was in the Australian winning free-style and medley relay teams. And she was second in the 400 m. free-style in 4:31.4, four seconds behind her team mate Karen Moras. Yet, despite these successes, her only Australian championship win prior going to Scotland was in the 400 m. medley in 1970.

LARSON, Lance (United States, 3 July 1940-). See DEVITT, John.

LARSSON, Gunnar (Sweden, 12 May, 1951–). Karl Gunnar Larsson, born in Malmo, won two Olympic, one World and three European titles between 1970 and 1973. He was an extremely versatile and talented swimmer and an exceptional competitor.

His medley victories at the 1972 Munich Olympics came in two of the most exciting races in the pool. He beat America's Tim McKee by two thousandths of a second over 400 m., with 4:31.981 to his rival's 4:31.983, having been 2.2 sec. behind McKee with the last 100 m., on free-style, to go. And he took the 200 m. by 1.2 sec. in a world record 2:07.17 having been three tenths down 50 m. out, again to McKee.

Larsson, who left Sweden to study at California State College, Long Beach (USA), where his coach was Don Gambril, had his first big successes at the European championships of 1970 in Barcelona. He won the 400 m. free-style and 200 m. medley in world records of 4:02.6 and 2:09.3 and the 400 m. medley in a European best of 4:36.2. He was also second in the 200 m. free-style.

The fact that two years earlier, at the Mexico Olympics, Larsson had failed to reach a single individual final and had a best 400 m. free-style time there of 4:25.0 underlined the importance of his American training to the fair-haired Swede.

His experience in the U.S. helped to sharpen his competitive instincts which were the spur to his final victory before retirement, at the first World championships in Belgrade in 1973. On his form before this event Larsson looked unlikely to reach a final. Sheer spirit took him to victory in great style in the 200 m. medley.

LEE, Sammy (United States, 1 Aug, 1920–). A little man but with colossal diving talent, Sammy Lee won the Olympic highboard title and a bronze medal in the springboard at the 1948 Olympics. Four years later, now Doctor Lee, he retained his highboard crown in Helsinki–the first man to win this event at successive Games.

Born in Fresno, California, of Korean parents, Lee graduated top of his class at the Benjamin Franklin High School in Los Angeles, where he was chosen as the school's top athlete in 1939. He won his first American titles (highboard and springboard) in 1942 and, after giving up diving upon entering medical college in 1943, he returned to win the highboard crown again in 1946.

The first American-born Oriental to win an Olympic gold medal for the United States, Dr. Lee received the Sullivan Award as America's outstanding amateur athlete in 1953. He was coach to the American diving team at the Rome Olympics where his pupil Bob Webster won the highboard title (which he retained in 1964). Dr. Lee's professional specialization is in diseases of the ear–very much an occupational hazard of divers.

LIFE SAVING, See ROYAL LIFE SAVING SOCIETY.

LIGUE EUROPÉENNE DE NATATION. The European Swimming League,

known internationally by the abbreviation of its French title, L.E.N., was founded in 1927 in order to control and manage the European championships which had been held for the first time, experimentally, in Budapest, the previous year.

The L.E.N. recognizes its own regional list of records and has international technical committees similar to those of the F.I.N.A. As well as the European championships, held normally every four years, L.E.N. also organizes a variety of other regional events (see European Cups etc.)

LONG COURSE. The term 'long course' is used to distinguish between performances set in international-size pools of 50 m. and those swum in shorter baths. The distinction is necessary because the extra turns in a 'short course' pool give a time advantage (see TURNS). All World, European and Commonwealth records now have to be set long course and all major swimming competitions are held in 50 m. pools.

LONG DISTANCE SWIMMING. This branch of swimming demands the same arduous training as all other branches of aquatics. It further demands the physical ability to maintain effort and to withstand cold, and sometimes rough water, for prolonged periods–and the mental ability to persevere where currents, tidal streams and wind drifts seem to have stopped progress altogether. Finally, long distance swimming requires courage, for example, to go through a pitch black night, fog, weed, flotsam, occasional oil fuel patches, swarms of jellyfish and maritime traffic.

There are two organizations in Britain primarily concerned with long distance swimming–the British Long Distance Swimming Association and the Channel Swimming Association, (see Channel Swimming).

The BLDSA organise the following annual British championships (the mile distances are given in brackets): Trentham Gardens Lake (3), Lake Bala (6), Torbay (7½) and Windermere (10¼). The Association also hold, periodically, an event in Loch Lomond (22) and a quadrennial international championship in Windermere (16). Clubs and associations affiliated to the BLDSA stage some 50 other open championships over distances between 2 and 20 miles. These range over the British Isles from the Shannon to the Tay and from Rathlin Sound to Clacton. Apart from these races, there are two BLDSA junior events over 2 and 3 miles and a 3½-mile veterans event.

The CSA observes (or investigates) and ratifies all successful swims across the Straits of Dover. Similarly, many local clubs and associations issue certificates in their own locality e.g. the Morecambe Cross Bay Swimming Association, the Solent Swimming club, the Essex Long Distance S.A. Where no local sponsoring authority exists, the BLDSA will ratify and award certificates for legitimately observed and timed swims of more than 5 miles.

In the U.S—although there is a 4-mile AAU championship for men and a 3-miler for women—the amateur side of the sport is not nearly as active as in Britain. The professional side, however, flourishes as it does also in Canada.

The World Professional Marathon Swimming Federation is based in Chicago. This organisation compiles and keeps marathon records as well as monitoring uniformity of conduct in professional marathon championships. The Marathon Swimming Hall of Fame is an integral part of the Swimming Hall of Fame at Fort Lauderdale, Florida (see HALL OF FAME).

In a short article it is impossible to name all the excellent US swimmers who have so enriched the sport. At this point of time Denis Matuch, the secretary of WPMSF, is outstanding. He became a professional swimmer in 1960 and immediately won the 10-mile Lake Michigan championship. Next year the distance was increased to 12 miles and he again won it as well as the 36½ miles Chicago to Waukegan race. He topped the US professional rankings for nearly a decade.

Florence Chadwick, the top woman marathon swimmer in the world through the 1950s, set brilliant records for individual swims right around the world e.g. The Channel, the Bosporus, Dardanelles, Bristol Channel, etc.

Greta Andersen (see ANDERSEN, Greta) was a superb competitive performer who often, as in the Butlin races of 1957 and 1958, beating all the men. Ted Erikson, first American to swim the English Channel both ways (1965) slashed 13 hours off the previous record.

Although modern distance swimming was given initial impetus in Britain, Canada and the United States, many other countries now hold national and international championships. In the continuing absence of Olympic recognition for a marathon, several influential countries are currently discussing the setting up of an amateur long distance championship of the world.

Long distance swimming was probably first chronicled in the legend of Leander swimming nightly across the Hellespont to meet Hero—1¼ miles each way. Much later, the Sicilians boasted a local athlete said to have swum for five days and five nights i.e. for 120 hours. Nowadays, the best endurance record is 168 hours by Charles Zibbelman in the USA.

In the early nineteenth century, Lord Byron gave the sport some impetus by several distance swims. But modern marathon history dates from Matthew Webb's 1875 Channel swim (see WEBB, MATTHEW). In 1884, Horace Davenport (see DAVENPORT, HORACE) swam from Southsea to Ryde; in 1907 'Professor' Stearne crossed Morecambe Bay and in 1911 James Foster was the first man to conquer Windermere. This last achievement is a good basis for comparing modern standards with those of the past.

In common with sprint swimming—and these days the longest Olympic event 1,500 m., has almost become a sprint—distance norms have improved enormously over the years. The records for Lake Windermere, which is non-tidal and minimally affected by weather, form an excellent yardstick to measure these great improvements. They show a most interesting and regular trend resulting, in turn, from better stroke techniques, virtual abolition of feeding stops, fiercer competition and expert attendance from qualified BLDSA pilot-lifesavers.

		hr.	min.
1911	Foster, James (Oldham)	11	29
1933	Humphreys, John (Preston)	10	04
1934	Daly, Charles (Denton)	6	22
1955	Oldman, Fred (Huddersfield)	5	53
1955	Slater, John (Halifax)	5	20
1958	Forsberg, Gerald (London)	5	19
1965	Lake, Geoffrey (Harrow)	5	17
1966	Gray, Elaine (St.Albans)	4	39

1967	Van Scheyndel, Jan (Neth)		
	(Neth)	4	36
1968	Van Scheyndel, Jan		
	(Neth)	4	07

LONSBROUGH, Anita (Great Britain, 10 Aug. 1941–). Anita Lonsbrough's seven-year career (1958–64) brought seven gold, three silver and two bronze medals in major Games. She held the Olympic, European and Commonwealth breast-stroke titles at the same time and was a feared competitor throughout the swimming world.

Yet she turned to her medal-winning breast-stroke only nine months before competing in the 1958 Commonwealth Games in Cardiff where she won the 220 y. in 2:53.5 and a second gold in England's world record-breaking medley relay team, just two months after her first appearance for Britain. Before this, the Yorkshire girl had been a club standard free-styler of little consequence.

Her finest performance was in the 1960 Olympics in Rome where, in a brilliant tactical race, she took the 200 m. title in world record time (2:49.5). She beat German's Wiltrud Urselmann by half a second, having taken the lead only in the last few metres.

Miss Lonsbrough was the silver medallist in the European 200 m. championship in 1958 and a medley relay bronze medal-winner. Four years later, she completed her hat-trick of titles by winning the European championship in Leipzig, a silver in the 400 m. medley and a medley relay bronze. And in the Perth Commonwealth Games that year she retained her 220 y. title, won the new 110 y. breaststroke and 440 y. medley events and a medley relay silver.

Anita, from Huddersfield, had to train mostly on her own. As a result she knew she had only herself to rely upon in her races. Finding morning racing difficult unless she got up hours before, she set her alarm for 4 a.m. in Rome so that she would be mentally and physically ready for the 10 a.m. heats. And she followed this pattern throughout her career.

As well as her medal triumphs, she broke four world breast-stroke records: 200 m. 2:50.3 (1959); 2:49.5 (1960); 220 y. 2:52.2 and 2:51.7 (1962). Then, having established herself without question as the world's No.1, she returned successfully to free-style and also took up the difficult medley individual.

In addition to her five **A.S.A.** breaststroke titles (220 y. 1958–62), she won the 440 y. medley (1963, '64), 220 y. free-style (1963) and was second in the 110 y. (1963) and 440 y. (1963/64). Her only disappointment was at never being allowed to swim in a free-style relay team in a major Games.

She ended her career after the Tokyo Olympics as British medley record holder (440 y. 5:36.8), with an M.B.E., having been voted 'Sportswoman of the Year' in two national polls in each of 1960 and '62 and the B.B.C. 'Sports Personality of the Year' in 1962. Anita is married to former British Olympic cyclist Hugh Porter, who won the world professional pursuit championship in 1968, '70, '72 and '73 (the only man to win this title four times) and received the M.B.E. in 1973.

LUDGROVE, Linda (Great Britain, 8 Sept. 1947–). The Commonwealth's top back-stroker at the 1962–66 Games, Linda Kay Ludgrove won five golds and a silver–and only Australia's great Dawn Fraser won more Commonwealth Games golds. At 15, in 1962, Linda took the 110 y. title in 1:11.1, having equalled her world record of 1:10.9 in a heat, the 220 y. in 2:35.2, equalling the world record she had set in a heat, and a silver in the medley relay. In Jamaica, in 1966, she retained her individual titles in 1:09.2, having set a Games record of 69.0 in a heat, and 2:28.5, again a world record. And she helped England to a world record-breaking win (4:40.6) in the medley relay. The Sports Writers' Association picked her as their top sportswoman of that year.

The South London blonde won a silver and two bronze medals at European championships (1962 & '66), was sixth in the 100 m. at the 1964 Olympics and broke five yards world records.

McCORMICK, Pat (United States, 12 May 1930–). Double diving gold medallist at the 1952 Olympics, Pat McCormick born Pat Keller, set herself a tough task in 1956 when she decided to try to get into the United States team and defend her titles in Melbourne only five months after the birth of her son. But this great competitor always rose to the big occasion. Coached by her airline pilot husband Glenn, she accomplished all she had set out to do. Her second double gold success–the only one in the diving history of the Olympics–came with her victories in the springboard by 16.47 points and the highboard by 3.19. This achievement earned her a place in the Swimming Hall of Fame, the first woman diver to be honoured.

Three times Pan American champion (highboard in 1951 and both titles in 1955), Mrs. McCormick kept fit for her Melbourne challenge before her son was born by swimming half a mile a day to within two days of his arrival. She won seventy-seven national championships and was named 'The Babe Zaharias Woman Athlete of the Year', 'The Helm's Hall North American Athlete of the Year', 'The Associated Press Woman Athlete of the Year' and 'The A.A.U.'s Sullivan Award Amateur Athlete of the Year'.

McGREGOR, Bobby (Great Britain, 3 Apr. 1944–). If nature ever designed a classic sprinter it was Robert Bilsland McGregor, from Falkirk, Scotland. Tall, broad shouldered, slim hipped, Bobby had all the natural advantages and ability to match. He became 100 m. champion of Europe in Utrecht in 1966 in one of the most astonishing races ever seen.

At the start, Russia's Leonid Ilichev wobbled and Horst Gregor of East Germany took a blatant flyer, while McGregor was left standing on his block, convinced the race would be called back. But, to the utter disbelief of everybody, the race went on. From a seemingly hopeless position, McGregor, unbelievably was ahead at the turn and he went on to win by six-tenths in 53.7 from Ilichev.

But the real horror of that starting incident was that McGregor had never won a major title. He had been second to Canada's Dick Pound in the 1962 Commonwealth Games sprint . . . second, by one-tenth, to America's Don Schollander in the 1964 Olympics . . . and second to Mike Wenden of Australia in the 1966 Commonwealth Games.

McGregor, coached by his father David, a former British Olympic (1936) water-polo player, competed at the 1968 Mexico Games–but his final university examinations in architecture and unsympathetic handling by British team officials put paid to his medal hopes. He was, in fact, fourth in the 100 m. in 53.5, the same time as in 1964, and half a second behind bronze medallist Mark Spitz.

McGregor, Scotland's hero, won the A.S.A. 110 y. title six times (1962–64 and 1966–68 . . . he did not swim in 1965) and the 220 y. title twice. He was second to Don Havens (USA) in the World Student Games 100 m. in 1967. He broke the world 110 y. record five times in three years, his final 53.5 (worth 53.2 for 100 m.) in 1966 being his best time. He was honoured with an M.B.E. for his swimming achievements.

MADISON, Helene (United States, 19 June 1913-27 Nov. 1970). Winner of the 1932 Olympic 100 and 400 m. in 66.8 (a world best long course time) and 5:28.5 (a world record) and anchor swimmer in the world record-breaking American relay team, Helene Madison, from Seattle, was the supreme freestyler of her era. In 1930–31 she broke the world record for every distance, with one exception–for 800 m. and technically she should have been the first record-holder for this too–and in the end she was.

The 880 y. for women came into the world record-book in 1919 (see EDERLE, GERTRUDE) but marks for the 15 ft. 4 in. shorter 800 m. (for men and women) were not accepted until the 1930s. On

6 July 1930, Helene, as the seventh record-breaker, set a world 880 y. mark of 11:41.2 in a 55 y. bath at Long Beach. On 23 August 1931, Yvonne Goddard of France clocked 12:18.8 for 800 m. in a 50 m. Paris pool and this time was ratified by F.I.N.A. as the first world record for the distance. In fact, the American girl's 880 y. time was at least equal to 11:37.0 for metres which makes it all the more strange that her July 1930 time was not also accepted for metres.

But this tale has a happy, even though belated, ending. In 1973, 43 years after her great 880 y. swim, the F.I.N.A. re-examined their world record lists, removed the time of Miss Godard and also a performance by Laura Kight (US) in 1933 in favour of Miss Madison's much superior effort.

The fifteen other world record distances that fell to Miss Madison, five of them twice, in sixteen months and thirteen days, were: 100 y. (60.8 and 60.0, the first level minute); 100 m. (68.0, 66.0); 200 m. (2:34.6); 220 y. (2:35.0, 2:34.8); 300 y. (3:41.6, 3:39.0); 300 m. (3:59.5); 400 m. (5:31.0); 440 y. (5:39.4, 5:31.0); 500 y. (6:16.4); 500m. (7:12.0); 880 y. (11:41.2); 1,000 y. (13:23.6); 1,000 m. (14:44.8); 1,500 m. (23:17.2); 1,760 y. (24:34.6).

Miss Madison won all four United States titles (100, 440, 880 and 1,760 y.) in 1930 and '31. After only three years at the top, but with so much to show for them, Helene Madison bowed out of swimming at the Los Angeles Olympics with her three gold medals and her twenty-first world record (5:28.5 for 400 m.) on 13 August 1932 at 19 years and 2 months young.

MAGIC MARKS. Swimming, like athletics with its four-minute mile, has magic marks that fire the imagination. Two of the modern era that will be long remembered were achieved by Australian girls, Dawn Fraser and Lorraine Crapp.

On 25 Aug. 1956 Miss Crapp took the world marks for 400 m. and 440 y. below the mythical five-minute barrier—and this sixteen years after Denmark's Ragnhild Hveger had come within one-tenth of five minutes. In one fabulous swim, the Sydney girl clocked 4:50.8 and 4:52.4 and on the way broke the world records for 200 m. and 220 y.

And 16 years after this another Australian, Shane Gould (see GOULD, Shane), took the world record under 4:20.0 with 4:19.04 in winning one of her three gold medals at the 1972 Olympic Games.

On 27 Oct. 1962 Miss Fraser swam 110 y. in 59.9, which was also a world record for the two feet shorter 100 m.

Johnny Weissmuller (USA) was the first man to break the minute for 100 m. (58.6), in Alameda on 9 July 1922. This improved the world record of 1920 Olympic champion Duke Kahanamoku by 1.8 sec. The powerful Weissmuller also was the first to swim 400 m. in under five minutes. He did this in the 25 y. Yale University pool on 6 Mar. 1923 when his 4:57.0 improved his own world mark by 9.6 seconds.

Fifty years later, swimming in a 50 m. pool in Belgrade, America's Rick DeMont (see DeMONT, Rick) went under 4 min. to win the first world 400 m. championship.

Don Schollander was the two minute-breaker. In Los Angeles on 27 July 1963, the fair-haired American clocked 1:58.8 for 200 m. to clip 1½ seconds from the three-month-old time of Australia's Bob Windle.

Of course, the longer the race, the greater the improvement. And minute-breaking has been a feature of the history of swimming's longest Olympic event, the 1,500 m. In sixty-one years, seven minute barriers have been broken.

First under twenty-two minutes was Sweden's Arne Borg (21:53.3 on 8 July 1923) . . . under twenty-one minutes went Australia's Boy Charlton (20:06.6 on 7 July 1924). It was Arne Borg again for the first sub-twenty-minute mark (19:07.2 on 2 Sept. 1927) and that stood for eleven years until Japan's Tomikatsu Amano clocked 18:58.8 on 10 Aug. 1938.

After eighteen years and World War II, Murray Rose (Australia) returned 17:59.5—but it took only six more years for seventeen minutes to be broken, by America's Roy Saari (16:58.7 on 2 Sept. 1964). And on 23 Aug. 1970 John Kinsella (USA), then 17, sailed under sixteen minutes (15:57.1).

The women's assault on the 1,500 m. world record has been equally astonishing. Miss Hveger was the first girl under twenty-two and twenty-one minutes (21:45.7 in 1938 and 20:57.0 in 1941). Australia's Ilsa Konrads broke twenty minutes with 19:25.7 in 1959 and three years later America's Carolyn House returned 18:44.0 for the fourth minute-breaking performance in twenty-four years. And Debbie Meyer, in the second of her four world record swims over the distance, clocked 17:50.2 in 1967.

It took only six more years for a girl to break 17 min. This was the redoubtable Shane Gould who on 11 Feb. 1973 in Adelaide clocked 16:56.9. And 1½ years later another Australian, tiny Jenny Turrall, 14, from Sydney, whose fifth successive world mark in nine months was 16:33.94, was nearly half way towards breaking 16 min.

Tom Mann (USA) broke the minute for 100 m. back-stroke on the first leg of the Olympic relay in Tokyo in 1964 (59.5). The 100 m. butterfly minute went in 1960 when Lance Larson (USA) clocked 59.0.

In 1961 Ted Stickles (USA) bettered 5 min. for 400 m. and 440 y. medley with 4:55.6 and 4:57.1 respectively in Los Angeles. Just 12 years later an East German girl, Gudrun Wegner emulated the feat of Stickles with her 1973 world championships winning time of 4:57.51.

American relay teams went through two barriers during the 1964 Games ... under four minutes for 4 x 100 m. medley (Tom Mann, Bill Craig, Fred Schmidt and Steve Clarke) with 3:58.4 on 16 Oct. and under eight minutes for 4 x 200 m. free-style (Clarke, Saari, Gary Ilman and Schollander) with 7:52.1 on 18 Oct.

And, during their final build-up for the 1972 Olympics, America's girls (Kim Peyton, Sandy Neilson, Jane Barkman and Shirley Babashoff) went under 4 min. for 4 x 100 m. free-style with 3:58.11 in Knoxville.

Other magic mark breakers were:

1902 Freddy Lane (Aus), 100 y. free-style under 1 min. (59.6).
1912 Percy Courtman (GB), 200 m. breast-stroke under 3 min. (2:56.6)
1934 Willy den Ouden (Neth), 100 y. free-style under 1 min. (59.8)
1935 Shozo Makino (Japan), 800 m. free-style under 10 min. (9:55.8)
1937 Jopie Waalberg (Neth), 200 m. breast-stroke under 3 min. (2:58.0)
1938 Al Vanderweghe (USA), 100 y. back-stroke under 1 min (59.4)

1944 Alan Ford (USA), 100 m. free-style under 50 sec. (49.7)
1947 Keith Carter (USA), 100 y. butterfly under 1 min. (59.4)–this was five years before butterfly was officially recognized.
1950 John Marshall (Aus), one mile under 20 min. (19:49.4)
1959 John Konrads (Aus), 800 m./880 y. under 9 min. (8:59.6)
1960 Lance Larson (USA), 100 m. butterfly under 1 min. (59.0)
1960 Jane Cedergvist (Swe), 800 m. under 10 min. (9:55.6)
1960 Anita Lonsbrough (GB), 200 m. breast-stroke (l/c) under 2:50.0 (2:49.5)
1971 Ann Simmons (USA), 800 m. free-style under 9 min. (8:59.4)
1972 Melissa Belote (USA), 200 m. back-stroke under 2:20.0 (2:19.19)
1973 David Wilkie (GB), 200 m. breast-stroke under 2:20.0 (2:19.28)
1974 Ulrike Tauber (E.Ger), 200 m. medley under 2:20.0 (2:18.97)
1974 Andras Hargitay (Hun), 400 m. medley under 4:30.0 (4:28.89)

MARKOVITS, Kalman (Hungary, 26 Aug. 1931–). A descendant of a Hungarian count, Kalman Markovits won Olympic gold medals for water-polo in 1952 and '56 and a bronze in 1960. The world's best half-back of his era, Markovits was also in Hungary's European championship winning teams in 1954, '58 and '62. Former manager of a producers' co-operative, he became coach to the Hungarian water-polo team for the 1968 Mexico Games. His first wife was Katalin Szoke, Olympic and European 100 m. champion in 1952 and '54 respectively.

MARSHALL, John (Australia, 1 Feb. 1930–30 Jan. 1957). Marshall's rise to world class was phenomenal. He was runner-up in his first race, over 110 y. (1:19.0) in 1946, yet the next year, thanks to his first coach Tom Donnet, he won four Australian titles–220, 440, 880 and 1,650 y.

In 1948 he won the silver in the 1,500 m. and the bronze in the 400 m. at the London Olympics. Bob Kiphuth of Yale University and coach to the American team was so impressed with Marshall–'a potential world-beater' he called him–

that he arranged for the Melbourne boy to study at Yale.

There Kiphuth transformed Marshall's technique so effectively that in 1950 and '51 the Australian broke nineteen world records, including 2:04.6 (200 m.), 2:05.5 (220 y.), 4:26.9 (400 m.), 4:36.4 to 4:28.1 (440 y., six marks in thirteen months), 5:12.0 (500 y.), 5:43.8 (500 m.) 9:37.5 (880 y.) and 19:49.4 (mile).

For all his record-breaking, the quiet modest Marshall was never able to emulate in an Olympics his promise of 1948.

He swam in the 1952 and 1956 Games, the latter on butterfly. But the next year he was killed in a motor accident after a tyre had burst.

MASTENBROEK, Rie (Netherlands, 26 Feb. 1919–). Hendrika Mastenbroek won three gold medals in the 1936 Olympics during her short and successful career. These were for the 100 m. in which she beat Jeannette Campbell (Arg) by 0.5 in 65.9, the 400 m. in which her 5:26.4 was 1.1 faster than Denmark's Ragnhild Hveger and the 4 x 100 m. relay. She missed a fourth gold in the 100 m. back-stroke by finishing 0.3 behind her team-mate Dina Senff

Coached by the famous Dutchwoman Ma Braun, Rie trained in the Rotterdam canals for distance and in 25 m. indoor baths for sprinting. She had a tremendous rise to fame, for in 1934, her first year outside Rotterdam regional competitions, she won the European 400 m. free-style and 100 m. back-stroke titles, came second in the 100 m. and was a member of the Dutch winning relay squad.

Her seven world records–one for free-style and six for back-stroke–include 5:29.1 for 440 y. (1936), 1:15.8 (100 m. back-stroke), 2:49.6 (150 y. ba), 5:48.8 (400 m. ba). She was honoured by the Hall of Fame (1968).

MATTHES, Roland (East Germany, 17 Nov. 1950–). The Rolls Royce of swimming is not an extravagant description of Matthes who went unbeaten through seven years of major back-stroke competition from September 1967 to August 1974. And that record included all five 100 and 200 m. double victories–at the Olympics of 1968 and '72, the World championships of 1973 and the European championships of 1970/'74.

Consistently head and shoulders, perhaps a body length or more, faster than his rivals, the title of 'the greatest back-stroke swimmer of all time' surely belongs to this slim, quiet man from Erfurt.

Yet the fact that Matthes had to bow, eventually, to America's John Naber over 100 and 200 m. in Concord, California at the end of the 1974 season finally came as no surprise, though Naber did not approach the East German's world record times.

In fact, Naber beat a Matthes worn out by the incessant responsibility of being East Germany's star man swimmer, not only for back-stroke but also for butterfly and free-style.

Matthes came out to represent his country again at the 1975 world championships in Cali, Colombia where he retained his 100 m. back-stroke title. But the effort left him grey and drawn. And two days later, in the 200 m., he could only manage fourth. It was the first time in eight years the East German had been beaten in a major competition–yet the winner, Zoltán Verrasztó (Hun) was more than three seconds slower than Matthes at his best. Only later was it known Matthes had been ill with stomach trouble.

Being in a class on his own did not make Roland over-confident. Indeed he suffered all the anxieties of lesser competitors when the big events came along. Yet his deceptively languid stroke with hidden power, which as he went into top gear could leave his rivals floundering, made him the winner before he pushed away from the wall at the start. He could cover a 50 m. lap of the pool in eight to ten strokes less than any of his rivals.

His flexibility of speed was demonstrated during the final of the 200 m. at the Mexico Olympics of 1968. He was only third at half distance and at the last turn was fifth. At exactly the right instant he speeded his stroke tempo just a fraction to glide ahead to win by one second from Mitch Ivey (USA) in 2:09.6

For the record, Matthes took the 100 m. world record from 58.4 to 56.30 and the 200 m. from 2:07.9 to 2:01.87 between 1967 and 1973.

MEDICA, Jack (United States, 5 Oct. 1914–). Medica, from Seattle, Washington State, won the Olympic 400 m.

gold and silvers in the 1,500 m. and relay at the 1936 Berlin Games. As a one-man team representing the University of Washington in the N.C.A.A. championships, he won three events (the maximum allowed)-three times in a row to place his university third, behind the big squads from Michigan and Iowa, in the points-scoring table.

Winner of ten A.A.U. titles, Medica set eleven world records from 200 m. to one mile, of which his best times were: 2:07.2 (200 m., which stood for nine years, 2:07.9 (220 y.), 3:04.4 (300 y.), 3:21.6 (300 m.), 4:38.7 (400 m., unbroken for seven years), 4:40.8 (440 y.), 5:16.3 (500 y.), 5:57.8 (500 m.), 10:15.4 (880 y.), 1,000 y. (11:37.4), 20:58.8 (one mile, stood for eight years).

MEDLEY SWIMMING. Medley swimming, as the name suggests, is an event in which the competitor or team uses a variety of strokes in equal parts during the course of a race.

In medley relays the order of swimming is back-stroke, breast-stroke, butterfly and free-style. In individual medley, to balance the load for the single swimmer, butterfly—the most tiring stroke—comes first followed by back-stroke, breast-stroke and free-style. In both events, and in the absence of technical rules covering front-crawl (see FREE-STYLE and FRONT-CRAWL), free-style is held to mean any stroke other than back-stroke, breast-stroke or butterfly and, therefore, is invariably front-crawl.

The Americans pioneered individual medley racing as the ultimate test of the complete swimmer in the 1930s, long before it became a world event. As a result, the swimmers of the United States dominated the event when it was added to the Olympic programme in 1964.

Medley individual world records began in 1952 but medley relay swimming began earlier.

The Commonwealth Games included this event in the programme in 1934, the European championships in 1958 and the Olympic Games in 1960. World medley relay records were ratified from 1946. Prior to the separation of breast-stroke and butterfly in 1952 (see BREAST STROKE and BUTTERFLY) medley events were for three strokes—back-

stroke, breast-stroke and free-style—and teams of three.

MELVILLE CLARK, NATIONAL MEMORIAL TROPHY (England's 'Diving Club of the Year'). This trophy, presented in memory of Gordon Melville Clark, former national diving champion and chairman of the A.S.A. diving committee, is awarded each year to the English club scoring the most place points in diving championships. From 1951 until 1973 the trophy was for men or women. From 1974 it was for men only following the presentation of a special trophy for women divers (see WHITE, Belle, National Memorial Trophy). Winners:

1951—60	Highgate (men)
1961	Isleworth Penguins (women)
1962	Highgate (men)
1963	Highgate (men)—Isleworth Penguins (women) (tie)
1964—69	Highgate (men)
1970	Hillingdon (women)
1971	Coventry (women)
1972	Hillingdon (women)—Coventry (women) (tie)
1973	Coventry (women)
1974	Highgate
1975	Highgate

METROPOLITAN SWIMMING ASSOCIATION. The Metropolitan Swimming Association, or, as it was known originally, the Associated Metropolitan Swimming Clubs and then the London Swimming Association, was founded on 7 Jan. 1869 following a swimming congress held at the German Gymnasium in King's Cross, London, under the presidency of Mr. E.G. Ravenstein.

This amalgamation of London clubs received a chorus of approval, but was given almost invisible active support. Its influence was purely local and its development hampered by lack of funds. Early in Feb. 1874 the title of the association was again changed to the Swimming Association of Great Britain, in order to include all the clubs in the country. In 1884, following a break-away led by the Otter Club of London, a rival body, the Amateur Swimming Union, was set up. A desperate struggle for supremacy went on until 1886 when the S.A.G.B. and A.S.U. agreed to dissolve in order to found the Amateur Swimming Association (q.v.)

METRIC/LINEAR CONVERSIONS.

Although almost all the world now measures in metres, there are many swimming baths, particularly in the United Kingdom, which are still linear in length. The simple conversion is that 100 m. is two feet shorter than 110 y. But the precise conversions, based on one inch equalling 2.54 cm., are:

91.44 m.	=	100 y.
100 m.	=	109 y. 1 ft. 1in
100.584 m.	=	110 y.
200 m.	=	218 y. 2 ft. 2 in.
201.168 m.	=	220 y.
400 m.	=	437 y. 1 ft. 4 in.
402.363 m.	=	440 y.
800 m.	=	874 y. 2 ft. 8 in.
804.672 m	=	880 y.
1,500 m.	=	1,640 y. 1 ft. 3 in.
1,508.760 m.	=	1,650 y.
1,609.344 m.	=	1,760 y. (mile)

METRIC/LINEAR TIME CONVERSIONS.

There are arbitrary international conventions for converting times for yards distances to those for the shorter metric distances and viceversa. In the list below, the first figure is for a man of good quality national standard and the second for a woman of similar standard. However, the times of a woman of world record calibre would convert more closely to the first figure while those for a man of world class could warrant an even smaller conversion time.

Style	Yards	Seconds − / +	Metres
Free-style	110	0.3 / 0.4	100
	220	0.7 / 0.8	200
	440	1.7 / 1.9	400
	880	3.5 / 4.0	800
	1,650	6.5 / 7.5	1,500
Back-stroke	110	0.4 / 0.5	100
	220	0.9 / 1.0	200
Breast-stroke	110	0.5 / 0.5	100
	220	1.0 / 1.1	200
Butterfly	110	0.4 / 0.5	100
	220	0.9 / 1.1	200
Individual medley	220	0.9 / 1.1	200
	440	1.9 / 2.1	400
Free-style relay	4 x 110	1.2 / 1.6	4 x 110
	4 x 220	2.8 / 3.2	4 x 200
Medley relay	4 x 110	1.6 / 1.9	4 x 110

MEYER, Debbie (United States, 14 Aug. 1952–). Typifying everything American in looks, personality and swimming, talented Deborah Meyer, from Sacramento, California, won three individual golds—the first competitor in the pool to do this at a single Games—at the 1968 Olympics. She took the new 200 m. title in 2:10.5, half a second ahead of 100 m. champion Jan Henne . . . the 400 m. in 4:31·8, with another team-mate Linda Gustavson (4:35·5) second . . . and she became the first 800 m. champion in 9:24·0, which was 11·7 faster than the third American runner-up Pam Kruse. And Debbie, of the Arden Hills Club, achieved all this despite being ill most of her time in Mexico with the inglorious local stomach infection.

If her Mexico racing was marvellous, the record-breaking performances of this girl who puts up man-style times have been breath-taking. In two years and five weeks (9 July 1967 to 17 Aug. 1969) Debbie set fifteen free-style world marks from 200 to 1,500 m. These included taking the 400 m., in four bites, from 4:32·6 to 4:24·5 (in thirteen months) . . . the 800 m. from 9:35·8 to 9:10·4 . . . and the 1,500 m. from 18:11·1 to 17:19·9 (nearly a minute off in two years)!

As a comparison, her 4:24·5 would have beaten Australia's Murray Rose by 2·8 sec. for the gold in the 1956 Olympic 400 m. final. Debbie's world 1,500 mark (17:19·9) was 39·0 faster than Rose in winning the Melbourne title and only 0·3 slower than John Konrads' 1960 Olympic winning time.

Pan American 400 and 800 m. champion in 1967 (4:32.6 and 9:22.8) she was named that year, by Tass News Agency, as 'Woman Athlete of the Year'.

Miss Meyer won the United States 400 and 1,500 m. outdoor titles four successive years (1967–70) and the 400 m. medley in 1969. In August, 1970 she reduced her world mark for 400 m. free-style to 4:24.3.

MILTON FAMILY, Freddie (Great Britain, 2 Oct. 1906–). **Irene Pirie** (Canada, 10 June 1914–), **Tony** (Great Britain, 22 Mar. 1938–). The Miltons, father, mother and son, all competed in the Olympic Games . . . a rare hat-trick this is any sport and only one other family in swimming (see GYARMATI FAMILY) are known to have done it.

First to gain the honour was Irene Pirie, from Ontario, who was in the 1932 Games. Four years later, in Berlin, Frederick George Matt Milton played waterpolo for Britain, while Irene, who had married Freddie the previous summer, again swam for Canada.

A further 24 years onwards, in 1960, their son Hamilton Pirie Matt—better known as Tony—was in the British fourth placed 4 x 200 m. relay squad, who broke the European record in Rome.

To finish this family story, Irene's brother Bob, two years her junior, was also in the 1936 Canadian Olympic team.

MORAS, Karen (Australia, 6 Jan. 1954 —). A bronze medal in the 400 m. and fourth place in the 800 m. in the 1968 Olympics at 14 were the first successes of Karen Moras, one of six Moras children, all members of the Forbes and Ursula Carlile Swim School in Ryde, New South Wales.

Early in 1970, Karen twice beat America's triple Olympic gold medallist Debbie Meyer in Sydney and in the Australian championships she won three titles—the 400 m. in 4:26.3 (only 1.7 outside Miss Meyer's world mark) and 200 m. in 2:09.8, both Commonwealth records and then clocked 9:09.1 for 800 m. and her first world mark.

Miss Moras reduced her world 800 m. time to 9:02.4 in winning the first of her three titles in the 1970 Commonwealth Games by 40 metres. She also won the 200 and 400 m.

MORTON, Lucy (Great Britain, 23 Feb. 1898—). The first British woman to win an individual Olympic swimming title was Lucy Morton of Blackpool, who took a surprise gold in the 200 m. breaststroke in 1924 at the age of 26. She was only the second string as world recordholder Irene Gilbert was Britain's real hope.

Fate helped the Briton for Holland's Marie Baron, who had the fastest heat time (3:22.6) was disqualified for a faulty turn. America's Agnes Geraghty was ahead after 150 m., followed by Miss Morton and third string Gladys Carson. But over the last 50 m. Miss Morton fought ahead to win by 0.8 in 3:33.2, a Games record, with Miss Carson third (3:35.4) and Irene Gilbert (who had been ill) a shadow of her world record self fifth (3:38.0).

The north of England woman never held the world record for her Olympic gold medal distance though she twice set 200 y. figures—3:11.4 as the first holder in 1916 and 3:06.0 in 1920. She must have had a good chance of a gold in 1920 . . . but there were no breaststroke events for women in the Antwerp Games.

Lucy also was a talented back-stroker —in the days of the old English double over-arm and frog leg-kick style—and was the first holder of the world record for 150 y. (2:17.0, 1916). She was the first A.S.A. champion for 150 y. backstroke and 200 y. breast-stroke in 1920. Married in 1927, Mrs. Heaton, *nee* Morton, taught swimming to Blackpool children for many years and has continued her interest in the sport as an official.

MUIR, Karen (South Africa, 16 Sept. 1952–). The youngest competitor in any sport to break a world record, Karen Yvette Muir was only 12 years, 10 months and 25 days young on 10 Aug. 1965 when she took seven-tenths off the 110 y. back-stroke time of Britain's Linda Ludgrove. Karen's 68.7 in a heat of the A.S.A. junior championship at Blackpool compared most favourably with the world 100 m. record of America's Cathy Ferguson—67.7 (equal to 68.2 for 110 y.) in winning the 1964 Olympic title, and the painfully shy, skinny South African, who had been brought to England 'for experience' and had no real idea of how to start or turn, showed this performance was no fluke by taking the final in 68.9.

Such exceptional talent deserved Olympic golds in Mexico. But South Africa were excluded from the 1968 Games where the back-stroke events were won by Americans: Kaye Hall in the 100 m. in 66.2 (breaking Karen's latest 100 m. mark by two-tenths, though the time was equivalent only to the Kimberley girl's 110 y. world mark of 66.7) and Pokey Watson in the 200 m. in 2:24.8 (against Karen's world record that year of 2:23.8).

Karen made many tours overseas—to Europe and the United States. Each time she returned with fresh honours. She was awarded the Helms Trophy for Africa and the South African President's Award of Merit. She won 22 South African championships, for free-style and medley as well as back-stroke, set 15 national records and won three United States back-stroke titles: 100 m. in 1968 and 200 m. in 1966 and '68.

MUNOZ, Felipe (Mexico, 3 Feb. 1951 —). Mexico's only swimming champion in the history of the Olympics, the roof was almost exploded off his home Mexico City pool in 1968 when Felipe Munoz touched half a second ahead of the Russian favourite Vladimir Kosinsky in the 200 m. breast-stroke. It was fortunate that the rest of the placings in this eight man final were clear cut and that the electrical timing and judging machine did not break down, for as Munoz finished every single Mexican at the poolside quit officiating and stood up and cheered.

Munoz, only the sixth fastest before the Games, was a national hero afterwards.

He is known affectionately as 'Tibio' or 'luke-warm' because his father comes from Aguascalientes ('hot water') and his mother from the village of Rio Frio ('cold river'). But there was nothing tepid about his swimming that memorable October evening.

NATIONAL COLLEGIATE ATHLETICS ASSOCIATION (USA) CHAMPIONS. The N.C.A.A. champion-

ships for men, instituted in 1937, are considered to be the finest and most highly competitive short course meeting in the world. They are open to teams from recognized United States colleges and universities.

The institution of a top team award increased the already tense excitement of this annual fixture at which the most successful squad in recent years has been Indiana University, who won six years in succession (1968-1973) and finished runners up behind the University of Southern California, in 1977 and 1975.

The venues and dates since 1960 are:

1960	Southern Methodist University, Dallas, Texas	24–26 March
1961	University of Seattle, Washington	23–25 March
1962	Ohio State University, Columbus, Ohio	30–31 March
1963	N. Caroline State Univ., Raleigh, N. Carolina	28–30 March
1964	Yale University, New Haven, Connecticut	26–28 March
1965	University of Iowa, Ames, Iowa	25–27 March
1966	Air Force Academy, Colorado	24–26 March
1967	East Lansing, Michigan	23–25 March
1968	Dartmouth, Hanover, New Hampshire	28–30 March
1969	Indiana University, Bloomington, Indiana	27–29 March
1970	Salt Lake City, Utah	26–28 March
1971	University of Iowa, Ames, Iowa	25–27 March
1972	Military Academy, West Point, New York	23–25 March
1973	Knoxville, Tennessee	22–24 March
1974	Long Beach, California	28–30 March
1975	Cleveland State University, Ohio	27–29 March

50 y. Free-style
1960	Hunter	21.9
1961	Legacki, Frank	21.4
1962	Jackman, Steve	21.1
1963	Jackman, Steve	21.2
1964	Austin, Mike	21.0
1965	Clark, Steve	21.2
1966	Kennen, James van	21.3
1967	Zorn, Zac	21.12
1968	Zorn, Zac	20.99
1969	Frawley, Dan	21.04
1970	Edgar, Dave	20.94
1971	Edgar, Dave	20.30
1972	Edgar, Dave	20.44
1973	Trembley, John	20.33
1974	Trembley, John	20.23
1975	Bottom, Joe	20.11

100 y. Free-style
1960	Lusk	49.4
1961	Jackman, Steve	50.6
1962	Jackman, Steve	47.5
1963	Lindberg, Per-Ola	47.1
1964	Clark, Steve	46.3
1965	Clark, Steve	46.1
1966	Roth, Donald	46.8
1967	Walsh, Ken	45.67
1968	Zorn, Zac	45.45
1969	Heath, Francis	46.24
1970	Edgar, Dave	46.06
1971	Edgar, Dave	44.69
1972	Edgar, Dave	45.00
1973	Trembley, John	45.09
1974	Bottom, Joe	45.06
1975	Skinner, Jonty	43.92

200 y. Free-style
1960*	Winters, Frank	2:04.3
1961*	Rose, Murray (Aus)	2:00.6
1962*	Spreitzer	2:00.9
1963	Clark, Steve	1:46.3
1964	Clark, Steve	1:44.4
1965	Saari, Roy	1:42.9
1966	Saari, Roy	1:44.6
1967	Buckingham, Greg	1:41.46
1968	Schollander, Don	1:42.04
1969	Spitz, Mark	1:39.53

1970	Bello, Juan (Peru)	1:42.70
1971	McConica, Jim	1:39.75
1972	Heidenreich, Jerry	1:38.35
1973	McConica, Jim	1:39.62
1974	Montgomery, Jim	1:39.18
1975	McDonnell, George	1:38.04
	* = 220 y.	

500 y. Free-style

1960*	Rousanvelle, Dennis	4:28.8
1961*	Rose, Murray (Aus)	4:17.9
1962*	Rose, Murray (Aus)	4:20.0
1963	Konrads, John (Aus)	4:50.7
1964	Saari, Roy	4:45.8
1965	Saari, Roy	4:43.6
1966	Saari, Roy	4:50.5
1967	Buckingham, Greg	4:37.16
1968	Charlton, Greg	4:38.24
1969	Spitz, Mark	4:33.48
1970	Burton, Mike	4:37.29
1971	Kinsella, John	4:27.39
1972	Kinsella, John	4:24.49
1973	Kinsella, John	4:27.59
1974	Naber, John	4:26.85
1975	Naber, John	4:20.45
	* = 440 y.	

1,650 y. Free-style

1960*	Chase	17:48.7
1961*	Rose, Murray (Aus)	17:21.8
1962*	Rose, Murray (Aus)	17:26.2
1963	Konrads, John (Aus)	17:24.0
1964	Saari, Roy	16:49.5
1965	Saari, Roy	16:39.9
1966	Saari, Roy	17:08.1
1967	Burton, Mike	16:17.59
1968	Burton, Mike	15:59.34
1969	Fassnacht, Hans (W Ger)	15:54.21
1970	Burton, Mike	16:10.59
1971	Kinsella, John	15:26.51
1972	Kinsella, John	15:33.58
1973	Kinsella, John	15:32.66
1974	Tingley, Jack	15:29.28
1975	Bruner, Mike	15:16.54
	* = 1,500 m.	

100 y. Back-stroke

1960	Bittick, Charles	54.4
1961	Bittick, Charles	53.9
1962	Schaefer, Louis	53.9
1963	Bennett, Bob	53.8
1964	Bennett, Bob	53.1
1965	Dilley, Gary	52.6
1966	Dilley, Gary	52.3
1967	Hickcox, Charles	53.17
1968	Hickcox, Charles	52.18
1969	Haywood, Fred	52.44

1970	Barbiere, Larry	51.9
1971	Esteva, Santiago (Sp)	51.71
1972	Gilbert, Paul	51.29
1973	Stamm, Mike	50.91
1974	Naber, John	50.51
1975	Naber, John	49.94

200 y. Back-stroke

1960	Bittick, Charles	2:00.1
1961	Bittick, Charles	1:57.1
1962	Schaefer, Louis	1:58.8
1963	Bartsch, Edward	1:57.8
1964	Graef, Jed	1:56.2
1965	Dilley, Gary	1:56.2
1966	Dilley, Gary	1:56.4
1967	Hickcox, Charles	1:55.30
1968	Hickcox, Charles	1:54.66
1969	Hickcox, Charles	1:53.67
1970	Ivey, Mitch	1:52.80
1971	Hall, Gary	1:50.60
1972	Campbell, Charles	1:50.55
1973	Stamm, Mike	1:50.56
1974	Naber, John	1:48.95
1975	Naber, John	1:46.82

100 y. Breast-stroke

1960	Peterson	1:03.1
1961	Nelson, Dick	1:02.1
1962	Nelson, Dick	1:01.7
1963	Green/Nelson (tie)	1:02.3
1964	Craig, William	59.9
1965	Craig, William	1:00.3
1966	Scheerer, P	1:00.4
1967	Merten, Ken	58.54
1968	Nesbit, Richard	59.11
1969	McKenzie, Don	58.36
1970	Job, Brian	57.58
1971	Job, Brian	57.24
1972	Bruce, Tom	56.99
1973	Hencken, John	57.11
1974	Wilkie, David (GB)	56.72
1975	Hencken, John	56.59

200 y. Breast-stroke

1960	Clark, Ronald	2:17.6
1961	Clark, Ronald	2:13.4
1962	Luken, Virgil	2:16.8
1963	Hull	2:17.0
1964	Craig, William	2:12.1
1965	Tretheway, T	2:10.4
1966	Anderson, Wayne	2:14.2
1967	Merten, Ken	2:07.99
1968	Long, Phil	2:11.72
1969	Dirksen, Michael	2:08.62
1970	Job, Brian	2:06.00
1971	Job, Brian	2:03.39
1972	Job, Brian	2:02.59

1973	Wilkie, David (GB)	2:03.47	1974	Furniss, Steve	1:51.52
1974	Hencken, John	2:01.74	1975	Tyler, Fred	+1:50.62
1975	Hencken, John	2:00.83			

+ Tyler, Fred and Engstrand, Lee were both timed at 1:50.628, but Tyler was given the victory on the ten-thousandths of a second placing.

100 y. Butterfly

1960	Troy, Mike	53.1
1961	Gillanders, David	52.9
1962	Spencer	52.5
1963	Richardson, Walter	51.6
1964	Richardson, Walter	50.2
1965	Schmidt, Fred	51.0
1966	Riker, Phil	51.1
1967	Wales, Ross	50.26
1968	Russell, Doug	49.57
1969	Spitz, Mark	49.69
1970	Spitz, Mark	49.82
1971	Spitz, Mark	49.42
1972	Spitz, Mark	47.98
1973	Trembley, John	48.68
1974	Trembley, John	48.71
1975	Rolan, Jeff	48.95

200 y. Butterfly

1960	Troy, Mike	1:58.8
1961	Gillanders, David	1:58.6
1962	Wolfe	1:58.0
1963	McDonough, Ed	1:57.3
1964	Schmidt, Fred	1:53.5
1965	Schmidt, Fred	1:51.4
1966	Robie, Carl	1:53.8
1967	Robie, Carl	1:52.59
1968	Houser, Phil	1:52.55
1969	Ferris, John	1:49.61
1970	Burton, Mike	1:51.60
1971	Spitz, Mark	1:50.10
1972	Spitz, Mark	1:46.89
1973	Hall, Gary	1:48.48
1974	Backhaus, Robin	1:47.00
1975	Backhaus, Robin	1:47.16

200 y. Individual medley

1960	Larson, Lance	2:03.2
1961	Kelso, Jack (Can)	2:02.9
1962	Mull	2:02.3
1963	Mull	2:01.6
1964	Saari, Roy	1:56.7
1965	Hopper, R	1:58.1
1966	Utley, Bill	1:58.5
1967	Roth, Dick	1:56.09
1968	Hickcox, Charles	1:52.56
1969	Hickcox, Charles	1:54.43
1970	Heckl, Frank	1:55.21
1971	Hall, Gary	1:52.20
1972	Hall, Gary	1:51.50
1973	Furniss, Steve	1:51.38

400 m. Individual medley

1963	Townsend, Ed	4:22.5
1964	McGeagh, Richard	4:16.4
1965	Robie, Carl	4:16.6
1966	Webb, Ken	4:19.8
1967	Roth, Dick	4:12.11
1968	Utley, Bill	4:10.85
1969	Fassnacht, Hans (W Ger)	4:07.66
1970	Hall, Gary	4:09.31
1971	Hall, Gary	3:58.25
1972	Hall, Gary	3:58.71
1973	Furniss, Steve	3:55.16
1974	Furniss, Steve	3:57.80
1975	Engstrand, Lee	3:57.86

Highboard diving

1967	Sitzberger, Ken	572.65
1968	Russell, Keith	494.55
1969	Henry, Jim	574.68
1970	Henry, Jim	550.55
1971	Boggs, Phil	552.93
1972	Lincoln, Craig	545.44
1973	Moore, Tim	539.61
1974	McAllister, Richard	526.41
1975		

Springboard diving

1960	Hall, Sam	510.35
1961	Vitucci, Lou	491.65
1962	Vitucci, Lou	506.45
1963	Vitucci, Lou	496.90
1964		
1965	Sitzberger, Ken	565.05
1966	Wrightson, Bernie	538.90
1967	Sitzberger, Ken	510.25
1968	Henry, Jim	512.05
1969	Henry, Jim	531.06
1970	Henry, Jim	487.56
1971	Finneran, Michael	520.98
1972	Smith, T	503.25
1973	Moore, Tim	487.90
1974	Moore, Tim	494.25
1975	Moore, Tim	508.71

Top Teams

1965	Univ. of S. California 285	
1966	Univ. of S. California 302	
1967	Stanford University 275; Univ. of S. California 260	
1968	Indiana University 346; Yale University 253	

1969   Indiana University 427;
       Stanford University 196
1970   Indiana University 332;
       Univ. of S. California 235
1971   Indiana University 351;
       Univ. of S. California 260
1972   Indiana University 390;
       Univ, of S. California 371
1973   India University 358;
       Univ. of Tennessee 294
1974   Univ. of S. California 339;
       Indiana University 338
1975   Univ. of S. California 344;
       Indiana University 274

NEILSON, Sandra (United States, 20 March, 1956-   ). Not a breaker of world records, nor a multi-winner of national titles, Sandy Neilson produced her shock 100 m. free-style victories on the big occasions; in her case, at the 1971 Pan-American and 1972 Olympic Games.

Not in the U.S.A. top ten sprinters in 1970, freckle-faced Sandy came through a year later to win the Pan-American title, in Cali, Colombia, by half a second and also collected a gold and silver from the free-style and medley relays.

She was only the third string 100 m. competitor at the Munich Olympics, yet on the day she was a clear winner (58.59) and she got golds from both relays. For the record, her only U.S.A. championship success was the Indoor 100 y. in 1971.

NETHERLANDS   CHAMPIONS. See DUTCH CHAMPIONS.

NEW   ZEALAND   AMATEUR SWIMMING ASSOCIATION. Swimming on an organized basis in New Zealand began in 1880 when, on 11th Oct, at a meeting at the home of Mr. Arthur Francis, the Christchurch Amateur Swimming Club was formed.

The N.Z.A.S.A.—after the English A.S.A., the second national governing body in the swimming world—was formally constituted on 4 Jan. 1890 through the efforts of Mr. Roland St. Clair. Rows between the North and South Islands led to the formation of a rival organization in the North Island, known as the New Zealand Amateur Swimming Association Registered. Peace was finally achieved on 21 Mar. 1904. There were eight affiliated clubs in 1892, though it is believed another eight were in existence. By the 1970s there were more than 200 clubs.

NEW   ZEALAND   CHAMPIONS. New Zealand championships have been held since 1890 on a centralized basis and the venues and winners since 1946 are:

1946	Napier
1947	Nelson
1948	Dunedin
1949	Auckland
1950	Auckland
1951	Timaru
1952	Hamilton
1953	Invercargill
1954	Wanganui
1955	Lower Hutt
1956	Greymouth
1957	Auckland
1958	Christchurch
1959	Napier
1960	Blenheim
1961	Tauranga
1962	Nae Nae
1963	Auckland
1964	Blenheim
1965	Dunedin
1966	Napier
1967	Christchurch
1968	New Plymouth
1969	Auckland
1970	Dunedin
1971	Palmerston North
1972	Dunedin
1973	Dunedin
1974	Christchurch
1975	Christchurch
1976	Dunedin

110 y. Free-style (instituted 1890)

1946*	Hatchwell, Bob	58.4
1947*	Hatchwell, Bob	55.2
1948*	Barry, Lyall	55.2
1949*	Ballantyne, Donald	1:00.2
1950*	Barry, Lyall	55.4
1951*	Keesing, Neil	59.0
1952*	Amos, Michael	56.4
1953*	Amos, Michael	57.0
1954*	Blackwood, Jim	58.2
1955*	Amos, Michael	55.6
1956*	Ramsey, Darryl	56.3
1957	Snoep, Otto	1:02.2
1958	Ramsey, Darryl	1:02.0
1959*	Dann, Graham	55.6
1960	Hatch, Peter	1:01.4
1961*	Hatch, Peter	52.6
1962	Hatch, Peter	59.0
1963	Hatch, Peter	57.8
1964	Hatch, Peter	58.7
1965	Walker, Robbie	57.6

1966	Walker, Robbie	58.1
1967	Smith, Glen	57.9
1968	O'Carroll, Paddy	56.7
1969	Curry, Ian	56.6
	* = 100 y.	

100 m. Free-style
1970	Borrie, Michael	55.6
1971	Campbell, Graham	57.8
1972	Herring, Colin	54.3
1973	Borrie, Michael	55.4
1974	Naylor, Brett	56.14
1975	Naylor, Brett	54.84

220 y. Free-style
1946	Chambers, Ned	2:27.0
1947	Barry, Lyall	2:23.8
1948	Chambers, Noel	2:20.4
1949	Lucas, Buddy	2:27.2
1950	Amos, Michael	2:20.0
1951	Stanley, Jack	2:33.0
1952	Amos, Michael	2:26.0
1953	Hamilton, John	2:22.3
1954	Hamilton, John	2:22.9
1955	Hamilton, John	2:19.9
1956	Harker, Reg	2:21.6
1957	Lucas, Buddy	2:19.8
1958	McGuinness, John	2:20.3
1959	Smith, Bill	2:14.5
1960	Dann, Graham	2:18.6
1961	Hatch, Peter	2:15.8
1962	Hatch, Peter	2:13.7
1963	Dalton, Terry	2:09.5
1964	Walker, Robbie	2:10.2
1965	Walker, Robbie	2:07.1
1966	Walker, Robbie	2:09.4
1967	Campbell, Graham	2:10.8
1968	Smith, Glen	2:07.0
1969	Kindred, Alan	2:05.5

200 m. Free-style
1970	Borrie, Michael	2:01.8
1971	Kindred, Alan	2:05.8
1972	Herring, Colin	2:03.2
1973	Borrie, Michael	2:02.8
1974	Naylor, Brett	1:59.50
1975	Naylor, Brett	1:57.70

440 y. Free-style (instituted 1890)
1946	Chambers, Noel	5:45.4
1947	Chambers, Noel	5:24.0
1948	Chambers, Noel	5:03.4
1949	Lucas, Buddy	5:20.0
1950	Lucas, Buddy	5:03.4
1951	Lucas, Buddy	5:03.2
1952	Jarvis, John	5:14.6
1953	Jarvis, John	5:08.2

1954	Hamilton, John	5:08.6
1955	Jarvis, John	5:00.1
1956	Flynn, John	5:04.4
1957	Lucas, Buddy	5:03.8
1958	McFadden, Colin	4:57.4
1959	McFadden, Colin	4:49.9
1960	Monteith, Graham	4:53.9
1961	Crowder, Brian	4:48.7
1962	Dalton, Terry	4:46.4
1963	Dalton, Terry	4:34.6
1964	Walker, Robbie	4:37.9
1965	Walker, Robbie	4:31.0
1966	Walker, Robbie	4:35.0
1967	Kindred, Alan	4:38.6
1968	Kindred, Alan	4:32.8
1969	Kindred, Alan	4:24.8

400 m. Free-style
1970	Kindred, Alan	4:26.5
1971	Kindred, Alan	4:25.2
1972	Treffers, Mark	4:17.2
1973	Craig, Martin	4:18.5
1974	Treffers, Mark	4:11.88
1975	Naylor, Brett	4:06.29

1,650 y. Free-style (instituted 1953)
1953	Jarvis, John	20:43.7
1954	Hamilton, John	20:43.5
1955	Jarvis, John	20:04.7
1956	Flynn, John	20:13.8
1957	Lucas, Buddy	20:16.1
1958	McFadden, Colin	20:01.9
1959	McFadden, Colin	19:30.9
1960	Monteith, Graham	19:40.5
1961	Crowder, Brian	19:33.6
1962	Monteith, Graham	19:22.4
1963	Dalton, Terry	18:26.0
1964	Walker, Robbie	18:31.6
1965	Walker, Robbie	18:18.4
1966	Walker, Robbie	18:33.9
1967	Kindred, Alan	18:30.0
1968	Kindred, Alan	18:34.8
1969	Kindred, Alan	17:42.6

1,500 m. Free-style
1970	Treffers, Mark	17:24.5
1971	Treffers, Mark	17:26.2
1972	Treffers, Mark	16:32.4
1973	Treffers, Mark	17:01.2
1974	Treffers, Mark	16:41.89
1975	Naylor, Brett	16:14.09

110 y. Back-stroke (instituted 1938)
1946*	Cliff, Clive	1:06.6
1947*	Mathieson, Peter	1:06.2
1948*	Wilson, Trevor	1:05.8
1949*	Mathieson, Peter	1:07.0

1950*	Mathieson, Peter	1:07.6
1951*	Hurring, Lincoln	1:06.6
1952*	Hurring, Lincoln	1:03.6
1953*	Hurring, Lincoln	1:02.6
1954*	Hamilton, Neil	1:07.0
1955*	Hamilton, Neil	1:06.1
1956*	Tansley, Mark	1:05.8
1957	Tansley, Mark	1:11.0
1958	Tansley, Mark	1:11.2
1959*	Robertson, Bill	1:03.5
1960	Hurring, Lincoln	1:08.7
1961*	Robertson, Bill	1:01.1
1962	Robertson, Bill	1:08.6
1963	Robertson, Bill	1:07.2
1964	O'Carroll, Paddy	1:07.4
1965	O'Carroll, Paddy	1:06.8
1966	O'Carroll, Paddy	1:05.7
1967	O'Carroll, Paddy	1:05.3
1968	O'Carroll, Paddy	1:04.0
1969	O'Carroll, Paddy	1:05.4
	* = 100 y.	

100 m. Back-stroke

1970	Bond, Barnett	1:05.4
1971	McConnochie, John	1:04.5
1972	Williams, John (Aus)	1:03.4
1973	Carter, Jimmy (GB)	1:04.2
1974	Thorogood, Philip	1:04.12
1975	Bullock, Ian	1:03.44

220 y. Back-stroke (instituted 1960)

1960	Robertson, Bill	2:31.6
1961	Robertson, Bill	2:27.5
1962	Robertson, Bill	2:28.7
1963	Robertson, Bill	2:26.0
1964	Seagar, Allan	2:26.4
1965	Seagar, Allan	2:22.3
1966	Seagar, Allan	2:23.8
1967	Brown, Hilton	2:24.1
1968	O'Carroll, Paddy	2:20.8
1969	Bond, Barmett	2:22.0

200 m. Back-stroke

1970	Bond, Barnett	2:19.5
1971	Knowles, Barry	2:23.7
1972	Williams, John (Aus)	2:16.2
1973	Gray, Roy	2:20.7
1974	Thorogood, Philip	2:15.62
1975	Bullock, Ian	2:16.37

110 y. Breast-stroke (instituted 1939)

1946*	Shanahan, John	1:14.4
1947*	Shanahan, John	1:12.2
1948*	Shanahan, John	1:10.0
1949*	Callan, Colin	1:14.8
1950*	Shanahan, John	1:10.0
1951*	Shaw, J.	1:15.0
1952*	Doms, John	1:14.0

1953*	Doms, John	1:13.6
1954*	Doms, John	1:12.0
1955*	Doms, John	1:11.9
1956*	Martlew, Gary	1:15.2
1957	Hilt, Con	1:19.8
1958	Hilt, Con	1:19.5
1959*	Hilt, Con	1:08.1
1960	Hilt, Con	1:18.5
1961*	Hilt, Con	1:09.1
1962	Graham, Tony	1:18.7
1963	Graham, Tony	1:15.6
1964	Ruzio-Saban, Gjoko	1:12.9
1965	Graham, Tony	1:12.0
1966	Graham, Tony	1:13.1
1967	Graham, Tony	1:12.9
1968	Johnstone, Ivan	1:14.0
1969	Graham, Tony	1:14.2
	* = 100 y.	

100 m. Breast-stroke

1970	Graham, Tony	1:14.3
1971	Pater, Bert	1:17.6
1972	Johnstone, Ivan	1:13.4
1973	Lewis, Brent	1:13.0
1974	Lewis, Brent	1:13.74
1975	Novak, R	1:12.64

220 y. Breast-stroke (instituted 1906)

1946	Dowse, Desmond	3:06.4
1947	Shanahan, John	3:00.8
1948	Shanahan, John	2:58.0
1949	Callan, Colin	3:10.2
1950	Shanahan, John	2:58.0
1951	Dowse, Desmond	3:02.6
1952	Doms, John	2:58.6
1953	Doms, John	2:57.0
1954	Doms, John	2:57.6
1955	Doms, John	2:56.8
1956	McDonald, Ian	2:59.8
1957	Hilt, Con	2:57.2
1958	Brittendon, Garry	2:57.4
1959	Hilt, Con	2:48.2
1960	Hilt, Con	2:58.1
1961	Graham, Tony	2:48.5
1962	Graham, Tony	2:51.5
1963	Graham, Tony	2:45.2
1964	Ruzion-Saban, Gjoko	2:46.1
1965	Graham, Tony	2:38.4
1966	Graham, Tony	2:39.0
1967	Graham, Tony	2:42.4
1968	Graham, Tony	2:44.7
1969	Graham, Tony	2:43.3

200 m. Breast-stroke

1970	Graham, Tony	2:42.9
1971	Pater, Bert	2:45.2
1972	Johnstone, Ivan	2:40.7
1973	Lewis, Brent	2:38.8

| 1974 | Lewis, Brent | 2:37.44 |
| 1975 | Novak, R | 2:35.66 |

110 y. Butterfly

1948*	Shanahan, John	1:08.6
1949*	Logan, Tom	1:30.0
1950*	Callan, Colin	1:09.4
1951*	Callan, Colin	1:11.0
1952*	Callan, Colin	1:09.4
1953*	Callan, Colin	1:10.3
1954*	Logan, Tom	1:10.8
1955*	Davies, John	1:06.4
1956*	Hilt, Con	1:06.3
1957	Hilt, Con	1:14.5
1958	Cruikshank, Dennis	1:12.0
1959*	Morse. Blake	1:03.1
1960	Hatch, Peter	1:09.5
1961*	Hatch, Peter	58.5
1962	Gerrard, David	1:04.8
1963	Gerrard, David	1:02.2
1964	Hatch, Peter	1:02.4
1965	Gerrard, David	1:01.8
1966	Gerrard, David	1:03.2
1967	Gerrard, David	1:02.3
1968	Gerrard, David	1:02.1
1969	Campbell, Graham	1:01.2

* = 100 y.

100 m. Butterfly

1970	Campbell, Graham	1:01.1
1971	Campbell, Graham	1:01.6
1972	Toomey, Michael	1:00.7
1973	Toomey, Michael	59.9
1974	Coutts, John	59.95
1975	Coutts, John	59.06

220 y. Butterfly (instituted 1948)

1948	Shanahan, John	3:07.8
1949	Dowse, Desmond	No time
1950	Shanahan, John	2:57.6
1951	Callan, Colin	3:06.6
1952	Dowse, Desmond	3:04.0
1953	Dowse, Desmond	3:10.8
1954	Dowse, Desmond	3:08.7
1955	Hilt, Con	3:03.6
1956	Hilt, Con	3:01.0
1957	Hilt, Con	3:05.6
1958	Cruikshank, Dennis	2:53.4
1959	Hilt, Con	2:50.0
1960	Gerrard, David	2:39.6
1961	Gerrard, David	2:30.3
1962	Gerrard, David	2:26.4
1963	Gerrard, David	2:16.5
1964	Gerrard, David	2:18.2
1965	Gerrard, David	2:17.4
1966	Gerrard, David	2:19.3
1967	Gerrard, David	2:16.7
1968	Gerrard, David	2:19.0
1969	Gerrard, David	2:18.7

200 m. Butterfly

1970	Barfoot, Alan	2:21.2
1971	Graham, Campbell	2:19.6
1972	Coutts, John	2:16.1
1973	Plummer, Warren (Aus)	2:14.0
1974	Coutts, John	2:10.69
1975	Coutts, John	2:09.45

Individual medley (instituted 1947)

1947	Jarvis, J. (100 y.)	1:05.6
1948	Shanahan, J. (100 y.)	1:04.8
1949	Logan. T. (100 y.)	1:08.6
1950	Callan, C. (133 1/3 y.)	2:03.8
1951	Branch, D. (133 1/3 y.)	1:52.0
1952	Hurring, Lincoln (100 y.)	1:07.0
1953	Hurring, Lincoln (100 y.)	1:06.1
1954	Blackwood, J. (100 y.)	1:06.0
1955	Todd, J. (100 y.)	1:04.6
1956	Harker, R. (400 y.)	5:17.5
1957	Harker, R. (440 y.)	5:51.0
1958	Harker, R. (440 y.)	5:54.6
1959	McDonald, I. (400 y.)	5:24.9
1960	Hatch, P. (220 y.)	2:42.2
1961	Seagar, Allan (266 2/3 y.)	3:10.0

220 y. Individual medley

1962	Seagar, Allan	2:24.7
1963	Seagar, Allan	2:23.3
1964	Seager, Allan	2:23.8
1969	Bond, Barnett	2:25.2

200 m. Individual medley

1970	Bond, Barnett	2:22.9
1971	McConnochie, John	2:21.1
1972	Portier, Buddy (Aus)	2:18.8
1973	Carter, Jimmy (GB)	2:18.0
1974	Fogel, Ashley	2:19.83
1975	Treffers, Mark	2:16.10

440 y. Individual medley

1962	Seagar, Allan	5:34.5
1963	Seagar, Allan	5:12.6
1964	Seagar, Allan	5:14.4
1965	Seagar, Allan	5:06.8
1966	Seagar, Allan	5:08.1
1967	Seagar, Allan	5:10.4
1968	Seagar, Allan	5:13.5
1969	Bond, Barnett	5:15.7

400 m. Individual medley

1970	Bond, Barnett	5:05.7
1971	McConnochie, John	5:07.4
1972	Portier, Buddy (Aus)	4:52.1
1973	Plummer, Warren (Aus)	4:52.8
1974	Treffers, Mark	4:51.17
1975	Treffers, Mark	4:44.13

WOMEN

110 y. Free-style (instituted 1912)

1946*	Casey, Betty	1:09.8
1947*	Casey, Betty	1:07.0
1948*	Casey, Betty	1:04.8
1949*	Casey, Betty	1:04.8
1950*	Jacobi, Kristin	1:03.8
1951*	Jacobi, Kristin	1:06.4
1952*	Roe, Marion	1:05.2
1953*	Roe, Marion	1:03.8
1954*	Roe, Marion	1:03.6
1955*	Roe, Marion	59.8
1956*	Roe, Marion	59.4
1957	Hunter, Jennifer	1:09.4
1958	Hunter, Jennifer	1:07.7
1959*	Bell, Alison	1:03.2
1960	Bell, Alison	1:07.9
1961*	Moore, Lesley	1:02.4
1962	Moore, Lesley	1:07.5
1963	McMillan, Alison	1:05.7
1964	McMillan, Alison	1:05.6
1965	McMillan, Alison	1:06.0
1966	McMillan, Alison	1:07.6
1967	Hall, Koreen	1:06.8
1968	Wright, Judith	1:06.0
1969	Crawford, Felicity	1:04.4

* = 100 y.

100 m. Free-style

1970	Crawford, Felicity	1:04.2
1971	Whiting, Cathy	1:04.1
1972	Gould, Shane (Aus)	59.7
1973	Booth, Sharon (Aus)	1:02.2
1974	Albury, Karol	1:03.20
1975	Perrott, Rebeca	1:00.11

220 y. Free-style (instituted 1924)

1946	Casey, Betty	2:49.6
1947	Casey, Betty	2:46.0
1948	Casey, Betty	2:44.8
1949	Casey, Betty	2:45.2
1950	Jacobi, Kristin	2:45.8
1951	Griffin, Winifred	2:43.4
1952	Menzies, Margaret	2:43.8
1953	Griffin, Winifred	2:36.0
1954	Roe, Marion	2:36.1
1955	Griffin, Winifred	2:30.4
1956	Roe, Marion	2:25.4
1957	Griffin, Winifred	2:31.6
1958	Bell, Alison	2:33.2
1959	Hunter, Jennifer	2:32.3
1960	Bell, Alison	2:30.6
1961	Moore, Lesley	2:30.3
1962	Moore, Lesley	2:27.3
1963	Nicholson, Shirley	2:27.0
1964	McMillan, Alison	2:23.0
1965	McMillan, Alison	2:24.2

1966	Macrae, Margaret	2:25.7
1967	Amies, June	2:25.7
1968	Shipston, Tui	2:21.9
1969	Shipston, Tui	2:17.7

200 m. Free-style

1970	Wright, Judith	2:21.8
1971	Wright, Judith	2:16.9
1972	Gould, Shane (Aus)	2:07.7
1973	Rickard, Virginia (Aus)	2:11.1
1974	Calder, Allison	2:14.79
1975	Perrott, Rebeca	2:07.36

440 y. Free-style (instituted 1921)

1946	Casey, Betty	6:09.0
1947	Casey, Betty	6:01.2
1948	Holman, Maureen	5:54.8
1949	Casey, Betty	6:02.0
1950	McKenzie, Helen	5:51.4
1951	Griffin, Winifred	5:59.0
1952	Holman, Maureen	5:44.4
1953	Griffin, Winifred	5:34.2
1954	Griffin, Winifred	5:35.3
1955	Griffin, Winifred	5:22.3
1956	Roe, Marion	5:13.7
1957	Griffin, Winifred I	5:29.4
1958	Bell, Alison	5:30.6
1959	Hunter, Jennifer	5:25.2
1960	Hunter, Jennifer	5:24.8
1961	Moore, Lesley	5:15.2
1962	Moore, Lesley	5:10.5
1963	Nicholson, Shirley	5:09.8
1964	Nicholson, Shirley	5:10.8
1965	McMillan, Alison	5:20.5
1966	Woonton, Suzanne	5:07.6
1967	Myers, Diane	5:06.7
1968	Shipston, Tui	4:59.1
1969	Shipston, Tui	4:53.1

400 m. Free-style

1970	Wright, Judith	4:53.0
1971	Parkhouse, Jaynie	4:47.1
1972	Comerford, Jane (Aus)	4:36.5
1973	Rickard, Virginia (Aus)	4:33.6
1974	Kennedy, Suzanne	4:38.41
1975	Calder, Allison	4:26.57

880 y. Free-style (instituted 1967)

1967	Myers, Diane	10:45.3
1968	Shipston, Tui	10:33.0
1969	Shipston, Tui	10:11.6

800 m. Free-style

1970	Wright, Judith	9:55.1
1971	Parkhouse, Jaynie	9:45.7
1972	Rickard, Virginia (Aus)	9:25.5
1973	Rickard, Virginia (Aus)	9:15.8

1974	Hunter, Susan	9:29.59
1975	Calder, Allison	9:04.72

110 y. Back-stroke (instituted 1929)

1946*	Lane, Ngaire	1:13.4
1947*	Lane, Ngaire	1:12.0
1948*	Lane, Ngaire	1:12.4
1949*	Lane, Ngaire	1:12.0
1950*	Stewart, Jean	1:13.6
1951*	Stewart, Jean	1:10.0
1952*	Stewart, Jean	1:08.0
1953*	Stewart, Jean	1:09.7
1954*	Stewart, Jean	1:13.0
1955*	Wilson, Moira	1:15.4
1956*	Stewart, Jean	1:09.1
1957	Gould, Phillipa	1:14.8
1958	Gould, Phillipa	1:13.8
1959*	Norman, Lynette	1:07.8
1960	Norman, Lynette	1:15.8
1961*	Norman, Lynette	1:06.9
1962	Macrae, Margaret	1:14.8
1963	Macrae, Margaret	1:15.2
1964	Macrae, Margaret	1:15.7
1965	Macrae, Margaret	1:14.7
1966	Macrae, Margaret	1:15.3
1967	Stirling, Glenda	1:13.1
1968	Stirling, Glenda	1:10.2
1969	Stirling, Glenda	1:12.9
	* = 100 y.	

100 m. Back-stroke

1970	Stirling, Glenda	1:10.5
1971	Stirling, Glenda	1:10.1
1972	Rickard, Virginia (Aus)	1:09.8
1973	Hunter, Susan	1:09.3
1974	Hunter, Susan	1:09.04
1975	Rodahl, Monique	1:07.16

220 y. Back-stroke (instituted 1938)

1946	Lane, Ngaire	3:00.6
1947	Lane, Ngaire	3:01.6
1948	Lane, Ngaire	3:03.0
1949	Lane, Ngaire	2:57.6
1950	Stewart, Jean	2:58.2
1951	Stewart, Jean	2:56.0
1952	Stewart, Jean	2:47.2
1953	Stewart, Jean	2:53.4
1954	Stewart, Jean	2:54.9
1955	Wilson, Moira	2:59.9
1956	Gould, Phillipa	2:44.3
1957	Gould Phillipa	2:42.0
1958	Gould, Phillipa	2:43.0
1959	Norman, Lynette	2:42.2
1960	Norman, Lynette	2:44.0
1961	Norman, Lynette	2:42.5
1962	Macrae, Margaret	2:40.3
1963	Macrae, Margaret	2:41.6
1964	Macrae, Margaret	2:41.0

1965	Macrae, Margaret	2:41.1
1966	Macrae, Margaret	2:43.2
1967	Macrae, Margaret	2:38.9
1968	Stirling, Glenda	2:33.8
1969	Stirling, Glenda	2:34.4

200 m. Back-stroke

1970	Stirling, Glenda	2:32.7
1971	Stirling, Glenda	2:33.4
1972	Rickard, Virginia (Aus)	2:28.5
1973	Rickard, Virginia (Aus)	2:25.2
1974	Hunter, Susan	2:27.64
1975	Rodahl, Monique	2:22.34

110 y. Breast-stroke (instituted 1939)

1946*	Pasalich, Marie	1:27.6
1947*	Smith, Helen	1:26.4
1948*	Forsyth, Heather	1:23.8
1949*	Teague, Maureen	1:26.6
1950*	Sweeney, Margaret	1:25.6
1951*	Currie, Rae	1:27.4
1952*	Currie, Rae	1:26.0
1953*	Currie, Rae	1:25.0
1954*	Currie, Rae	1:22.9
1955*	Currie, Rae	1:23.1
1956*	Orbell, Lindley	1:22.4
1957	Sawyers, Kay	1:32.0
1958	Sawyers, Kay	1:28.3
1959*	Sawyers, Kay	1:19.0
1960	Sawyers, Kay	1:28.6
1961*	Sawyers, Kay	1:18.2
1962	Haddon, Vivien	1:22.5
1963	Haddon, Vivien	1:21.6
1964	Haddon, Vivien	1:24.8
1965	Jonas, Barbara	1:26.9
1966	Haddon, Vivien	1:25.2
1967	Deal, Christine	1'23,9
1968	McRae, Donna	1:22.4
1969	McRae, Donna	1:23.6
	* = 100 y.	

100 m. Breast-stroke

1970	Hill, Margaret	1:23.4
1971	Noble, Vivien	1:22.3
1972	Lowe, Jane	1:21.1
1973	Whitfield, Beverley (Aus)	1:17.8
1974	Lowe, Jane	1:19.41
1975	Reynolds, M	1:18.88

220 y. Breast-stroke (instituted 1924)

1946	Pasalich, Marie	3:27.8
1947	Shaw, Nola	3:29.4
1948	Forsyth, Heather	3:23.2
1949	Sweeney, Margaret	3:24.6
1950	Forsyth, Heather	3:27.4
1951	Currie, Rae	3:22.4
1952	Currie, Rae	3:23.8

1953	Currie, Rae	3:18.4
1954	Currie, Rae	3:13.5
1955	Currie, Rae	3:14.1
1956	Orbell, Lindley	3:14.6
1957	Sawyers, Kay	3:17.8
1958	Sawyers, Kay	3:12.2
1959	Sawyers, Kay	3:07.1
1960	Sawyers, Kay	3:08.1
1961	Sawyers, Kay	3:05.0
1962	Haddon, Vivien	2:59.9
1963	Haddon, Vivien	2:56.3
1964	Haddon, Vivien	2:59.5
1965	Jonas, Barbara	3:06.4
1966	Haddon, Vivien	3:02.9
1967	Smith, Lesley	3:02.1
1968	Smith, Lesley	2:55.3
1969	Williams, Beth	2:57.6

200 m. Breast-stroke

1970	Williams, Beth	2:59.0
1971	Noble, Vivien	2:58.5
1972	Lowe, Jane	2:57.7
1973	Whitfield, Beverley (Aus)	2:46.2
1974	Lowe, Jane	2:51.12
1975	Lowe, Jane	2:49.75

110 y. Butterfly (institited 1948)

1948*	Forsyth, Heather	1:25.6
1949*	Bridson, Norma	1:27.8
1950*	Bridson, Norma	1:25.0
1951*	Bridson, Norma	1:25.8
1952*	Currie, Rae	1:28.2
1953*	Stewart, Jean	1:28.0
1954*	Cleaver, Judith	1:29.2
1955*	Currie, Rae	1:22.2
1956*	Orbell, Lindley	1:24.4
1957	Staveley, Tessa	1:22.8
1958	Staveley, Tessa	1:19.6
1959*	McCleary, Helen	1:08.6
1960	McCleary, Helen	1:15.4
1961*	Phillips, Marilyn	1:10.2
1962	Rogers, Helen	1:16.0
1963	Nicholson, Shirley	1:15.2
1964	Nicholson, Shirley	1:15.3
1965	Kerr, Heather	1:16.4
1966	Kerr, Heather	1:13.2
1967	Kerr, Heather	1:13.9
1968	Whittleson, Sandra	1:10.8
1969	Shipston, Tui	1:09.5
	* = 100 y.	

100 m. Butterfly

1970	Whiting, Cathy	1:12.4
1971	Whiting, Cathy	1:07.5
1972	Wallis, Julie (Aus)	1:07.2
1973	Wallis, Julie (Aus)	1:09.6
1974	Legerwood, Debbie	1:09.89
1975	Rodahl, Monique	1:05.68

220 y. Butterfly (instituted 1966)

1966	Kerr, Heather	2:43.4
1967	Kerr, Heather	2:38.5
1968	Whittleson, Sandra	2:36.8
1969	Shipston, Tui	2:29.5

200 m. Butterfly

1970	Williams, Beth	2:29.8
1971	Whiting, Cathy	2:35.7
1972	Comerford, Jane (Aus)	2:27.4
1973	Hunter, Susan	2:29.1
1974	Legerwood, Debbie	2:25.98
1975	Rowe, Lynne	2:20.80

Individual medley (instituted 1947)

1947	Hobson, O. (100 y.)	1:21.4
1948	Bridson, Norma (100 y.)	1:14.0
1949	Bridson, Norma (100 y.)	1:16.8
1950	Bridson, Norma (133 1/3 y.)	
		2:20.8
1951	Wilson, M. (133 1/3 y.)	2:03.6
1952	Wilson, M. (100 y.)	1:13.8
1953	Wilson, M. (100 y.)	1:14.9
1954	Jones, B. (100 y.)	1:15.9
1955	Wilson, M.	1:16.4
1956	Duthie, J. (400 y.)	6:07.4
1957	Staveley, Tessa (440 y.)	6:44.0
1958	Staveley, Tessa (440 y.)	6:30.3
1959	Staveley, Tessa (400 y.)	5:35.5
1960	McCleary, Helen (220 y.)	2:55.2
1961	Phillips, M. (266 2/3 y.)	3:40.8

220 y. Individual medley (instituted 1966)

1966	Macrae, Margaret	2:45.0
1967	Shipston, Tui	2:40.2
1968	Shipston, Tui	2:39.1
1969	Shipston, Tui	2:37.2

200 m. Individual medley

1970	Hunter, Susan	2:38.4
1971	Hunter, Susan	2:38.2
1972	Gould, Shane (Aus)	2:28.5
1973	Hunter, Susan	2:30.6
1974	Hunter, Susan	2:31.41
1975	Rodahl, Monique	2:26.48

440 y. Individual medley (instituted 1962)

1962	Rogers, Helen	6:13.7
1963	Nicholson, Shirley	6:12.5
1964	Nicholson, Shirley	6:07.6
1965	Macrae, Margaret	5:49.2
1967	Shipston, Tui	5:40.2
1968	Shipston, Tui	5:35.4
1969	Shipston, Tui	5:28.7

400 m. Individual medley

1970	Hunter, Susan	5:34.0
1971	Hunter, Susan	5:29.2
1972	Hunter, Susan	5:19.1
1973	Hunter, Susan	5:16.2
1974	Hunter, Susan	5:13.33
1975	Hunter, Susan	5:06.63

NORELIUS, Martha (United States, 20 Jan. 1908-55). The first woman to win the Olympic gold for the same event at successive Games—the 400 m. in 1924 at 16 and in 1928 (plus a relay gold that year). Born in Stockholm and raised in America, she was coached by her father Charles, who represented Sweden at the 1906 Interim Games, and later by L. de B. Handley.

Miss Norelius set seventeen world records between 28 Feb. 1926 and 27 Aug. 1928 of which the best times were: 200 m./220 y. 2:40.6, 400 m. 5:39.2, 880 y. 12:17.8 and 1.500 m. 23:44.6, After a seven-year reign as the queen of American swimming, she turned professional in 1929 following her suspension by the A.A.U. for swimming an exhibition in the same pool with professionals.

As a professional, she won the $10,000 ten-mile Wrigley Marathon in Toronto where she met and married Joe Wright, silver medal winner for Canada in the double sculls in the 1928 Olympics. The darling of the social set, Martha was considered to be the first woman to swim like the men. Her front crawl was similar to Johnny Weismuller's, with a high head position, arched back and heavy six-beat leg kick.

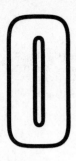

aica in 1966 where he retained his Commonwealth titles in world record times though six weeks before the Games he was 30 lb. overweight and out of training.

O'Brien broke four world records: 110 y. (68.6 and 68.2), 200 m. (2:27.8, his Olympic winning time that stood for four years) and 220 y. (2:28.0, in Jamaica and worth 2:27.0 for 200 m. and so better than his metric record).

OLYMPIC GAMES. The earliest celebration of the ancient Olympic Games of which there is a record is that of July 776 B.C. The ancient Games were ended in A.D. 392 by the decree of the Roman Emperor Theodosius. The first Games of the modern era were organized in Greece, the home of the old Games, fifteen centuries later as a result of the idealism and energy of a Frenchman, Baron Pierre de Coubertin. Dates and venues:

O'BRIEN, Ian, (Australia, 3 Mar. 1947-). Olympic 200 m. breast-stroke champion in 1964 and four times champion of the Commonweatlh—for the 110 and 220 y. breast-stroke in 1962 and '66. Ian O'Brien from Wellington, New South Wales, was a redoubtable competitor. He demonstrated this particularly in Jam-

No.	Venue and course	Dates of	Year
I	Athens, Greece (open sea)	6–15 April	1896
II	Paris, France (river Seine)	11–19 Aug.	1900
III	St. Louis, U.S.A. (artificial lake)	5–7 Sept.	1904
Interim	Athens, Greece	22 April–2 May	1906
IV	London, England (100 m. pool inside the athletics stadium)	13–25 July	1908
V	Stockholm, Sweden (100 m. salt water course in sheltered harbour)	6–15 July	1912
VI	Berlin, Germany	Not held	1916
VII	Antwerp, Belgium (100 m. pool)	22–29 Aug.	1920
VIII	Paris, France (50 m. outdoor)	13–20 July	1924
IX	Amsterdam, Netherlands (50 m. outdoor)	4–11 Aug.	1928
X	Los Angeles (50 m. outdoor)	6–13 Aug.	1932
XI	Berlin, Germany (50 m. outdoor)	8–15 Aug.	1936
XII	Helsinki, Finland	Not held	1940
XIII	No venue	Not held	1944
XIV	London, England (50 m. indoor)	30 July–7 Aug.	1948
XV	Helsinki, Finland (50 m. outdoor)	25 July–2 Aug.	1952
XVI	Melbourne, Australia (50 m. indoor)	30 Nov–6 Dec.	1956
XVII	Rome, Italy (50 m. outdoor)	25 August–3 Sept.	1960
XVIII	Tokyo, Japan (50 m. indoor)	11–18 Oct.	1964
XIX	Mexico City, Mexico (50 m. indoor)	17–26 Oct.	1968
XX	Munich, West Germany (50 m.	27 August–4 Sept.	1972
XXI	Montreal, Canada (50 m. indoor)	18–27 July	1976
XXII	Moscow, USSR (50 m. indoor)	10–24 Aug. (Provisional)	1980

OLYMPIC GAMES CHAMPIONS.

Swimming for men was included in the first Games of the modern era, in Athens in 1896. Two events for women—100 and 4 x 100 m. free-style—were added for Stockholm in 1912. The water-polo tournament was first held in 1900 and diving began at the Olympics of 1904.

The only swimmer to win the same individual title at three successive Games is Dawn Fraser (Aus)—100 m. in 1956, 60 and 64; The first to win four golds at a single Games is Don Schollander (USA) —100, 400, 4 x 100 and 4 x 200 m. in 1964. Debbie Meyer (USA) was the first to take three individual titles at the same Games—200, 400 and 800 m. in 1968 (but the 200 and 800 m. were new events).

But Mark Spitz (USA) made Olympic history in 1972 when he won seven gold medals in Munich—100 and 200 m. for free-style and butterfly and three men's relays—a feat never before achieved in any other sport in the programme of the Games.

After the failure of the 1904 Games in St. Louis, which some critics blamed on thoughtless and incompetent arrangements by the American organizers, and the very few visiting competitors, European Olympic leaders pressed for a sports festival for their athletes, most of whom had been unable to participate in the United States.

Greece, the home of the Ancient Olympic Games and hosts to the first Games of the modern era in 1896, offered to stage such a meeting. In fact, their event in Athens in 1906—which has become known as the Interim Games—proved as big a disappointment as St. Louis and attracted only a few national representatives.

Opinions are divided whether the results of the Interim Games should be included in the lists of official Olympic Games medal winners. For the sake of continuity, and taking into account that there was little to choose between St. Louis and the second Athens meeting, the 1906 results are included here.

MEN

100 m. Free-style

1896	Hajós, Alfréd (Hun)	1:22.2
1904*	Halmay, Zóltan (Hun)	1:02.8
1906	Daniels, Charles (USA)	1:13.4
1908	Daniels, Charles (USA)	1:05.6
1912	Kahanamoku, Duke (USA)	1:03.4
1920†	Kahanamoku, Duke (USA)	1:01.4
1924	Weismuller, Johnny (USA)	59.0
1928	Weismuller, Johnny (USA)	58.6
1932	Miyazaki, Yasuji (Jap)	58.2
1936	Csik, Ferenc (Hun)	57.6
1948	Ris, Wally (USA)	57.3
	Ford, Alan (USA)	57.2
	Kádas, Géza (Hun)	58.1
1952	Scholes, Clarke (USA)	57.4
	Suzuki, Hiroshi (Jap)	57.4
	Larsson, Goran (Swe)	58.2
1956	Henricks, Jon (Aus)	55.4
	Devitt, John (Aus)	55.8
	Chapman, Gary (Aus)	56.7
1960	Devitt, John (Aus)	55.2
	Larson, Lance (USA)	55.2
	Santos, Manuel dos (Braz)	55.4
1964	Schollander, Don (USA)	53.4
	McGregor, Bobby (GB)	53.5
	Klein, Hans-Joachim (Ger)	54.0
1968	Wenden, Mike (Aus)	52.2
	Walsh, Ken (USA)	52.8
	Spitz, Mark (USA)	53.0
1972	Spitz, Mark (USA)	51.22
	Heidenreich, Jerry (USA)	51.65
	Bure, Vladimir (USSR)	51.77

* = 100 y. (91.44 m.)

† The final was re-swum after a protest by Herald (Aus) against Ross (USA)—the latter did not take part in the second final. The medal places remained unchanged. Kahanamoku had won the first final in 1:00.4 (world record).

200 m. Free-style

1900	Lane, Freddy (Aus)	2:52.2
1904*	Daniels, Charles (USA)	2:44.2
1908-64	Event not held	
1968	Wenden, Mike (Aus)	1:55.2
	Schollander, Don (USA)	1:55.8
	Nelson, John (USA)	1:58.1
1972	Spitz, Mark (USA)	1:52.78
	Genter, Steve (USA)	1:53.73
	Lampe, Werner (W Ger)	1:53.99

* = 220 y. (291.17 m.)

400 m. Free-style

1896*	Neumann, Paul (Aut)	8:12.6
1904†	Daniels, Charles (USA)	6:16.2
1906	Scheff, Otto (Aut)	6:22.8
1908	Taylor, Henry (GB)	5:36.8
1912	Hodgson, George (Can)	5:24.4

1920	Ross, Norman (USA)	5:26.6
1924	Weissmuller, Johnny (USA)	
		5:04.2
1928	Zorilla, Alberto (Arg)	5:01.6
1932	Crabbe, Buster (USA)	4:48.4
1936	Medica, Jack (USA)	4:44.5

1948	Smith, Bill (USA)	4:41.0
	McLane, Jimmy (USA)	4:43.4
	Marshall, John (Aus)	4:47.4
1952	Boiteaux, Jean (Fr)	4:30.7
	Konno, Ford (USA)	4:31.3
	Ostrand, Per-Ola (Swe)	4:35.2
1956	Rose, Murray (Aus)	4:27.3
	Yamanaka, Tsuyoshi (Jap)	4:30.4
	Breen, George (USA)	4:32.5
1960	Rose, Murray (Aus)	4:18.3
	Yamanaka, Tsuyoshi (Jap)	4:21.4
	Konrads, John (Aus)	4:21.8
1964	Schollander, Don (USA)	4:12.2
	Wiegand, Frank (Ger)	4:14.9
	Wood, Allan (Aus)	4:15.1
1968	Burton, Mike (USA)	4:09.0
	Hutton, Ralph (Can)	4:11.7
	Mosconi, Alain (Fr)	4:13.3

1972	Cooper, Brad (Aus)††	4:00.27
	Genter, Steve (USA)	4:01.94
	McBreen, Tom (USA)	4:02.64

* = 500 m. (564.83 y)

† = 440 y. (402. 336 m.)

†† DeMont, Rick (USA) touched first in 4:00.26 but was disqualified by the IOC Medical Commission

1,500 m. Free-style
1896*	Hajós, Alfréd (Hun)	18:22.2
1900†	Jarvis, John (GB)	13:40.2
1904††	Rausch, Emil (Ger)	27:18.2
1906††	Taylor, Henry (GB)	28:28.0
1908	Taylor, Henry (GB)	22:48.4
1912	Hodgson, George (Can)	22:00.0
1920	Ross, Norman (USA)	22:23.2
1924	Charlton, Boy (Aus)	20:06.6
1928	Borg, Arne (Swe)	19:51.8
1932	Kitamura, Kusuo (Jap)	19:12.4
1936	Terada, Noboru (Jap)	19:13.7

1948	McLane, Jimmy (USA)	19'18.5
	Marshall, John (Aus)	19:31.3
	Mitro, Gyorgy (Hun)	19:43.2
1952	Konno, Ford (USA)	18:30.3
	Hashizume, Shiro (Jap)	18:41.4
	Okamoto, Tetsuo (Braz)	18:51.3

1956	Rose, Murray (Aus)	17:58.9
	Yamanaka, Tsuyoshi (Jap)	
		18:00.3
	Breen, George (USA)	18'08.2
1960	Konrads, John (Aus)	17:19.6
	Rose, Murray (Aus)	17:21.7
	Breen, George (USA)	17:30.6
1964	Windle, Bob (Aus)	17:01.7
	Nelson, John (USA)	17:03.0
	Wood, Allan (Aus)	17:07.7
1968	Burton, Mike (USA)	16:38.9
	Kinsella, John (USA)	16:57.3
	Brough, Greg (Aus)	17:04.7

1972	Burton, Mike (USA)	15:52.58
	Windeatt, Graham (Aus)	15:58.48
	Northway, Doug (USA)	16:09.25

* = 1,200 m. (1,312.333 y.)
† = 1,000 m. (1,093.612y.)
†† = 1 mile (1,609.34 m.)

100 m. Back-stroke
1904*	Brack, Walter (Ger)	1:16.8
1908	Bieberstein, Arno (Ger)	1:24.6
1912	Hebner, Harry (USA)	1:21.2
1920	Kealoha, Warren (USA)	1:15.2
1924	Kealoha, Warren (USA)	1:13.2
1928	Kojac, George (USA)	1:08.2
1932	Kiyokawa, Masaji (Jap)	1:08.6
1936	Kiefer, Adolf (USA)	1:05.9

1948	Stack, Allen (USA)	1:06.4
	Cowell, Bob (USA)	1:06.5
	Vallerey, Georges (Fr)	1:07.8
1952	Oyakawa, Yoshinobu (USA)	
		1:05.4
	Bozon, Gilbert (Fr)	1:06.2
	Taylor, Jack (USA)	1:06.4
1956	Theile, David (Aus)	1:02.2
	Monckton, John (Aus)	1:03.2
	McKinney, Frank (USA)	1:04.5
1960	Theile, David (Aus)	1:01.9
	McKinney, Frank (USA)	1:02.1
	Bennett, Bob (USA)	1:02.3
1964	Event not held	
1968	Matthes, Roland (E Ger)	58.7
	Hickcox, Charles (USA)	1:00.2
	Mills, Ronnie (USA)	1:00.5

1972	Matthes, Roland (E Ger)	56.58
	Stamm, Mike (USA)	57.70
	Murphy, John (USA)	58.35

* = 100 y. (91.44 m.)

200 m. Back-stroke
1900	Hoppenberg, Ernst (Ger)	2:47.0

1904-60 Event not held

1964	Graef, Jed (USA)	2:10.3
	Dilley, Gary (USA)	2:10.5
	Bennett, Bob (USA)	2:13.1
1968	Matthes, Roland (E Ger)	2:09.6
	Ivey, Mitch (USA)	2:10.6
	Horsley, Jack (USA)	2:10.9

1972	Matthes, Roland (E Ger)	2:02.82
	Stamm, Mike (USA)	2:04.09
	Ivey, Mitch (USA)	2:04.33

100 m. Breast-stroke
1968	McKenzie, Don (USA)	1:07.7
	Kosinsky, Vladimir (USSR)	1:08.0
	Pankin, Nikolay (USSR)	1:08.0

1972	Taguchi, Nobutaka (Jap)	1:04.94
	Bruce, Tom (USA)	1:05.43
	Hencken, John (USA)	1:05.61

200 m. Breast-stroke
1908	Holman, Frederick (GB)	3:09.2
1912	Bathe, Walther (Ger)	3:01.8
1920	Malmroth, Hakan (Swe)	3:04.4
1924	Skelton, Robert (USA)	2:56.6
1928	Tsuruta, Yoshiyuki (Jap)	2:48.8
1932	Tsuruta, Yoshiyuki (Jap)	2:45.5
1936	Hamuro, Tetsuo (Jap)	2:41.5

1948	Verdeur, Joseph (USA)	Bu2:39.3
	Carter, Keith (USA)	Bu2:40.2
	Sohl, Robert (USA)	Bu2:43.9
1952	Davies, John (Aus)	Bu2:34.4
	Stassforth, Bowen (USA)	
		Bu2:34.7
	Klein, Herbert (Ger)	Bu2:35.9
1956	Furukawa, Masaru (Jap)	
		Uw2:34.7
	Yoshimura, Masahiro (Jap)	
		Uw2:36.7
	Junitschev, Charis (USSR)	
		Uw2:36.8
1960	Mulliken, Bill (USA)	2:37.4
	Osaki, Yoshihiko (Jap)	2:38.0
	Mensonides, Wieger (Neth)	2:39.7
1964	O'Brien, Ian (Aus)	2:27.8
	Prokopenko, Georgy (USSR)	
		2:28.2
	Jastremski, Chet (USA)	2:29.6
1968	Munoz, Felipe (Mex)	2:28.7
	Kosinsky, Vladimir (USSR)	
		2:29.2
	Job, Brian (USA)	2:29.9

1972	Hencken, John (USA)	2:21.55
	Wilkie, David (GB)	2:23.67
	Taguchi, Nobutaka (Jap)	2:23.88

100 m. Butterfly
1968	Russell, Doug (USA)	55.9
	Spitz, Mark (USA)	56.4
	Wales, Ross (USA)	57.2

1972	Spitz, Mark (USA)	54.27
	Robertson, Bruce (Can)	55.56
	Heidenreich, Jerry (USA)	55.74

200 m. Butterfly
1956	Yorzyk, Bill (USA)	2:19.3
	Ishimoto, Takashi (Jap)	2:23.8
	Tumpek, Gyorgy (Hun)	2:23.9
1960	Troy, Mike (USA)	2:12.8
	Hayes, Neville (Aus)	2:14.6
	Gillanders, David (USA)	2:15.3
1964	Berry, Kevin (Aus)	2:06.6
	Robie, Carl (USA)	2:07.5
	Schmidt, Fred (USA)	2:09.3
1968	Robie, Carl (USA)	2:08.7
	Woodroffe, Martyn (GB)	2:09.0
	Ferris, John (USA)	2:09.3

1972	Spitz, Mark (USA)	2:00.70
	Hall, Gary (USA)	2:02.86
	Backhaus, Robin (USA)	2:03.23

200 m. Individual medley*
1968	Hickcox, Charles (USA)	2:12.0
	Buckingham, Greg (USA)	2:13.0
	Ferris, John (USA)	2:13.3

1972	Larsson, Gunnar (Swe)	2:07.17
	McKee, Tim (USA)	2:08.37
	Furniss, Steve (USA)	2:08.45

*Not in the programme of the 1976 Montreal Games.

400 m. Individual medley
1964	Roth, Dick (USA)	4:45.4
	Saari, Roy (USA)	4:47.1
	Hetz, Gerhard (Ger)	4:51.0
1968	Hickcox, Charles (USA)	4:48.4
	Hall, Gary (USA)	4:48.7
	Holthaus, Michael (W Ger)	4:51.4

1972	Larsson, Gunnar (Swe)	*4:31.98
	McKee, Tim (USA)	*4:31.98
	Hargitay, Andras (Hun)	4:32.70

*Larsson 4:31.981/McKee 4:31.983

4 x 100 m. Free-style*
1964	United States	3:33.2

(Clark, Steve; Austin, Mike; Ilman, Gary, Schollander, Don)

Germany   3:37.2
(Loffler, Horst; Wiegand, Frank; Jac-
obsen, Uwe; Klein, Hans-Joachim)
Australia   3:39.1
(Dickson, David; Doak, Peter; Ryan,
John; Windle, Bob)

1968 United States   3:31.7
(Zorn, Zac; Rerych, Steve; Spitz,
Mark; Walsh, Ken)
     Soviet Union   3:34.2
(Belits-Geiman, Semeòn; Mazanov, Vic-
tor; Kulikov, Georgy; Ilichev, Leonid)
     Australia   3:34.7
(Rogers, Greg; Windle, Bob; Cusack,
Robert; Wenden, Mike)

1972 United States   3:26.42
(Edgar, Dave; Murphy, John; Heiden-
reich, Jerry; Spitz, Mark)
     Soviet Union   3:29.72
(Bure, Vladimir; Mazanov, Viktor;
Aboimov, Viktor; Grivennikov, Igor)
     East Germany   3:32.42
(Matthes, Roland; Hartung, Wilfried;
Bruch, Peter; Unger, Lutz)

*Not in the programme of the 1976
Montreal Games.

4 x 200 m. Free-style
1906* Hungary   16:52.4
(Onódy, József; Hajós, Henrik; Kiss
Géza; Halmay, Zoltán)
1908 Great Britain   10:55.6
(Derbyshire, Rob; Radmilovic, Paul;
Foster, William; Taylor, Henry)
1912 Australasia†   10:11.6
(Healy, Cecil; Champion, Malcolm;
Boardman, Leslie; Hardwick, Harold)
1920 United States   10:04.4
(McGillivray, Perry; Kealoha, Pua;
Ross, Norman; Kahanamoku, Duke)
1924 United States   9:53.4
(O'Connor, Wally; Glancy, Harry;
Breyer, Ralph; Weissmuller, Johnny)
1928 United States   9:36.2
(Clapp, Austin; Laufer, Walter; Kojac,
George; Weissmuller, Johnny)
1932 Japan   8:58.4
(Miyazaki, Yasuji; Yusa, Masanori;
Yokoyama, Takashi; Toyoda, Hisa-
kichi)
1936 Japan   8:51.5
(Yusa Masanori; Sugiura, Shigeo; Tag-
uchi, Masaharu; Arai, Shigeo)

1948 United States   8:46.0
(Ris, Wally; McLane, Jimmy; Wolf,
Wallace; Smith, Bill)
     Hungary   8:48.4

(Szathmári, Elemér; Mitró, György;
Nyéki, Imre; Kádas, Géza)
     France   9:08.0
(Bernardo, Joseph; Padou, Henry jun;
Cornu, Rene; Jany, Alex)
1952 United States   8:31.1
(Moore, Wayne; Woolsey, Bill; Konno,
Ford; McLane, Jimmy)
     Japan   8:33.5
(Suzuki, Hiroshi; Hamaguchi, Yosh-
ihiro; Goto, Toru; Tanikawa, Teijiro)
     France   8:45.9
(Bernardo, Joseph; Eminente, Aldo;
Jany, Alex; Boiteux, Jean)
1956 Australia   8:23.6
(O'Halloran, Kevin; Devitt, John;
Rose, Murray; Henricks, Jon)
     United States   8:31.5
(Hanley, Dick; Breen George; Wool-
sey, Bill; Konno, Ford)
     Soviet Union   8:34.7
(Sorokin, Vitaly; Strujanov, Vladimir;
Nikolaiev, Gennadi; Nitikin, Boris)
1960 United States   8:10.2
(Harrison, George; Blick, Dick; Troy,
Mike; Farrell, Jeff)
     Japan   8:13.2
(Fukui, Makoto; Ishii, Hiroshi; Yam-
anaka, Tsuyoshi; Fujimoto, Tatsuo)
     Australia   8:13.8
(Dickson, David; Devitt, John; Rose,
Murray; Konrads, John)
1964 United States   7:52.1
(Clark, Steve; Saari, Roy; Ilman, Gary;
Schollander, Don)
     Germany††   7:59.3
(Gregor, Horst-Gunther; Hetz, Ger-
hard; Wiegand, Frank; Klein, Hans-
Joachim)
     Japan   8:03.8
(Fukui, Makoto; Iwasaki, Kunihiro;
Shoji, Toshio; Okabe, Yukaiki)
1968 United States   7:52.3
(Nelson, John; Rerych, Steve; Spitz,
Mark; Schollander, Don)
     Australia   7:53.7
(Rogers, Greg; White, Graham; Windle,
Bob; Wenden, Mike)
     Soviet Union   8:01.6
(Bure, Vladimir; Belits-Geiman, Se-
meòn; Kulikov, Georgy; Ilichev, Leo-
nid)

1972 United States   7:35.78
(Kinsella, John; Tyler, Fred; Genter,
Steve; Spitz, Mark)

West Germany 7:41.69
(Steinbach, Klaus; Lampe, Werner; Vosseler, Hans-Guenter; Fassnacht, Hans)
Soviet Union 7:45.75
(Grivennikov, Igor; Mazanov, Victor; Kulikov, Georgy; Ilichev, Leonid)

* 4 x 250 m. (273.39 y.)

+Australasian team was Healy, Boardman and Hardwick of Australia and Champion from New Zealand.

††Combined German team; Hetz and Klein (W Ger); Gregor and Wiegand (E Ger)

4 x 100 medley relay

1960 United States 4:05.4
(McKinney, Frank; Hait, Paul; Larson, Lance; Farrell, Jeff)
Australia 4:12.0
(Theile, David; Gathercole, Terry; Hayes, Neville; Shipton, Geoff)
Japan 4:12.2
(Tomita, Kazuo; Hirakida, Koichi; Osaki, Yoshihiko; Shimizu, Keigo)

1964 United States 3:38.4
(Mann, Tom; Craig, Bill; Schmidt, Fred; Clark, Steve)
Germany* 4:01.6
(Kuppers, Ernst-Joachim; Henninger, Egon; Gregor, Horst-Gunther; Klein, Hans-Joachim)
Australia 4:02.3
(Reynolds, Peter; O'Brien, Ian; Berry, Kevin; Dickson, David)

1968 United States 3:54.9
(Hickcox, Charles; McKenzie, Don; Russell, Doug; Walsh, Ken)
East Germany 3:57.5
(Matthes, Roland; Henninger, Egon; Gregor, Horst-Gunther; Wiegand, Frank)
Soviet Union 4:00.7
(Gromak, Yuri; Kosinsky, Vladimir; Nemschilov, Vladimir; Ilichev, Leonid)

1972 United States 3:48.16
(Stamm, Mike; Bruce, Tom; Spitz, Mark; Heidenreich, Jerry)
East Germany 3:52.12
(Matthes, Roland; Katzur, Klaus; Floeckner, Hartmut; Unger, Lutz)
Canada 3:52.26
(Fish, Erik; Mahony, Bill; Robertson, Bruce; Kasting, Bob)

* Combined German team; Kuppers and Klein (W Ger), Henninger and Gregor (E Ger).

Springboard diving

1908	Zürner, Albert (Ger)	85.5
1912	Gunther, Paul (Ger)	79.23
1920	Kuehn, Louis (USA)	675.4
1924	White, Albert (USA)	696.4
1928	Desjardins, Pete (USA)	185.04
1932	Galitzen, Micky (USA)	161.38
1936	Degener, Dickie (USA)	163.57

1948	Harlan, Bruce (USA)	163.64
	Anderson, Miller (USA)	157.29
	Lee, Sammy (USA)	145.52
1952	Browning, Skippy (USA)	205.29
	Anderson, Miller (USA)	199.84
	Clotworthy, Bob (USA)	184.92
1956	Clotworthy, Bob (USA)	159.56
	Harper, Don (USA)	156.23
	Capilla, Joaquin (Mex)	150.69
1960	Tobian, Gary (USA)	170.00
	Hall, Sammy (USA)	167.08
	Botella, Juan (Mex)	162.30
1964	Sitzberger, Ken (USA)	159.90
	Gorman, Frank (USA)	157.63
	Andreasen, Larry (USA)	143.77
1968	Wrightson, Bernie (USA)	170.15
	Dibiasi, Klaus (It)	159.74
	Henry, Jim (USA)	158.09
1972	Vasin, Vladimir·(USSR)	594.09
	Cagnotto, Giorgio (It)	591.63
	Lincoln, Craig (USA)	577.29

Highboard diving

1904*	Sheldon, George (USA)	12.66
1906*	Walz, Gottlob (Ger)	156.00
1908*	Johansson, Hjalmar (Swe)	83.75
1912	Adlerz, Erik (Swe)	73.94
1920	Pinkson, Clarence (USA)	100.67
1924	White, Albert (USA)	97.46
1928	Desjardins, Pete (USA)	98.74
1932	Smith, Harold 'Dutch' (USA)	124.80
1936	Wayne, Marshall (USA)	113.58

1948	Lee, Sammy (USA)	130.05
	Harlan, Bruce (USA)	122.30
	Capilla, Joaquin (Mex)	113.52
1952	Lee, Sammy (USA)	156.28
	Capilla, Joaquin (Mex)	145.21
	Haase, Gunther (Ger)	141.31
1956	Capilla, Joaquin (Mex)	152.44
	Tobian, Gary (USA)	152.41
	Connor, Richard (USA)	149.79
1960	Webster, Robert (USA)	165.56
	Tobian, Gary (USA)	165.25
	Phelps, Brian (GB)	157.13

1964	Webster, Robert (USA)	148.58
	Dibiasi, Klaus (It)	147.54
	Gompf, Tom (USA)	146.57
1968	Dibiasi, Klaus (It)	164.18
	Gaxiola, Alvaro (Mex)	154.49
	Young, Ed (USA)	153.93
1972	Dibiasi, Klaus (It)	504.12
	Rydze, Dick (USA)	480.75
	Cagnotto, Giorgio (It)	475.83

* = Plain diving

Water polo

1900 Great Britain (Manchester
    Osborne S.C.)
    (Robertson, Arthur; Coe, Thomas;
    Robinson, Eric; Kemp, Peter; Wilkinson, George; Derbyshire, Rob; Lister,
    William)

1904 United States (New York AC)
    (Van Cleef, George; Goodwin, Leo;
    Handley, Louis B.de; Hesser, David;
    Ruddy, Joseph; Steen, James; Bratton, David)

1908 Great Britain
    (Smith, Charles; Nevinson, George;
    Cornet, George; Radmilovic, Paul;
    Wilkinson, George; Thould, Thomas;
    Forsyth, Eric)

1912 Great Britain
    (Smith, Charles; Cornet, George;
    Bugbee, Charles; Hill, Arthur; Wilkinson, George; Radmilovic, Paul; Bentham, Isaac)

1920 Great Britain
    (Smith, Charles; Radmilovic, Paul;
    Bugbee, Charles; Purcell, Norman;
    Jones, Christopher; Peacock, William;
    Dean, William)

1924 France
    (Dujardin, Paul; Padou, Henri; Rigal
    Georges; Deborgie, Albert; Delberghe,
    Noel; Desmettre, Robert; Mayaud,
    Albert)

1928 Germany
    (Rademacher, Erich; Gunst, Fritz;
    Cordes, Otto; Benecke, Emil; Rademacher, Joachim; Bahre, Karl; Amann,
    Max; Blank, Johannes; Protze, Karl-
    Heinz; Kuhne, Otto; Atmer, Heinrich)

1932 Hungary
    (Brody, Gyorgy; Ivady, Sandor; Hommonai, Marton; Halasy, Oliver; Vertesy, Jozsef; Nemeth, Janos; Keseru II,
    Alajos; Barta, Istvan; Sarkany, Miklos;
    Keseru I, Ferenc; Bozsi, Mihaly)

1936 Hungary
    (Brody, Gyorgy; Hazai, Kalman;
    Hommonai, Marton; Halasy, Oliver;
    Brandi, Jeno; Nemeth, Janos; Bozsi,
    Mihaly; Molnar, Istvan; Kutasi,
    Gyorgy; Tarics, Sandor; Sarkany,
    Miklos)

1948 Italy
    (Bunocore, Pasquale; Bulgarelli,
    Emilio; Rubini, Cesare; Ognio, Geminio; Arena, Ermenegildo; Ghira, Aldo;
    Pandolfini, Tullio; Maioni, Mario;
    Fabiano, Luigi; Pandolfini, Gianfranco; Toribolo, Alfredo)
    Hungary
    Holland

1952 Hungary
    (Jeney, Laszlo; Vizvary, Gyorgy;
    Gyarmati, Deszo; Karpati, Gyorgy;
    Antal, Robert; Fabian, Deszo; Szittya,
    Karloy; Lemhenyi, Deszo; Hasznos,
    Istvan; Martin, Miklos; Markovits,
    Kalman; Bolvari, Antal; Szivos, Istvan)
    Yugoslavia
    Italy

1956 Hungary
    (Boros, Otto; Gyarmati, Dezso;
    Mayer, Mihaly; Markovits, Kalman;
    Bolvari, Antal; Zador, Ervin; Karpati,
    Gyorgy; Jeney, Laszlo; Hevesi, Istvan;
    Kanisza, Tivadar; Szivos, Istvan)
    Yugoslavia
    Soviet Union

1960 Italy
    (Ambron, Amedeo; Bardi, Danio;
    D'Altrui, Guiseppe; Gionta, Salvatore;
    Lavoratori, Franco; Lonzi, Gianni;
    Manelli, Luigi; Parmegiani, Rosario;
    Pizzo, Eraldo; Rossi, Dante; Spinelli,
    Brunello; Guerrini, Giancarlo)
    Soviet Union
    Hungary

1964 Hungary
    (Ambrus, Miklos; Felkai, Laszlo;
    Konrad, Janos; Domotor, Zoltan;
    Kanisza, Tividar; Rusoran, Peter; Karpati, Gyorgy; Garmati, Deszo; Pocsik,
    Denes; Mayer, Mihaily; Bodnar
    Andras; Boros, Otto)
    Yugoslavia
    Soviet Union

1968 Yugoslavia
    (Stipanic, Karlo; Trumbic, Ivo; Bonacic, Ozren; Marovic, Urcs; Lopanty,
    Ronald; Jankovic, Zorna; Poljak, Miroslav; Dabovic, Djean; Perisic, Djordjie; Sandic, Mirko; Hebel, Zoravko)

Soviet Union
Hungary

1972 Soviet Union
(Akimov, Anatoly; Barkelov, Alexei;
Dolgushin, Aleksandr; Dreval, Alek-
sandr; Goliaev, Vadim; Kabanov, Alek-
sandr; Melnikov, Nikolay; Ossipov,
Leonid; Shidlovski, Aleksandr; Shmu-
dski, Vladimir; Sobchenko, Vyaches-
lav)
Hungary
United States

WOMEN

100 m. Free-style
1912	Durack, Fanny (Aus)	1:22.2
1920	Bleibtrey, Ethelda (USA)	1:13.6
1924	Lackie, Ethel (USA)	1:12.4
1928	Osipowich, Albina (USA)	1:11.0
1932	Madison, Helene (USA)	1:06.8
1936	Mastenbroek, Rie (Neth)	1:05.9
1948	Andersen, Greta (Den)	1:06.3
	Curtis, Ann (USA)	1:06.5
	Vaessen, Marie-Louise (Neth)	
		1:07.6
1952	Szöke, Katalin (Hun)	1:06.8
	Termeulen, Hanni (Neth)	1:07.0
	Temes, Judit (Hun)	1:07.1
1956	Fraser, Dawn (Aus)	1:02.0
	Crapp, Lorraine (Aus)	1:02.3
	Leech, Faith (Aus)	1:05.1
1960	Fraser, Dawn (Aus)	1:01.2
	Saltza, Chris von (USA)	1:02.8
	Steward, Natalie (GB)	1:03.1
1964	Fraser, Dawn (Aus)	59.5
	Stouder, Sharon (USA)	59.9
	Ellis, Kathy (USA)	1:00.8
1968	Henne, Jan (USA)	1:00.0
	Pedersen, Sue (USA)	1:00.3
	Gustavson, Linda (USA)	1:00.3
1972	Neilson, Sandy (USA)	58.59
	Babashoff, Shirley (USA)	59.02
	Gould, Shane (Aus)	59.06

200 m. Free-style
1968	Meyer, Debbie (USA)	2:10.5
	Henne, Jan (USA)	2:11.0
	Barkman, Jane (USA)	2:11.2
1972	Gould, Shane (Aus)	2:03.56
	Babashoff, Shirley (USA)	2:04.33
	Rothhammer, Keena (USA)	
		2:04.92

400 m. Free-style
1920*	Bleibtrey, Ethelda (USA)	4:34.0
1924	Norelius, Martha (USA)	6:02.2
1928	Norelius, Martha (USA)	5:42.8
1932	Madison, Helene (USA)	5:28.5
1936	Mastenbroek, Rie (Neth)	5:26.4
1948	Curtis, Ann (USA)	5:17.8
	Harup, Karen (Den)	5:21.2
	Gibson, Cathy (GB)	5:22.5
1952	Gyenge, Valéria (Hun)	5:12.1
	Novák, Eva (Hun)	5:13.7
	Kawamoto, Evelyn (USA)	5:14.6
1956	Crapp, Lorraine (Aus)	4:54.6
	Fraser, Dawn (Aus)	5:02.5
	Ruuska, Sylvia (USA)	5:07.1
1960	Saltza, Chris von (USA)	4:50.6
	Cederqvist, Jane (Swe)	4:53.9
	Lagerberg, Tina (Neth)	4:56.9
1964	Duenkel, Ginny (USA)	4:43.3
	Ramenofsky, Marilyn (USA)	
		4:44.6
	Stickles, Terri (USA)	4:47.2
1968	Meyer, Debbie (USA)	4:31.8
	Gustavson, Linda (USA)	4:35.5
	Moras, Karen (Aus)	4:37.0
1972	Gould, Shane (Aus)	4:19.04
	Calligaris, Novella (It)	4:22.44
	Wegner, Gudrun (E Ger)	4:23.11

* 300 m. (328.08 y.)

800 m. Free-style
1968	Meyer, Debbie (USA)	9:24.0
	Kruse, Pam (USA)	9:35.7
	Ramirez, Maria Teresa (Mex)	
		9:38.5
1972	Rothhammer, Keena (USA)	
		8:53.68
	Gould, Shane (Aus)	8:56.39
	Calligaris, Novella (It)	8:57.46

100 m. Back-stroke
1924	Bauer, Sybil (USA)	1:23.2
1928	Braun, Maria (Neth)	1:22.0
1932	Holm, Eleanor (USA)	1:19.4
1936	Senff, Dina (Neth)	1:18.9
1948	Harup, Karen (Den)	1:14.4
	Zimmerman, Suzanne (USA)	
		1:16.0
	Davies, Judy-Joy (Aus)	1:16.7
1952	Harrison, Joan (SAf)	1:14.3
	Wielema, Geertje (Neth)	1:14.5
	Stewart, Jean (NZ)	1:15.8

1956	Grinham, Judy (GB)	1:12.9
	Cone, Carin (USA)	1:12.9
	Edwards, Margaret (GB)	1:13.1
1960	Burke, Lynn (USA)	1:09.3
	Steward, Natalie (GB)	1:10.8
	Tanaka, Satoko (Jap)	1:11.4
1964	Ferguson, Cathy (USA)	1:07.7
	Caron, Christine (Fr)	1:07.9
	Duenkel, Ginny (USA)	1:08.0
1968	Hall, Kaye (USA)	1:06.2
	Tanner, Elaine (Can)	1:06.7
	Swagerty, Kaye (USA)	1:08.1
1972	Belote, Melissa (USA)	1:05.78
	Gyarmati, Andrea (Hun)	1:06.26
	Atwood, Susie (USA)	1:06.34

200 m. Back-stroke

1968	Watson, Pokey (USA)	2:24.8
	Tanner, Elaine (Can)	2:27.4
	Hall, Kaye (USA)	2:28.9
1972	Belote, Melissa (USA)	2:19.19
	Atwood, Susie (USA)	2:20.38
	Gurr, Donna-Marie (Can)	2:23.22

100 m. Breast-stroke

1968	Bjedov, Djurdjica (Yug)	1:15.8
	Prozumenshikova, Galina (USSR)	1:15.9
	Wichman, Sharon (USA)	1:16.1
1972	Carr, Cathy (USA)	1:13.58
	Stepanova, Galina* (USSR)	1:14.99
	Whitfield, Beverley (Aus)	1:15.73

* nee Prozumenshikova

200 m. Breast-stroke

1924	Morton, Lucy (GB)	3:33.2
1928	Schrader, Hilde (Ger)	3:12.6
1932	Dennis, Clare (Aus)	3:06.3
1936	Maehata, Hideko (Jap)	3:03.6
1948	Vliet, Nel van (Neth)	2:57.2
	Lyons, Nancy (Aus)	2:57.7
	Novak, Eva (Hun)	3:00.2
1952	Székely, Éva (Hun)	Bu2:51.7
	Novak, Éva (Hun)	2:54.4
	Gordon, Elenor (GB)	2:57.6
1956	Happe, Ursula (Ger)	2:53.1
	Székely, Éva (Hun)	2:54.8
	Ten Elsen, Eva-Marie (Ger)	2:55.1
1960	Lonsbrough, Anita (GB)	2:49.5
	Urselmann, Wiltrud (Ger)	2:50.0
	Göbel, Barbara (Ger)	2:53.6
1964	Prozumenshikova, Galina (USSR)	2:46.4

	Kolb, Claudia (USA)	2:47.5
	Babanina, Svetlana (USSR)	2:48.6
1968	Wichman, Sharon (USA)	2:44.4
	Bjedov, Djurdjica (Yug)	2:46.4
	Prozumenshikova, Galina (USSR)	2:47.0
1972	Whitfield, Beverley (Aus)	2:41.71
	Schoenfield, Dana (USA)	2:42.05
	Stepanova, Galina* (USSR)	2:42.36

* nee Prozumenshikova

100 m. Butterfly

1956	Mann, Shelley (USA)	1:11.0
	Ramey, Nancy (USA)	1:11.9
	Sears, Mary-J (USA)	1:14.4
1960	Schuler, Carolyn (USA)	1:09.5
	Heemskerk, Marianne (Neth)	1:10.4
	Andrew, Jan (Aus)	1:12.2
1964	Stouder, Sharon (Aus)	1:04.7
	Kok, Ada (Neth)	1:05.6
	Ellis, Kathy (USA)	1:06.0
1968	McClements, Lyn (Aus)	1:05.5
	Daniel, Ellie (USA)	1:05.8
	Shields, Susan (USA)	1:06.2
1972	Aoki, Mayumi (Jap)	1:03.34
	Beier, Roswitha (E Ger)	1:03.61
	Gyarmati, Andrea (Hun)	1:03.73

200 m. Butterfly

1968	Kok, Ada (Neth)	2:24.7
	Lindner, Helga (E Ger)	2:24.8
	Daniel, Ellie (USA)	2:25.9
1972	Moe, Karen (USA)	2:15.57
	Colella, Lynn (USA)	2:16.34
	Daniel, Ellie (USA)	2:16.74

200 m. Individual medley*

1968	Kolb, Claudia (USA)	2:24.7
	Pedersen, Sue (USA)	2:28.8
	Henne, Jan (USA)	2:31.4
1972	Gould, Shane (Aus)	2:23.07
	Ender, Kornelia (E Ger)	2:23.59
	Vidali, Lynn (USA)	2:24.06

* Not in the programme for the 1976 Montreal Games.

400 m. Indivudual medley

1964	Varona, Donna de (USA)	5:18.7
	Finneran, Sharon (USA)	5:24.1
	Randall, Martha (USA)	5:24.2
1968	Kolb, Claudia (USA)	5:08.5
	Vidali, Lynn (USA)	5:22.2
	Steinbach, Sabine (E Ger)	5:25.3

1972	Neall, Gail (Aus)	5:02.07
	Cliff, Leslie (Can)	5:03.57
	Calligaris, Novella (It)	5:03.99

4 x 100 m. Free-style relay

1912 Great Britain   5:52.8
(Moore, Bella; Fletcher, Jennie; Speirs, Annie; Steer, Irene)

1920 United States   5:11.6
(Woodbridge, Margaret; Schroth, Frances; Guest, Irene; Bleibtrey Ethelda)

1924 United States   4:58.8
(Ederle, Gertrude; Donnelly, Euphrasia; Lackie, Ethel; Wehselau, Mariechen)

1928 United States   4:47.6
(Lambert, Adelaide; Garatti, Eleanora; Osipowich, Albina; Norelius, Martha)

1932 United States   4:38.0
(McKim, Josephine; Johns, Helen; Saville-Garatti, Eleanora; Madison, Helene)

1936 Netherlands .   4:36.0
(Selbach, Johanna; Wagner, Catherina; Ouden, Willy den; Mastenbroek, Rie)

- -

1948 United States   4:29.2
(Corridon, Marie; Kalama, Thelma, Helser, Brenda; Curtis, Ann)
Denmark   4:29.6
(Riise, Esa; Harup, Karen; Andersen, Greta; Carstensen, Fritze)
Netherlands   4:31.6
(Schumacher, Irma; Marsman, Margot; Vaessen, Marie-Louise; Termeulen, Hanni)

1952 Hungary   4:24.4
(Novák, Ilona; Temes, Judit; Novák, Eva; Szöke, Katalin)
Netherlands   4:29.0
(Linssen (nee Vaessen), Marie-Louise; Voorn, Koosje van; Termeulen, Hanni; Heijting (nee Schumacher), Irma)
United States   4:30.1
(La Vine, Jackie; Stepan, Marilee; Alderson, Joan; Kawamoto, Evelyn)

1956 Australia   4:17.1
(Fraser, Dawn; Leech, Faith; Morgan, Sandra; Crapp, Lorraine)
United States   4:19.2
(Ruuska, Sylvia; Mann, Shelley; Simmons, Nancy; Rosazza, Joan)
South Africa   4:25.7
(Myburgh, Jeanette; Roberts, Susan; Myburgh, Natalie; Abernathy, Moira)

1960 United States   4:08.9
(Spillane, Joan; Stobs, Shirley; Wood, Carolyn; Saltza, Chris von)
Australia   4:11.3
(Fraser, Dawn; Konrads, Ilsa; Crapp, Lorraine; Colqhoun, Alva)
Germany*   4:19.7
(Steffin, Christel; Pechstein, Heidi; Weiss, Gisela; Brunner, Ursula)

1964 United States   4:03.8
(Stouder, Sharon; Varona, Donna de; Watson, Lillian "Pokey"; Ellis, Kathy)
Australia   4:06.9
(Thorn, Robyn; Murphy, Janice; Bell, Lyn, Fraser, Dawn)
Netherlands   4:12.0
(Wildt, Pauline van der; Beumer, Catharina; Weerdenburg, Win; Terpstra, Erica)

1968 United States   4:02.5
(Barkman, Jane; Gustavson, Linda; Pedersen, Sue; Henne, Jan)
East Germany (GDR)   4:05.7
(Wetzko, Gabriele; Krause, Roswitha; Schmuck, Uta; Grunert, Martina)
Canada   4:07.2
(Coughlan, Angela; Corson, Marilyn, Tanner, Elaine; Lay, Marion)

- -

1972 United States   3:55.19
(Neilson, Sandy; Kemp, Jenny, Barkman, Jane; Babashoff, Shirley)
East Germany   3:55.55
(Wetzko, Gabriele; Eife, Andrea; Sehmisch, Elke; Ender, Kornelia)
West Germany   3:57.93
(Weber, Jutta; Reineck, Heidi; Beckmann, Gudrun; Steinbach, Angela)

* Combined German team: Steffin, Pechstein and Weiss (E Ger); Brunner (W Ger).

4 x 100 m. Medley relay

1960 United States   4:41.1
(Burke, Lynn; Kempner, Pat; Schuler, Carolyn; Saltza, Chris von)
Australia   4:45.9
(Wilson, Marilyn; Lassig, Rosemary; Andrew, Jan; Fraser, Dawn)
Germany*   4:47.6
(Schmidt, Ingrid; Küper, Ursula; Fuhrmann, Barbel; Brunner, Ursula)

1964 United States   4:33.9
(Ferguson, Cathy; Goyette, Cynthia; Stouder, Sharon; Ellis, Kathy)
Netherlands   4:37.0
(Winkel, Corrie; Bimolt. Kleine; Kok Ada; Terpstra, Erica)

Soviet Union   4:39.2
(Savelieva, Tatyana; Babanina, Svet-
lana; Devjatova, Tatyana; Ustinova,
Natalia)

1968 United States   4:28.3
(Hall, Kaye; Ball, Catie; Daniel, Ellie;
Pedersen, Susan)
      Australia   4:30.0
(Watson, Lyn; Playfair, Judy; Mc-
Clements, Lyn; Steinbeck, Janet)
      West Germany   4:36.4
(Kraus, Angelika; Frommater, Uta;
Hustede, Heiki; Reineck, Heidi)
- -
1972 United States   4:20.75
(Belote, Melissa; Carr, Cathy; Dear-
durff, Deena; Neilson, Sandy)
      East Germany   4:24.91
(Herbst, Christine; Vogel, Renate;
Beier, Roswitha; Ender, Kornelia)
      West Germany   4:26.46
(Pielen, Silke; Eberle, Verena; Beck-
mann, Gudrun; Reineck, Heidi)

* Combined German team: Schmidt, Ku-
per, and Fuhrmann (E Ger); Brunner
(W Ger).

Springboard diving
1920 Riggin, Aileen (USA)   539. 9
1924 Becker, Elizabeth (USA)   474.50
1928 Meany, Helen (USA)   78.62
1932 Coleman, Georgia (USA)   87.52
1936 Gestring, Marjorie (USA)   89.27
- -
1948 Draves, Vickie (USA)   108.74
      Olsen Zoe-Ann (USA)   108.23
      Elsener, Patricia   101.30
1952 McCormick, Pat (USA)   147.30
      Moreau, Mady (Fr)   139.34
      Jensen (nee Olsen) Zoe-Ann
      (USA)   127.57
1956 McCormick, Pat (USA)   142.36
      Stunyo, Jeanne (USA)   125.89
      MacDonald, Irene (Can)   121.40
1960 Krämer, Ingrid (Ger)   155.81
      Pope (nee Myers), Paula (USA)
                                  141.24
      Ferris, Elizabeth (GB)   139.09
1964 Engel (nee Krämer) Ingrid (Ger)
                                  145.00
      Collier, Jeanne (USA)   138.36
      Willard, Patsy (USA)   138.18
1968 Gossick, Sue (USA)   150.77
      Pogoscheva, Tamara (USSR)
                                  145.30
      O'Sullivan, Keala (USA)   145.23

1972 King, Micki (USA)   450.03
      Knape, Ulrika (Swe)   434.19
      Janicke, Marina (E Ger)   430.92

Highboard diving
1912* Johanasson, Greta (Swe)   39. 9
1920* Fryland-Clausen, Stefani (Den)
                                    34. 6
1924* Smith, Caroline (USA)   33. 2
1928 Pinkston (nee Becker),
      Elizabeth (USA)   31.60
1932 Poynton, Dorothy (USA)   40.26
1936 Hill (nee Poynton), Dorothy
      (USA)   33.93
- -
1948 Draves, Vicky (USA)   68.87
      Elsener, Patricia (USA)   66.28
      Christoffersen, Birte (Den) 66.04
1952 McCormick, Pat (USA)   79.37
      Myers, Paula (USA)   71.63
      Irwin (nee Stover), Juno (USA)
                                   70.40
1956 McCormick, Pat (USA)   84.85
      Irwin (nee Stover), Juno (USA)
                                   81.64
      Myers, Paula (USA)   81.58
1960 Krämer, Ingrid (Ger)   91.28
      Pope (nee Myers), Paula (USA)
                                   88.94
      Krutova, Ninel (USSR)   86.99
1964 Bush, Lesley (USA)   99.80
      Engel (nee Krämer), Ingrid
      (Ger)   98.45
      Alekseyeva, Galina (USSR)   97.60
1968 Duchkova, Milena (Czech)   109.59
      Lobanova, Natalia (USSR)   105.14
      Peterson, Ann (USA)   101.11
1972 Knape, Ulrika (Swe)   390.00
      Duchkova, Milena (Czech)   370.92
      Janicke, Marina (E Ger)   360.54

    * Plain diving

Events no longer in the Olympic programme.

MEN

50 y. Free-style
1904 Halmay, Zoltan (Hun)   *28.0
*After swim-off with Scott Leary (USA)

880 y. Free-style
1904 Rausch, Emil (Ger)   13:11.4

4,000 m. Free-style
1900 Jarvis, John (GB)   58:24.0

400 m. Breast-stroke
1904 Zacharias, Georg (Ger) *7:23.6
1912 Bathe, Walther (Ger) 6:29.6
1920 Malmroth, Hakan (Swe) 6:31.8
* = 440 y.

100 m. For sailors (of ships anchored in the port of Pireus)
1896 Malokinis, Jean (Gre) 2:20.4

Obstacle swimming
1900 Lane, Freddy (Aus) 2:28.4

60 m. Under-water swimming
1900 Vendeville, Charles de (Fr) 1:53.4

Plunging
1904 Dickey, Paul (USA) 62' 6''

4 x 50 y. Free-style relay
1904 New York A.C. (USA)* 2:04.6
(Ruddy, Joseph; Goodwin, Leon; Handley, Louis de B. Daniels, Charles)

*The only Games when non-national teams have been allowed to participate.

200 m. Team Swimming*
1900 Germany 19 pts.
(Hoppenberg, Ernst; Hainle, Max; Von Petersdorff, Herbert; Schone, Max; Frey, Julius)

*Each man swam 200 m. and points were awarded according to the placings of each individual competitor.

Plain High Diving
1912 Alderz, Erik (Swe) 40.00
1920 Wallman, Arvid (USA) 7 pts.
1924 Eve, Richmond (Aus) 160.00

OLYMPIC GAMES, DEVELOP-MENT OF THE PROGRAMME. For details of events at each games see table on page 169.

OLYMPIC GAMES RECORDS. This list of records set during Olympic swimming competitions has been based on an original manuscript drawn up be Sebastian Salinas Abril, a Vice-President of F.I.N.A.

h = heat. s = semi-final. f = final.

MEN

100 m. Free-style
1:22.2 f Hajós, Alfréd (Hun) 1896
1:13.4 f Daniels, Charles (USA) 1906
1:08.2 h Halmay, Zoltan (Hun) 1908
1:05.6 f Daniels, Charles (USA) 1908
1:04.8 h McGillivray, Perry (USA) 1912
1:02.6 h Kahanamoku, Duke (USA)
1912
1:02.4 s Kahanamoku, Duke (USA)
1912
1:01.8 h Kahanamoku, Duke (USA)
1920
1:01.4 s Kahanamoku, Duke (USA)
1920
1:00.4 *f Kahanamoku, Duke (USA)
1920
59.0 f Weissmuller, Johnnny (USA)
1924
58.6 h Weissmuller, Johnny (USA)
1928
58.0 s Miyasaka, Yasugi (Jap) 1932
57.6 h Fick, Peter (USA) 1936
57.5 h Taguchi, Masaharu (Jap) 1936
57.3 f Ris, Wally (USA) 1948
57.1 s Scholes, Clarke (USA) 1952
56.8 h Patterson, Floyd (USA) 1956
55.7 s Henricks, Jon (Aus) 1956
55.4 f Henricks, Jon (Aus) 1956
55.2 f Devitt, John (Aus) 1960
54.0 h Ilman, Gary (USA) 1964
53.9 s Ilman, Gary (USA) 1964
53.4 f Schollander, Don (USA) 1964
52.9 s Wenden, Mike (Aus) 1968
52.2 f Wenden, Mike (Aus) 1968
- -
51.22f Spitz, Mark (USA) 1972

* Time recorded in first final but race re-swum after protest, Kahanamoku won second final in 1:01.4.

200 m. Free-style *
2:25.5 f Lane, Freddy (Aus) 1900
1:59.5 h Nelson, John (USA) 1968
1:59.3 h Wenden, Mike (Aus) 1968
1:55.2 f Wenden, Mike (Aus) 1968
- -
1:52.78f Spitz, Mark (USA) 1972

*Not in the Olympic programme between 1900 and 1968.

400 m. Free-style*
6:16.2 f†Daniels, Charles (USA) 1904
5:48.8 h Battersby, Sydney (GB) 1908
5:42.2 h Taylor, Henry (GB) 1908
5:40.6 h Scheff, Otto (Aus) 1908
5:36.8 f Taylor, Henry (GB) 1908
5:36.0 h Hardwick, Harold (Aus) 1912

OLYMPIC GAMES, DEVELOPMENT OF THE PROGRAMME: NUMBER OF EVENTS AT EACH GAMES

	1896	1900	1904	1908	1912	1920	1924	1928	1932	1936	1948	1952	1956	1960	1964	1968	1972	1976
MEN																		
Free-style individual	3	3	6	3	3	3	3	3	3	3	3	3	3	3	3	4	4	4
Free-style relay	-	1	1	1	1	1	1	1	1	1	1	1	1	1	2	2	2	1
Back-stroke	-	1	1	1	1	1	1	1	1	1	1	1	1	1	1	2	2	2
Breast-stroke	-	-	1	1	2	2	1	1	1	1	1	1	1	1	1	2	2	2
Butterfly	-	-	-	-	-	-	-	-	-	-	-	-	1	1	1	2	2	2
Medley individual	-	-	-	-	-	-	-	-	-	-	-	-	-	-	1	2	2	1
Medley relay	-	-	-	-	-	-	-	-	-	-	-	-	-	1	1	1	1	1
Diving	-	-	2	2	3	3	3	2	2	2	2	2	2	2	2	2	2	2
Water-Polo	-	1	1	1	1	1	1	1	1	1	1	1	1	1	1	1	1	1
Miscellaneous*	1	2	-	-	-	-	-	-	-	-	-	-	-	-	-	-	-	-
TOTAL	4	8	12	9	11	11	10	9	9	9	9	9	10	11	13	18	18	16
WOMEN																		
Free-style individual	-	-	-	-	1	2	2	2	2	2	2	2	2	2	2	4	4	4
Free-style relay	-	-	-	-	1	1	1	1	1	1	1	1	1	1	1	1	1	1
Back-stroke	-	-	-	-	-	-	1	1	1	1	1	1	1	1	1	2	2	2
Breast-stroke	-	-	-	-	-	-	1	1	1	1	1	1	1	1	1	2	2	2
Butterfly	-	-	-	-	-	-	-	-	-	-	-	-	1	1	1	2	2	2
Medley individual	-	-	-	-	-	-	-	-	-	-	-	-	-	-	1	2	2	1
Medley relay	-	-	-	-	-	-	-	-	-	-	-	-	-	1	1	1	1	1
Diving	-	-	-	-	1	2	2	2	2	2	2	2	2	2	2	2	2	2
TOTAL	-	-	-	-	3	5	7	7	7	7	7	7	8	9	10	16	16	15
GRAND TOTAL	4	8	12	9	14	16	17	16	16	16	16	16	18	20	23	34	34	31

* A race for sailors (1896), an obstacle race and plunging (1900).

5:34.0 h Healy, Cecil (Aus) 1912
5:25.4 s Hodgson, George (Can) 1912
5:24.4 f Hodgson, George (Can) 1912
5:22.4 h Breyer, Ralph (USA) 1924
5:22.2 h Weissmuller, Johnny (USA) 1924
5:13.6 s Weissmuller, Johnny (USA) 1924
5:04.2 f Weissmuller, Johnny (USA) 1924
5:01.6 f Zorilla, Alberto (Arg) 1928
4:53.2 h Yokayama, Takashi (Jap) 1932
4:51.4 s Yokayama, Takashi (Jap) 1932
4:48.4 f Crabbe, Buster (USA) 1932
4:45.5 h Uto, Shumpei (Jap) 1936
4:44.5 f Medica, Jack (USA) 1936
4:42.2 h McLane, Jimmy (USA) 1948
4:41.0 f Smith, Bill (USA) 1948
4:38.6 h Ostrand, Per-Ola (Swe) 1952
4:33.1 s Boiteux, Jean (Fr) 1952
4:30.7 f Boiteux, Jean (Fr) 1952
4:27.3 f Rose, Murray (Aus) 1956
4:21.0 h Yamanaka, Tsuyoshi (Jap) 1960
4:19.2 h Somers, Alan (USA) 1960
4:18.3 f Rose, Murray (Aus) 1960
4:17.2 h Wiegand, Frank (Ger) 1964
4:15.8 h Schollander, Don (USA) 1964
4:12.2 f Schollander, Don (USA) 1964
4:09.0 f Burton, Mike (USA) 1968

4:06.59h Gingsjö, Bengt (Swe) 1972
4:05.89h Genter, Steve (USA) 1972
4:04.59h Cooper, Brad (Aus) 1972
4:00.27f Cooper, Brad (Aus)†† 1972

*A 500 m. event was held in 1896

† 440 y.

†† DeMont, Rick (USA) touched first in
4:00.26 (Olympic record) but was disqualified by the IOC Medical Commission.

1,500 m. Free-style*
25:02.6 h Radmilovic, Paul (GB) 1908
23:45.8 h Beaurepaire, Frank (Aus) 1908
23:42.8 h Battersby, Sydney (GB) 1908
23:24.4 h Taylor, Henry (GB) 1908
22:54.0 s Taylor, Henry (GB) 1908
22:48.4 f Taylor, Henry (GB) 1908
22:23.0 h Hodgson, George (Can) 1912
22:00.0 f Hodgson, George (Can) 1912
21:20.4 h Charlton, Boy (Aus) 1924
21:11.4 h Borg, Arne (Swe) 1924
20:06.6 f Charlton, Boy (Aus) 1924
19:51.8 f Borg, Arne (Swe) 1928
19:51.6 s Kitamura, Kusuo (Jap) 1932
19:38.7 s Makino, Shozo (Jap) 1932
19:12.4 f Kitamura, Kusuo (Jap) 1932

18:34.0 h Hashizume, Shiro (Jap) 1952
18:30.0 f Konno, Ford (USA) 1952
18:04.1 h Rose, Murray (Aus) 1956
17:52.9 h Breen, George (USA) 1960
17:46.6 h Yamanaka, Tsuyoshi (Jap) 1960
17:32.0 h Rose, Murray (Aus) 1960
17:19.6 f Konrads, John (Aus) 1960
17:15.9 h Windle, Bob (Aus) 1964
17:01.7 f Windle, Bob (Aus) 1964
16:38.9 f Burton, Mike (USA) 1968

16:34.63h Fassnacht, Hans (W Ger) 1972
15:59.63h Windeatt, Graham (Aus) 1972
15:52.58f Burton, Mike (USA) 1972

*The long distance races prior to 1908
were held over a variety of different
distances (see OLYMPIC GAMES)

100 m. Back-stroke*
1:25.6 h Bieberstein, Arno (Ger) 1908
1:24.6 f Bieberstein, Arno (Ger) 1908
1:21.0 h Hebner, Harry (USA) 1912
1:20.8 s Hebner, Harry (USA) 1912
1:17.8 h Kegeris, Ray (USA) 1920
1:14.8 h Kealoha, Warren (USA) 1920
1:13.4 h Kealoha, Warren (USA) 1924
1:13.2 f Kealoha, Warren (USA) 1924
1:09.2 h Kojac, George (USA) 1928
1:08.2 f Kojac, George (USA) 1928
1:06.9 h Kiefer, Adolph (USA) 1936
1:06.8 s Kiefer, Adolph (USA) 1936
1:05.9 f Kiefer, Adolph (USA) 1936
1:05.7 s Oyakawa, Yoshinobu (USA) 1952
1:05.4 f Oyakawa, Yoshinobu (USA) 1952
1:04.2 h Christophe, Robert (Fr) 1956
1:03.4 h Monckton, John (Aus) 1956
1:02.2 f Theile, David (Aus) 1956
1:02.0 h Bennett, Bob (USA) 1960
1:01.9 f Theile, David (Aus) 1960
1:01.0 h Matthes, Roland (E Ger) 1968
58.7 f Matthes, Roland (E Ger) 1968

58.63h Stamm, Mike (USA) 1972
58.15h Ivey, Mitch (USA) 1972
57.99s Ivey, Mitch (USA) 1972
56.58f Matthes, Roland (E Ger) 1972

* Not held in 1964

200 m. Back-stroke*
2:47.0 f Hoppenberg, Ernst (Ger) 1900
2:16.1 h Bennett, Bob (USA) 1964
2:14.7 h Fukushima, Shigeo (Jap) 1964
2:14.5 h Graef, Jed (USA) 1964
2:14.2 h Dilley, Gary (USA) 1964
2:13.8 s Dilley, Gary (USA) 1964
2:13.7 s Graef, Jed (USA) 1964

2:10.3 f Graef, Jed (USA)   1964
2:09.6 f Matthes, Roland (E Ger)   1968

- -

2:07.51h Stamm, Mike (USA)   1972
2:06.62h Matthes, Roland (E Ger)   1972
2:02.82f Matthes, Roland (E Ger)   1972

*Not in the Olympic programme between 1904–1960

100 m. Breast-stroke
1:08.9 h Pankin, Nikolay (USSR)   1968
1:08.1 h McKenzie, Don (USA)   1968
1:07.9 h Kosinsky, Vladimir (USSR) 1968
1:07.7 f McKenzie, Don (USA)   1968

- -

1:05.89h Chatfield, Mark (USA)   1972
1:05.68s Hencken, John (USA)   1972
1:05.13s Taguchi, Nobutaka (Jap)   1972
1:04.94f Taguchi, Nobutaka (Jap)   1972

200 m. Breast-stroke
3:10.6 h Holman, Frederick (GB)   1908
3:10.0 s Holman, Frederick (GB)   1908
3:09.2 f Holman, Frederick (GB)   1908
3:07.4 h Lutzow, Wilhelm (Ger)   1912
3:03.7 h Bathe, Walther (Ger)   1912
3:02.2 s Bathe, Walther (Ger)   1912
3:01.8 f Bathe, Walther (Ger)   1912
2:56.0 h Skelton, Robert (USA)   1924
2:52.0 h Rademacher, Erich (Ger)   1928
2:50.0 h Tsuruta, Yoshijuki (Jap)   1928
2:49.2 s Tsuruta, Yoshijuki (Jap)   1928
2:48.8 f Tsuruta, Yoshijuki (Jap)   1928
2:46.2 h Tsuruta, Yoshijuki (Jap)   1932
2:44.9 s Koike, Reizo (Jap)   1932
2:42.5 h Hamuro, Tetsuo (Jap)   1936
2:41.5 f Hamuro, Tetsuo (Jap)   1936

- -

2:40.0 h Verdeur, Joe (USA)   Bu1948
2:39.3 f Verdeur, Joe (USA)   Bu1948
2:38.9 h Komadel, L. (Czech)   Bu1952
2:36.8 h Holan, Gerry (USA)   Bu1952
2:34.4 f Davies. John (Aus)   Bu1952

- -

2:36.1*h Furukawa, Masaru (Jap)
                                     Uw1956
2:34.7 f Furukawa, Masaru (Jap)
                                     Uw1956

- -

2:38.0†h Mulliken, Bill (USA)   1960
2:37.2 s Mulliken, Bill (USA)   1960
2:31.4 h O'Brien, Ian (Aus)   1964
2:30.1 h Henninger, Egon (Ger)   1964
2:28.7 s O'Brien, Ian (Aus)   1964
2:27.8 f O'Brien, Ian (Aus)   1964

- -

2:26.32h Katzur, Klaus (E Ger)   1972
2:23.45h Taguchi, Nobutaka (Jap)   1972
2:21.55 f Hencken, John (USA)   1972

*Olympic record standard adjusted after breast-stroke was separated from butter-fly.

†Olympic record standard adjusted after under-water swimming was disallowed in breast-stroke (see BREAST-STROKE)

100 m. Butterfly
57.3 h Russell, Doug (USA)   1968
55.9 s Russell, Doug (USA)   1968

- -

54.27f Spitz, Mark (USA)   1972

200 m. Butterfly
2:18.6 h Yorzyk, Bill (USA)   1956
2:15.5 h Troy, Mike (USA)   1960
2:12.8 f Troy, Mike (USA)   1960
2:10.0 h Robie, Carl (USA)   1964
2:09.3 s Robie, Carl (USA)   1964
2:06.6 f Berry, Kevin (Aus)   1964

- -

2:03.70h Hall, Gary (USA)   1972
2:03.11h Backhaus, Robin (USA)   1972
2:02.11h Spitz, Mark (USA)   1972
2:00.70f Spitz, Mark (USA)   1972

200 m. Individual medley
2:16.1 h Hickcox, Charles (USA)   1968
2:14.6 h Ferris, John (USA)   1968
2:12.0 f Hickcox, Charles (USA)   1968

- -

2:10.88h Hargitay, András (Hun)   1972
2:09.70h Larsson, Gunnar (Swe)   1972
2:07.17 f Larsson, Gunnar (Swe)   1972

400 m. Individual medley
4:52.0 h Robie, Carl (USA)   1964
4:45.4 f Roth, Dick (USA)   1964

- -

4:37.51h Hargitay, András (Hun)   1972
4:34.99h Larsson, Gunnar (Swe)   1972
4:31.98f Larsson, Gunnar (Swe)   1972

WOMEN

100 m. Free-style
1:29.8 h Moore, Bella (GB)   1912
1:23.6 h Curwen, Daisy (GB)   1912
1:19.8 h Durack, Fanny (Aus)   1912
1:18.0 h Schroth, Frances (USA)   1920
1:14.4 h Bleibtrey, Ethelda (USA)   1920
1:13.6 f Bleibtrey, Ethelda (USA)   1920
1:12.2 h Wehselau, Mariechen (USA)
                                       1924
1:11.4 h Garatti, Eleanor (USA)   1928
1:11.0 f Osipowich, Albina (USA)   1928
1:09.0 h Cooper, Joyce (GB)   1932
1:08.9 h Madison, Helene (USA)   1932
1:08.5 h Saville (nee Garatti),
           Eleanor (USA)   1932

1:07.6	s	Ouden, Willy den (Neth)	1932
1:06.8	f	Madison, Helene (USA)	1932
1:06.4	h	Mastenbroek, Rie (Neth)	1936
1:05.9	f	Mastenbroek, Rie (Neth)	1936
1:05.5	h	Temes, Judit (Hun)	1952
1:03.4	h	Crapp, Lorraine (Aus)	1956
1:02.4	h	Fraser, Dawn (Aus)	1956
1:02.0	f	Fraser, Dawn (Aus)	1956
1:01.9	h	Saltza, Chris von (USA)	1960
1:01.4	s	Fraser, Dawn (Aus)	1960
1:01.2	f	Fraser, Dawn (Aus)	1960
1:00.6	h	Fraser, Dawn (Aus)	1964
59.9	s	Fraser, Dawn (Aus)	1964
59.5	f	Fraser, Dawn (Aus)	1964

- -

59.47h	Patoh, Magdolna (Hun)	1972
59.44h	Gould, Shane (Aus)	1972
59.05s	Babashoff, Shirley (USA)	1972
58.59f	Neilson, Sandy (USA)	1972

200 m. Free-style

2:13.1	h	Meyer, Debbie (USA)	1968
2:10.5	f	Meyer, Debbie (USA)	1968

- -

2:08.12	h	Marshall, Ann (USA)	1972
2:07.48	h	Rothhammer, Keena (USA)	1972
2:07.05	h	Eife, Andrea (E Ger)	1972
2:03.56	f	Gould, Shane (Aus)	1972

400 m. Free-style

6:12.2	h	Ederle, Gertrude (USA)	1924
6:02.2	f	Norelius, Martha (USA)	1924
5:45.4	h	Norelius, Martha (USA)	1928
5:42.8	f	Norelius, Martha (USA)	1928
5:40.9	h	Kight, Lenore (USA)	1932
5:28.5	f	Madison, Helene (USA)	1932
5:28.0	h	Hveger, Ragnhild (Den)	1936
5:26.4	f	Mastenbroek, Rie (Neth)	1936
5:25.7	s	Harup, Karen (Den)	1948
5:17.8	f	Curtis, Ann (USA)	1948
5:16.6	h	Kawamoto, Evelyn (USA)	1952
5:12.1	f	Gyenge, Valéria (Hun)	1952
5:07.6	h	Shriver, Marley (USA)	1956
5:02.5	h	Fraser, Dawn (Aus)	1956
5:00.2	h	Crapp, Lorraine (Aus)	1956
4:54.6	f	Crapp, Lorraine (Aus)	1956
4:53.6	h	Saltza, Chris von (USA)	1960
4:50.6	f	Saltza, Chris von (USA)	1960
4:48.6	h	Duenkel, Ginny (USA)	1964
4:47.7	h	Ramenofsky, Marilyn (USA)	1964
4:43.3	f	Duenkel, Ginny (USA)	1964
4:35.0	h	Meyer, Debbie (USA)	1968
4:31.8	f	Meyer, Debbie (USA)	1968

- -

4:27.53h	Wylie, Jenny (USA)	1972
4:24.14h	Calligaris, Novella (It)	1972
4:19.04f	Gould, Shane (Aus)	1972

800 m. Free-style

9:42.8	h	Meyer, Debbie (USA)	1968
9:38.3	h	Moras, Karen (Aus)	1968
9:24.0	f	Meyer, Debbie (USA)	1968

- -

8:59.69h	Rothhammer, Keena (USA)	1972
8:53.68f	Rothhammer, Keena (USA)	1972

100 m. Back-stroke

1:24.0	h	Bauer, Sybil (USA)	1924
1:23.3	f	Bauer, Sybil (USA)	1924
1:22.0	h	King, Ellen (GB)	1928
1:21.6	h	Braun, Marie (Neth)	1928
1:18.3	h	Holm, Eleanor (USA)	1932
1:16.6	h	Senff, Dina (Neth)	1936
1:15.6	h	Harup, Karen (Den)	1948
1:15.5	s	Harup, Karen (Den)	1948
1:14.4	f	Harup, Karen (Den)	1948
1:13.8	h	Wielema, Geertje (Neth)	1952
1:13.1	h	Grinham, Judy (GB)	1956
1:13.0	h	Edwards, Margaret (GB)	1956
1:12.9	f	Grinham, Judy (GB)	1956
1:12.0	h	Ranwell, Lorna (SAf)	1960
1:09.4	h	Burke, Lynn (USA)	1960
1:09.3	f	Burke, Lynn (USA)	1960
1:08.9	h	Duenkel, Ginny (USA)	1964
1:08.8	h	Ferguson, Cathy (USA)	1964
1:08.5	h	Caron, Christine (Fr)	1964
1:07.7	f	Ferguson, Cathy (USA)	1964
1:07.6	h	Tanner, Elaine (Can)	1968
1:07.4	s	Tanner, Elaine (Can)	1968
1:06.2	f	Hall, Kaye (USA)	1968

- -

1:06.08s	Belote, Melissa (USA)	1972
1:05.78f	Belote, Melissa (USA)	1972

200 m. Back-stroke

2:31.1	h	Hall, Kaye (USA)	1968
2:30.9	h	Tanner, Elaine (USA)	1968
2:29.2	h	Watson, Pokey (USA)	1968
2:24.8	f	Watson, Pokey (USA)	1968

- -

2:22.13h	Atwood, Susie (USA)	1972
2:20.58h	Belote, Melissa (USA)	1972
2:19.19f	Belote, Melissa USA	1972

100 m. Breast-stroke (instituted 1968)

1'18.8	h	Ball, Catie (USA)	1968
1:17.7	h	Bjedov, Djurdjica (Yug)	1968
1:17.4	h	Norbis, Ana-Maria (Urug)	1968
1:16.8	s	Wichman, Sharon (USA)	1968
1:16.7	s	Norbis, Ana-Maria (Urug)	1968
1:15.8	f	Bjedov, Djurdjica (Yug)	1968

- -

1:15.00s	Carr, Cathy (USA)	1972
1:13.58f	Carr, Cathy (USA)	1972

200 m. Breast-stroke (instituted 1924)

3:27.6	h Geraghty, Agnes (USA)	1924
3:11.6	h Schrader, Hilder (Ger)	1928
3:11.2	s Schrader, Hilde (Ger)	1928
3:08.2	h Dennis, Clare (Aus)	1932
3:06.3	f Dennis, Clare (Aus)	1932
3:02.9	h Genenger, Martha (Ger)	1936
3:01.9	h Maehata, Hideko (Jap)	1936
3:01.2	h Székely, Eva (Hun)	Bu1948
2:57.4	h Vliet, Nel van (Neth)	1948
2:57.0	s Vliet, Nel van (Neth)	1948
2:54.0	h Novák, Eva (Hun)	1952
2:51.7	f Székely, Eva (Hun)	Bu1952
2:54.1*h	Happe, Ursula (Ger)	1956
2:53.1	f Happe, Ursula (Ger)	1956
2:54.2†h	Göbel, Barbara (Ger)	1960
2:53.3	h Lonsbrough, Anita (GB)	1960
2:52.0	h Urselmann, Wiltrude (Ger)	1960
2:49.5	f Lonsbrough, Anita (GB)	1960
2:48.6	h Grimmer, Barbara (Ger)	1964
2:46.4	f Prozumenshikova, Galina (USSR)	1964
2:44.4	f Wichman, Sharon (USA)	1968
2:43.13h	Kaczanda, Agnes (Hun)	1972
2:41.71f	Whitfield, Beverley (Aus)	1972

*Olympic record standard adjusted after breast-stroke was separated from butterfly.

+Olympic record standard adjusted after under-water swimming was disallowed in breast-stroke (see BREAST-STROKE)

100 m. Butterfly

1:11.2	h Mann, Shelley (USA)	1956
1:11.0	f Mann, Shelley (USA)	1956
1:09.8	h Schuler, Carolyn (USA)	1960
1:09.5	f Schuler, Carolyn (USA)	1960
1:07.8	h Ellis, Kathy (USA)	1964
1:07.5	h Varona, Donna de (USA)	1964
1:07.0	h Stouder, Sharon (USA)	1964
1:05.6	s Stouder, Sharon (USA)	1964
1:04.7	f Stouder, Sharon (USA)	1964
1:04.01h	Gyarmati, Andrea (Hun)	1972
1:04.00h	Aoki, Mayumi (Jap)	1972
1:03.80s	Gyarmati, Andrea (Hun)	1972
1:03.34f	Akoi, Mayumi Jap)	1972

200 m. Butterfly

2:33.0	h Giebel, Diana (USA)	1968
2:29.4	h Daniel, Ellie (USA)	1968
2:29.1	h Hewitt, Toni (USA)	1968
2:26.3	h Kok, Ada (Neth)	1968
2:24.7	f Kok, Ada (Neth)	1968
2:18.32h	Kother, Rosemarie (E Ger)	1972
2:17.18h	Daniel, Ellie (USA)	1972
2:15.57f	Moe, Karen (USA)	1972

200 m. Individual medley

2:33.2	h Steinbach, Sabine (E Ger)	1968
2:31.5	h Nishigawa, Yoshima (Jap)	1968
2:28.8	h Kolb, Claudia (USA)	1968
2:24.7	f Kolb, Claudia (USA)	1968
2:23.07f	Gould, Shane (Aus)	1972

400 m. Individual medley

5:30.6	h Lonsbrough, Anita (GB)	1964
5:27.8	h Randall, Martha (USA)	1964
5:26.8	h Holletz, Veronika (Ger)	1964
5:24.2	h Varona, Donna de (USA)	1964
5:18.7	f Varona, Donna de (USA)	1964
5:17.2	h Kolb, Claudia (USA)	1968
5:08.5	f Kolb, Claudia (USA)	1968
5:06.96h	Stoltze, Evelyn (E Ger)	1972
5:02.97f	Neall, Gail (Aus)	1972

OUDEN, Willy den (Netherlands, 1 Jan. 1918-). The darling of Dutch swimming before World War II, Willeminjte den Ouden was femininity itself out of the water and a flashing mermaid in it.

At 13, at the 1931 European championships, she was second in the 100 m. and won a gold in the 4 x 100 m. relay. She was again second in the 100 m. at the Olympic Games the following year and took another silver in Holland's relay squad. Her great year was 1934 when she became champion of Europe for her favourite 100 m., was second in the 400 m. equal on time with her team-mate winner Rie Mastenbroek (5:27.4) and helped Holland retain the relay title.

Willy's only disappointing big occasion was the 1936 Olympics. In February she had set a world 100 m. record of 64.6 (which stood for 20 years). But she was three seconds slower in Berlin and placed fourth. There was a consolation with a relay gold and she won a third European relay medal, a silver, at the 1938 championships.

Her 13 individual world records included a 59.8 for 100 y. which made her the fastest girl under the minute.

PAN AMERICAN GAMES. Instituted in 1951 as a multi-sports "little Olympics", the Pan American Games has done a great deal to assist the development of swimming particularly among the countries of South America.

The most medals at a single Pan-Am went to Frank Heckl (USA) with six golds and a silver. He won the 100 and 200 m. free-style, 100 m. butterfly, was a member of America's first-placed teams in all three relays and came second in the 200 m. medley in Cali, Colombia in 1971.

The venues and winners are:

No.	Venue	Dates	
I	Buenos Aires, Argentina	25 Feb. – 8 Mar.	1951
II	Mexico City, Mexico	12 Mar. – 26 Mar.	1955
III	Chicago, U.S.A.	27 Aug. – 7 Sept.	1959
IV	Sao Paulo, Brazil	21 Apr. – 28 Apr.	1963
V	Winnipeg, Canada	22 July – 5 Aug.	1967
IV	Cali, Colombia	6 Aug. – 11 Aug.	1971
VII	Mexico City, Mexico	12 Oct. – 24 Oct.	1975

MEN

100 m. Free-style
1951	Cleveland, Dick (USA)	58.8
	Gora, Ron (USA)	59.9
	Silveiro, Nicasio (Cuba)	1:00.1
1955	Scholes, Clark (USA)	57.7
	Park, George (Can)	58.7
	Wooley, Carl (USA)	59.3
1959	Farrell, Jeff (USA)	56.3
	Follett, Elton (USA)	57.2
	Woolsey, Bill (USA)	57.6
1963	Clark, Steve (USA)	54.7
	Jackman, Steve (USA)	54.8
	Sherry, Dan (Can)	56.1
1967	Havens, Don (USA)	53.79
	Zorn, Zac (USA)	53.97
	Gilchrist, Sandy (Can)	54.85
1971	Heckl, Frank (USA)	52.80
	Diniz-Aranha, José (Braz)	53.74
	Kasting, Bob (Can)	53.76
1975	Abbott, Rick (USA)	51.96
	Babashoff, Jack (USA)	52.26
	Robertson, Bruce (Can)	53.44

200 m. Free-style
1967	Schollander, Don (USA)	1:56.0
	Hutton, Ralph (Can)	1:58.4
	Arango, Julio (Col)	2:01.7
1971	Heckl, Frank (USA)	1:56.3
	McConica, Jim (USA)	1:58.1
	Hutton, Ralph (Can)	1:59.8
1975	Delgado, Jorge (Ecu)	1:55.4
	DeMont, Rick (USA)	1:55.9
	Favero, Rex (USA)	1:57.0

400 m. Free-style
1951	Okamoto, Tetsuo (Braz)	4:52.4
	Heusner, Bill (USA)	4:54.5
	Gutierrez, Tonatiuh (Mex)	4:57.2
1955	McLane, Jimmy (USA)	4:51.3
	Moore, Wayne (USA)	4:53.4
	Kramer, Oscar (Arg)	4:56.1
1959	Breen, George (USA)	4:31.4
	Harrison, George (USA)	4:31.8
	Lenz, Eugene (USA)	4:34.9
1963	Saari, Roy (USA)	4:19.3
	Schollander, Don (USA)	4:23.3
	Gilchrist, Sandy (Can)	4:29.1

967	Charlton, Greg (USA)	4:10.23
	Hutton, Ralph (Can)	4:11.88
	Burton, Mike (USA)	4:15.74
971	McConica, Jim (USA)	4:08.97
	Genter, Steve (USA)	4:13.05
	Hutton, Ralph (Can)	4:15.75
975	Northway, Doug (USA)	4:00.51
	Hackett, Bobby (USA)	4:03.38
	Madruga, Djan (Bra)	4:06.83

,500 m. Free-style

951	Okamoto, Tetsuo (Braz)	19:23.3
	Gutiérrez, Tonatiuh (Mex)	19:24.5
	Fierro, Efren (Mex)	19:57.4
955	McLane, Jimmy (USA)	20:04.0
	Kramer, Oscar (Arg)	20:09.9
	Arango, Gilberto (Mex)	20:37.2
959	Somers, Alan (USA)	17:53.2
	Breen, George (USA)	17:55.0
	Heinrich, Gary (USA)	18:30.6
963	Saari, Roy (USA)	17:26.2
	Gilchrist, Sandy (Can)	17:58.9
	Hutton, Ralph (Can)	18:08.6
967	Burton, Mike (USA)	16:44.40
	Hutton, Ralph (Can)	16:51.81
	Strenk, Andy (USA)	17:03.43
971	Miles, Pat (USA)	16:32.03
	McBreen, Tom (USA)	16:32.99
	García, Guillermo (Mex)	16:45.56
975	Hackett, Bobby (USA)	15:53.10
	Hartloff, Paul (USA)	15:57.32
	Madruga, Djan (Bra)	16:30.08

00 m. Back-stroke

951	Stack, Allen (USA)	1:08.0
	Galvao, Pedro (Arg)	1:08.3
	Jones, Burwell (USA)	1:09.8
955	McKinney, Frank (USA)	1:07.1
	Galvao, Pedro (Arg)	1:07.8
	Baarcke, Buddy (USA)	1:07.8
959	McKinney, Frank (USA)	1:03.6
	Bittick, Charles (USA)	1:04.2
	Schaefer, Louis (USA)	1:05.3
963	Bartsch, Edward (USA)	1:01.5
	Bittick, Charles (USA)	1:02.1
	Olivera, A. P. (Braz)	1:03.2
967	Hickcox, Charles (USA)	1:01.19
	Haywood, Fred (USA)	1:02.45
	Shaw, Jim (Can)	1:02.87
971	Nash, Mel (USA)	59.84
	Murphy, John (USA)	1:01.00
	Kennedy, Bill (Can)	1:01.35

1975	Rocca, Peter (USA)	58.31
	Jackson, Bob (USA)	58.90
	Arantes, Rómulo (Bra)	59.16

200 m. Back-stroke

1967	Hutton, Ralph (Can)	2:12.5
	Hickcox, Charles (USA)	2:13.05
	Goettsche, Charles (USA)	2:15.94
1971	Campbell, Charles (USA)	2:07.09
	McKee, Tim (USA)	2:07.87
	Hawes, John (Can)	2:14.72
1975	Harrigan, Don (USA)	2:06.09
	Scarth, Mike (Can)	2:09.50
	Jackson, Bob (USA)	2:10.18

100 m. Breast-stroke

1967	Fiolo, José (Braz)	1:07.52
	Webb, Russell (USA)	1:09.13
	Merten, Ken (USA)	1:09.32
1971	Chatfield, Mark (USA)	1:06.75
	Job, Brian (USA)	1:07.93
	Fiolo, Jose (Braz)	1:07.94
1975	Colella, Rick (USA)	1:06.02
	Dowler, Lawrence (USA)	1:06.41
	Fiolo, José (Bra)	1:08.12

200 m. Breast-stroke

1951	Nimo, Domínguez (Arg)	2:43.8
	Jordan, W. (Braz)	2:47.3
	Stassforth, Bowen (USA)	2:47.6
1955	Nimo, Domínguez (Arg)	2:46.9
	Sanguily, Manuel (Cuba)	2:48.3
	Ocampo, Walter (Mex)	2:50.7
1959	Mulliken, Bill (USA)	2:43.1
	Nakasone, Ken (USA)	2:43.2
	Sanguily, Manuel (Cuba)	2:44.3
1963	Jastremski, Chet (USA)	2:35.4
	Merten, Ken (USA)	2:38.4
	Kelso, Jack (Can)	2:41.4
1967	Fiolo, José (Braz)	2:30.42
	Momsen, Bob (USA)	2:31.01
	Merten, Ken (USA)	2:34.17
1971	Colella, Rick (USA)	2:27.12
	Muñoz, Felipe (Mex)	2:27.22
	Job, Brian (USA)	2:28.11
1975	Colella, Rick (USA)	2:24.00
	Heinbuch, Dave (Can)	2:28.96
	Lozono, Gustavo (Mex)	2:29.28

100 m. Butterfly

1967	Spitz, Mark (USA)	56.29
	Wales, Ross (USA)	57.04
	Nicolao, Alberto (Arg)	58.63

1971	Heckl, Frank (USA)	56.92
	Heidenreich, Jerry (USA)	57.30
	MacDonald, Byron (Can)	58.40
1975	Currington, Mike (USA)	56.09
	Jagenburg, Greg (USA)	56.13
	Robertson, Bruce (Can)	56.80

200 m. Butterfly

1955	Rios, Eulalio (Mex)	2:39.8
	Ocampo, Walter (Mex)	2:40.3
	Yorzyk, Bill (USA)	2:42.5
1959	Gillanders, Dave (USA)	2:18.0
	Troy, Mike (USA)	2:18.3
	Rios, Eulalio (Mex)	2:22.5
1963	Robie, Carl (USA)	2:11.3
	Schmidt, Fred (USA)	2:13.3
	Nicolao, Luís (Arg)	2:16.1

1967	Spitz, Mark (USA)	2:06.42
	Arusoo, Tom (Can)	2:10.70
	Burton, Mike (USA)	2:13.26
1971	Delgardo, Jorge (Ecu)	2:06.41
	Orr, Charles (USA)	2:08.39
	Vigil, Augusto (Peru)	2:09.90
1975	Jagenburg, Greg (USA)	2:03.42
	Gregg, Steve (USA)	2:04.06
	Delgado, Jorge (Ecu)	2:05.11

200 m. Individual medley

1967	Russell, Doug (USA)	2:13.22
	Utley, Bill (USA)	2:13.68
	Gilchrist, Sandy (Can)	2:16.61
1971	Furniss, Steve (USA)	2:10.82
	Heckl, Frank (USA)	2:12.11
	Muñoz, Felipe (Mex)	2:16.28
1975	Furniss, Steve (USA)	2:09.77
	Currington, Mike (USA)	2:10.17
	Sawchuk, Bill (Can)	2:11.63

400 m. Individual medley

1967	Utley, Bill (USA)	4:48.12
	Webb, Ken (USA)	4:50.89
	Gilchrist, Sandy (Can)	4:55.60
1971	Furniss, Steve (USA)	4:42.69
	Marmolejo, Ricardo (Mex)	4:49.04
	Colella, Rick (USA)	4:49.30
1975	Furniss, Steve (USA)	4:40.38
	Colella, Rick (USA)	4:40.91
	Marmolejo, Ricardo (Mex)	4:43.89

4 x 100 m. Free-style relay

| 1967 | United States | 3:34.08 |

(Walsh, Ken; Fitzmaurice, Mike; Spitz, Mark, Schollander, Don)

| | Canada | 3:40.82 |
| | Argentina | 3:45.50 |

| 1971 | United States | 3:32.1 |

(Edgar, Dave; Genter, Steve; Heidenreich, Jerry; Heckl, Frank)

| | Canada | 3:38.3 |
| | Brazil | 3:42.4 |

| 1975 | United States | 3:27.6 |

(Babashoff, Jack; Runie, Art; Gratten, Mike; Abbott, Rick)

| | Canada | 3:36.2 |
| | Mexico | 3:39.1 |

4 x 200 m. Free-style relay

| 1951 | United States | 9:00.6 |

(Gora, Ron; Jones, Burwell; Cleveland, Dick; Heusner, Bill)

| | Brazil | 9:13.0 |
| | Argentina | 9:15.5 |

| 1955 | United States | 9:00.0 |

(Smith, Bill; Yorzyk, Bill; Moore, Wayne; McLane, Jimmy)

| | Argentina | 9:09.0 |
| | Canada | 9:12.2 |

| 1959 | United States | 8:22.7 |

(Blick, Richard; Sintz, Peter; Rounsavelle, Dennis; Winters, Frank)

| | Mexico | 8:56.4 |
| | Canada | 9:00.4 |

| 1963 | United States | 8:16.9 |

(Ilman, Gary; McDonough, Ed; Lyons, Dave; Townsend, Ed)

| | Canada | 8:33.0 |
| | Brazil | 8:41.4 |

| 1967 | United States | 8:00.4 |

(Schollander, Don; Hickcox, Charles; Charlton, Greg; Spitz, Mark)

| | Canada | 8:07.1 |
| | Argentina | 8:19.4 |

| 1971 | United States | 7:45.8 |

(Heidenreich, Jerry; McConica, Jerry; Genter, Steve; Heckl, Frank)

| | Canada | 8:04.7 |
| | Brazil | 8:08.4 |

| 1975 | United States | 7:50.9 |

(DeMont, Rick; Favero, Rex; Horner, Brad; Curington, Mike)

| | Canada | 8:00.8 |
| | Brazil | 8:02.3 |

3 x 100 m. Medley relay

| 1951 | United States | 3:16.9 |

(Stack, Allen; Stassforth, Bowen; Cleveland, Dick)

| | Argentina | 3:20.7 |
| | Mexico | 3:22.5 |

4 x 100 m. Medley relay

1955	United States	4:29.1
	(McKinney, Frank; Maguire, Fred; Baarcke, Buddy; Scholes, Clark)	
	Argentina	4:33.4
	Mexico	4:35.5
1959	United States	4:14.9
	(McKinney, Frank; Nakasone, Ken; Troy, Mike; Farrell, Jeff)	
	Canada	4:23.3
	Mexico	4:25.0
1963	United States	4:05.6
	(McGeagh, Dick; Craig, Bill; Richardson, Bill; Kirby, N.)	
	Argentina	4:17.3
	Canada	4:17.4

- -

1967	United States	3:59.31
	(Russell, Doug; Webb, Russell; Spitz, Mark; Walsh, Ken)	
	Canada	4:04.29
	Brazil	4:06.64
1971	United States	3:56.08
	(Murphy, John; Job, Brian; Heidenreich, Jerry; Heckl, Frank)	
	Canada	4:00.53
	Brazil	4:02.94
1975	United States	3:53.81
	(Rocca, Peter; Colella, Rick; Currington, Mike; Babashoff, Jack)	
	Canada	3:58.95
	Brazil	3:59.05

Springboard diving

1951	Capilla, Joaquín (Mex)	201.716
	Anderson, Miller (USA)	199.66
	Lee, Sammy (USA)	191.916
1955	Capilla, Joaquín (Mex)	175.76
	Coffey, Arthur (USA)	160.09
	Clotworthy, Bob (USA)	157.41
1959	Tobian, Gary (USA)	161.40
	Hall, Sammy (USA)	160.08
	Webster, Robert (USA)	148.90
1963	Dinsley, Tom (Can)	154.40
	Gilbert, Richard (USA)	154.17
	Sitzberger, Ken (USA)	148.88
1967	Wrightson, Bernie (USA)	166.95
	Russell, Keith (USA)	163.61
	Escobar, Raul (Col)	137.80
1971	Finneran, Michael (USA)	551.57
	Lincoln, Craig (USA)	537.18
	Robinson, Jose (Mex)	506.58
1975	Moore, Tim (USA)	579.75
	Boggs, Phil (USA)	576.36
	Giron, Carlos (Mex)	562.69

Highboard diving

1951	Capilla, Joaquín (Mex)	159.966
	Lee, Sammy (USA)	153.533
	Anderson, Miller (USA)	136.566
1955	Capilla, Joaquín (Mex)	172.33
	Clotworthy, Bob (USA)	160.62
	Tobian, Gary (USA)	152.21
1959	Gaxiola, Alvaro (Mex)	168.77
	Harper, Don (USA)	164.44
	Botella, Juan (Mex)	162.71
1963	Webster, Robert (USA)	164.12
	Gaxiola, Alvaro (Mex)	158.97
	Capilla, Ricardo (Mex)	139.56
1967	Young, Winn (USA)	154.93
	Rivera, Luís de (Mex)	141.39
	Henad, Diego (Col)	139.85
1971	Earley, Rick (USA)	479.09
	Rydze, Dick (USA)	470.46
	Henad, Diego (Col)	450.30
1975	Giron, Carlo (Mex)	532.83
	Moore, Tim (USA)	529.47
	Vosler, Kent (USA)	507.60

WOMEN

100 m. Free-style

1951	Geary, Sharon (USA)	1:08.4
	Lavine, Jackie (USA)	1:09.9
	Shultz, Ana Marie (Arg)	1:10.6
1955	Stewart, Helen (Can)	1:07.7
	Werner, Wander (USA)	1:07.7
	Grant, Virginia (Can)	1:08.3
1959	Saltza, Chris von (USA)	1:03.8
	Spillane, Joan (USA)	1:05.7
	Botkin, Molly (USA)	1:05.7
1963	Stickles, Terri (USA)	1:02.8
	Stewart, Mary (Can)	1:03.3
	Ellis, Kathy (USA)	1:03.5

- -

1967	Bricker, Erika (USA)	1:00.89
	Lay, Marion (Can)	1:01.02
	Watson, Pokey (USA)	1:01.43
1971	Neilson, Sandra (USA)	1:00.06
	Coughlan, Angela (Can)	1:01.15
	James, Karen (Can)	1:01.88
1975	Peyton, Kin (USA)	58.24
	Sterkel, Jill (USA)	58.57
	Quirk, Jill (Can)	58.92

200 m. Free-style

1951	Shultz, Ana Marie (Arg)	2:32.4
	Mullen, Betty (USA)	2:32.3*
	Holt, Eileen (Arg)	2:36.5

1955	Werner, Wander (USA)	2:32.5
	Gonzalis, Liliana (Arg)	2:32.9
	Aranda, Gilda (Mex)	2:33.6
1959	Saltza, Chris von (USA)	2:18.5
	Stobbs, Shirley (USA)	2:22.9
	Spillane, Joan (USA)	2:23.0
1963	Johnson, Robyn (USA)	2:17.5
	Stickles, Terri (USA)	2:18.4
	Pomfret, Pat (Can)	2:28.4
1967	Kruse, Pam (USA)	2:11.91
	Lay, Marion (Can)	2:14.68
	Coughlan, Angela (Can)	2:15.66
1971	Peyton, Kim (USA)	2:09.62
	Coughlan, Angela (Can)	2:10.56
	Angulo, Olga de (Col)	2:14.34
1975	Peyton, Kim (USA)	2:04.57
	Amundrud, Gail (Can)	2:05.67
	Jardin, Ann (Can)	2:07.68

400 m. Free-style

1951	Shultz, Ana Marie (Arg)	5:26.7
	Green, Carolyn (USA)	5:33.1
	Coutinho, Piedad (Braz)	5:33.6
1955	Wittall, Beth (Can)	5:32.4
	Green, Carolyn (USA)	5:34.7
	Tait, Carol (USA)	5:34.9
1959	Saltza, Chris von (USA)	4:55.9
	Ruuska, Sylvia (USA)	5:03.4
	Graham, Donna (USA)	5:03.5
1963	Finneran, Sharon (USA)	4:52.7
	Johnson, Robyn (USA)	4:56.1
	Pomfret, Pat (Can)	5:20.4
1967	Meyer, Debbie (USA)	4:32.64
	Kruse, Pam (USA)	4:42.81
	Coughlan, Angela (Can)	4:48.88
1971	Simmons, Ann (USA)	4:26.19
	Strong, Jill (USA)	4:36.15
	Coughlan, Angela (Can)	4:38.86
1975	Heddy, Kathy (USA)	4:23.01
	Wickstrand, Kathie (USA)	4:27.66
	Oliver, Mich (Can)	4:30.20

800 m. Free-style

1967	Meyer, Debbie (USA)	9:22.9
	Pedersen, Sue (USA)	9:38.4
	Coughlan, Angela (Can)	9:48.6
1971	Calhoun, Cathy (USA)	9:15.19
	Enze, Cindy (USA)	9:32.15
	Ramirez, María T. (Mex)	9:44.32
1975	Weinberg, Wendy (USA)	9:05.47
	Montgomery, Mary (USA)	9:06.70
	Stenhouse, Jan (Can)	9:17.86

100 m. Back-stroke

1951	O'Brien, Maureen (USA)	1:18.5
	Donahue, Sheila (USA)	1:20.5
	Bruggeman, Magda (Mex)	1:21.4
1955	Fisher, Leonore (Can)	1:16.7
	O'Connor, Coralie (USA)	1:17.8
	Gill, Cynthia (USA)	1:17.9
1959	Cone, Carin (USA)	1:12.2
	Barber, Sara (Can)	1:12.3
	Kluter, Chris (USA)	1:12.4
1963	Harmar, Nina (USA)	1:11.5
	Ferguson, Cathy (USA)	1:31.1
	Weir, Eileen (Can)	1:14.5
1967	Tanner, Elaine (Can)	1:07.32
	Hall, Kaye (USA)	1:09.76
	Cazalet, Shirley (Can)	1:11.33
1971	Gurr, Donna-Marie (Can)	1:07.18
	Atwood, Sue (USA)	1:07.51
	Halay, Jill (USA)	1:08.49
1975	Chenard, Lyne (Can)	1:06.59
	Boone, Rosemary (USA)	1:07.18
	Kemp, Jenny (USA)	1:07.29

200 m. Back-stroke

1967	Tanner, Elaine (Can)	2:24.44
	Moore, Kendis (USA)	2:30.38
	Ferguson, Cathy (USA)	2:32.48
1971	Gurr, Donna-Marie (Can)	2:24.73
	Atwood, Sue (USA)	2:26.48
	Darby, Barbara (USA)	2:30.73
1975	Wennerstrom, Donna (USA)	
		2:19.93
	Chenard, Lyne (Can)	2:21.36
	Gibson, Cheryl (Can)	2:22.68

100 m. Breast-stroke

1967	Ball, Catie (USA)	1:14.80
	Norbis, Ana Marie (Uru)	1:15.95
	Goyette, Cynthis (USA)	1:19.39
1971	Dockerill, Sylvia (Can)	1:18.63
	Kurtz, Linda (USA)	1:19.30
	Colella, Lynn (USA)	1:19.72
1975	Siering, Laura (USA)	1:15.17
	Morey, Marcia (USA)	1:16.25
	Stuart, Marian (Can)	1:16.40

200 m. Breast-stroke

1951	Turnbull, Dorotea (Arg)	3:08.4
	Rhode, Beatriz (Arg)	3:10.3
	Pence, Carol (USA)	3:14.7
1955	Elsenius, Mary-L (USA)	3:08.4
	Sears, Mary-J (USA)	3:09.0
	Rhode, Beatriz (Arg)	3:09.4

1959	Warner, Ann (USA)	2:56.8
	Kempner, Patty (USA)	3:00.1
	Bancroft, Anne (USA)	3:01.3
1963	Driscoll, Alice (USA)	2:56.2
	Whipple, Roby (USA)	2:57.7
	Wilmink, Marjon (Can)	3:00.0
1967	Ball, Catie (USA)	2:42.18
	Kolb, Claudia (USA)	2:48.93
	Norbis, Ana Maria (Uru)	2:50.70
1971	Colella, Lynn (USA)	2:50.03
	Wright, Jane (Can)	2:50.96
	Urueta, Leonor (Mex)	2:52.72
1975	Siering, Laura (USA)	2:42.35
	Baker, Joanna (Can)	2:42.96
	Morey, Marcia (USA)	2:45.58

100 m. Butterfly

1955	Wittall, Beth (Can)	1:16.2
	Mullen, Betty (USA)	1:16.5
	Mann, Shelley (USA)	1:17.7
1959	Collins, Becky (USA)	1:09.5
	Ramey, Nancy (USA)	1:10.4
	Botkin, Molly (USA)	1:12.3
1963	Ellis, Kathy (USA)	1:07.6
	Stewart, Mary (Can)	1:08.9
	Worley, Kim (USA)	1:11.6
1967	Daniel, Ellie (USA)	1:05.24
	Tanner, Elaine (Can)	1:05.35
	Corson, Marilyn (Can)	1:07.68
1971	Deardurff, Deena (USA)	1:06.22
	Cliff, Leslie (Can)	1:07.77
	Burle, Lucy (Braz)	1:08.79
1975	Wright, Camille (USA)	1:02.71
	Tosdal, Peggy (USA)	1:03.37
	Quirk, Wendy (Can)	1:05.07

200 m. Butterfly

1967	Kolb, Claudia (USA)	2:25.49
	Davis, Lee (USA)	2:26.74
	Corson, Marilyn (Can)	2:30.54
1971	Colella, Lynn (USA)	2:23.11
	Jones, Alice (USA)	2:28.10
	Smith, Susan (Can)	2:32.60
1975	Wright, Camille (USA)	2:18.57
	Gibson, Cheryl (Can)	2:21.95
	Ribeiro, Rosemary (Bra)	2:22.47

200 m. Individual medley

1967	Kolb, Claudia (USA)	2:26.06
	Pedersen, Sue (USA)	2:30.91
	Dowler, Sandra (Can)	2:36.18
1971	Cliff, Leslie (Can)	2:30.03
	Atwood, Sue (USA)	2:30.29
	Plaistead, Cindy (USA)	2:33.23

1975	Heddy, Kathy (USA)	2:22.22
	Franks, Jenny (USA)	2:23.37
	Gibson, Cheryl (Can)	2:25.54

400 m. Individual medley

1967	Kolb, Claudia (USA)	5:09.68
	Pedersen, Sue (USA)	5:21.57
	Corson, Marilyn (Can)	5:36.75
1971	Cliff, Leslie (Can)	5:13.31
	Plaistead, Cindy (USA)	5:13.64
	Atwood, Sue (USA)	5:13.75
1975	Heddy, Kathy (USA)	5:06.05
	Gibson, Cheryl (Can)	5:06.87
	Franks, Jenny (USA)	5:08.08

4 x 100 m. Free-style

1951	United States	4:37.1
	(Green, Carolyn; Geary, Sharon; Lavine, Jackie; Mullen, Betty)	
	Argentina	4:38.1
	Brazil	5:03.6
1955	United States	5:11.6
	(Kluter, Gretchen; Green, Carolyn; Roberts, Judith; Werner, Wanda)	
	Canada	4:38.1
	Argentina	4:43.7
1959	United States	4:17.5
	(Botkin, Molly; Spillane, Joan; Stobbs, Shirley; Saltza, Chris von)	
	Canada	4:31.9
	Mexico	4:37.0
1963	United States	4:15.7
	(MacCleary, E.; Ellis, Kathy; Templeton, M.; Varona, Donna de)	
	Canada	4:31.7
	Brazil	4:34.3
1967	United States	4:04.57
	(Fordyce, Wendy; Gustavson, Linda; Carpinelli, Pam; Kruse, Pam)	
	Canada	4:09.73
	Puerto Rico	4:26.56
1971	United States	4:04.20
	(Neilson, Sandra; Fordyce, Wendy; McKitterick, Kathy; Skrifvars, Lynn)	
	Canada	4:10.52
	Brazil	4:15.24
1975	United States	3:53.31
	(Heddy, Kathy; Brown, Bonnie; Sterkel, Jill; Peyton, Kim)	
	Canada	3:54.95
	Brazil	4:12.20

3 x 100 m. Medley relay

1951	United States	3:49.3

(O'Brien, Maureen; Pence, Carol; Geary, Sharon)

	Argentina	3:59.7
	Mexico	4:13.2

4 x 100 m. Medley relay

1955	United States	5:11.6

(O'Connor, Coralie; Sears, Mary-J; Mullen, Betty; Werner, Wanda)

	Canada	5:12.2
	Argentina	5:30.5

1959	United States	4:44.6

(Cone, Carin; Bancroft, Anne; Collins, Becky; Saltza, Chris von)

	Canada	4:58.7
	Mexico	5:18.7

1963	United States	4:49.1

(Duenkel, Ginny; Goyette, Cynthia; Stouder, Sharon; Varona, Donna de)

	Canada	4:52.5
	Venezuela	5:11.8

- -

1967	United States	4:29.97

(Moore, Kendis; Ball, Catie, Daniel; Ellie; Fordyce, Wendy)

	Canada	4:40.88
	Uruguay	4:49.27

1971	Canada	4:35.50

(Gurr, Donna-Marie; Wright, Jane; Cliff, Leslie; Coughlan, Angela)

	United States	4:36.73
	Mexico	4:45.18

1975	United States	4:22.34

(Boone, Rosemary; Morey, Marcia; Wright, Camille; Peyton, Kim)

	Canada	4:24.84
	Brazil	4:37.67

Springboard diving

1951	Cunningham, Mary (USA)	131.93
	McCormick, Pat (USA)	128.08
	Castillo, Dolores (Guat)	109.94
1955	McCormick, Pat (USA)	142.42
	Stunyo, Jeanne (USA)	137.41
	Houghton, Emily (USA)	133.12
1959	Pope (nee Meyers), Paula (USA)	139.23
	Lenzi, Joel (USA)	137.62
	Dudeck, Barbara (USA)	131.21
1963	McAlister, Barbara (USA)	144.31
	Stewart, Judy (Can)	135.63
	Willard, Pasty (USA)	131.00
1967	Gossick, Sue (USA)	150.41
	King, Micki (USA)	147.34
	McDonald, Kathy (Can)	142.40

1971	Carruthers, Elizabeth (Can)	435.24
	King, Micki (USA)	432.51
	Boys, Beverley (Can)	425.01
1975	Chandler, Denise (USA)	427.62
	Carruthers, Elizabeth (Can)	424.62
	McIngvale (nee Potter), Cynthia (USA)	407.87

Highboard diving

1951	McCormick, Pat (USA)	65.71
	Rios, Carlotta (Mex)	65.13
	Cunningham, Mary (USA)	51.53
1955	McCormick, Pat (USA)	94.05
	Irwin (nee Stover), Juno (USA)	80.32
	Pesado, Margarita (Mex)	65.74
1959	Pope (nee Myers), Paula (USA)	97.13
	Irwin (nee Stover), Juno (USA)	90.64
	Sparling, Tahiea (USA)	87.86
1963	Cooper, Linda (USA)	100.35
	Poulsen, Nancy (USA)	96.07
	Adamses, Maria (Mex)	86.70
1967	Bush, Lesley (USA)	108.20
	Boys, Beverley (Can)	103.09
	Peterson, Ann (USA)	98.28
1971	Robertson, Nancy (Can)	375.12
	Boys, Beverley (Can)	363.57
	Lipman, Debby (USA)	362.01
1975	Nutter, Janet (Can)	162.00
	Ely, Janet (USA)	147.45
	Cuthbert, Linda (Can)	144.03

Synchronized swimming solo

1975	Buzonas (nee Johnson), Gail (USA)	139.70
	Fortier, Sylvia (Can)	138.37
	Guardia, Lourdes de la (Cub)	112.66

Synchronized swimming duet

1975	Curren, Robin/ Norrish, Amanda (USA)	135.46
	Stewart, Carol/ Wilkin, Laura (Can)	131.39
	Martinez, Sara/ Foyo, Alicia (Cub)	109.71

Synchronized swimming team

1975	United States	135.31
	Canada	129.47
	Mexico	108.63

PHELPS, Brian (Great Britain. 21 Apr. 1944-). Diving is not a sport for records, yet the career of Brian Phelps from East Ham is studded with them. He was the youngest man to win a European diving championship—at 14, for highboard in 1958. He was the only champion, swimmer or diver, to defend a title four years later—and he won again. He was the youngest man to represent Britian and he had won more gold medals (four) at the Commonwealth Games than any other diver, man or woman, until Don Wagstaffe (Aus) emulated him in 1970/74.

Phelps, the perfectionist with the ideal competitive temperament, was the first British man in thirty-six years—and only the second ever—to win an Olympic diving medal. This was in 1960, when he took the bronze on the highboard in Rome. He dived also in the 1964 Olympics for sixth place.

His first appearance for Britain was against Italy on 3 Aug. 1957—he was then 13 years 3 months and 12 days old and he had to learn two difficult voluntary dives in a hurry in order to compete. The same year, he won the first of his fourteen A.S.A. titles, the high plain.

The next year, although having hospital treatment for a badly strained shoulder, he was second in the Commonwealth highboard for England, only 3.3 points behind Scotland's veteran Peter Heatly. Six weeks later, Phelps was champion of Europe, having beaten men old enough to be his father and he won by the tremendous margin of 7.17 points.

It was harder in the 1962 Europeans in Leipzig but Mr. Consistency Phelps kept his highboard crown. But in 1966, in Utrecht, after a row over judging, he had to bow to Italy's Klaus Dibiasi, who went on to become Olympic champion in 1968.

Phelps appeared in three Commonwealth Games and in 1962 and '66 added four golds—for the springboard and highboard diving doubles—to his 1958 silver. He was undefeated from the highboard in Britain from 1958-66, winning the A.S.A. title eight times (he could not compete through injury in 1963). He was also springboard champion 1960-62 and took the plain diving in 1957 (at 13), 1960 and 1961.

PINKSTON, Clarence (United States, 2 Feb. 1900-61) and **BECKER**, Betty (6 Mar. 1903-). Husband and wife Olympic champions, Clarence from Wichita, Kansas, won the 1920 highboard title and was runner-up in the springboard in Antwerp and four years later won the two diving bronze medals. He married Betty Becker from Philadelphia after her springboard gold and highboard silver successes in the 1924 Paris Olympics and coached his wife to her second Olympic crown, on the highboard, in 1928. Clarence was honoured by the Hall of Fame in 1966 and Betty a year later—a truly remarkable family double.

PIRIE, Irene (Canada), see MILTON FAMILY.

PLUNGING. A plunge is the shallow dive used by competitors to start all races except back-stroke (in which competitors start in the water). The perfect starting dive requires the greatest amount of forward momentum and the minimum amount of submergence.

This principle is also important in distance-plunging competitions which were most popular in Britain until the 1940s because there were no age barriers to hamper success. The competitor took a standing plunge from a firm take-off, then floated motionless, face downwards, until his breath gave out or 60 seconds had elapsed, whichever was the shorter. No progressive actions were allowed except the impetus from the dive. Championships were decided on the best distance of three attempts.

Plunging was held only once in the Olympics, in 1904, when America, with a preponderance of entries in all events, took all three medals. W. E. Dickey, the winner, plunged 62 ft. 6 in. which compared unfavourably with the 75 ft. 4 in. of John Jarvis in taking the A.S.A. title that year, but who did not go to St. Louis.

PLUNGING, A.S.A. CHAMPIONS. Plunging championships were instituted in 1883 and discontinued in 1947 after two breaks during World Wars I and II. Of the fifty-two championships held, Frank Parrington won eleven times between 1926 and 1939, W. Allason ten (1896-1922) and W. Taylor eight (1895-

1906). The full list of champions is:

		ft.	in.
1883	Clarke T.H.	63	2
1884	Davenport, Horace	64	8
1885	Davenport, Horace	72	10½
1886	Davenport, Horace	67	11½
1887	Blake, G.A.	73	10½
1888	Blake, G.A.	71	3
1889	Blake, G.A.	73	5
1890	Blake, G.A.	69	3
1891	Blake, G.A.	67	3
1892	Wilson, H.A.	59	6
1893	Dadd, S.T.	64	3
1894	McHugh, J.	64	4
1895	Taylor, W.	65	3
1896	Allason, W.	73	4
1897	Allason, W.	68	11
1898	Taylor, W.	78	9
1899	Taylor, W.	73	9
1900	Taylor, W.	75	11
1901	Taylor, W.	78	0
1902	Allason, W.	73	10
1903	Taylor, W.	74	0
1904	Jarvis, John	75	4
1905	Taylor, W.	75	7
1906	Taylor, W.	82	7
1907	Allason, W.	75	10½
1908	Allason, W.	78	7
1909	Allason, W.	74	2¾
1910	Allason, W.	79	0
1911	Allason, W.	81	5
1912	Smith, W.H.M.	69	1¾

1913	Davison, H.	73	3
1914-19	No events		
1920	Davison, H.	71	9
1921	Allason, W.	78	6
1922	Allason, W.	73	8½
1923	Beaumont, Arthur	75	11
1924	Beaumont, Arthur	75	5
1925	Wilson, William	74	3½
1926	Parrington, Frank	85	6
1927	Parrington, Frank	80	9
1928	Parrington, Frank	81	0
1929	Parrington, Frank	85	4
1930	Beaumont, Arthur	85	10
1931	Beaumont, Arthur	85	9½
1932	Beaumont, Arthut	80	11
1933	Parrington, Frank	84	6
1934	Parrington, Frank	84	1½
1935	Parrington, Frank	84	0
1936	Parrington, Frank	80	6
1937	Parrington, Frank	80	7¾
1938	Parrington, Frank	81	7½
1939	Parrington, Frank	76	2½
1940-45	No events		
1946	Snow, J.C.	76	4½
1947	Discontinued		

POYNTON, Dorothy (see HILL [nee POYNTON], Dorothy).

PROSUMENSHIKOVA, Galina (USSR). See STEPANOVA, GALINA.

RADMILOVIC, Paul (Great Britain, 5 Mar. 1886-1968). The Olympic record of Paul (Paulo) Radmilovic is one of the most amazing in the history of organized swimming. He competed in five Olympic Games from 1908 to 1928 (London, Stockholm, Antwerp, Paris and Amsterdam) and in the 1906 Interim Games in Athens. And he won gold medals at three of them.

He was a member of the British waterpolo team who won in London in 1908 and captained the gold medal teams in 1912 and 1920. He was also in the winning 4 x 200 m. relay squad in 1908. Had the war not stopped the holding of the 1916 Games, Raddy, as he was best known, must have achieved a record number of appearances (and gold medals) in the pool.

Raddy, whose father was Greek and mother Irish, was in international swimming for thirty years—from the age of 16 to 45. He won nine A.S.A. championships from 100 y. to 5 miles and the span of his successes was remarkable. He took the sprint in 1909 in 61.0; the 440 y. in 1925 (5:41.2); the 880 y. in 1926 (11:57.4); one mile in 1925, '26, '27 (best time 24:27.0 in 1925 and '26); the long distance (five miles in the River Thames) in 1907 and 1925 and 1926 (best time 1 hr. 5:06.4 in 1925). There were twenty years between his first and last long distance victories and in 1926 he was 40.

His Welsh championship winning record was equally impressive. He won the 100 y. title fifteen times between 1901 and 1922 (with six races cancelled because of the war and W. J. Kimber winning in 1921). The 220 and 440 y. championships were not instituted until 1927, when Raddy was 41, yet he won

the quarter in 1929 in a championships record of 5:44.2 that stood until 1938. He was the first winner of the 880 y. (1910) and won for the sixth time in 1929.

A scratch golfer, an outstanding footballer, Welshman Raddy, born in Cardiff but who lived most of his life in Weston-super-Mare, continued to swim for sheer pleasure almost until the day he died. At 78 he was still swimming a quarter-mile each day. He was honoured by the Hall of Fame in 1967.

RAUSCH, Emil (Germany, 11 Sept. 1882-15 Feb. 1954). The last man to win an Olympic gold medal swimming side-stroke, Rausch won the 880 and mile at the 1904 Games, in 13:11.4 and 26:18.2, and came third in the 220 y. He also won a silver medal in Germany's relay team at the 1906 Interim Games. He won national titles between 1900 and 1910 for distances from 100 to 7,500 m. and was awarded a gold honour medal for helping to promote life-saving in England.

RAWLS, Katherine (United States, 14 June 1918-). Probably the world's greatest all-round aquatic performer, Katherine Rawls was a fine diver—bronze medallist from the springboard at the 1932 Olympics (at 14) and again in 1936. She was a remarkable swimmer—a bronze medal in the American freestyle relay squad in the 1936 Games was just one of her achievements. And had the medley individual event existed outside America in her days she must have been Olympic champion.

The oldest and best of the Rawls sisters from Fort Lauderdale—baby Peggy was in shows at 18 months, and there were Dorothy and Evelyn (who made United States national relay teams)—Katherine was a girl before her time. She twice won four titles at national championships—the first woman to do so. The first was in 1933 with the improbable combination of springboard diving, 200 m. breast-stroke, 880 y. free-style and 300 m. medley (before the days of butterfly). She won thirty-three national titles—more than any other woman—in the days when there were only seven individual women's events, against the twelve of the modern era.

Katherine never held a world record, but she was undefeated in individual medley events for eight years (1932-39) and her performances were looked upon as world bests. World War II and a fascination for flying spelt the end of her pool career. She became one of the world's top women flyers and one of the original twenty-five glamorous women pilots who ferried planes to combat zones for the Air Transport Command.

RECORDS. There are records for all levels of swimming, from world and continental, national and area, junior and down to the youngest age groups (see AGE GROUP). There are Games and championship records, i.e., the best performances in competition during the Olympic, Commonwealth or Pan-American Games or the World and European championships. There are records for individual and relay events and for all recognized strokes and distances.

Generally, records are classified under the headings of long course (see LONG COURSE) and short course (see SHORT COURSE). At the upper echelon (World, European, Commonwealth, etc.) only long course metric records are recognized. At other levels there are usually short and long course lists.

The world record list, which is the basis of all other records and ranking lists of importance, was cut to a tidy thirty-one events during the F.I.N.A. Congress at the 1968 Mexico Olympics to be operative from 1 Jan. 1969 as follows:

Men: 100, 200, 400, 800, 1,500, 4 x 100 and 4 x 200 m. free-style, 100 and 200 m. back-stroke, breast-stroke and butterfly and 200, 400 and 4 x 100 m. medley = 16.

Women: 100, 200, 400, 800, 1,500, and 4 x 100 m. free-style, 100 and 200 m. back-stroke, breast-stroke and butterfly and 200, 400 and 4 x 100 m. medley = 15.

RELAY RACING. This is a team competition in which squads—normally four —race successively in order to produce an aggregate time. Relays are excellent tests of the strength of a country or a club.

At the take-over between swimmers 1 and 2, 2 and 3 and 3 and 4, the incoming racer must have touched the wall before the feet of the out-going teammate have lost touch with the starting block. Failure to do this is described as a 'flyer' and results in disqualification. Only the first swimmer, who starts on the gun, can set an individual record in a relay.

Relay events were in the Olympics first in 1904 when there was a 4 x 50 y. free-style race for men, but only clubs sides from the United States took part. It was in 1906, at the Interim Games in Athens, that the standard 4 x 200 m. event was first contested and was won by Hungary. In 1912 a 4 x 100 m. event for women was included and Britain were the winners.

In 1960, 4 x 100 m. medley relays for men and women were added to the Olympic programme, but before this there had been medley relay events in the Commonwealth Games (from 1934) and the European championships (1958).

Despite the early start of relay racing, it was not until 1932 that world relay records by national teams were recognized with the ratification of the Olympic winning times of Japan's men (4 x 200 m., 8:58.4) and America's women (4 x 100 m., 4:38.0).

REYNOLDS. Peter (Australia, 17 June 1945-). An Olympic medley relay bronze medallist in 1964, Reynolds from New South Wales, had his best year in 1966 when, in the Commonwealth Games in Jamaica, he won four gold medals.

Reynolds took the 220 y. back-stroke and 440 y. medley in world record times (2:12.0 and 4:50.8), the 110 y. back-stroke (62.4) and swam in Australia's 4 x 220 y. free-style team, who broke the world record (7:59.5) and became the first squad to go under eight minutes. Reynolds would have won a record five golds in one Games had not the Australian team been disqualified for a 'flying' take-over in the 4 x 110 y. medley, having been inside the world record in touching finish.

RICHTER, Ulrike (East Germany, 17 June, 1952-). An outstanding back-stroker, Ulrike Richter set six world records—more than any other swimmer— in 1974. She reduced the 100 m. time by 1½ sec. to 1:02.98 in four swims in seven weeks and improved the 200 m. figures by 1.8 sec. to 2:17.35.

She beat America's Olympic double

champion Melissa Belote (see BELOTE, Melissa) to win the 1973 World 100 m. title in Belgrade where her opening world record back-stroke leg in the medley relay set her team on the way to an amazing nine sec. victory over the United States.

In Vienna, in 1947, she beat her team-mate Ulrike Tauber (see TAUBER, Ulrike) into second place by two sec. over 100 m. and 1½ sec. over 200 m. and won a third gold in the medley relay.

Yet, amazingly, the year before she burst on the scene to become World champion, Tauber had not swum fast enough on either distance to get into the world's top 50 ranking lists for 1972.

RIGGIN, Aileen (United States, 2 May 1906-). Winner of the first Olympic springboard diving title for women, Aileen Riggin was a tiny child and had just passed her fourteenth birthday in 1920 when she beat her team-mate Helen Wainwright by 5.8 points for the gold medal. At the time, she was the youngest Olympic champion. America's Marjorie Gestring took Aileen's 'babe' record in 1936 when she also won the springboard title, three months before her fourteenth birthday (see GESTRING, MARJORIE).

Four years after this remarkable feat, Aileen became the first competitor in the history of the Games to win medals for swimming and diving . . . by coming third in the 100 m. back-stroke (1:28.2) as well as winning the silver for spring-board diving.

Aileen, born in Newport, Rhode Island, was high point woman for swim-ming and diving at a United States championships meeting, won three out-door and one indoor springboard titles and was a member of two teams who won American relay titles. She made the first under-water and slow-motion swim-ming and diving films for Grantland Rice in 1922 and '23.

She turned professional in 1926, toured the world, appeared in many Hollywood pictures, helped to coach and starred in Billy Rose's first Aqua-cade, at the 1937 Cleveland Exposition, and wrote articles for many of the prestige women's magazines.

RITTER, R. Max (Germany/United States, 7 Nov. 1886-23 May 1974). A leader of world swimming, Richard Max Ritter played a unique part in the develop-ment of the sport since the foundation of F.I.N.A. in 1908 (see FEDERATION INTERNATIONALE DE NATATION AMATEUR).

Born in Magdeburg, the son of a well-to-do manufacturer, Ritter spent the years of 1905-09 in London, during which he swam for Germany in the 1908 Olympics, reaching the semi-finals of the back-stroke. He was the spokesman for Germany at the F.I.N.A. founding meet-ing and also swam for the country of his birth in the 1912 Olympics. Follow-ing high school, he had gone into the chemical business and after his spell in London his job took him to the United States. By 1916 he was an American citizen, building up a cloth dyeing and finishing company and becoming a millionaire.

But before leaving Germany in 1904, he took his first step in swimming ad-ministration by founding the successful Hellas Club in his home town. In America, he became a member of the New York Athletic Club and continued to race and play polo. By 1936 he was the United States representative on the F.I.N.A. Bureau and in 1946 he took on the dual office of Hon. Secretary and Treasurer. The two-year financial steward-ship of this astute business man resulted in a much improved F.I.N.A. bank balance. He continued as secretary until 1952, was elected president in 1960 and an honorary member in 1964.

He pioneered—and often paid for out of his own pocket—many projects for the betterment of swimming, in-cluding the Ritter judging machine (de-velopment costs around $10,000), the first machine in swimming to record the finishing order of a race on a paper tape. Nor surprisingly, Ritter was the first swimming administrator to be honoured by the Hall of Fame (1965).

ROBIE, Carl (United States, 12 May 1945-). At 23 and considered to be past his best, Robie rocked the swimming world by winning the 1968 Olympic 200 m. butterfly gold while his fancied team-mate Mark Spitz, the world record-holder, finished last in the final. Robie's victory in Mexico was carefully and quietly planned. Four years earlier, he had missed golds in Tokyo in two events —200 m. butterfly (2nd) and 400 m. medley (4th)—having been the fastest qualifier for the final in each event. In 1968 he went for one event only and in a predicted American medal hat trick Robie had been put down for the bronze. He entered the final as an equal fourth fastest qualifier, but in the big race he was leading at 100 m. and he beat off the late challenge from Britain's Martyn Woodroffe to win by three-tenths in 2:08.7.

Robie played a part in two eras of top ranking swimming—an unusual achievement particularly for an American. He broke his first world record on 19 Aug. 1961—200 m. butterfly in 2:12.6. He trimmed this to 2:12.4 and 2:10.8 in separate races on the same day, (11 Aug. 1962) and to 2:08.2 a year later. He won the Pan-American 200 m. butterfly title in 1963, but was not in the United States team to defend his crown four years later. Then he came back to his greatest triumph in Mexico.

ROSE, Murray (Australia, 6 Jan. 1939-). British born Murray Rose, who emigrated with his parents to Australia as a baby, became the youngest triple Olympic gold medallist in 1956 when he won the 400 and 1,500 m. and was a member of the Australian world record-breaking winning 4 x 200 m. squad. He made history again in 1960 when he became the first man to win a distance title, in this case the 400 m., at successive Games. With a silver in the 1,500 m. and a bronze in the free-style relay in Rome. Rose's Olympic medal tally was four golds, a silver and a bronze.

Rose certainly would have swum in a third Olympics, in Tokyo in 1964, but for a row with officials of the Australian Swimming Union. They demanded that Rose return from the United States to take part in national trials and refused to pick him when he said he could not come. Rose's answer, in the months before the Games, was to break the world records for 880 y. and 1,500 m. And still Australia would not add him to the team.

He swam in only one Commonwealth Games, in 1962, when he won the 440 and 1,650 y. titles and two more golds in the free-style relays. His nine world records included three for 400 m. (first = 4:25.9 in 1957/last = 4:13.4 in 1962). 440 y. (4:27.1, 1957), 800 m. (8:51.3, 1962), 880 y. (9:34.2, 1956 and 8:55.5, 1964), 1,500 m. (17:59.5, 1956, and

17:01.8, 1964).

The Rose family came from Nairn in the Scottish Highlands and trace their origins back to Hugh de Ros, one of the early Scottish barons. Rose's ancestors fought for Bonnie Prince Charlie at Culloden in 1746 and the family have their own tartan, coat of arms and the motto 'Constant and True'.

In Australia, the family lived in Double Bay, a fashionable Sydney resort. But Murray finished his education at the University of Southern California where he graduated in drama and television in 1962. He was raised from birth on a diet which excluded meat, fish, poultry, refined flour and sugar. Wheatgerm, honey and seaweed were some of his substitute foods.

American coaches called Rose 'the greatest swimmer ever . . . greater even than Johnny Weissmuller'. He was awarded, by the American Amateur Athletic Union in 1962, a special trophy (given to only one other individual in history) for his major contribution to sport. The same year he received the Helms Foundation World Trophy. He featured on a postage stamp issued by the Dominican Republic, was entertained on the royal yacht *Britannia* by the Queen and Prince Philip and, in 1965, was one of the first swimmers to be honoured by the Hall of Fame.

ROSS, Norman (United States, 2 May, 1896-19 June 1953). Winner of three golds at the 1920 Olympics, Ross was an outstanding swimmer, but also a showman, a leader and a brave man, as his decoration by General Pershing during World War I indicates.

His Olympic victories in Antwerp were in the 400, 1,500 and 4 x 200 m. relay, just a year after he had taken five firsts at the 1919 Allied War Games.

Ross broke 14 world records . . . led the American team revolt during the 1920 Games over the transport (a troop carrier) which had brought them to Belgium and which the squad were determined would not be used to take them home again . . . married a Hawaiian Princess . . . and became America's first classical disc jockey.

ROTH, Dick (United States, 26 Sept. 1947-). Richard Roth's special claim to fame, in addition to winning the 400

m. medley at the 1964 Tokyo Olympics, was that he earned his gold medal in a world record 4:45.4 despite the fact that he had an appendix attack the night before his final. Told he must have an emergency operation, he said: 'Not until after the race'.

The winning time of Roth, from the amazingly-successful Santa Clara Swim Club, remained in the world record book for almost four years until Russia's Andrei Dunaev was able to trim one-tenth off the American's Tokyo mark.

Roth won six United States outdoor medley titles—the 200 m. (1963-65) in the days before world records were recognized for this distance and 400 m. (1964-66). But like so many talented American stars, he retired young, at 19, with perhaps his best swimming years ahead of him.

ROTHHAMMER, Keena (United States, 26 Feb. 1957-). Miss All-America from Little Rock, Arkansas, with her dark hair and vivacious personality—that's Keena Rothhammer, the 1972 Olympic 800 m. champion and winner of the 200 m. at the 1973 World championships.

A talented free-styler with a racing range from 200 to 1,500 m., Rothhammer's performances were unpredictable, except that she always won something. In Munich she was America's third string for 800 m. with a best time of 9:04.67, yet she took the gold medal in a world record 8:53.68. She was the first string for the 400 m. and came sixth. And she was the U.S. second-best for 200 m. and held this place for the bronze behind her American team-mate Shirley Babashoff and the winner Shane Gould of Australia (see biographies).

It was a similar story at the World championships in Belgrade. Keena was the 200 m. second string and came first. She was first string and world record-holder (4:08.07) for 400 m. and came second. And in her Olympic gold medal 800 m. she didn't win a medal at all.

Sadly Keena retired from swimming—at the ripe old age of 16 years six months.

ROYAL LIFE SAVING SOCIETY. The Life Saving Society was formed in 1891 to reduce the annual toll of 2,000 lives lost by drowning in the United Kingdom by publicising the causes of such deaths, by encouraging everyone to learn to swim and by teaching competent swimmers individual methods of rescuing a drowning person.

The work of the Society quickly attracted the attention of Royalty and in 1904 the Society was granted permission to use the title "Royal".

Meanwhile the Society had visited several countries in Europe where life saving societies soon sprang up. It was not long before visits were made to the various Dominions and Colonies who soon took up the work and formed their own Scoieties, or branches of the United Kingdom Society.

The aims of the R.L.S.S. were laid down in a charter of 1924. Those aims remain valid today and are expressed in the Society's work which is (a) the teaching of water safety (b) the teaching of individual rescue methods (c) the teaching of resuscitation (d) the provision of rescue teams or lifeguards. Emphasis varies from country to country according to circumstances. The work is largely carried on by volunteers whose aim is to see that every competent swimmer is a trained life saver.

Since 1891 over nine million graded tests have been taken successfully with a steadily increasing yearly total. Proper teaching and testing are very important since an attempt at rescue by an untrained person whose skill does not match his courage may end in a double tragedy.

The four aspects of the Society's work are directed at the public who frequent inland waters as well as the sea since they can never be fully supervised and an individual acting on his own initiative and without aids may well be the only one capable of preventing a tragedy. It is important to forestall tragedy, hence the need to alert the general public, particularly the young, many of whom drown before they have a chance to learn to swim.

The various water safety tests, life saving tests and resuscitation training provide a series of skills that can be started in childhood and lead to qualifications enabling life savers to give a voluntary service to the community through the life guard clubs. The value of the Society's training is shown by the fact that despite an ever increasing use of water for recreation the number of drownings has been reduced to well under 1,000 annually.

Now the Society is truly a Commonwealth Society, under the grand presidency of H.R.H. Princess Alexandra who succeeded the Earl of Mountbatten of Burma in 1973. National Societies are controlled by the Commonwealth Council from the headquarters in London. They are:

United Kingdom. 50 branches in England, Wales, Scotland and Ireland and 12 overseas branches and 19 honorary overseas representatives virtually encircling the globe.

Canada. Ten branches covering all but the more remote and virtually uninhabited areas.

Australia. Nine branches covering the whole of the continent. Paupa, New Guinea and Fiji.

New Zealand. 15 branches throughout the Dominion.

Malaysia. The branch covers the whole of the country.

RYAN, Noel (Australia, 1912-69). Winner of four Commonwealth gold medals, Noel Ryan died doing what he liked most—swimming. He collapsed after competing in a half-mile race at Manly Beach, Sydney, age 57.

His Commonwealth victories were at the first Games in 1930, when he won the 440 y. in 4:39.8, seven sec. ahead of New Zealand's George Bridson and the 1,500 y. (18.55.4), again beating Bridson, this time by 45.6. In 1935, he beat England's Norman Wainwright, for the 440 y. gold (5:03.0) and Canada's Bob Pirie, with Wainwright third, in the 1,500 y. (18:25.4−30 sec. faster than in 1930). Only one man swimmer, Ian O'Brien, the Olympic breast-stroke champion (see O'BRIEN, IAN) had won more Commonwealth golds prior to 1970, when Mike Wenden (see WENDEN, MIKE) brought his tally to seven in Edinburgh.

Ryan won fifteen Australian titles and had his best times on his last victories: 100 y., 1934 (55.8); 220 y., 1931, '37 (2:18.2); 440 y., 1931, '33, '37 (5:00.2), 880 y., 1929, '31, '33, '34 (10.29.2); mile, 1928, '29, '31, '33, '34 (21:36.6).

SALTZA, Chris von (United States, 13 Jan. 1944-). Susan Christine von Saltza, who is still recognized as a baroness in the 'Who's Who' of Swedish nobility, was in 1957 the first star to spring from the then new American age-group programme, set up following the heavy United States defeats at the hands of Australia in the 1956 Melbourne Olympics.

The tangible proof of her talent, ability and willingness to work, are the three golds and a silver she won at the 1960 Rome Olympics in which she was first in the 400 m. (4:50.6) and America's world record-breaking medley and free-style relay teams and second (62.8), 1.6 behind Australia's Dawn Fraser in the 100 m.

Yet it was for back-stroke and not free-style that Chris won her first United States outdoor title, at 13, for 220 y. in 2:40.2 (1957). She won again in 1958, over 200 m. in a world record 2:37.4. On free-style, Chris was first in the 100 m.–110 y. 1958-60. 200 m./ 220 y. and 400 m./440 y. in 1959/60 . . . limited to three individual events at each meeting, she could not have won many more.

At the 1959 Pan-American Games, her medal haul was five golds for the 100 m. (63.8), 200 m. (2:18.5), 400 m. (4:55.9) and 4 x 100 m. free-style and medley relays. She broke about seventy-five American records for seventeen different distances on back-stroke, free-style and individual medley and the world 400 m. mark (4:44.5) in the 1960 United States Olympic trials.

Chris, whose Prussian forebears migrated to Sweden 700 years ago, and whose grandfather Count Philip came to the United States at the turn of the century, was a pupil of George Haines at Santa Clara, California. Haines first saw her as an untutored 11-year-old. He told her to kick a few lengths in a 20 y. pool until he could attend to her. A hundred and forty-four lengths later he remembered her . . . but Haines didn't forget Chris von Saltza again.

SCHOLLANDER, Don (United States, 30 Apr. 1946-). The first swimmer to win four golds at one Olympic Games, Donald Arthur Schollander looked and swam like a dream come true—fast, flat and with feeling. It was also so effortless, so beautiful that it was hard to realize he was going so fast.

His Games was Tokyo 1964 when he won the 100 m. by one-tenth from Britain's Bobby McGregor in 53.4, though Schollander had said: 'I'm not really a sprinter.' He took the 400 m. by 2.7 from East Germany's Frank Wiegand in a world record 4:12.2. Swimming even pace throughout, Schollander's first 200 m. was 2:05.7, he came back in 2:06.5 and his final 100 m. (61.7) was only 1.3 slower than his first . . . it was masterly.

Schollander won two relay golds in the 4 x 100 and 4 x 200 m. free-style. America broke world records both times and with 7:52.1 for the longer relay became the first nation to get inside the 8-minute barrier. Schollander's 'split' as an anchor man was 1:55.6, two seconds faster than the thirty-one other men in the race.

The free-style leg in the medley relay was decided by trial in Tokyo before the start of the Games and went to Steve Clark, who had not won a place in the USA team for the individual sprint. Clark had a 'split' of 52.4 in anchoring America to their third relay world record-breaking success.

A law student at Yale University, Schollander, from Oregon, but who did most of his swimming with George Haines at Santa Clara, failed to qualify in the 1968 American trials for the right to defend his 100 and 400 m. titles in Mexico. Instead he earned his place in the 200 m.–which was last in the Olympic programme in 1900, though there was a 220 y. event in 1904–with a world record 1:54.3. And though Mike Wenden beat him for the gold (see WENDEN, Mike) the Australian could not beat Schollander's world mark.

The 200 m. was undoubtedly Schollander's best distance. The 5 ft. 11 in. and 173 lb. student broke the world record for this eight times in five years ... being the first to break the two-minute barrier with 1:58.8 on 27 July 1963, through to his 1:54.3 on 30 Aug. 1968. He also won the Pan-American 200 m. title in 1967 along with two more relay golds. The better of his two 400 m. world records was his Olympic winning 4:12.2 in 1964 and he was in eight world record-breaking American free-style relay teams though never in a medley squad that set a world time.

SCOTTISH AMATEUR SWIMMING ASSOCIATION.

The early minutes of the S.A.S.A. have been lost, but it is agreed that the first meeting of club delegates was held in the Bible Society's Room, 5 St. Andrew Square, Edinburgh, on 28 Jan. 1888. But there were clubs in Scotland long before this time. The records of Bon-Accord A.S.C. (Aberdeen), instituted on 26 Apr. 1862–and one of the world's longest surviving clubs–give proof that there were clubs in Aberdeen and other cities of Scotland before then, though these clubs do not exist today.

The first available information relating to an organized body is found in the minutes of the Dunfermline/Carnegie Club, of 17 Sept. 1877, when Mr. W. Wilson of Glasgow–a noted swimming pioneer–invited the club to join the Association of Swimming Clubs of Scotland. On 17 Apr. 1886, a further letter resulted in the proposal that the name of the Association should be the Scottish Amateur Swimming Association.

SCOTTISH CHAMPIONS

MEN

110 y. Free-style (instituted 1888 for 100 y.)

1946*	MacDonald, Ian	59.0
1947*	Harrop, Trevor	56.1
1948*	Harrop, Trevor	55.4
1949*	Wardrop, Jack	55.6
1950*	Wardrop, Jack	53.6
1951*	Wardrop, Jack	52.6
1952*	Wardrop, Jack	52.2
1953*	Welsh, Doug	54.0
1954*	Spence, Ian	55.0
1955*	Welsh, Doug	54.9
1956*	Murphy, Ron	55.0
1957*	Hill, Jimmy	54.7
1958*	Still, Athole	54.8
1959*	Black, Ian	52.0
1960*	Black, Ian	52.7
1961	McGregor, Bobby	59.2
1962	McGregor, Bobby	57.8
1963	McGregor, Bobby	57.5
1964	McGregor, Bobby	55.9
1965	Black, Gordon	57.9
1966	McGregor, Bobby	54.9
1967	McGregor, Bobby	54.4
1968	McGregor, Bobby	54.6
1969	MacGregor, Alistair	58.4
1970†	Shore, Martin	57.0
1971	Shore, Martin	57.9

* = 100 y.   † = 100 m.

100 m. Free-style

1972	Shore, Martin	56.0
1973	Hewit, Gordon	57.22
1974	Mills, Wilson	56.57
1975	Downie, Gordon	55.76

220 y. Free-style (instituted 1888)

1946	MacDonald, Ian	2:24.3
1947	MacDonald, Ian	2:22.2
1948	Wardrop, Jack	2:22.4
1949	Wardrop, Jack	2:24.2
1950	Wardrop, Jack	2:20.0
1951	Wardrop, Jack	2:17.2
1952	Wardrop, Jack	2:10.0
1953	Sreenan, Bob	2:19.4
1954	Still, Athole	2:16.4
1955	Baillie, Jack	2:20.8
1956	Baillie, Jack	2:18.2
1957	Murphy, Ron	2:15.0
1958	Black, Ian	2:08.2
1959	Black, Ian	2:07.2
1960	Black, Ian	2:07.3
1961	Thomas, Frank	2:16.9
1962	Gallacher, Ian	2:16.0
1963	McGregor, Bobby	2:12.4
1964	McGregor, Bobby	2:09.8
1965	Black, Gordon	2:11.4
1966	McGregor, Bobby	2:06.1
1967	McGregor, Bobby	2:08.9
1968	McGregor, Bobby	2:06.5
1969	MacGregor, Alastair	2:11.4
1970*	Souter, Gordon	2:08.1
1971	Souter, Gordon	2:07.7

* = 200 m.

200 m. Free-style

1972	Souter, Gordon	2:04.2
1973	Hewit, Gordon	2:05.62
1974	Hewit, Gordon	2:02.50
1975	Downie, Gordon	1:59.28

440 y. Free-style (instituted 1890)

1946	Heatly, Peter	5:43.6
1947	Wardrop, Jack	5:15.9
1948	Wardrop, Jack	5:17.0
1949	Wardrop, Jack	5:12.9
1950	Wardrop, Jack	5:07.2
1951	Wardrop, Jack	4:55.9
1952	Wardrop, Jack	4:41.9
1953	Sreenan, Bob	4:54.1
1954	Sreenan, Bob	4:50.8
1955	Sreenan, Bob	4:49.1
1956	Baillie, Jack	5:05.0
1957	Baillie, Jack	5:00.3
1958	Black, Ian	4:37.2
1959	Black, Ian	4:50.3
1960	Black, Ian	4:30.6
1961	Sreenan, Bob	4:50.8
1962	Gallacher, Ian	4:50.5
1963	Wilson, Jim	4:54.4
1964	Galletly, Alex	4:44.3
1965	Galletly, Alex	4:41.6
1966	Wilson, Jim	4:42.9
1967	Wilson, Jim	4:37.3
1968	McClatchey, John	4:37.0
1969	McClatchey, John	4:39.3
1970*	Souter, Gordon	4:32.8
1971	Devlin, Alex	4:39.6

* = 400 m.

400 m. Free-style

1972	Wilkie, David	4:25.2
1973	Carter, Jimmy	4:13.53
1974	McClatchey, Alan	4:20.63
1975	McClatchey, Alan	4:08.55

880 m. Free-style (instituted 1892)

1946	Heatly, Peter	11:50.0
1947	MacDonald, Ian	11:11.9
1948	Wardrop, Jack	10:53.7
1949	Wardrop, Jack	11:22.2
1950	Wardrop, Jack	11:29.2
1951	Wardrop, Jack	10:08.0
1952	Wardrop, Jack	9:57.3
1953	Sreenan, Bob	10:32.4
1954	Sreenan, Bob	10:06.7
1955	Sreenan, Bob	10:21.2
1956	Sreenan, Bob	10:12.0
1957	Baillie, Jack	10:30.0
1958	Black, Ian	9:31.6
1959	Black, Ian	9:52.8
1960	Black, Ian	10:11.0
1961	Sreenan, Bob	10:08.5
1962	Sreenan, Bob	9:58.4
1963	Wilson, Jim	10:20.6
1964	Wilson, Jim	10:10.1
1965	Galletley, Alex	9:49.5
1966	Wilson, Jim	9:51.4
1967	Wilson, Jim	9:47.8

1968	Henderson, Eric	9:47.0
1969	Henderson, Eric	10:10.2
1970*	Souter, Gordon	9:34.7
1971	Souter, Gordon	9:33.7

* = 800 m.

800 m. Free-style

1972	Devlin, Alex	9:19.1
1973	Carter, Jimmy	9:18.50
1974	Taylor, Colin	9:40.36
1975	Carter, Jimmy	8:41.78

1,650 y. Free-style (Instituted 1964)

1964	Wilson, Jim	20:19.5
1965	Galletly, Alex	19:21.6
1966	Wilson, Jim	19:56.1
1967	Henderson, Eric	18:50.4
1968	Henderson, Eric	18:44.4
1969	Henderson, Eric	19:01.7
1970*	Devlin, Alex	18:37.8
1971	Scott, Allan	18:14.6

* = 1,500 m.

1,500 m. Free-style

1972	Devlin, Alex	17:33.6
1973	Connor, James	17:37.07
1974	McClatchey, Alan	17:37.82
1975	McClatchey, Alan	17:13.7*

110 y. Back-stroke (instituted 1913 for 100 y. In 1924 increased to 150 y.)

1946*	Harrop, Trevor	1:44.0
1947*	Wardrop, Bert	1:50.9
1948†	Wardrop, Bert	1:05.0
1949†	Wardrop, Bert	1:04.1
1950†	Wardrop, Bert	1:03.4
1951†	Wardrop, Bert	1:03.2
1952†	Wardrop, Bert	1:03.6
1953†	Burns, Ronnie	1:04.2
1954†	Robson, Tom	1:02.1
1955†	Burns, Ronnie	1:01.5
1956†	Burns, Ronnie	1:01.3
1957†	Robson, Tom	1:03.1
1958†	Hill, Jimmy	1:03.2
1959†	Hill, Jimmy	1:02.4
1960†	Harrower, Andy	1:01.4
1961	Not held	
1962	Not held	
1963	Littlejohn, Gary	1:07.9
1964	Smart, Ian	1:06.5
1965	Smart, Ian	1:07.0
1966	Nelson, Casey	1:06.3
1967	Smart, Ian	1:06.5
1968	Smart, Ian	1:06.8
1969	Simpson, Hammy	1:06.4
1970‡	Simpson, Hammy	1:07.4
1971	Simpson, Hammy	1:05.0

* = 150 y.   † = 100 y.   ‡ = 100 m.

100 m. Back-stroke

1972	Simpson, Hammy	1:04.9
1973	Wilkie, David	1:02.61
1974	Riach, Eddie	1:03.49
1975	Carter, Jimmy	1:00.74

220 y. Back-stroke (instituted 1961)

1961	Harrower, Andy	2:29.1
1962	Harrower, Andy	2:30.0
1963	Nelson, Casey	2:30.9
1964	Smart, Ian	2:26.5
1965	Smart, Ian	2:26.7
1966	Nelson, Casey	2:25.9
1967	Smart, Ian	2:25.8
1968	Smart, Ian	2:26.2
1969	Simpson, Hammy	2:25.2
1970*	Simpson, Hammy	2:25.0
1971	Simpson, Hammy	2:21.1

* = 200 m.

200 m. Back-stroke

1972	Simpson, Hammy	2:19.6
1973	Hughes, Ian	2:17.43
1974	Riach, Eddie	2:22.71
1975	Carter, Jimmy	2:09.07

110 y. Breast-stroke (instituted 1963)

1963	More, Ian	1:15.6
1964	More, Ian	1:14.3
1965	Young, Archie	1:17.6
1966	Leckie, Stuart	1:15.9
1967	Young, Archie	1:14.0
1968	Young, Archie	1:15.0
1969	Young, Archie	1:14.4
1970*	Wilkie, David	1:13.4
1971	Stirton, Gordon	1:14.8

* = 100 m.

100 m. Breast-stroke

1972	Wilkie, David	1:10.4
1973	Thompson, Alan	1:09.94
1974	Stirton, Gordon	1:12.80
1975	Crorkin, Colin	1:11.73

220 y. Breast-stroke (instituted 1913 for 200 y.)

1946*	Service, John	2:38.6
1947*	Service, John	2:34.0
1948*	Service, John	2:33.4
1949*	Calder, Ally	2:45.6
1950*	Service, John	2:42.0
1951*	Spence, Ian	Bu2:35.0
1952*	Spence, Ian	Bu2:35.4
1953*	Service, John	2:34.5
1954*	Service, John	2:29.8
1955*	Spence, Ian	2:37.7
1956*	Percy-Robb, Ian	2:31.0
1957*	Percy-Robb, Ian	2:29.6
1958*	Percy-Robb, Ian	2:36.0
1959*	MacTaggart, Jimmy	2:32.9
1960*	Crawford, Alastair	2:35.8
1961	Braund, R. W.	2:54.2
1962	Cowie, Cleave	2:45.8
1963	More, Ian	2:42.4
1964	More, Ian	2:44.8
1965	Leckie, Stuart	2:52.4
1966	Young, Archie	2:49.4
1967	Young, Archie	2:47.5
1968	Stirton, Gordon	2:52.8
1969	Stirton, Gordon	2:51.5
1970†	Wilkie, David	2:39.4
1971	Stirton, Gordon	2:43.6

* = 200 y.   † = 200 m.

200 m. Breast-stroke

1972	Wilkie, David	2:38.4
1973	Wilkie, David	2:29.50
1974	Stirton, Gordon	2:40.47
1975	Riach, Fraser	2:38.36

110 y. Butterfly (instituted 1963)

1963	McGregor, Bobby	1:03.5
1964	Harrower, Andy	1:02.9
1965	Henderson, Eric	1:02.7
1966	Henderson, Eric	1:02.6
1967	Brown, Downie	1:02.8
1968	Henderson, Eric	1:02.9
1969	Henderson, Eric	1:02.9
1970*	Henderson, Eric	1:01.5
1971	Henderson, Eric	1:03.3

* = 100 m.

100 m. Butterfly

1972	Shore, Martin	1:02.9
1973	Milne, Graham	1:01.19
1974	Hewit, Gordon	1:00.89
1975	McClatchey, Alan	1:00.37

220 y. Butterfly (instituted 1954 for 200 y.)

1954*	Smith, Hamilton	2:32.5
1955*	Smith, Hamilton	2:35.5
1956*	Smith, Hamilton	2:32.0
1957*	Smith, Hamilton	2:31.6
1958*	Black, Ian	2:09.9
1959*	Black, Ian	2:08.6
1960*	Black, Ian	2:09.7
1961	Blyth, Ian	2:27.2
1962	Blyth, Ian	2:25.9
1963	Harrower, Andy	2:31.0
1964	Henderson, Eric	2:21.9
1965	Henderson, Eric	2:17.7
1966	Henderson, Eric	2:23.4
1967	Henderson, Eric	2:22.7
1968	Henderson, Eric	2:20.4

The happy United States 4 x 100 m. free-style relay team; (*left to right*)
Joe Bottom, John Murphy, Mel Nash and man-of-the-meet Jim Montgomery after their victory at the first World championships in Belgrade in
1973. David Wilkie, of Britain, (*below*) on the way to retaining his 200 m.
breast-stroke title in decisive fashion at the 1975 World championships in
Cali, where he also took the 100 m. crown

Canada's Commonwealth double champion Bill Mahony giving his team badge to the Queen after Her Majesty had presented him with his second gold medal at the 1970 Games in Edinburgh

John Devitt, the controversial Australian winner of the Olympic 100 m. free-style title in Rome in 1960. He is here with Lance Larson, who was placed second, and bronze medalist Manuel dos Santos (Brazil)

(*top*) Start of the 100 y. free-style final at the 1904 Olympics. On the extreme left of the raft, which moved as the men dived in, is Zoltán Halmay (Hungary), the eventual champion. Next is America's Charles Daniels (second in the final) and fourth from the left is US bronze medallist Scott Leary. (*centre*) The finish, with Halmay touching well ahead. (*bottom*) White City, London, where the 1908 Olympics were in a pool in the middle of the stadium. Winner of the 200 m. breast-stroke was Britain's Frederick Holman (*left*), followed by team-mate William Robinson (*centre*) with Pontus Hansson (Sweden, *right*) third

An all-American trio who made a tremendous impact on world swimming in the 1960s—Catie Ball (*left*), the world breast-stroke record-breaker; Pokey Watson (*centre*), the 1968 Olympic 200 m. back-stroke champion and Debbie Meyer (*right*), who in Mexico City that year became the first swimmer to win three individual golds at the same Games

Roland Matthes of East Germany, the greatest back-stroke swimmer the world has ever seen. Olympic double champion in 1968 and 1972, European double champion in 1970 and 1974, and winner of three titles in World championships.

Australia's teenage free-style world record-breakers: Steve Holland, the World 1,500 m. champion in 1973, and Jenny Turrall, 1975 World 800 m. champion

Judy Grinham (*centre*), the first Briton to be Olympic, European and Commonwealth champion and world-record holder at the same time. She is here with her team-mate Margaret Edwards (*left*) and New Zealand's Phillipa Gould after the girls had finished in this order in the 1958 Commonwealth Games 110 y. back-stroke. The bespectacled Ada Kok, Holland's great butterflyer *(below)*, broke world records and won Olympic medals in the 1960s (with Enith Brigitha, the Dutch pool star of the 1970s)

The World championships "nursery". Introducing a trio of medal winners whose combined ages totalled only 44 years. *(Left to right)* Birgit Treiber (East Germany), 15, Nancy Garapick (Canada), 13 and Ulrike Richter (East Germany), 16, who were first, second and third respectively in the 200 m. back-stroke in Cali in 1975

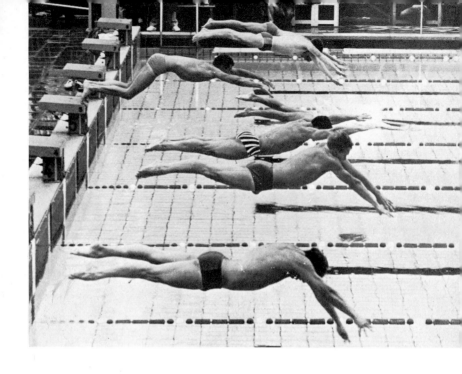

The right and the wrong of swimming starts. *(Above)* the near-disaster in Utrecht in 1966 when Bobby McGregor (GB), in lane 5, was left on the block yet still managed to win the European 100 m. free-style title. *(Below)* all away in a line, chasing gold at the World championships in Cali in 1975

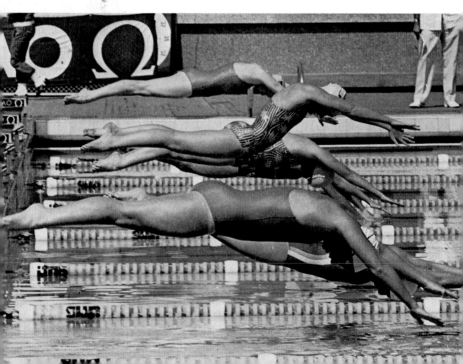

1969	Henderson, Eric	2:18.7
1970†	Henderson, Eric	2:16.7
1971	Henderson, Eric	2:20.4
	* = 200 y. † = 200 m.	

200 m. Butterfly

1972	Henderson, Eric	2:15.5
1973	Henderson, Eric	2:14.21
1974	Hewit, Gordon	2:12.48
1975	McClatchey, Alan	2:10.63

220 y. Individual medley (instituted 1968)

1968	Black, Gordon	2:28.4
1969	Henderson, Eric	2:29.0
1970*	MacGregor, Alastair	2:27.3
1971	Simpson, Hammy	2:25.8
	* = 200 m.	

200 m. Individual medley

1972	Wilkie, David	2:15.3
1973	Devlin, Alex	2:21.63
1974	McClatchey, Alan	2:21.01
1975	McClatchey, Alan	2:17.85

440 y. Medley (instituted 1952 for 300 y. and increased to 400 y. in 1956 after separation of breast-stroke and butterfly)

1952*	Spence, Ian	3:52.4
1953*	Cargill, T.	4:03.0
1954*	Spence, Ian	3:56.6
1955*	Spence, Ian	3:59.2
1956†	Spence, Ian	5:22.6
1957†	Black, Ian	4:59.0
1958†	Black, Ian	5:04.7
1959†	Black, Ian	4:48.6
1960†	Black, Ian	4:57.3
1961	Blyth, Ian	5:36.2
1962	Blyth, Ian	5:28.3
1963	Harrower, Andy	5:38.2
1964	Harrower, Andy	5:38.8
1965	Henderson, Eric	5:24.4
1966	Henderson, Eric	5:26.9
1967	Henderson, Eric	5:19.4
1968	Henderson, Eric	5:20.9
1969	Henderson, Eric	5:24.6
1970‡	Henderson, Eric	5:18.1
1971	Connor, James	5:16.7
	* = 300 y. † = 400 y. ‡ = 400 m.	

400 m. Individual medley

1972	Wilkie, David	5:08.8
1973	Devlin, Alex	4:57.29
1974	Riach, Eddie	5:00.90
1975	Carter, Jimmy	4:41.45

Highboard diving (instituted 1947)

1947	Heatly, Peter
1948	No contest
1949	Heatly, Peter
1950	Heatly, Peter
1951	Heatly, Peter
1952	Berry, Geoff
1953	Heatly, Peter
1954	Heatly, Peter
1955	Heatly, Peter
1956	Heatly, Peter
1957	Heatly, Peter
1958	Heatly, Peter
1959	Davidson, Brian
1960	Davidson, Brian
1961	Davidson, Brian
1962	Davidson, Brian
1963	Davidson, Brian
1964	Davidson, Brian
1965	Campbell, Maurice
1966	Davidson, Brian
1967	Campbell, Maurice
1968	Campbell, Maurice
1969	Not held
1970	Campbell, Maurice
1971	Not held
1972	Downs, Danny
1973	Downs, Danny
1974	Downs, Danny
1975	Hurst, Ronnie

3 m. Springboard diving (instituted 1936)

1946	Heatly, Peter
1947	Heatly, Peter
1948	Heatly, Peter
1949	Heatly, Peter
1950	Heatly, Peter
1951	Heatly, Peter
1952	Berry, Geoff
1953	Heatly, Peter
1954	Heatly, Peter
1955	Heatly, Peter
1956	Heatly, Peter
1957	Heatly, Peter
1958	Law, William
1959	Davidson, Brian
1960	Davidson, Brian
1961	Davidson, Brian
1962	Law, William
1963	Davidson, Brian
1964	Davidson, Brian
1965	Campbell, Maurice
1966	Davidson, Brian
1967	Davidson, Brian
1968	Campbell, Maurice
1969	Campbell, Maurice
1970	Campbell, Maurice
1971	Black, Ian
1972	Black, Ian

1973	Downs, Danny
1974	Downs, Danny
1975	Black, Ian

1 m. Springboard diving (instituted 1951)

1951	Heatly, Peter
1952	Heatly, Peter
1953	Heatly, Peter
1954	Heatly, Peter
1955	Heatly, Peter
1956	Heatly, Peter
1957	Law, William
1958	Law, William
1959	Davidson, Brian
1960	Law, William
1961	Davidson, Brian
1962	Davidson, Brian
1963	Davidson, Brian
1964	Law, William
1965	Campbell, Maurice
1966	Campbell, Maurice
1967	Davidson, Brian
1968	Campbell, Maurice
1969	Campbell, Maurice
1970	Campbell, Maurice
1971	Black, Ian
1972	Downs, Danny
1973	Downs, Danny
1974	Downs, Danny
1975	Downs, Danny

WOMEN

110 y. Free-style (instituted 1907 for 100 y.)

1946*	Munro, Margaret	1:05.4
1947*	Riach, Nancy	1:03.2
1948*	Gibson, Cathie	1:02.4
1949*	Turner, Elizabeth	1:03.5
1950*	Girvan, Margaret	1:05.4
1951*	Gibson, Cathie	1:02.8
1952*	Melville, Dorothy	1:04.2
1953*	Hogben, Frances	1:04.7
1954*	Gibson, Cathie	1:03.6
1955*	MacDonald, Flora	1:04.9
1956*	Girvan, Margaret	1:03.7
1957*	Girvan, Margaret	1:02.3
1958*	Harris, Christine	1:03.2
1959*	Rae, Nan	1:00.7
1960*	Harris, Christine	1:00.3
1961	Rae, Nan	1:06.2
1962	Watt, Sheila	1:09.0
1963	Nicol, Pat	1:07.6
1964	Stewart, Eleanor	1:07.1
1965	Kellock, Fiona	1:06.1
1966	Kellock, Fiona	1:05.2
1967	Kellock, Fiona	1:04.9
1968	Kellock, Fiona	1:04.4
1969	Brown, Moira	1:06.9

1970	Brown, Moira	1:04.6
1971	Mackie, Andrea	1:06.0

* = 100 y.   † = 100 m.

100 m. Free-style

1972	McGlashan, Morag	1:03.5

1973	McGlashan, Morag	1:02.09
1974	Fraser, Fiona	1:02.65
1975	Walker, Diane	1:02.73

220 y. Free-style (instituted 1891 for 200 y.)

1946*	Gibson, Cathie	2:19.5
1947*	Gibson, Cathie	2:18.6
1948*	Gibson, Cathie	2:18.3
1949*	Gibson, Cathie	2:25.4
1950*	Girvan, Margaret	2:24.6
1951*	Gibson, Cathie	2:20.8
1952*	Gibson, Cathie	2:23.9
1953*	Melville, Dorothy	2:24.9
1954*	Girvan, Margaret	2:21.2
1955	Hogben, Frances	2:44.2
1956	Girvan, Margaret	2:38.6
1957	Girvan, Margaret	2:36.5
1958	Girvan, Margaret	2:36.0
1959	Rae, Nan	2:27.3
1960	Rae, Nan	2:27.7
1961	Rae, Nan	2:26.3
1962	Nicol, Pat	2:32.2
1963	Nicol, Pat	2:29.8
1964	Stewart, Eleanor	2:28.5
1965	Kellock, Fiona	2:26.9
1966	Kellock, Fiona	2:27.9
1967	Kellock, Fiona	2:25.2
1968	Kellock, Fiona	2:28.1
1969	Brown, Moira	2:28.8
1970†	Hogg (Davidson) Sally	2:19.8
1971	Mackie, Andrea	2:22.0

* = 200 y.   † = 200 m.

200 m. Free-style

1972	Brown, Moira	2:17.9

1973	Simpson, Debbie	2:14.21
1974	Walker, Diane	2:13.90
1975	Gibson, Graeme	2:13.15

440 y. Free-style (instituted 1931)

1946	Riach, Nancy	5:55.4
1947	Gibson, Cathie	5:29.2
1948	Gibson, Cathie	5:29.9
1949	Girvan, Margaret	5:45.7
1950	Girvan, Margaret	5:46.3
1951	Gibson, Cathie	5:38.6
1952	Melville, Dorothy	5:45.7
1953	Girvan, Margaret	5:41.5
1954	Girvan, Margaret	5:31.0
1955	Hogben, Frances	5:53.3
1956	Hogben, Frances	5:45.7

1957	Girvan, Margaret	5:30.4
1958	Rae, Nan	5:23.8
1959	Rae, Nan	5:06.6
1960	Rae, Nan	5:16.2
1961	Rae, Nan	5:10.5
1962	Watt, Sheila	5:28.8
1963	Nicol, Pat	5:29.8
1964	Nicol, Pat	5:13.2
1965	Kellock, Fiona	5:16.6
1966	Kellock, Fiona	5:15.0
1967	Kellock, Fiona	5:02.4
1968	Fenton, Margaret	5:17.4
1969	Fenton, Margaret	5:15.1
1970*	Mackie, Andrea	4:51.8
1971	Mackie, Andrea	4:58.3

* = 400 m.

400 m. Free-style

1972	Brown, Moira	4:47.0

1973	Simpson, Debbie	4:43.88
1974	Walker, Diane	4:39.95
1975	Walker, Diane	4:32.8*

880 y. Free-style (instituted 1967)

1967	Fenton, Margaret	10:45.5
1968	Fenton, Margaret	11:09.4
1969	Mackie, Andrea	11:01.1
1970*	Hogg (Davidson), Sally	10:08.0
1971	Mackie, Andrea	10:23.2

* = 800 m.

800 m. Free-style

1972	Brown, Moira	9:56.7

1973	Walker, Diane	9:40.51
1974	Walker, Diane	9:30.60
1975	Walker, Diane	9:31.45

110 y. Back-stroke (instituted 1924 for 150 y. Reduced to 100 y. 1948)

1946*	Gibson, Cathie	1:51.1
1947*	Gibson, Cathie	1:50.0
1948†	Gibson, Cathie	1:10.0
1949†	Girvan, Margaret	1:12.6
1950†	McDowall, Margaret	1:09.2
1951†	McDowall, Margaret	1:08.9
1952†	McDowall, Margaret	1:09.4
1953†	McDowall, Margaret	1:08.3
1954†	McDowall, Margaret	1:10.0
1955†	McDowall, Margaret	1:12.0
1956†	McDowall, Margaret	1:08.0
1957†	McDowall, Margaret	1:08.8
1958†	McDowall, Margaret	1:09.3
1959†	Johnstone, Frances	1:12.8
1960†	Campbell, Louise	1:10.0
1961	Campbell, Louise	1:16.4
1962	Campbell, Louise	1:13.9
1963	Campbell, Louise	1:14.9
1964	Mays, Lorraine	1:16.1

1965	Robertson, Bobby	1:17.8
1966	Robertson, Bobby	1:14.0
1967	Robertson, Bobby	1:13.8
1968	Robertson, Bobby	1:15.5
1969	Armour, Linda	1:16.4
1970‡	Armour, Linda	1:14.8
1971	Ross, Jean	1:14.6

* = 150 y.   † = 100 y.   ‡ = 100 m.

100 m. Back-stroke

1972	Fordyce, Gillian	1:14.0

1973	Wickham, Kim	1:13.41
1974	Fordyce, Gillian	1:10.60
1975	Gray, Elaine	1:13.05

220 y. Back-stroke (instituted 1963)

1963	Campbell, Louise	2:42.4
1964	Mays, Lorraine	2:44.3
1965	Campbell, Louise	2:46.5
1966	Robertson, Bobby	2:39.9
1967	Robertson, Bobby	2:39.9
1968	Fenton, Margaret	2:42.7
1969	Armour, Linda	2:44.4
1970*	Armour, Linda	2:40.7
1971	Armour, Linda	2:38.1

* = 200 m.

200 m. Back-stroke

1972	Fordyce, Gillian	2:40.5

1973	Fordyce, Gillian	2:33.95
1974	Fordyce, Gillian	2:34.01
1975	Simpson, Debbie	2:36.24

110 y. Breast-stroke (instituted 1963)

1963	Baxter, Ann	1:23.9
1964	Baxter, Ann	1:20.7
1965	McLeod, Margaret	1:23.7
1966	Baxter, Ann	1:21.4
1967	Baxter, Ann	1:22.0
1968	McLeod, Margaret	1:25.3
1969	Stewart, Kathie	1:24.4
1970*	Wilson, Pam	1:21.8
1971	Walker, Diane	1:22.2

* = 100 m.

100 m. Breast-stroke

1972	Walker, Diane	†1:20.5

1973	Lornie, Jayne	1:20.96
1974	Dickie, Sandra	1:16.46
1975	Dickie, Sandra	1:19.74

220 y. Breast-stroke (instituted 1924 for 200 y.)

1946*	Bolton, Margaret	3:05.0
1947*	Gordon, Elenor	2:56.8
1948*	Gordon, Elenor	2:53.0
1949*	Gordon, Elenor	2:56.0

1950*	Gordon, Elenor	2:50.6
1951*	Gordon, Elenor	2:44.1
1952*	Gordon, Elenor	2:45.3
1953*	Gordon, Elenor	2:44.9
1954*	Gordon, Elenor	2:41.8
1955*	Gordon, Elenor	2:46.2
1956*	Gordon, Elenor	2:46.7
1957*	Gordon, Elenor	2:41.2
1958*	Turnbull, Alison	2:51.5
1959*	Turnbull, Alison	2:48.0
1960*	Turnbull, Alison	2:44.5
1961	Turnbull, Alison	2:58.0
1962	Turnbull, Alison	3:00.1
1963	Baxter, Ann	3:02.5
1964	Baxter, Ann	2:59.3
1965	Baxter, Ann	3:03.2
1966	Baxter, Ann	2:57.5
1967	Baxter, Ann	2:56.8
1968	Blyth, Ann	3:05.1
1969	Walker, Diane	3:08.1
1970†	Wilson, Pam	2:55.8
1971	Walker, Diane	2:43.6

* = 200 y.   † = 200 m.

200 m. Breast-stroke

1972	Walker, Diane	†2:53.6
1973	Lornie, Jayne	2:52.22
1974	Dickie, Sandra	2:48.02
1975	Dickie, Sandra	2:52.4*

†Wilson, Pam touched first in 1:20.4 and 2:51.0 respectively in these combined senior and junior championships finals. But as she had only entered the junior events, the senior titles were awarded to the second fastest swimmer (Walker) who had been entered in both senior and junior events. The rules have since been changed so that this anomalous situation cannot occur again.

110 y. Butterfly (instituted 1954 for 100 y.)

1954*	Laird, Heather	1:24.6
1955*	MacDonald, Flora	1:16.1
1956*	MacDonald, Flora	1:15.7
1957*	Watt, Sheila	1:09.8
1958*	Watt, Sheila	1:10.9
1959*	Watt, Sheila	1:06.7
1960*	Watt, Sheila	1:06.0
1961	Watt, Sheila	1:15.6
1962	Watt, Sheila	1:13.5
1963	Stewart, Eleanor	1:14.0
1964	Stewart, Eleanor	1:11.7
1965	Stewart, Eleanor	1:12.0
1966	Stewart, Eleanor	1:11.5
1967	Kellock, Fiona	1:14.7
1968	Brown, Moira	1:13.6
1969	Brown, Moira	1:16.4
1970†	Brown, Moira	1:10.7
1971	Ross, Louise	1:12.7

* = 100 y.   † = 100 m.

100 m. Butterfly

1972	Brown, Moira	1:11.5
1973	Wickham, Kim	1:09.41
1974	Wickham, Kim	1:08.39
1975	Simpson, Debbie	1:08.21

220 y. Butterfly (instituted 1963)

1963	Watt, Sheila	2:51.8
1964	Stewart, Eleanor	2:50.9
1965	Stewart, Eleanor	2:55.4
1966	Stewart, Eleanor	2:51.2
1967	McCallum, Margaret	2:54.7
1968	Brown, Moira	2:51.0
1969	Brown, Moira	2:52.2
1970*	Brown, Moira	2:38.1
1971	Ross, Louise	2:39.5

* = 200 m.

200 m. Butterfly

1972	Brown, Moira	2:28.8
1973	Ross, Louise	2:30.44
1974	Simpson, Debbie	2:25.76
1975	Simpson, Debbie	2:28.66

220 y. Individual medley (instituted 1968)

1968	Fenton, Margaret	2:47.5
1969	Brown, Moira	2:45.5
1970*	Wilson, Pam	2:39.4
1971		

* = 200 m.

200 m. Individual medley

1972	Walker, Diane	2:33.4
1973	McGlashan, Morag	2:39.55
1974	Dickie, Sandra	2:29.48
1975	Dickie, Sandra	2:30.62

440 y. Individual medley (instituted 1952 for 300 y. and increased to 400 y. in 1956 after separation of breast-stroke and butterfly).

1952*	Taylor, J.	4:07.9
1953*	Taylor, J.	4:15.4
1954*	MacDonald, Flora	4:12.3
1955*	MacDonald, Flora	4:22.5
1956†	MacDonald, Flora	6:06.0
1957†	Watt, Sheila	5:42.6
1958†	Watt, Sheila	5:49.4
1959†	Mays, Karen	5:30.2
1960†	Mays, Karen	5:31.8
1961	Mays, Karen	6:07.0

1962	Watt, Sheila	6:09.5	
1963	Mays, Karen	6:11.1	
1964	Mays, Karen	6:07.3	
1965	Stewart, Eleanor	6:08.9	
1966	Stewart, Eleanor	6:03.2	
1967	Fenton, Margaret	5:52.5	
1968	Fenton, Margaret	6:07.0	
1969	Fenton, Margaret	6:02.6	
1970‡	Wilson, Pam	5:41.2	
1971	Walker, Diane	5:34.2	

* = 300 y.   † = 400 y.   ‡ = 400 m.

400 m. Individual medley

1972	Walker, Diane	5:23.6
1973	Lornie, Jayne	5:27.89
1974	Simpson, Debbie	5:15.49
1975	Simpson, Debbie	5:17.31

Highboard diving (instituted 1950)

1950	Mitchell, Sheila
1951	Mitchell, Sheila
1952	Mitchell, Sheila
1953	Melville, Elsie
1954	Melville, Elsie
1955	Melville, Elsie
1956	Melville, Elsie
1957	Melville, Elsie
1958	No contest
1959	Melville, Elsie
1960	Melville, Elsie
1961	Melville, Elsie
1962	Melville, Elsie
1963	Melville, Elsie
1964	Rossi, Sylvia
1965-69	Events not held
1970	Graham, Carol
1971	Not held
1972	Graham, Carol
1973	Hotson, Fiona
1974	Hotson, Fiona
1975	Hotson, Fiona

Springboard diving (instituted 1951)

1951	Marrian, Valerie
1952	Melville, Elsie
1953	Melville, Elsie
1954	Melville, Elsie
1955	Marrian, Valerie
1956	Melville, Elsie
1957	Melville, Elsie
1958	Marrian, Valerie
1959	Melvile, Elsie
1960	Melville, Elsie
1961	Melville, Elsie
1962	Melville, Elsie
1963	Melville, Elsie
1964	Alston, M.
1965	Philip, Linda

1966	Melville, Elsie
1967	McCarroll, Anne
1968	McCarroll, Anne
1969	McCarroll, Anne
1970	McCarroll, Anne
1971	Graham, Carol
1972	Graham, Carol
1973	Hotson, Fiona
1974	Hotson, Fiona
1975	Hotson, Fiona

1 m. Springboard diving (instituted 1950)

1950	Mitchell, Sheila
1951	Mirchell, Sheila
1952	Mitchell, Sheila
1953	Marrian, Valerie
1954	Melville, Elsie
1955	Melville, Elsie
1956	Melville, Elsie
1957	Melville, Elsie
1958	Marrian, Valerie
1959	Melville, Elsie
1960	Melville, Elsie
1961	Rossi, Sylvia
1962	Melville, Elsie
1963	Melville, Elsie
1964	Rollo, Joy
1965	Philip, Linda
1966	Philip, Linda
1967	Philip, Linda
1968	McCarroll, Anne
1969	McCarroll, Anne
1970	McCarroll, Anne
1971	Cooper, Carol
1972	Hotson, Fiona
1973	Ogden, Lesley
1974	Ogden, Lesley
1975	Hotson, Fiona

SEMI-FINALS. There was a time when semi-finals as well as heats and finals were the rule in swimming, irrespective of the number of competitors in the event. Nowadays, in events like the Olympics, it is the generally accepted practice to have semi-finals only for events for 100 metres and then only if there are more than thirty-two entries—requiring more than four heats in the eight-lane bath.

SHAW, Tim (United States, 8 Nov. 1957-). Shaw, from Long Beach, California, became only the second man in history to hold the world records for 200, 400 and 1,500 m. free-style at the same time—the first being John Konrads of Australia (see KONRADS, John). The American, then 16, achieved his feat in four days of fine swimming at Concord, California in August 1974. Then he won the U.S. Outdoor titles for 400 m. in 3:54.69—having also broken the world record with 3:56.96 in a heat—the 200 m. in 1:51.66 and 1,500 m. in 16:31.75. These achievements earned him the F.I.N.A. Prize Eminence for that year.

The following year, at the World championships in Cali, Colombia, Shaw was the top man swimmer, with victories in the 200, 400 and 1,500 m. free-style, but missed a fourth gold because his team-mate Bruce Furniss took a 'flying' take over from him in the 4 x 200 m. relay. The U.S. squad were disqualified and lost the golds and a world record.

There was some consolation for Shaw and Furniss (see FURNISS BROTHERS) the following month when they swam in a Long Beach team who broke the world record in winning the American National title.

In 1975 Shaw broke five more individual world free-style records: the 400 m. (3:53.95 and 3:53.31) and 800 m. (8:13.68 and 8:09.06) twice and for 1,500 m. (15:20.91).

SHORT COURSE. The term 'short course' refers to any pool shorter than the international-size 50 m. The phrase acquired special significance from 1 May 1957 when F.I.N.A. eliminated all 'short course' marks from their world record book (see LONG COURSE and WORLD RECORDS). However, many countries hold short course events, particularly in the winter and recognize short course national records. In short course races, competitors obtain a time advantage because of the extra turns (see TURNS).

SLADE, Betty (Great Britain, 18 June 1921-   ). European springboard diving champion in 1938, Betty Joyce Slade, from Ilford, Essex, was a tiny girl with the flexible body of an acrobat who fought like a giant at the Empire Pool, Wembley, to win her gold. She dropped an early dive, scoring only 2's and 3's (out of ten), yet pulled back to win by 1.32 points from Germany's Gerda Daumerlang.

She was ninth in the springboard at the 1936 Olympics but was not chosen for the Commonwealth Games in Sydney early in 1938, though she had twice won

(1936/37) the A.S.A. springboard title and went on to win it twice more (1938/39) and the highboard in 1939. She turned professional and toured Britain and many parts of the world giving diving shows in swimming pools and on the stage into a tank.

SOVIET UNION CHAMPIONS. See U.S.S.R. CHAMPIONS.

SPEARHEAD PRINCIPLE. The spearhead or arrow formation is a fairly modern system, applied particularly to swimming, in which competitors qualifying for semi-finals or finals are placed in lanes according to the times they recorded in the heats or semi-finals.

In an eight-lane bath, the fastest competitor goes in lane 4. the second fastest in lane 5, and the others in order in lanes 3, 6, 2, 7, 1, 8. In a six-lane bath the order is lanes 3, 4, 2, 5, 1, 6. The reasons for this are two-fold—to give the best racers the opportunity to see each other and also to help the judges in their difficult job of visually deciding the order of finish. With the development of electrical timing and judging machines (see TIMING) the second reason is becoming less important.

Until the 1968 Olympics, the allocation of lanes for heats was not done on the spearhead principle. The lanes were drawn at random after the division of competitors into heats of equal standard; i.e. with each heat containing an equal number of fast and slow swimmers. Since that time however, the spearhead principle operated for heats, based on pre-Games times, as well as for semi-finals and finals.

SPITZ, Mark Andrew (United States, 10 Feb. 1950-   ). There has only ever been one Mark Spitz in Olympic history, one competitor who has won seven gold medals at a single Games. And his unique feat in Munich in 1972 is unlikely ever to be repeated.

Spitz won his medals in this order . . . 200 m. butterfly and 4 x 100 m. free-style (Aug. 28); 200 m. free-style (29); 100 m. butterfly and 4 x 200 m. free-style (31); 100 m. free-style (Sept 3); 4 x 100 m. medley (4). All his victories, four individual and three in relays, were in world record times.

With this tally, plus the two relay

golds and a 100 m. free-style bronze at the 1968 Games in Mexico, Spitz turned professional immediately after Munich with a total of ten medals, nine of them gold. Only one man has won more Olympic golds and that was America's Ray Ewry (10), who took the now discontinued standing take-off events for high and long jump (4 each, 1900, '04, '06, '08) and triple jump (2, 1900 and '04).

In Munich the brilliant and talented Spitz, from Modesto, California, had matured considerably from the nervy and temperamental boy who had tipped himself to win six golds in Mexico City and failed to measure up to his own forecast. Yet even the new Spitz was a loner, concerned largely with his own performance and hardly the Pin Up boy of the U.S. men's squad, though a Spitz poster with his seven golds hung around his neck later became a collector's item.

This dark-haired, superbly-built athlete also won five titles at the 1967 Pan-American Games in Winnipeg—100 and 200 m. butterfly and three relays. He broke 26 individual world records, of which his first, on 25 June, 1967—strangely—was for 400 m. free-style, the event he soon gave up in favour of shorter races.

His world record total was made up as follows . . . free-style: 100 m. (three, 51.9 to 51.22 between 1970 and '72), 200 m. (four, 1:54.3 in '68 to 1:52.78 in '72), 400 m. (three, best 4:07.7 in June '68)—butterfly: 100 m. (seven, 56.3 to 54.27 from 1967-72) and 200 m. (2:06.4 to 2:00.70, 1967-72). He was also in six U.S. teams who broke relay world records.

Spitz, who was put under special security guard in Munich after the assassination of some Israeli athletes, because it was feared he could be next on the list for the terrorists, moved into big money contracts on the strength of his Olympic achievements. He is reputed to have earned millions rather than thousands of dollars.

SPRINGBOARD DIVING
Springboards are 1 m. and 3 m. above the level of the water and there are separate competitions for the two boards. In major competitions, the dives are almost always from the 3 m. board because of the higher tariff values.

The international test for men is five required dives, selected from five groups and six voluntary dives from five groups. The test for women is five required and five voluntary dives. In each case, the required dives, which may be performed in (a), (b) or (c) positions are forward dive, back dive, reverse dive, inward dive and forward dive half-twist. (see DIVING).

STARTS. A much neglected aspect of swimming in many countries is the art of starting. The speed with which a competitor can move from a static position on the bath-side (or in the water at the bath-end in the case of back-stroke) into flowing action can cut vital tenths of seconds off the total racing time.

The starting procedure in swimming is simple and false starts need not happen unless there is a deliberate effort on the part of competitors to steal a 'flyer'. For all events except back-stroke the start is from a dive. The competitors line up behind their starting blocks or line. If raised blocks are used—which may be from 0.5 to 0.75 m. above the water surface—on a signal from the referee the competitors step on to the back surface of the block and remain there. On the command from the starter of 'Take your marks', the competitors immediately step forward to the front of the block or line, bend forward into their pre-dive positions and remain stationary. When all competitors are still, the starter gives the starting signal (a shot, klaxon, whistle or voice command) and the race is off.

An innovation of the 1970s was the "grab" start for all but back-stroke races. In using this style the swimmer bends down to grasp securely the starting block with his hands and thus can lean, and then push away strongly on the starting signal. This technique eliminates a great deal of extraneous movement and allows for a secure balance at the crucial moment before the start. The "grab" properly used can be the fastest of all the starts.

In back-stroke, the competitors line up in the water, facing the starting end, with their hands placed on the starting grips. Their feet, including the toes, must be under the surface of the water and standing in or on the gutter or bending the toes over the lip of the gutter is prohibited. On the 'Take your marks' command, the swimmers assume their push away position and their hands must not release the starting grip until the starting signal has been given.

The starter calls back the competitors at the first or second false start i.e. if any competitor moves before his time. If there are a third or more false starts in the same heat, no matter if by the same or another swimmer, then the person making that false start is disqualified.

A blatant occasion when the starter allowed a race to continue although a number of competitors had taken flyers was during the final of the European 100 m. free-style championship in Utrecht in 1966. It almost cost Britain's Bobby McGregor the gold medal (see McGREGOR, Bobby and picture facing page 193).

STEPANOVA, Galina (USSR, 26 Nov. 1948-). This outstanding breast-stroke swimmer competed at three Olympics and took a medal from each of her five races (a gold, two silvers and two bronzes). Her most successful Games was her first, in 1964 when, known by her famous maiden name of Prozumenshikova, she was the only European to win a swimming title.

She won the 200 m. in Tokyo by 1.2 seconds from America's Claudia Kolb in 2:46.4 (an Olympic record) but the victory margin was unimportant for she looked a winner all the way. In Mexico four years later it was a different story for the heavy and powerful Miss P., was affected more by the altitude than her lighter rivals. She lost the 100 m. title by one-tenth (1:15.9) to Djurdjica Bjedov (Yugo) and only fighting spirit enabled her to win the bronze for 200 m. by one-tenth, from her team-mate Alla Grebennikova. Galina collapsed after this race and was carried to the dressing-rooms by a small and most heroic Mexican.

It was a slimmer, trimmer Galina, now Mrs. Stepanova and a mother, who appeared in Munich in 1972. She stormed into the lead in the 200 m. final and was nearly two seconds ahead at half distance. With just over 50 m. to go, she still held what looked to be an unbeatable lead. Then, suddenly and despite all her experience, the Russian woman 'died'. It was heart-breaking to watch as first

Australia's Beverley Whitfield (see WHITFIELD, Beverley) and then America's Dana Schoenfield overtook her, though Stepanova just managed to hold on for the bronze.

In the 100 m. she could not match the speed of Cathy Carr (USA) and had to settle again for the silver medal that had been her prize in Mexico.

She was undefeated in European championship events, winning the 200 m. in Utrecht in 1966 and Barcelona '70 and the 100 m. at her second championships, the first time this event was in the programme. And her fine breast-stroke legs in the medley relay at these two meetings gave the Soviet Union the silver medals.

Galina held the world 100 m. record for five months in 1966 (1:15.7), but four times set figures for 200 m., of which her first at Blackpool on April 11, 1964 was also a mark for 220 y. Her best times were 1:14.6 for 100 m. (Minsk, 13 Aug. 1971) and 2:40.7 for 200 m. (her 1970 Barcelona winning performance). She retired from international competition after the Munich Olympics.

STEWART SISTERS. (Canada), **Helen** (1939-) and **Mary** (1946-). The Stewart sisters, Helen and Mary, have a proud family swimming record. Helen first got the Stewart name into the medal lists at the 1954 Commonwealth Games in her home city of Vancouver where she won a silver in Canada's free-style relay team. A year later, she won the Pan-American 100 m. title (67.7) in Mexico City. In 1956 Helen clocked 57.6 for 100 y.–a world record, but one that was never ratified–and reached the semi-finals of the 100 m. at the Melbourne Olympics. Her last big swim occasion was, after her marriage, at the 1959 Pan-American Games in Chicago where she won a silver again in the free-style relay.

Mary, seven years younger and very much inspired by her sister, appeared on the international swimming scene at Chicago Pan-American's where she placed sixth in the 100 m. butterfly (1:22.2) at 13. A tiny 5 ft. 3 in, and 7 st. 12 lb. mermaid, Mary showed her power and potential at the 1960 Olympics by being a surprise finalist in the 100 m. free-style (65.5, 8th) having clocked 64.2 in a semi-final to rob Australia's famous Ilsa Konrads of a place in the last eight.

It was back to butterfly in 1961 and world records for 100 m. (68.8) and 110 y. (69.0) and election as Canada's 'Woman Athlete of the Year'—with 135 votes to the 94 of her nearest rival. She clipped the world marks to 67.3 in 1962 with her time over the longer 110 y. distance and at the Perth Commonwealth Games (1962) she won the 110 y. butterfly gold and a bronze in Canada's medley relay team.

At the 1963 Pan-American Games in Sao Paulo, Brazil, Mary missed putting her name two below Helen's in the list of 100 m. free-style winners. She was second, 0.5 behind Terri Stickles (USA) but her 63.3 was 4.4 faster than her sister's gold medal effort eight years earlier. Mary was second too in the 100 m. butterfly (68.9), won two more silvers in the relays and for good measure came sixth in the 100 m. back-stroke.

Mary, whose father William was born in Aberdeen and went to Canada in 1921, competed in the A.S.A. championships at Blackpool in 1963 and came first in the 110 y. butterfly. And she bowed out of swimming almost where she had begun—with eighth place in the 1964 Olympics—this time for butterfly and not free-style.

STOUDER, Sharon (United States, 9 Nov. 1948-). Slim Sharon Stouder from Glendora, California, pulled off the shock victory of the 1964 Olympics in beating the hot favourite, Ada Kok of Holland, in the 100 m. butterfly. She won by 0.9 in 64.7, beating the Dutch girl's world record by 0.4. And though Miss Kok (see KOK, ADA). regained her world record with 64.5 the next year, Sharon's Olympic winning time was still the second fastest of all time as swimming moved into the 1970s.

The American, only 15, came close to a second, even more astonishing, victory in the 100 m. free-style. She chased Dawn Fraser (see FRASER, DAWN) to within four-tenths, and though the Australian achieved her historic third successive victory, Sharon, in clocking 59.9, became only the second woman in the world to break the minute. This talented 5 ft. 8 in. and 9 st. 9 lb. fairhaired schoolgirl added two more golds to her Tokyo tally in the free-style and

medley relays.

A medley relay gold medallist—she swam the butterfly leg—in America's winning team at the 1963 Pan-American Games in Sao Paulo—Sharon won three titles at the 1964 United States outdoor championships. She took the 100 m. freestyle (60.4), 100 m. butterfly (65.4) and broke her own world record in winning the 200 m. butterfly in 2:26.4.

SWEDISH CHAMPIONS. Sweden, one of the eight founder nations of F.I.N.A., have always been advanced thinkers in the development of swimming. They were among the pioneers of badge schemes to further the popularity of the sport for recreation as well as competition. Appropriately, women's events were introduced into the Olympic swimming programme at the 1912 Games in Stockholm.

Arne Borg (see BORG, ARNE) was the dominating figure at the first two European championships (1926/27) and, in the modern era, Gunnar Larsson (see LARSSON, GUNNAR) proved himself one of the outstanding medley swimmers in the world.

Larsson's versatility earned him 21 National titles—for free-style, back-stroke, butterfly and medley. And though he never won a breast-stroke title, he was the Swedish record-holder for 200 m.

MEN

100 m. Free-style

1960	Lindberg, Per-Ola	56.8
1961	Lindberg, Per-Ola	56.5
1962	Lindberg, Per-Ola	56.4
1963	Lindberg, Per-Ola	55.5
1964	Lindberg, Per-Ola	55.7
1965	Eriksson, Lester	56.2
1966	Eriksson, Lester	55.9
1967	Jansson, Göran	55.2
1968	Eriksson, Lester	55.1
1969	Larsson, Gunnar	56.1
1970	Larsson, Gunnar	55.3
1971	Jansson, Göran	54.9
1972	Gingsjö, Bengt	54.7
1973	Zarnowiecki, Bernt	54.36
1974	Zarnowiecki, Bernt	54.04
1975	Zarnowiecki, Bernt	54.50

200 m. Free-style

1960	Lindberg, Per-Ola	2:08.3
1961	Lindberg, Per-Ola	2:09.2
1962	Lindberg, Per-Ola	2:05.7

1963	Lundin, Jan	2:02.7	
1964	Svensson, Mats	2:02.6	
1965	Eriksson, Lester	2:04.0	
1966	Eriksson, Lester	2:01.8	
1967	Eriksson, Lester	2:00.8	
1968	Eriksson, Lester	1:58.2	
1969	Larsson, Gunnar	2:00.2	
1970	Larsson, Gunnar	2:01.1	
1971	Larsson, Gunnar	1:56.6	
1972	Gingsjö, Bengt	1:58.4	
1973	Zarnowiecki, Bernt	1:57.54	
1974	Gingsjö, Bengt	1:57.31	
1975	Gingsjö, Bengt	1:55.97	

400 m. Free-style

1960	Bengtsson, Lars-Eric	4:34.6
1961	Ekman, Sten	4:35.0
1962	Rosendhal, Hans	4:32.1
1963	Lundin, Jan	4:26.3
1964	Rosendhal, Hans	4:22.2
1965	Eriksson, Lester	4:26.1
1966	Lundin, Jan	4:24.9
1967	Holst, Sven von	4:21.3
1968	Larsson, Gunnar	4:11.8
1969	Larsson, Gunnar	4:15.8
1970	Larsson, Gunnar	4:11.5
1971	Larsson, Gunnar	4:04.9
1972	Larsson, Gunnar	4:07.8
1973	Bellbring, Anders	4:05.33
1974	Petersson, Peter	4:05.62
1975	Gingsjö, Bengt	4:04.04

1,500 m. Free-style

1960	Bengtsson, Lars-Erik	18:25.5
1961	Ekman, Sten	18:33.8
1962-64	Not held	
1965	Feil, Peter	18:20.6
1966	Bengtsson, Glen	17:57.5
1967	Feil, Peter	17:25.2
1968	Feil, Peter	17:03.0
1969	Holst, Sven von	17:19.4
1970	Larsson, Gunnar	16:41.5
1971	Bellbring, Anders	16:33.4
1972	Bellbring, Anders	16:29.8
1973	Bellbring, Anders	16:10.38
1974	Pettersson, Peter	16:24.77
1975	Pettersson, Peter	16:18.19

100 m. Back-stroke

1960	Almstedt, Bengt-Olov	1:06.7
1961-64	Not held	
1965	Tegeback, Hans	1:05.0
1966	Tegeback, Hans	1:04.6
1967	Tegeback, Hans	1:02.6
1968	Tegeback, Hans	1:03.2
1969	Tegeback, Hans	1:02.8
1970	Tegeback, Hans	1:01.8

1971	Zetterlund, Svante	1:01.9
1972	Sandberg, Anders	1:01.5
1973	Zetterlund, Svante	1:01.02
1974	Zetterlund, Svante	1:01.98
1975	Brandén, Mikael	1:00.22

200 m. Back-stroke (instituted 1962)

1962	Almstedt, Bengt-Olov	2:23.4
1963	Lundin, Jan	2:23.3
1964	Sjöblom, Leif	2:22.1
1965	Ferm, Olle	2:20.4
1966	Ferm, Olle	2:19.6
1967	Ljungberg, Hans	2:16.7
1968	Ljungberg, Hans	2:17.6
1969	Larsson, Gunnar	2:14.3
1970	Larsson, Gunnar	2:15.1
1971	Zetterlund, Svante	2:13.0
1972	Sandberg, Anders	2:12.4
1973	Eriksson, Leif	2:13.02
1974	Eriksson, Leif	2:10.57
1975	Brandén, Mikael	2:08.16

100 m. Breast-stroke

1960	Lundin, Roland	1:15.6
1961	Lundin, Roland	1:15.5
1962	Lundin, Roland	1:16.0
1963	Lundin, Roland	1:16.5
1964	Kindblom, Hakan	1:15.0
1965	Jonsson, Thomas	1:14.0
1966	Jonsson, Thomas	1:11.2
1967	Jonsson, Thomas	1:11.5
1968	Jonsson, Thomas	1:10.1
1969	Jonsson, Thomas	1:10.1
1970	Jonsson, Thomas	1:10.8
1971	Eriksson, Göran	1:10.2
1972	Häggquist, Anders	1:10.9
1973	Eriksson, Göran	1:10.73
1974	Christiansen, Glen	1:08.99
1975	Christiansen, Glen	1:08.23

200 m. Breast-stroke

1960	Lindström, Tommie	2:39.3
1961	Lindström, Tommie	2:42.6
1962	Lundin, Roland	2:44.5
1963	Eriksson, Ulf	2:43.3
1964	Finsson, Björn	2:42.1
1965	Jonsson, Thomas	2:42.1
1966	Jonsson, Thomas	2:36.1
1967	Jonsson, Thomas	2:35.1
1968	Jonsson, Thomas	2:36.8
1969	Jonsson, Thomas	2:34.2
1970	Jonsson, Thomas	2:35.6
1971	Eriksson, Göran	2:34.6
1972	Kensen, Tomas	2:36.7

1973	Norling, Anders	2:34.42
1974	Andersson, Stefan	2:28.99
1975	Christiansen, Glen	2:27.14

100 m. Butterfly (instituted 1965)

1965	Eriksson, Ingvar	1:01.4
1966	Eriksson, Ingvar	1:00.5
1967	Eriksson, Ingvar	59.8
1968	Eriksson, Ingvar	1:00.2
1969	Westergren, Bo	59.5
1970	Westergren, Bo	1:00.1
1971	Ljunggren, Hans	1:00.1
1972	Berglund, Per	1:00.6

1973	Berglund, Per	59.43
1974	Kasting, Bob (Can)	58.50
1975	Gingsjö, Bengt	58.72

200 m. Butterfly

1960	Bengtsson, Hakan	2:28.0
1961	Bengtsson, Hakan	2:26.3
1962	Bengtsson, Hakan	2:25.0
1963	Eriksson, Ingvar	2:18.4
1964	Eriksson, Ingvar	2:21.7
1965	Feil, Peter	2:18.1
1966	Feil, Peter	2:14.6
1967	Eriksson, Ingvar	2:09.4
1968	Feil, Peter	2:08.0
1969	Larsson, Gunnar	2:15.7
1970	Feil, Peter	2:11.5
1971	Gingsjö, Bengt	2:11.3
1972	Gingsjö, Bengt	2:10.5

1973	Bellbring, Anders	2:07.51
1974	Bellbring, Anders	2:06.11
1975	Bellbring, Anders	2:05.69

200 m. Individual medley (instituted 1965)

1965	Ljungberg, Hans	2:21.7
1966	Ljunberg, Hans	2:21.5
1967	Ljungberg, Hans	2:17.4
1968	Ljungberg, Hans	2:17.2
1969	Larsson, Gunnar	2:15.7
1970	Larsson, Gunnar	2:16.0
1971	Larsson, Gunnar	2:12.4
1972	Larsson, Gunnar	2:13.4

1973	Larsson, Gunnar	2:14.05
1974	Bellbring, Anders	2:14.50
1975	Gingsjö, Bengt	2:13.01

400 m. Individual medley (instituted 1961)

1961	Lundin, Jan	5:30.0
1962	Ekman, Sten	5:19.8
1963	Lundin, Jan	5:13.2
1964	Ferm, Olle	5:12.0
1965	Ferm, Olle	5:07.0
1966	Feil, Peter	5:06.8

1967	Ljungberg, Hans	4:54.6
1968	Ljungberg, Hans	4:51.8
1969	Ljungberg, Hans	4:50.6
1970	Larsson, Gunnar	4:45.7
1971	Larsson, Gunnar	4:40.5
1972	Gingsjö, Bengt	4:45.6

1973	Bellbring, Anders	4:44.74
1974	Gingsjö, Bengt	4:45.10
1975	Gingsjö, Bengt	4:40.57

WOMEN

100 m. Free-style

1960	Larsson, Karin	1:04.5
1961	Grubb, Karin	1:06.1
1962	Hagberg, Ann-Christine	1:04.4
1963	Hagberg, Ann-Christine	1:02.7
1964	Lilja, Ann-Charlott	1:04.2
1965	Hagberg, Ann-Christine	1:03.2
1966	Hagberg, Ann-Christine	1:02.9
1967	Berglund, Elizabeth	1:03.5
1968	Andersson, Lotten	1:02.6
1969	Kock, Vera	1:03.8
1970	Berglund, Elizabeth	1:02.1
1971	Zarnowieki, Anita	1:02.7
1972	Zarnowieki, Anita	1:01.9

1973	Olsson, Diana	1:01.17
1974	Olsson, Diana	59.97
1975	Persson, Ylva	1:00.07

200 m. Free-style (instituted 1967)

1967	Kock, Vera	2:19.0
1968	Berglund, Elizabeth	2:16.1
1969	Wikman, Gunilla	2:16.9
1970	Zarnowiecki, Anita	2:15.0
1971	Johansson, Irwi	2:15.3
1972	Johansson, Irwi	2:13.5

1973	Johansson, Irwi	2:11.43
1974	Lundberg, Gunilla	2:10.55
1975	Anderson, Eva	2:10.86

400 m. Free-style

1960	Cederqvist, Jane	4:55.3
1961	Cederqvist, Jane	4:56.0
1962	Ljunggren, Elizabeth	5:01.8
1963	Ljunggren, Elizabeth	4:48.9
1964	Ljunggren, Elizabeth	4:54.1
1965	Lilja, Ann-Charlotte	4:51.3
1966	Lilja, Ann-Charlotte	4:55.3
1967	Ljunggren, Elizabeth	4:46.2
1968	Berglund, Elizabeth	4:48.9
1969	Jonsson, Gunilla	4:47.5
1970	Jonsson, Gunilla	4:42.2
1971	Jonsson, Gunilla	4:45.3
1972	Johansson, Irwi	4:41.9

1973	Johansson, Irwi	4:33.41
1974	Sundeborg, Marie	4:30.85
1975	Martensson, Pia	4:34.54

800 m. Free-style (instituted 1967)

1967	Ljunggren, Elizabeth	9:53.7
1968	Gustavsson, Ingrid	9:56.9
1969	Kock, Vera	10:02.4
1970	Jonsson, Gunilla	9:51.1
1971	Jonsson, Gunilla	9:50.3
1972	Gunsten, Else	9:41.1
1973	Gunsten, Else	9:31.11
1974	Gunsten, Else	9:22.85
1975	Ottosson, Pia	9:25.38

100 m. Back-stroke

1960	Sergerström, Bibbi	1:14.3
1961	Sergerström, Bibbi	1:13.2
1962	Stridh, Marianne	1:15.4
1963	Haagman, Birgitta	1:14.4
1964	Haagman, Birgitta	1:13.8
1965	Haagman, Birgitta	1:11.8
1966	Hiljebäck, Yvonne	1:12.8
1967	Hiljebäck, Yvonne	1:11.6
1968	Hiljebäck, Yvonne	1:12.2
1969	Folkeson, Eva	1:11.6
1970	Folkeson, Eva	1:10.9
1971	Folkeson, Eva	1:10.6
1972	Zarnowiecki, Anita	1:10.8
1973	Olsson, Diana	1:09.01
1974	Olsson, Diana	1:07.88
1975	Lundberg, Gunilla	1:08.22

200 m. Back-stroke (instituted 1965)

1965	Bengtsson, Lena	2:38.4
1966	Bengtsson, Lena	2:37.9
1967	Hammarsten, B-M.	2:34.9
1968	Hiljebäck, Yvonne	2:37.2
1969	Folkeson, Eva	2:36.6
1970	Folkeson, Eva	2:34.4
1971	Zarnowiecki, Anita	2:32.1
1972	Zarnowiecki, Anita	2:29.6
1973	Olsson, Diana	2:26.99
1974	Olsson, Diana	2:27.44
1975	Lundberg, Gunilla	2:27.19

100 m. Breast-stroke

1960	Eriksson, Barbro	1:23.4
1961	Eriksson, Barbro	1:25.4
1962	Olsson, Christina	1:25.2
1963	Berg, Agneta	1:25.3
1964	Israelsson, Monica	1:23.7
1965	Israelsson, Monica	1:21.7
1966	Lahti, Britt-Marie	1:21.9
1967	Brage, Yvonne	1:20.0
1968	Brage, Yvonne	1:19.5

1969	Brage, Yvonne	1:18.7
1970	Brage, Yvonne	1:19.6
1971	Smedh, Btitt-Marie	1:18.9
1972	Smedh, Britt-Marie	1:18.3
1973	Smedh, Britt-Marie	1:17.17
1974	Petersson, Jeanette	1:16.56
1975	Petersson, Jeanette	1:15.75

200 m. Breast-stroke

1960	Eriksson, Barbro	2:55.7
1961	Eriksson, Barbro	3:00.7
1962	Sjöström, Marianne	3:01.6
1963	Kallerhult, Kristina	3:00.2
1964	Israelsson, Monica	3:00.2
1965	Brage, Yvonne	2:57.2
1966	Brage, Yvonne	2:54.9
1967	Brage, Yvonne	2:52.3
1968	Brage, Yvonne	2:51.0
1969	Brage, Yvonne	2:47.2
1970	Brage, Yvonne	2:47.4
1971	Brage, Yvonne	2:49.4
1972	Smedh, Britt-Marie	2:46.1
1973	Smedh, Britt-Marie	2:43.86
1974	Smedh, Britt-Marie	2:44.05
1975	Roos, Ann-Sofi	2:42.76

100 m. Butterfly

1960	Larsson, Kristina	1:14.7
1961	Stenbäck, Karin	1:10.9
1962	Stenbäck, Karin	1:10.4
1963	Stenbäck, Karin	1:10.9
1964	Andersson, Lotten	1:11.0
1965	Andersson, Lotten	1:11.5
1966	Gustavsson, Ingrid	1:10.2
1967	Gustavsson, Ingrid	1:09.2
1968	Andersson, Lotten	1:09.3
1969	Hjort, Elizabeth	1:10.3
1970	Wikner, Eva	1:09.0
1971	Wikner, Eva	1:07.1
1972	Wikner, Eva	1:06.8
1973	Andersson, Gunilla	1:07.24
1974	Andersson, Gunilla	1:06.38
1975	Andersson, Gunilla	1:04.07

200 m. Butterfly (instituted 1967)

1967	Gustavsson, Ingrid	2:34.4
1968	Gustavsson, Ingrid	2:31.5
1969	Wikner, Eva	2:40.2
1970	Wikner, Eva	2:34.9
1971	Wikner, Eva	2:29.8
1972	Wikner, Eva	2:29.7
1973	Andersson, Gunilla	2:26.32
1974	Andersson, Gunilla	2:23.82
1975	Andersson, Gunilla	2:19.95

200 m. Individual medley (first held 1961)

1961	Larsson, Karin	2:46.2
1962-64	Not held	
1965	Julander, Britt	2:41.3
1966	Andersson, Lotten	2:39.2
1967	Gustavsson, Ingrid	2:38.1
1968	Brage, Yvonne	2:41.3
1969	Zarnowiecki, Anita	2:37.4
1970	Zarnowiecki, Anita	2:33.9
1971	Zarnowiecki, Anita	2:33.0
1972	Zarnowiecki, Anita	2:30.0
1973	Olsson, Diana	2:30.34
1974	Olsson, Diana	2:26.83
1975	Zarnowiecki, Anita	2:28.77

400 m. Individual medley (instituted 1962)

1962	Ljunggren, Elizabeth	5:44.6
1963	Ljunggren, Elisabeth	5:35.4
1964	Ljunggren, Elisabeth	5:43.3
1965	Berglund, Elisabeth	5:43.1
1966	Ljunggren, Elisabeth	5:41.2
1967	Gustavsson, Ingrid	5:38.8
1968	Gustavsson, Ingrid	5:38.3
1969	Wikman, Gunilla	5:36.5
1970	Zarnowiecki, Anita	5:26.1
1971	Zarnowiecki, Anita	5:25.7
1972	Zarnowiecki, Anita	5:21.5
1973	Zarnowiecki, Anita	5:18.39
1974	Zarnowiecki, Anita	5:13.20
1975	Zarnowiecki, Anita	5:13.15

SWIMMING. The eight letters spelling 'Swimming' cover a wide range of aquatic activities. In the competitive sense, which is what this book is about, the word swimming includes not only speed racing, but also diving, water-polo, sychronized and long-distance swimming.

But water and the ability to swim have many other associations. There are recreational swimming (some call it bathing), water-skiing and sub-aqua diving. There are rowing, sailing and canoeing for which the ability to keep afloat is a prime safety requirement, though, unfortunately, all too many still go on the water without the insurance of being able to protect their lives should they unexpectedly go into the water.

In a world whose surface is two-thirds water, the importance of swimming cannot be over-emphasised. And the health-giving, recreational and life-saving aspects are as important as the glamour ones of competition, records and medals.

America's noted coach Bob Kiphuth (see KIPHUTH, BOB) summed up the sport he loved like this: 'Swimming contributes to the physical and organic growth and development of the body, aids social development through intensive participation under leadership, helps the psychological development of children through the satisfaction of achievement and is a pleasurable leisure-time hobby.' And that, in fact, is what swimming is all about.

SYNCHRONIZED SWIMMING. This form of swimming became recognized internationally in 1952. Although many countries organize national championships for synchronized swimming, it is the only one of the F.I.N.A. approved events which is not included in the Olympic programme although it is in the world championships and European championships (from 1977).

Synchronized swimmers are almost always female. They must have the speed of a racer, the acrobatic mobility of a diver, the grace of a ballerina, the stamina of a water-polo player and a feeling for music.

A competition consists of a stunt (figures) section and a free routine section. It is very similar, in fact, to an ice-skating competition. The stunts have tariff values similar to those for diving (see DIVING) and the points awarded after elimination of the highest and lowest marks, are multiplied by the tariff (degree of difficulty) (see DIVING JUDGING).

There are four stunt categories:

1. Ballet leg—in which one leg is extended vertically at a $90°$ angle to the horizontal body at some stage in the movement.
2. Dolphin head first and foot first—in which the body traverses the circumference of an imaginary circle about eight feet in diameter, beginning in a back layout position and then continuing in a head first or foot first direction.
3. Somersault, front and back—in which the body rotates (somersaults) about a lateral axis.
4. Diverse—containing a different variety of movements other than those in categories 1 to 3.

In the judging of the stunts, the judges look for a slow, high and controlled movements with each section of the stunt defined clearly and uniform in timing. Points are awarded from 0 to 10, using ½ points, on the following basis: completely failed = 0; unsatisfactory = ½ to 2½; deficient = 3 to 4½; satisfactory = 5 to 6½; good = 7 to 8½; excellent = 9 to 10.

The free-routine section, as in ice-skating, is performed to music. The competitors incorporate any of the 77 listed stunts or strokes and/or parts thereof. Competitors must restrict their routines to a five minute maximum time, including a maximum of 20 seconds of deck movements before entry into the water. For routines, the judging is in two parts:

1. Execution–to cover the performance of the figures, strokes and/or parts thereof from the stand point of perfection.

2. Composition–including difficulty and variety of strokes, figures and hybrids, interpretation of music, manner of presentation, pool pattern and synchronization.

There are three competetive sections in routine competitions–solo, duet and team. A team is made up of at least four swimmers. In scoring, teams with more than four swimmers are allowed a half point for each additional swimmer up to a maximum of eight, (i.e. an extra 2 points for a team of eight).

In competition, during the stunt section plain dark bathing suits and white caps must be worn. For the free-routines, competitors may wear more colourful costumes and appropriate head pieces.

SZÉKELY, Éva (Hungary), see GYARMATI FAMILY.

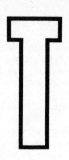

110 y. butterfly. Her tally included the 440 y. free-style, sprint back-stroke and distance butterfly and both medleys.

Her best times were for free-style 61.5 (100 m.), 2:14.8 (200 m.), 4:43.8 (400 m.) . . . for back-stroke 66.7 (100 m.) and 2:24.5 (200 m.) . . . for butterfly 65.4 (100 m.) and 2:29.9 (200 m.) . . . for medley 2:31.8 (200 m.) and 5:26.3 (400 m.).

TARIFF VALUES IN DIVING. See DIVING

TAUBER, Ulrike (East Germany, 16 June, 1958-). This schoolgirl's first appearance in the East German senior team was at the European championships 'in Vienna in 1974. And she returned home with four medals and two world records from eight days of superswimming.

Ulrike won the 200 and 400 m. medley by the astonishingly big margins of five and six seconds respectively in world figures of 2:18.97 and 4:52.42. She also won the silver medals, behind her team-mate Ulrike Richter (see RICHTER, Ulrike), in the 100 and 200 m. back-stroke. These achievements led to her being named the World's No. 1 woman Swimmer of 1974.

The following year, Ulrike reduced her world 200 and 400 m. medley records to 2:18.83 and 4:52.20. She won the world title for the longer event at the World championships in Cali, Colombia, but had to settle for the silver in the 200 m., behind America's Kathy Heddy, in returning a time 1½ seconds outside her best.

TAYLOR, Henry, (Great Britain, 17 Mar. 1885-28 Feb. 1951). Happy Henry Taylor, from Oldham, Lancashire, was a swashbuckling athlete and the aquatic marvel of 1906-08. He won the mile and was second in the 400 m. at the Interim Games of 1906 in Athens. And he won the 400 and 1,500 m. at the 1908 London Olympics in world record times of 5:36.8 (7.4 ahead of Australia's Frank Beaurepaire) and 22:48.4 (beating his team-mate Syd Battersby by 2.8) as well as a gold in the free-style relay.

A member of the Chadderton club, Taylor, an orphan, was raised by his brother. He worked in the cotton mills and trained during his lunch break and

TANNER, Elaine (Canada, 22 Feb. 1951-). Canada's 'Mighty Mouse'; Elaine Tanner, 5 ft. 2 in. of power-packed versatility, was the most successful woman swimmer at the 1966 Commonwealth Games at 15. She won four golds and three silvers and broke two world records.

Her titles came in the 110 and 220 y. butterfly (66.8 and 2:29.9) and the 440 y. medley (5:26.3) and the 4 x 110 y. free-style, the Canadians setting a world record (4:10.8) in beating Australia by three-tenths. Elaine was second to England's Linda Ludgrove in both the 110 and 220 y. back-stroke and won her third silver in the medley relay (behind England's world record-breaking team).

In fact, her greatest successes were for back-stroke. She won the 100 and 200 m. on this style at the 1967 Pan-American Games in Winnipeg, both in world record times (67.3 and 2:24.4) and clipped her shorter distance mark to 67.1 on the first leg of the medley relay in which Canada came second to the United States. She was also second in the 100 m. butterfly and 4 x 100 m. free-style and fourth in the 100 m. free-style and 200 m. butterfly.

Elaine, from Vancouver, who spent some time in California with her English-born parents, made her final big-time appearance at the Mexico Olympics where she was second in both the 100 and 200 m. back-stroke and won a bronze in the free-style relay.

Her national championship successes were equally impressive. In 1965 she was the Canadian, American and British sprint butterfly champion. She took seventeen Canadian titles between 1965 and 1968, including four successive years for the 200 m./220 y. back-stroke and 100 m./

in the evening in any water he could find—in canals, streams and in the baths on dirty-water (and cheaper) day. His one excursion into business—having mortgaged all his silver cups to find the stake —was a failure and his last job was as a pool attendant at the Chadderton baths where he had done so much of his swimming in his youth as a 'boy who loved his swimming more than anything in his life'.

Taylor had won his Interim Games medals before he became champion of England. He won fifteen A.S.A. titles: 440 y. (1906, '07), 500 y. (1906, '07, '08, '11), 880 y. (1906, '07, '11), one mile (1906, '07, '11) and long distance (1909, '12 and '20). This last success was at the age of 35, the year he also played water-polo for England. As well as his 1908 400 and 1,500 m. Olympic Games world records, which were the first for the distances, Taylor was the first official holder of the 880 y. world mark. In 1969, the year of the centenary of the A.S.A., Taylor was honoured by the Hall of Fame.

Amazingly, Taylor's Olympic successes continued for two more Games, separated by World War I. At Stockholm in 1912 and Antwerp in 1920, he was a member of Britain's teams who were third in the free-style relay event, a feat he had also achieved back in 1906.

THEILE, David (Australia, 17 Jan. 1938-   ). Winner of the Olympic 100 m. back-stroke title in 1956 and '60, Dr. David Theile from Brisbane was a quiet, unobtrusive type except when he was actually swimming and then he was a danger man. His first victory, in Melbourne, was in a world record 62.2, one second ahead of his team-mate John Monckton. In Rome, having missed the 1958 Commonwealth Games and dropped a little out of the limelight, he came back to beat America's Frank McKinney for the individual gold by 0.2 and to win a silver in the new medley relay event.

Theile began competitive swimming at 9, won the Australian junior back-stroke title in 1954. The following year he took the men's 110 y. crown—his 67.4 taking 0.5 off Percy Oliver's national record set the year David was born. He kept the title in 1956, rested from swimming during the first two years of his medical studies, then won again in 1959/60.

Essentially a sprinter, Theile never won championships nor broke records for 200 m. or 220 y. But he took the Australian 100 y. mark from 60.8 to 57.7 in two years and the 100 m. from 65.4— breaking another 1938 record of Oliver— to 62.2.

Theile, a graduate of the University of Queensland and a Fellow of the Royal Australian College of Surgeons, was honoured by the Hall of Fame in 1968 during his time in London as a lecturer in surgery.

TIME CONVERSIONS, see METRIC/ LINEAR TIME CONVERSIONS.

TIMING. Until recent years, all swimming timing has been done by human watch-holders (time-keepers) holding precision stop-watches, graduated to one fifth or one-tenth—the latter being more common these days—of a second. Now, with the development of electrical timing machines, capable of recording even to thousandths of a second, the problems of human judges sorting out extremely close finishes with their vision obscured by the flurry of water have been largely eliminated.

A swimmer must be clocked by three manual time-keepers for a world record —and indeed for most national and other records—to be ratified. If at least two watches agree, then this is the accepted time. If all three differ, then the middle time is accepted.

In 1970, F.I.N.A. ruled that automatic timing (and judging) equipment should take precedence over the decisions of human timers (and judges). Two years later, the world authority went a step further in deciding to ratify world records to hundredths of a second, while still accepting times to tenths where no electrical timing facilities were available.

But even before this, at the Olympic Games of 1964 and '68, highly-sophisticated and expensive electrical equipment, recording to thousandths and even ten thousandths of a second, had been used to determine placings. Taking science to the 'enth degree, this resulted at the Tokyo Games ('64) in Gary Ilman (USA) losing the 100 m. free-style bronze to Germany's Hans-Joachim Klein by one thousandths of a second.

And at the 1972 Munich Games, where overhead television cameras were installed above every lane as a back-up system, Tim McKee (USA) lost the gold medal in the 400 m. medley by two thousandths of a second to Gunnar Larsson of Sweden (see LARSSON, GUNNAR). The men were given the same official time of 4:31.98, but Larsson stopped the electrical clock at 4:31.981 to the 4:31.983 of his rival.

In hindsight it was decided that to go to such extremes in order to find a single winner, to split competitors who virtually touch together and whom the eye could not separate, was unreasonable and unfair. So in 1973 F.I.N.A. agreed that times and placings in future would be determined only to hundredths of a second and that competitors whose times were equal to hundredths, no matter about the thousandths, would be adjudged to have dead-heated.

Good time-keeping is all important in swimming, for progression from heats to semi-finals and to finals is determined by time and not by placings.

TROY, Mike (United States, 3 Oct. 1940-   ). Pain was Mike Troy's watchword—he had it written in foot-high letters on the wall of his room at Indiana University, Indianapolis. And pain in training beyond what his body thought it could bear brought an improvement of 3.6 sec. in a year and the Olympic 200 m. butterfly title in a world record 2:12.8 at the 1960 Rome Games. His time was 7½ secs. better than Bill Yorzyk's gold medal effort at the 1956 Olympics, and Troy beat Australia's Neville Hayes by 1.8 with his American team-mate David Gillanders third (2:15.3). Troy was also a member of America's winning 4 x 200 m. free-style relay team.

The year before, Troy had come second in the Pan-American 200 m. butterfly (2:18.3), 0.3 behind Gillanders. And he won a gold in the medley relay.

Like so many American swimmers, Troy's time at the top was short—from 1958-60—during which he played havoc with the world record for his speciality 200 m. event. On 11 July 1959 he set two marks (2:19.0 and 2:16.4—the latter in winning the first of his two United States outdoor titles). The following summer he clipped back further with 2:13.4 (United States championship), 2:13.2 and his Rome record of 2:12.8. He also won the United States 100 m.

title in 1958 (62.8).

TSURUTA, Yoshijuki (Japan, 1 Oct. 1903-   ). The only man to win the Olympic 200 m. breast-stroke title at successive Games, Tsuruta, from Kogosima, the second of nine sons, achieved his feat at the 1928 (Amsterdam) and 1932 (Los Angeles) Games.

His victory, at the age of 24, in Holland, by 1.8 sec. (2:48.8) over reigning world record-holder Erich Rademacher (Ger)' gave Japan their first Olympic swimming gold medal and the inspiration of his achievement sent the Japanese team home convinced that what one could do all could do.

Four years later the sun indeed rose for Japan. In Los Angeles they shocked the normally all-conquering hosts by winning 11 out of the possible 16 swimming medals and five of the six titles.

TURNS. In swimming, there are rules to govern the way in which competitors turn for each of the four styles. They are: **Free-style**—the touch on the wall can be made by any part of the body, a hand touch is not obligatory, and other than this the competitor can turn as he wants. **Back-stroke**—the swimmer must remain on his back until the foremost part of his body has touched. He may turn beyond the vertical in executing the turn, but must have returned past the vertical on to his back before the feet leave the wall. **Breast-stroke**—the touch (and finish) must be with both hands simultaneously on the same level and with the shoulders in the horizontal position and the swimmer must not do more than one leg kick and one arm pull before surfacing after the turn. **Butterfly**—the touch is the same as for breast-stroke and the swimmer may take only one arm pull under the water before surfacing. **Medley individual**—there is no specific international rule to cover turns in medley, but it generally accepted that the swimmer goes into the turn and touch covered by the rules of the stroke he is using at that time, but comes out covered by the rule of the stroke he is about to start.

Good turns give a tremendous time advantage and it is for this reason that most record lists now distinguish between long course (50 m. pools) and short course (less than 50 m. and usually 25 m. pools) performances.

The time gain has been put at 0.7 sec. for each turn. Thus a 400 m. race in a 25 m. course has fifteen turns compared to the seven in a 50 m. pool, and a time advantage of 8 x 0.7 sec. = 5.6 sec.

TURRALL, Jenny (Australia, 14 May, 1960-   ). This tiny dark-haired girl from Ryde, N.S.W., whose vital statistics then were 5 ft. 2 in. (157 cm) and 94 lb. (42.5k), was only 13 at the end of 1973 when she broke her first world record. This was for the longest racing distance of 1,500 m. and she clocked 16:49.9. Nine months and four more world record-breaking performances later, she had cut this to 16:33.94 (in winning the U.S.A. Outdoor title), a time that would have given her the Olympic men's crown as recently as 1968.

Carefree Jenny, who swims faster and faster as her races progress, picked up four medals, including a gold for 400 m., at the Commonwealth Games in January 1974, plus a world mark for 800 m. (8:50.1).

Her "reverse split" ability—i.e. her unusual ability to cover the last half a race faster than the first—brought the little Australian her first world title in Cali, Colombia in 1975 when she moved from seventh after 100 m., fifth at 200 m. and second at 400 m. to a four seconds victory of America's Heather Greenwood in the 800 m.

Miss Turrall's winning 8:44.75, just 1.27 sec. outside the world record she had set in London in March of that year, was a superb performance, bearing in mind that the competition was held at an altitude of 1,003 m. above sea-level. She also took second place in the 400 m. and reached the final of the 200 m. free-style.

TYERS, Jack (Great Britain). A prolific winner of A.S.A. championships, the career of Tyers, from Manchester Osborne Club (now defunct), was coming near its end as the first Olympic Games were held in Athens in 1896. But as one of the pioneers of England's early world swimming supremacy, the competitive record of this remarkable man is an important mile-stone in the history of swimming.

In 1896, he won the A.S.A. 100 y. title in 61.4 (equivalent at most to 68.0 for 100 m.) and 500 y. in 6:55.8 (worth about 7:36.0 for 500 m.)—times which must have won him medals in Athens had Britain entered a team.

Tyers won twenty-nine A.S.A. championships between 1892 and 1897, including all seven free-style titles in 1893 and '94. In these six years he was undefeated over 100 and 220 y., his best winning times being 61.4 (1896) and 2:38.8 (1897) respectively. He won the 440 and 500 y. and mile four successive times (1893-96) and his fastest efforts were 6:08.8 (1895), 4:45.0 (1894) and 26:46.0 (1896). He took the 880 y. in 1893-95 (fastest 13:41.0, 1893) and the long distance twice (1893, '94). He also played water-polo in three winning England teams, against Scotland in 1893 and 1895, the latter occasion as captain, and against Ireland in 1895 when England scored 12 goals without conceding one.

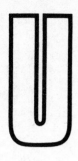

UNITED STATES CHAMPIONS.

The championships of the United States of America are organized by the national men's and women's swimming committees of the Amateur Athletic Union of the United States which controls altogether ten sports.

At the beginning, however, it was the New York Athletic Club who took the initiative. They organized a one mile championship in 1877 which was won by R. Wiessenborn in 44:44¼. The event was held again in 1878, then there was nothing until 1883 when four races (100, 440 and 880 y. and mile) took place.

Five championships for women were held in 1916—440 and 880 y., mile and long distance swimming and platform diving.

UNITED STATES DIVING CHAMPIONS.

A platform diving championship for men was instituted in 1909 and was won in the first three years by George Gaidzik, who had been third and the best American diver at the 1908 London Olympics. A women's platform event began in 1916.

There are two main championship meetings, the Indoor which very often are held in conjunction with the Indoor swimming championships (see UNITED STATES INDOOR CHAMPIONS) in the spring and the Outdoor (see UNITED STATES OUTDOOR CHAMPIONS) as the highlight of the summer season.

Divers from the United States have a record second to none in Olympic competition. Up to the Munich Games in 1972 they had won 39 of the 58 titles and 104 out of the 175 medals (there being two bronzes awarded for the men's highboard in 1904).

The winners of the Indoor and Outdoor championships since 1960 are:

MEN

Highboard diving (Indoor)

1964	Gompf, Tom	498.00
1965	Knorr, Charles	472.25
1966	Knorr, Charles	456.80
1967	Russell, Keith	548.90
1968	Andreason, Larry	445.38
1969	Rydze, Dick	549.39
1970	Dibiasi, Klaus (It)	479.79
1971	Rydze, Dick	470.10
1972	Rydze, Dick	501.00
1973	McFarland, Steve	460.77
1974	McFarland, Steve	486.21
1975	Moore, Tim	522.89

Springboard diving (Indoor)

1960	Gerlach, Jozsef	446.65
1961	O'Brien, Ronald	529.55
1962	Gilbert, Rick	542.55
1963	Gilbert, Rick	522.40
1964	Sitzberger, Ken	476.35
1965	Gilbert, Rick	562.55
1966	Wrightson, Bernie	591.85
1967	Russell, Keith	509.70
1968	Young, Winn	456.15
1969	Young, Winn	559.68
1970	Henry, Jim	543.24
1971	Finneran, Mike	552.78
1972	Boggs, Phil	551.82
1973	Boggs, Phil	531.75
1974	Boggs, Phil	547.20
1975	Boggs, Phil	596.82

1m Springboard diving (Indoor)

1960	Hall, Sam	440.10
1961	Vittucci, Lou	509.95
1962	Webster, Robert	463.96
1963	Gilbert, Rick	466.35
1964	Sitzberger, Ken	482.30
1965	Sitzberger, Ken	519.65
1966	Knorr, Charles	507.90
1967	Rivera, Luis de (Mex)	516.70
1968	Henry, Jim	484.05
1969	Henry, Jim	506.25
1970	Henry, Jim	519.63
1971	Lincoln, Craig	546.72
1972	Dunfield, Don	531.18
1973	Moore, Tim	501.81
1974	Moore, Tim	517.65
1975	Moore, Tim	553.68

WOMEN

Highboard diving (Indoor)

1964	Talmage, Barbara	307.10
1965	King, Micki	304.55
1966	Willard, Patsy	281.80
1967	Simms, Patty	266.25
1968	Bush, Lesley	288.27
1969	Boys, Beverley (Can)	361.11
1970	Loken, Lani	338.55
1971	King, Micki	362.61
1972	Knape, Ulrika (Swe)	370.56
1973	Lipman, Debbie	354.45
1974	Ely, Janet	327.75
1975	Irish, Carrie	346.83

Springboard diving (Indoor)

1960	MacDonald, Irene (Can)	353.85
1961	Lenzi, Joel	450.30
1962	O'Connell, (nee Lenzi) Joel	416.10
1963	McAllister, Barbara	425.35
1964	Talmage, Barbara	383.35
1965	O'Connell, (nee Lenzi) Joel	438.25
1966	Gossick, Sue	433.60
1967	Gossick, Sue	416.40
1968	Bush, Lesley	407.01
1969	Potter, Cynthia	447.51
1970	Potter, Cynthia	472.08
1971	King, Micki	393.45
1972	Potter, Cynthia	429.54
1973	Potter, Cynthia	486.75
1974	Chandler, Jenni	459.33
1975	Irish, Carrie	511.41

1m Springboard diving (Indoor)

1960	Willard, Patsy	339.55
1961	Lenzi, Joel	454.70
1962	Willard, Patsy	357.50
1963	Willard, Patsy	415.85
1964	Talmage, Barbara	409.05
1965	O'Connell (nee Lenzi) Joel	415.15
1966	O'Connell (nee Lenzi) Joel	423.95
1967	Bush, Lesley	443.10
1968	O'Sullivan, Keala	415.89
1969	Potter, Cynthia	442.26
1970	Potter, Cynthia	440.58
1971	Potter, Cynthia	427.20
1972	King, Micki	436.08
1973	King, Micki	436.08
1974	Loock, Christine	459.09
1975	Chandler, Jenni	446.49

MEN

Highboard diving (Outdoor)

1960	Tobian, Gary	466.40
1961	Harper, Don	482.40
1962	Webster, Robert	472.75
1963	Gompf, Tom	443.65
1964	Webster, Robert	470.55
1965	Wrightson, Bernie	452.40
1966	Gilbert, Rick	577.45
1967	Russell, Keith	576.95
1968	Young, Winn	494.07
1969	Rydze, Dick	552.96
1970	Earley, Rick	597.15
1971	Rydze, Dick	655.52
1972	Earley, Rick,	490.74
1973	Moore, Tim	519.90
1974	Russell, Keith	546.84
1975	Vosler, Kent	545.34

Springboard diving (Outdoor)

1960	Hall, Sam	477.80
1961	Vogel, John	485.50
1962	Vittucci, Lou	487.25
1963	Andreason, Larry	537.90
1964	Wrightson, Bernie	489.10
1965	Wrightson, Bernie	550.65
1966	Gilbert, Rick	552.45
1967	Russell, Keith	557.10
1968	Wrightson, Bernie	552.03
1969	Henry, Jim	515.88
1970	Lincoln, Craig	556.53
1971	Henry, Jim	569.04
1972	Finneran, Mike	556.29
1973	Boggs, Phil	578.73
1974	Russell, Keith	625.05
1975	Boggs, Phil	619.89

1m Springboard diving (Outdoor)

1964	Wrightson, Bernie	522.35
1965	Wrightson, Bernie	494.50
1966	Wrightson, Bernie	503.45
1967	Henry, Jim	489.85
1968	Henry, Jim	595.89
1969	Henry, Jim	510.69
1970	Henry, Jim	550.95
1971	Brown, Mike	548.49
1972	Dunfield, Don	524.61
1973	Finneran, Mike	498.96
1974	Moore, Tim	555.36
1975	Moore, Tim	529.95

WOMEN

Highboard diving (Outdoor)

1960	Irwin (nee Stover), Juno	83.13
1961	McAllister, Barbara	288.50
1962	Cooper, Linda	281.00
1963	Talmage, Barbara	307.95
1964	Willard, Patsy	300.95

1965	Bush, Lesley	345.65
1966	Teeples, Shirley	377.05
1967	Bush, Lesley	377.10
1968	Peterson, Ann	314.58
1969	King, Micki	411.57
1970	Potter, Cynthia	396.03
1971	Potter, Cynthia	430.56
1972	Ely, Janet	389.55
1973	Kepler, Deborah	370.38
1974	York, Teri (Can)	362.19
1975	Ely, Janet	384.81

Springboard diving (Outdoor)

1960	Willard, Patsy	381.10
1961	Lenzi, Joel	453.80
1962	McAllister, Barabra	416.45
1963	Collier, Jeanne	450.80
1964	Talmage, Barbara	446.60
1965	King, Micki	463.05
1966	Gossick, Sue	456.50
1967	King, Micki	466.90
1968	Adair, Jerrie	431.58
1969	King, Micki	472.86
1970	King, Micki	460.80
1971	Potter, Cynthia	508.05
1972	Potter, Cynthia	427.23
1973	Irish, Carrie	445.32
1974	Loock, Christine	522.89
1975	McIngvale (nee Potter) Cynthia	
		465.42

1m Springboard (Outdoor)

1964	Willard, Patsy	441.55
1965	O'Connell, Joel Lenzi	450.95
1966	O'Connell, Joel Lenzi	452.75
1967	King, Micki	407.80
1968	Potter, Cynthia	439.02
1969	Potter, Cynthia	463.95
1970	Potter, Cynthia	419.25
1971	Potter, Cynthia	463.09
1972	Potter, Cynthia	446.82
1973	Potter, Cynthia	431.18
1974	Potter, Cynthia	491.34
1975	McIngvale (nee Potter) Cynthia	
		483.78

UNITED STATES INDOOR CHAMPIONS. These championships are held short course (see SHORT COURSE) in 25 y. baths at the end of the winter season and are one of the reasons why American starting and turning techniques are second to none. But although the championships are known as "The Indoors" they have been held outdoors on occasions.

Championships for men started around 1901 and for women about 1916. At the beginning, the events were held singly at different venues around the country. It was not until the mid-1920's that centralized meetings, over three or four days, were instituted.

The venues and dates of the meetings since 1960 are:

MEN

1960	New Haven, Connecticut	31 March – 2 April
1961	New Haven, Connecticut	30 March – 1 April
1962	Bartlesville, Oklahoma	5–7 April
1963	New Haven, Connecticut	20–23 March
1964	Bartlesville, Oklahoma	2–4 April
1965	New Haven, Connecticut	1–3 April
1966	Brandon, Florida	7–9 April
1967	Dallas, Texas	6–8 April
1968	Greenville, North Carolina	11–13 April

WOMEN

1960	Bartlesville, Oklahoma	14–16 April
1961	Hialeah, Florida	6–8 April
1962	Sacramento, California	19–21 April
1963	Berea, Ohio	28–31 March
1964	Pittsburgh, Pennsylvania	16–19 April
1965	City of Commerce, California	15–18 April
1966	Bartlesville, Oklahoma	15–17 April
1967	Fairview Park, Ohio	13–15 April
1968	Pittsburgh, Pennsylvania	17–20 April

JOINT (Men and women)

1969	Long Beach, California	10–13 April
1970	Cincinnati, Ohio	9–12 April
1971	Pullman, Washington	7–10 April
1972	Dallas, Texas	5–8 April
1973	Cincinnati, Ohio	4–7 April
1974	Dallas, Texas	10–13 April
1975	Cincinnati, Ohio	9–12 April
1976*	Long Beach, California	8–11 April

*in 50 m. pool in preparation for 1976 Olympic Games

The champions since 1960 are.

MEN

100 y. Free-style
1960	Farrell, Jeff	48.2
1961	Clark, Steve	46.8
1962	Jackman, Steve	48.3
1963	Jackman, Steve	46.5
1964	Clark, Steve	47.1
1965	Clark, Steve	45.6
1966	Rerych, Steve	47.5
1967	Havens, Don	46.0
1968	Havens, Don	45.67
1969	Havens, Don	45.92
1970	Edgar, Dave	45.15
1971	Heckl, Frank	45.56
1972	Spitz, Mark	45.10
1973	Knox, Ken	45.26
1974	Bottom, Joe	44.84
1975	Coan, Andy	44.50

200 y. Free-style
1960*	Farrell, Jeff	2:00.2
1961*	Clark, Steve	2:00.0
1962*	Saari, Roy	1:58.6
1963	Schollander, Don	1:44.4
1964	Schollander, Don	1:42.6
1965	Schollander, Don	1:41.7
1966	Schollander, Don	1:42.8
1967	Schollander, Don	1:41.2
1968	Burrell, Bill	1:43.46
1969	Heckl, Frank	1:42.29
1970	Kinsella, John	1:40.76
1971	Heckl, Frank	1:40.55
1972	Genter, Steve	1:39.23
1973	McDonnell, Tim	1:40.04
1974	Krumpholtz, Kurt	1:39.47
1975	Shaw, Tim	1:38.35

*= 220 y.

500 y. Free-style
1960*	Somers, Alan	4:22.6
1961*	Rose, Murray (Aus)	4:18.2
1962*	Saari, Roy	4:14.6
1963	Saari, Roy	4:48.2
1964	Schollander, Don	4:44.5
1965	Robie, Carl	4:44.1
1966	Buckingham, Greg	4:41.1
1967	Burton, Mike	4:37.0
1968	Charlton, Trevor	4:37.29
1969	Fassnacht, Hans (W Ger)	4:32.99
1970	Kinsella, John	4:27.13
1971	Kinsella, John	4:28.84
1972	Kinsella, John	4:28.29
1973	Tingley, Jack	4:26.86
1974	Shaw, Tim	4:23.50
1975	Shaw, Tim	4:22.57

*= 440 y.

1,650 y. Free-style
1960*	Breen, George	18:00.8
1961*	Rose, Murray (Aus)	17:43.7
1962*	Saari, Roy	16:54.1
1963	Saari, Roy	16:52.1
1964	Saari, Roy	16:49.3
1965	Saari, Roy	16:40.8
1966	Burton, Mike	16:27.3
1967	Burton, Mike	16:08.0
1968	Southwood, Charles	16:24.98
1969	Burton, Mike	15:40.10
1970	Kinsella, John	15:35.93
1971	Kinsella, John	15:42.38
1972	Kinsella, John	15:31.30
1973	Tingley, Jack	15:19.41
1974	Bruner, Mike	15:15.33
1975	Naber, John	15:09.51

*= 1,500 m.

100 y. Back-stroke
1960	Bittick, Charles	54.4
1961	Bittick, Charles	53.4
1962	Bennett, Bob	54.1
1963	Bittick, Charles	53.3
1964	Bennett, Bob	53.7
1965	Mann, Tom	52.5
1966	McGeagh, Richard	53.9
1967	Haywood, Fred	52.6
1968	Hickcox, Charles	52.51

1969	Haywood, Fred	52.26
1970	Stamm, Mike	51.17
1971	Stamm, Mike	51.52
1972	Stamm, Mike	51.86
1973	Naber, John	51.36
1974	Naber, John	50.41
1975	Naber, John	50.36

200 y. Back-stroke

1960*	Bittick, Charles	2:13.1
1961*	Bittick, Charles	2:09.7
1962*	Stock, Tom	2:09.0
1963	Bittick, Charles	1:55.9
1964	Bartsch, Edward	1:56.3
1965	Mann, Tom	1:56.8
1966	Hickcox, Charles	1:58.9
1967	Mader, Mark	1:54.4
1968	Hickcox, Charles	1:54.93
1969	Hall, Gary	1:52.00
1970	Hall, Gary	1:51.42
1971	Stamm, Mike	1:52.26
1972	Stamm, Mike	1:51.03
1973	Naber, John	1:50.48
1974	Naber, John	1:49.70
1975	Naber, John	1:48.13
	* = 220 y.	

100 y. Breast-stroke

1960	Nelson, Dick	1:02.4
1961	Jastremski, Chet	59.6
1962	Jastremski, Chet	59.1
1963	Jastremski, Chet	58.5
1964	Craig, Bill	1:00.1
1965	Scheerer, P	1:00.4
1966	Anderson, Wayne	1:01.0
1967	Merten, Ken	58.9
1968	Merten, Ken	58.83
1969	Job, Brian	58.11
1970	Job, Brian	57.02
1971	Job, Brian	57.75
1972	Job, Brian	57.50
1973	Chatfield, Mark	57.36
1974	Hencken, John	55.50
1975	Hencken, John	56.16

200 y. Breast-stroke

1960*	Mulliken, Bill	2:34.8
1961*	Jastremski, Chet	2:26.7
1962*	Jastremski, Chet	2:25.3
1963	Jastremski, Chet	2:09.0
1964	Matsumoto, Kenjiro	2:09.7
1965	Merten, Ken	2:11.8
1966	Merten, Ken	2:12.5
1967	Merten, Ken	2:10.4
1968	Job, Brian	2:08.09
1969	Job, Brian	2:07.34
1970	Job, Brian	2:04.03

1971	Job, Brian	2:04.04
1972	Job, Brian	2:02.36
1973	Colella, Rick	2:03.18
1974	Colella, Rick	2:01.43
1975	Hencken, John	2:00.89
	* = 220 y.	

100 y. Butterfly

1960	Troy, Mike	53.1
1961	Legacki, Frank	51.9
1962	Schulhof, Larry	52.1
1963	Richardson, Walter	1:02.6
1964	Richardson, Walter	50.8
1965	Nicolao, Luis (Arg)	50.9
1966	Wales, Ross	51.3
1967	Spitz, Mark	49.9
1968	Spitz, Mark	49.72
1969	Wales, Ross	50.54
1970	Spitz, Mark	49.10
1971	Heckl, Frank	49.59
1972	Spitz, Mark	48.76
1973	Robertson, Bruce (Can)	49.59
1974	Baxter, Steve	49.51
1975	Hall, Gary	48.86

200 y. Butterfly

1960*	Troy, Mike	2:12.4
1961*	Troy, Mike	2:10.9
1962*	Schulhof, Larry	2:10.7
1963	Schmidt, Fred	1:55.2
1964	Schmidt, Fred	1:53.8
1965	Robie, Carl	1:52.9
1966	Robie, Carl	1:54.9
1967	Spitz, Mark	1:50.6
1968	Spitz, Mark	1:51.50
1969	Burton, Mike	1:52.63
1970	Hall, Gary	1:50.54
1971	Hall, Gary	1:48.44
1972	Spitz, Mark	1:49.01
1973	Backhaus, Robin	1:49.55
1974	Backhaus, Robin	1:47.27
1975	Jagenburg, Greg	1:47.28
	* = 220 y.	

200 y. Individual medley

1960	McGill, John	2:03.3
1961	Stickles, Ted	2:02.1
1962	Jastremski, Chet	1:59.4
1963	Jastremski, Chet	1:58.5
1964	Roth, Dick	1:58.2
1965	Saari, Roy	1:56.2
1966	Utley, Bill	1:57.8
1967	Utley, Bill	1:55.9
1968	Hickcox, Charles	1:53.30
1969	Johnson, David	1:56.22
1970	Hall, Gary	1:54.65
1971	Larsson, Gunnar (Swe)	1:53.37

1972	Hall, Gary	1:53.13
1973	Furniss, Steve	1:51.59
1974	Engstrand, Lee	1:51.28
1975	Engstrand, Lee	1:50.31

400 y. Individual medley

1960	Harrison, George	4:28.6
1961	Bittick, Charles	4:23.7
1962	Stickles, Ted	4:18.1
1963	Saari, Roy	4:16.6
1964	Roth, Dick	4:13.2
1965	Buckingham, Greg	4:08.9
1966	Roth, Dick	4:15.5
1967	Roth, Dick	4:09.5
1968	Hall, Gary	4:10.07
1969	Hall, Gary	4:00.85
1970	Hall, Gary	3:59.66
1971	Larsson, Gunnar (Swe)	4:01.50
1972	Hall, Gary	3:58.09
1973	Szuba, Tom	3:57.78
1974	Colella, Rick	3:57.19
1975	Hargitay, Andras (Hun)	3:54.91

Top Teams

1960 Univ. of S. California 79; New Haven 64
1961 Univ. of S. California 74; New Haven 44½
1962 N. Carolina AC and Univ. of S. California Freshmen 34 (tied)
1963 Indiana Univ. 91; Univ, of S California 51
1964 Univ. of S. California 83
1965 Univ. of S. California 74
1966 Univ. of S. California 119
1967 Santa Clara SC 65; Indiana Univ. 63
1968 Indiana Univ. 334; Santa Clara SC 269
1969 Univ. of S. California 400; Yale Univ. 209
1970 Santa Clara SC 286; Univ of S. California 249
1971 Indiana Univ. 561; Univ. of S. California 550
1972 Univ. of S. California 607; Indiana Univ. 596
1973 Univ. of S. California 666; Indiana Univ. 255
1974 Univ. of S. California 564; Univ, of Washington 347.
1975 Univ. of S. California 474; Indiana Unic. 306

WOMEN

100 y. Free-style

1960	Saltza, Chris von	56.3
1961	Saltza, Chris von	55.8
1962	Johnson, Robyn	55.5
1963	Stickles, Terri	55.3
1964	Stouder, Sharon	54.2
1965	Hallock, Jean	54.3
1966	Randall, Martha	53.6
1967	Brickner, Erica	53.3
1968	Barkman, Jane	52.1
1969	Fordyce, Wendy	52.80
1970	Fordyce, Wendy	52.89
1971	Neilson, Sandra	53.27
1972	Shaw, Barbara	52.10
1973	Babashoff, Shirley	52.15
1974	Heddy, Kathy	50.89
1975	Babashoff, Shirley	50.97

200 y. Free-style

1960*	Saltza, Chris von	2:38.4
1961*	Saltza, Chris von	2:39.0
1962*	Johnson, Robyn	2:34.6
1963*	Stickles, Terri	2:34.7
1964*	Stickles, Terri	2:32.0
1965	Estes, Penny	1:58.2
1966	Randall, Martha	1:56.9
1967	Watson, Lillian (Pokey)	1:54.1
1968	Meyer, Debbie	1:52.1
1969	Gustavson, Linda	1:54.48
1970	Fordyce, Wendy	1:55.58
1971	Spitz, Nancy	1:55.83
1972	Peyton, Kim	1:52.49
1973	Rothhammer, Keena	1:50.51
1974	Babashoff, Shirley	1:48.79
1975	Babashoff, Shirley	1:49.52
	* = 250 y.	

500 y. Free-style

1960	Saltza, Chris von	5:37.7
1961	Saltza, Chris von	5:32.9
1962	Johnson, Robyn	5:27.2
1963	Finneran, Sharon	5:23.4
1964	Stickles, Terri	5:19.2
1965	Caretto, Patty	5:15.6
1966	Kruse, Pam	5:15.5
1967	Kruse, Pam	5:06.9
1968	Meyer, Debbie	4:54.1
1969	King, Vicki	5:01.65
1970	Meyer, Debbie	5:00.77
1971	Meyer, Debbie	5:02.78
1972	Rothhammer, Keena	4:57.87
1973	Rothhammer, Keena	4:52.52
1974	Babashoff, Shirley	4:47.34
1975	Babashoff, Shirley	4:50.95

1,650 y. Free-style

1964	Finneran, Sharon	18:31.5
1965	Caretto, Patty	18:03.6
1966	Finneran, Sharon	18:10.9
1967	Meyer, Debbie	17:38.1
1968	Meyer, Debbie	17:04.4
1969	Meyer, Debbie	17:04.40
1970	Meyer, Debbie	16:54.64
1971	Meyer, Debbie	17:11.83
1972	Harshbarger, Jo	16:59.33
1973	Gould, Shane (Aus)	16:46.65
1974	Hazen, Karen	16:28.37
1975	Harshbarger, Jo	16:27.11

100 y. Back-stroke

1960	Burke, Lynn	1:03.0
1961	Harmer, Nina	1:04.2
1962	Varona, Donna de	1:04.0
1963	Harmer, Nina	1:02.6
1964	Ferguson, Cathy	1:01.5
1965	Ferguson, Cathy	1:00.9
1966	Tanner, Elaine (Can)	1:00.7
1967	Hall, Kaye	1:01.6
1968	Hall, Kaye	59.3
1969	Atwood, Sue	58.80
1970	Atwood, Sue	58.75
1971	Atwood, Sue	58.22
1972	Atwood, Sue	58.75
1973	Stimpson, Linda	58.50
1974	Stimpson, Linda	57.30
1975	Vandeweghe, Tauna	58.12

200 y. Back-stroke

1960	Burke, Lynn	2:16.7
1961	Saltza, Chris von	2:19.9
1962	Varona, Donna de	2:17.9
1963	Duenkel, Ginny	2:14.9
1964	Ferguson, Cathy	2:12.8
1965	Ferguson, Cathy	2:13.2
1966	Humbarger, Judy	2:11.8
1967	Moore, Kendis	2:10.2
1968	Hall, Kaye	2:10.8
1969	Atwood, Sue	2:07.51
1970	Atwood, Sue	2:05.88
1971	Atwood, Sue	2:06.07
1972	Atwood, Sue	2:04.01
1973	Belote, Melissa	2:05.49
1974	Cook, Wendy (Can)	2:04.00
1975	Garapick, Nancy (Can)	2:02.84

100 y. Breast-stroke

1960	Rogers, Susan	1:12.8
1961	Dellekamp, Jean	1:12.9
1962	Whipple, Roby	1:13.3
1963	Goyette, Cynthia	1:11.7
1964	Kolb, Claudia	1:09.3
1965	Goyette, Cynthia	1:09.0
1966	Ball, Catie	1:07.4
1967	Ball, Catie	1:06.6
1968	Wichman, Sharon	1:07.4
1969	Wichman, Sharon	1:07.06
1970	Brecht, Kim	1:06.55
1971	Colella, Lynn	1:06.74
1972	Vidali, Lynn	1:07.00
1973	Carr, Cathy	1:06.10
1974	Morey, Marcia	1:05.53
1975	Dunson, Kim	1:05.25

200 y. Breast-stroke

1960*	Rogers, Susan	3:14.6
1961*	Rogers, Susan	3:19.9
1962*	Hopkins, Andrea	3:15.2
1963*	Whipple, Roby	3:14.7
1964*	Goyette, Cynthia	3:09.1
1965	Goyette, Cynthia	2:26.4
1966	Goyette, Cynthia	2:25.6
1967	Ball, Catie	2:25.2
1968	Wichman, Sharon	2:25.2
1969	Brecht, Kim	2:24.44
1970	Kurtz, Linda	2:23.02
1971	Colella, Lynn	2:21.93
1972	Colella, Lynn	2:22.39
1973	Colella, Lynn	2:20.59
1974	Colella, Lynn	2:19.77
1975	Morey, Marcia	2:18.77

* = 250 y.

100 y. Butterfly

1960	Ramey, Nancy	1:00.3
1961	Ellis, Kathy	1:01.7
1962	Stewart, Mary (Can)	59.2
1963	Ellis, Kathy	59.2
1964	Ellis, Kathy	58.8
1965	Stouder, Sharon	58.0
1966	Tanner, Elaine (Can)	58.7
1967	Davis, Lee	58.4
1968	Daniel, Ellie	58.3
1969	Daniel, Ellie	58.39
1970	Colella, Lynn	58.07
1971	Deardurff, Deena	57.06
1972	Deardurff, Deena	57.16
1973	Deardurff, Deena	56.44
1974	Tosdal, Peggy	55.91
1975	Deardurff, Deena	55.70

200 y. Butterfly

1960	Collins, Becky	2:16.9
1961	Collins, Becky	2:18.4
1962	Finneran, Sharon	2:16.8
1963	Worley, Kim	2:15.3
1964	Varona, Donna de	2:10.5
1965	Pitt, Sue	2:09.6
1966	Davis, Lee	2:11.5
1967	Davis, Lee	2:07.9
1968	Daniel, Ellie	2:06.6
1969	Daniel, Ellie	2:06.65
1970	Colella, Lynn	2:03.93
1971	Jones, Alice	2:03.97
1972	Moe, Karen	2:03.34
1973	Gould, Sharon (Aus)	2:02.72
1974	Lee, Valerie	2:00.84
1975	Lee, Valerie	2:00.70

200 y. Individual medley

1961	Varona, Donna de	2:19.3
1962	Varona, Donna de	2:18.9
1963	Varona, Donna de	2:15.0
1964	Varona, Donna de	2:12.4
1965	Hallock, Jeanne	2:14.2
1966	Barkman, Jane	2:13.8
1967	Kolb, Claudia	2:09.7
1968	Kolb, Claudia	2:08.5
1969	Vidali, Lynn	2:09.21
1970	Vidali, Lynn	2:10.98
1971	Atwood, Sue	2:10.10
1972	Bartz, Jenny	2:08.22
1973	Cliff, Leslie (Can)	2:06.75
1974	Heddy, Kathy	2:05.06
1975	Franks, Jenni	2:04.74

400 y. Individual medley

1960	Ruuska, Sylvia	4:57.0
1961	Collins, Becky	4:55.5
1962	Finneran, Sharon	4:52.9
1963	Varona, Donna de	4:47.3
1964	Varona, Donna de	4:42.9
1965	Finneran, Sharon	4:47.4
1966	Finneran, Sharon	4:49.4
1967	Pedersen, Sue	4:37.0
1968	Kolb, Claudia	4:33.2
1969	Vidali, Lynn	4:36.78
1970	Meyer, Debbie	4:34.23
1971	Atwood, Sue	4:34.80
1972	Atwood, Sue	4:28.85
1973	Gould, Shane (Aus)	4:27.11
1974	Franks, Jenni	4:26.22
1975	Franks, Jenni	4:24.51

Top teams

1960	Santa Clara SC 83; Berkeley SC and Los Angeles AC 40 (tied)
1961	Multnomah AC 57½; Ann Arbor (Mich) SC 44½
1962	Santa Clara SC 46; Cleveland SC 38
1963	Santa Clara SC 113½; Los Angeles AC 38
1964	Santa Clara SC 130½
1965	City of Commerce SC 159
1966	Santa Clara SC 94
1967	Santa Clara SC 136; Arden Hills SC 59
1968	Santa Clara SC 455; Arden Hills SC 196
1969	Santa Clara SC 320½; Lakewood AC 234½
1970	Santa Clara SC 327; Lakewood AC 211
1971	Santa Clara SC 498; Phillips "66" 333
1972	Santa Clara SC 649; Lakewood AC 284
1973	Santa Clara SC 326; Cincinnati Marlins 194
1974	Santa Clara SC 323; Mission Viejo Nadadores 258
1975	Mission Viejo Nadadores 283; Santa Clara SC 217

UNITED STATES OUTDOOR CHAMPIONS. These championships are held long course (see LONG COURSE) in the summer. As with the Indoor championships, the events were held singly at different venues, but from the mid-1920s they have been organized as centralized meetings, over three or four days.

The venues and dates since 1960 are:

MEN			
	1960	Toledo, Ohio	22–24 July
	1961	Los Angeles, California	18–20 Aug
	1962	Cayahoga Falls, Ohio	10–12 Aug
	1963	Oak Park, Illinois	9–11 Aug

WOMEN			
	1960	Indianapolis, Indiana	14–17 July
	1961	Philadelphia, Pennsylvania	10–13 Aug
	1962	Chicago, Illinois	16–19 Aug
	1963	High Point, North Carolina	14–17 Aug

JOINT (Men and Women)

1964	Los Altos, California	30 July – 2 Aug
1965	Maumee, Ohio	11–15 Aug
1966	Lincoln, Nebraska	18–21 Aug
1967	Oak Park, Illinois (Men)	11–13 Aug
	Philadelphia, Pa (Women)	17–20 Aug
1968	Lincoln, Nebraska	1–4 Aug
1969	Lousville, Kentucky	8–14 Aug
1970	Los Angeles, California	20–23 Aug
1971	Houston, Texas	25–28 Aug
1972*	Chicago, Illinois	2–6 Aug
1973	Louisville, Kentucky	22–25 Aug
1974	City of Concord, California	20–25 Aug
1975	Kansas City, Kansas	20–23 Aug
1975	Philadelphia, Pennsylvania	12–15 Aug

*No championships were held in 1972 but the results of the Olympic trials for that year have been included for continuity.

MEN

100 m. Free-style

1946	Smith, Bill	59.0
1947	Ris, Wally	58.5
1948	Nugent, Robert	58.9
1949	Gibe, Robert	58.2
1950*	Cleveland, Dick	58.2
1951	Cleveland, Dick	58.2
1952*	Cleveland, Dick	58.4
1953	Cleveland, Dick	57.2
1954	Cleveland, Dick	57.5
1955	Gideonse, Hendrick	57.6
1956	Hanley, Richard	56.3
1957	Hanley, Richard	57.3
1958	Henricks, Jon (Aus)	55.8
1959	Farrell, Jeff	59.6
1960	Farrell, Jeff	54.8
1961	Clark, Steve	54.4
1962	Clark, Steve	54.4
1963	Clark, Steve	54.9
1964	Schollander, Don	54.0
1965	Roth, Donald	53.8
1966	Schollander, Don	53.5
1967	Schollander, Don	53.3
1968	Spitz, Mark	53.6
1969	Havens, Don	52.5
1970	Heckl, Frank	52.5
1971	Spitz, Mark	52.45
1972	Spitz, Mark	51.91
1973	Montgomery, Jim	52.95
1974	Hickcox, Tom	52.16
1975	Montgomery, Jim	51.04

* = 110 y.

200 m. Free-style

1946	Smith, Bill	2:14.4
1947	Smith, Bill	2:12.6
1948	Gilbert, Edward	2:16.9
1949	Hamaguchi, Yoshiro (Jap)	2:11.0
1950*	McLane, Jimmy	2:10.5
1951	Moore, Wayne	2:08.4
1952*	Woolsey, William	2:13.2
1953	Moore, Wayne	2:09.0
1954	Konno, Fred	2:10.6
1955	Woolsey, William	2:08.2
1956	Woolsey, William	2:06.6
1957	Hanley, Richard	2:08.4
1958	Henricks, Jon (Aus)	2:05.2
1959	Farrell, Jeff	2:06.9
1960	Farrell, Jeff	2:03.2
1961	Yamanaka, Tsuyoshi (Jap)	2:00.4
1962	Schollander, Don	2:00.4
1963	Schollander, Don	1:59.0
1964	Schollander, Don	1:57.6
1965	Ilman, Gary	1:59.0
1966	Schollander, Don	1:56.2
1967	Schollander, Don	1:55.7
1968	Spitz, Mark	1:57.0
1969	Fassnacht, Hans (W Ger)	1:56.5
1970	Spitz, Mark	1:54.6
1971	Spitz, Mark	1:54.74
1972	Spitz, Mark	1:53.58
1973	Montgomery, Jim	1:53.69
1974	Shaw, Tim	1:51.66
1975	Furniss, Bruce	1:50.32

* = 220 y.

400 m. Free-style

1946	McLane, Jimmy	4:49.5
1947	McLane, Jimmy	4:41.9
1948	McLane, Jimmy	4:53.5
1949	Furuhashi, , Hironashin (Jap)	4:33.3
1950*	Marshall, John (Aus)	4:39.3
1951	Moore, Wayne	4:35.8
1952*	Konno, Fred	4:48.0
1953	Konno, Fred	4:39.8
1954	Woolsey, William	4:43.3
1955	Konno, Fred	4:38.7

1956	Breen, George	4:37.6
1957	Breen, George	4:35.1
1958	Rose, Murray (Aus)	4:24.5
1959	Somers, Alan	4:30.6
1960	Somers, Alan	4:21.9
1961	Yamanaka, Tsuyoshi (Jap)	4:17.5
1962	Rose, Murray (Aus)	4:17.2
1963	Schollander, Don	4:17.7
1964	Schollander, Don	4:12.7
1965	Nelson, John	4:14.1
1966	Schollander, Don	4:11.6
1967	Charlton, Greg	4:09.8
1968	Hutton, Ralph (Can)	4:06.5
1969	Fassnacht, Hans (W Ger)	4:04.0
1970	Kinsella, John	4:02.8

1971	McBreen, Tom	4:02.08
1972	McBreen, Tom	4:00.70
1973	DeMont, Rick	4:00.14
1974	Shaw, Tim	3:59.69
1975	Shaw, Tim	3:53.31
	* = 440 y	

1,500 m. Free-style

1946	McLane, Jimmy	19:23.1
1947	McLane, Jimmy	19:57.5
1948	Taylor, Jack	19:48.1
1949	Furuhashi, Hironoshin (Jap)	
		18:29.9
1950*	Marshall, John (Aus)	20:08.6
1951	Konno, Ford	18:46.3
1952*	Konno, Ford	20:47.1
1953	Konno, Ford	19:20.0
1954	Konno, Ford	19:07.1
1955	Onekea, George	18:52.3
1956	Breen, George	18:27.6
1957	Breen, George	18:17.9
1958	Rose, Murray (Aus)	18:06.4
1959	Somers, Alan	17:51.3
1960	Breen, George	17:33.5
1961	Saari, Roy	17:29.8
1962	Rose, Murray (Aus)	17:16.7
1963	Saari, Roy	17:34.6
1964	Rose, Murray (Aus)	17:01.8
1965	Krause, Steve	16:58.6
1966	Burton, Mike	16:41.6
1967	Burton, Mike	16:34.1
1968	Burton, Mike	16:29.4
1969	Burton, Mike	16:04.5
1970	Kinsella, John	15:57.1

1971	Burton, Mike	16:09.66
1972	DeMont, Rick	15:52.91
1973	DeMont, Rick	15:51.02
1974	Shaw, Tim	15:31.75
1975	Hackett, Bobby	15:29.36
	* = one mile	

100 m. Back-stroke

1946	Holiday, Harry	1:08.0
1947	Stack, Allen	1:07.8
1948	Stack, Allen	1:07.7
1949	Stack, Allen	1:07.1
1950*	Stack, Allen	1:08.2
1951	Thomas, Jack	1:07.4
1952*	Oyakawa, Yashinobu	1:05.7
1953	Oyakawa, Yashinobu	1:06.8
1954	Wiggins, Albert	1:07.2
1955	Oyakawa, Yashinobu	1:05.3
1956	Oyakawa, Yashinobu	1:05.9
1957	McKinney, Frank	1:04.5
1958	McKinney, Frank	1:04.5
1959	McKinney, Frank	1:03.6
1960	Stock, Tom	1:02.9
1961	Bennett, Robert	1:01.3
1962	Stock, Tom	1:00.9
1963	McGeagh, Richard	1:01.7
1964	McGeagh, Richard	1:01.6
1965	Mann, H. Thompson	1:00.5
1966	Hickcox, Charles	1:01.0
1967	Hickcox, Charles	59.7
1968	Barbiere, Larry	1:00.9
1969	Ivey, Mitch	1:00.2
1970	Stamm, Mike	58.5

1971	Nash, Mel	59.28
1972	Ivey, Mitch	58.61
1973	Stamm, Mike	59.35
1974	Naber, John	58.12
1975	Naber, John	57.35
	* = 110 y.	

200 m. Back-stroke (instituted 1953)

1953	Oyakawa, Yoshinobu	2:29.9
1954	Wiggins, Albert	2:31.0
1955	Oyakawa, Yoshinobu	2:26.1
1956	McKinney, Frank	2:24.5
1957	McKinney, Frank	2:21.7
1958	McKinney, Frank	2:20.8
1959	McKinney, Frank	2:17.9
1960	Stock, Tom	2:16.0
1961	Stock, Tom	2:11.5
1962	Stock, Tom	2:10.9
1963	Stock, Tom	2:12.4
1964	Bennett, Robert	2:15.7
1965	Mann, H. Thompson	2:12.4
1966	Hickcox, Charles	2:12.4
1967	Hickcox, Charles	2:12.3
1968	Horsley, Jack	2:12.2
1969	Hall, Gary	2:06.6
1970	Stamm, Mike	2:06.3

1971	Campbell, Charles	2:07.14
1972	Ivey, Mitch	2:06.57
1973	Naber, John	2:05.67
1974	Naber, John	2:03.50
1975	Naber, John	2:02.52

100 m. Breast-stroke (Instituted 1952)

1952*	Holan, Jerry	Bu1:09.2
1953	Dudeck, John	Bu1:08.4
1954-55	Event not held	
1956	Hughes, Robert	1:11.2
1957	Hughes, Robert	1:12.1
1958	Sanguilly, Manuel (Cuba)	1:15.9
1959	Sanguilly, Manuel (Cuba)	1:14.6
1960	Jastremski, Chet	1:12.4
1961	Jastremski, Chet	1:07.5
1962	Jastremski, Chet	1:08.2
1963	Craig, William	1:10.2
1964	Jastremski, Chet	1:10.0
1965	Trethewey, Tom	1:08.3
1966	Merten, Ken	1:08.9
1967	Merten, Ken	1:08.7
1968	Dirksen, Mike	1:08.8
1969	Fiolo, Jose (Braz)	1:06.9
1970	Job, Brian	1:06.5
1971	Dahlberg, Peter	1:06.91
1972	Hencken, John	1:05.99
1973	Hencken, John	1:05.17
1974	Hencken, John	1:04.38
1975	Colella, Rick	1:05.95

    * = 110 y.

200 m. Breast-stroke

1946	Verduer, Joe	Bu2:44.2
1947	Verduer, Joe	Bu2:38.4
1948	Verduer, Joe	Bu2:48.7
1949	Verduer, Joe	Bu2:36.3
1950*	Brawner, Robert	Bu2:41.0
1951	Davies, John (Aus)	Bu2:35.8
1952*	Stassforth, Bowen	Bu2:34.7
1953	Hawkins, David (Aus)	Bu2:37.9
1954	Fadgen, Richard	2:49.5
1955	Mattson, Robert	2:46.8
1956	Fadgen, Richard	2:45.8
1957	Sanguilly, Manuel (Cuba)	2:44.0
1958	Rumpel, Norbert (W Ger)	2:47.8
1959	Clark, Ronald	2:45.6
1960	Fogarasey, Peter	2:38.8
1961	Tremewan, Cary	2:36.0
1962	Jastremski, Chet	2:30.0
1963	Merten, Ken	2:34.5
1964	Jastremski, Chet/	
	Craig, William (tie)	2:31.8
1965	Jastremski, Chet	2:30.7
1966	Merten, Ken	2:31.2
1967	Merten, Ken	2:30.8
1968	Job, Brian	2:31.2
1969	Dirksen, Mike	2:26.9
1970	Job, Brian	2:23.5
1971	Colella, Rick	2:25.05
1972	Job, Brian	2:23.27

1973	Henchen, John	2:20.52
1974	Hencken, John	2:18.93
1975	Colella, Rick	2:21.32

    * = 220 y.

100 m. Butterfly. (Instituted 1954)

1954	Fadgen, Richard	1:07.4
1955	Event not swum	
1956	Wiggins, Albert	1:04.2
1957	Wiggins, Albert	1:02.8
1958	Troy, Mike	1:02.8
1959	Larson, Lance	1:01.1
1960	Larson, Lance	58.7
1961	Schmidt, Fred	58.6
1962	Spencer, Edwin	58.9
1963	Richardson, Walter	58.8
1964	Richardson, Walter	57.5
1965	Nicolao, Luis (Arg)	57.8
1966	Spitz, Mark	58.1
1967	Spitz, Mark	56.7
1968	Spitz, Mark	57.0
1969	Russell, Douglas	56.0
1970	Spitz, Mark	56.1
1971	Spitz, Mark	55.30
1972	Spitz, Mark	54.56
1973	Backhaus, Robin	56.81
1974	Bottom, Mike	55.50
1975	Baxter, Steve	55.29

200 m. Butterfly (Instituted 1955)

1955	Yorzyk, Bill	2:29.1
1956	Yorzyk, Bill	2:24.3
1957	Yorzyk, Bill	2:22.0
1958	Yorzyk, Bill	2:22.5
1959	Troy, Mike	2:16.4
1960	Troy, Mike	2:13.4
1961	Robie, Carl	2:12.6
1962	Robie, Carl	2:10.8
1963	Robie, Carl	2:08.8
1964	Robie, Carl	2:09.2
1965	Robie, Carl	2:07.7
1966	Houser, Philip	2:09.9
1967	Spitz, Mark	2:06.4
1968	Robie, Carl	2:08.9
1969	Burton, Mike	2:06.5
1970	Hall, Gary	2:05.0
1971	Spitz, Mark	2:03.89
1972	Spitz, Mark	2:01.53
1973	Gregg, Steve	2:04.11
1974	Bruner, Mike	2:01.69
1975	Jagenburg, Greg	2:00.73

200 m. Individual medley (instituted 1959)

1959	Larson, Lance	2:24.7
1960	Stickles, Ted	2:22.1
1961	Stickles, Ted	2:15.9

1962	Stickles, Ted	2:16.2
1963	Roth, Dick	2:16.0
1964	Roth, Dick	2:15.5
1965	Roth, Dick	2:14.9
1966	Buckingham, Greg	2:12.4
1967	Buckingham, Greg	2:11.3
1968	Bello, Juan (Peru)	2:14.1
1969	Hall, Gary	2:09.6
1970	Hall, Gary	2:09.5
1971	Hall, Gary	2:10.07
1972	Hall, Gary	2:09.30
1973	Carper, Stan	2:08.58
1974	Furniss, Steve	2:08.26
1975	Furniss, Bruce	2:06.08

400 m. Individual medley

1946*	Holiday, Harry	3:58.8
1947*	Verdeur, Joe	3:59.2
1948*	Verdeur, Joe	4:00.0
1949*	Verdeur, Joe	3:53.7
1950†	Thomas, James	3:55.1
1951*	Jones, Burwell	3:52.3
1952†	Jones, Burwell	3:54.8
1953*	Jones, Burwell	3:46.2
1954	Jones, Burwell	5:29.0
1955	Harrison, George	5:23.3
1956	Yorzyk, Bill	5:19.0
1957	Heinrich, Gary	5:15.6
1958	Brunell, Frank	5:20.6
1959	Barton, William	5:14.6
1960	Rounsanvelle, Dennis	5:04.5
1961	Stickles, Ted	4:55.6
1962	Stickles, Ted	4:51.5
1963	Stickles, Ted	4:55.0
1964	Roth, Dick	4:48.6
1965	Roth, Dick	4:49.2
1966	Roth, Dick	4:47.9
1967	Williams, Peter	4:50.8
1968	Hall, Gary	4:48.0
1969	Hall, Gary	4:33.9
1970	Hall, Gary	4:31.0
1971	Hall, Gary	4:33.11
1972	Hall, Gary	4:30.81
1973	Colella, Rick	4:32.38
1974	Furniss, Steve	4:30.56
1975	Hannula, Dave	4:31.35

* = 300 m.   † = 330 y.

WOMEN

100 m. Free-style

1946	Helser, Brenda	1:07.2
1947	Curtis, Ann	1:07.0
1948	Curtis, Ann	1:08.0
1949*	Kalama, Thelma	1:10.9
1950	Lavine, Jackie	1:10.0
1951	Geary, Sharon	1:07.6
1952	No championship meeting	

1953*	Roberts, Judy	1:07.9
1954	Alderson, Judy	1:06.1
1955	Werner, Wanda	1:06.1
1956*	Werner, Wanda	1:06.3
1957*	Fraser, Dawn (Aus)	1:03.9
1958	Von Saltza, Chris	1:03.5
1959*	Von Saltza, Chris	1:04.8
1960	Von Saltza, Chris	1:01.6
1961	Johnson, Robyn	1:03.2
1962	Johnson, Robyn	1:02.2
1963	Johnson, Robyn	1:01.5
1964	Stouder, Sharon	1:00.4
1965	Watson, L. 'Pokey'	1:00.7
1966	Watson, L. 'Pokey'	59.9
1967	Barkman, Janie	59.8
1968	Barkman, Janie	1:00.1
1969	Pedersen, Sue	59.7
1970	Schilling, Cindy	1:00.4
1971	Johnson, Linda	1:00.03
1972	Kemp, Jenny	58.63
1973	Babashoff, Shirley	58.77
1974	Peyton, Kim	58.22
1975	Babashoff, Shirley	57.48

* = 110 y.

200 m. Free-style (Instituted 1958)

1958	Botkin, Molly	2:23.2
1959*	Von Saltza, Chris	2:21.1
1960	Von Saltza, Chris	2:15.1
1961	House, Carolyn	2:18.9
1962	House, Carolyn	2:14.6
1963	Johnson, Robyn	2:15.6
1964	Hallock, Jeanne	2:13.3
1965	Randall, Martha	2:12.3
1966	Watson, L. 'Pokey'	2:10.5
1967	Kruse, Pam	2:09.7
1968	Wetzel, Eadie	2:08.8
1969	Pedersen, Sue	2:07.8
1970	Simmons, Ann	2:09.6
1971	Johnson, Linda	2:08.03
1972	Babashoff, Shirley	2:05.21
1973	Babashoff, Shirley	2:04.63
1974	Babashoff, Shirley	2:02.94
1975	Babashoff, Shirley	2:02.39

* = 220 y.

400 m. Free-style

1946	Curtis, Ann	5:26.7
1947	Curtis, Ann	5:21.5
1948	Curtis, Ann	5:26.2
1949*	Kalama, Thelma	5:41.2
1950	Kalama, Thelma	5:30.9
1951	Hobelmann, Barbara	5:21.6
1952	No championship meeting	
1953*	Meulenkamp, Delia	5:22.2
1954	Green, Carolyn	5:14.7
1955	Gray, 'Dougie'	5:16.1

1956*	Shriver, Marley	5:13.8
1957*	Crapp, Lorraine (Aus)	5:08.5
1958	Ruuska, Sylvia	5:04.1
1959*	Von Saltza, Chris	4:59.4
1960	Von Saltza, Chris	4:46.9
1961	House, Carolyn	4:52.5
1962	House, Carolyn	4:45.3
1963	Johnson, Robyn	4:46.8
1964	Ramenofsky, Marilyn	4:41.7
1965	Randall, Martha	4:39.2
1966	Randall, Martha	4:38.0
1967	Meyer, Debbie	4:29.0
1968	Meyer, Debbie	4:26.7
1969	Meyer, Debbie	4:26.4
1970	Meyer, Debbie	4:24.3
1971	Simmons, Ann	4:24.82
1972	Rothhammer, Keena	4:21.99
1973	Rothhammer, Keena	4:18.07
1974	Babashoff, Shirley	4:15.77
1975	Babashoff, Shirley	4:15.63

* = 440 y.

800 m. Free-style

1946	Curtis, Ann	11:26.3
1947	Curtis, Ann	11:21.8
1948	Curtis, Ann	11:37.2
1949*	Kleinschmidt, Catherine	11:48.1
1950	Green, Carolyn	11:28.3
1951	Green, Carolyn	11:15.5
1952	No championship meeting	
1953*	Green, Carolyn	11:15.2
1954	Green, Carolyn	10:49.9
1955	Green, Carolyn	10:45.3
1956*	Ruuska, Sylvia	10:54.5
1957*	Ruuska, Sylvia	10:45.8
1958	Event discontinued	

* = 880 y.

1,500 m. Free-style

1946	Curtis, Ann	22:08.1
1947	Sahner, Merilyn	22:23.1
1948	Mallory, Joan	22:58.4
1949*	Lutyens, Jean	24:34.5
1950	Hobelman, Barbara	22:25.7
1951	Green, Carolyn	21:48.3
1952	No championship meeting	
1953*	Green, Carolyn	23:03.4
1954	Green, Carolyn	21:80.5
1955	Green, Carolyn	21:15.4
1956†	Green, Carolyn	21:30.2
1957*	Murray, Carolyn	22:13.7
1958	Ruuska, Sylvia	20:34.6
1959*	Ruuska, Sylvia	21:38.9
1960	House, Carolyn	19:45.0
1961	House, Carolyn	19:46.3
1962	House, Carolyn	18:44.0
1963	Duenkel, Virginia	18:57.9
1964	Caretto, Patty	18:30.5
1965	Caretto, Patty	18:23.7

1966	Caretto, Patty	18:12.9
1967	Meyer, Debbie	17:50.2
1968	Meyer, Debbie	17:38.5
1969	Meyer, Debbie	17:19.9
1970	Meyer, Debbie	17:28.4
1971	Calhoun, Cathy	17:19.20
1972†	Harshbarger, Jo	8:53.83
1973	Harshbarger, Jo	16:54.14
1974	Turrall, Jenny (Aus)	16:33.94
1975	Greenwood, Heather	16:47.11

* = one mile † = 1,650 y.
‡ = 800 m. (Olympic trial)

100 m. Back-stroke

1946	Zimmerman, Suzanne	1:18.0
1947	Zimmerman, Suzanne	1:17.6
1948	Zimmerman, Suzanne	1:16.4
1949*	Jensen, Barbara	1:20.3
1950	O'Brien, Maureen	1:17.9
1951	Freeman, Mary	1:18.8
1952	No championship meeting	
1953*	Stark, Barbara	1:16.6
1954	Mann, Shelley	1:15.5
1955	Cone, Carin	1:15.6
1956*	Cone, Carin	1:14.5
1957*	Cone, Carin	1:13.6
1958	Cone, Carin	1:13.3
1959*	Cone, Carin	1:13.3
1960	Burke, Lynn	1:10.2
1961	Harmar, Nina	1:11.0
1962	De Varona, Donna	1:10.4
1963	Ferguson, Cathy	1:09.2
1964	Ferguson, Cathy	1:09.2
1965	Caron, Christine (Fr)	1:08.1
1966	Fairlie, Ann (SAf)	1:07.9
1967	Moore, Kendis	1:09.2
1968	Muir, Karen (SAf)	1:06.9
1969	Atwood, Sue	1:06.0
1970	Atwood, Sue	1:06.2
1971	Atwood, Sue	1:06.72
1972	Belote, Melissa	1:07.08
1973	Belote, Melissa	1:05.72
1974	Moffit, Margie	1:04.68
1975	Jezek, Linda	1:04.70

* = 110 y.

200 m. Back-stroke

1946	Zimmerman, Suzanne	2:48.7
1947	Zimmerman, Suzanne	2:49.0
1948	Zimmerman, Suzanne	2:48.3
1949*	Jensen, Barbara	2:54.9
1950	O'Brien, Maureen	2:51.2
1951	Freeman, Mary	2:49.8
1952	No championship meeting	
1953*	Stark, Barbara	2:45.7
1954	Stark, Barbara	2:47.9
1955	Cone, Karin	2:45.6

1956*	Cone, Carin	2:43.8
1957*	Von Saltza, Chris	2:40.2
1958	Von Saltza, Chris	2:37.4
1959*	Cone, Carin	2:37.9
1960	Burke, Lynn	2:33.5
1961	Harmer, Nina	2:35.0
1962	Duenkel, Virginia	2:32.1
1963	Duenkel, Virginia	2:30.8
1964	Ferguson, Cathy	2:29.2
1965	Ferguson, Cathy/	
	Humbarger, Judy (tie)	2:28.0
1966	Muir, Karen (SAf)	2:26.4
1967	Moore, Kendis	2:28.1
1968	Muir, Karen (SAf)	2:24.3
1969	Atwood, Sue	2:21.5
1970	Atwood, Sue	2:22.0
1971	Atwood, Sue	2:22.91
1972	Belote, Melissa	2:21.77
1973	Belote, Melissa	2:20.75
1974	Cook, Wendy (Can)	2:18.81
1975	Belote, Melissa	2:18.16

* = 220 y.

100 m. Breast-stroke

1946	Wilson, Jeanne	1:26.2
1947	Van Vleit, Nel (Neth)	1:21.6
1948	Wilson, Jeanne	1:28.9
1949*	Pence, Carol	1:25.8
1950	Cornell, Judy	1:23.1
1951	Cornell, Judy	1:21.0
1952	No championship meeting	
1953*	Peters, Gail	Bu1:18.0
1954–55	Event not held	
1956*	Sears, Mary-Jane	1:22.7
1957*	Elsenius, Mary-Lou	1:24.9
1958	Ordogh, Susie (Hun)	1:23.8
1959*	Hargreaves, Marianne	1:22.4
1960	Warner, Ann	1:23.4
1961	Barnhard, Dale	1:22.6
1962	Urslemann, Wiltrud (W Ger)	
		1:20.6
1963	Dellekamp, Jean	1:20.7
1964	Kolb, Claudia	1:19.0
1965	Kolb, Claudia	1:17.1
1966	Ball, Catie	1:16.4
1967	Ball, Catie	1:14.6
1968	Ball, Catie	1:15.7
1969	Brecht, Kim	1:15.7
1970	Kurtz, Linda	1:16.7
1971	Nickloff, Diane	1:16.71
1972	Carr, Cathy	1:15.17
1973	Morey, Marcia	1:16.04
1974	Morey, Marcia	1:15.09
1975	Morey, Marcia	1:13.55

* = 110 y.

200 m. Breast-stroke

1946	Merkie, Nancy	3:15.0
1947	Van Vliet, Nel (Neth)	2:58.6
1948	Wilson, Jeanne	3:17.7
1949*	Kawamoto, Evelyn	3:14.5
1950	Kawamoto, Evelyn/	
	Hulton, Marce (tie)	3:10.2
1951	Pence, Carol	3:09.2
1952	No championship meeting	
1953*	Peters, Gail	Bu3:01.1
1954	Sears, Mary-Jane	3:07.4
1955	Sears, Mary-Jane	3:01.4
1956*	Sears, Mary-Jane	2:59.0
1957*	Elsenius, Mary-Lou	3:04.8
1958	Ordogh, Susie (Hun)	2:58.6
1959*	Warner, Ann	3:02.4
1960	Warner, Ann	2:53.3
1961	Dellekamp, Jean	2:56.7
1962	Urselmann, Wiltrud (W Ger)	
		2:53.3
1963	Dellekamp, Jean	2:53.4
1964	Kolb, Claudia	2:49.8
1965	Kolb, Claudia/	
	Goyette, Cynthia (tie)	2:48.6
1966	Ball, Catie	2:44.4
1967	Ball, Catie	2:39.4
1968	Ball, Catie	2:40.9
1969	Brecht, Kim	2:45.4
1970	Clevenger, Claudia	2:46.7
1971	Clevenger, Claudia	2:45.72
1972	Schoenfield, Dana	2:43.71
1973	Colella, Lynn	2:41.63
1974	Morey, Marcia	2:39.90
1975	Morey, Marcia	2:39.43

* = 220 y.

100 m. Butterfly (Instituted 1954)

1954	Mann, Shelley	1:17.0
1955	Mullen, Betty	1:15.0
1956*	Mann, Shelley	1:11.8
1957*	Ramey, Nancy	1:11.3
1958	Ramey, Nancy	1:10.3
1959*	Collins, Becky	1:11.2
1960	Collins, Becky	1:10.8
1961	Doerr, Susan	1:08.2
1962	Stewart, Mary (Can)	1:07.6
1963	Ellis, Kathy	1:06.5
1964	Stouder, Sharon	1:05.4
1965	Pitt, Susan	1:06.2
1966	Pitt, Susan	1:07.0
1967	Daniel, Ellie	1:05.7
1968	Daniel, Ellie	1:06.9
1969	Durkin, Virginia	1:05.9
1970	Jones, Alice	1:04.1
1971	Deardurff, Deena	1:05.03
1972	Deardurff, Deena	1:04.08
1973	Deardurff, Deena	1:03.85

1974	Deardurff, Deena	1:02.77
1975	Wright, Camille	1:02.90
	* = 110 y.	

200 m. Butterfly (Instituted 1956)

1956*	Mann, Shelley	2:44.4
1957*	Wilson, Jane	2:47.6
1958	Ruuska, Sylvia	2:43.6
1959*	Collins, Becky	2:37.0
1960	Collins, Becky	2:36.8
1961	Collins, Becky	2:32.8
1962	Finneran, Sharon	2:31.2
1963	Finneran, Sharon	2:31.8
1964	Stouder, Sharon	2:26.4
1965	Moore, Kendis	2:26.3
1966	Davis, Lee	2:27.2
1967	Hewitt, Toni	2:23.6
1968	Hewitt, Toni	2:24.2
1969	Colella, Lynn	2:21.6
1970	Jones, Alice	2:19.3
1971	Daniel, Ellie	2:18.40
1972	Moe, Karen	2:16.62
1973	Colella, Lynn	2:18.34
1974	Lee, Valerie	2:16.52
1975	Lee, Valerie	2:15.07
	* = 220 y.	

200 m. Individual medley (Instituted 1961)

1961	De Varona, Donna	2:35.0
1962	De Varona, Donna	2:33.3
1963	De Varona, Donna	2:31.8
1964	De Varona, Donna	2:29.9
1965	Kolb, Claudia	2:30.8
1966	Kolb, Claudia	2:27.8
1967	Kolb, Claudia	2:25.0
1968	Kolb, Claudia	2:27.5
1969	Vidali, Lynn	2:26.2
1970	Vidali, Lynn	2:26.1
1971	Nishigawa, Yoshimi (Jap)	2:26.00
1972	Vidali, Lynn	2:24.46
1973	Heddy, Kathy	2:25.41
1974	Heddy, Kathy	2:22.47
1975	Heddy, Kathy	2:19.93

400 m. Individual medley

1946*	Merki, Nancy	4:29.9
1947*	Merki, Nancy	4:32.9
1948*	Jensen, Barbara	4:31.3
1949*	Kawamoto, Evelyn	4:27.5
1950*	Kawamoto, Evelyn	4:29.0
¹951†	Kawamoto, Evelyn	4:33.0

1952	No championship meeting	
1953†	Peters, Gail	4:21.7
1954	Gillett, Marie	6:06.9
1955	Gillett, Marie	6:01.5
1956‡	Mann, Shelley	5:52.5
1957‡	Ruuska, Sylvia	5:49.5
1958	Ruuska, Sylvia	5:43.7
1959‡	Ruuska, Sylvia	5:40.2
1960	De Varona, Donna	5:36.5
1961	De Varona, Donna	5:34.5
1962	Finneran, Sharon	5:25.4
1963	De Varona, Donna	5:24.5
1964	De Varona, Donna	5:17.7
1965	Olcese, Mary-Ellen	5:19.6
1966	Kolb, Claudia	5:15.5
1967	Kolb, Claudia	5:08.2
1968	Pedersen, Sue	5:10.3
1969	Meyer, Debbie	5:08.6
1970	Atwood, Sue	5:07.3
1971	Bartz, Jenny	5:08.38
1972	Montgomery, Mary	5:04.96
1973	Bartz, Jenni	5:08.73
1974	Franks, Jenni	5:00.51
1975	Franks, Jenni	4:53.86
	* = 330 y. † = 300 m. ‡ = 440 y.	

U.S.S.R. CHAMPIONS. The first Soviet Union championships were held in 1921 but it was not for another 38 years that a national swimming federation was founded, the events before 1959 have been organized by the swimming secrion of the national all-sports body.

The first Russian Olympic swimming champion was Galina Prozumenshikova (see STEPANOVA, Galina) who took the 200 m. breast-stroke title in 1964. And it is for producing outstanding breast-stroke competitors, like Vladimir Minashkin, Leonid Kolesnikov, Georgy Prokopenko, Vladimir Kosinsky and Nikolay Pankin, who were all world record-breakers, that the Soviet Union has made its greatest impact on the sport.

In the European championships, the Soviet Union's men were the most successful swimming nation in 1958, '62, '66 and '74. Their combined men's and women's team were top diving country in 1966 and '72.

The venues and winners of championships since 1960 are:

1960	Moscow	8−12 July
1961	Lvov	5−9 Sept
1962	Kharkov	7−10 Aug.
1963	Moscow	13−17 Aug.
1964	Moscow	5−9 Sept.
1965	Kharkov	27−31 Aug.
1966	Moscow	8−14 July
1967	Moscow	1−5 July
1968	Tzahkadzoz	3−9 Sept.
1969	Kharkov (men)	
	Moscow (women)	1−5 Aug.
1970	Lvov	4−8 Aug.
1971	Moscow	27−31 July
1972	Moscow	6−16 Aug.
1973	Rostov-na-Donu	24−31 July
1974	Erevan-Kharkov	2−6 July
1975	Moscow	6−9 June

MEN

100 m. Free-style

1960	Morgachev, Petr	57.7
1961	Konoplev, Victor	57.7
1962	Konoplev, Victor	56.6
1963	Konoplev, Victor	56.4
1964	Shuvalov, Vladimir	55.4
1965	Ilichev, Leonid	56.0
1966	Ilichev, Leonid	54.6
1967	Ilichev, Leonid	53.9
1968	Ilichev, Leonid	53.9
1969	Ilichev, Leonid	54.1
1970	Ilichev, Leonid	53.4
1971	Bure, Vladimir	52.9
1972	Bure, Vladimir	52.5
1973	Bure, Vladimir	52.6
1974	Bure, Vladimir	52.8
1975	Bure, Vladimir	51.80

200 m. Free-style

1962	Luzkovsky, Igor	2:06.4
1963	Not held	
1964	Belits-Geiman, Semeòn	2:03.4
1965	Not held	
1966	Ilichev, Leonid	1:58.4
1967	Ilichev, Leonid	1:57.6
1968	Ilichev, Leonid	1:59.9
1969	Ilichev, Leonid	2:00.1
1970	Kulikov, Georgy	1:57.7
1971	Bure, Vladimir	1:58.1
1972	Grivennikov, Igor	1:56.1
1973	Bure, Vladimir	1:56.2
1974	Samsonov, Aleksandr	1:55.0
1975	Krylov, Andrey	1:54.44

400 m. Free-style

1960	Nikitin, Boris	4:32.3
1961	Androsov, Gennady	4:37.8
1962	Paramonov, Aleksandr	4:35.3
1963	Belits-Geiman, Semeòn	4:26.5
1964	Belits, Geiman, Semeòn	4:24.8
1965	Belits-Geiman, Semeòn	4:20.0
1966	Pletnev, Aleksandr	4:15.9
1967	Belits-Geiman, Semeòn	4:13.2
1968	Belits-Geiman, Semeòn	4:21.7
1969	Belits-Geiman, Semeòn	4:17.4
1970	Samsonov, Aleksandr	4:09.0
1971	Samsonov, Aleksandr	4:10.3
1972	Bure, Vladimir	4:07.3
1973	Bure, Vladimir	4:06.3
1974	Samsonov, Aleksandr	4:06.5
1975	Samsonov, Aleksandr	4:01.89

1,500 m. Free-style

1960	Androsov, Gennady	18:17.5
1961	Lavrinenko, Vladimir	18:43.6
1962	Pikalov, Petr	18:20.2
1963	Pikalov, Petr	17:44.8
1964	Dunaev, Andrey	17:49.6
1965	Pletnev, Aleksandr	17:19.0
1966	Pletnev, Aleksandr	17:07.1
1967	Belits-Geiman, Semeòn	16:52.7
1968	Bure, Vladimir	17:25.6
1969	Dunaev, Andrey	17:05.2
1970	Belits-Geiman, Semeòn	17:04.2
1971	Dunaev, Andrey	17:01.1
1972	Samsonov, Aleksandr	16:31.3
1973	Evgrafov, Igor	16:28.2
1974	Parinov, Valentin	16:33.4
1975	Evgrafov, Igor	16:05.30

100 m. Back-stroke

1960	Siymar, Veiko	1:03.3
1961	Not held	
1962	Barbier, Leonid	1:02.7
1963	Not held	
1964	Mazanov, Victor	1:03.8
1965	Not held	
1966	Mazanov, Victor	1:01.2
1967	Gromak, Yury	1:01.3
1968	Mazanov, Victor	1:00.9
1969	Mazanov, Victor	1:02.0
1970	Grivennikov, Igor	1:01.8
1971	Grivennikov, Igor	1:00.4
1972	Grivennikov, Igor	1:00.1
1973	Potiakin, Igor	1:00.4
1974	Potiakin, Igor	1:01.0
1975	Potiakin, Igor	1:00.86

200 m. Back-stroke (Instituted 1961)

1961	Barbier, Leonid	2:16.3
1962	Barbier, Leonid	2:19.6
1963	Mazanov, Victor	2:17.6
1964	Mazanov, Victor	2:16.7
1965	Mazanov, Victor	2:15.7
1966	Mazanov, Victor	2:15.3
1967	Gromak, Yury	2:14.5
1968	Dobroskokin, Leonid	2:15.8
1960	Dvorkin, Vladimir	2:15.5
1970	Davidor, Grigory	2:14.6
1971	Dobroskokin, Leonid	2:12.5
1972	Doborskokin, Leonid	2:11.5
1973	Rodionov, Stanislav	2:11.4
1974	Potiakin, Igor	2:13.2
1975	Omelchenko, Igor	2:10.49

100 m. Breast-stroke

1960	Kolesnikov, Leonid	1:12.1
1961	Kolesnikov, Leonid	1:11.1
1962	Prokopenko, Georgy	1:09.9
1963	Prokopenko, Georgy	1:06.9
1964	Not held	
1965	Not held	
1966	Prokopenko, Georgy	1:07.8
1967	Kosinsky, Vladimir	1:08.0
1968	Mihailov, Eugeny	1:08.9
1969	Pankin, Nikolay	1:06.8
1970	Morchuckov, Igor	1:07.9
1971	Pankin, Nikolay	1:06.2
1972	Stulikov, Victor	1:06.4
1973	Kriukin, Mihail	1:05.5
1974	Pankin, Nikolay	1:05.4
1975	Pankin, Nikolay	1:05.44

200 m. Breast-stroke

1960	Prokopenko, Georgy	2:38.0
1961	Kolesnikov, Leonid	2:35.6
1962	Karetnikov, Ivan	2:32.8

1963	Karetnikov, Ivan	2:31.9
1964	Prokopenko, Georgy	2:29.6
1965	Prokopenko, Georgy	2:31.0
1966	Tutakaev, Aleksandr	2:29.8
1967	Kosinsky, Vladimir	2:29.7
1968	Mihailov, Eugeny	2:30.0
1969	Pankin, Nikolay	2:28.8
1970	Mihailov, Eugeny	2:28.0
1971	Pankin, Nikolay	2:26.9
1972	Pankin, Nikolay	2:24.2
1973	Kriukin, Mihail	2:24.9
1974	Pankin, Nikolay	2:25.2
1975	Pankin, Nikolay	2:24.17

100 m. Butterfly

1960	Kiselev, Grigory	1:02.6
1961	Kuzmin, Valentin	1:03.1
1962	Markelov, Evgeny	1:02.9
1963	Kuzmin, Valentin	1:00.4
1964	Not held	
1965	Not held	
1966	Kuzmin, Valentin	59.8
1967	Gordeev, Aleksandr	58.5
1968	Nemshilov, Vladimir	58.7
1969	Nemshilov, Vladimir	59.4
1970	Nemshilov, Vladimir	58.3
1971	Nemshilov, Vladimir	58.4
1972	Sharigrin, Victor	58.5
1973	Nemshilov, Vladimir	57.9
1974	Nemshilov, Vladimir	58.7
1975	Dombrovsky, Vadim	57.79

200 m. Butterfly

1960	Kuzmin, Valentin	2:81.1
1961	Kuzmin, Valentin	2:18.9
1962	Kuzmin, Valentin	2:16.6
1963	Kuzmin, Valentin	2:18.7
1964	Kuzmin, Valentin	2:12.0
1965	Djatlov, Stanislav	2:16.4
1966	Kuzmin, Valentin	2:11.0
1967	Kuzmin, Valentin	2:11.3
1968	Kuzmin, Valentin	2:11.9
1969	Konov, Sergey	2:11.6
1970	Sharigin, Victor	2:08.7
1971	Sharigin, Victor	2:08.1
1972	Sharigin, Victor	2:09.2
1973	Nemshilov, Vladimir	2:08.5
1974	Nemshilov, Vladimir	2:10.2
1975	Avtouchenko, Andrei	2:03.87

200 m. Individual medley (Instituted 1966)

1966	Dunaev, Andrey	2:17.6
1967	Kravchenko, Vladimir	2:16.9
1968	Kravchenko, Vladimir	2:18.0
1969	Kravchenko, Vladimir	2:15.1
1970	Kravchenko, Vladimir	2:14.2

1971	Kravchenko, Vladimir	2:13.0
1972	Suharev, Mihail	2:11.3
1973	Zakarov, Sergey	2:11.7
1974	Zakarov, Sergey	2:11.5
1975	Smirnov, Andrei	2:07.95

400 m. Individual medley (Instituted 1962)

1962	Androsov, Gennady	5:12.3
1963	Androsov, Gennady	5:02.1
1964	Efimov, Aleksandr	5:03.3
1965	Dunaev, Andrey	4:57.8
1966	Dunaev, Andrey	4:50.2
1967	Dunaev, Andrey	4:47.2
1968	Kravchenko, Vladimir	5:03.7
1969	Dunaev, Andrey	4:47.8
1970	Dunaev, Andrey	4:48.1
1971	Dunaev, Andrey	4:45.7
1972	Suharev, Mihail	4:39.3
1973	Zaharov, Sergey	4:39.7
1974	Zaharov, Sergey	4:40.8
1975	Smirnov, Andrey	4:36.04

WOMEN

100 m. Free-style

1960	Voog, Ulvi	1:06.5
1961	Samovarova, Galina	1:07.1
1962	Luzhkovskaja, Marina	1:06.3
1963	Luzhkovskaja, Marina	1:05.1
1964	Ustinova, Natalia	1:03.5
1965	Sosnova, Tamara	1:03.7
1966	Sipchenko, Natalia	1:04.3
1967	Rudenko, Antonina	1:02.3
1968	Ustinova, Natalia	1:03.0
1969	Sinitzina, Galina	1:03.3
1970	Zolotnitzkaja, Tatjana	1:02.2
1971	Tereshina, Trina	1:02.4
1972	Zolotnitzkaja, Tatjana	1:01.3
1973	Shelofastova, Tamara	1:00.8
1974	Shelofastova, Tamara	1:01.3
1975	Kobsova, Lubov	1:00.02

200 m. Free-style (Instituted 1966)

1966	Bistrova, Natalia	2:20.2
1967	Rudenko, Antonia	2:18.5
1968	Sosnova, Tamara	2:20.3
1969	Zolotnitzkaja, Tatjana	2:19.4
1970	Zolotnitzkaja, Tatjana	2:13.9
1971	Tereshina, Trina	2:16.4
1972	Zolotnitzkaja, Tatjana	2:11.3
1973	Shelofastova, Tamara	2:10.4
1974	Zolotnitzkaja, Tatjana	2:12.5
1975	Vlasova, Irina	2:09.44

400 m. Free-style

1960	Voog, Ulvi	5:15.5
1961	Viktorova, Larisa	5:20.5
1962	Mihailova, Natalia	5:11.4
1963	Mihailova, Natalia	5:05.6
1964	Sosnova, Tamara	5:00.9
1965	Sosnova, Tamara	4:56.6
1966	Sosnova, Tamara	4:59.0
1967	Sosnova, Tamara	4:50.7
1968	Not held	
1969	Kravchenko (nee Sosnova)	4:58.0
1970	Kudashova, Olga	4:48.8
1971	Suhovtzeva, Nina	4:45.9
1972	Zolotnitzkaja, Tatjana	4:40.6
1973	Shelofastova, Tamara	4:36.0
1974	Popova, Natalia	4:32.2
1975	Malutina, Marina	4:26.62

800 m. Free-style (Instituted 1966)

1966	Sosnova, Tamara	10:12.8
1967	Sosnova, Tamara	10:02.0
1968	Not held	
1969	Kravchenko (nee Sosnova)	10.13.3
1970	Kudashova, Olga	9:51.5
1971	Petruseva, Olga	9:45.9
1972	Suhovtzeva, Nina	9:47.5
1973	Burmenskaja, Elena	9:30.1
1974	Popova, Natalia	9:22.7
1975		

100 m. Back-stroke

1960	Viktorova, Larisa	1:11.7
1961	Viktorova, Larisa	1:14.1
1962	Viktorova, Larisa	1:13.6
1963	Viktorova, Larisa	1:11.3
1964	Savelieva, Tatjana	1:12.2
1965	Savelieva, Tatjana	1:12.1
1966	Savelieva, Tatjana	1:11.2
1967	Anashkina, Vera	1:11.2
1968	Lekveishvili, Tinatin	1:10.7
1969	Lekveishvili, Tinatin	1:10.8
1970	Lekveishvili, Tinatin	1:09.0
1971	Lekveishvili, Tinatin	1:08.0
1972	Ershova, Natalia	1:07.9
1973	Ershova, Natalia	1:09.4
1974	Stavko, Nadezhda	1:09.0
1975	Stavko, Nadezhda	1:07.67

200 m. Back-stroke (Instituted 1966)

1966	Mihailova, Natalia	2:31.7
1967	Savelieva, Tatjana	2:31.4
1968	Savelieva, Tatjana	2:35.5
1969	Burbello, Ludmila	2:33.3
1970	Lekveishvili, Tinatin	2:29.2
1971	Lekveishvili, Tinatin	2:28.7

1972	Lekveishvili, Tinatin	2:26.5		1969	Kostitzina (nee Devjatova),	
1973	Golovanova, Trina	2:27.0			Tatjana	1:08.6
1974	Stavko, Nadezhda	2:26.5		1970	Vaskevich, Victorija	1:07.7

1975	Stavko, Nadezhda	2:23.02

100 m. Breast-stroke

1960	Maurer, Eva	1:21.8
1961	Egorova, Valeria	1:21.9
1962	Egorova, Valeria	1:22.8
1963	Not held	
1964	Babanina, Svetlana	1:18.0
1965	Not held	
1966	Prozumenshikova, Galina	1:17.7
1967	Prozumenshikova, Galina	1:15.9
1968	Prozumenshikova, Galina	1:16.1
1969	Grebennikova, Alla	1:18.8
1970	Stepanova, Galina*	1:17.0
1971	Stepanova, Galina*	1:15.7
1972	Porubajko, Ludmila	1:16.9
1973	Rusanova, Lubov	1:16.3
1974	Fetisova, Trina	1:16.8

1975	Rusanova, Lubov	1:14.30

200 m. Breast-stroke

1960	Maurer, Eva	2:57.1
1961	Egorova, Kaleria	2:56.4
1962	Egorova, Kaleria	2:55.2
1963	Prozumenshikova, Galina	2:53.2
1964	Babanina, Svetlana	2:47.2
1965	Prozumenshikova, Galina	2:49.4
1966	Prozumenshikova, Galina	2:47.8
1967	Prozumenshikova, Galina	2:42.2
1968	Prozumenshikova, Galina	2:43.0
1969	Grebennikov, Alla	2:50.4
1970	Stepanova, Galina*	2:42.4
1971	Stepanova, Galina*	2:42.8
1972	Stepanova, Galina*	2:43.3
1973	Porubajko, Ludmila	2:43.8
1974	Yurtchenia, Marina	2:45.9

1975	Yurtchenia, Marina	2:41.14
	*nee Prozumenshikova	

100 m. Butterfly

1960	Pozniak, Valentina	1:13.7
1961	Pozniak, Valentina	1:13.1
1962	Egorova, Galina	1:11.8
1963	Jakovleva, Valentina	1:11.1
1964	Egorova, Ludmila	1:11.3
1965	Devjatova, Tatjana	1:11.0
1966	Devjatova, Tatjana	1:09.4
1967	Devjatova, Tatjana	1:10.7
1968	Devjatova, Tatjana	1:06.9

1971	Vaskevich, Victorija	1:07.9
1972	Ustimenko, Irina	1:06.6
1973	Meerzon, Aleksandra	1:07.3
1974	Meerzon, Aleksandra	1:05.7

1975	Shelofastova, Tamara	1:05.31

200 m. Butterfly (Instituted 1966)

1966	Devjatova, Tatjana	2:37.3
1967	Devjatova, Tatjana	2:36.4
1968	Not held	
1969	Kostitzina (nee Devjatova),	
	Tatjana	2:35.8
1970	Kabanova, Natalia	2:28.9
1971	Tutaeva, Valentina	2:30.1
1972	Meerzon, Aleksandra	2:29.1
1973	Meerzon, Aleksandra	2:25.7
1974	Popova, Natalia	2:20.1

1975	Popova, Natalia	2:19.30

200 m. Individual medley (Instituted 1966)

1966	Hazieva, Ludmila	2:38.6
1967	Zaharova, Larisa	2:33.7
1968	Zaharova, Larisa	2:31.1
1969	Milenina, Ludmila	2:34.3
1970	Milenina, Ludmila	2:31.1
1971	Petrova, Nina	2:31.2
1972	Petrova, Nina	2:27.1
1973	Uzhkurajtite, Birute	2:30.8
1974	Popova, Natalia	2:24.4

1975	Malutina, Marina	2:26.00

400 m. Individual medley (Instituted 1962)

1962	Babanina, Svetlana	5:52.2
1963	Babanina, Svetlana	5:49.4
1964	Devjatova, Tatjana	5:46.4
1965	Devjatova, Tatjana	5:42.0
1966	Hazieva, Ludmila	5:33.2
1967	Zaharova, Larisa	5:32.2
1968	Zaharova, Larisa	5:32.9
1969	Milenina, Ludmila	5:30.5
1970	Milenina, Ludmila	5:21.1
1971	Petrova, Nina	5:22.1
1972	Uzhkurajtite, Birute	5:14.6
1973	Popova, Natalia	5:16.3
1974	Popova, Natalia	5:04.4

1975	Malutina, Marina	5:02.72

VARONA, Donna de (United States, 26 Apr. 1947-). At 13, the youngest of the American team at the 1960 Olympics, Donna Dee—as she was known—won two golds, for 400 m. medley and free-style relay, at the Tokyo Games four years later.

Her versatility was reflected in her almost complete dominance of the world 400 m. medley record list from 1960. She cut this time back from 5:35.5 to 5:14.9 in four years, her last mark in Aug. 1964 standing until 1967. She set her first world record only weeks before the Rome Olympics, and had the medley event been in the programme at that time Donna must have become the youngest Olympic swimming champion.

One of the most photographed of American women athletes, dark-haired Donna was cover girl on *Life, Time, Saturday Evening Post* and twice on *Sports Illustrated.* She was also the first 'queen' of the Hall of Fame who honoured her beauty as well as her swimming talent in 1965. In 1964 Donna was voted America's outstanding woman athlete in any sport and she demonstrated her magnificent swimming talents in Australia, New Zealand, Germany, Japan, Netherlands, Peru, Brazil, England and Italy.

VARSITY MATCH. The meetings between Oxford and Cambridge—the longest-standing annual swimming fixture in the world—began in 1891 with a water-polo game between the two universities. Oxford won 4—1. The next year (1892) a swimming contest was added. And the two senior British universities have met at swimming and water-polo every year since, except during World Wars I and II. Of the 74 swimming matches to 1975, Cambridge have won 48, Oxford 21 and 5 were drawn. In the 75 water-polo games, Cambridge have come out top in 39 to the 23 victories of Oxford and 13 drawn.

VOGEL, Renate (East Germany, 30 June, 1955-). World breast-stroke double champion (100/200 m.), with a third gold for good measure in the medley relay in Belgrade in 1973, Renate Vogel had to settle for the 100 m. silver and a medley relay gold at the European championships in Vienna a year later.

Her defeat at the hands of West Germany's Christel Justen, who became the only non-East German winner of a women's title in Austria, was a tremendous shock. All the more so because Justen, who won in 1:12.55, also took away the world mark of 1:12.91 which Vogel had set in a heat.

The medal, of course, was lost for ever, but within ten days Vogel had regained her time supremacy with a 1:12.28 in Concord, Calif., where she beat U.S.A. champion Marcia Morey by 1½ sec. Renate's first big-event appearance was the 1972 Olympics where she won a silver in East Germany's medley relay team.

WARDROP TWINS, Jack and Bert (Great Britain, 26 May 1932-). John Caldwell Wardrop, called Jack and his ten-minutes younger brother Robert, called Bert, were probably the only twins to have swum in an Olympics (1952). Certainly Jack was the first British man to break a world record in forty years in 1954, when he cut 11.1 off the 440 y. medley mark (4:41.7) in the United States Indoor championships at Yale University. He went on to set four more world times, of which his first for 220 y. free-style (2:03.9) was never claimed on his behalf. But he took this and the record for 200 m. on 4 Mar. 1955 in clocking 2:03.4 for the longer yards distance. A month later, again in a United States Indoor meeting, he reduced his 400 y. medley time a further 4.8 to 4:36.9.

The twins swam at the 1952 Olympics and 1954 European championships and British Empire and Commonwealth Games (where they won bronze medals for Scotland in the 3 x 110 y. medley relay). Jack was also in the 1948 and '56 Olympic teams.

Jack won twelve A.S.A. titles in four years including all the free-style ones in 1952 (100, 220, 440, 880 y. and mile). He was as talented on back-stroke but, at 12, had tossed with Bert the styles they would swim and thus not have to race against each other. He won twenty-one Scottish titles between 1947–52, including the 440 y. six successive years (1947-52) and the 220 and 880 y. five times each (1948-52). Before going to America, he held all nine British free-style records from 100 y. to mile and was the first Briton to break the minute for 100 m. (59.3).

Bert won the A.S.A. 100 y. back-stroke in 1952 and was Scottish champion from 1947-52.

WATER-POLO. It is agreed the world over that Britain were the founders of the game of water-polo. Efforts were made from 1870 to draw up a code of rules for a game called at that time football-in-the-water, but it was not until 1885, after considerable pioneering work and pressure from Scotland and the clubs in the Midlands of England, that the Swimming Association of Great Britain, later to become the Amateur Swimming Association recognized the game as being under their jurisdiction.

Even then different and very primitive rules for play were used around the country. And some of them were odd indeed. There were no goal posts, a goal —called a 'touch down'—being scored by a swimmer placing the ball with both hands anywhere along the full width of the bath end or pontoon. And the goal-keeper—often there were two in the same team—used to stand out of the water and would jump on any players from the rival side who looked likely to score goals. This nearly resulted in a fatal accident in Portsmouth harbour where J. Mayger, later to become President of the Midland Counties A.S.A. (1892) got pushed under a pontoon during a desperate scrimmage—rugby-sounding language this—and was nearly insensible by the time he was found and rescued.

Scotland, whose William Wilson had drawn up a code of rules in 1877, were the first to use goal-posts (1879) which were similar to those used in football. And slowly a common set of rules, from trial and error, were formulated.

With all this pioneering work, it is not surprising that British teams dominated the early Olympic tournaments. Represented by the Manchester Osborne Club, Britain won the first water-polo golds at the 1900 Games in Paris. The 1904 tournament in St. Louis was contested by club teams from the United States and was won by the New York Athletic Club. Britain were successful again in 1908, 1912 and 1920 and it was not until 1924 in Paris, the scene of their first world victory, that they had to bow to Hungary 6–7 in the first round after three periods of extra time. The Magyars in their turn were beaten by Belgium who lost to France who won the tournament. Hungary were second to Germany in 1928 and then went on to win five of the next seven Olympic competitions (1932, '36, '52, '56, '64), coming second in 1948 and third in 1960 when Italy were the winners. Hungary were third again in 1968 when Yugoslavia and Russia finished ahead of them and second behind the Soviet Union in 1972. (See OLYMPIC GAMES CHAMPIONS). The Hungarians were successful at the first World championships in 1973 and won their ninth European title in 1974.

WATER-POLO, A.S.A. CLUB CHAMPIONS.

This, the first water-polo championship in the world, was instituted in 1888. Entries were meagre at the beginning because of the expense of travelling around the country for matches. The Midlands club Burton, one of the first to adopt the new ball games (1877) as a club pastime, won three of the first four championships (1888, '89, '91) and were beaten finalists in 1890.

The reign of the Manchester Osborne Club began in 1894 and they were decisive winners through to 1901, except in 1900 when the entire club team were busy representing Britain and winning the first Olympic water-polo championship in Paris. Soon after this the club was disbanded, the members moving either to Wigan or Hyde Seal. These two clubs continued to dominate English water-polo until World War I.

Plaistow United had a long run of victories, winning eight times in eleven years (1928-31, 1935-38), during which time, also representing Essex, they won the county title (see later) seven times (1931, 1933-38).

In the post World War II era, the London club, Ploytechnic had eight victories in 17 years (1956/57, '60, '63, '69-'72).

WATER-POLO, A.S.A. COUNTY CHAMPIONS.

The County championship was instituted in 1896. The early rounds were played on a regional basis, but despite this the North of England dominated the competition, claiming one of the teams in the final right through to 1923. Lancashire won the first eight championships and thirteen in all up to World War I.

This regional system, that had kept Cheshire out of the final in the years when Lancashire were the top northern county, bedevilled the championship until 1965. Middlesex, Surrey and Essex, for a long time three of the best county sides, were all to often in the same sub-division of the southern group and only one could go forward.

The system from 1965 provided for the top seven teams to be seeded and exempted from preliminary rounds. They, with the winner of the qualifying competition, were drawn into groups of four, playing all-against-all tournaments at centralized venues, the top two teams going forward to a final league of four. This new system produced a much fairer result. However, after the 1971 championship had been completed, the event was discontinued.

WATER-POLO, HOME INTERNATIONAL MATCHES.

The first known international water-polo match of any kind was played between England and Scotland at the Kensington baths, London, on 28 July 1890. There was no conformity of rules and as England were the hosts, the match was contested under their rules which permitted 'ducking'. The Englishmen, although heavier and speedier were sadly lacking in skill and strategy and the Scots, who concentrated on playing the ball not the man, won easily, 4–0. The teams on that hisortic occasion were: Scotland–C. W. Donald (Edinburgh University, goal; G. S. Bryson (Dennistoun) and S. D. Cawood (Victoria), backs; A. Strauss (Southern), captain, half-back; J. Bissland (Leander), A. Whyte (Victoria) and S. Capie (Dennistoun), forwards. England–F. Browne (Burton-on-Trent), goal; W. G. Carrey (Amateur) and H. F. Clark (Stroud Green), backs; J. F. Genders (Nautilus), half-back; J. Finegan (Liverpool Sefton) and W. Henry (Zephyr) (see HENRY WILLIAM,) and J. I. Mayger (Burton-on-Trent), captain, forwards.

England and Scotland played annually until 1901 while Ireland, who lost their first game with England (1895, 0–12) and Wales, who were defeated by Scotland in 1897 (3–2) were also producing teams. By 1906 a home international programme had been devised in which each of the four teams played each other on a two-year cycle. Except during war years; this system continued until 1962. During this era, England won 29 of the 32 matches against Scotland, were never beaten by Ireland and had one draw and no defeats against Wales. Scotland lost to Ireland six times out of 27 meetings and had 16 wins and three draws (out of 26 matches) against Wales.

Then the format of the home international water-polo matches was changed to an annual four-county competition on na all-play-all league basis. England won on each occasion up to 1970, except in 1967 when they did not participate in protest over the Welsh choice of venue (Maindee bath, Newport) which did not conform to the conditions of the tournament as regards the depth of water. The event was discontinued in 1972.

WATER-POLO RULES. For many years, the pattern set by Britain in the early days, with teams of seven playing in positions similar to those in Association Football, was followed internationally. The players were not allowed to move once the referee's whistle had been blown for an infringement until the free throw had been taken. This static play eventually detracted from the excitement and popularity of the game.

The rules were changed after the 1948 Olympics to allow free movement after the whistle, except for the player taking the throw, and this revived interest in water-polo. But the rule whereby a major offender or offenders could be ordered from the water until a goal had been scored—which at the 1936 Olympics had resulted in a large part of one match being contested between one team with three players and a goal-keeper left in the water and the other with two players and a goal-keeper—remained in the laws.

The most significant rule changes came in the 1960s. In 1966 a system of penalty points for major fouls was devised by which a free throw and a penalty point was given against the offending team but the offender was not ordered out of the water. After a side had received three penalty points against them, a penalty shot at goal was awarded to the other side. The weakness of this idea was demonstrated in the final of the Olympic tournament in 1968 when, at the end of full time in the match between Yugoslavia and Russia a total of 73 penalty points had been awarded—the teams, in fact, having played for them as the easiest way to score goals.

As a result, the International Water-Polo Committee faced up to the fact that they had to penalize offending teams by making them play a man short. Thus, for a major foul, the player concerned is now ordered from the water for one minute or until a goal has been scored, whichever time is the shorter.

Also, in an effort to deal with gamesmanship, the I.W.P.C. decreed that teams keeping possession of the ball for more than 45 sec. without shooting at their opponent's goal, were guilty of time-wasting. The penalty for this is a free throw.

A team consists of seven players, one of whom must be the goalkeeper, and four reserves, who may be used as substitutes. The duration of a match is four periods of five minutes each of actual play, with two minute intervals between quarters.

WATSON, Lynn (Australia, 22 Nov. 1952-   ). A medley relay silver medallist, at 15, in the 1968 Olympic Games, Lynn Watson, for Western Australia, won four gold medals at the 1970 Commonwealth Games.

She took the 100 and 200 m. backstroke, setting a Commonwealth record in the latter of 2:22.9. She broke her own Australian 100 m. record for the fourth time during the Games with 66.8 to send her team on the way to victory in the 4 x 100 m. medley relay and had the best split (60.6) in Australia's winning freestyle relay squad. Her back-stroke performances showed considerable improvement on her 69.1 and 2:29.5 in coming sixth and fourth respectively in the individual events in the Mexico Olympics.

WATSON, Pokey (United States, 11 July 1950-   ). Christened Lillian Debra, but known the swimming world over by the unflattering nickname of 'Pokey', Miss Watson was one of only three girl swimmers in the American team at the Mexico Olympics who competed in the 1964 Games in Tokyo.

Her first Olympic appearance was at 14 and she won a free-style relay gold. Then it was the 1967 Pan-American Games and a bronze in the 100 m. freestyle (61.5) and fourth in the 200 m. (2:19.1). With three United States freestyle outdoor titles to her credit—100 m. in 1965 (60.7) and '66 (59.9) and the

200 m. in 1966 (2:10.5, a world record that stood for exactly a year)—it was slightly surprising to see her in Mexico in the 200 m. back-stroke. She had never won a United States outdoor back-stroke title, though she was second behind Karen Muir in 1968 when the South African, whose country had been excluded from the 1968 Olympics, broke the world 200 m. record with 2:24.3 (see MUIR, KAREN).

But Pokey, born in Mineola, New York but living in California and a member of the Santa Clara Club, knew what she was about in Mexico. And she won the gold (2:28.8) by the handsome margin of 2.6 from Canada's Elaine Tanner, having been 1.3 down at half distance.

WEBB, Captain Matthew (Great Britain, 19 Jan. 1848-24 July 1883). Matthew Webb earned his place in immortality on 25 Aug. 1875 when, after 21 hrs. and 45 min. in the water, he stepped on to the Calais beach as the first to swim across the English Channel. It took until 1911 for another man (London's Tom Burgess) to emulate this heroic feat and until 1934 before Webb's time was beaten (by Ted Temme of England).

Webb left from Admiralty Pier, Dover, at 12.56 on 24 Aug., 3¼ hr. before high water, on a 15 ft. 10 in tide. In the first 1¾ hr., he was swept 1½ miles to the west of his direct route to France. In the next 5¼ hr., he was swept 8½ miles on an eastern drift, parallel with the distant French coast. Between 20.00 on the Tuesday and 03.00 on the Wednesday morning, Webb again was taken 2½ miles west of his course. Then seven hours in a north-east stream drifted him 7¼ miles to the east and closer and closer to France. It took him ¾ hr. in slack water under Calais Pier to finish.

The shortest distance from England to France (Dover to Cap Gris Nez) is 17¾ nautical miles and Dover to Calais is 21¼ miles. Webb, who swam through three tides, plus 1¾ hours in a south-west stream at the start and about ¾ hour in slack water at the finish, actually swam 39½ miles.

Webb, 5 ft. 8 in. and 14½ st., was rubbed with porpoise oil before the start and for the first 15 hr. the weather was splendid, the sea, 65°, smooth as glass, the sun obscured by a haze during the day, and a three-quarter moon to light his way at night.

The worst time was from 3 a.m. on 25 Aug. when drowsiness had to be overcome and the water was rough. At this time, Webb was only 4½ miles off Cap Gris Nez, but had not the strength then to fight the N.E. stream and strike directly for land. Had he been able to go forward he could have landed between 07.00 and 08.00. As it was, he finally landed in Calais at 10.40.

Webb, fortified by beer, brandy and beef tea, swam very high on the water on his breast, with slow and steady arm strokes and powerful leg action, averaging about twenty cycles a minute. He was accompanied by a lugger and two rowing boats and a posse of journalists, who were undisputed witnesses to the veracity of his feat.

Born at Dawley, Shropshire, one of 12 children, Webb learned to swim at eight. During his seafaring career, serving aboard the Cunard ship "Russia", sailing between New York and London, jumped overboard in heavy seas in a vain attempt to save a shipmate. For this he was awarded the Stanhope Gold Medal for the bravest deed of the year of 1874.

He had a good breast-stroke, but was not a fast swimmer, even measured against those days, and he had spent a seafaring life for some years before his Channel success, which was, in fact, his second attempt. On 12 Aug. 1875 he swam for seven hours but had drifted so far off course that he retired.

Eight years after his epic achievement, in an attempt to bolster lagging attendances at his vaudeville act, he tried for immortality a second time by swimming across the rapids just above Niagara Falls. But this 'impossible' feat proved indeed to be impossible and Webb was drowned. He is buried at Niagara Falls, Ontario, Canada, but Captain Matthew Webb will for ever be remembered.

WEISSMULLER, Johnny (United States, 2 June 1904-   ). A Tarzan of swimming indeed was Johnny Weissmuller, who was voted 'The Greatest Swimmer of the half century' by 250 sports writers in 1950. He won five Olympic gold medals and a bronze and broke twenty-four world records.

His high-riding stroke, with its pull-and-push arm stroke, independent head

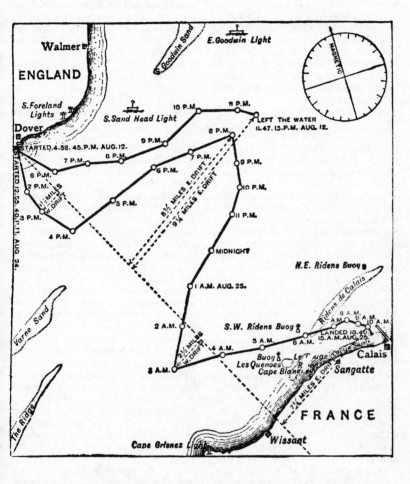

Map showing the routes of Captain Matthew Webb's Channel swims in August 1875. His first, unsuccessful, attempt started on the afternoon of 12 Aug. and was abandoned 6 hr. 48 min. 30 sec. later, after Webb had covered 13½ miles but had drifted 9¼ miles off his course. His second, successful, attempt began just before 1 p.m. on 24 Aug. and finished 21 hr. 44 min. 35 sec. after he had entered the water at Dover as he stepped on to the French soil under Calais Pier, on 25 Aug. The dotted line shows the shortest route as the crow might fly. (This map originally appeared in the *Field* but is reproduced from the Badminton Book of Swimming 1894).

turning action for breathing and deep flutter leg-kick, was revolutionary and had a tremendous influence on the development of the crawl throughout the world.

Weissmuller won the 100 and 400 m. free-style at the 1924 Games in Olympic records of 59.0 and 5:04.2, a third gold in the 4 x 200 m. relay and a bronze in water-polo. In Amsterdam in 1928, he retained his sprint title, again in a Games record (59.6) and won his fifth Olympic gold in the relay.

Johnny's first world records were set on 25 Mar. 1922, when he was 17, for 300 y. and 300 m. (3:16.6 and 3:35.2) and his next, on 20 Apr. of that year, was for 150 y. back-stroke (1:45.4). But of his records for all eleven free-style distances on the books in his time, his best remembered and admired achievements were his 51.0 for 100 y. (his fifth successive mark) on 5 Apr. 1927, which stood for seventeen years; 58.6 for 100 m. on 9 July 1922—the first man to break the minute and he did it in a 100 y.-long pool—and his subsequent 57.4 for 100 m. (25 m. pool) on 17 Feb. 1924 which stood for ten years.

But there were many more Weissmuller world marks that took nearly a decade to be bettered . . . his 2:08.0 for 200 m. in Apr. 1927, which improved his own five-year-old record by 7.6 sec. (and was set on the same day he clocked 51.0 for 100 y.) stood for seven years . . . so did his 220 y. time of 2:09.0, set during the same swim . . . and so, too, did his 300 m. mark. And it took a man as great as Arne Borg of Sweden to trim Weissmuller's 4:57.0 (the first man under five minutes) for 400 m. and 440 y. and his 5:47.6 and 6:24.2 for 500 y. and 500 m. Johnny got back the 440 y. record from Borg on 25 Aug. 1927. It was to be his last world mark. He clocked 4:52.0, racing in a 110 y. pool in Honolulu, and though the time did not break Borg's metric mark of 4:50.3 (25 y. bath) it was equivalently much faster. In fact, it was worth 4:47.3 for 400 m. in a 50 m. pool, whereas Borg's time was equal to 4:57.3 over a 50 m. course. Weissmuller's 440 y. time was not bettered for six years. When he was 36, Johnny, born in Chicago swam 100 y. in 48.5 as a professional in Billy Rose's World Fair Aquacade.

Invited to take a screen test for the film part of Tarzan, Weissmuller said 'no thanks'. Bribed with promises that he could meet Greta Garbo and lunch with Clark Gable, Johnny agreed. There were 150 husky young men trying out also, and after his test the disinterested Johnny took off for Oregon and his job as a swim-suit salesman. That he got the part is film history—but it nearly lost him his name. The producer, obviously not a sports fan, said: 'Johnny Weissmuller, that's too long, it won't go on the posters, we'll have to change it.' Then somebody told him just who Weissmuller was! And the swimming Tarzan was born.

WELSH AMATEUR SWIMMING ASSOCIATION. The W.A.S.A. was founded in 1896 in Cardiff, where an indoor bath, the first in Wales, had been built that year. Before this there had been active clubs in Newport, Swansea, and at Penarth, who had been playing water-polo for a number of years. But it was the energetic Cardiff club who had the drive to form a national association.

The first secretary was Jack Coppock, the second eldest of nine water-polo playing brothers. Seven Coppocks used to make up a team and the other two played for the opposition—who usually lost.

WELSH CHAMPIONS. The first Welsh championship was held in 1897— 100 y. free-style for men. In the early days, this title was almost exclusively the property of Paul Radmilovic (see RADMILOVIC, PAUL) who won it fifteen times between 1901 and 1922, with the races from 1914-19 (5) cancelled because of the war. This left one year (1912) when 'Raddy' did not win in more than two decades. A 100 y. free-style for women was instituted in 1905; four years after England held their first women's championship.

Since 1953, the majority of the Welsh championships have been held at centralized venues as follows:

Year	Venue
1953	Maindee
1954	Bargoed
1955	Barry
1956	Tenby
1957	Pwllheli
1958	Cardiff*
1959	Cardiff*
1960	Maindee
1961	Rhyl

1962	Neath
1963	Maindee
1964	Cardiff*
1965	Afan Lido
1966	Ebbw Vale
1967	Afan Lido
1968	Afan Lido
1969	Afan Lido
1970	Maindee
1971-75	Afan Lido (50 m.)

*Wales Empire Pool

The winners, since 1946, are:

MEN

110 y. Free-style (instituted 1897)

1946*	Huxtable, Graham	1:00.0
1947*	Webb, Roy	58.0
1948*	Mail, Arthur	1:00.8
1949*	Webb, Roy	58.2
1950*	Casa-Grande, Roger	58.0
1951*	Casa-Grande, Roger	56.4
1952*	Casa-Grande, Roger	58.2
1953*	Casa-Grande, Roger	57.7
1954*	Newman, Bernard	54.5
1955*	Newman, Bernard	54.3
1956*	Newman, Bernard	58.6
1957	Edwards, Mike	1:03.3
1958	Newman, Bernard	1:02.8
1959	Hansard, Chris	1:02.8
1960*	Hansard, Chris	55.5
1961	Morgan, Glyn	1:02.5
1962	Hansard, Chris	1:02.7
1963*	Hansard, Chris	53.5
1964	Lewis, Alun	59.3
1965	Lewis, Alun	58.9
1966	Jones, Roddy	57.5
1967	Ross, Keith	59.7
1968	Moran, Kevin	59.0
1969	Woodroffe, Martyn	56.6
1970*	Sheard, David	53.5

* = 100 y.

100 m. Free-style

1971	Moran, Kevin	57.1
1972	Moran, Kevin	58.5
1973	Moran, Kevin	56.8
1974	Lewis, Clive	57.2
1975	Gibson, Alan (Eng)	58.0

220 y. Free-style (instituted 1927)

1946	Bates, Harry (Eng)	2:24.8
1947	Summers, Tony/Webb, Roy	
		2:33.4
1948	Summers, Tony	2:24.4
1949	Summers, Tony	2:37.7
1950	Casa-Grande, Roger	2:26.2
1951	Williams, Eugene	2:22.5

1952	Williams, Eugene	2:29.1
1953	Casa-Grande, Roger	2:25.9
1954	Stevens, Alban	2:28.6
1955	Newman, Bernard	2:20.6
1956	Newman, Bernard	2:33.2
1957	Edwards, Mike	2:22.1
1958	Edwards, Mike	2:20.9
1959	Jenkins, Brian	2:18.2
1960	Flook, Brian	2:23.0
1961	Flook, Brian	2:25.2
1962	Lewis, Alun	2:21.8
1963	Jones, Roddy	2:19.0
1964	Lewis, Alun	2:15.7
1965	Lewis, Alun	2:13.5
1966	Moran, Kevin	2:10.9
1967	Moran, Kevin	2:13.8
1968	Moran, Kevin	2:11.0
1969	Woodroffe, Martyn	2:05.1
1970	Maher, Sean	2:10.4

200 m. Free-style

1971	Maher, Sean	2:07.9
1972	Maher, Sean	2:05.2
1973	Jones, Rowland	2:07.2
1974	Dunne, David (Eng)	2:08.6
1975	Hewit, Gordon (Sco)	2:04.6

440 y. Free-style (instituted 1927)

1946	Bates, Harry (Eng)	5:24.8
1947	Summers, Tony	No time
1948	Geary, S.	No time
1949	Williams, Eugene	5:44.0
1950	Williams, Eugene	5:25.6
1951	Williams, Eugene	5:06.3
1952	Casa-Grande, Roger	5:18.4
1953	Williams, Eugene	5:20.2
1954	Stevens, Alban	5:32.8
1955	Thomas, C.	5:46.6
1956	Morgan, Glyn	5:32.8
1957	Edwards, Mike	5:10.0
1958	Edwards. Mike	5:04.8
1959	Jenkins, Brian	4:56.5
1960	Flook, Brian	5:01.4
1961	Flook, Brian	5:20.0
1962	Flook, Brian	5:04.9
1963	Flook, Brian	5:04.4
1964	Lewis, Alun	4:55.7
1965	Lewis, Gethin	4:47.3
1966	Lewis, Gethin	4:50.4
1967	Lewis, Gethin	4:45.2
1968	Woodroffe, Martyn	4:39.9
1969	Woodroffe, Martyn	4:23.2
1970	Maher, Sean	4:40.5

400 m. Free-style

1971	Maher, Sean	4:31.9
1972	Maher, Sean	4:25.7
1973	Jones, Rowland	4:29.0
1974	Trenchard, David	4:32.7
1975	Hewit, Gordon (Sco)	4:26.6

800 y. Free-style (instituted 1910)

1946	Lewis, Trevor	No time
1947	Mail, Arthur	No time
1948	Mail, Arthur	No time
1949	Not held	
1950	Davies, Ken	No time
1951	Casa-Grande, Roger	12:16.9
1952	Casa-Grande, Roger	11:46.2
1953	Casa-Grande, Roger	11:57.0
1954	Landey, R.	15:07.4
1955	Bebell, D.	13:34.0
1956	Morgan, Glyn	12:25.2
1957	Morgan, Glyn	11:55.0
1958	Flook, Brian	11:25.0
1959	Flook, Brian	10:50.4
1960	Flook, Brian	11:10.0
1961	Flook, Brian	10:29.1
1962	Wooding, Trevor	10:53.2
1963	Flook, Brian	11:06.0
1964	Lewis, Gethin	10:29.5
1965	Lewis, Gethin	10:28.5
1966	Elliott, Terry (Eng)	10:54.9
1967	Jones, Larry	10:03.5
1968	Jones, Jarry	10:00.0
1969	Maher, Sean	9:48.0
1970	Maher, Sean	9:48.9

800 m. Free-style

1971	Trenchard, David	9:55.5
1972	Trenchard, David	9:44.4
1973	Trenchard, David	9:23.0
1974	Trenchard, David	9:22.4
1975	Weaver, K.	9:25.6

One mile (instituted 1925)

1946	Mail, Arthur	No time
1947	Summers, Tony	No time
1948	Summers, Tony	No time
1949	Not held	
1950	Not held	
1951	Williams, Eugene	25:00.0
1952	Casa-Grande, Roger	23:22.5
1953	Casa-Grande, Roger	24:43.0
1954	Mutch, Alf	32:27.5
1955	Thomas, C.	25:08.0
1956	Morgan, Glyn	23:51.5
1957	Flook, Brian	25:54.0
1958	Flook, Brian	22:36.0
1959	Flook, Brian	22:17.0
1961	Flook, Brian	23:11.6
1962	Flook, Brian	22:42.7
1963	Flook, Brian	22:41.6
1964	Lewis, Gethin	21:35.1
1965	Williams, Peter	21:22.6
1966	Lewis, Gethin	20:55.8
1967	Jones, Larry	20:26.2
1968	Jones, Larry	21:25.8
1969	Maher, Sean	20:35.3
1970	Maher, Sean	19:51.5

1,500 m. Free-style

1971	Trenchard, David	18:33.5
1972	Richards, Martin	18:21.2
1973	Trenchard, David	18:10.6
1974	Trenchard, David	18:00.1
1975	Parker, David (Eng)	17:07.1

110 y. Back-stroke (instituted 1924 for 100 y.)

1946*	Brockway, John	1:04.8
1947*	Summers, Tony	1:03.8
1948*	Brockway, John	1:02.2
1949*	Brockway, John	1:02.0
1950*	Brockway, John	1:01.5
1951*	Stevens, Alban	1:04.6
1952*	Stevens, Alban	1:07.4
1953*	Brockway, John	1:02.7
1954*	Stevens, Alban	1:07.6
1955*	Brockway, John	1:01.0
1956*	Brockway, John	1:07.9
1957	Stevens, Alban	1:12.4
1958	Brockway, John	1:01.1
1959	Birchenhough, Ian	1:11.9
1960*	Jones, Roddy	1:01.0
1961	Stevens, Alban	1:12.8
1962	Jones, Roddy	1:08.8
1963*	Jones, Roddy	1:00.8
1964	Wooding, Trevor	1:07.1
1965	Jones, Roddy	1:05.1
1966	Jones, Roddy	1:05.4
1967	Richards, Mike	1:06.0
1968	Richards, Mike	1:03.5
1969	Richards, Mike	1:05.2
1970*	Richards, Mike	57.3
	* = 100 y.	

100 m. Back-stroke

1971	Lewis, Clive	1:06.0
1972	Richards, Mike	1:02.7
1973	Jones, Rowland	1:05.2
1974	Culverwell, Nigel	1:04.0
1975	Bunce, Steve (Eng)	1:02.5

220 y. Back-stroke (instituted 1962)

1962	Jones, Roddy	2:28.6
1963*	Jones, Roddy	2:13.5
1964	Jones, Roddy	2:28.7
1965	Thwaites, Geoff (Eng)	2:29.3
1966	Jones, Roddy	2:26.0
1967	Jones, Roddy	2:23.5
1968	Richards, Mike	2:18.7
1969	Richards, Mike	2:24.6
1970*	Roberts, Keith	2:08.5
	* = 200 y.	

200 m. Back-stroke

1971	Maher, Sean	2:26.2
1972	Jones, Rowland	2:20.3
1973	Jones, Rowland	2:20.1

| 1974 | Culverwell, Nigel | 2:19.2 |
| 1975 | Bunce, Steve (Eng) | 2:15.8 |

110 y. Breast-stroke (instituted 1966)
1966	Tiffany, Trevor	1:14.0
1967	Davies, Keith	1:16.2
1968	Woodroffe, Martyn	1:15.4
1969	Carty, Mark	1:13.2
1970*	Carty, Mark	1:04.0

* = 100 y.

100 m. Breast-stroke
1971	Carty, Mark	1:14.2
1972	Mills, D.	1:16.5
1973	Davies, Vivian	1:13.1
1974	Cometson, David	1:14.2
1975	Atkinson, Leigh	1:11.6

220 y. Breast-stroke (instituted 1924 for 200 y.)
1946*	Langley, Bill	3:01.0
1947*	Williams, John	2:57.6
1948*	Davies, Brian	2:49.8
1949*	Williams, John	2:52.8
1950*	Davies, Graham	2:51.0
1951*	Dudley, Terry	2:44.6
1952*	Read, John	2:46.3
1953*	Read, John	2:41.8
1954*	Read, John	2:43.5
1955*	Bevan, John	2:44.1
1956*	Bevan, John	2:43.2
1957	Bevan, John	2:58.2
1958	Bevan, John	2:50.4
1959	Cooke, Davies, Terry	2:51.7
1960	Beavan, John	2:49.0
1961	Beavan, John	2:59.6
1962	Beavan, John	2:47.6
1963*	Jenkins, Hugh	2:30.9
1964	Jenkins, Hugh	2:51.2
1965	Jenkins, Hugh	2:51.7
1966	Davies, Keith	2:49.6
1967	Davies, Keith	2:48.8
1968	Morgan, Trevor	2:48.2
1969	Morgan, Trevor	2:46.4
1970*	Johnson, Nigel	2:23.2

* = 200 y.

200 m. Breast-stroke
1971	Henning, Robert	2:52.6
1972	Jones, Rowland	2:47.4
1973	Davies, Vivian	2:36.9
1974	Cometson, David	2:43.6
1975	Atkinson, Leigh	2:49.0

110 y. Butterfly (instituted 1966)
1966	Woodroffe, Martyn	1:03.0
1967	Woodroffe, Martyn	1:01.2
1968	Woodroffe, Martyn	59.8

| 1969 | Woodroffe, Martyn | 59.1 |
| 1970* | Godfrey, Peter | 56.1 |

* = 100 y.

100 m. Butterfly
1971	Maher, Sean	1:00.9
1972	Maher, Sean	1:00.8
1973	Maher, Sean	1:01.2
1974	Jones, Alan	1:02.2
1975	Hewit, Gordon (Sco)	1:00.3

220 y. Butterfly (instituted 1953 for 200 y.)
1953*	Dudley, Terry	2:39.4
1954*	Read, John	2:46.2
1955*	Taylor, Gareth	3:01.9
1956*	Read, John	2:52.4
1957	Evans, Richard	3:00.5
1958	Evans, Richard	2:50.6
1959	Hewitt, John	2:52.0
1960	O'Brien, M.	2:45.6
1961	Harber, Mike	3:01.5
1962	Jenkins, Brian	2:22.3
1963*	Jenkins, Brian	2:03.9
1964	Williams, G.	2:41.0
1965	Woodroffe, Martyn	2:30.7
1966	Woodroffe, Martyn	2:22.4
1967	Woodroffe, Martyn	2:18.0
1968	Woodroffe, Martyn	2:12.5
1969	Woodroffe, Martyn	2:14.2
1970*	Maher, Sean	2:10.6

* = 200 y.

200 m. Butterfly
1971	Maher, Sean	2:13.5
1972	Maher, Sean	2:11.8
1973	Maher, Sean	2:22.1
1974	Godfrey, Peter	2:22.9
1975	Hewit, Gordon (Sco)	2:15.3

Individual medley (instituted 1954, various distances)
1954*	Stevens, Alban	1:43.8
1955†	Stevens, Alban	2:33.1
1956†	Newman, Bernard	2:43.4
1957‡	Stevens, Alban	2:53.4
1958‡	Stevens, Alban	2:49.9
1959‡	Evans, Richard	2:46.9
1960*	Stevens, Alban	1:33.6
1961†	Stevens, Alban	2:16.0
1962+	Jones, Roddy	1:38.5
1963*	Jones, Roddy	1:27.4
1964†	Jones, Roddy	2:38.1
1965†	Thwaites, Geoff (Eng)	2:31.8

* = 133 1/3 y.   † = 200 y.
‡ = 220 y.   + = 136 2/3 y.

220 y. Individual medley (instituted 1969)

1969	Woodroffe, Martyn	2:23.8
1970*	Maher, Sean	2:59.7
	* = 266 2/3 y.	

200 m. Individual medley

1971	Maher, Sean	2:24.7
1972	Jones, Rowland	2:22.9
1973	Davies, Vivian	2:21.0
1974	Trenchard, David	2:26.3
1975	Trenchard, David	2:23.2

440 y. Individual medley (instituted 1966)

1966	Woodroffe, Martyn	5:17.2
1967	Woodroffe, Martyn	5:14.0
1968	Woodroffe, Martyn	4:59.4
1969	Woodroffe, Martyn	5:09.0
1970*	Maher, Sean	4:38.4
	* = 400 y.	

400 m. Individual medley

1971	Maher, Sean	5:08.6
1972	Jones, Rowland	5:03.5
1973	Jones, Rowland	5:01.5
1974	Trenchard, David	5:08.8
1975	Trenchard, David	5:11.0

WOMEN

110 y. Free-style (instituted 1905 for 100 y.)

1946*	Grande, Mary	1:09.6
1947*	Linton, Pip	1:06.4
1948*	Linton, Pip	1:06.0
1949*	Linton, Pip	1:05.4
1950*	Linton, Pip	1:03.1
1951*	Linton, Pip	1:03.4
1952*	Linton, Pip	1:04.5
1953*	Linton, Pip	1:04.7
1954*	Dallimore, Vida	1:06.2
1955*	Linton, Pip	1:05.2
1956*	Francis, Geraldine	1:10.6
1957	Hooper, Jocelyn	1:12.2
1958	Hooper, Jocelyn	1:10.3
1959	Hooper, Jocelyn	1:09.5
1960*	Redwood, Sidney	1:01.0
1961	Hooper, Jocelyn	1:11.6
1962	Hooper, Jocelyn	1:10.7
1963*	Phillips, Glenda	1:01.2
1964	Hooper, Jocelyn	1:10.5
1965	Phillips, Glenda	1:08.1
1966	Phillipa, Glenda	1:07.0
1967	Phillips, Glenda	1:07.1
1968	Wheeler, Anne	1:06.2
1969	Wheeler, Anne	1:06.7
1970*	Davies, Christine	57.9
	* = 100 y.	

100 m. Free-style

1971	Hurn, Sally	1:05.7
1972	Hurn, Sally	1:04.9
1973	Whiting, Cathy (NZ)	1:03.6
1974	Walker, Kim	1:03.2
1975	Howells, Marcia	1:02.4

220 y. Free-style (instituted 1927)

1946	James, S.	3:09.0
1947	Linton, Pip	2:42.5
1948	Dowsell, Margaret	3:11.0
1949	Linton, Pip	2:45.7
1950	Linton, Pip	2:47.4
1951	Linton, Pip	2:41.9
1952	Linton, Pip	2:48.2
1953	Linton, Pip	2:41.6
1954	Dallimore, Vida	2:56.0
1955	Linton, Pip	2:42.1
1956	Francis, Geraldine	2:54.4
1957	Francis, Geraldine/Hooper, Jocelyn (tie)	2:41.1
1958	Hooper, Jocelyn	2:37.7
1959	Hooper, Jocelyn	2:37.4
1960	Hooper, Jocelyn	2:38.2
1961	Hooper, Jocelyn	2:42.9
1962	Hooper, Jocelyn	2:41.2
1963	Phillips, Glenda	2:31.9
1964	Phillips, Glenda	2:30.5
1965	Phillips, Glenda	2:29.6
1966	Phillips, Glenda	2:28.1
1967	Phillips, Glenda	2:28.9
1968	Bowen, Bernadette	2:29.9
1969	Bowen, Bernadette	2:28.0
1970	Hurn, Sally	2:27.4

200 m. Free-style

1971	Jones, Sue	2:21.5
1972	Hurn, Sally	2:22.5
1973	Hurn, Sally	2:17.8
1974	Hurn, Sally	2:20.2
1975	James, Mandy	2:15.5

440 y. Free-style (instituted 1927)

1946	Westacott, Marion	7:00.0
1947	Linton, Pip	6:02.0
1948	Linton, Pip	No time
1949	Linton, Pip	6:30.4
1950	Linton, Pip	5:50.1
1951	Linton, Pip	5:49.8
1952	Linton, Pip	6:07.6
1953	Linton, Pip	5:47.7
1954	Dallimore, Vida	5:56.4
1955	Linton, Pip	5:48.2
1956	Francis, Geraldine	6:34.6
1957	Francis, Geraldine	6:07.7
1958	Francis, Geraldine	5:49.4
1959	Francis, Geraldine	5:35.8
1960	Francis, Geraldine	5:40.5
1961	Hooper, Jocelyn	5:56.5

1962	Hooper, Jocelyn	5:41.3
1963	Hooper, Jocelyn	5:40.4
1964	Bowen, Bernadette	5:39.3
1965	Mitrenko, Susan	5:40.4
1966	Phillips, Glenda	5:41.1
1967	Bowen, Bernadette	5:27.3
1968	Bowen, Bernadette	5:17.4
1969	Bowen, Bernadette	5:12.6
1970	Jones, Sue	5:17.8

400 m. Free-style

1971	Jones, Sue	5:05.7
1972	Hurn, Sally	5:08.8
1973	Hurn, Sally	4:53.7
1974	Hurn, Sally	4:52.5
1975	James, Mandy	4:44.8

880 y. Free-style (instituted 1937)

1946	Westacott, Marion	No time
1947-49	Not held	
1950	Dowsell, Margaret	No time
1951	Dallimore, Vida	No time
1952	Not held	
1953*	Dallimore, Vida	12:50.7
1954	Jones, F.	19:12.3
1955	Hughes, Christine	13:49.1
1956*	Francis, Geraldine	13:53.0
1957	Francis, Geraldine	12:18.0
1958	Francis, Geraldine	12:09.0
1959	Hooper, Jocelyn	13:14.5
1960	Hooper, Jocelyn	12:37.4
1961*	Hooper, Jocelyn	12:19.0
1962	Hooper, Jocelyn	11:55.8
1963	Hooper, Jocelyn	11:44.4
1964	Bowen, Barnadette	12:17.4
1965	Phillips, Glenda	10:48.4
1966	Phillips, Glenda	11:03.5
1967	Bowen, Bernadette	11:41.8
1968	Bowen, Bernadette	11:19.6
1969	Jones, Sue	10:41.3
1970	Jones, Sue	10:35.2

* = open water

800 m. Free-style

1971	Jones, Sue	10:32.7
1972	Hurn, Sally	10:23.5
1973	Hurn, Sally	10:06.2
1974	James, Mandy	9:57.0
1975	James, Mandy	10:16.6

One mile (instituted 1925)

1946	Vittle, Pat	No time
1947	No result available	
1948	Dowsell, Margaret	No time
1949	Not held	
1950	No result available	
1951	Dallimore, Vida	No time
1952	No result available	
1953	Dallimore, Vids	26:37.1

1954	Not held	
1955	Hughes, Christine	27:36.3
1956	Francis, Geraldine	27:48.5
1957*	Francis, Geraldine	27:46.0
1958*	Francis, Geraldine	30:12.0
1959	Hooper, Jocelyn	26:59.1
1960	Francis, Geraldine	24:48.8
1961	Hooper, Jocelyn	25:55.1
1962	Hooper, Jocelyn	24:55.8
1963	Bowen, Bernadette	24:56.2
1964	Bowen, Bernadette	25:01.5
1965	Phillips, Glenda	22:15.1
1966	Bowen, Bernadette	24:18.6
1967	Bowen, Bernadette	24:26.6
1968	Bowen, Bernadette	23:19.1
1969	Bowen, Bernadette	23:06.5
1970	Jones, Sue	22:15.8

* = open water

1,500 m. Free-style

1971	Jones, Sue	20:30.7
1972	Hurn, Sally	20:00.8
1973	Hurn, Sally	19:53.6
1974	Hurn, Sally	19:35.7
1975	Biddle, D.	19:28.2

110 y. Back-stroke (instituted 1925 for 100 y.)

1946*	Vittle, Pat	1:15.0
1947*	Vittle, Pat	No time
1948*	Vittle, Pat	No time
1949*	Daymond, Rosina	1:17.0
1950*	Seaborne, Shirley	1:17.0
1951*	Daymond, Rosina	1:13.8
1952*	Crossman, Judy	1:16.5
1953*	Crosswaite (Daymond), Rosina	1:16.4
1954*	Dallimore, Vida	1:18.8
1955*	Dewar, Lesley	1:14.8
1956*	Davies, Diane	1:17.3
1957	Davies, Diane	1:24.4
1958	Dixon, Joyce	1:22.7
1959	Dixon, Joyce	1:20.4
1960*	Dixon, Joyce	1:08.2
1961	Dixon, Joyce	1:21.1
1962	Ford, Carol	1:18.4
1963*	Ford, Carol	1:08.2
1964	Lawson, Janice	1:18.6
1965	Lawson, Janice	1:19.6
1966	Lawson, Janice	1:19.5
1967	Lawson, Janice	1:17.9
1968	Lawson, Janice	1:16.6
1969	Lawson, Janice	1:15.1
1970*	Williams, Avis	1:07.0

* = 100 y.

100 m. Back-stroke

| 1971 | Davies, Elizabeth | 1:12.8 |
| 1972 | Walker, Kim | 1:12.2 |

1973	Walker, Kim	1:11.5
1974	Kelly, Margaret (Eng)	1:09.0
1975	Culverwell, Louise	1:10.3

220 y. Back-stroke (instituted 1966)

1966	Lawson, Janice	2:52.0
1967	Lawson, Janice	2:49.1
1968	Lawson, Janice	2:52.1
1969	Lawson, Janice	2:48.7
1970*	Hiron, Carol	2:27.6

* = 200 y.

200 m. Back-stroke

1971	Davies, Elizabeth	2:41.2
1972	Walker, Kim	2:38.5
1973	Moseley, Jane (Eng)	2:34.8
1974	Kelly, Margaret (Eng)	2:29.3
1975	Walker, Kim	2:32.4

110 y. Breast-stroke (instituted 1966)

1966	Willett, Yvonne	1:22.4
1967	Bevan, Julie	1:22.9
1968	Davies, Christine	1:25.2
1969	Davies, Christine	1:26.4
1970*	Wells, Pat	1:12.6

* = 100 y.

100 m. Breast-stroke

1971	Beavan (nee Wells), Pat	1:20.5
1972	Stephenson, L.	1:25.4
1973	Beavan, Pat	1:20.1
1974	Adams, Anne	1:21.6
1975	Phipps, Tina	1:21.7

220 y. Breast-stroke (instituted 1925 for 200 y.)

1946*	Wade, Pat	3:04.0
1947*	Wade, Pat	3:20.0
1948	Dowsell, Margaret	3:00.2
1949*	Dowsell, Margaret	3:05.8
1950*	Dowsell, Margaret	3:02.0
1951*	Libby, Diana	3:00.6
1952	Lewis, Margaret	2:57.4
1953*	Lewis, Margaret	3:00.3
1954*	Lewis, Margaret	2:58.0
1955*	Libby, Diana	2:55.0
1956*	Libby, Diana	3:02.5
1957	Howells, Gilliam	3:15.3
1958	Howells, Gillian	3:05.5
1959	Shaddick, Cynthia	3:05.5
1960	Shaddick, Cynthia	3:02.8
1961	Shaddick, Cynthia	3:14.2
1962	Shaddick, Cynthia	3:04.3
1963*	Lemare, Janet	2:48.9
1964	Phillips, Kathryn	3:09.1
1965	Edwards, Ceinwen	3:03.6
1966	Willett, Yvonne	3:00.1
1967	Bevan, Julie	2:59.3

1968	Edwards, Ceinwen	3:00.3
1969	Edwards, Ceinwen	3:01.1
1970*	Davies, Christine	2:37.5

* = 200 y.

200 m. Breast-stroke

1971	Beavan (nee Wells), Pat	2:51.3
1972	Arentson, G.	3:03.9
1973	Beavan, Pat	2:49.1
1974	Phipps, Tina	2:57.2
1975	Ball, Debbie	2:55.2

110 y. Butterfly (instituted 1954)

1954*	Lewis, Margaret	1:20.1
1955*	Lewis, Margaret	1:21.5
1956*	Phillips, J.	1:30.7
1957	Francis, Geraldine	1:28.4
1958	Francis, Geraldine	1:23.9
1959	Francis, Geraldine	1:24.0
1960*	Howells, Gillian	1:13.0
1961	Howells, Gillian	1:17.5
1962	Phillips, Glenda	1:12.7
1963*	Phillips, Glenda	1:07.2
1964	Hooper, Jocelyn	1:24.4
1965	Phillips, Glenda	1:12.7
1966	Phillips, Glenda	1:12.7
1967	Phillips, Glenda	1:12.0
1968	Phillips, Glenda	1:12.8
1969	Adams (Phillips) Glenda	1:11.0
1970*	Davies, Christine	1:08.0

* = 100 y.

100 m. Butterfly

1971	Williams, Avis	1:13.7
1972	Hurn, Sally	1:13.4
1973	Whiting, Cathy (NZ)	1:08.5
1974	Adams, Anne	1:08.1
1975	Hurn, Sally	1:08.8

220 y. Butterfly (instituted 1969)

| 1969 | Adams (Phillips), Glenda | 2:48.0 |
| 1970* | Bull, Francis | 2:39.8 |

* = 200 y.

200 m. Butterfly

1971	Williams, Avis	2:52.4
1972	Hurn, Sally	2:43.9
1973	Williams, Caryn	2:37.4
1974	John, Penny	2:30.9
1975	John, Penny	2:28.8

Individual medley (instituted 1954, various distances)

1954*	Dallimore, Vida	1:48.6
1955†	Lewis, Margaret	2:59.0
1956†	Davies, Diane	3:08.0
1957‡	Francis, Geraldine	3:03.9
1958‡	Francis, Geraldine	3:01.0

1959‡ Hooper, Jocelyn   3:03.1
1960* Hooper, Jocelyn   1:40.1
1961† Hooper, Jocelyn   2:21.4
1962+ Phillips, Glenda   1:44.9
1963* Phillips, Glenda   1:34.6
1964‡ Hooper, Jocelyn   2:57.7
1965‡ Phillipa, Glenda   2:46.4
       * = 133 1/3 y.   † = 200 y.
       ‡ = 220 y.   + = 136 2/3 y.

200 m. Individual medley
1971   Jones, Sue   2:44.7
1972   Adams, Anne   2:43.3
1973   John, Penny   2:36.1
1974   Adams, Anne   2:34.7
1975   John, Penny   2:34.0

220 y. Individual medley (instituted 1969)
1969   Comins, Jackie   2:45.9
1970* Davies, Christine   3:20.5
       * = 266 2/3 y.

440 y. Individual medley (instituted 1966)
1966   Phillips, Glenda   5:56.5
1967   Phillips, Glenda   5:55.7
1968   Phillips, Glenda   5:59.0
1969   Comins, Jackie   5:58.5
1970* Evans, Janet   5:44.0
       * = 400 y.

400 m. Individual medley
1971   Jones, Sue   5:50.0
1972   Adams, Anne   5:54.0
1973   John, Penny   5:29.5
1974   John, Penny   5:29.6
1975   James, Mandy   5:23.4

WENDEN, Michael (Australia, 17 Nov. 1949-). Australia's 'Swimming Machine' Mike Wenden did not so much swim as attack the water, but he slaughtered the might of America in the 1968 Olympics in winning the 100 and 200 m. In the sprint, he beat Ken Walsh by six-tenths in 52.2, a world record. His victim in the 200 m. was the 1964 quadruple gold medal winner Don Schollander. Six-tenths was the victory margin again, with Wenden clocking 1:55.2.

Wenden versus Schollander was a battle of the extremes—a contrast of the classic against the unorthodox. The sandy-haired Australian was the rough-stroking, tough, animated windmill. The sleek, gold-haired American the immaculate, effortless, flowing stylist. In the end, Wenden using ten to fifteen strokes more per

length than his rival, was just too strong.

For all that Wenden's stroke looked wrong on the surface, underwater, where it counted, his command of the alien element, the power of his pull and the co-ordination of his arm cycle made him 100 per cent effective. And his preparations for Mexico were almost super-human. He covered between 12,000 to 15,000 m. a day—distances no sprinter had ever done before. And the effect could be seen in the fitness of his body, 12 st. but without an ounce of excess weight.

The Australian's Mexico haul also included a silver and a bronze in the 4 x 200 and 4 x 100 m. relays in which his last leg 'splits' were 1:54.3 and 51.7. There was no medal from the medley relay, but Wenden's anchor leg was covered in an amazing 51.4, worth probably under 52.0 from a standing start.

For his great achievements Wenden received the O.B.E.

Wenden competed in three Commonwealth Games (1966, '70 and '74) and finally hung up his trunks to dry with a record Commonwealth medal tally of eight golds, four silvers and a bronze.

WEST GERMAN CHAMPIONS. Germany, the pre-World War II nation, were one of the eight founder members of FINA, but their membership of the International Federation was lapsed following the 1939-45 War. In 1950, when FINA readmitted Germany, separate affiliations for the German Federal Republic (West Germany) and the German Democratic Republic (East Germany) were accepted (see EAST GERMAN CHAMPIONS).

The first Olympic champion from the new West German Federation was Ursula Happe, winner of the 200 m. breaststroke at the Melbourne Games of 1956, when the I.O.C. still required that the two Germanys compete as a single nation.

The first outstanding all-round West German champion was the American-trained Hans Fassnacht, winner of three gold and three silver medals at the 1970 European championships (see FASSNACHT, Hans). At the 1974 European meeting in Vienna, Peter Nocke took five golds, for the 100 and 200 m. freestyle and as anchor man in all three relays.

The venues and winners of the West German championships since 1960 are:

1960	West Berlin
1961	Reutlingen
1962	Würzburg
1963	Gladbeck
1964	West Berlin
1965	Itzehoe
1966	Sindelfingen
1967	Essen
1968	Berlin
1969	Einbeck
1970	Würselen
1971	Wattenschied
1972	Munich
1973	Bonn-Bad Godesberg
1974	Regensburg
1975	Hannover
1976	Berlin

MEN

100 m. Free-style

1960	Jacobsen, Uwe	58.2
1961	Jacobsen, Uwe	57.4
1962	Klein, Hans-Joachim	55.6
1963	Jacobsen, Uwe	56.4
1964	Klein, Hans-Joachim	55.3
1965	Klein, Hans-Joachim	54.7
1966	Kremer, Wolfgang	55.3
1967	Kremer, Wolfgang	55.0
1968	Kremer, Wolfgang	54.1
1969	Kremer, Wolfgang	55.0
1970	Kremer, Wolfgang	54.7
1971	Schiller, Gerhard	54.5
1972	Steinbach, Klaus	53.4
1973	Steinbach, Klaus	53.07
1974	Nocke, Peter	52.28
1975	Nocke, Peter	52.17

200 m. Free-style

1960	Klein, Hans-Joachim	2:05.4
1961	Hetz, Gerhard	2:04.7
1962/5	Not held	
1966	Schilling, Olaf von	2:01.9
1967	Fassnacht, Hans	2:02.1
1968	Kremer, Wolfgang	1:59.4
1969	Lampe, Werner	2:04.2
1970	Lampe, Werner	1:58.3
1971	Lampe, Werner	1:57.1
1972	Steinbach, Klaus	1:56.0
1973	Lampe, Werner	1:56.80
1974	Nocke, Peter	1:54.60
1975	Nocke, Peter	1:53.70

400 m. Free-style

1960	Klein, Hans-Joachim	4:32.0
1961	Hetz, Gerhard	4:40.8
1962	Hetz, Gerhard	4:41.8
1963	Hetz, Gerhard	4:25.9
1964	Hetz, Gerhard	4:24.5
1965	Kirschke, Holger	4:25.0
1966	Kirschke, Holger	4:21.6
1967	Fassnacht, Hans	4:21.7
1968	Fassnacht, Hans	4:17.4
1969	Lampe, Werner	4:20.3
1970	Lampe, Werner	4:18.4
1971	Lampe, Werner	4:07.2
1972	Lampe, Werner	4:08.6
1973	Lampe, Werner	4:10.89
1974	Lampe, Werner	4:08.76
1975	Lampe, Werner	4:05.20

1,500 m. Free-style

1960	Hetz, Gerhard	18:23.7
1961	Hetz, Gerhard	18:06.3
1962	Hetz, Gerhard	17:31.7
1963	Hetz, Gerhard	18:30.5
1964	Hetz, Gerhard	18:03.0
1965	Kirschke, Holger	17:43.3
1966	Meeuw, Folkert	17:29.7
1967	Fassnacht, Hans	17:45.8
1968	Krammel, Werner	18:07.2
1969	Lampe, Werner	17:11.7
1970	Lampe, Werner	16:23.9
1971	Lampe, Werner	16:40.8
1972	Rosenkranz, Peter	16:34.8
1973	Lampe, Werner	16:41.31
1974	Geisler, Hans-Joachim	16:42.15
1975	Lampe, Werner	16:20.57

100 m. Back-stroke

1960	Kuppers, Ernst-Joachim	1:06.0
1961	Kuppers, Ernst-Joachim	1:06.0
1962/5	Not held	
1966	Kuppers, Ernst-Joachim	1:03.3
1967	Kuppers, Ernst-Joachim	1:04.1
1968	Blechert, Reinhard	1:02.6
1969	Blechert, Reinhard	1:02.8
1970	Beckmann, Ralf	1:01.8
1971	Beckmann, Ralf	1:02.3
1972	Weber, Andreas	1:01.8
1973	Steinbach, Klaus	1:00.22
1974	Steinbach, Klaus	1:00.63
1975	Steinbach, Klaus	59.50

200 m. Back-stroke

1960	Kuppers, Ernst-Joachim	2:23.1
1961	Kuppers, Ernst-Joachim	2:21.2
1962	Kuppers, Ernst-Joachim	2:18.0
1963	Kuppers, Ernst-Joachim	2:17.0
1964	Kuppers, Ernst-Joachim	2:14.8
1965	Blechert, Reinhard	2:18.1
1966	Kuppers, Ernst-Joachim	2:18.6
1967	Butterbrodt, Karl	2:21.6
1968	Butterbrodt, Karl	2:15.1

1969	Blechert, Reinhard	2:17.7
1970	Verweyen, Norbert	2:14.4
1971	Verweyen, Norbert	2:16.2
1972	Verweyen, Norbert	2:14.6
1973	Schlag, Bodo	2:15.73
1974	Steinbach, Klaus	2:10.7
1975	Steinbach, Klaus	2:09.62

100 m. Breast-stroke (Instituted 1966)

1966	Donners, Willy	1:11.1
1967	Betz, Gregor	1:12.1
1968	Betz, Gregor	1:08.8
1969	Betz, Gregor	1:09.5
1970	Aretz, Thomas	1:08.3
1971	Kusch, Walter	1:07.1
1972	Kusch, Walter	1:05.9
1973	Kusch, Walter	1:06.82
1974	Kusch, Walter	1:07.54
1975	Kusch, Walter	1:06.64

200 m. Breast-stroke

1960	Troger, Hans-Joachim	2:40.9
1961	Gross, Jan	2:43.1
1962	Mrazek, Holm	2:39.5
1963	Donners, Willy	2:40.1
1964	Roos, Joachim	2:36.9
1965	Fries, Fred	2:36.6
1966	Donners, Willy	2:36.6
1967	Barth, Claus	2:33.8
1968	Gunther, Michael	2:31.7
1969	Betz, Gregor	2:35.1
1970	Kusch, Walter	2:30.4
1971	Kusch, Walter	2:28.2
1972	Kusch, Walter	2:25.7
1973	Kusch, Walter	2:28.13
1974	Kusch, Walter	2:28.46
1975	Kusch, Walter	2:25.77

100 m. Butterfly (Instituted 1966)

1966	Stoklasa, Lutz	1:01.2
1967	Stoklasa, Lutz	1:00.3
1968	Stoklasa, Lutz	58.0
1969	Stoklasa, Lutz	59.2
1970	Lampe, Hans	57.9
1971	Stoklasa, Lutz	58.5
1972	Lampe, Hans	58.6
1973	Meeuw, Folkert	58.49
1974	Meeuw, Folkert	58.47
1975	Stoklasa, Lutz	57.57

200 m. Butterfly

1960	Zierold, Hans	2:24.0
1961	Lotter, Hermann	2:25.9
1962	Hetz, Gerhard	2:18.0
1963	Freitag, Werner	2:19.5
1964	Lotter, Hermann	2:15.1
1965	Freitag, Werner	2:13.0

1966	Meeuw, Folkert	2:15.5
1967	Stoklasa, Lutz	2:13.9
1968	Stoklasa, Lutz	2:08.9
1969	Meeuw, Folkert	2:12.6
1970	Meeuw, Folkert	2:08.9
1971	Mack, Walter	2:08.7
1972	Meeuw, Folkert	2:07.6
1973	Meeuw, Folkert	2:06.53
1974	Kraus, Michael	2:07.63
1975	Kraus, Michael	2:05.73

200 m. Individual medley (Instituted 1967)

1967	Schiller, Jurgen	2:20.9
1968	Holthaus, Michael	2:13.9
1969	Holthaus, Michael	2:18.1
1970	Aretz, Thomas	2:14.8
1971	Becker, Klaus Uwe	2:18.1
1972	Steinbach, Klaus	2:13.2
1973	Weiss, Matthias	2:15.10
1974	Konneker, Jurgen	2:12.74
1975	Konneker, Jurgen	2:12.56

400 m. Individual medley (Instituted 1962)

1962	Hetz, Gerhard	5:15.5
1963	Hetz, Gerhard	5:05.3
1964	Hetz, Gerhard	5:08.5
1965	Kirschke, Holger	5:03.7
1966	Schiller, Jurgen	5:00.6
1967	Holthaus, Michael	4:58.3
1968	Holthaus, Michael	4:44.0
1969	Holthaus, Michael	4:50.4
1970	Holthaus, Michael	4:54.9
1971	Hillemeyer, Wolfgang	4:56.2
1972	Holthaus, Michael	4:51.7
1973	Geisler, Hans-Joachim	4:44.20
1974	Geisler, Hans-Joachim	4:40.05
1975	Geisler, Hans-Joachim	4:35.17

WOMEN

100 m. Free-style

1960	Brunner, Ursel	1:04.8
1961	Brunner, Ursel	1:05.3
1962	Brunner, Ursel	1:05.8
1963	Brunner, Ursel	1:05.4
1964	Beierlein, Traudi	1:04.1
1965	Dick, Gisela	1:05.1
1966	Dick, Gisela	1:04.9
1967	Langheinrich, Ruth	1:03.6
1968	Reineck, Heidimarie	1:03.4
1969	Reineck, Heidimarie	1:03.3
1970	Reineck, Heidimarie & Meister, Doris (tie)	1:02.7
1971	Reineck, Heidimarie	1:02.1

1972	Webber, Jutta	:00.6
1973	Weber, Jutta	1:00.06
1974	Steinbach, Angela	1:00.48
1975	Weber, Jutta	58.53

200 m. Free-style (Instituted 1967)

1967	Langheinrich, Ruth	2:21.3
1968	Reineck, Heidimarie	2:19.5
1969	Heinze, Kathy	2:19.9
1970	Reineck, Heidimarie	2:18.3
1971	Schutz, Uta	2:15.8
1972	Weber, Jutta	2:12.0
1973	Weber, Jutta	2:09.75
1974	Schwarzfeldt, Barbara	2:09.41
1975	Weber, Jutta	2:08.23

400 m. Free-style

1960	Brunner, Ursel	5:08.2
1961	Brunner, Ursel	5:18.3
1962	Brunner, Ursel	5:11.2
1963	Brunner, Ursel	5:07.8
1964	Hettling, Margit	5:00.4
1965	Hettling, Margit	5:13.1
1966	Hetting, Margit	5:03.3
1967	Hettling, Margit	5:07.2
1968	Reineck, Heidimarie	5:00.5
1969	Romer, Ursula	4:52.8
1970	Romer, Ursula	4:51.0
1971	Schutz, Uta	4:45.7
1972	Schutz, Uta	4:38.1
1973	Schutz, Uta	4:34.28
1974	Schutz, Uta	4:32.34
1975	Wagner, Helga	4:29.86

800 m. Free-style (Instituted 1966)

1966	Hettling, Margit	10:45.6
1967	Hettling, Margit	10:29.6
1968	Gerlach, Ulrike	10:28.2
1969	Budenbender, Petra	10:09.7
1970	Romer, Ursula	9:55.6
1971	Schutz, Uta	9:47.0
1972	Schutz, Uta	9:34.0
1973	Wagner, Helga	9:31.68
1974	Schutz, Uta	9:21.38
1975	Wagner, Helga	9:12.69

100 m. Back-stroke

1960	Schmidt, Helga	1:13.9
1961	Schmidt, Helga	1:15.0
1962	Schmidt, Helga	1:15.7
1963	Schmidt, Helga	1:14.9
1964	Neuber (nee Schmidt) Helga	1:12.0
1965	Bothe, Gisela	1:16.5
1966	Olbrisch, Jutta	1:15.2
1967	Meister, Doris	1:13.6

1968	Kraus, Angelika	1:10.2
1969	Kraus, Angelika	1:11.7
1970	Kraus, Angelika	1:09.1
1971	Pielen, Silke	1:07.3
1972	Pielen, Silke	1:08.0
1973	Grieser, Angelika	1:08.44
1974	Grieser, Angelika	1:06.75
1975	Grieser, Angelika	1:08.07

200 m. Back-stroke

1960	Schmidt, Helga	2:42.5
1961	Schmidt, Helga	2:45.8
1962/66	Not held	
1967	Kraus, Angelika	2:39.0
1968	Kraus, Angelika	2:35.2
1969	Kraus, Angelika	2:34.0
1970	Kraus, Angelika	2:27.1
1971	Kraus, Angelika	2:27.0
1972	Kober, Annegret	2:26.0
1973	Grieser, Angelika	2:24.82
1974	Grieser, Angelika	2:23.57
1975	Grieser, Angelika	2:25.15

100 m. Breast-stroke (Instituted 1966)

1966	Goss, Kata	1:20.1
1967	Frommater, Uta	1:18.4
1968	Frommater, Uta	1:16.5
1969	Frommater, Uta	1:18.0
1970	Gross, Kathe	1:20.0
1971	Eberle, Verena	1:18.4
1972	Sierck, Dagmar	1:18.2
1973	Nows, Petra	1:17.05
1974	Rehak, Dagmar	1:15.75
1975	Askamp, Gabriele	1:14.50

200 m. Breast-stroke

1960	Urslemann, Wiltrud	2:50.6
1961	Urslemann, Wiltrud	2:54.4
1962	Urslemann, Wiltrud	2:50.5
1963	Urslemann, Wiltrud	2:52.1
1964	Hoffmann, Martha	2:48.8
1965	Frommater, Uta	2:55.1
1966	Hoffmann, Martha	2:54.5
1967	Frommater, Uta	2:50.3
1968	Frommater, Uta	2:46.0
1969	Frommater, Uta	2:48.5
1970	Sobek, Monika	2:50.0
1971	Eberle, Verena	2:46.1
1972	Eberle, Verena	2:44.8
1973	Nows, Petra	2:47.39
1974	Rehak, Dagmar	2:42.96
1975	Rehak, Dagmar	2:44.71

100 m. Butterfly

| 1960 | Haase, Herta | 1:14.8 |
| 1961 | Brunner, Ursel | 1:16.2 |

1962	Brunner, Ursel	1:13.3
1963	Hustede, Heike	1:09.6
1964	Hustede, Heike	1:09.9
1965	Hustede, Heike	1:10.2
1966	Hustede, Heike	1:08.1
1967	Rutten, Monika	1:10.3
1968	Hustede, Heike	1:07.3
1969	Heinze, Kathy	1:09.8
1970	Nagel (nee Hustede), Heike	
		1:07.4
1971	Nagel (nee Hustede), Heike	
		1:06.5
1972	Nagel (nee Hustede), Heike	
		1:05.7
1973	Beckmann, Gudrun	1:04.68
1974	Beckmann, Gudrun	1:04.39
1975	Beckmann, Gudrun	1:04.90

200 m. Butterfly (Instituted 1967)

1967	Langenberg, Helga	2:44.7
1968	Hustede, Heike	2:28.3
1969	Heinze, Kathy	2:32.7
1970	Mack, Helga	2:40.9
1971	Nagel (nee Hustede), Heike	
		2:26.0
1972	Nagel, (nee Hustede), Heike	
		2:27.6
1973	Schutz, Uta	2:27.56
1974	Schwarzfeldt, Barbara	2:22.08
1975	Schwarzfeldt, Barbara	2:21.76

200 m. Individual medley

1967	Matzdorf, Heli	2:41.2
1968	Matzdorf, Heili	2:33.7
1969	Heinze, Kathy	2:35.6
1970	Stelter, Annemarie	2:34.1
1971	Mack, Helga	2:31.9
1972	Boxberger, Helmi	2:31.1
1973	Bormann, Karin	2:30.17
1974	Neumann, Birgit	2:28.03
1975	Neumann, Birgit	2:26.99

400 m. Individual medley

1962	Brunner, Ursel	5:51.3
1963	Brunner, Ursel	5:49.1
1964	Olbrisch, Jutta	5:38.5
1965	Hustede, Heike	5:46.6
1966	Hustede, Heike	5:40.4
1967	Lochter, Brigitte	5:52.0
1968	Matzdorf, Heli	5:31.1
1969	Toll, Brigitte	5:38.7
1970	Mack, Helga	5:34.9
1971	Mack, Helga	5:26.4
1972	Neimann, Helga	5:21.8
1973	Schutz, Uta	5:17.66
1974	Schutz, Uta	5:12.75
1975	Neumann, Birgit	5:15.05

WETZKO, **Gabriele** (East Germany, 28 Aug. 1954-   ). An Olympic silver medallist at 14, in the 4 x 100 m. free-style, fourth in the 200 m. (2:12.3) and fifth in the 400 m. (4:40.2) at the 1968 Olympics, Gabriele, from Leipzig, became the first European woman to swim 100 m. in under a minute (59.6) in Budapest on 23 Aug. 1969.

In that year she also set European records for 200 m. (2:08.9) and 400 m. (4:36.1), was a member of the East German squad who broke the world mark for 4 x 100 m. medley and won the 100 and 400 m. European Youth titles.

Tall (1 m. 64 cm.) and slim, Wetzko belied her build in the water where she showed tremendous power and speed. In the European championships of 1970 she won the 100 and 200 m. free-style titles and was the architect of East Germany's victories in the free-style and medley relays. She equalled, for the second time, her European record (59.6) in winning the sprint and clipped this time to 59.3, the fastest time in the world in 1970, on the first leg of the free-style relay. She also broke her own European 200 m. records with 2:08.2

But her finest performance was her anchor leg in the medley relay in which she turned a 3.7 sec. deficit behind the Soviet Union into a 1.2 sec. world record breaking victory (4:00.8) with a split of 58.2. Even allowing for the advantage of a flying take-over (about 0.5 sec.) this was equivalently inside the 58.9 world record of Australia's Dawn Fraser (see FRASER, Dawn).

At the 1972 Olympic Games in Munich, Gabriele, now near the end of her fine swimming career, still only missed a bronze in the 100 m. free-style by a tenth of a sec. and she bowed out with a silver in the free-style relay.

WHITE, **Belle** (Great Britain, 1 Sept, 1894-7 July, 1972). The honour of being the first Briton to win an Olympic diving medal is just one achievement of Isabella Mary White, of London, who among other feats, was also the first British diver to win a European championship. The fact that fifteen years divided these successes is some indication of Belle's tremendous courage, talent and ability.

Belle had been diving for eight years before women's events were included in the Olympic programme in 1912. She had trained carefully for her big occasion, even going to Sweden to practise on their fine wooden highboards the year before the Games. And her reward in Stockholm was the bronze medal.

In 1927, just before her thirty-third birthday, she won the European high board title in Bologna with 36.04 points. Between these two successes, she had competed in the Olympics of 1920 (4th) and 1924 (6th). And she made her fourth Olympic appearance in 1928 but did not reach the last six.

A good swimmer as well as a diver, she won the Swedish 'Magistern' in 1911 which was a test of both swimming and diving. There were no A.S.A. diving championships then—in fact, the first one was not until 1924 for highboard, which Belle won and went on doing so until 1929. She was also the first winner, in 1916, of the Ladies Plain Diving Bath championship organized by the Amateur Diving Association (later to become part of the A.S.A.) and she won this nine times.

Her only local highboard facility in the early days was in the men's pool at the Highgate Ponds to which women were admitted, as a concession, on one day a week. Much of her training for her competitions from 33-foot boards, was done from tiny platforms attached to unsteady ladders, rising from the end of seaside piers at Brighton and Clacton! Still enthusiastic, still interested, Belle stayed on in her sport as an official and committee-woman until her death at the age of 77.

WHITE, BELLE, NATIONAL MEMORIAL TROPHY. Presented by friends after the death of Belle White, Britain's first Olympic and European diving medallist (see WHITE, Belle), this trophy is awarded each year to England's most successful club in women's competitions. (see MELVILLE CLARK, NATIONAL MEMORIAL TROPHY), Winners:

1974	Coventry	26 points
1975	Coventry	11 points

WHITFIELD, Beverley (Australia, 15 June, 1954-). Though already a Commonwealth double breast-stroke champion, bonny Bev Whitfield (5' 4"/163cm and 124 lb/56.7k) was a long way from being a potential medallist at the 1972 Munich Olympics. In fact, she wasn't in the top six for either of her events.

Yet on the day when the favourite Galina Stepanova (see STEPANOVA, Galina) "blew up", it was the determined Whitfield who came bursting through to win the 200 m. crown in a Games record (2:41.71). And to show it was no fluke, she took the bronze in the 100 m.

Her Commonwealth titles were won in Edinburgh in 1970, where she twice edged out England's Dorothy Harrison, over 100 and 200 m., and helped Australia to victory in the medley relay. Four years later, in Christchurch, Beverley had to settle for silvers in the 200 m. and the medley relay.

WIEGAND, Frank (East Germany, 15 Mar. 1943-). Voted 'Swimmer of the Championships' at the 1966 Europeans in Utrecht, Frank Wiegand set a world mark for 400 m. free-style (4:11.1) and European figures for 400 m. medley (4:47.9) in winning these titles and he added a third gold and two silvers in East German relay teams.

But the best season for this soldier from Rostock was 1964 when he was second by 2.7 to Don Schollander in the Olympic 400 m. free-style in 4:14.9 and was a member of the combined East/West German team who won the silvers in the 4 x 100 and 4 x 200 m. free-style relays.

Wiegand swam in three Olympics—as a relay man (medalless) in 1960, and for relays again in 1968 when his team won the silvers in the medley. He was also a medallist in the 1962 European championships—400 m. free-style (3rd), 4 x 100 m. medley (1st) and 4 x 200 m. free-style (3rd).

His best times for free-style were: 53.7 (100 m.); 1:57.8 (200 m.); 4:11.1 (400 m.); 9:03.8 (800 m.) and for medley: 2:13.5 (200 m.) and 4:47.9 (400 m.). All but his 100 m. were world marks.

WILKIE, David (Great Britain, 8 March, 1954-). A fierce and highly-motivated competitor, Scotland's David Wilkie was undefeated in all major races over 200 m. breast-stroke between 1973 and 1975. His seven golds, two silvers and two bronze medals from World, European and Commonwealth events in these three years made him Britain's most successful man swimmer since Henry

Taylor (see TAYLOR, Henry) in 1908.

He "found" himself at the Olympics of 1972 when he was the surprise silver-medallist in the 200 m. breast-stroke, behind America's John Hencken (see HENCKEN, John). That success changed David's whole way of life. He left boarding school in Edinburgh to take up a valuable scholarship at the University of Miami, Florida, where as well as studying, he learned what big-time swimming was all about.

He learned well enough to win the World 200 m. breast-stroke title from Hencken in world record time (2:19.28) in Belgrade in 1973 and take the 200 m. medley bronze. At the 1974 Europeans in Vienna he won the 200 m. breast-stroke and medley titles (the latter in a world record 2:06.32) and also led Britain to the silvers in the medley relay.

And the next year, in Cali, Colombia, the Colombo (Ceylon) born Aberdonian, won both World breast-stroke championships in majestic style. He retained his 200 m. crown by 5½ metres in 2:18.23, just two hundredths outside Hencken's world record, and won the 100 m. by 1½ metres from Olympic champion Nobutaka Taguchi of Japan (1:04.26) plus a bronze in the medley relay.

These times were European and Commonwealth records and the fastest by any man in 1975. And for all this, and his three victories in the Europa Cup, Wilkie was voted "Sportsman of the Year" by members of the Sports Writers' Association of Great Britain.

Wilkie's first taste of success was at the 1970 Commonwealth Games in Edinburgh where, as a newcomer, he managed to snatch a bronze in the 200 m. breast-stroke. He won this title and the 200 m. medley in Christchurch, as well as a silver in the 100 m. breast-stroke, in 1974, the year he was honoured with an M.B.E. in the Queen's Birthday honour's list.

David's medal tally could have been greater but for some strange mental lapses which cost him dear. In Belgrade, he could have won the 200 m. medley, but a careless turn, which sent him crashing head-on into the bath end, dropped him to third place. In Christchurch, he had to bow to England's David Leigh in the 100 m. breast-stroke because he had not taken the meet seriously enough.

And in Vienna, he threw away a certain gold in the 100 m. During the heats, tall, dark and good-looking David (6′ 1″/185cm and 162lb/70½k) stopped swimming after the dive-in, having mistaken the sound of a horn in the crowd for a false start re-call signal. He didn't qualify for the final.

Despite his success, it was also third-time unlucky for Wilie in Cali. As joint world record-holder he was expected to win a third gold in the 200 m. medley but did not qualify for the final. Exhaustion from a needless journey from Miami to Majorca for an unimportant Scottish international before returning across the Atlantic finally overtook him and he was six seconds outside his best in his heat.

WILKINSON, Diana (Great Britain, 17 Mar. 1944-   ). Stockport's Diana Wilkinson was only 13 years, 3 months and 4 days in 1957 when she competed against Germany in Liverpool. And three months later she had become the youngest winner of the A.S.A. women's 110 y. title (65.7).

Diana's great year was 1958 when she swam in the Commonwealth Games in Cardiff and anchored England's medley relay team to victory. Her last-leg free-style rival was Olympic champion Dawn Fraser—and Diana's three team-mates, Judy Grinham, Anita Lonsbrough and Christine Godsen knew they would have to swim their hearts out to give their 14 year-old last girl the big lead to withstand the challenge of the Australian. They did, and Diana swam one second faster than she had ever done before to touch 1.0 ahead. England's 4:54.0 was not only a world record for the yards distance but also for 4 x 100 m.

Good team girl Diana won ten major Games medals, five each in European championships (1958/62) and Commonwealth Games (1958/62/66) . . . but except for a silver medal in the 100 m. free-style at the 1962 European championships, with the same time as the winner, all the rest were for relays. She also took part in the 1960 and '64 Olympics.

She was the first British girl to swim 100 y. in under a minute (9 Aug. 1957—57.3) for which she was elected England's 'Swimmer of the Year'. She was also the *Daily Express* 'Sportswoman of the Year' in 1957—at 13. Diana won seven A.S.A. titles: 110 y. (1957, 1961-64) and 220 y. (1961/62). A number of times she swam in British teams with her brother Chris, who in 1961-62 won the A.S.A. 220 y. breast-stroke title.

WILLIAMS, Esther (United States). Esther Williams, from Los Angeles, might have been an Olympic swimming champion. Instead she became an aquatic film star. American 100 m. free-style champion in 1939 (69.0), Esther's Olympic hopes were blasted by World War II. So she was one of seventy-five girls who auditioned for the female lead opposite Johnny Weissmuller in the 1940 San Francisco World's Fair Aquacade. Johnny wanted someone tall, picked Esther from the crowd and that was the end of her amateur swimming career and the start of her movie fame.

WINDLE, Bob (Australia, 7 Nov. 1944-). A relay reserve at 15, Olympic 1,500 m. champion four years later and a double relay medallist four years after, that is Robert George Windle's proud achievement.

Windle's victory in Tokyo was something of a surprise for his pre-Games times did not challenge those of his American rivals. But, on the day, he was too good for everyone and he proved it with his Games record of 17:01.7 and victory by 1.3 sec. And to show his versatility, he also won a bronze medal in Australia's 4 x 100 m. free-style relay squad.

In Mexico Windle's fine competitive temperament enabled him to rise to the occasion and come sixth in the 200 m. and help Australia to the silver medals in the 4 x 200 m. and bronzes in the 4 x 100 m. free-style relays, with personal 'splits' of 1:59.7 and 53.7.

Between these three Olympics, Windle from Sydney swam successfully in two Commonwealth Games. In 1962, he was third in the 440 y. (4:23.1), second in the 1,650 y. (17:44.5) and first with the 4 x 220 y. relay squad. In 1966, he won the 440 y. (4:15.0) and got two more golds in the 4 x 110 and 4 x 220 y. relays.

Although his big successes were for the longer distances, his only world records were for 200 m. (2:00.3, 1963 and 220 y. (2:01.1, 1964). He won eleven Australian titles: 100 m./220 y. and 400 m./440 y. (1962-64), 880 y. (1963 and 1,500 m./1,650 y. (1961-64).

WOLSTENHOLME, Celia (Great Britain, 18 May 1915-). Commonwealth 200 y. breast-stroke champion in 1930 (2:54.8), Celia Wolstenholme from Manchester was not the favourite for the European 200 m. crown the following year—her fellow-Mancunian Margery Hinton having broken the world record only five weeks before the championships opened in Magdeburg. But it was second string Celia who won in 3:16.2 with Margery third.

Celia broke world records for 220 y. (2:56.0 and 2:54.6) and 400 m. (6:41.4) breast-stroke, all in 1930—the year she won her only A.S.A. breast-stroke title. Her younger sister Beatrice (Beatie) won two bronze medals for free-style in 1934 —in relays at the Commonwealth Games and European championships—and four A.S.A. free-style titles: 220 y. (1933) and 440 y. (1933-35).

WOODROFFE, Martyn (Great Britain, 8 Sept. 1950-). Dour determination, talent and hard training took Martyn from Cardiff, to the silver in the 200 m. butterfly (2:09.0) at the 1968 Olympics—the only Briton to win a swimming medal in Mexico.

But Woodroffe's swimming talents were not confined to his Olympic medal style. In 1969 he was the fastest Briton at the A.S.A. championships for eight of the thirteen events: free-style—220 y. 2:01.5, 440 y. 4:19.6 (British record 400 m.), 880 y. 9:05.4; 1,650 y. 17:34.0; butterfly—110 y. 59.2, 220 y. 2:09.9; medley—220 y. 2:17.6 and 440 y. 4:55.1. That year he also won the international invitation 200 m. butterfly in Santa Clara California, in a European record of 2:07.8 and set British marks for 100 m. butterfly (58.8) and 400 m. medley (4:49.5) plus a 200 m. medley mark (2:17.1) in Wurtzburg.

WORLD CHAMPIONS. F.I.N.A. took eight years to turn their World championships dream into a fact, in Belgrade from 1—9 Sept. 1973. For the first time, too, synchronized swimming competitions were in the programme of a major meet together with the Olympic disciplines of swimming, diving and water-polo.

The first championships were fitted into an already heavily congested major swimming programme. However, from 1978 (after holding their second championships in 1975, in Cali, Colombia), F.I.N.A.'s own meeting went on a four-year rota in the even years between Olympic Games with the L.E.N.-organised European meetings taking the odd years immediately following an Olympics.

Kornelia Ender (see ENDER, Kornelia) of East Germany won the trophy for the outstanding competitor, man or woman, at the first and second championships, her tally of four golds and a silver at each of the 1973 and 1975 meetings giving her a grand total of eight golds and two silvers.

But the most gold-medalled swimmer at a single meeting was Jim Montgomery (USA) who took five, in the 100, 200, 4 x 100 and 4 x 200 m. free-style and 4 x 100 m. medley in Belgrade.

The venues and dates of the world championships are:

No.	Venue	Date	
I	Belgrade, Yugoslavia	1–9 Sept.	1973
II	Cali, Colombia	18–27 July	1975
III	Berlin, West Germany		1978

MEN
100 m. Free-style

1973	Montgomery, Jim (USA)	51.70
	Rousseau, Michael (Fra)	52.08
	Wenden, Michael (Aus)	52.22

1975	Coan, Andy (USA)	51.25
	Bure, Vladimir (USSR)	51.32
	Montgomery, Jim (USA)	51.44

200 m. Free-style

1973	Montgomery, Jim (USA)	1:53.02
	Krumpholz, Kurt (USA)	1:53.61
	Pyttel, Roger (E Ger)	1:53.97

1975	Shaw, Tim (USA)	1:51.04
	Furniss, Bruce (USA)	1:51.72
	Brinkley, Brian (GB)	1:53.56

400 m. Free-style

1973	DeMont, Rick (USA)	3:58.18
	Cooper, Brad (Aus)	3:58.70
	Gingsjö, Bengt (Swe)	4:00.27

1975	Shaw, Tim (USA)	3:54.88
	Furniss, Bruce (USA)	3:57.71
	Pfütze, Frank (E Ger)	4:01.10

1,500 m. Free-style

1973	Holland, Steve (Aus)	15:31.85
	De Mont, Rick (USA)	15:35.44
	Cooper, Brad (Aus)	15:45.04

1875	Shaw, Tim (USA)	15:28.92
	Goodell, Brian (USA)	15:39.00
	Parker, David (GB)	15:58.21

100 m. Back-stroke

1973	Matthes, Roland (E Ger)	57.47
	Stamm, Mike (USA)	58.77
	Wanja, Lutz (E Ger)	59.08

1975	Matthes, Roland (E Ger)	58.15
	Murphy, John (USA)	58.34
	Nash, Mel (USA)	58.38

200 m. Back-stroke

1973	Matthes, Roland (E Ger)	2:01.87
	Verraszto, Zoltan (Hun)	2:05.89
	Naber, John (USA)	2:06.61

1975	Verraszto, Zoltan (Hun)	2:05.05
	Tonelli, Mark (Aus)	2:05.78
	Hove, Paul (USA)	2:06.49

100 m. Breast-stroke

1973	Hencken, John (USA)	1:04.02
	Kriukin, Mihail (USSR)	1:04.61
	Taguchi, Nobutaka (Jap)	1:05.61

1975	Wilkie, David (GB)	1:04.26
	Taguchi, Nobutaka (Jap)	1:05.04
	Leigh, David (GB)	1:05.32

200 m. Breast-stroke

1973	Wilkie, David (GB)	2:19.28
	Hencken, John (USA)	2:19.95
	Taguchi, Nobutaka (Jap)	2:23.11

1975	Wilkie, David (GB)	2:18.23
	Colella, Rick (USA)	2:21.60
	Pankin, Nikolai (USSR)	2:21.75

100 m. Butterfly

1973	Robertson, Bruce (Can)	55.69
	Bottom, Joe (USA)	56.37
	Backhaus, Robin (USA)	56.42

1975	Jagenburg, Greg (USA)	55.63
	Pyttel, Roger (E Ger)	56.04
	Forrester, Bill (USA)	56.07

200 m. Butterfly

1973	Backhaus, Robin (USA)	2:03.32
	Gregg, Steve (USA)	2:03.58
	Floeckner, Hartmut (E Ger)	
		2:03.84
1975	Forrester, Bill (USA)	2:01.95
	Pyttel, Roger (E Ger)	2:02.22
	Brinkley, Brian (GB)	2:02.47

200 m. Individual medley

1973	Larsson, Gunnar (Swe)	2:08.36
	Carper, Stan (USA)	2:08.43
	Wilkie, David (GB)	2:08.84
1975	Hargitay, András (Hun)	2:07.72
	Furniss, Steve (USA)	2:07.75
	Smirnov, Andrey (USSR)	2:08.52

400 m. Individual medley

1973	Hargitay, András (Hun)	4:31.11
	Strachan, Rod (USA)	4:33.50
	Colella, Rick (USA)	4:34.68
1975	Hargitay, András (Hun)	4:32.57
	Smirnov, Andrey (USSR)	4:35.63
	Geisler, Hans-Joachim (W Ger)	
		4:36.40

4 x 100 m. Free-style relay

1973 United States   3:27.18
(Nash, Mel; Bottom, Joe; Montgomery, Jim; Murphy, John)
USSR   3:31.36
(Grivennikov, Igor; Aboimov; Krivtstov; Bure, Vladimir)
East Germany   3:32.03
(Matthes, Roland; Pyttel, Roger; Bruch, Peter; Floeckner, Hartmut)

1975 United States   3:24.85
(Furniss, Bruce; Montgomery, Jim; Coan, Andy; Murphy, John)
West Germany   3:29.55
(Steinbach, Klaus; Braunleder, Dirk; Meier, Kersten; Nocke, Peter)
Italy   3:31.85
(Pangaro, Roberto; Barelli, Paolo; Zei, Claudio, Guarducci, Marcello)

4 x 200 m. Free-style relay

1973 United States   7:33.22
(Krumpholz, Kurt; Backhaus, Robin, Klatt, Richard; Montgomery, Jim)
Australia   7:43.65
(Kulasalu, John; Badger, Stephen; Cooper, Brad; Wenden, Michael)
West Germany   7:43.68
(Steinbach, Klaus; Lampe, Werner; Nocke, Peter; Meeuw, Folkert)

1975* West Germany   7:39.44
(Steinbach, Klaus; Lampe, Werner; Geisler, Hans-Joachim; Nocke, Peter)
Great Britain   7:42.55
(McClatchey, Alan; Jameson, Gary; Downie, Gordon; Brinkley, Brian)
USSR   7:43.58
(Samsonov, Alksandr; Ribakov, Anatoli; Aboimov, Viktor; Krylov, Andrey)

*United States (Backhaus, Robin. Montgomery, Jim; Shaw, Tim; Furniss, Bruce) touched first in a world record 7:30.35 but were disqualified for a flying takeover between their third and fourth men.

4 x 100 m. Medley relay

1973 United States   3:49.49
(Stamm, Mike; Hencken, John. Bottom, Joe; Montgomery, Jim)
East Germany   3:53.24
(Matthes, Roland; Glas, Jurgen; Floeckner, Hartmut; Pyttel, Roger)
Canada   3:56.37
(MacKenzie, Ian; Hrdlitschka, Peter; Robertson, Bruce; Phillips, Brian)

1975 United States   3:49.00
(Murphy, John; Colella, Rick; Jagenburg, Greg; Coan, Andy)
West Germany   3:51.85
(Steinbach, Klaus; Kusch, Walter; Kraus, Michael; Nocke, Peter)
Great Britain   3:52.80
(Carter, Jimmy; Wilkie, David; Brinkley, Brian; Downie, Gordon)

Springboard diving

1973	Boggs, Phil (USA)	618.57
	Dibiasi, Klaus	615.18
	Russell, Keith (USA)	579.48
1975	Boggs, Phil (USA)	597.12
	Dibiasi, Klaus (Ita)	588.21
	Strakhov, Vicheslav (USSR)	
		577.59

Highboard diving

1973	Dibiasi, Klaus (It)	559.53
	Russell, Keith (USA)	523.74
	Hoffmann, Falk (E Ger)	492.15
1975	Dibiasi, Klaus (It)	547.98
	Mikhailin, Nikolay (USSR)	532.95
	Giron, Carlos (Mex)	529.71

Water-polo

1973 Hungary
(Molnár, Endre; Farago, Tamas; Gorgenyi, Istvan; Bodnär, András; Sárosi, Laszlo; Szivos, Istvan; Konrad, Ferenc;

Kasas, Z.; Csapo, Gabor; Balla, B.;
Czeryenyak, Tibor)
  USSR
  Yugoslavia

1975 USSR
(Klebanov, Anatoli; Gorshkov, Sergei;
Dreval, Aleksandr; Dolguchin, Alek-
sandr; Romanchuk, Vitaliy; Kabanov,
Aleksandr; Barkalov, Alexei; Melmi-
kov, Nicolai; Rodionov, Aleksandr;
Rozhkov, Vitaliy; Zaharov, Aleksandr)
  Hungary
  Italy

WOMEN

100 m. Free-style
1973	Ender, Kornelia (E Ger)	57.54
	Babashoff, Shirley (USA)	*58.87
	Brigitha, Enith (Neth)	*58.87

*Babashoff 58.876/Brigitha 58.879

1975	Ender, Kornelia (E Ger)	56.50
	Babashoff, Shirley (USA)	57.81
	Brigitha, Enith (Neth)	58.20

200 m. Free-style
1973	Rothhammer, Keena (USA)	2:04.99
	Babashoff, Shirley (USA)	2:05.33
	Eife, Andrea (E Ger)	2:05.52
1975	Babashoff, Shirley (USA)	2:02.50
	Ender, Kornelia (E Ger)	2:02.69
	Brigitha, Enith (Hol)	2:03.92

400 m. Free-style
1973	Greenwood, Heather (USA)	4:20.28
	Rothhammer, Keena (USA)	4:21.50
	Calligaris, Novella (It)	4:21.78
1975	Babashoff, Shirley (USA)	4:16.87
	Turrall, Jenny (Aus)	4:17.88
	Heddy, Kathy (USA)	4:18.03

800 m. Free-style
1973	Calligaris, Novella (It)	8:52.97
	Harshbarger, Jo (USA)	8:55.56
	Wegner, Gudrun (E Ger)	9:01.82
1975	Turrall, Jenny (Aus)	8:44.75
	Greenwood, Heather (USA)	8:48.88
	Babashoff, Shirley (USA)	8:53.22

100 m. Back-stroke
1973	Richter, Ulrike (E Ger)	1:05.42
	Belote, Melissa (USA)	1:06.11
	Cook, Wendy (Can)	1:06.27
1975	Richter, Ulrike (E Ger)	1:03.30
	Treiber, Birgit (E Ger)	1:04.34
	Garapick, Nancy (Can)	1:04.73

200 m. Back-stroke
1973	Belote, Melissa (USA)	2:20.52
	Brigitha, Enith (Neth)	2:22.15
	Gyarmati, Andrea (Hun)	2:22.48
1975	Treiber, Birgit (E Ger)	2:15.46
	Garapick, Nancy (Can)	2:16.09
	Richter, Ulrike (E Ger)	2:18.76

100 m. Breast-stroke
1973	Vogel, Renate (E Ger)	1:13.74
	Rusanova, Lubov (USSR)	1:15.42
	Schuchardt, Brigitte (E Ger)	1:15.82
1975	Anke, Hannelore (E Ger)	1:12.72
	Mazereeuw, Wijda (Hol)	1:14.29
	Morey, Marcia (USA)	1:15.00

200 m. Breast-stroke
1973	Vogel, Renate (E Ger)	2:40.01
	Anke, Hannelore (E Ger)	2:40.49
	Colella, Lynn (USA)	2:41.71
1975	Anke, Hannelore (E Ger)	2:37.25
	Mazereeuw, Wijda (Hol)	2:37.50
	Linke, Karla (E Ger)	2:38.10

100 m. Butterfly
1973	Ender, Kornelia (E Ger)	1:02.53
	Kother, Rosemarie (E Ger)	1:02.68
	Aoki, Mayumi (Jap)	1:03.73
1975	Ender, Kornelia (E Ger)	1:01.24
	Kother, Rosemarie (E Ger)	1:01.80
	Wright, Camille (USA)	1:02.79

200 m. Butterfly
1973	Kother, Rosemarie (E Ger)	2:13.76
	Beier, Roswitha (E Ger)	2:16.77
	Colella, Lynn (USA)	2:19.53
1975	Kother, Rosemarie (E Ger)	2:13.82
	Lee, Valerie (USA)	2:14.89
	Wuschek, Gabriele (E Ger)	2:15.96

200 m. Individual medley
1973	Hubner, Angela (E Ger)	2:20.51
	Ender, Kornelia (E Ger)	2:21.21
	Heddy, Kathy (USA)	2:23.84
1975	Heddy, Kathy (USA)	2:19.80
	Tauber, Ulrike (E Ger)	2:20.40
	Franke, Angela (E Ger)	2:20.81

400 m. Individual medley
1973 Wegner, Gudrun (E Ger)   4:57.51
     Franke, Angela (E Ger)   5:00.37
     Calligaris, Novella (It)   5:02.02

1975 Tauber, Ulrike (E Ger)   4:52.76
     Linke, Karla (E Ger)   4:57.83
     Heddy, Kathy (USA)   5:00.46

4 x 100 m. Free-style relay
1973 East Germany   3:52.45
    (Ender, Kornelia; Eife, Andrea; Hubner, Angela; Eichner, Sylvia)
    United States   3:55.52
    (Peyton, Kim; Heddy, Kathy; Greenwood, Heather; Babashoff, Shirley)
    West Germany   3:58.88
    (Weber, Jutta; Reineck, Heidi; Beckmann, Gudrun; Steinbach, Angela)

1975 East Germany   3:49.37
    (Ender, Kornelia; Krause, Barbara; Hempel, Claudia; Brückner, Ute)
    United States   3:50.74
    (Heddy, Kathy; Reeser, Karen; Rowell, Kelly; Babashoff, Shirley)
    Canada   3:56.76
    (Amundrud, Gail; Quirk, Jill; Smith, Becky; Jardin, Ann)

4 x 100 m. Medley relay
1973 East Germany   4:16.84
    (Richter, Ulrike; Vogel, Renate; Kother, Rosemarie; Ender, Kornelia)
    United States   4:25.80
    (Belote, Melissa; Morey, Marcia; Deardurff, Deena; Babashoff, Shirley)
    West Germany   4:26.57
    (Grieser, Angelika; Nows, Petra; Beckmann, Gudrun; Weber, Jutta)

1975 East Germany   4:14.74
    (Richter, Ulrike; Anke, Hannelore; Kother, Rosemarie; Ender, Kornelia)
    United States   4:20.47
    (Jezek, Linda; Morey, Marcia; Wright, Camille; Babashoff, Shirley)
    Netherlands   4:21.45
    (Eijk, Paula van; Mazereeuw, Wijda; Damen, José; Brigitha, Enith)

Springboard diving
1973 Kohler, Christine (E Ger) 442.17
     Knape, Ulrika (Swe)   434.19
     Janicke, Marina (E Ger)   428.33

1975 Kalinina, Irina (USSR)   489.81
     Volynkina, Tatiana (USSR)
                       473.37
     Loock, Christine (USA)   466.92

Highboard diving
1973 Knape, Ulrika (Swe)   406.77
     Duchkova, Milena (Czech) 387.18
     Kalinina, Irina (USSR)   381.42

1975 Ely, Janet (USA)   403.89
     Kalinina, Irina (USSR)   387.99
     Knape, Ulrika (Swe)   387.90

Synchronized swimming solo
1973 Andersen, Teresa (USA) 120.460
     Carrier, JoJo (Can)   112.534
     Hasumi, Junko (Jap)   104.183

1975 Buzonas (nee Johnson) Gail
     (USA)   133.083
     Fortier, Sylvie (Can)   130.866
     Unezaki, Yasuko (Jap)   126.616

Synchronized swimming duet
1973 Andersen, Teresa/
     Johnson, Gail (USA)   116.891
     Carrier, JoJo/
     Ramsay, Mado (Can)   111.917
     Fujiwara, Masako/
     Fujiwara, Yasuko (Jap) 107.702

1975 Curren, Robin/
     Norrish, Amanda (USA) 129.433
     Wilkin, Laura/
     Stuart, Carol (Can)   127.733
     Fujiwara, Yasuko/
     Fujiwara, Masako (Jap) 126.099

Synchronized swimming team
1973 United States   117.617
    (Andersen, Teresa; Baross, Susan; Curren, Robin; Douglass, Jackie; Johnson, Gail; Moore, Dana; Norrish, Amanda; Randell, Suzanne)
    Canada   112.918
    (Calkins, Michelle; Hambrook, Frances; Humphrey, Debbie; Nicholl, Lorraine; Page, Gail; Stuart, Carol, Thomas, Susan; Wilkin, Laura)
    Japan   107.311
    (Fujiwara, Masako; Fujiwara, Yasuko; Hasumi, Junko; Unezaki, Yasuko)

1975 United States   128.812
    (Buzonas (nee Johnson), Gail; Baross, Susan; Norrish, Amanda; Curren, Robin; Barone, Michelle; Tyron, Pam; Longo, Mary Ellen; Shelley, Linda)
    Canada   125.129
    (Fortier, Sylvie; Boucher, Jocelyne; Anderson, Kiki; Luzon, Danielle; Bidard, Linda; Poulin, Marie; Verret, Judy; Anderson, Robin)
    Japan   123.691
    (Unezaki, Yasuko; Fujiwara, Yasuko; Fujiwara, Masako; Fujiwara, Masae; Sugawara, Junko; Ishii, Yuki)

Top Nations

Swimming (Men)

1973	United States	204
	East Germany	97
	Australia	74
1975	United States	178
	Great Britain	86
	West Germany	80

Swimming (Women)

1973	East Germany	193
	United States	142
	Holland	45
1975	East Germany	191
	United States	150
	Canada	75

Diving (Men)

1973	Italy	26
	United States	25
	Soviet Union	13
1975	United States	22
	Italy	21
	USSR	15

Diving (women)

1973	East Germany	22
	Sweden	21
	United States	11
1975	USSR	28
	United States	20
	East Germany	7

Synchronized swimming

1973	United States	45
	Canada	35
	Japan	30
1975	United States	45
	Canada	35
	Japan	30

WORLD RECORDS. After sixty years of chopping and changing, a single, tidy list of world records became established in 1968 (operative from 1 Jan. 1969) when F.I.N.A. settled for thirty-one metric distances and long-course (see LONG COURSE) times only for their record book. Thus sixteen events for men and fifteen for women emerged from the 105 distances which had been in and out of the list since official world records were first recognized in 1908.

Of the records of the modern era, eight for men (100, 200, 400, 1,500 m. free-style, 100 and 200 m. back-stroke

and 100 and 200 m. breast-stroke) and one for women (100 m. free-style) were among the original list of 1908 when F.I.N.A. ratified not only the best of that year but also certain authenticated times set previously. At that time, world records for distances under 800 m. could be set in pools of any length over 25 y., and it was possible for times to be taken mid-course not just at the bath end.

The first cutting back of record distances was in 1948 when out went the little-raced 300 y., 300 m., 1,000 y., 1,000 m. free-style, 400 m. back-stroke and 400 m. breast-stroke. Four years later saw the elimination of 500 y. and 500 m. free-style, 150 y. back-stroke and, with the separation of breast-stroke and butterfly (to give four styles of swimming), the 3 x 100 y. and m. medley relays.

The traditional English linear distances (100, 200, 400 y. and mile) went out on 1 May 1957, being replaced by multiples of 110 y. (the 1 ft. 11 in. longer linear equivalent of metric distance). At this time, F.I.N.A. also decided that only long course performances would be accepted for all distances and that times taken mid-course without a bath-end touch would not be recognised (ie a 200 m. time in a 55 y. pool on the way to 220 y.).

During the 1968 Olympics all records for yards distances were thrown out and, a year later, it was decided that record-equalling performances would be ratified. On 21 Aug. 1972, retrospectively to 1 Jan. of that year, F.I.N.A. decided to accept records timed to 1/100th of a second while still retaining 1/10th times.

In the build-up of world record lists, there have been a number of anomalies. Early retrospective ratification of records was not consistent. Freddy Lane of Australia (see LANE, FREDDY) was the first man to swim 100 y. in under a minute (Oct. 1902–59.6), but this was not ratified although his 2:28.6 for 220 y. on 18 Aug. 1902 was.

There were wonderful Australian record performances, ahead of his era, by Barney Kieran (see KIERAN, BARNEY) between 1904-06). But the one to be approved as a world mark was the 6:07.2 for 500 y. which Kieran set in Leeds, England.

There were failures, too, to ratify early 220, 440 and 880 y. marks also as

metric records when such times were
faster than the approved times for the
shorter 200, 400 and 800 m. distances.
This error, in fact, was finally corrected
by F.I.N.A. in 1973 and '74. In Lane's
case, whose 220 y. time (see Page 255)
— the earliest record to be ratified—should
also have gone into the 200 m. list, the
action came 72 years after the deed.

Ladislav Hauptman (Czech), a former
honorary member of the world body, in
his Golden Book of F.I.N.A. reported
that, in the first 50 years of the Federation, 1,059 world records were approved
—581 for men and 478 for women. The
1,000th mark was on July 7, 1957 by
Japan's Takashi Ishimoto (1:01.3 for
100 m. butterfly).

On 19 July, 1958, the very day of
F.I.N.A.'s 50th anniversary, the occasion
was celebrated with a world record. This
was the 4:17.4 for 4 x 100 y. free-style
by Australia during the British Empire
Games in Cardiff. It is doubtful whether
the swimmers concerned (Lorraine Crapp,
Sandra Moran, Alva Colquhoun and Dawn
Fraser) were aware of their symbolic
achievement.

For a world record to be ratified by
F.I.N.A. the following conditions must
be observed:
1. The performance must be in a 50 m.
pool, with still water, in a scratch competition or individual race against time,
held in public and announced publicly
by advertisement at least three clear days

before the race or the attempt is to be
made.
2. No pacemaking shall be permitted,
nor may any device be used or plan adopted which has that effect.
3. The measurement of the course must
be certified correct by a surveyor or
other qualified official appointed, or
approved by, the governing body of the
country in which it is situated.
4. Members of relay teams must be of
the same nationality.
5. Timing must be in accordance with
F.I.N.A. rules (see TIMING).

In the following lists, dotted lines have
been introduced to show the different
stages in the development of F.I.N.A.
records:
a) the separation of breast-stroke and
butterfly on 1 Jan. 1953 (in breast-stroke
lists only);
b) the discontinuation of under-water
swimming in breast-stroke on 30 April
1957 (breast-stroke lists only);
c) the start of the long-course lists on 1
May 1957. F.I.N.A. used a number of
different formulas to determine the first
records and these are indicated in the
appropriate place in each list;
d) the start of the 1/100th of a second
timing for record purposes. Where an
asterisk (*) appears in the place of the
second decimal point in this section of
the record lists the star indicates that the
time was taken to 1/10th of a second; in
earlier sections it indicates a short course
performance.

MEN

100 m. Free-style

1:05.8*	Halmay, Zoltan (Hun)	Vienna	3 Dec. 1905
1:05.6	Daniels, Charles (USA)	London	July 1908
1:02.8*	Daniels, Charles (USA)	New York	15 Apr. 1910
1:02.4*	Bretting, Kurt (Ger)	Brussels	6 Apr. 1912
1:01.6	Kahanamoku, Duke (USA)	Hamburg	20 July 1912
1:01.4	Kahanamoku, Duke (USA)	New York	9 Aug. 1918
1:00.4	Kahanamoku, Duke (USA)	Antwerp	24 Aug. 1920
58.6	Weissmuller, Johnny (USA)	Alameda	9 July 1922
57.4*	Weissmuller, Johnny (USA)	Miami	17 Feb. 1924
56.8*	Fick, Peter (USA)	New Haven	2 Mar. 1934
56.6*	Fick, Peter (USA)	New Haven	5 Mar. 1935
56.4*	Fick, Peter (USA)	New Haven	11 Feb. 1936
55.9*	Ford, Alan (USA)	New Haven	13 Apr. 1944
55.8*	Jany, Alex (Fra)	Mentone	15 Sept. 1947
55.4*	Ford, Alan (USA)	New Haven	29 June 1948
54.8*	Cleveland, Dick (USA)	New Haven	1 Apr. 1954
54.6†	Devitt, John (Aus)	Brisbane	28 Jan. 1957

The time by Devitt (above) remained in the list

54.6†	Devitt, John (Aus)	Brisbane	28 Jan. 1957
54.4	Clark, Steve (USA)	Los Angeles	18 Aug. 1961
53.6	Santos, Manuel dos (Braz)	Rio de Janiero	20 Sept. 1961
52.9	Gottvalles, Alain (Fra)	Budapest	13 Sept. 1964
52.6	Walsh, Ken (USA)	Winnipeg	27 July 1967
52.6e	Zorn, Zac (USA)	Long Beach	2 Sept. 1968
52.2	Wenden, Mike (Aus)	Mexico City	19 Oct. 1968
51.9	Spitz, Mark (USA)	Los Angeles	23 Aug. 1970
51.47	Spitz, Mark (USA)	Chicago	5 Aug. 1972
51.22	Spitz, Mark (USA)	Munich	3 Sept. 1972
51.12	Montgomery, Jim (USA)	Long Beach	21 June 1975
51.11	Coan, Andy (USA)	Fort Lauderdale	3 Aug. 1975
50.59	Montgomery, Jim (USA)	Kansas City	23 Aug. 1975

†In December 1956, F.I.N.A. provisionally designated the 55.4 by Henricks, Jon (Aus) in winning the Olympic title in Melbourne on 30 Nov. 1956 as the first record in the new long-course list. Devitt subsequently became the last record holder in the old list and the first holder in the new list.

200 m. Free-style

2:28.6*y†	Lane, Freddy (Aus)	Weston-s-Mare	18 Aug. 1902
2:26.8*y†	Halmay, Zoltan (Hun)	Budapest	28 June 1908
2:25.4*y†	Daniels, Charles (USA)	Pittsburg	26 Mar. 1909
2:21.6*y	Ross, Norman (USA)	San Francisco	24 Nov. 1916
2:19.8*y	Cann, Tedford (USA)	Detroit	10 Apr. 1920
2:15.6*y	Weissmuller, Johnny (USA)	Honolulu	26 May 1922
2:15.2*y	Weissmuller, Johnny (USA)	McKeesport	9 Dec. 1925
2:08.0*	Weissmuller, Johnny (USA)	Ann Arbor	5 Apr. 1927
2:07.2*	Medica, Jack (USA)	Chicago	12 Apr. 1935
2:06.2*	Smith, Bill (USA)	Columbus	12 Feb. 1944
2:05.4*	Jany, Alex (Fra)	Marseille	20 Sept. 1946
2:04.6*	Marshall, John (Aus)	New Haven	31 Mar. 1950
2:03.9*	Konno, Ford (USA)	Columbus	27 Feb. 1954
2:03.4*	Wardrop, Jack (GB)	Columbus	8 Mar. 1955
2:01.5*	Hanley, Dick (USA)	Minneapolis	8 Mar. 1957

Minimum time 2:05.2

2:04.8y	Konrads, John (Aus)	Sydney	18 Jan. 1958
2:03.2y	Konrads, John (Aus)	Sydney	5 Mar. 1958
2:03.0	Yamanaka, Tsuyoshi (Jap)	Osaka	22 Aug. 1958
2:02.2y	Konrads, John (Aus)	Sydney	16 Jan. 1959
2:01.5	Yamanaka, Tsuyoshi (Jap)	Osaka	26 July 1959
2:01.2	Yamanaka, Tsuyoshi (Jap)	Osaka	24 June 1961
2:01.1	Yamanaka, Tsuyoshi (Jap)	Tokyo	6 Aug. 1961
2:00.4	Yamanaka, Tsuyoshi (Jap)	Los Angeles	20 Aug. 1961
2:00.3	Windle, Bob (Aus)	Tokyo	21 Apr. 1963
1:58.8	Schollander, Don (USA)	Los Angeles	27 July 1963
1:58.5	Schollander, Don (USA)	Tokyo	17 Aug. 1963
1:58.4	Schollander, Don (USA)	Osaka	24 Aug. 1963
1:58.2	Klein, Hans-Joachim (W Ger)	Dortmund	24 May 1964
1:57.6	Schollander, Don (USA)	Los Altos	1 Aug. 1964
1:57.2	Schollander, Don (USA)	Los Angeles	29 July 1966
1:56.2	Schollander, Don (USA)	Lincoln	19 Aug. 1966
1:56.0	Schollander, Don (USA)	Winnipeg	29 July 1967
1:55.7	Schollander, Don (USA)	Oak Park	12 Aug. 1967
1:54.3	Schollander, Don (USA)	Long Beach	30 Aug. 1968
1:54.3e	Spitz, Mark (USA)	Santa Clara	12 July 1969
1:54.2	Spitz, Mark (USA)	Leipzig	4 Sept. 1971

1:53.5	Spitz, Mark (USA)	Minsk	10 Sept. 1971
1:52.78	Spitz, Mark (USA)	Munich	29 Aug. 1972
1:51.66	Shaw, Tim (USA)	Concord	23 Aug. 1974
1:51.41	Furniss, Bruce (USA)	Long Beach	18 June 1975
1:50.89	Furniss, Bruce (USA)	Long Beach	18 June 1975
1:50.32	Furniss, Bruce (USA)	Kansas City	21 Aug. 1975

† The following ratified times, which were inferior to the performances for the longer 220 y. (201.168 m.) by Lane (1902), Halmay ('08) and Daniels ('09), have been deleted and the earlier and faster times of the above named have been introduced into the world 200 m. record list:

2:31.6*	Scheff, Otto (Aut)	Vienna	11 Nov. 1908
2:30.0*	Beaurepaire, Frank (Aus)	Exeter	9 Sept. 1910
2:25.4*	Daniels, Charles (USA)	Pittsburg	28 Mar. 1911

400 m. Free-style

5:36.8	Taylor, Henry (GB)	London	16 July 1908
5:26.4*y†	Battersby, Syd (Eng)	Seacombe	26 Oct. 1908
5:23.0*y†	Beaurepaire, Frank (Aus)	Budapest	8 June 1910
5:21.6*	Hatfield, Jack (Eng)	London	26 Sept. 1912
5:14.6*	Ross, Norman (USA)	Los Angeles	9 Oct. 1919
5:14.4*	Ross, Norman (USA)	Brighton Beach	25 Sept. 1921
5:11.8*	Borg, Arne (Swe)	Stockholm	22 June 1922
5:06.6	Weissmuller, Johnny (USA)	Honolulu	22 June 1922
4:57.0*	Weissmuller, Johnny (USA)	New Haven	6 Mar. 1923
4:54.7*	Borg, Arne (Swe)	Stockholm	9 Dec. 1923
4:50.3*	Borg, Arne (Swe)	Stockholm	11 Sept. 1925
4:47.0*	Taris, Jean (Fra)	Paris	16 Apr. 1931
4:46.4	Makino, Shozo (Jap)	Tokyo	14 Aug. 1933
4:38.7*	Medica, Jack (USA)	Honolulu	30 Aug. 1934
4:38.5*	Smith, Bill (USA)	Honolulu	13 May 1941
4:35.2	Jany, Alex (Fra)	Monte Carlo	12 Sept. 1947
4:34.6	Furuhashi, Hironashin (Jap)	Tokyo	24 July 1949
4:33.3	Furuhahsi, Hironashin (Jap)	Los Angeles	18 Aug. 1949
4:33.1*	Marshall, John (Aus)	New Haven	11 Mar. 1950
4:29.5*	Marshall, John (Aus)	New Haven	1 Apr. 1950
4:26.9*	Marshall, John (Aus)	New Haven	24 Mar. 1951
4:26.7*	Konno, Ford (USA)	New Haven	3 Apr. 1954
4:25.9	Rose, Murray (Aus)	Sydney	12 Jan. 1957

The 4:25.9 by Rose (above) was a mid-course time and could not be considered for the new long course list. F.I.N.A. took Rose's winning time at the Olympic Games as the first record in the new list.

4:27.0	Rose, Murray (Aus)	Melbourne	27 Oct. 1956
4:25.9y	Konrads, John (Aus)	Sydney	15 Jan. 1958
4:21.8y	Konrads, John (Aus)	Melbourne	18 Feb. 1958
4:19.0y	Konrads, John (Aus)	Sydney	7 Feb. 1959
4:16.6	Yamanaka, Tsuyoshi (Jap	Osaka	26 July 1959
4:15.9y	Konrads, John (Aus)	Sydney	23 Feb. 1960
4:13.4	Rose, Murray (Aus)	Chicago	17 Aug. 1962
4:12.7	Schollander, Don (USA)	Los Altos	31 July 1964
4:12.2	Schollander, Don (USA)	Tokyo	15 Oct. 1964
4:11.8	Nelson, John (USA)	Lincoln	18 Aug. 1966
4:11.6	Schollander, Don (USA)	Lincoln	18 Aug. 1966
4:11.1	Wiegand, Frank (E Ger)	Utrecht	25. Aug 1966
4:10.6	Spitz, Mark (USA)	Heywood	25 June 1967
4:10.6	Mosconi, Alain (Fra)	Monaco	2 July 1967
4:09.2	Mosconi, Alain (Fra)	Monaco	4 July 1967

4:08.8	Spitz, Mark (USA)	Santa Clara	7 July 1967
4:08.2	Charlton, Greg (USA)	Tokyo	28 Aug. 1967
4:07.7	Spitz, Mark (USA)	Heywood	23 June 1968
4:06.5	Hutton, Ralph (Can)	Lincoln	1 Aug. 1968
4:04.0	Fassnacht, Hans (W Ger)	Louisville	14 Aug. 1969
4:02.8	Kinsella, John (USA)	Los Angeles	20 Aug. 1970
4:02.6	Larsson, Gunnar (Swe)	Barcelona	7 Sept. 1970
4:02.1	McBreen, Tom (USA)	Houston	25 Aug. 1971
4:01.7*	Cooper, Brad (Aus)	Brisbane	12 Feb. 1972
4:00.11	Krumpholz, Kurt (USA)	Chicago	4 Aug. 1972
3:58.18	DeMont, Rick (USA)	Belgrade	6 Sept. 1973
3:56.96	Shaw, Tim (USA)	Concord	22 Aug. 1974
3:54.69	Shaw, Tim (USA)	Concord	22 Aug. 1974
3:53.95	Shaw, Tim (USA)	Long Beach	19 June 1975
3:53.31	Shaw, Tim (USA)	Kansas City	20 Aug. 1975

† The following ratified times, which were inferior to the performances for the longer 440 y. (402.336) by Battersby (1908) and Beaurepaire (1910), have been deleted and the earlier and faster times of the above named have been introduced into the world 400 m. record list:

5:35.8	Battersby, Sydney (Eng)	London	21 Sept. 1911
5:29.0	Kenyery, Alajos (Hun)	Magdeburg	21 Apr. 1912
5:28.4	Torres, Bela las (Hun)	Budapest	5 June 1912
5:24.4	Hodgson, George (Can)	Stockholm	13 July 1912

800 m. Free-style

11:25.4y†	Taylor, Henry (Eng)	Runcorn	21 July 1906
11:24.2y†	Ross, Norman (USA)	Sydney	10 Jan. 1920
11:05.2y†	Charlton, Boy (Aus)	Sydney	13 Jan. 1923
10:51.8y†	Charlton, Boy (Aus)	Sydney	19 Jan. 1924
10:43.6y†	Borg, Arne (Swe)	Honolulu	11 Apr. 1924
10:37.4y†	Borg, Arne (Swe)	Harnus	25 Aug. 1925
10:32.0y†	Charlton, Boy (Aus)	Sydney	8 Jan. 1927
10:22.2y†	Weissmuller, Johnny (USA)	Honolulu	27 July 1927
10:19.6	Taris, Jean (Fra)	Paris	30 May 1930
10:17.2	Taris, Jean (Fra)	Cannes	9 June 1931
10:16.6	Makino, Shozo (Jap)	Osaka	30 Aug. 1931
10:15.6	Taris, Jean (Fra)	Cannes	21 June 1932
10:08.6	Makino, Shozo (Jap)	Tokyo	25 June 1933
10:01.2	Makino, Shozo (Jap)	Tokyo	16 Sept. 1934
9:55.8	Makino, Shozo (Jap)	Tokyo	15 Sept. 1935
9:50.9	Smith, Bill (USA)	Honolulu	24 July 1941
9:45.6	Furuhashi, Hironashin (Jap)	Tokyo	26 June 1949
9:45.0	Hashizume, Shiro (Jap)	Los Angeles	16 Aug. 1949
9:40.7	Furuhashi, Hironashin (Jap)	Los Angeles	16 Aug. 1949
9:35.5	Furuhashi, Hironashin (Jap)	Los Angeles	19 Aug. 1949
9:30.7	Konno, Ford (USA)	Honolulu	7 July 1951
9:16.7	Breen, George (USA)	New Haven	27 Oct. 1956

The 9:16.7 by Breen (above) was a mid-course time and could not be considered for the new long course list. F.I.N.A. took Breen's 9:19.2 for 880 y. in the same swim as the first record of this list.

9:19.2y	Breen, George (USA)	New Haven	27 Oct. 1956
9:17.7y	Konrads, John (Aus)	Sydney	11 Jan. 1958
9:14.6y	Konrads, John (Aus)	Melbourne	22 Feb. 1958
8:59.6y	Konrads, John (Aus)	Sydney	10 Jan. 1959
8:51.5	Rose, Murray (Aus)	Los Altos	26 Aug. 1962
8:47.4	Belitz-Geiman, Semeón (USSR)	Kharkov	3 Aug. 1966

8:47.3	Bennett, John (Aus)	Sydney	16 Jan. 1967
8:46.8	Mosconi, Alain (Fra)	Monaco	5 July 1967
8:42.0	Luyce, Francis (Fra)	Dinard	21 July 1967
8:43.3	Burton, Mike (USA)	Long Beach	3 Sept. 1968
8:28.8	Burton, Mike (USA)	Louisville	17 Aug. 1969
8:28.6	Windeatt, Graham (Aus)	Sydney	3 Apr. 1971

8:23.8*	Cooper, Brad (Aus)	Sydney	12 Jan. 1972
8:17.6*	Holland, Steve (Aus)	Brisbane	5 Aug. 1973
8:16.27	Holland, Steve (Aus)	Belgrade	8 Sept. 1973
8:15.88	Holland, Steve (Aus)	Christchurch	1 Feb. 1974
8:15.02	Holland, Steve (Aus)	Christchurch	25 Jan. 1975
8:13.68	Shaw, Tim (USA)	Long Beach	21 June 1975
8:09.60	Shaw, Tim (USA)	Mission Viejo	12 July 1975
8:06.27	Holland, Steve (Aus)	Sydney	27 Feb. 1976
8:02.91	Holland, Steve (Aus)	Sydney	29 Feb. 1976

† Ratified as records for the longer 880 y. (804.672 m.) before 800 m. records were recognized in 1930.

1,500 m. Free-style

22:48.4	Taylor, Henry (Eng)	London	25 July 1908
22:00.0	Hodgson, George (Can)	Stockholm	10 July 1912
21:35.3	Borg, Arne (Swe)	Gothenburg	8 July 1923
21:15.0	Borg, Arne (Swe)	Sydney	30 Jan. 1924
21:11.4	Borg, Arne (Swe)	Paris	13 July 1924
20:06.6	Charlton, Boy (Aus)	Paris	15 July 1924
20:04.4	Borg, Arne (Swe)	Budapest	18 Aug. 1926
19:07.2	Borg, Arne (Swe)	Bologna	2 Sept. 1927
18:58.8	Amano, Tomikatsu (Jap)	Tokyo	10 Aug. 1938
18:35.7	Hashizume, Shiro (Jap)	Los Angeles	16 Aug. 1949
18:19.0	Furuhashi, Hironashin (Jap)	Los Angeles	16 Aug. 1949
18:05.9	Breen, George (USA)	New Haven	3 May 1956
17:59.5	Rose, Murray (Aus)	Melbourne	30 Oct. 1956
17:52.9	Breen, George (USA)	Melbourne	5 Dec. 1956

Breen's record (above) set in a heat of the Olympics remained in the list

17:52.9	Breen, George (USA)	Melbourne	5 Dec. 1956
17:28.7y	Konrads, John (Aus)	Melbourne	22 Feb. 1958
17:11.0y	Konrads, John (Aus)	Sydney	27 Feb. 1960
17:05.5	Saari, Roy (USA)	Tokyo	17 Aug. 1963
17:01.8	Rose, Murray (Aus)	Los Altos	2 Aug. 1964
16:58.7	Saari, Roy (USA)	New York	2 Sept. 1964
16:58.6	Krause, Steve (USA)	Maumee	15 Aug. 1965
16:41.6	Burton, Mike (USA)	Lincoln	21 Aug. 1966
16:34.1	Burton, Mike (USA)	Oak Park	13 Aug. 1967
16:28.1	Echevarria, Guillermo (Mex)	Santa Clara	7 July 1968
16:08.5	Burton, Mike (USA)	Long Beach	3 Sept. 1968
16:04.5	Burton, Mike (USA)	Louisville	17 Aug. 1969
15:57.1	Kinsella, John (USA)	Los Angeles	23 Aug. 1970

15:52.91	DeMont, Rick (USA)	Chicago	6 Aug. 1972
15:52.58	Burton, Mike (USA)	Munich	4 Sept. 1972
15:37.8*	Holland, Steve (Aus)	Brisbane	5 Aug. 1973
15:31.85	Holland, Steve (Aus)	Belgrade	8 Sept. 1973
15:31.75	Shaw, Tim (USA)	Concord	25 Aug. 1974
15:27.79	Holland, Steve (Aus)	Christchurch	25 Jan. 1975
15:20.91	Shaw, Tim (USA)	Long Beach	21 June 1975
15:10.59	Holland, Steve (Aus)	Sydney	27 Feb. 1976

100 m. Back-stroke

1:20.8*	Wechesser, Maurice (Belg)	Schaerbeck	2 Oct. 1910
1:18.8*	Baronyi, Andras (Hun)	Budapest	17 July 1911
1:18.4*	Schiele, Oskar (Ger)	Brussels	6 Apr. 1912
1:15.6*	Fahr, Otto (Ger)	Magdeburg	29 Apr. 1912
1:14.8	Kealoha, Warren (USA)	Antwerp	22 Aug. 1920
1:12.6*	Kealoah, Warren (USA)	Honolulu	17 Oct. 1922
1:12.4	Kealoha, Warren (USA)	Honolulu	13 Apr. 1924
1:11.4*	Kealoha, Warren (USA)	Honolulu	19 June 1926
1:11.2	Laufer, Walter (USA)	Berlin	20 June 1926
1:10.2*	House, P.A. (USA)	New Haven	22 Mar. 1927
1:09.0	Kojac, George (USA)	Detroit	23 June 1928
1:08.2	Kojac, George (USA)	Amsterdam	9 Aug. 1928
1:07.4*	Vandeweghe, Albert (USA)	Honolulu	23 July 1934
1:07.0*	Kiefer, Adolph (USA)	Berlin	20 Oct. 1935
1:06.2*	Kiefer, Adolph (USA)	Krefeld	22 Oct. 1935
1:04.9*	Kiefer, Adolph (USA)	Breslau	9 Nov. 1935
1:04.8*	Kiefer, Adolph (USA)	Detroit	18 Jan. 1936
1:04.0*	Stack, Allen (USA)	New Haven	23 June 1948
1:03.6*	Stack, Allen (USA)	New Haven	4 Feb. 1949
1:03.3*	Bozon, Gilbert (Fra)	Troyes	26 Dec. 1952
1:02.8*	Oyakawa, Yoshinobu (USA)	New Haven	1 Apr. 1954
1:02.1*	Bozon, Gilbert (Fra)	Troyes	27 Feb. 1955

Winning time by Theile at Olympic Garnes taken as first record.

1:02.2	Theile, David (Aus)	Melbourne	6 Dec. 1956
1:01.5y	Monckton, John (Aus)	Melbourne	15 Feb. 1958
1:01.3	Bennett, Bob (USA)	Los Angeles	19 Aug. 1961
1:01.0	Stock, Tom (USA)	Cuyahoga Falls	11 Aug. 1962
1:00.9	Stock, Tom (USA)	Cuyahoga Falls	12 Aug. 1962
1:00.8	Kuppers, Ernst-Joachim (W Ger)	Dortmund	28 Aug. 1964
1:00.0	Mann, Tom (USA)	New York	3 Sept. 1964
59.6	Mann, Tom (USA)	Tokyo	16 Oct. 1964
59.5	Russell, Doug (USA)	Tokyo	28 Aug. 1967
59.3	Hickcox, Charles (USA)	Tokyo	28 Aug. 1967
59.1	Hickcox, Charles (USA)	Tokyo	31 Aug. 1967
58.4	Matthes, Roland (E Ger)	Leipzig	21 Sept. 1967
58.0	Matthes, Roland (E Ger)	Mexico City	26 Oct. 1968
57.8	Matthes, Roland (E Ger)	Wurzburg	23 Aug. 1969
56.9	Matthes, Roland (E Ger)	Barcelona	8 Sept. 1970
56.7	Matthes, Roland (E Ger)	Leipzig	4 Sept. 1971

56.3*	Matthes, Roland (E Ger)	Moscow	9 Apr. 1972
56.30e	Matthes, Roland (E Ger)	Munich	4 Sept. 1972

200 m. Back-stroke

3:04.4	Schiele, Oskar (Ger)	Charlottenburg	27 June 1909
2:59.8*	Arnold, George (Ger)	Magdeburg	3 Jan. 1910
2:56.4*	Weckesser, Maurice (Belg)	Schaerbeck	18 Oct. 1910
2:50.6*	Pentz, Hermann (Ger)	Magdeburg	11 Mar. 1911
2:48.4*	Fahr, Otto (Ger)	Magdeburg	3 Apr. 1912
2:47.1	Laufer, Walter (USA)	Bremen	24 June 1926
2:44.9	Laufer, Walter (USA)	Nurnberg	11 July 1926
2:38.8*	Laufer, Walter (USA)	Magdeburg	13 July 1926
2:37.8	Irie, Toshio (Jap)	Tamagawa	14 Oct. 1928
2:32.2*	Kojac, George (USA)	New Haven	16 June 1930
2:27.8*	Vandeweghe, Albert (USA)	Honolulu	30 Aug. 1934
2:24.0*	Kiefer, Adolph (USA)	Chicago	11 Apr. 1935
2:23.0*	Kiefer, Adolph (USA)	Honolulu	23 May 1941

2:22.9*	Holiday, Harry (USA)	Detroit	18 May 1943
2:19.3*	Kiefer, Adolph (USA)	Annapolis	4 Mar. 1944
2:18.5*	Stack, Allen (USA)	New Haven	4 May 1949
2:18.3*	Bozon, Gilbert (Fra)	Algiers	26 June 1953

Minimum time 2:20.2

2:18.8y	Monckton, John (Aus)	Sydney	15 Jan. 1958
2:18.4y	Monckton, John (Aus)	Melbourne	18 Feb. 1958
2:17.9	McKinney, Frank (USA)	Los Altos	12 July 1959
2:17.8	McKinney, Frank (USA)	Osaka	25 July 1959
2:17.6	Bittick, Charles (USA)	Los Angeles	26 June 1960
2:16.0	Stock, Tom (USA)	Toledo	24 July 1960
2:13.2	Stock, Tom (USA)	Chicago	2 July 1961
2:11.5	Stock, Tom (USA)	Los Angeles	20 Aug. 1961
2:10.9	Stock, Tom (USA)	Cuyahoga Falls	10 Aug. 1962
2:10.3	Graef, Jed (USA)	Tokyo	13 Oct. 1964
2:09.4	Hickcox, Charles (USA)	Tokyo	29 Aug. 1967
2:07.9	Matthes, Roland (E Ger)	Leipzig	8 Nov. 1967
2:07.5	Matthes, Roland (E Ger)	Leipzig	14 Aug. 1968
2:07.4	Matthes, Roland (E Ger)	Santa Clara	12 July 1969
2:06.6	Hall, Gary (USA)	Louisville	14 Aug. 1969
2:06.4	Matthes, Roland (E Ger)	Berlin	29 Aug. 1969
2:06.3	Stamm, Mike (USA)	Los Angeles	20 Aug. 1970
2:06.1	Matthes, Roland (E Ger)	Barcelona	11 Sept. 1970
2:05.6	Matthes, Roland (E Ger)	Leipzig	3 Sept. 1971

2:02.8*	Matthes, Roland (E Ger)	Leipzig	10 July 1972
2:02.82e	Matthes, Roland (E Ger)	Munich	2 Sept. 1972
2:01.87	Matthes, Roland (E Ger)	Belgrade	7 Sept. 1973

100 m. Breast-stroke

1:24.0*	Baronyi, Andras (Hun)	Vienna	17 Nov. 1907
1:22.6*	Coubert, Felicien (Belg)	Brussels	30 Sept. 1909
1:21.8*	Goldi, Odon (Hun)	Budapest	12 June 1910
1:18.4*	Bathe, Walther (Ger)	Magdeburg	2 Oct. 1910
1:17.8	Bathe, Walther (Ger)	Budapest	18 Dec. 1910
1:16.8*	Lutzow, Wilhelm (Ger)	Magdeburg	24 May 1921
1:16.2*	Sipos, Marton (Hun)	Budapest	24 Sept. 1922
1:15.9*	Rademacher, Erich (Ger)	Leipzig	5 Apr. 1925
1:15.6*	Faust, Heinz (Ger)	Strasbourg	5 Dec. 1926
1:14.0*	Spence, Walter (USA)	New York	28 Oct. 1927
1:13.6*	Cartonnet, Jacques (Fra)	Paris	20 May 1932
1:13.0*	Cartonnet, Jacques (Fra)	Paris	8 Feb. 1933
1:12.4*	Cartonnet, Jacques (Fra)	Paris	4 Feb. 1933
1:10.8*	Higgins, John (USA)	New Haven	Bu22 Feb. 1935
1:10.0*	Higgins, John (USA)	New Haven	Bu3 Mar. 1936
1:09.8*	Cartonnet, Jacques (Fra)	Toulouse	Bu6 Aug. 1937
1:09.5*	Balke, Joachim (Ger)	Bremen	Bu12 Nov. 1938
1:07.3*	Hough, Dick (USA)	New Haven	Bu15 Apr. 1939
1:07.2*	Meshkov, Leonid (USSR)	Moscow	Bu20 Dec. 1949
1:07.0*	Meshkov, Leonid (USSR)	Minsk	Bu23 Feb. 1950
1:06.8*	Meshkov, Leonid (USSR)	Moscow	Bu17 Apr. 1950
1:06.6*	Meshkov, Leonid (USSR)	Moscow	Bu7 Jan. 1951
1:06.5*	Meshkov, Leonid (USSR)	Moscow	Bu5 May 1951
1:05.8*	Klein, Herbert (Ger)	Nordeney	Bu17 Feb. 1952

Minimum time 1:12.0

| 1:11.9* | Minashkin, Vladimir (USSR) | Leningrad | Uw11 Feb. 1953 |
| 1:11.2* | Minashkin, Vladimir (USSR) | Leningrad | Uw23 Feb. 1953 |

1:10.9*	Petrusewicz, Marek (Pol)	Wroclaw	Uw18 Oct. 1953
1:10.5*	Minashkin, Vladimir (USSR)	Stockholm	Uw24 Feb. 1954
1:09.8*	Petruswwicz, Marek (Pol)	Wroclaw	Uw23 May 1954
1:08.2*	Furukawa, Masaru (Jap)	Tokyo	Uw1 Oct. 1955

Minimum time 1:13.0

1:12.7	Svozil, Viteslav (Czech)	Piestany	1 May 1957
1:11.6	Lieh-Yung, Chi (China)	Canton	1 May 1957
1:11.5	Minashkin, Vladimir (USSR)	Leipzig	15 Sept. 1957
1:11.4	Kolesnikov, Leonid (USSR)	Moscow	5 May 1961
1:11.1	Jastremski, Chet (USA)	Chicago	2 July 1961
1:10.8	Tittes, Gunter (E Ger)	Berlin	5 July 1961
1:10.7	Jastremski, Chet (USA)	Tokyo	28 July 1961
1:10.0	Jastremski, Chet (USA)	Tokyo	30 July 1961
1:09.5	Jastremski, Chet (USA)	Osaka	3 Aug. 1961
1:07.8	Jastremski, Chet (USA)	Los Angeles	20 Aug. 1961
1:07.5	Jastremski, Chet (USA)	Los Angeles	20 Aug. 1961
1:07.4	Prokopenko, Georgy (USSR)	Baku	26 Mar. 1964
1:06.9	Prokopenko, Georgy (USSR)	Moscow	3 Sept. 1964
1:06.7	Kosinsky, Vladimir (USSR)	Leningrad	8 Nov. 1967
1:06.4	Fiolo, Jose (Braz)	Rio de Janiero	19 Feb. 1968
1:06.2	Pankin, Nicolay (USSR)	Moscow	18 Apr. 1968
1:05.8	Pankin, Nicolay (USSR)	Magdeburg	20 Apr. 1969

1:05.68	Hencken, John (USA)	Munich	29 Aug. 1972
1:05.13	Taguchi, Nobutaka (Jap)	Munich	29 Aug. 1972
1:04.94	Taguchi, Nobutaka (Jap)	Munich	30 Aug. 1972
1:04.35	Hencken, John (USA)	Belgrade	4 Sept. 1973
1:04.02	Hencken, John (USA)	Belgrade	4 Sept. 1973
1:03.88	Hencken, John (USA)	Concord	31 Aug. 1974

200 m. Breast-stroke

3:09.2	Holman, Frederick (Eng)	London	18 Aug. 1908
3:08.3*	Andersson, Robert (Swe)	Stockholm	18 Apr. 1909
3:00.8*	Coubert, Felicien (Belg)	Schaerbeck	2 Oct. 1910
2:56.6*	Courtman, Percy (Eng)	Garston	28 July 1914
2:54.4*	Rademacher, Erich (Ger)	Amsterdam	12 Nov. 1922
2:52.6*	Skelton, Robert (USA)	Milwaukee	21 Mar. 1924
2:50.4*	Rademacher, Erich (Ger)	Magdeburg	7 Apr. 1924
2:48.0*	Rademacher, Erich (Ger)	Brussels	11 Mar. 1927
2:45.0*	Tsuruta, Yoshiyuki (Jap)	Kyoto	27 July 1929
2:44.6*	Spence, Leonard (USA)	Chicago	2 Apr. 1931
2:44.0*	Spence, Leonard (USA)	New Haven	1 Apr. 1932
2:42.6*	Cartonnet, Jacques (Fra)	Paris	8 Feb. 1933
2:42.4*	Sietas, Erwin (Ger)	Dusseldorf	16 Mar. 1935
2:39.6*	Cartonnet, Jacques (Fra)	Paris	4 May 1935
2:37.2*	Kasley, Jack (USA)	New Haven	Bu28 Mar. 1936
2:36.8*	Nakache, Alfred (Fra)	Marseilles	Bu6 July 1941
2:35.6*	Verdeur, Joe (USA)	Bainbridge	Bu5 Apr. 1946
2:35.0*	Verdeur, Joe (USA)	New Haven	Bu15 Feb. 1947
2:32.0*	Verdeur, Joe (USA)	New Haven	Bu14 Feb..1948
2:30.5*	Verdeur, Joe (USA)	New Haven	Bu2 Apr. 1948
2:30.0*	Verdeur, Joe (USA)	New Haven	Bu28 June 1948
2:28.3*	Verdeur, Joe (USA)	New Haven	Bu31 Mar. 1950
2:27.3*	Klein, Herbert (Ger)	Munich	Bu9 June 1951

Minimum time 2:38.0

| 2:37.4* | Gleie, Knud (Den) | Copenhagen | 14 Feb. 1953 |
| 2:36.6* | Furukawa, Masaru (Jap) | Tokyo | Uw10 Apr. 1954 |

2:35.4*	Furukawa, Masaru (Jap)	Tokyo	Uw10 Apr. 1954
2:35.2*	Tanaka, Mamoru (Jap)	Tokyo	Uw17 Sept. 1954
2:33.7	Furukawa, Masaru (Jap)	Tokyo	Uw5 Aug. 1955
2:31.0*	Furukawa, Masaru (Jap)	Tokyo	Uw1 Oct. 1955

Minimum time 2:40.0

2:36.5y	Gathercole, Terry (Aus)	Townsville	28 June 1958
2:33.6	Jastremski, Chet (USA)	Tokyo	28 July 1961
2:29.6	Jastremski, Chet (USA)	Los Angeles	19 Aug. 1961
2:28.2	Jastremski, Chet (USA)	New York	30 Aug. 1964
2:27.8	O'Brien, Ian (Aus)	Tokyo	15 Oct. 1964
2:27.4	Kosinsky, Vladimir (USSR)	Kalev	3 Apr. 1968
2:26.5	Pankin, Nicolay (USSR)	Minsk	22 Mar. 1969
2:25.4	Pankin, Nicolay (USSR)	Magdeburg	19 Apr. 1969
2:23.5	Job, Brian (USA)	Los Angeles	22 Aug. 1970

2:22.79	Hencken, John (USA)	Chicago	5 Aug. 1972
2:21.55	Hencken, John (USA)	Munich	2 Sept. 1972
2:20.52	Hencken, John (USA)	Louisville	24 Aug. 1973
2:19.28	Wilkie, David (GB)	Belgrade	6 Sept. 1973
2:18.93	Hencken, John (USA)	Concord	24 Aug. 1974
2:18.21	Hencken, John (USA)	Concord	1 Sept. 1974

100 m. Butterfly
Minimum time 1:05.8

1:04.3*	Tumpek, Gyorgy (Hun)	Budapest	31 May 1953
1:03.7*	Tumpek, Gyorgy (Hun)	Budapest	8 May 1954
1:02.3	Tumpek, Gyorgy (Hun)	Budapest	1 Aug. 1954
1:02.1*	Tumpek, Gyorgy (Hun)	Szehesfehervar	20 Nov. 1954
1:02.0*	Tumpek, Gyorgy (Hun)	Budapest	21 Dec. 1954
1:01.5*	Wiggins, Albert (USA)	New Haven	2 Apr. 1955

Minimum time 1:03.5

1:03.4	Tumpek, Gyorgy (Hun)	Budapest	26 May 1957
1:01.5	Ishimoto, Takashi (Jap)	Kurume	16 June 1957
1:01.3	Ishimoto, Takashi (Jap)	Tokyo	7 July 1957
1:01.2	Ishimoto, Takashi (Jap)	Tokyo	6 Sept. 1957
1:01.0	Ishimoto, Takashi (Jap)	Kochi	14 Sept. 1958
1:00.1	Ishimoto, Takashi (Jap)	Los Angeles	29 June 1958
59.0	Larson, Lance (USA)	Los Angeles	26 June 1960
58.7	Larson, Lance (USA)	Toledo	24 July 1960
58.6	Schmidt, Fred (USA)	Los Angeles	20 Aug. 1961
58.4	Nicolao, Luis (Arg)	Rio de Janiero	24 Apr. 1962
57.0	Nicolao, Luis (Arg)	Rio de Janiero	27 Apr. 1962
56.3	Spitz, Mark (USA)	Winnipeg	31 July 1967
56.3e	Russell, Doug (USA)	Tokyo	29 Aug. 1967
55.7	Spitz, Mark (USA)	Berlin	7 Oct. 1967
55.6	Spitz, Mark (USA)	Long Beach	30 Aug. 1968
55.0	Spitz, Mark (USA)	Houston	25 Aug. 1971

54.72	Spitz, Mark (USA)	Chicago	4 Aug. 1972
54.56	Spitz, Mark (USA)	Chicago	4 Aug. 1972
54.27	Spitz, Mark (USA)	Munich	31 Aug. 1972

200 m. Butterfly
Minimum time 2:27.3 (based on former 200 m. breast-stroke record by Klein, Herbert (Ger) on 9 June, 1951 using the butterfly style).

2:21.6*	Nagasawa, Jiro (Jap)	Tokyo	17 Sept. 1954
2:20.8*	Ishimoto, Takashi (Jap)	Tokyo	1 Oct. 1955
2:19.3*	Nagasawa, Jiro (Jap)	New Haven	14 Mar. 1956

2:16.7*	Yorzyk, Bill (USA)	Winchendon	14 Apr. 1956

Minimum time 2:19.0

2:19.0	Troy, Mike (USA)	Los Altos	11 July 1959
2:16.4	Troy, Mike (USA)	Los Altos	11 July 1959
2:15.0	Troy, Mike (USA)	Evansville	10 July 1960
2:13.4	Troy, Mike (USA)	Toledo	23 July 1960
2:13.2	Troy, Mike (USA)	Detroit	4 Aug. 1960
2:12.8	Troy, Mike (USA)	Rome	2 Sept. 1960
2:12.6	Robie, Carl (USA)	Los Angeles	19 Aug. 1961
2:12.5y	Berry, Kevin (Aus)	Melbourne	20 Feb. 1962
2:12.4	Robie, Carl (USA)	Cuyahoga Falls	11 Aug. 1962
2:10.8	Robie, Carl (USA)	Cuyahoga Falls	11 Aug. 1962
2:09.7y	Berry, Kevin (Aus)	Melbourne	23 Oct. 1962
2:08.4y	Berry, Kevin (Aus)	Sydney	12 Jan. 1963
2:08.2	Robie, Carl (USA)	Tokyo	18 Aug. 1963
2:06.9	Berry, Kevin (Aus)	Sydney	29 Feb. 1964
2:06.6	Berry, Kevin (Aus)	Tokyo	18 Oct. 1964
2:06.4	Spitz, Mark (USA)	Winnipeg	26 July 1967
2:06.4e	Spitz, Mark (USA)	Oak Park	12 Aug. 1967
2:06.0	Ferris, John (USA)	Tokyo	30 Aug. 1967
2:05.7	Spitz, Mark (USA)	Berlin	8 Oct. 1967
2:05.4	Spitz, Mark (USA)	Los Angeles	22 Aug. 1970
2:05.0	Hall, Gary (USA)	Los Angeles	22 Aug. 1970
2:03.9	Spitz, Mark (USA)	Houston	27 Aug. 1971
2:03.9e	Spitz, Mark (USA)	Houston	27 Aug. 1971
2:03.3	Fassnacht, Hans (W Ger)	Landskrona	31 Aug. 1971
2:01.87	Spitz, Mark (USA)	Chicago	2 Aug. 1972
2:01.53	Spitz, Mark (USA)	Chicago	2 Aug. 1972
2:00.70	Spitz, Mark (USA)	Munich	28 Aug. 1972

200 m. Individual medley

Minimum time 2:13.0

2:12.4	Buckingham, Greg (USA)	Lincoln	21 Aug. 1966
2:11.3	Buckingham, Greg (USA)	Oak Park	23 Aug. 1967
2:10.6	Hickcox, Charles (USA)	Long Beach	31 Aug. 1968
2:09.6	Hall, Gary (USA)	Louisville	17 Aug. 1969
2:09.5	Hall, Gary (USA)	Los Angeles	23 Aug. 1970
2:09.3	Larsson, Gunnar (Swe)	Barcelona	12 Sept. 1970
2:09.30e	Hall, Gary (USA)	Chicago	6 Aug. 1972
2:07.17	Larsson, Gunnar (Swe)	Munich	3 Sept. 1972
2:06.32	Wilkie, David (GB)	Vienna	24 Aug. 1974
2:06.32e	Furniss, Steve (USA)	Concord	1 Sept. 1974
2:06.08	Furniss, Bruce (USA)	Kansas City	23 Aug. 1975

400 m. Individual medley

5:48.5	O'Neill, Frank (Aus)	Sydney	17 Jan. 1953
5:43.0	O'Neill, Frank (Aus)	Sydney	24 Feb. 1953
5:38.7*	Kettesy, Gusztav (Hun)	Budapest	24 Apr. 1953
5:35.6*	Lucien, Maurice (Fra)	Troys	24 Apr. 1953
5:32.1	Kettesy, Gusztav (Hun)	Budapest	26 July 1953
5:31.0*	Andsberg, Jan (Swe)	Lund	29 Oct. 1953
5:27.3*	Lucien, Maurice (Fra)	Reims	18 Mar. 1954
5:18.3*	Spengler, Alfred (E Ger)	Dresden	22 Apr. 1954
5:15.4*	Stroujanov, Vladimir (USSR)	Minsk	2 Oct. 1954
5:09.4*	Androsov, Gennady (USSR)	Lvov	10 Mar. 1957
5:08.3*	Stroujanov, Vladimir (USSR)	Moscow	17 Mar. 1957

Minimum time 5:22.0

5:12.9	Stroujanov, Vladimir (USSR)	Moscow	20 Oct. 1957
5:08.8y	Black, Ian (GB)	Cardiff	6 June 1959
5:07.8	Harrison, George (USA)	Los Angeles	24 June 1960
5:05.3	Harrison, George (USA)	Los Angeles	24 June 1960
5:04.5	Rounsavelle, Dennis (USA)	Toledo	22 July 1960
5:04.3	Stickles, Ted (USA)	Chicago	1 July 1961
4:55.6	Stickles, Ted (USA)	Los Angeles	18 Aug. 1961
4:53.8	Hetz, Gerhard (W Ger)	Moscow	24 May 1962
4:51.4	Stickles, Ted (USA)	Chicago	30 June 1962
4:51.0y	Stickles, Ted (USA)	Louisville	12 July 1962
4:50.2	Hetz, Gerhard (W Ger)	Tokyo	12 Oct. 1963
4:48.6	Roth, Dick (USA)	Los Altos	31 July 1964
4:45.4	Roth, Dick (USA)	Tokyo	14 Oct. 1964
4:45.3	Dunaev, Andrei (USSR)	Tallinen	3 Apr. 1968
4:45.1	Buckingham, Greg (USA)	Santa Clara	6 July 1968
4:43.3	Hall, Gary (USA)	Los Angeles	20 July 1968
4:39.0	Hickcox, Charles (USA)	Long Beach	30 Aug. 1968
4:38.7	Hall, Gary (USA)	Santa Clara	11 July 1969
4:33.9	Hall, Gary (USA)	Louisville	15 Aug. 1969
4:31.0	Hall, Gary (USA)	Los Angeles	21 Aug. 1970

- -

4:30.81	Hall, Gary (USA)	Chicago	3 Aug. 1972
4:28.89	Hargitay, Andras (Hun)	Vienna	20 Aug. 1974

4 x 100 m. Free-style Relay

4:10.2	Budapest University, Hungary	Budapest	26 June 1937

(Kiss, Zoltan; Dienes, Gyula; Lengyel, Arpad; Csik, Ferenc)

4:06.6	Hungary	Budapest	15 Aug. 1937

(Zolyomi, Gyula; Korosi, Istvan; Grof, Odon; Csik, Ferenc)

4:03.6*	Bremischer, Germany	Bremen	5 Mar. 1938

(Heibel, Hermann; Freese, Hans; Askamp, Edward; Fischer, Helmuth)

4:02.4*	City of Berlin, Germany	Copenhagen	1 Apr. 1938

(Wille, Otto; Birr, Werner; Plath, Werner; Eckenbrecher, Kurt von)

4:02.0*	Hungary	Budapest	14 July 1938

(Zolomi, Gyula; Csik, Ferenc; Korosi, Istvan; Grof, Odon)

3:59.2	United States	Berlin	20 Aug. 1938

(Hirose, T.; Jaretz, O.; Wolf, Paul; Fick, Peter)

3:54.4*	Yale University, United States	New Haven	8 Mar. 1940

(Sanburn, W.; Pope, E.; Duncan, R.; Johnson, H)

3:50.8*	Yale University, United States	New Haven	18 Mar. 1942

(Johnson, H,; Kelly, R.; Pope, E.; Lilley, F)

3:48.6*	New Haven S.C., United States	New Haven	29 June 1948

(Ford, Alan; Hueber, E.; Dooley, F.; Johnson, H)

3:47.9*	Yale University, United States	New Haven	19 Mar. 1951

(Thoman, Dick; Sheff, D.; Farnsworth, W.; Reid, R)

3:46.8	Japan	Tokyo	6 Aug. 1955

(Suzsuki, Hiroshi; Tani, A.; Goto, Toro; Koga, M.)

- -

The time by Japan (above) retained in list

3:46.8	Japan	Tokyo	6 Aug. 1955

(Suzsuki, Hiroshi; Tani, A.; Goto, Toro; Koga, M.)

3:46.3	Australia	Brisbane	3 May 1958

(Chapman, Gary; Konrads, John; Shipton, Geoff; Devitt, John)

3:44.4	United States	Tokyo	21 July 1959

(Follett, Ed.; Larson, Lance; Farrell, Jeff; Alkire, Joe)

3:42.5	France	Thionville	10 Aug. 1962

(Gottvalles, Alain; Gropaiz, Gerard; Curtillet, Jean-Pierre; Christophe, Robert)

3:39.9	Santa Clara S.C., United States	Los Altos	4 July 1963

(Clark, Steve; Schoenmann, N.; Schollander, Don; Townsend, Ed)

3:36.1	United States	Tokyo	18 Aug. 1963

(Clark, Steve; McDonough, R.; Ilman, Gary; Townsend, Ed)

3:33.2	United States	Tokyo	14 Oct. 1964

(Clark, Steve; Austin, Mike; Ilman, Gary; Schollander, Don)

3:32.6	United States	Tokyo	28 Aug. 1967

(Walsh, Ken; Zorn, Zac; Havens, Don; Charlton, Greg)

3:32.5	United States	Long Beach	3 Sept. 1968

(Zorn, Zac; Rerych, Steve; Walsh, Ken; Schollander, Don)

3:31.7	United States	Mexico City	17 Oct. 1968

(Zorn, Zac; Rerych, Steve; Spitz, Mark; Walsh, Ken)

3:28.8	Los Angeles S.C., United States	Los Angeles	23 Aug. 1970

(Havens, Don; Weston, Mike; Frawley, Bill; Heckl, Frank)

3:28.84e	United States	Munich	28 Aug. 1972

(Fairbank, David; Conelly, Gary; Heidenreich, Jerry; Edgar, David)

3:26.42	United States	Munich	28 Aug. 1972

(Edgar, David; Murphy, John; Heidenreich, Jerry; Spitz, Mark)

3:25.17	United States	Concord	1 Sept. 1974

(Coan, Andy; Montgomery, Jim; Bottom, Mike; Hickcox, Tom)

3:24.85	United States	Cali	23 July 1975

(Furniss, Bruce; Montgomery, Jim; Coan, Andy; Murphy, John)

4 x 200 m. Free-style relay

8:58.4	Japan	Los Angeles	9 Aug. 1932

(Miyazaki, Yasuji; Yokoyama, Takashi; Yusa, Masanori; Toyoda, Hisakichi)

8:52.2	Japan	Tokyo	19 Aug. 1935

(Yusa, Masanori; Makino, Shozo; Isharada, S.; Negami, H.)

8:51.5	Japan	Berlin	11 Aug. 1936

(Yusa, Masanori; Sugiura, Shiego; Arai, Shigeo; Taguchi, Masaharu)

8:46.0	United States	London	3 Aug. 1948

(Ris, Wally; Wolf, Wallace; McLane, Jimmy; Smith, Bill)

8:45.4	Tokyo S.C., Japan	Los Angeles	18 Aug. 1949

(Hamaguchi, Yoshihiro; Maruyama, S.; Murayama, S.; Furuhashi, Hironashin)

8:43.2*	Yale University, United States	New Haven	24 Feb. 1950

(Farnsworth, W.; Munson, L.; Blum, J.; Reid, R.)

8:40.6*	Tokyo S.C., Japan	Marilaia	2 Apr. 1950

(Hamaguchi, Yoshihiro; Murayama, S.; Hashizume, Shiro; Furuhashi, Hironashin)

8:33.0*	France	Marseilles	2 Aug. 1951

(Bernardo, Joseph; Biloch, Willy; Boiteux, Jean; Jany, Alex)

8:29.4*	Yale University, United States	New Haven	16 Feb. 1952

(Moore, Wayne; McLane, Jimmy; Sheff, D.; Thoman, Dick)

8:24.5*	U.S.S.R.	Moscow	4 Nov. 1956

(Nikitin, Boris; Strujanov, Vladimir; Nikolaev, Gennadi; Sorokin, Vitali)

8:23.6	Australia	Melbourne	3 Dec. 1956

(O'Halloran, Kevin; Devitt, John; Rose, Murray; Henricks, Jon)

The winning time by Australia (above) at the Olympic Games remained in the list.

8:23.6	Australia	Melbourne	3 Dec. 1956

(O'Halloran, Kevin; Devitt, John; Rose, Murray; Henricks, Jon)

8:21.6	Japan	Tokyo	22 July 1959

(Umenoto, T.; Fujimoto, Tatsuo; Fukui, Makoto; Yamanaka, Tsuyoshi)

8:18.7	Japan	Osaka	26 July 1959

(Yamanaka, Tsuyoshi; Fukui, Makoto; Kenjo, K.; Fujimoto, Tatsuo)

8:17.0	Indianapolis A.C., United States	Toledo	23 July 1960

(Sintz, Peter; Breen, George; Somers, Alan; Troy, Mike)

| 8:16.6y | Australia | Townsville | 6 Aug. 1960 |

(Henricks, John; Dickson, David; Konrads, John; Rose, Murray)

| 8:10.2 | United States | Rome | 1 Sept. 1960 |

(Harrison, George; Blick, Dick; Troy, Mike; Farrell, Jeff)

| 8:09.8 | Japan | Tokyo | 21 Apr. 1963 |

(Fujimoto, Tatsuo; Yamanaka, Tsuyoshi; Okabe, Y.; Fukui, Makato)

| 8:07.6 | Santa Clara S.C., United States | Illinois | 10 Aug. 1963 |

(Townsend, Ed; Wall, Mike; Clark, Steve; Schollander, Don)

| 8:03.7 | United States | Tokyo | 9 Aug. 1963 |

(Schollander, Don; McDonough, R.; Townsend, Ed; Saari, Roy)

| 8:01.8 | United States | Los Angeles | 28 Sept. 1964 |

(Mettler, W.; Wall, Mike; Lyons, Dave; Schollander, Don)

| 7:52.1 | United States | Tokyo | 18 Oct. 1964 |

(Clark, Steve; Saari, Roy; Ilman, Gary; Schollander, Don)

| 7:52.1e | Santa Clara S.C., United States | Oak Park | 12 Aug. 1967 |

(Ilman, Gary; Spitz, Mark; Wall, Mike; Schollander, Don)

| 7:50.8 | Australia | Edinburgh | 24 July 1970 |

(Rogers, Greg; Devenish, Bill; White, Graham; Wenden, Mike)

| 7:48.0 | United States | Tokyo | 28 Aug. 1970 |

(Kinsella, John; McBreen, Tom; Hall, Gary; Lambert, Mark)

| 7:45.8 | United States | Cali | 9 Aug. 1971 |

(Heidenreich, Jerry; Genter, Steve; McConica, Jim; Heckl, Frank)

| 7:43.3 | United States | Minsk | 10 Sept. 1971 |

(Spitz, Mark; Heidenreich, Jerry; Tyler, Fred; McBreen, Tom)

| 7:35.78 | United States | Munich | 31 Aug. 1972 |

(Kinsella, John; Tyler, Fred; Genter, Steve; Spitz, Mark)

| 7:33.22 | United States | Belgrade | 7 Sept. 1973 |

(Krumpholz, Kurt; Backhaus, Robin; Klatt, Richard; Montgomery, Jim)

| 7:30.54 | Long Beach S.C. United States | Kansas City | 22 Aug. 1975 |

(Favero, Rex; Shaw, Tim; Furniss, Steve; Furniss, Bruce)

4 x 100 m. Medley relay

| 4:39.2* | S.K. Poseidon, Sweden | Halsingborg | 22 Feb. 1953 |

(Hellsing, Gustaf; Brock, Lennart; Dahl, Roy; Westesson, Hakan)

| 4:32.2* | France | Charleroi | 22 Mar. 1953 |

(Bozon, Gilbert; Dumesnil, Pierre; Lucien, Maurice; Jany, Alex)

| 4:31.5* | Racing Club de France (France) | Troyes | 1 Apr. 1953 |

(Violas, A.; Dumesnil, Pierre; Arene, Julian; Eminente, Aldo)

| 4:30.8* | Sweden | Lund | 17 Apr. 1953 |

(Hellsing, Gustaf; Brock, Lennart; Larsson, Goran; Ostrand, Per-Ola)

| 4:27.8* | Sweden | Boras | 24 Apr. 1953 |

(Hellsing, Gustaf; Brock, Lennart; Larsson, Goran; Ostrand, Per-Ola)

| 4:24.8* | U.S.S.R. | Moscow | 13 May 1953 |

(Lopatine, V.; Minaschkin, Vladimir; Skriptschenkov, P.; Balandin, Lev)

| 4:21.3* | U.S.S.R. | Moscow | 26 Jan. 1954 |

(Soloviev, V.; Minaschkin, Vladimir; Skriptschenkov, P.; Balandin, Lev)

| 4:19.0* | Soviet Union | Stockholm | 24 Feb. 1954 |

(Soloviev, V.; Minaschkin, Vladimir; Skriptschenkov, P.; Balandin, Lev)

| 4:18.1 | Hungary | Budapest | 5 Aug. 1954 |

(Magyar, Laszlo, Utassy, Sandor; Tumpek, Gyorgy; Nyeki, Imre)

| 4:17.2* | Japan | Tokyo | 17 Sept. 1954 |

(Hase, K; Tanaka, M; Nagasawa, J; Tani, A)

| 4:15.7 | Japan | Osaka | 13 Aug. 1955 |

(Hase, K; Furukawa, Masaru; Ishimoto, T; Koga, M)

| 4:14.8* | U.S.S.R. | Moscow | 14 Aug. 1956 |

(Kuvaldin, G; Minaschkin, Vladimir; Strujanov, Vladimir; Balandin, Lev)

Minimum time 4:18.0

4:17.8	Japan	Tokyo	7 Sept. 1957

(Tomita, Kazuo; Furukawa, Masaru; Ishimoto, Takashi; Ishiharo, Katsuki)

4:17.2	Japan	Tokyo	28 May 1958

(Hase, K; Furukawa, Masaru; Ishimoto, Takashi; Koga, M)

4:14.2y	Australia	Cardiff	25 July 1958

(Monckton, John; Gathercole, Terry; Wilkinson, Brian; Devitt, John)

4:10.4	Australia	Osaka	22 Aug. 1958

(Monckton, John; Gathercole, Terry; Wilkinson, Brian; Devitt, John)

4:09.2	Indianapolis A.C., United States	Toledo	24 July 1960

(McKinney, Frank; Jastremski, Chet; Troy, Mike; Sintz, Peter)

4:08.2	United States	Rome	27 Aug. 1960

(Bennett, Bob; Hait, Paul; Gillanders, David; Clark, Steve)

4:05.4	United States	Rome	1 Sept. 1960

(McKinney, Frank; Hait, Paul; Larson, Lance; Farrell, Jeff)

4:03.0	Indianapolis A.C., United States	Los Angeles	20 Aug. 1961

(Stock, Tom; Jastremski, Chet; Schulhof, Larry; Sintz, Peter)

4:01.6	Indianapolis A.C., United States	Cuyahoga Falls	12 Aug. 1962

(Stock, Tom; Jastremski, Chet; Schmidt, Fred; Sintz, Peter)

4:00.1	United States	Osaka	24 Aug. 1963

(McGeagh, Dick; Craig, Bill; Richardson, W.; Clark, Steve)

3:58.4	United States	Tokyo	16 Oct. 1964

(Mann, Tom; Craig, Bill; Schmidt, Fred; Clark, Steve)

3:57.2	National University Team, United States	Tokyo	31 Aug. 1967

(Hickcox, Charles; Merten, Ken; Russell, Doug; Walsh, Ken)

3:56.5	East Germany	Leipzig	7 Nov. 1967

(Matthes, Roland; Henninger, Egon; Gregor, Horst; Wiegand, Frank)

3:54.9	United States	Mexico City	26 Oct. 1968

(Hickcox, Charles; McKenzie, Don; Russell, Doug; Walsh, Ken)

3:54.4	East Germany	Barcelona	8 Sept. 1970

(Matthes, Roland; Katzur, Klaus; Poser, Udo; Unger, Lutz)

3:50.4	United States	Liepzig	3 Sept. 1971

(Campbell, Charles; Dahlberg, Peter; Spitz, Mark; Heidenreich, Jerry)

- -

3:48.16	United States	Munich	4 Sept. 1972

(Stamm, Mike; Bruce, Tom; Spitz, Mark; Heidenreich, Jerry)

WOMEN

100 m. Free-style

1:35.0*	Gerstung, Martha (Ger)	Magdeburg	18 Oct. 1906
1:26.6*	Guttenstein, C. (Belg)	Schaerbeck	2 Oct. 1910
1:24.6*	Curwen, Daisy (Eng)	Liverpool	29 Sept. 1911
1:20.6*	Curwen, Daisy (Eng)	Birkenhead	10 June 1912
1:19.8	Durack, Fanny (Aus)	Stockholm	9 July 1912
1:18.8	Durack, Fanny (Aus)	Hamburg	21 July 1912
1:16.2	Durack, Fanny (Aus)	Sydney	6 Feb. 1915
1:13.6	Bleibtrey, Ethelda (USA)	Antwerp	25 Aug. 1920
1:12.8	Ederle, Gertrude (USA)	Newark	30 June 1923
1:12.2	Wehselau, Mariechen (USA)	Paris	19 July 1924
1:10.0*	Lackie, Ethel (USA)	Toledo	28 Jan. 1926
1:09.8	Garratti, Eleanora (USA)	Honolulu	7 Aug. 1929
1:09.4	Osipowich, Albina (USA)	San Fransisco	25 Aug. 1929
1:08.0*	Madison, Helene (USA)	Miami Beach	14 Mar. 1930
1:06.6*	Madison, Helene (USA)	Boston	20 Apr. 1931
1:06.0*	Ouden, Willy den (Neth)	Antwerp	9 July 1933
1:05.4*	Ouden, Willy, den (Neth)	Amsterdam	24 Feb. 1934
1:04.8*	Ouden, Willy den (Neth)	Rotterdam	15 Apr. 1934
1:04.6*	Ouden, Willy den (Neth)	Amsterdam	27 Feb. 1936
1:04.5	Fraser, Dawn (Aus)	Sydney	21 Feb. 1956
1:04.2*	Gastelaars, Cockie (Neth)	Amsterdam	3 Mar. 1956

1:04.0*	Gastelaars, Cockie (Neth)	Schiedam	14 Apr. 1956
1:03.3	Fraser, Dawn (Aus)	Townsville	25 Aug. 1956
1:03.2	Crapp, Lorraine (Aus)	Sydney	20 Oct. 1956
1:02.4	Crapp, Lorraine (Aus)	Melbourne	25 Oct. 1956
1:02.0	Fraser, Dawn (Aus)	Melbourne	1 Dec. 1956

Winning time by Fraser (above) at Olympic Games remained in the list

1:02.0	Fraser, Dawn (Aus)	Melbourne	1 Dec. 1956
1:01.5y	Fraser, Dawn (Aus)	Melbourne	18 Feb. 1958
1:01.4y	Fraser, Dawn (Aus)	Cardiff	21 July 1958
1:01.2	Fraser, Dawn (Aus)	Schiedam	10 Aug. 1058
1:00.2y	Fraser, Dawn (Aus)	Sydney	23 Feb. 1960
1:00.0y	Fraser, Dawn (Aus)	Melbourne	23 Oct. 1962
59.9y	Fraser, Dawn (Aus)	Melbourne	27 Oct. 1962
59.5y	Fraser, Dawn (Aus)	Perth	24 Nov. 1962
58.9	Fraser, Dawn (Aus)	Sydney	29 Feb. 1964
58.9e	Gould, Shane (Aus)	London	30 Apr. 1971

58.5*	Gould, Shane (Aus)	Sydney	8 Jan. 1972
58.25	Ender, Kornelia (E Ger)	E. Berlin	13 July 1973
58.12	Ender, Kornelia (E Ger)	Utrecht	18 Aug. 1973
57.61	Ender, Kornelia (E Ger)	Belgrade	8 Sept.1973
57.54	Ender, Kornelia (E Ger)	Belgrade	9 Sept. 1973
57.51	Ender, Kornelia (E Ger)	Rostock	4 July 1974
56.96	Ender, Kornelia (E Ger)	Vienna	19 Aug. 1974
56.38	Ender, Kornelia (E Ger)	Dresden	14 Mar. 1975
56.22	Ender, Kornelia (E Ger)	Cali	26 July 1975

200 m. Free-style

2:56.0*y†	Durack, Fanny (Aus)	Manly	4 Mar. 1915
2:47.6*y	Boyle, C. (USA)	New Brighton	25 Aug. 1921
2:45.2*	Ederle, Gertrude (USA)	Brooklyn	4 Apr. 1923
2:40.6*y	Norelius, Martha (USA)	Miami	28 Feb. 1926
2:34.6*	Madison, Helene (USA)	St. Augustine	6 Mar. 1930
2:28.6*	Ouden, Willy den (Neth)	Rotterdam	3 May 1933
2:27.6*y	Ouden, Willy den (Neth)	Dundee	5 May 1934
2:25.3*	Ouden, Willy den (Neth)	Copenhagen	8 Sept. 1935
2:24.6*	Veen, Rie van (Neth)	Rotterdam	26 Feb. 1938
2:21.7*	Hveger, Ragnhild (Den)	Aarthus	11 Sept. 1938
2:20.7	Fraser, Dawn (Aus)	Sydney	25 Feb. 1956
2:19.3	Crapp, Lorraine (Aus)	Townsville	25 Aug. 1956
2:18.5	Crapp, Lorraine (Aus)	Sydney	20 Oct. 1956

Minimum time 2:18.5 (based on former record by Crapp on way to 440 y. in a 55 y. bath but now ruled out because the time was taken mid-course).

2:17.7y	Fraser, Dawn (Aus)	Adelaide	10 Feb. 1958
2:14.7y	Fraser, Dawn (Aus)	Melbourne	22 Feb. 1958
2:11.6y	Fraser, Dawn (Aus)	Sydney	27 Feb. 1960
2:10.5	Watson, Pokey (USA)	Lincoln	19 Aug. 1966
2:09.7	Kruse, Pam (USA)	Philadelphia	19 Aug. 1967
2:09.5	Pedersen, Sue (USA)	Santa Clara	6 July 1968
2:08.8	Wetzel, Eadie (USA)	Lincoln	2 Aug. 1968
2:06.7	Meyer, Debbie (USA)	Los Angeles	24 Aug. 1968
2:06.5	Gould, Shane (Aus)	London	1 May 1971
2:05.8	Gould, Shane (Aus)	Sydney	26 Nov. 1971

2:05.21	Babashoff, Shirley (USA)	Chicago	4 Aug. 1972
2:03.56	Gould, Shane (Aus)	Munich	1 Sept. 1972
2:03.22	Ender, Kornelia (E Ger)	Vienna	22 Aug. 1974

2:02.94	Babashoff, Shirley (USA)	Concord	23 Aug. 1974
2:02.94e	Babashoff, Shirley (USA)	Concord	31 Aug. 1974
2:02.27	Ender, Kornelia (E Ger)	Dresden	15 Mar. 1975

† The ratified time of 2:56.4 by Dorfner, O. (USA) in Alameda on 21 July, 1918, which was inferior to the performance for the longer 220 y. (201.168 m.) by Durack (1915), has been deleted and the earlier and faster time has been introduced into the world 200 m. record list.

400 m. Free-style

6:30.2y	Bleibtrey, Ethelda (USA)	New York	16 Aug. 1919
6:16.6*y	James, Hilda (Eng)	Leeds	29 July 1921
5:53.2	Ederle, Gertrude (USA)	Indianapolis	4 Aug. 1922
5:51.4y	Norelius, Martha (USA)	Coral Gables	23 Jan. 1927
5:49.6	Norelius, Martha (USA)	New York	30 June 1928
5:42.8	Norelius, Martha (USA)	Amsterdam	6 Aug. 1928
5:39.2*	Norelius, Martha (USA)	Vienna	27 Aug. 1928
5:31.0*	Madison, Helene (USA)	Seattle	3 Feb. 1931
5:28.5	Madison, Helene (USA)	Los Angeles	13 Aug. 1932
5:16.0*	Ouden, Willy den (Neth)	Rotterdam	12 July 1934
5:14.2*	Hveger, Ragnhild (Den)	Copenhagen	10 Feb. 1937
5:14.0*	Hveger, Ragnhild (Den)	Gand	3 Oct. 1937
5:12.4*	Hveger, Ragnhild (Den)	Magdeburg	14 Nov. 1937
5:11.0*	Hveger, Ragnhild (Den)	Copenhagen	12 Dec. 1937
5:08.2*	Hveger, Ragnhild (Den)	Copenhagen	16 Jan. 1938
5:06.1*	Hveger, Ragnhild (Den)	Copenhagen	1 Aug. 1938
5:05.4*	Hveger, Ragnhild (Den)	Svendborg	8 Sept. 1940
5:00.1*	Hveger, Ragnhild (Den)	Copenhagen	15 Sept. 1940
4:50.8	Crapp, Lorraine (Aus)	Townsville	25 Aug. 1956
4:47.2	Crapp, Lorraine (Aus)	Sydney	20 Oct. 1956

Minimum time 4:47.2 (based on former record by Crapp on way to 440 y. in a 55 y. bath but now ruled out because the time was taken mid-course)

4:45.4y	Konrads, Ilsa (Aus)	Sydney	9 Jan. 1960
4:44.5	Saltza, Chris von (USA)	Detroit	5 Aug. 1960
4:42.0	Ramenofsky, Marilyn (USA)	Los Altos	11 July 1964
4:41.7	Ramenofsky, Marilyn (USA)	Los Altos	1 Aug. 1964
4:29.5	Ramenofsky, Marilyn (USA)	New York	31 Aug. 1964
4:39.2	Randall, Martha (USA)	Maumee	14 Aug. 1965
4:38.0	Randall, Martha (USA)	Monaco	26 Aug. 1965
4:36.8	Kruse, Pam (USA)	Ft. Lauderdale	30 June 1967
4:36.4	Kruse, Pam (USA)	Santa Clara	7 July 1967
4:32.6	Meyer, Debbie (USA)	Winnipeg	27 July 1967
4:29.0	Meyer, Debbie (USA)	Philadelphia	18 Aug. 1967
4:26.7	Meyer, Debbie (USA)	Lincoln	1 Aug. 1968
4:24.5	Meyer, Debbie (USA)	Los Angeles	25 Aug. 1968
4:24.3	Meyer, Debbie (USA)	Los Angeles	20 Aug. 1970
4:22.6	Moras, Karen (Aus)	London	30 Apr. 1971
4:21.2	Gould, Shane (Aus)	Santa Clara	9 July 1971
4:19.04	Gould, Shane (Aus)	Munich	30 Aug. 1972
4:18.07	Rothhammer, Keena (USA)	Louisville	22 Aug. 1973
4:17.33	Greenwood, Heather (USA)	Santa Clara	28 June 1974
4:15.77	Babashoff, Shirley (USA)	Concord	22 Aug. 1974
4:14.76	Babashoff, Shirley (USA)	Long Beach	20 June 1975

800 m. Free-style

13:19.0y†	Ederle, Gertrude (USA)	Indianapolis	17 Aug. 1919
12:58.2y†	McGary, Ethel (USA)	Detroit	6 Aug. 1925
12:56.0y†	McGary, Ethel (USA)	Indianpolis	15 Aug. 1925
12:47.2y†	Norelius, Martha (USA)	Philadelphia	7 Aug. 1926
12:17.8y†	Norelius, Martha (USA)	Massapaqua	31 July 1927
12:03.8y†	McKim, Josephine (USA)	Honolulu	10 Aug. 1929
11:41.2y††	Madison, Helene (USA)	Long Beach	6 July 1930
11:34.4y	Kight, Laura (USA)	Manhattan Beach	21 July 1935
11:11.7	Hveger, Ragnhild (Den)	Copenhagen	3 July 1936
10:52.5	Hveger, Ragnhild (Den)	Copenhagen	13 Aug. 1941
10:42.4	Gyenge, Valeria (Hun)	Budapest	28 June 1953
10:30.9	Crapp, Lorraine (Aus)	Sydney	14 Jan. 1956

Minimum time 10:30.9 (based on former record by Crapp on way to 880 y. but now ruled out because time was taken mid-course)

10:17.7y	Konrads, Ilsa (Aus)	Sydney	9 Jan. 1958
10:16.2y	Konrads, Ilsa (Aus)	Melbourne	20 Feb. 1958
10:11.8y	Konrads, Ilsa (Aus)	Townsville	13 June 1958
10:11.4y	Konrads, Ilsa (Aus)	Hobart	19 Feb. 1959
9:55.6	Cederqvist, Jane (Swe)	Uppsala	17 Aug. 1960
9:51.6	House, Carolyn (USA)	Los Altos	26 Aug. 1962
9:47.3	Caretto, Patty (USA)	Los Altos	30 July 1964
9:36.9	Finneran, Sharon (USA)	Los Angeles	28 Sept. 1964
9:35.8	Meyer, Debbie (USA)	Santa Clara	9 July 1967
9:22.9	Meyer, Debbie (USA)	Winnipeg	29 July 1967
9:19.0	Meyer, Debbie (USA)	Los Angeles	21 July 1968
9:17.9	Meyer, Debbie (USA)	Lincoln	4 Aug. 1968
9:10.4	Meyer, Debbie (USA)	Los Angeles	28 Aug. 1968
9:09.1	Moras, Karen (Aus)	Sydney	1 Mar. 1970
9:02.4	Moras, Karen (Aus)	Edinburgh	18 July 1970
8:59.4	Simmons, Ann (USA)	Minsk	10 Sept. 1971
8:58.1	Gould, Shane (Aus)	Sydney	3 Dec. 1971

8:53.83	Harshbarger, Jo (USA)	Chicago	6 Aug. 1972
8:53.68	Rothhammer, Keena (USA)	Munich	3 Sept. 1972
8:52.97	Calligaris, Novella (It)	Belgrade	9 Sept. 1973
8:50.1*	Turrall, Jenny (Aus)	Sydney	5 Jan. 1974
8:47.66	Harshbarger, Jo (USA)	Concord	25 Aug. 1974
8:47.59	Harshbarger, Jo (USA)	Concord	31 Aug. 1974
8:43.48	Turrall, Jenny (Aus)	London	31 Mar. 1975

† Ratified as records for the longer 880 y. (804.672 m.) before 800 m. records were recognised in 1930.

†† The following ratified times, which were inferior to the performance for the longer 880 y. by Madison (1930), have been deleted and the earlier and faster time of the above named has been introduced into the world 800 m. record list.

12:18.8	Godard, Yvonne (Fra)	Paris	23 Aug. 1931
11:44.3	Kight, Laura (USA)	Jones Beach	23 July 1933

1,500 m. Free-style

25:06.6	Wainwright, Helen (USA)	Manhattan Beach	19 Aug. 1922
24:07.6	McGary, Ethel (USA)	Coral Gables	31 Dec. 1925
24:00.2	Mayne, Edith (Eng)	Exmouth	15 Sept. 1926
23:44.6	Norelius, Martha (USA)	Massapaqua	28 July 1927
23:17.2	Madison, Helene (USA)	New York	15 July 1931
22:36.7	Frederiksen, G. (Den)	Copenhagen	26 June 1936

21:45.7	Hveger, Ragnhild (Den)	Helsingor	3 July 1938
21:10.1	Hveger, Ragnhild (Den)	Helsingor	11 Aug. 1940
20:57.0	Hveger, Ragnhild (Den)	Copenhagen	20 Aug. 1941
20:45.6	Nijs, Lenie de (Neth)	Utrecht	23 July 1955
20:22.8	Koster, Jans (Neth)	Utrecht	21 Aug. 1956

Time of Koster remained in list.

20:22.8	Koster, Jans (Neth)	Utrecht	21 Aug. 1956
20:03.1	Koster, Jans (Neth)	Hilversum	27 July 1957
19:25.7y	Konrads, Ilsa (Aus)	Sydney	14 Jan. 1959
19:23.6	Cederqvist, Jane (Swe)	Uppsala	8 Sept. 1960
19:02.8	Rylander, Margareta (Swe)	Uppsala	27 June 1961
18:44.0	House, Carolyn (USA)	Chicago	16 Aug. 1962
18:30.5	Caretto, Patty (USA)	Los Altos	30 July 1964
18:23.7	Caretto, Patty (USA)	Los Altos	12 Aug. 1965
18:12.9	Caretto, Patty (USA)	Lincoln	21 Aug. 1966
18:11.1	Meyer, Debbie (USA)	Santa Clara	9 July 1967
17:50.2	Meyer, Debbie (USA)	Philadelphia	20 Aug. 1967
17:31.2	Meyer, Debbie (USA)	Los Angeles	21 July 1968
17:19.9	Meyer, Debbie (USA)	Louisville	17 Aug. 1969
17:19.2	Calhoun, Cathy (USA)	Houston	28 Aug. 1971
17:00.6	Gould, Shane (Aus)	Sydney	12 Dec. 1971

16:56.9*	Gould, Shane (Aus)	Adelaide	11 Feb. 1973
16:54.14	Harshbarger, Jo (USA)	Louisville	25 Aug. 1973
16:49.9*	Turrall, Jenny (Aus)	Sydney	9 Dec. 1973
16:48.2*	Turrall, Jenny (Aus)	Sydney	9 Jan. 1974
16:43.4*	Turrall, Jenny (Aus)	Sydney	12 July 1974
16:39.28	Turrall, Jenny (Aus)	Mission Viejo	3 Aug. 1974
16:33.94	Turrall, Jenny (Aus)	Concord	25 Aug. 1974

100 m. Back-stroke

1:36.7	Hart, Doris (Eng)	Gothenburg	6 July 1923
1:35.0	Mullerova, J. (Czech)	Prague	29 July 1923
1:26.6	Bauer, Sybil (USA)	Newark	8 Aug. 1923
1:22.4*	Bauer, Sybil (USA)	Miami	6 Jan. 1924
1:22.0*	Turk, Willy van den (Neth)	Rotterdam	10 July 1927
1:21.6	Braun, Marie (Neth)	Amsterdam	11 Aug. 1928
1:21.4*	Braun, Marie (Neth)	Brussels	20 Apr. 1929
1:21.0*	Braun, Marie (Neth)	Gravenhage	27 Nov. 1929
1:20.6*	Mealing, Bonnie (Aus)	Sydney	27 Feb. 1930
1:18.6*	Harding, Phyllis (GB)	Wallasey	30 May 1932
1:18.2	Holm, Eleanor (USA)	Jones Beach	16 July 1932
1:16.8*	Mastenbroek, Rie (Neth)	Dusseldorf	25 Nov. 1934
1:16.3	Holm, Eleanor (USA)	Chicago	15 Jan. 1935
1:15.8*	Mastenbroek, Rie (Neth)	Amsterdam	27 Feb. 1936
1:15.7*	Senff, Dina (Neth)	Copenhagen	8 Sept. 1936
1:15.4*	Senff, Dina (Neth)	Copenhagen	10 Sept. 1936
1:13.6*	Senff, Dina (Neth)	Dusseldorf	25 Oct. 1936
1:13.5*	Kint, Cor (Neth)	Copenhagen	1 Nov. 1938
1:13.2*	Feggelen, Iet van (Neth)	Amsterdam	10 Nov. 1938
1:13.0*	Feggelen, Iet van (Neth)	Gravenhage	12 Nov. 1938
1:12.9*	Feggelen, Iet van (Neth)	Antwerp	26 Nov. 1938
1:10.9*	Kint, Cor (Neth)	Rotterdam	22 Sept. 1939

Winning time by Grinham at Olympic Games taken as first record.

1:12.9	Grinham, Judy (GB)	Melbourne	5 Dec. 1956
1:12.5y	Gould, Phillipa (NZ)	Auckland	12 Mar. 1958
1:12.4y	Edwards, Margaret (GB)	Cardiff	19 Apr. 1958

1:12.3	Velsen, Ria van (Neth)	Nijmegen	20 July 1958
1:11.9	Grinham, Judy (GB)	Cardiff	23 July 1958
1:11.7	Velsen, Ria van (Neth)	Waalwijk	26 July 1959
1:11.4	Cone, Carin (USA)	Chicago	6 Sept. 1959
1:11.0	Velsen, Ria van (Neth)	Leipzig	12 June 1960
1:10.9	Velsen, Ria van (Neth)	Maastricht	10 July 1960
1:10.1	Burke, Lynn (USA)	Indianapolis	17 July 1960
1:10.0	Burke, Lynn (USA)	Detroit	4 Aug. 1960
1:09.2	Burke, Lynn (USA)	Detroit	5 Aug. 1960
1:09.0	Burke, Lynn (USA)	Rome	2 Sept. 1960
1:08.9	Varona, Donna de (USA)	Los Angeles	28 July 1963
1:08.6	Caron, Christine (Fra)	Paris	14 June 1964
1:08.3	Duenkel, Ginny (USA)	Los Angeles	28 Sept.1964
1:07.7	Ferguson, Cathy (USA)	Tokyo	14 Oct. 1964
1:07.4	Fairlie, Ann (SAf)	Beziers	23 July 1966
1:07.3	Tanner, Elaine (Can)	Winnipeg	27 July 1967
1:07.1	Tanner, Elaine (Can)	Winnipeg	30 July 1967
1:06.7	Muir, Karen (SAf)	Kimberley	30 Jan. 1968
1:06.4	Muir, Karen (SAf)	Paris	6 Apr. 1968
1:06.2	Hall, Kaye (USA)	Mexico City	23 Oct. 1968
1:05.6	Muir, Karen (SAf)	Utrecht	6 July 1969
1:05.39	Richter, Ulrike (E Ger)	Utrecht	18 Aug. 1973
1:04.99	Richter, Ulrike (E Ger)	Belgrade	4 Sept. 1973
1:04.78	Cook, Wendy (Can)	Christchurch	31 Jan. 1974
1:04.43	Richter, Ulrike (E Ger)	Rostock	8 July 1974
1:04.09	Richter, Ulrike (E Ger)	Vienna	22 Aug. 1974
1:03.03	Richter, Ulrike (E Ger)	Vienna	23 Aug. 1974
1:02.98	Richter, Ulrike (E Ger)	Concord	1 Sept. 1974
1:02.6	Richter, Ulrike (E Ger)	Tallinn	14 Mar. 1976

200 m. Back-stroke

3:06.8*	Bauer, Sybil (USA)	Brighton Beach	4 July 1922
3:03.8*	Bauer, Sybil (USA)	Miami	9 Feb. 1924
2:59.2*	Braun, Marie (Neth)	Brussels	24 Nov. 1928
2:58.8*	Holm, Eleanor (USA)	Buffalo	1 Feb. 1930
2:58.2*	Holm, Eleanor (USA)	New York	1 Mar. 1930
2:50.4*	Harding, Phyllis (Eng)	Wallasey	19 Sept. 1932
2:49.6*	Mastenbroek, Rie (Neth)	Amsterdam	20 Jan. 1935
2:48.7*	Holm, Eleanor (USA)	Toledo	3 Mar. 1936
2:44.6*	Senff, Dina (Neth)	Amsterdam	2 Feb. 1937
2:41.3*	Hveger, Ragnhild (Den)	Aarhus	14 Feb. 1937
2:41.0*	Kint, Cor (Neth)	Aarhus	17 Apr. 1938
2:40.6*	Feggelen, Iet van (Neth)	Dusseldorf	26 Oct. 1938
2:39.0*	Feggelen, Iet van (Neth)	Amsterdam	18 Dec. 1938
2:38.8*	Kint, Cor (Neth)	Rotterdam	29 Nov. 1939
2:35.3*	Wielema, Geertje (Neth)	Hilversum	2 Apr. 1950

Minimum time 2:42.8

2:39.9y	Gould, Phillipa (NZ)	Auckland	16 Jan. 1957
2:38.5y	Nijs, Lenie de (Neth)	Blackpool	17 May 1957
2:37.4	Saltza, Chris von (USA)	Topeka	1 Aug. 1958
2:37.1	Tanaka, Satoko (Jap)	Tokyo	12 July 1959
2:34.8	Tanaka, Satoko (Jap)	Tokyo	2 Apr. 1960
2:33.5	Burke, Lynn (USA)	Indianapolis	15 July 1960
2:33.3	Tanaka, Satoko (Jap)	Tokyo	23 July 1960
2:33.2	Tanaka, Satoko (Jap)	Tokyo	30 July 1961
2:32.1	Tanaka, Satoko (Jap)	Beppu	3 June 1962
2:31.6	Tanaka, Satoko (Jap)	Osaka	29 July 1962
2:29.6y	Tanaka, Satoko (Jap)	Sydney	10 Feb. 1963

2:29.6y	Tanaka, Satoko (Jap)	Sydney	10 Feb. 1963
2:28.9y	Tanaka, Satoko (Jap)	Perth	18 Feb. 1963
2:28.5y	Tanaka, Satoko (Jap)	Perth	21 Feb. 1963
2:28.2	Tanaka, Satoko (Jap)	Tokyo	4 Aug. 1963
2:27.4	Ferguson, Cathy (USA)	Los Angeles	28 Sept. 1964
2:27.1	Muir, Karen (SAf)	Beziers	25 July 1966
2:26.4	Muir, Karen (SAf)	Lincoln	18 Aug. 1966
2:24.4	Tanner, Elaine (Can)	Winnipeg	26 July 1967
2:24.1y	Muir, Karen (SAf)	Kimberley	26 Jan. 1968
2:23.8	Muir, Karen (SAf)	Los Angeles	21 July 1968
2:21.5	Atwood, Susie (USA)	Louisville	14 Aug. 1969

2:20.64	Belote, Melissa (USA)	Chicago	5 Aug. 1972
2:20.58	Belote, Melissa (USA)	Munich	4 Sept. 1972
2:19.19	Belote, Melissa (USA)	Munich	4 Sept. 1972
2:18.41	Richter, Ulrike (E Ger)	Rostock	7 July 1974
2:17.35	Richter, Ulrike (E Ger)	Vienna	25 Aug. 1974
2:16.33	Garapick, Nancy (Can)	Brantford	27 Apr. 1975
2:16.10	Treiber, Birgit (E Ger)	Wittenberg	6 June 1975
2:15.46	Treiber, Birgit (E Ger)	Cali	25 July 1975
2:13.5*	Stille, Antje (E Ger)	Tallinn	29 Feb. 1976
2:13.5*	Stille, Antje (E Ger)	Tallinn	Mar. 1976

100 m. Breast-stroke

1:37.6*	Bogaert, E. van den (Belg)	Brussels	22 July 1921
1:33.4*	Hart, Doris (Eng)	Aldershot	23 Aug. 1922
1:31.8*	Gilbert, Irene (Eng)	Rotherham	30 Oct. 1924
1:29.0*	Huneus, Erno (Ger)	Aachen	4 Oct. 1925
1:28.8*	Geraghty, Agnes (USA)	St. Augustine	13 Feb. 1926
1:26.3*	Muhe, Lotte (Ger)	Magdeburg	9 June 1928
1:26.2*	Jacobsen, Else (Den)	Copenhagen	10 Apr. 1932
1:26.0*	Jacobsen, Else (Den)	Stockholm	11 May 1932
1:24.6*	Dennis, Clare (Aus)	Unley	14 Feb. 1933
1:24.5*	Holzner, Johanna (Ger)	Copenhagen	15 Jan. 1935
1:23.4*	Holzner, Johanna (Ger)	Halle	16 Feb. 1936
1:22.8*	Christensen, V. (Den)	Dusseldorf	8 Mar. 1936
1:20.2*	Holzner, Johanna (Ger)	Plauen	13 Mar. 1936
1:19.8*	Grass, Gisela (Ger)	Leipzig	9 May 1943
1:19.4*	Vliet, Nel van (Neth)	Alost	29 July 1946
1:19.0*	Vliet, Nel van (Neth)	Den Haag	1 Aug. 1946
1:18.2*	Vliet, Nel van (Neth)	Arnhem	28 Apr. 1947
1:17.4*	Vallerey, Gisele (Fra)	Casablanca	Bu23 Apr. 1950
1:16.9*	Szekely, Eva (Hun)	Moscow	Bu9 May 1951

Minimum time 1:18.2 (based on van Vliet time on 28 Apr. 1947). No woman achieved this time prior to 1 May, 1957 when another adjustment was made in the system of breast-stroke records

Minimum time 1:21.0

1:20.3	Beyer, Karin (E Ger)	Berlin	20 July 1958
1:19.6	Beyer, Karin (E Ger)	Leipzig	12 Sept. 1958
1:19.1	Urselmann, Wiltrud (W Ger)	Zurich	12 Mar. 1960
1:19.0	Kuper, Ursela (E Ger)	Leipzig	14 July 1960
1:18.2	Gobel, Barbara (E Ger)	Rostock	1 July 1961
1:17.9	Kolb, Claudia (USA)	Los Angeles	11 July 1964
1:17.2	Babanina, Svetlana (USSR)	Moscow	3 Sept. 1964
1:16.5	Babanina, Svetlana (USSR)	Tashkent	11 May 1965
1:15.7	Prozumenshikova, Galina (USSR)	Lenin	17 July 1966

1:15.6	Ball, Catie (USA)	Ft. Lauderdale	28 Dec. 1966
1:15.6	Ball, Catie (USA)	Santa Clara	7 July 1967
1:14.8	Ball, Catie (USA)	Winnipeg	31 July 1967
1:14.6	Ball, Catie (USA)	Philadelphia	19 Aug. 1967
1:14.2	Ball, Catie (USA)	Los Angeles	25 Aug. 1968

1:13.58	Carr, Cathy (USA)	Munich	2 Sept. 1972
1:12.91	Vogel, Renate (E Ger)	Vienna	22 Aug. 1974
1:12.55	Justen, Christel (W Ger)	Vienna	23 Aug. 1974
1:12.28	Vogel, Renate (E Ger)	Concord	1 Sept. 1974

200 m. Breast-stroke

3:38.2	Bogaert, E. van der (Belg)	Antwerp	7 Aug. 1921
3:34.6*	Bogaert, E. van der (Belg)	Brussels	6 May 1922
3:31.4*	Bogaert, E. van der (Belg)	Antwerp	4 Oct. 1922
3:20.4*	Gilbert, Irene (Eng)	Rotherham	18 June 1923
3:20.2*	Murray, Erna (Ger)	Leipzig	5 Apr. 1925
3:19.1*	Hazelius, B. (Swe)	Stockholm	11 Aug. 1926
3:18.4*	Baron, Marie (Neth)	Brussels	24 Oct. 1926
3:16.6	Jacobsen, Else (Den)	Oslo	20 Aug. 1927
3:15.8*	Muhe, Lotte (Ger)	Magdeburg	15 Apr. 1928
3:12.8*	Baron, Marie (Neth)	Rotterdam	22 Apr. 1928
3:11.2	Muhe, Lotte (Ger)	Berlin	15 July 1928
3:10.6*	Hinton, Margery (Eng)	Manchester	20 July 1931
3:08.4*	Dennis, Clare (Aus)	Sydney	18 Jan. 1932
3:08.2*	Rocke, Lisa (Ger)	Leipzig	21 Apr. 1932
3:03.4*	Jacobsen, Else (Den)	Stockholm	11 May 1932
3:00.4*	Maehata, Hideko (Jap)	Tokyo	30 Sept. 1933
3:00.2*	Waalberg, Jopie (Neth)	Amsterdam	11 May 1937
2:58.0*	Waalberg, Jopie (Neth)	Zaandyk	27 June 1937
2:56.9*	Waalberg, Jopie (Neth)	Gand	2 Oct. 1937
2:56.0*	Lenk, Maria (Braz)	Rio de Janiero	8 Nov. 1939
2:52.6*	Vliet, Nel van (Neth)	Bilthoven	17 Aug. 1946
2:51.9*	Vliet, Nel van (Neth)	Amsterdam	29 Mar. 1947
2:49.2*	Vliet, Nel van (Neth)	Hilversum	20 July 1947
2:48.8*	Novak, Eva (Hun)	Szekesfehervar	21 Oct. 1950
2:48.5*	Novak, Eva (Hun)	Moscow	5 May 1951

Minimum time 2:48.5

| 2:46.4* | Haan, Ada den (Neth) | Naarden | 13 Nov. 1956 |

Minimum time 2:55.0

2:52.5y	Haan, Ada den (Neth)	Blackpool	18 May 1957
2:51.9	Haan, Ada den (Neth)	Rhenen	3 Aug. 1957
2:51.3	Haan, Ada den (Neth)	Rhenen	4 Aug. 1957
2:50.3	Lonsbrough, Anita (GB)	Waalwijk	25 July 1959
2:50.2	Urselmann, Wiltrud (W Ger)	Aachen	6 June 1960
2:49.5	Lonsbrough, Anita (GB)	Rome	27 Aug. 1960
2:48.0	Beyer, Karin (E Ger)	Budapest	5 Aug. 1961
2:47.7y	Prozumenshikova, Galina (USSR)	Blackpool	11 Apr. 1964
2:45.4	Prozumenshikova, Galina (USSR)	Berlin	17 May 1964
2:45.3	Prozumenshikova, Galina (USSR)	Groningen	12 Sept. 1965
2:40.8	Prozumenshikova, Galina (USSR)	Utrecht	22 Aug. 1966
2:40.5	Ball, Catie (USA)	Santa Clara	9 July 1967
2:39.5	Ball, Catie (USA)	Philadelphia	20 Aug. 1967
2:38.5	Ball, Catie (USA)	Los Angeles	26 Aug. 1968

2:37.89	Schott, Anne-Katrin (E Ger)	Rostock	6 July 1974
2:37.44	Linke, Karla (E Ger)	Vienna	19 Aug. 1974
2:34.99	Linke, Karla (E Ger)	Vienna	19 Aug. 1974

100 m. Butterfly
Minimum time 1:16.9 (based on former breast-stroke record by Szekely, Eva (Hun) in Moscow (9 May, 1951) which was swum on butterfly)

1:16.6	Langenau, Jutta (E Ger)	Turin	31 Aug. 1954
1:14.0*	Mann, Shelley (USA)	Richmond	4 Sept. 1954
1:13.8*	Kok, Mary (Neth)	Alkmaar	16 Apr. 1955
1:13.7*	Voorbij, Atie (Neth)	Naarden	14 July 1955
1:13.2*	Voorbij, Atie (Neth)	Algiers	28 Aug. 1955
1:13.1*	Voorbij, Atie (Neth)	Vlaardingen	21 Sept. 1955
1:11.9*	Voorbij, Atie (Neth)	Velsen	5 Feb. 1956
1:11.8*	Mann, Shelley (USA)	Tyler	7 July 1956
1:10.5*	Voorbij, Atie (Neth)	Hilversum	12 Nov. 1956

Minimum time 1:11.0

1:10.5	Voorbij, Atie (Neth)	Rhenen	4 Aug. 1957
1:09.6	Ramey, Nancy (USA)	Los Angeles	28 June 1958
1:09.1	Ramey, Nancy (USA)	Chicago	2 Sept. 1959
1:08.9	Andrew, Jan (Aus)	Tokyo	2 Apr. 1961
1:08.8	Stewart, Mary (Can)	Philadelphia	12 Aug. 1961
1:08.2	Doerr, Susan (USA)	Philadelphia	12 Aug. 1961
1:07.8	Doerr, Susan (USA)	Philadelphia	2 Aug. 1962
1:07.3y	Stewart, Mary (Can)	Vancouver	28 July 1962
1:06.5	Ellis, Kathy (USA)	N. Carolina	16 Aug. 1963
1:06.1	Kok, Ada (Neth)	Soestduinen	1 Sept. 1963
1:05.4	Stouder, Sharon (USA)	Los Altos	1 Aug. 1964
1:05.1y	Kok, Ada (Neth)	Blackpool	30 May 1964
1:04.7	Stouder, Sharon (USA)	Tokyo	16 Oct. 1964
1:04.5	Kok, Ada (Neth)	Budapest	14 Aug. 1965
1:04.1	Jones, Alice (USA)	Los Angeles	20 Aug. 1970

1:03.9*	Aoki, Mayumi (Jap)	Tokyo	21 July 1972
1:03.80	Gyarmati, Andrea (Hun)	Munich	31 Aug. 1972
1:03.34	Aoki, Mayumi)Jap)	Munich	1 Sept. 1972
1:03.05	Ender, Kornelia (E Ger)	E. Berlin	14 Apr. 1973
1:02.31	Ender, Kornelia (E Ger)	E. Berlin	14 July 1973
1:02.09	Kother, Rosemarie (E Ger)	Vienna	21 Aug. 1974
1:01.99	Kother, Rosemarie (E Ger)	Vienna	22 Aug. 1974
1:01.88	Kother, Rosemarie (E Ger)	Concord	1 Sept. 1974
1:01.33	Ender, Kornelia (E Ger)	Wittenberg	9 June 1975
1:01.24	Ender, Kornelia (E Ger)	Cali	24 July 1975

200 m. Butterfly
Minimum time 2:48.0

2:42.3*	Lagerberg, Tineke (Neth)	Naarden	12 Dec. 1956
2:38.1*	Lagerberg, Tineke (Neth)	Naarden	19 Mar. 1957

Minimum time 2:43.4

2:40.5	Ramey, Nancy (USA)	Los Angeles	29 June 1958
2:38.9	Lagerberg, Tineke (Neth)	Naarden	13 Sept. 1958
2:37.0y	Collins, Becky (USA)	Redding	19 July 1959
2:34.4	Heemskerk, Marianne (Neth)	Leipzig	12 June 1960
2:38.8	Collins, Becky (USA)	Philadelphia	13 Aug. 1961
2:31.2	Finneran, Sharon (USA)	Chicago	19 Aug. 1962
2:30.7	Finneran, Sharon (USA)	Los Altos	25 Aug. 1962
2:29.1	Pitt, Sue (USA)	Philadelphia	27 July 1963
2:28.1	Stouder, Sharon (USA)	Los Angeles	12 July 1964
2:26.4	Stouder, Sharon (USA)	Los Altos	2 Aug. 1964
2:26.3	Moore, Kendis (USA)	Maumee	15 Aug. 1965
2:25.8	Kok, Ada (Neth)	De Vliet	21 Aug. 1965

2:25.3	Kok, Ada (Neth)	Groningen	12 Sept. 1965
2:22.5	Kok, Ada (Neth)	Groningen	2 Aug. 1967
2:21.0y	Kok, Ada (Neth)	Blackpool	25 Aug. 1967
2:20.7	Moe, Karen (USA)	Santa Clara	11 July 1970
2:19.3	Jones, Alice (USA)	Los Angeles	22 Aug. 1970
2:18.6	Moe, Karen (USA)	Los Angeles	7 Aug. 1971
2:18.4	Daniel, Ellie (USA)	Houston	28 Aug. 1971
2:18.4e	Daniel, Ellie (USA)	Houston	28 Aug. 1971
2:18.4e	Daniel, Ellie (USA)	Minsk	10 Sept. 1971
2:16.62	Moe, Karen (USA)	Chicago	6 Aug. 1972
2:15.57	Moe, Karen (USA)	Munich	4 Sept. 1972
2:15.45	Kother, Rosemarie (E Ger)	Belgrade	8 Sept. 1973
2:13.76	Kother, Rosemarie (E Ger)	Belgrade	8 Sept. 1973
2:13.6*	Kother, Rosemarie (E Ger)	Tallinn	14 Mar. 1976

200 m. Individual medley

Minimum time 2:28.0

2:27.8	Kolb, Claudia (USA)	Lincoln	21 Aug. 1966
2:27.5	Kolb, Claudia (USA)	Santa Clara	8 July 1967
2:26.1	Kolb, Claudia (USA)	Winnipeg	30 July 1967
2:25.0	Kolb, Claudia (USA)	Philadelphia	18 Aug. 1967
2:23.5	Kolb, Claudia (USA)	Los Angeles	25 Aug. 1968
2:23.07	Gould, Shane (Aus)	Munich	28 Aug. 1972
2:23.01	Ender, Kornelia (E Ger)	E. Berlin	13 Apr. 1973
2:20.51	Hubner, Andrea (E Ger)	Belgrade	4 Sept. 1973
2:18.97	Tauber, Ulrike (E Ger)	Vienna	18 Aug. 1974
2:18.83	Tauber, Ulrike (E Ger)	Wittenberg	10 June 1975

400 m. Individual medley

5:50.4*	Szekely, Eva (Hun)	Budapest	10 Apr. 1953
5:47.3*	Kok, Mary (Neth)	Hilversum	28 Mar. 1955
5:40.8*	Szekely, Eva (Hun)	Budapest	13 July 1955
5:38.9*	Kok, Mary (Neth)	Hilversum	2 Dec. 1956

Minimum time 5:49.0

5:46.6	Ruuska, Sylvia (USA)	Los Angeles	27 June 1958
5:43.7	Ruuska, Sylvia (USA)	Topeko	1 Aug. 1958
5:41.1y	Ruuska, Sylvia (USA)	Melbourne	24 Feb. 1959
5:40.2y	Ruuska, Sylvia (USA)	Redding	17 July 1959
5:36.5	Varona, Donna de (USA)	Indianapolis	15 July 1960
5:34.5	Varona, Donna de (USA)	Philadelphia	11 Aug. 1961
5:29.7	Varona, Donna de (USA)	Los Altos	2 June 1962
5:27.4	Finneran, Sharon (USA)	Osaka	26 July 1962
5:24.7	Varona, Donna de (USA)	Osaka	26 July 1962
5:21.9	Finneran, Sharon (USA)	Osaka	28 July 1962
5:16.5	Varona, Donna de (USA)	Lima	10 Mar. 1964
5:14.9	Varona, Donna de (USA)	New York	30 Aug. 1964
5:11.7	Kolb, Claudia (USA)	Santa Clara	9 July 1967
5:09.7	Kolb, Claudia (USA)	Winnipeg	1 Aug. 1967
5:08.2	Kolb, Claudia (USA)	Philadelphia	19 Aug. 1967
5:04.7	Kolb, Claudia (USA)	Los Angeles	24 Aug. 1968
5:02.97	Neall, Gail (USA)	Munich	31 Aug. 1972
5:01.10	Franke, Angela (E Ger)	Utrecht	18 Aug. 1973
4:57.51	Wegner, Gudrun (E Ger)	Belgrade	6 Sept. 1973
4:52.42	Tauber, Ulrike (E Ger)	Vienna	21 Aug. 1974
4:52.20	Tauber, Ulrike (E Ger)	Wittenberg	7 June 1975

4 x 100 m. Free-style relay

4:38.0	United States	Los Angeles	12 Aug. 1932

(McKim, Josephine; Johns, Helen; Garatti-Saville, Eleanor; Madison, Helene)

4:33.3*	Netherlands	Rotterdam	14 Apr. 1934

(Selbach, Jopie; Timmermans, Annie; Mastenbroek, Rie; Den Ouden, Willy)

4:32.8*	Netherlands	Rotterdam	24 May 1936

(Selbach, Jopie; Mastenbroek, Rie; Wagner, Catherina; Den Ouden, Willy)

4:29.7*	Denmark	Copenhagen	8 Feb. 1938

(Svendsen, E; Kraft, Gunvor; Ove-Petersen, Birte; Hveger, Ragnhild)

4:27.6*	Denmark	Copenhagen	7 Aug. 1938

(Arndt, Eva; Kraft, Gunvor; Ove-Petersen, Birte; Hveger, Ragnhild)

4:27.2*	Hungary	Moscow	27 Apr. 1952

(Littomerisky, Maria; Novak, Eva; Szekely, Eva; Szoke, Katalin)

4:24.4	Hungary	Helsinki	1 Aug. 1952

(Novak, Ilona; Temes, Judith; Novak, Eva; Szoke, Katalin)

4:22.3	Australia	Sydney	20 Oct. 1956

(Crapp, Lorraine; Fraser, Dawn; Gibson, Margaret; Jackson, Barbara)

4:19.7	Australia	Melbourne	25 Oct. 1956

(Crapp, Lorraine; Fraser, Dawn; Leech, Faith; Gibson, Margaret)

4:17.1	Australia	Melbourne	6 Dec. 1956

(Fraser, Dawn; Leech, Faith; Morgan, Sandra; Crapp, Lorraine)

Winning time by Australia (above) at Olympic Games remained in the list

4:17.1	Australia	Melbourne	6 Dec. 1956

(Fraser, Dawn; Leech, Faith; Morgan, Sandra; Crapp, Lorraine)

4:16.2y	Australia	Townsville	6 Aug. 1960

(Fraser, Dawn; Colquhoun, Alva; Konrads, Ilsa; Crapp, Lorraine)

4:08.9	United States	Rome	3 Sept. 1960

(Spillane, Joan; Stobs, Shirley; Wood, Carolyn; Von Saltza, Chris)

4:08.5	Santa Clara S.C., United States	Los Altos	31 July 1964

(Stickles, Terri; Varona, Donna de; Watson, Pokey; Haroun, Judy)

4:07.6	United States	Los Angeles	28 Sept. 1964

(Allsup, Lynn; Stickles, Terri; Seidel, Kathy; Bricker, Eleanor)

4:03.8	United States	Tokyo	15 Oct. 1964

(Stouder, Sharon; Varona, Donna de; Watson, Pokey; Ellis, Kathy)

4:03.5	Santa Clara S.C., United States	Philadelphia	19 Aug. 1967

(Gustavson, Linda; Ryan, Nancy; Fritz, L; Watson, Pokey)

4:01.1	Santa Clara S.C., United States	Santa Clara	6 July 1968

(Gustavson, Linda; Watson, Pokey; Carpinelli, Pam; Henne, Jan)

4:00.8	East Germany	Barcelona	11 Sept. 1970

(Wetzko, Gabriele; Komor, Iris; Sehmisch, Elke; Schulze, Carola)

4:00.7	United States	Minsk	9 Sept. 1971

(Johnson, Linda; Deardurff, Deena; Babashoff, Shirley; Peyton, Kim)

3:58.11	United States	Knoxville	18 Aug. 1972

(Peyton, Kim; Neilson, Sandy; Barkman, Jane; Babashoff, Shirley)

3:58.11e	East Germany	Munich	30 Aug. 1972

(Eife, Andrea; Eichner, Sylvia; Sehmisch, Elke; Ender, Kornelia)

3:55.19	United States	Munich	30 Aug. 1972

Neilson, Sandy; Kemp, Jenny; Barkman, Jane; Babashoff, Shirley)

3:52.45	East Germany	Belgrade	8 Sept. 1973

(Ender, Kornelia; Eife, Andrea; Hubner, Andrea; Eichner, Sylvia)

3:51.99	United States	Concord	31 Aug. 1974

(Heddy, Kathy; Marshall, Anne; Peyton, Kim; Babashoff, Shirley)

3:49.37	East Germany	Cali	26 July 1975

(Ender, Kornelia; Krause, Barbara; Hempel, Claudia; Bruckner, Ute)

4 x 100 m. Medley relay

5:10.8	Hungary	Budapest	24 July 1953

(Hunyadfi, Magda; Killermann, Klara; Szekely, Eva; Gyenge, Valeria)

5:09.2	Hungary	Bucarest	10 Aug. 1953

(Hunyadfi, Magda; Killermann, Klara; Szekely, Eva; Gyenge, Valeria)

5:07.8	Hungary	Budapest	3 Aug. 1954

(Temes, Judit; Killermann, Klara; Littomeritzky, Maria; Szoke, Katalin)

5:06.2*	France	Marseilles	16 Aug. 1954

(Andre, Marie-Helene; Derommeleere, Francoise; Lusien, Odette; Arene, Josette)

5:02.1*	Netherlands	Rotterdam	27 Nov. 1954

(De Korte, Joke; Bruins, Rika; Kok, Mary; Wielema, Geertje)

5:00.1	Netherlands	Paris	17 July 1955

(Van Alphen; Jopie, Bruins, Rika; Voorbij, Atie; Balkenende, Hetty)

4:57.8	Hungary	Budapest	3 Sept. 1955

(Pajor, Eva; Szekely, Eva; Szekely, Rypsyma; Szoke, Katalin)

4:54.3*	De Robben S.C., Netherlands	Hilversum	19 Nov. 1956

(De Nijs, Lenie; Kroon, Rita; Voorbij, Atie; Kraan, Greetje)

4:53.1*	Netherlands	Zwolle	8 Dec. 1956

(De Korte, Joke; Den Haan, Ada; Largerberg, Tineke; Gastelaars, Cocky)

Minimum time 5:00.0

4:57.0y	Netherlands	Blackpool	18 May 1957

(Kraan, Greetje; Den Haan, Ada; Voorbij, Atie; Gastelaars, Cocky)

4:54.0y	England	Cardiff	25 July 1958

(Grinham, Judy; Lonsbrough, Anita; Gosden, Chris; Wilkinson, Diana)

4:52.9	Netherlands	Budapest	5 Sept. 1958

(De Nijs, Lenie; Den Haan, Ada; Voorbij, Atie; Gastelaars, Cocky)

4:51.5	Netherlands	Waalwijk	26 July 1959

(Van Velsen, Ria; Den Haan, Ada; Lagerberg, Tineke; Gastelaars, Cocky)

4:44.6	United States	Chicago	6 Sept. 1959

(Cone, Carin; Bancroft, Ann; Collins, Becky; Von Saltza, Chris)

4:41.1	United States	Rome	2 Sept. 1960

(Burke, Lynn; Kempner, Patty; Schuler, Carolyn; Von Saltza, Chris)

4:40.1	East Germany	Leipzig	23 Aug. 1962

(Schmidt, Ingrid; Gobel, Barbara; Noack, Ute; Pechstein, Heidi)

4:39.1	Netherlands	Groningen	28 June 1964

(Velsen, Ria van; Bimolt, Klenie; Kok, Ada; Terpstra, Erica)

4:38.1	Santa Clara S.C., United States	Los Altos	4 July 1964

(Haroun, Judy; Kolb, Claudia; Varona, Donna de; Watson, Pokey)

4:34.6	United States	Los Angeles	28 Sept. 1964

(Ferguson, Cathy; Goyette, Cynthia; Ellis, Kathy; Randall, Martha)

4:33.9	United States	Tokyo	18 Oct. 1964

(Ferguson, Cathy; Goyette, Cynthia; Stouder, Sharon; Ellis, Kathy)

4:30.0	United States	Winnipeg	30 July 1967

(Moore, Kendis; Ball, Catie; Daniel, Ellie; Fordyce, Wendy)

4:28.1	United States	Colorado Springs	14 Sept. 1968

(Hall, Kaye; Ball, Catie; Daniel, Ellie. Pedersen, Sue)

4:27.4	United States	Tokyo	1 Sept. 1970

(Atwood, Sue; Brecht, Kim; Jones, Alice; Schilling, Cindy)

4:27.3	United States	Minsk	11 Sept. 1971

(Atwood, Sue; Clevenger, Claudia; Daniel, Ellie; Johnson, Linda)

4:25.34	United States	Knoxville	18 Aug. 1972

(Atwood, Sue; Vidali, Lynn; Daniel, Ellie; Barkman, Jane)

4:20.75	United States	Munich	3 Sept. 1972

(Belote, Melissa; Carr, Cathy; Deardurff, Deena; Neilson, Sandy)

4:16.84	East Germany	Belgrade	4 Sept. 1973

(Richter, Ulrike; Vogel, Renate; Kother, Rosemarie; Ender, Kornelia)

4:13.78	East Germany	Vienna	24 Aug. 1974

(Richter, Ulrike; Vogel, Renate; Kother, Rosemarie; Ender, Kornelia)

Obsolete World Records (last date for recognition in brackets after event)

MEN

100 y. Free-style (1 May 1957)
55.4*	Daniels, Charles (USA)	1907	First
48.9*	Moore, Robin (USA)	1956	Last

110 y. Free-style (31 Dec. 1968)
55.2	Devitt, John (Aus)	1957	First
53.5	McGregor, Bobby (GB)	1966	Last

220 y. Free-style (31 Dec. 1968)
2:28.6*	Lane, Freddy (Aus)	1902	First
1:57.0	Schollander, Don (USA)	1966	Last

300 y. Free-style (31 Dec. 1948)
3:31.4*	Battersby, Syd (Eng)	1909	First
3:03.0*	Jany, Alex (Fra)	1948	Last

300 m. Free-style (31 Dec. 1948)
3:57.6*	Daniels, Charles (USA)	1910	First
3:21.0	Jany, Alex (Fra)	1947	Last

440 y. Free-style (31 Dec. 1968)
5:26.4*	Battersby, Syd (Eng)	1908	First
4:12.2	Charlton, Greg (USA)	1966	Last

500 y. Free-style (31 Dec. 1952)
6:07.2*	Kieran, Barney (Aus)	1905	First
5:12.0*	Marshall, John (Aus)	1950	Last

500 m. Free-style (31 Dec. 1952)
7:06.4*	Scheff, Otto (Aut)	1906	First
5:43.7*	Marshall, John (Aus)	1951	Last

880 y. Free-style (31 Dec. 1968)
11:25.4	Taylor, Henry (Eng)	1906	First
8:55.5	Rose, Murray (Aus)	1964	Last

1,000 y. Free-style (31 Dec. 1948)
13:34.8	Billington, David (Eng)	1905	First
11:37.4	Medica, Jack (USA)	1933	Last

1,000 m. Free-style (31 Dec. 1948)
15:50.8	Scheff, Otto (Aut)	1908	First
12:33.8	Amano, Tomikatsu (Jap)	1938	Last

1,650 y. Free-style (31 Dec. 1968)
17:28.7	Konrads, John (Aus)	1958	First
17:11.0	Konrads, John (Aus)	1960	Last

1,760 y. Free-style (1 May 1957)
25:24.4	Scheff, Otto (Aut)	1908	First
19:40.4	Breen, George (USA)	1956	Last

100 y. Back-stroke (1 May 1957)
59.4*	Vanderweghe, Albert (USA)	1939	First
55.7*	Oyakawa, Yoshinobu (USA)	1954	Last

110 y. Back-stroke (31 Dec. 1968)

1:01.5	Monckton, John (Aus)	1958	First
1:00.1	Matthes, Roland (E Ger)	1967	Last

150 y. Back-stroke (31 Dec. 1952

1:57.6*	Unwin, Fred (Eng)	1909	First
1:29.9*	Stack, Allen (USA)	1949	Last

220 y. Back-stroke (31 Dec. 1968)

2:18.8	Monckton, John (Aus)	1958	First
2:12.0	Reynolds, Peter (Aus)	1966	Last

400 m. Back-stroke (31 Dec. 1948)

6:46.0*	Meyboom, Hermann (Belg)	1910	First
5:03.9*	Stack, Allen (USA)	1948	Last

100 y. Breast-stroke (1 May 1957)

1:02.1*	Skinner, J. (USA)	1939	First
1:00.4*	Hughes, Robert (USA)	1956	Last

110 y. Breast-stroke (31 Dec. 1968)

1:13.5	Gathercole, Terry (Aus)	1958	First
1:08.2	O'Brien, Ian (Aus)	1966	Last

200 y. Breast-stroke (31 Dec. 1952)

2:41.8*	Baronyi, Andras (Hun)	1908	First
2:12.9*	Davies, John (Aus)	Bu1952	Last

220 y. Breast-stroke (31 December 1968)

2:38.8*	Gleie, Knud (Den)	1953	First
2:28.0	O'Brien, Aus)	1966	Last

400 m. Breast-stroke (31 Dec. 1948)

6:53.4	Zacharias, Georg (Ger)	1907	First
5:40.2*	Bonte, Bjorn (Neth)	1948	Last

500 m. Breast-stroke (31 Dec. 1948)

8:30.6	Zacharias, Georg (Ger)	1904	First
7:10.6*	Bonte, Bjorn (Neth)	1948	Last

100 y. Butterfly (1 May 1957)

57.3*	Baarcke, Larry (USA)	1954	First
54.3*	Wiggins, Albert (USA)	1957	Last

110 y. Butterfly (31 Dec. 1968)

1:03.8	Wilkinson, Brian (USA)	1958	First
56.3	Spitz, Mark (USA)	1967	Last

220 y. Butterfly (31 Dec. 1968)

2:26.1*	Drake, Phil (USA)	1955	First
2:08.4	Berry, Kevin (Aus)	1963	Last

220 y. Individual medley (31 Dec. 1968

2:14.0	(Standard time never achieved)	1964

400 y. Individual medley (1 May 1957)

4:52.8*	Jones, Burwell (USA)	1953	First
4:36.9*	Wardrop, Jack (GB)	1955	Last

440 y. Individual medley (31 Dec. 1968)

5:08.8	Black, Ian (GB)	1959	First
4:46.8	Holthaus, Michael (W Ger)	1968	Last

4 x 100 y. Free-style relay (1 May 1957)

3:31.4*	Michigan University (USA)	1937	First
3:18.3*	Yale University (USA)	1957	Last

4 x 110 y. Free-style relay (31 Dec. 1968)

3:47.3	Australia	1958	First
3:35.6	Australia	1966	Last

4 x 200 y. Free-style relay (1 May 1957)

8:38.8	Yale University (USA)	1934	First
7:39.9*	Yale University (USA)	1953	Last

4 x 200 y. Free-style relay (31 Dec. 1968)

8:24.5	Australia	1958	First
7:59.5	Australia	1966	Last

3 x 100 y. Medley relay (31 Dec. 1952)

2:57.6*	Yale University (USA)	1946	First
2:47.1*	Ohio State University (USA)	1952	Last

3 x 100 m. Medley relay (31 Dec. 1952)

3:20.7	Ohio State University (USA)	1946	First
3:07.0*	New Haven S.C. (USA)	1952	Last

4 x 110 y. Medley relay (31 Dec. 1968)

4:19.4	Australia	1958	First
4:03.2	Australia	1966	Last

WOMEN

100 y. Free-style (1 May 1957)

1:13.6*	Fletcher, Jennie (Eng)	1909	First
56.9	Fraser, Dawn (Aus)	1956	Last

110 y. Free-style (31 Dec. 1968)

1:02.4	Fraser, Dawn (Aus)	1958	First
59.5	Fraser, Dawn (Aus)	1962	Last

220 y. Free-style (31 Dec. 1968)

2:56.0*	Durack, Fanny (Aus)	1915	First
2:11.6	Fraser, Dawn (Aus)	1960	Last

300 y. Free-style (31 Dec. 1948)

4:33.2*	Neave, Vera (Eng)	1911	First
3:25.6*	Hveger, Ragnhild (Den)	1938	Last

300 m. Free-style (31 Dec. 1948)

5:57.6*	Zahoure, Berta (Aut)	1910	First
3:42.5*	Hveger, Ragnhild (Den)	1940	Last

440 y. Free-style (31 Dec. 1968)

6:30.2	Bleibtrey, Ethelda (USA)	1919	First
4:38.8	Wainwright, Kathy (Aus)	1966	Last

500 y. Free-style (31 Dec. 1952)

7:32.4	Durack, Fanny (Aus)	1915	First
5:53.0*	Hveger, Ragnhild (Den)	1942	Last

500 m. Free-style (31 Dec. 1952)

7:22.2	Ederle, Gertrude (USA)	1922	First
6:27.4*	Hveger, Ragnhild (Den)	1940	Last

880 y. Free-style (31 Dec. 1968)

13:19.0	Ederle, Gertrude (USA)	1919	First
9:44.1	Meyer, Debbie (USA)	1967	Last

1,000 y. Free-style (31 Dec. 1948)

14:58.4	Wainwright, Helen (USA)	1922	First
12:36.0	Hveger, Ragnhild (Den)	1938	Last

1,000 m. Free-style (31 Dec. 1948)

15:49.6	Mayne, Edith (Eng)	1926	First
13:54.4	Hveger, Ragnhild (Den)	1941	Last

1,650 y. Free-style (31 Dec. 1968)

19:25.7	Konrads, Ilsa (Aus)	1959	First
18:47.8	Coughlan, Angela (Can)	1968	Last

1,760 y. Free-style (1 May 1957)

26:08.0	Durack, Fanny (Aus)	1914	First
22:05.5	De Nijs, Lenie (Neth)	1955	Last

100 y. Back-stroke (1 May 1957)

1:05.1*	Kint, Cor (Neth)	1939	First
1:03.8*	Cone, Carin (USA)	1957	Last

110 y. Back-stroke (31 Dec. 1968)

1:13.5	Edwards, Margaret (GB)	1957	First
1:06.7	Muir, Karen (SAf)	1968	Last

150 y. Back-stroke (31 Dec. 1952)

2:17.0*	Morton, Lucy (GB)	1916	First
1:40.4*	Wielema, Geertje (Neth)	1951	Last

220 y. Back-stroke (31 Dec. 1968)

2:39.9	Gould, Phillipa (NZ)	1957	First
2:24.1	Muir, Karen (SAf)	1968	Last

400 m. Back-stroke (31 Dec. 1948)

6:24.8*	Bauer, Sybil (USA)	1922	First
5:38.2*	Hveger, Ragnhild (Den)	1941	Last

100 y. Breast-stroke (1 May 1957)

1:16.6*	Dillard, J. (USA)	1939	First
1:09.2*	Van Vliet, Nel (Neth)	1947	Last

110 y. Breast-stroke (31 Dec. 1968)

1:21.2	Lassig, Rose (Aus)	1960	First
1:17.0	Ball, Catie (USA)	1967	Last

200 y. Breast-stroke (31 Dec. 1952)

3:11.4*	Morton, Lucy (Eng)	1916	First
2:34.0*	Novak, Eva (Hun)	1950	Last

220 y. Breast-stroke (31 Dec. 1968)
2:52.5	Den Haan, Ada (Neth)	1957	First
2:46.9	Ball, Catie (USA)	1967	Last

400 m. Breast-stroke (31 Dec. 1948)
7:42.2*	Van Den Bogaert, E. (Belg)	1922	First
5:58.6*	Van Vliet, Nel (Neth)	1947	Last

500 m. Breast-stroke (31 Dec. 1948)
10:33.2	Welch, D. (Aus)	1930	First
7:41.0*	Van Vliet, Nel (Neth)	1946	Last

100 y. Butterfly (1 May 1957)
1:06.3*	Mann, Shelley (USA)	1954	First
1:01.9*	Ramey, Nancy (USA)	1957	Last

110 y. Butterfly (31 Dec. 1968)
1:11.3	Ramey, Nancy (USA)	1957	First
1:05.1	Kok, Ada (Neth)	1964	Last

220 y. Butterfly (31 Dec. 1968)
2:44.4*	Mann, Shelley (USA)	1956	First
2:21.0	Kok, Ada (Neth)	1967	Last

220 y. Individual medley (31 Dec. 1968)
2:29.0	(Standard time never achieved)	1964

400 y. Individual medley (1 May 1957)
5:10.5*	Kok, Mary (Neth)	1955	First
5:08.0*	Ruuska, Sylvia (USA)	1957	Last

440 y. Individual medley (31 Dec. 1968)
5:41.1	Ruuska, Sylvia (USA)	1959	First
5:25.1	Olcese, Mary-Ellen (USA)	1965	Last

4 x 100 y. Free-style relay (1 May 1957)
4:08.1*	Denmark	1939	First
3:56.8*	Lafayette S.C. (USA)	1956	Last

4 x 110 y. Free-style relay (31 Dec. 1968)
4:18.9	Australia	1958	First
4:10.8	Canada	1966	Last

3 x 100 y. Medley relay (31 Dec. 1952)
3:26.6*	Denmark	1947	First
3:18.1*	Lafayette S.C. (USA)	1952	Last

3 x 100 m. Medley relay (31 Dec. 1952)
3:46.3*	Netherlands	1946	First
3:35.9*	Netherlands	1950	Last

4 x 100 y. Medley relay (1 May 1957)
4:34.4*	Lafayette S.C. (USA)	1954	First
4:23.0*	Walter Reed S.C. (USA)	1956	Last

4 x 100 y. Medley relay (31 Dec. 1968)
4:57.0	Netherlands	1957	First
4:37.4	United States	1967	Last

YEADEN MEMORIAL TROPHY
(England's 'Swimmer of the Year'.) This trophy was presented to the A.S.A. by the five district associations to perpetuate the memory of T. M. Yeaden, honorary secretary of the A.S.A. from 1913-20, honorary treasurer 1921-36 and president in 1924, who died on 17 Jan. 1937. It has been awarded since 1938 to the English swimmer whose performance is judged the best of the year. Winners:

1938 Storey, Doris (Montague Butron)
1939 Wainwright, Norman (Hanley)
1940-46 Not awarded

1947 Romain, Roy (King's College)
1948 Hale, Jack (Hull Kingston)
1949 Wellington, Margaret (Beckenham)
1950 Wilkinson, Daphne (Sparkhill)
1951 Wilkinson, Daphne (Woolwich)
1952 Wilkinson, Daphne (Woolwich)
1953 Preece, Lillian (Wallasey)
1954 Symons, Pat (Northumberland)
1955 Symonds, Graham (Coventry)
1956 Grinham, Judy (Hampstead L)
1957 Wilkinson, Diana (Stockport)
1958 Grinham, Judy (Hampstead L)
1959 Lonsbrough, Anita (Huddersfield)
1960 Lonsbrough, Anita (Huddersfield)
1961 Wilkinson, Chris (Stockport)
1962 Ludgrove, Linda (St. James's L)
1963 Mitchell, Stella (Hampstead L)
1964 Mitchell, Stella (Hampstead L)
1965 Long, Elizabeth (Ilford)
1966 Kimber, Alan (Southampton)
1967 Williams, Sue (Exeter)
1968 Jackson, Alex (Peel, I.o.M.)
1969 Terrell, Ray (Southampton)
1970 Harrison, Dorothy (Hartlepool)
1971 Brinkley, Brian (Modernians)
1972 Brinkley, Brian (Modernians)
1973 Brinkley, Brian (Modernians)
1974 Brinkley, Brian (Modernians)
1975 Brinkley, Brian (Modernians)

INDEX